ANTI
THE BEAST REVEALED

Edward Hendrie

"Little children, it is the last time: and as ye have heard that antichrist shall come, even now are there many antichrists; whereby we know that it is the last time." (1 John 2:18)

Garrisonville, Virginia 22463

Copyright © 2015 by Edward Hendrie
All rights reserved.

ISBN: 978-0-9832627-8-7

EdwardHendrie@gmail.com

Other books from Great Mountain Publishing:

● Antichrist Conspiracy
● 9/11-Enemies Foreign and Domestic
● Solving the Mystery of BABYLON THE GREAT
● The Anti-Gospel
● Bloody Zion
● What Shall I Do to Inherit Eternal Life?
● Murder, Rape, and Torture in a Catholic Nunnery
● Rome's Responsibility for the Assassination of Abraham Lincoln

Available at:
www.antichristconspiracy.com
www.lulu.com
www.911enemies.com
www.mysterybabylonthegreat.net
www.antigospel.com
https://play.google.com
www.barnesandnoble.com
www.amazon.com.

The author is a contract staff member of the U.S. Department of State and as such is required to give the following disclaimer pursuant to the U.S. Department of State Foreign Affairs Manual, to wit: 3 FAM 4172.1-4. The views expressed in this book are those of the author in his private capacity and do not necessarily represent the views of the U.S. Department of State or any other entity of the U.S. Government.

Edward Hendrie rests on the authority of the Holy Bible alone for doctrine. He considers the Holy Bible to be the inspired and inerrant word of God. Favorable citation by Edward Hendrie to an authority outside the Holy Bible on a particular issue should not be interpreted to mean that he agrees with all of the doctrines and beliefs of the cited authority.

All Scripture references are to the Authorized (King James) Version of the Holy Bible, unless otherwise indicated.

Table of Contents

Introduction. 1

1   The Confession of the Antichrist. 4

2   Mystery of Iniquity. 13

3   That Man of Sin. 22

4   Ravening Wolves on the Prowl. 34

5   Satanic Ritual Abuse by Catholic Priests. 60

6   Speaking Lies in Hypocrisy. 77

7   Changing the Times and the Laws. 80

8   Many Shall Say "I Am Christ". 93

9   Signs and Lying Wonders. 99

10   Whosoever Sins Ye Remit, They Are Remitted. 107

11   Doctrines of Devils. 114

12   Putting Christ to an Open Shame. 116

13   The Dark Secret of the Catholic Liturgy. 137

14   The Antichrist Guarantees Heaven for the Jews. 157

15   The Antichrist is Caught Worshiping Lucifer. 166

16   A Hellish Stopover on the Way to Heaven. 181

17   Charging Admission to Enter Heaven. 185

18   Fire from Heaven. 190

19   Raping the Church. 194

20	Dethroning Caesar.	201
21	Sitting as God in the Temple of God.	203
22	Blessing Bloody Murder.	217
23	Denying that Jesus is the Christ.	224
24	The Attack of the Moon God.	236
25	The Perverse Effect of Religious Misogyny.	257
26	Common Root of Catholicism and Islam.	284
27	Proving the Awful Disclosures of Maria Monk.	294
28	Masonic Secret Agent.	344
29	The Torture Room.	352
30	The "Holy" Antichrist.	358
31	Supreme Druid.	362
32	Denying Christ Has Come in the Flesh.	364
33	Queen of Heaven.	372
34	The Little Horn.	388
35	Behold a White Horse.	404
36	Mark of the Beast.	409
37	Hiding the Antichrist.	422
38	Dual Destruction of the Antichrist.	431
39	Identifying the False Prophet.	434
40	The Image of the Beast Comes Alive.	455

41	The Great Harlot Seduces Protestant Churches. 485
42	The Antichrist Orchestrates the Killing of Lincoln. 508
43	The Antichrist Targets the USA. 545

Endnotes. 561

Introduction

This book compares the biblical prophecies about the antichrist with the historical evidence of the fulfillment of those prophecies. After reading this book, you will come to the ineluctable conclusion that the anticrhrist is here, now, among us. The prophesied son of perdition has come "after the working of Satan with all power and signs and lying wonders, And with all deceivableness of unrighteousness." 2 Thessalonians 2:10. This book documents that the antichrist has in fact given an esoteric confession to being the antichrst. You will read how the antichrist, who is now in the world, fulfills Daniel's prophecy of thinking to change the time and the laws, (Daniel 7:25) and Paul's prophecy of sitting "in the temple of God, shewing himself that he is God." (2 Thessalonians 2:4) You will learn who is the mysterious false prophet in the book of Revelation, and how he assists the antichrist in his spiritual warfare against God and man by introducing false doctrine into churches today.

This book is not written to criticize or offend those who are followers of the antichrist. I was at one time a member of that large deluded class of people. I was saved by the grace of God through faith in Jesus Christ out of the darkness of ignorance that is the religion of the antichrist. This book is written to warn those people who have been misled by the spiritual dissimulation of the antichrist so that they can obey the command of God to "come out of her, my people, that ye be not partakers of her sins, and that ye receive not of her plagues." (Revelation 18:4)

The spiritual success of the antichrist can be measured by the obstreperous vehemence of his defenders. The followers of the religion of the antichrist simply cannot believe that the true character of their spiritual leader is completely contrary to his public image. The deluded followers are ignorant of the devices of the devil and cannot imagine hypocrisy on such a grand scale. The antichrist finds the roots of his character in the hypocrisy of the scribes and Pharisees.

> We unto you, scribes and Pharisees, hypocrites! for ye are like unto whited sepulchres, which indeed appear beautiful outward, but are within full of dead men's bones, and of all uncleanness. Even so ye also outwardly appear righteous unto men, but within ye are full of hypocrisy and iniquity. (Matthew 23:27-28)

The antichrist, like the scribes and Pharisees before him, camouflages his villainous character behind a facade of righteousness. The antichrist is above all things an arch-practitioner of hypocrisy. What is hypocrisy but "behavior that does not agree with what someone claims to believe or feel."[1] Noah Webster probably defined hypocrisy best:

> 1. Simulation; a feigning to be what one is not; or dissimulation, a concealment of one's real character or motives. More generally, hypocrisy is simulation, or the assuming of a false appearance of virtue or religion; a deceitful show of a good character, in morals or religion; a counterfeiting of religion.
>
> Beware ye of the leaven of the Pharisees, which is hypocrisy. Luke 12:1.
>
> 2. Simulation; deceitful appearance; false pretense.
>
> Hypocrisy is the necessary burden of villainy.[2]

The antichrist's adeptness as a hypocrite is the reason for his evil success. Indeed, to be the antichrist, his evil character must be concealed beneath a disguise of piety. "And no marvel; for Satan himself is transformed into an angel of light. Therefore it is no great thing if his ministers also be transformed as the ministers of righteousness; whose end shall be according to their works." 2 Corinthians 11:14-15. The key to revealing the identity of the antichrist is to uncover his hypocrisy. Because the hypocrisy of the antichrist is so extreme, those who have been hoodwinked by his religious doctrines will be shocked to learn of it. This book exposes the concealed iniquity of the antichrist and juxtaposes it against his publicly proclaimed false persona of righteousness, thus bringing into clear relief that man of sin, the son of perdition, who is truly a ravening wolf in sheep's clothing, speaking lies in hypocrisy. *See* Matthew 7:15 and 1 Timothy 4:1-3.

Edward Hendrie
January 12, 2015

1 The Confession of the Antichrist

The first mention of the antichrist in scripture is made by Jesus Christ. "For many shall come in my name, saying, I am Christ; and shall deceive many." (Matthew 24:5) Jesus did not use the word antichrist, but he was clearly warning of "many" who would come claiming to be Christ. Jesus clarified his warning a few verses later when he stated: "For there shall arise false Christs, and false prophets, and shall shew great signs and wonders; insomuch that, if it were possible, they shall deceive the very elect." (Matthew 24:24) *See also*, Mark 13:22. Jesus warned of false (pseudo) Christs (plural). In identifying the antichrist, one should not look for one but rather "many," who will not only oppose Jesus Christ but also seek to take his place as Christ.

John builds on what Jesus had warned and for the first time in scripture comes out and calls the false Christ, antichrist. "Little children, it is the last time: and as ye have heard that antichrist shall come, even now are there many antichrists; whereby we know that it is the last time." 1 John 2:18. Notice the warning of John includes the point that even then there were many antichrists (plural). We know from what John and Jesus said that antichrist, while a singular noun, is intended to describe a person who occupies an office that is filled by "many" antichrists. Christian historian J. A. Wylie explains the significance of the title, antichrist, used by John. Wylie's sublime writing cannot be equaled, and so I will quote him directly:

> Who is Antichrist? It will help us to the right answer to this question if we shall first determine, *What* is Antichrist?
>
> Antichrist is an enemy who makes war with the Son of God. Of that there is no doubt. But what is the form of this war, and under what character does Antichrist carry it on? Does he wage it openly, or does he fight it under a mask? Does he take the field as an open rebel and a declared foe, or does he come as a friendly adherent who professes to bring support and help to the cause which, in reality, he seeks to undermine and destroy? To determine this point, let us look at the meaning of the word *Antichrist* as employed in Scripture.[3]

Wylie explains that the key to understanding who is the antichrist, is to first understand what the word antichrist means.

> The reader sees that the term is a composite one, being made up of two words *anti* and *Christ*. The name is one of new formation; being compounded, it would seem, for this very enemy, and by its etymology expressing more exactly and perfectly his character than any other word could. The precise question now before us is this —What is the precise sense of *anti* in this connection? Does it designate an enemy who says openly and truly, "I am *against* Christ." Or does it designate one who says plausibly, yet falsely, "I am *for* Christ." Which?[4] To determine this, let us look at the force given to this prefix by writers in both classic literature and Holy Scripture. First, the old classic writers. By these the preposition *anti* is often employed to designate a *substitute*. This is, in fact, a very common use of it in the classic writers. For instance, *anti-basileus*, he who is the *locum tenens* of a king, or as we now should say *viceroy*: *anti* having in this case the force of the English term *vice*. He who filled the place of consul

was *antihupatos*, pro-counsul. He who took the place of an absent guest at a feast was styled *antideipnos*. The preposition is used in this sense of the great Substitute Himself. Christ is said to have given Himself as an *antilutron*, a ransom in the stead of all. Classic usage does not require us to give only one sense to this word, and restrict it to one who seeks openly, and by force, to seat himself in the place of another, and by violent usurpation bring that other's authority to an end. We are at liberty to apply it to one who steals into the office of another under the mask of friendship; and while professing to uphold his interest, labours to destroy them.[5]

So the antichrist must be a man who cunningly and secretly works against Christ while coming in a line of "many" who comes in the guise of being in place of Christ. Antichrist, therefore, means one who takes the place of Christ while opposing him. Wylie explains why this cannot be any of the leaders of atheism or pantheism.

> Antichrist, then, is a *counterfeit*. But this one mark is not alone sufficient to identify the person on whom it is found as the great apostate. All deceit in religion is anti-Christian; the other marks must come along with this one to warrant us to say that we have found that pre-eminently wicked one, and that portentous combination of all evil that is to form the Antichrist. Yet this one mark enables us to test certain theories which have been advanced on this subject. If Antichrist must necessarily be a deceiver – a false Christ – then no Atheist or body of Atheists can be Antichrist. No Pantheist of body of Pantheists can be Antichrist. They are not deceivers; they are open enemies. They make war in defiance of God and Christ, and under the protestation that there is no such person as the Bible affirms filling the office of the world's Mediator and Saviour. They hold the whole affair to be an invention of priests. Antichrist dare make no such avowal. It would be fatal to him. Were he to affirm that Christianity is a fable, and out and out imposture, he

would cut away the ground from under his own feet. He would deny the very first postulate in his system; for there must first be a Christ before there can be an Antichrist.[6]

The antichrist does not openly oppose Christ, his opposition is surreptitious. The antichrist is a pretender. He is the leader of a phalanx of evil men, engaging in a spiritual battle against Christ by deceiving the unwary into believing they are ministers of righteousness.

> For such are false apostles, deceitful workers, transforming themselves into the apostles of Christ. And no marvel; for Satan himself is transformed into an angel of light. Therefore it is no great thing if his ministers also be transformed as the ministers of righteousness; whose end shall be according to their works. (2 Corinthians 11:13-15)

The antichrist is not a political leader who openly opposes Christ. The antichrist certainly opposes Christ, but he does it through dissimulation, under the guise of being an advocate of Christ. Wylie explains:

> And not less does this mark shut us up to the rejection of the theory which has been advanced with much earnestness and some plausibility, that Antichrist is a political character, or potentate, some frightfully tyrannical and portentously wicked King, who is to arise, and for a short space devastate the world by arms. This is an altogether different Antichrist from that Antichrist which prophecy foreshadows. He may resemble, nay, surpass him, in open violence, but he lacks the profound dissimulation under which Antichrist is to commit his atrocities. The rage of the mere tyrant is indiscriminately vented upon the world at large; Antichrist's rage is concentrated on one particular object and cause; nor with any propriety can such a one be said to sit in the "temple of God," the seat on which the mock-Christ specially delights to show himself. Prophecy absolutely refuses to see in

> either of these theories the altogether unique and over-topping system of hypocrisy, blasphemy, and tyranny which it has foretold. So far we are helped in our search. When we are able to put aside some of the false Antichrists, we come more within sight of the true one.[7]

There are many characters who oppose Christ, but in order for that person to be the antichrist, he must seek to replace Christ. If he is not a substitute, indeed a counterfeit Christ, he cannot be the antichrist. Wylie explains for that reason, a religious leader who opposes Christ without claiming to replace Christ cannot be the antichrist; so also a religious leader who ostensibly supports Christ without claiming to replace him cannot be the antichrist.

> Well, let us suppose that one or other of these notoriously wicked personages or systems has been put to the bar, on the charge of being the "adversary" predicted by John. "Who are you?" says the judge. "Are you a Vice-Christ? So you make a profession of Christianity, and under that pretext seek to undermine and destroy it? "No," replies the accused. "I am no counterfeit. Christ and His Gospel I hate; but I am an open enemy, I fight under no mask." Turning to the likeness drawn by Paul and John of Christ's great rival and opponent, and finding the outstanding and essential feature in the portrait absent in the accused, the judge would be constrained to say, "I do not find the charge proven. Go your way; you are not the Antichrist."

> Mohammedanism comes nearer than any other of the opposing systems to the Antichrist of the Bible; yet it falls a long way short of it. Mohamet did not disavow the mission of Jesus; on the contrary, he professed to hold Him in honour as a prophet. And in much the same way do His followers still feel towards Christ. But Islam does not profess to be an imitation of Christianity. Any counterfeit that can be discovered in Mohammedanism is partial and shadowy.[8]

Who is this antichrist warned of by Jesus and John? The answer is clear, because the antichrist has announced to the world his identity. The pope considers himself to be the "Vicar of Christ" (which means Vice-Christ), and it is this that identifies him as the antichrist. Pope Boniface VIII stated: "Therefore, of the one and only Church there is one body and one head, not two heads like a monster; that is, Christ and the **Vicar of Christ**, Peter and the successor of Peter."[9]

That quote from Pope Boniface VIII is purported to be an infallible pronouncement on the primacy of the pope over all rulers and authority on earth. Clearly, Pope Boniface is stating unequivocally that he and all popes in succession are the vicars of Christ. The world recognizes the pope as the vicar of Christ. Even the satanically subversive *Rolling Stone* magazine in a laudatory cover story on the newly installed Pope Francis called him, "Pope Francis, the 266th vicar of Jesus Christ on Earth."[10] J. A. Wylie describes the title, vicar of Christ, as the key to unlocking the identity of the antichrist.

> The Papacy holds in its name the key of its meaning. We shall make use of that key in unlocking its mystery and true character. The Papacy cannot complain though we adopt this line of interpretation. We do nothing more than use the key it has put into our hands.[11]

How is the title, vicar of Christ, the key to identifying the antichrist? The key is found in the meaning of vicar. The word vicar means one who acts in place of another. We derive the English word vice from vicar. For example the Vice President acts in place of the President during those times when the President himself cannot act. The Bible talks about one who would come and deceive the world into believing that he is in place of Christ. He is identified as the **antichrist.** The pope himself is acknowledging that he is the antichrist by claiming to be the vicar of Christ. Vicar of Christ means antichrist. Noah Webster defined the prefix "anti" as a preposition meaning not only against but also in place of the noun it precedes.[12] The Oxford English Dictionary[13] defines "anti" as meaning "opposite, against, in exchange, instead, representing, rivaling, simulating." Antichrist means one who is against Christ and at the same time purports to take the place of Christ. **Therefore, vicar of Christ = antichrist.**

Wylie explains: "Of all systems that ever were on the earth, or are now upon it, Romanism alone meets all the requirements of prophecy, and exhibits all the features of the Vice-Christ; and it does so with a completeness and a truthfulness which enable the man who permits himself to be guided by the statements of the Word of God on the one hand, and the facts of history on the other, to say at once, 'This is the Antichrist.'"[14]

Wylie elaborates on the significance of the title "Vicar of Christ" used by the popes of Rome and how that title reveals the papacy is the very office of the antichrist:

> The Apostle John, we have said, speaking of the apostacy, the coming of which he predicts, styles it the "Antichrist." And we have also said that the Papacy, speaking through its representative and head, calls itself the "Vicar of Christ." The first, "Antichrist," is a Greek word, the second, "Vicar," is an English word; but the two are in reality one, for both words have the same meaning. Antichrist translated into English is Vice-Christ, or Vicar of Christ; and Vicar of Christ, rendered into Greek is Antichrist–*Antichristos*. If we can establish this –and the ordinary use of the word by those to whom the Greek was a vernacular, is decisive on the point–we shall have no difficulty in showing that this is the meaning of the word "Antichrist,"–even a Vice-Christ. And if so, then every time the Pope claims to be the Vicar of Christ, he pleads at the bar of the world that he is the "Antichrist."[15]

The pope's claim to be the vicar of Christ continues to be the official position of the Catholic Church. For example, Pope John Paul II made the claim that the pope is the fulfilment of Christ's promise that he will be with us until the end of the world. John Paul II says that Jesus is personally present in his church through the office of the pope.

> Once again, concerning names: The Pope is called the 'Vicar of Christ.' This title should be considered within the entire context of the Gospel. Before ascending into heaven, Jesus said to the apostles: 'I am

with you always, until the end of the age' (Matthew 28:20). Though invisible, He is personally present in His Church. *Pope John Paul II.*[16]

Jesus' promise in Matthew 28:20 to be with his church until the end of the age is fulfilled by the Holy Ghost. It is the Holy Ghost, not the pope of Rome, through whom Jesus is present with us.

> These things have I spoken unto you, being yet present with you. **But the Comforter, which is the Holy Ghost, whom the Father will send in my name, he shall teach you all things, and bring all things to your remembrance, whatsoever I have said unto you.** (John 14:25-26)
>
> Nevertheless I tell you the truth; It is expedient for you that I go away: for **if I go not away, the Comforter will not come unto you; but if I depart, I will send him unto you.** (John 16:7)

Pope John Paul II's claim to be the fulfillment of the prophecy by Jesus that he would be with them until the end of the age reveals the pope as the deceiver, whom Christ warned of in Matthew when he said "many shall come in my name, saying, I am Christ." Matthew 24:5.

The case for the pope being the antchrist is so compelling that even informed Catholic theologians admit to the uncanny similarity of the pope to the prophesied antichrist. For example, the Catholic Encyclopedia (without admitting the pope is the antichrist) acknowledges that, because "the pope is an image of Christ, Antichrist must have some similarity to the Pope." That statement in the Catholic Encyclopedia comes as precipitously close to the edge as one can come to identifying the papal vicar of Christ as the antichrist, while at the same time denying that fact. The Encyclopedia avers that the "Antichrist simulates Christ," and therefore, "Antichrist must have some similarity to the Pope," since the pope claims to be "an image of Christ." The Catholic Encyclopedia maintains that the pope is not the antichrist, but at the same time avers that the antichrist must necessarily be just like the pope. The full quote is below:

The gibe, "If the Pope is not Antichrist, he has bad luck to be so like him", is really another argument in favour of the claims of the Pope; since Antichrist simulates Christ, and the Pope is an image of Christ, Antichrist must have some similarity to the Pope, if the latter be the true Vicar of Christ.[17]

2 Mystery of Iniquity

God through Paul, in 2 Thessalonians chapter 2, refers to the antichrist as that man of sin, the son of perdition.

> Let no man deceive you by any means: for that day shall not come, except there come a falling away first, and **that man of sin** be revealed, **the son of perdition**; Who opposeth and exalteth himself above all that is called God, or that is worshipped; so that he as God sitteth in the temple of God, shewing himself that he is God. (2 Thessalonians 2:3-4)

Later, in that same chapter, Paul refers to the spirit of the antichrist as the "mystery of iniquity" whose coming is after the working of Satan.

> For the **mystery of iniquity** doth already work: only he who now letteth will let, until he be taken out of the way. And then shall that Wicked be revealed, whom the Lord shall consume with the spirit of his mouth, and shall destroy with the brightness of his coming: Even him, **whose coming is after the working of Satan** with all power and signs and lying wonders. (2 Thessalonians 2:7-9)

The titles used to describe the coming antichrist are further clues to his identity and character. First, let us explore the moniker, "the mystery of iniquity." What does God mean by the mystery of iniquity? God gave a hint that the mystery of iniquity would be "after the working of Satan." Iniquity is the opposite of godliness. God uses the term "mystery of godliness" and explains in 1 Timothy chapter 3, that the mystery of godliness is, in part, that "God was manifest in the flesh."

> And without controversy great is the **mystery of godliness: God was manifest in the flesh,** justified in the Spirit, seen of angels, preached unto the Gentiles, believed on in the world, received up into glory. (1 Timothy 3:16)

Wylie eloquently explains how the contrasting attributes of the mystery of godliness reveals the mystery of iniquity.

> The "mystery of iniquity," which stands over against the "mystery of godliness" as its parallel and counterfeit, must be like it –like it in having its source outside the world, like it in its slow and gradual development, and like it in its final culmination. Of it, too, we must say it is not the development of a system only, it is the development of a person. It is the gathering together of all the principles of evil, and the marshalling of them into one organization or host, and their embodiment at last in a representative person or head –Antichrist. He was to be the grand outcome of the apostacy; not its mere ornamental head, but its executive. He was to guide its counsels, inspire its policy, execute its decrees; in short, he was to be the organ through which its terrible powers were to be put forth.
>
> This we take to be the ruling idea in the passage. Just as the "mystery of godliness" is not merely the manifestation of the system of godliness, but the manifestation of God Himself, so the "mystery of iniquity" is not merely the manifestation of the system

> of iniquity, but the manifestation of the person or author of iniquity. The prophecy brings before us two mysteries, the one the counterfeit in all points of the other. We have an invisible agent, even God, beneath the one; we have an invisible agent, even Satan, beneath the other. We have the one mystery culminating at last in an incarnation, "God manifest in the flesh." We see the other in like manner culminating in an incarnation, in a loose sense; for all its principles concentrate themselves in and show themselves to the world through its living head on earth, Antichrist. We may go even farther and say that there is as real an incarnation of the spirit and mind of Satan in the "mystery of iniquity," as there is of the spirit and mind of God in the "mystery of godliness." And as in Christ God and man meet; so in Antichrist, his counterfeit and rival, the human and the superhuman meet and act together earth-born man and arch-angel fallen.[18]

The mystery of godliness was spoken of by the prophets as they prophesied of the coming Christ. There were historical types of Christ manifested throughout history, revealed in the Old Testament. Those prophecies and types did not fully reveal the mystery of godliness. Wylie explains that the mystery of godliness remained largely a mystery until the veil was completely removed and godliness came full bloom in the world through the presence of Jesus Christ.

> Thus did the "mystery of godliness" work, unfolding and still unfolding itself as the ages passed on – the type growing ever the clearer, and the prophecy ever the fuller – till at last the "mystery" stepped out from behind the veil, and stood before the world, perfected, finished, and fully revealed in the person of Jesus of Nazareth, the Christ – "God manifest in the flesh;" and centering in His person, and flowing out from it, through His life and ministry and death, as rays from the sun, were all the glorious doctrines of the Gospel.[19]

Wylie explains how in like manner the mystery of iniquity was gradually developed but was not fully revealed until it came into full bloom before the world when the pope of Rome announced his entrance as the "vicar of Christ."

> Silently and stealthily this "mystery" pursued its course. For ages and for generations it too was a hidden mystery. Paul tells us that it was working in his day. This warrants us to say that Antichrist was then born, and was making trial of his infantile powers. The world did not hear his working, but Paul, by the spirit of prophecy did so, and sounded an alarm to the church. The Gnostics and other teachers of error that had gone forth into the world so early as Paul's day, were Antichrists, and those in especial who propagated the delusion that it was a phantom which the Jews seized, and crucified on Calvary. They seemed to admit the mission of Christ, yet they subverted the great end of His coming by denying His incarnation, and, by consequence, the whole work of redemption. But, though these teachers were anti-Christian, they were not the Antichrist. After them, Paul gave warning there should come one far mightier than they, "the latchet of whose shoes they were not worthy to loose." They were misgrown and misshapen Antichrists; their system of error was immature, and their power of attack contemptible, compared with that full-grown anti-Christianism which would stand up on after days, and say to the world, "I am Christ," and under that colour make war upon the true Christ. ...
>
> For what were the Caesars, king and priest of the Roman world, but types of that more terrible power, temporal and spiritual, that was to centre in the chair of the Popes? That colossal image he kept full in the world's view, till the "fulness of the time" for Antichrist's appearance had arrived, and then he withdrew the image, and brought forward the great reality, the "Man of Sin" now come to his full birth, though not as yet to his full stature, and he found for him a seat and throne on the Seven Hills.[20]

Since the antichrist is the opposite of God in character, but he seeks to replace God, then the mystery of iniquity must be the devil manifest in the flesh. It is notable that in the verses following God's explanation of the mystery of godliness in 1 Timothy, he explains that "in the latter times some shall depart from the faith, giving heed to seducing spirits, and doctrines of devils; Speaking lies in hypocrisy; having their conscience seared with a hot iron; Forbidding to marry, and commanding to abstain from meats." 1 Timothy 4:1-2. The Roman Catholic Church has embraced both the doctrine of forbidding Catholic priests to marry and forbidding the eating of meat on Friday during Lent.

So we see that the mystery of iniquity is the manifestation of the devil in the flesh. Are there other verses that support this interpretation? In John 6:70-71, Jesus referred to Judas as a devil. "Jesus answered them, Have not I chosen you twelve, and **one of you is a devil**? He spake of Judas Iscariot the son of Simon: for he it was that should betray him, being one of the twelve." (John 6:70-71) Was Judas a devil? In looking at the gospel of Luke we see that the devil (Satan) in fact entered into Judas prior to Judas' betrayal of Jesus. "**Then entered Satan into Judas** surnamed Iscariot, being of the number of the twelve." (Luke 22:3)

We see that the devil was manifest in the flesh when he entered into Judas. This interpretation is confirmed by John 17:12 where Jesus refers to Judas as **"the son of perdition."** "While I was with them in the world, I kept them in thy name: those that thou gavest me I have kept, and none of them is lost, but **the son of perdition**; that the scripture might be fulfilled." (John 17:12) The term "son of perdition" is the same term used in 2 Thessalonians 2:3 to describe the antichrist. "Let no man deceive you by any means: for that day shall not come, except there come a falling away first, and that man of sin be revealed, **the son of perdition**." (2 Thessalonians 2:3) The "son of perdition" is also described as "that man of sin" and "the mystery of iniquity" in 2 Thessalonians. They are all descriptions for the antichrist.

That man of sin, the son of perdition, described in 2 Thessalonians 2:3, can be none other than the pope of Rome. The mystery of iniquity, therefore, must be that the pope of Rome, who, being the son of perdition, is possessed by Satan. Just as Judas, who, also was the son of perdition and was possessed by Satan. As Christ was God manifest in the flesh, and is the "mystery of godliness," so also the antichrist is the devil manifest in the flesh and is the "mystery of iniquity."

The Roman Church teaches that Peter is the rock upon which God has built his church, and that the Pope, as the bishop of Rome, is Peter's successor, head of the church, and the "Vicar of Christ."[21] The Bible, however, is clear that Jesus Christ is the foundation and head of the church, not the pope. "And he is the head of the body, the church: who is the beginning, the firstborn from the dead; that in all things he might have the preeminence." (Colossians 1:18) So, the pope seeks to replace Christ as he opposes him. He is the antichrist.

Just as Judas, the son of perdition, pretended to be a loyal follower of Jesus as he worked to betray him (Luke 22:47-48), so the pope, who is also the son of perdition pretends to be a loyal follower of Jesus and is betraying his subjects into the lake of fire. Revelation 20:10, 15. The antichrist is the very opposite of Jesus; Jesus is the mystery of godliness, who is faithful and true and will never forsake us. Hebrews 13:5, Revelation 19:11.

The picture on this page is Pope John Paul II at the Sea of Galilee in Israel on March 24, 2000. Notice the satanic symbol of the upside down cross on the throne set up for the Pope. The Pope never misses an opportunity to blaspheme the Lord Jesus. It is not enough for him to blaspheme Chris via his devilish doctrines, he feels a need to also do so by the devilish symbolism of an upside down cross, which signifies a reversal of Christian doctrine, i.e., antichrist doctrine, it symbolizes a mockery and rejection of Jesus Christ.[22]

Pope John Paul II sitting on a throne depicting a satanic upside-down cross at the Sea of Galilee in Israel on March 24, 2000.

The Catholic Church never officially explained the upside-down cross, however, its agents on the internet explained that the upside-down cross is a symbol of Peter. The Catholic Church's mythology includes the story that Peter was crucified upside-down, although there is absolutely no evidence to support that claim.

One must be aware that all occult symbols have two meanings. One meaning is an open (exoteric) meaning that is for the general public, the other hidden (esoteric) meaning is only for those initiated into the secret doctrines. Russell R. Boedeker is an expert in occult symbolism. Boedeker is a 32nd degree Freemason and a Knight Command of the Court of Honour of the Scottish Rite of Freemasonry. He is also an instructor in the Portland Scottish Rite University and has developed and taught classes from the 1st through 8th and the 31st degree of Freemasonry. "His Masonic specialty and interest is in the field of esoteric symbolism."[23] Boedeker reveals that those who are newly initiated into Freemasonry are given explanations of symbols that are "meant to conceal the true meaning from the initiate."[24] Boedeker explains:

> The symbols of old from the ancient mysteries were not meant to reveal, but to conceal. When a new candidate was initiated into the lower levels of the ancient mysteries he was given an explanation of the symbols, but the explanation was erroneous and meant to mislead him; protecting the truth as only the adepts were allowed to know the true meaning of the mysteries.[25]

Albert Pike, who was (and still is) probably the most respected 19th century authority on Freemasonry, wrote in his treatise on Freemasonry, Morals and Dogma, that the occult symbols of Freemasonry have two meanings, one exoteric meaning, which is a cover for the true, esoteric meaning that is concealed and known only to the adepts. Pike states that "[t]here must always be a commonplace interpretation for the mass of Initiates, of the symbols that are eloquent to the Adepts."[26] Pike shamelessly explains that the public explanation of the symbols of Freemasonry are deceptions.

Masonry, like all the Religions, all the Mysteries,

> Hermeticism, and Alchemy, *conceals* its secrets from all except the Adepts and Sages, or the Elect, and uses false explanations and misinterpretations of its symbols to mislead those who deserve only to be misled; to conceal the Truth, which it calls light, and draw them away from it.[27] (italics in original)

Notice that Pike reveals that Freemasonry is in fact a religion, similar to the heathen mystery religions of antiquity. Pike further explains in Morals and Dogma that when one enters Freemasonry as an initiate, the higher order members lie to the new initiate about what the masonic words, symbols, and ceremonies really mean. It is only after the initiate progresses and proves himself that he is told the truth. At that point, he has progressed to become an "adept," worthy to know the satanic secrets of Freemasonry.

> The Blue Degrees are but the outer court or portico of the Temple. Part of the symbols are displayed there to the Initiate, but he is intentionally misled by false interpretations. It is not intended that he shall understand them; but it is intended that he shall imagine he understands them. Their true explication is reserved for the Adepts, the Princes of Masonry.[28]

Roman Catholicism is the ultimate mystery religion. Virtually every Roman Catholic symbol has a hidden meaning, known only to the adepts. In the case of the upside-down cross on John Paul II's throne, the open meaning is that the upside-down cross represents Peter; the hidden meaning, understood by occult practitioners is that the upside-down cross mocks the crucifixion of Jesus and is a rejection of his teachings.

The Catholic explanation for the upside-down cross loses weight in light of a picture of Pope Paul II while he was still a cardinal. He had not yet been elevated to Peter's mythical seat, yet he is seen in a trip to Chicago wearing a vestment bearing the symbol of an upside-down double-cross.

The double-cross is an occult symbol of premeditated betrayal. Even today, when someone is betrayed by a premeditated plan, they are said to have been "double-crossed." Cardinal Wojtyla was not yet pope, and therefore had no standing to claim symbolic identification with the Catholic mythology of Peter's upside-down crucifixion. It was certainly fitting, however, for another reason, that Cardinal Wojtyla was wearing an upside-down double-cross on his vestment. It not only symbolized his rejection of Jesus Christ, but also his intent on double-crossing his followers. The upside-down double-cross depicted accurately his attitude toward Christ. That picture is truly worth a thousand words. His earlier use of the upside-down double-cross on his vestments, indicates that the later upside-down cross depicted on his papal throne was simply a continuation of his practice of using esoteric satanic symbols. His earlier use of satanic symbolism also undermines the claim that the later satanic symbol on his throne symbolized Peter's alleged upside-down crucifixion.

Cardinal Wojtyla (later elected Pope John Paul II) wearing a vestment bearing a satanic upside-down double-cross.

One of the reasons that Babylon the Great, the Mother of Harlots and Abominations of the Earth is called "Mystery" is that she embodies the mystery of iniquity. The mystery of iniquity is that the antichrist is the devil manifest in the flesh. The pope, therefore, must be possessed by Satan himself.

3 That Man of Sin

Paul refers to the coming antichrist as "that man of sin." "Let no man deceive you by any means: for that day shall not come, except there come a falling away first, and that **man of sin** be revealed, the son of perdition." (2 Thessalonians 2:3) Ian Paisley explains the significance of the title, "man of sin."

> The apostle Paul completes the portrait of the Antichrist by styling him the "Man of Sin and Son of Perdition."
>
> Christ is the Man of Holiness, the only truly holy man this earth has ever seen. "That Holy Thing." Said the angel (Luke 1:35). "The Holy Child Jesus," said Luke (Acts 4:27). The apostle Paul witnessed that He was "Holy, harmless, undefiled, separate from sinners" (Heb. 9:26).
>
> The Pope, the Vicar of Christ, is the Man of Sin. He has invented sin, he has taught sin, he has enticed sin, established iniquity by a law, he trades in sins and has grown rich through the sins of Christendom. Sin is the Pope's work. Sin is the Pope's being. Popery is the incarnation of sin as the Gospel is the incarnation of holiness.

> The policy of the Pope as the Antichrist is not to deny truth but to pervert truth.
>
> He perverts the commandments of God and converts them into sin. He perverts the sacraments of Christ and converts them into sin. He perverts the offices of the church and converts them into sin. There is not a doctrine of the Bible which the Pope does not pervert and thus deny. King Jeroboam made Israel to sin. The Pope has made the world to sin.[29]

What does Paisley mean when he says that the pope invents sin? He means that the pope calls that which is righteous - sin. Indeed, the pope has determined that the gospel of Jesus Christ is sin. That is not hyperbole. The official doctrine of the Roman Catholic Church is that it is a sin to abide by the gospel of Jesus Christ. For example, in the Holy Scriptures, the point is made time and again that works are the fruit of salvation. Those same works, however, do not themselves merit salvation. Salvation is the unmerited gift of God.

> But God, who is rich in mercy, for his great love wherewith he loved us, Even when we were dead in sins, hath quickened us together with Christ, (by grace ye are saved;) And hath raised us up together, and made us sit together in heavenly places in Christ Jesus: That in the ages to come he might shew the exceeding riches of his grace in his kindness toward us through Christ Jesus. **For by grace are ye saved through faith; and that not of yourselves: it is the gift of God: Not of works, lest any man should boast.** For we are his workmanship, created in Christ Jesus unto good works, which God hath before ordained that we should walk in them. (Ephesians 2:4-10)

There is nothing man can do to earn salvation through works. Faith itself is not by the power of one's own will. It is a gift of God.

> But as many as received him, to them gave he power to become the sons of God, even to them that believe on

> his name: **Which were born, not of blood, nor of the will of the flesh, nor of the will of man, but of God**. (John 1:12-13)

The gospel of Jesus Christ is that our sins are remitted once and for all by the sacrifice of Jesus on the cross. We are saved by grace alone through faith alone in Jesus Christ. Once saved from the punishment of sin by Christ's sacrifice on the cross, there is no more sacrifice needed for our sins.

> By the which will **we are sanctified through the offering of the body of Jesus Christ once for all**. And every priest standeth daily ministering and offering oftentimes the same sacrifices, which can never take away sins: But this man, after he had offered one sacrifice for sins for ever, sat down on the right hand of God; From henceforth expecting till his enemies be made his footstool. For by one offering he hath perfected for ever them that are sanctified. Whereof the Holy Ghost also is a witness to us: for after that he had said before, This is the covenant that I will make with them after those days, saith the Lord, I will put my laws into their hearts, and in their minds will I write them; **And their sins and iniquities will I remember no more. Now where remission of these is, there is no more offering for sin**. (Hebrews 10:10-18)

However, the Catholic Church invents a sin where there is no sin. The official Catholic doctrine is that the gospel of salvation by grace alone through faith alone is sin. The papacy places a hellish curse on anyone who says that good works do not earn salvation. Council of Trent Canon XXIV states:

> If anyone say that the justice received is not preserved and also increased before God through good works; but that the said works are merely the fruits and signs of justification obtained, but not a cause of the increase thereof, let him be anathema.[30]

The gospel of Jesus Christ is that our sins are remitted once and for all by the sacrifice of Jesus on the cross. There is no more sacrifice needed for our sins. Hebrews 10:10-18. Catholic doctrine, however, curses anyone who states that Christ's one sacrifice on the cross is sufficient atonement to remit all of the sins of God's elect. *See* COUNCIL OF TRENT, SESSION VI, DECREE ON JUSTIFICATION, Canon XXX, January 13, 1547.

The theme of the Holy Bible is that sins are remitted for all time by the grace of God, not by any works that we perform. Salvation by the grace of God is mutually exclusive of salvation by the works of man. Neither can there be a mixture of grace and works. Romans 4:18; 11:6. All who preach the false gospel of works are under a curse from God (Galatians 1:8-9), which is effectual, unlike the Catholic curses. Read this author's book, *The Anti-Gospel: The Perversion of Christ's Grace Gospel,* for more information on the false gospel with which the agents of the papacy have infected the Protestant churches.

Salvation by grace, by its very meaning, excludes the possibility of any works that would merit salvation. "And if by grace, then is it no more of works: otherwise grace is no more grace. But if it be of works, then is it no more grace: otherwise work is no more work." (Romans 11:6) Abraham did not work for salvation, he believed God, and it was counted to him for righteousness.

> What shall we say then that Abraham our father, as pertaining to the flesh, hath found? For if Abraham were justified by works, he hath whereof to glory; but not before God. For what saith the scripture? **Abraham believed God, and it was counted unto him for righteousness. Now to him that worketh is the reward not reckoned of grace, but of debt. But to him that worketh not, but believeth on him that justifieth the ungodly, his faith is counted for righteousness.** Even as David also describeth the blessedness of the man, unto whom God imputeth righteousness without works, Saying, Blessed are they whose iniquities are forgiven, and whose sins are covered. Blessed is the man to whom the Lord will not impute sin. (Romans 4:1-8)

Those who believe in Jesus are cleansed not just from some sin but from all sin. That truth comes from God's word, and Christ is the word that became flesh. John 1:1,14.

> But if we walk in the light, as he is in the light, we have fellowship one with another, and **the blood of Jesus Christ his Son cleanseth us from all sin.** (1 John 1:7)

> The next day John seeth Jesus coming unto him, and saith, **Behold the Lamb of God, which taketh away the sin of the world.** (John 1:29)

The Catholic Church invents yet another sin and curses anyone who believes that Jesus paid the whole penalty for sin. That Jesus is the lamb of God who came to earth to take away the sins of the world is the heart of the Gospel. The Council of Trent Cannon XII states:

> If anyone saith that God always remits the whole punishment together with the guilt, and that the satisfaction of penitents is no other than the faith whereby they apprehend that Christ has satisfied for them; let him be anathema.[31]

The pope invents sin by heaping curses on all adherents of the gospel truth that Jesus Christ offered himself once for the remission of all the sins of his elect. Council of Trent Canon XXX states:

> If anyone saith that, after the grace of justification has been received, to every penitent sinner the guilt is remitted, and the debt of the eternal punishment is blotted out in such a way that there remains not any debt of temporal punishment to be discharged either in this world, or in the next in Purgatory, before the entrance to the Kingdom of Heaven can be opened (to him); let him be anathema.[32]

The Catholic curses from the Council of Trent on those who believe the gospel are still the official doctrines of the Catholic Church today. What better proof that the pope of Rome is the man of sin than that he makes it a sin to abide by the gospel. Cursing the gospel is cursing Christ; Christ is the Word who became flesh. John 1:1,14. All believers are disciples of Jesus Christ and collectively make up his Church. Christ's church is his body. Colossians 1:18. Cursing Christ's disciples is the same as cursing Christ. Acts 22:7.

> Ye know that ye were Gentiles, carried away unto these dumb idols, even as ye were led. Wherefore I give you to understand, that **no man speaking by the Spirit of God calleth Jesus accursed**: and that no man can say that Jesus is the Lord, but by the Holy Ghost. (1 Corinthians 12:2-3)

God laughs at the curses of the Church of Rome. "He that sitteth in the heavens shall laugh: the Lord shall have them in derision." (Psalms 2:4) The curses of the Roman Church are ineffectual, but God does not take blasphemy lightly. The Roman doctrine is a perversion of the gospel, and that organization and any others that follow its example are under the curse of God. God has placed a curse on anyone who corrupts the gospel of Christ, and unlike the Catholic curses, God's curse is effectual. "But though we, or an angel from heaven, preach any other gospel unto you than that which we have preached unto you, let him be accursed. As we said before, so say I now again, If any man preach any other gospel unto you than that ye have received, let him be accursed." (Galatians 1:8-9)

Some might think that Vatican Council II has changed the direction of the Catholic church, that it is no longer the bloodthirsty harlot of abominations that it once was. Vatican II is in reality a deadly deception. In Vatican II, Protestant Christians who were formerly referred to as "heretics" are now called "separated brethren." This Jesuitical deception becomes apparent when it is realized that Vatican II did not repeal a single papal bull or anathema issued against Christians by past Popes or Vatican councils. In fact, Vatican II reaffirmed the canons and decrees of previous councils, including the Second Council of Nicea, the Council of Florence, and the Council of Trent.[33] The Council of Trent alone accounted for over 100 anathemas against Christians and Christian beliefs.

Christians are still under the countless curses of the Roman Catholic Church, and the "Holy Office" that carried out the many previous inquisitions is still in operation. Just as a leopard cannot change his spots neither can the Vatican change its evil ways. "Can the Ethiopian change his skin, or the leopard his spots? then may ye also do good, that are accustomed to do evil." Jeremiah 13:23. The Catholic Church never changes. The official doctrine of the Catholic Church remains that there is no salvation outside the Roman Catholic Church. In the eyes of the Roman Church Protestant Christians are hell bound, yet they call us "separated brethren." Section 846 of the 1994 Catechism of the Catholic Church states emphatically that no person who knowingly refuses to join the Catholic Church or who leaves the Catholic Church can ever be saved, if they do so "knowing that the Catholic Church was founded as necessary by God through Christ."[34] That curse of damnation is aimed directly at informed Christians, who reject the legitimacy of the Roman Church.

In fact, in the official Vatican statement, *Dominus Iesus*,[35] the Catholic Church states that "ecclesial communities" that do not recognize the Eucharist mystery are not truly churches at all. That pronouncement alone makes it clear that the Catholic Church was being disingenuous when it stated in Vatican Council II that the Vatican considered Protestant Christians "separated brethren." *Dominus Iesus* was written by the Vatican's chief expert on doctrine, Cardinal Josef Ratzinger (Pope Benedict XVI), and it was ratified by Pope John Paul II, with the following purportedly infallible pronouncement: "The Sovereign Pontiff John Paul II, at the Audience of June 16, 2000, granted to the undersigned Cardinal Prefect of the Congregation for the Doctrine of the Faith, with sure knowledge and by his apostolic authority, ratified and confirmed this Declaration, adopted in Plenary Session and ordered its publication."

Not only does the pope reveal himself as the man of sin by claiming righteousness is sin, he confirms his identity as the man of sin by claiming that sin is righteousness. God commands us to keep from idols. Exodus 20:4-5; 1 John 5:21. The papacy authorizes, indeed encourages, the worship of idols. The Vatican instructs its Catholics to bow down to idols of the saints. The papacy curses those who oppose bowing down to idols.[36] The papal curse presumably includes a curse upon God. What more could the pope do to deserve the title of "that man of sin." The papal curse is ineffectual. The pope is under a curse from God, and God's curse is effectual. "Woe unto them that call evil good, and good evil; that put darkness for light, and light for darkness; that put bitter for sweet, and sweet for bitter!" (Isaiah 5:20)

Ian Paisley states that the pope "trades in sins and has grown rich through the sins." What does it mean to trade in sin? The pope trades in sin through a schedule of tax payments in order to grant absolution for sins. Pope John XXII (1244-1334) instituted the following schedule of fees for absolution of sin: Priests who wish to keep a concubine can do so if they pay seventy six francs, and one sou; a woman who is carrying on an adulterous relationship may continue in the adultery if she pays the pope eighty-seven francs, three sous; the husband who is taking part in the adultery shall pay the same tax; if either of the adulterous couple have committed incest with their children, they are to add six francs to the tax; absolution and assurance that the crimes of rapine, arson, and robbery will not be pursued requires the payment of one hundred thirty one francs, seven sous; absolution for the simple murder of a layman is taxed at fifteen francs, four sous, eight deniers; if the assassin has slain several persons on the same day, he shall pay no more; a husband who has rudely struck his wife shall pay into the chancellery three francs, four sou; if a man kills his wife, he shall pay seventeen francs, fifteen sous; if a man has killed his wife to marry another woman, he shall pay an additional tax of thirty-two francs, nine sous; all who have assisted the husband in the murder shall be absolved upon the payment of two francs per head; absolution can be obtained for murdering ones own child upon the payment of seventeen francs; if both the father and mother act in concert in killing their child, together they must pay twenty seven francs, one sou; the tax to obtain absolution for murdering a brother, sister, mother, or father, requires the payment of seventeen francs, fifteen sou.[37]

It is notable that along with the list of taxes for absolution are contained the following taxes: a converted heretic shall pay two hundred and sixty nine francs for his absolution; the son of a burned heretic, or one put to death by any torture, shall not be reinstated to the Catholic Church until he has paid into the chancellory two hundred and eighteen francs, seventeen sous.[38]

Barbara Aho explains that "[t]he word 'Vatican' literally means 'Divining Serpent,' and is derived from Vatis=Diviner and Can=Serpent. Vatican City and St. Peter's Basilica were built on the ancient pagan site called in Latin *vaticanus mons or vaticanus collis*, which means hill or mountain of prophecy. Coins minted in Vatican City often bear the inscription 'CITTÁ DEL VATICANO', which means City of Prophecy."[39] It is notable that the book of prophecy, Revelation, identifies the serpent, who is the namesake for the Vatican: "And the great dragon was cast out, that old serpent, called the Devil, and Satan, which deceiveth the whole world: he was cast out into the earth, and his angels were cast out with him." (Revelation 12:9) The serpent (a/k/a the dragon) gave his power to the beast. "And they worshipped the dragon which gave power unto the beast: and they worshipped the beast, saying, Who is like unto the beast? who is able to make war with him?" (Revelation 13:4)

It is no wonder, therefore, that the Vatican means divining serpent. The bible explains that Babylon the Great who rides the beast has "become the habitation of devils, and the hold of every foul spirit, and a cage of every unclean and hateful bird." (Revelation 18:2) That explains why "Vatican City has the highest crime rate in the world."[40] The man of sin is not only surrounded by sin, he dwells in sin. Indeed, he wallows in sin. Mark Binelli, in an article praising Pope Francis published in *Rolling Stone* magazine, had to acknowledge some of the historic evils committed by the man of sin.

> Writing of the Church under Clement VI, elected in 1342, Petrarch described prostitutes "swarm[ing] on the papal beds," adding, "I will not speak of adultery, seduction, rape, incest; these are only the prelude to their orgies." Norwich quotes the writer Gerard Noel on Pope Innocent VIII, who "grew grossly fat and increasingly inert, being able, toward the end of his life, to take for nourishment no more than a few drops of milk from the breast of a young woman."[41]

It was revealed in 2013 in *The Independent* that the Vatican is the landlord for a sodomite bathhouse. What is particularly damning is that Cardinal Ivan Dias "enjoys a 12-room apartment on the first-floor of the imposing palazzo, at 2 Via Carducci, just yards from the ground floor entrance to the steamy flesh pot. There are 18 other Vatican apartments in the block, many of which house priests."[42]

It is not a coincidence that there are 18 Vatican apartments on the street with the sodomite bathhouse. As reported in *The Guardian* and the Italian newspaper *La Republica*:

> A potentially explosive report has linked the resignation of Pope Benedict XVI to the discovery of a network of gay prelates in the Vatican, some of whom – the report said – were being blackmailed by outsiders.
>
> The pope's spokesman declined to confirm or deny the report, which was carried by the Italian daily newspaper *La Republica*.
>
> The paper said the pope had taken the decision on 17 December that he was going to resign – the day he received a dossier compiled by three cardinals delegated to look into the so-called "Vatileaks" affair.[43]

With the rampant sexual immorality at the Vatican, it is not surprising to find the pope voicing a lenient attitude toward sodomite priests. *The New York Times* reported "brief remarks by Pope Francis suggesting that he would not judge priests for their sexual orientation." Pope Francis stated that "if someone is gay and he searches for the Lord and has good will, who am I to judge?"[44]

Indeed, it seems that the Vatican is beginning to make a doctrinal shift toward accepting sodomite relationships. A recent preliminary report issued in October 2014 during a Vatican General Assembly of the Synod of Bishops presided over by Pope Francis was hailed as a breakthrough by some gay-rights groups.[45] The BBC reported that *relatio post disceptationem*, "[a] preliminary report written by bishops during a Vatican synod said homosexuals had 'gifts and qualities to offer.'"[46] John Thavis, who is a journalist specializing in the Vatican and author of *The Vatican Diaries*, which was a New York Times best-seller, characterized the bishop's report as an "earthquake."[47] The preliminary report states that "[h]omosexuals have gifts and qualities to offer to the Christian community," and asks the rhetorical question of whether the Catholic church can accept and value their sexual orientation.[48] Thavis pointed out that "[a]t least one bishop asked what happened to the concept of sin. The word "sin" appears only rarely in the 5,000-word *relatio*."[49] Clearly, the Vatican is going soft on the sin of sodomy. Of course, that is no surprise to those who know the real character of the Vatican.

The preliminary report was not approved in a final vote, which required the affirmation of two-thirds of the bishops.[50] The preliminary report, however, can be seen as a first step toward approval of the sodomite lifestyle. Steps have already been taken by the pope to clear out the opposition to the official doctrinal approval of sodomy. Conservative Catholic Cardinals and Bishops who oppose the liberal moves of Pope Francis on the sodomy issue are being demoted. This is being done to send a message that the Catholic clergy that they had better go along with the liberal changes in the official doctrines of the church on sodomites in the church. *MSN News* reported one recent example: "Cardinal Raymond Burke, the conservative American who holds the top position in the Vatican's justice system, on Friday told BuzzFeed he was being demoted. Burke, a former archbishop of St Louis, has publicly challenged Pope Francis on issues including abortion and homosexuality."[51] A day after the preliminary report of the Synod of Bishops was issued "Burke expressed concern, and said a great number of synod fathers had objected to the contents of the report."[52] Apparently, Pope Francis was displeased with the push-back he was receiving from the Roman Curia and decided to make an example of Burke by demoting him.

God's views on sodomy are contrary to the pope's and bishops' more lenient (or rather sinful) views. "Thou shalt not lie with mankind, as with womankind: it is abomination." (Leviticus 18:22) The prevalence of vile affections within the ranks of the Catholic priests is not surprising when viewed in light of God's word, and what God has said about those who corrupt the gospel. The reprobate minds of the priests have been seared by sin.

> Because that, when they knew God, they glorified him not as God, neither were thankful; but became vain in their imaginations, and their foolish heart was darkened. Professing themselves to be wise, they became fools, And changed the glory of the uncorruptible God into an image made like to

corruptible man, and to birds, and fourfooted beasts, and creeping things. Wherefore God also gave them up to uncleanness through the lusts of their own hearts, to dishonour their own bodies between themselves: Who changed the truth of God into a lie, and worshipped and served the creature more than the Creator, who is blessed for ever. Amen. **For this cause God gave them up unto vile affections: for even their women did change the natural use into that which is against nature: And likewise also the men, leaving the natural use of the woman, burned in their lust one toward another; men with men working that which is unseemly, and receiving in themselves that recompence of their error which was meet.** (Romans 1:21-27)

4 Ravening Wolves on the Prowl

The man of sin presides over the most abominable sins, which have permeated every level of the Roman Catholic Church. The man of sin traffics in the sin of pederasty. The victims of this sin-trafficking, whose lives have been destroyed, are cast off by the Vatican to live a life of suffering. Most of the victims are young boys. A research study by John Jay College revealed that between 1950 and 2002, 81 percent of the victims of molestation by Catholic priests were male.[53] The inescapable conclusion is that the vast majority of Catholic priests who engage in molestation of minors are homosexuals. The Catholic priesthood is the host of a predatory sodomite subculture, which preys, for the most part, on young boys.

The pope has tried to distance himself from the pervasive sexual abuse by his priests. He has taken the pubic stance that the perpetrators were wayward priests who were not properly disciplined by their individual bishops.[54] The pope has expressed a guarded reproof of his priests' predation.

An example of the half-hearted reproval is the speech that Pope Benedict XVI gave on December 20, 2010. In that speech, Pope Benedict XVI implied that the child molestation by priests is wrong; however, he "blamed the scandal on child pornography, sexual tourism and the moral relativism of the 1970s."[55] In essence, he was making excuses for the priests' inexcusable behavior. He made the appalling statement in his speech that "in the 1970s, paedophilia was seen as a natural thing for men and children."[56] Roberto Mirabile, the head of an Italian anti-pedophilia campaign group, La Caramella Buona, said: "When Benedict puts priestly abuse in this context, it sounds like he is trying to justify it."[57] Pope Benedict XVI was clearly trying to justify it. There are no ifs, ands, or buts about it.

Pope Benedict was suggesting that we must understand the deviant predatory behavior of priests, because in the 1970's society viewed that behavior as "natural for men and children." According to Pope Benedict's twisted moral code, the priests' depravity was justified, because there were some in society who thought that behavior was acceptable. Based on that logic, one could justify any depravity, simply by finding some fringe element of society that accepts deviant behavior.

Benedict's statement was not only inane, it was a purposefully deceptive mischaracterization of history. Since the time of Christ, through to the Protestant Reformation, and on to today, pedophilia has been viewed as deviantly sinful behavior. If anything, pedophilia was viewed with more disgust and aversion in the 1970's than it is today. Pope Benedict's statement reveals him as a deceiver and a reprobate sociopath. Devil possession tends to do that to people.

Benjamin Radford explains the savage moral turpitude of Pope Benedict's reasoning:

> Pope Benedict used his annual speech to Rome's cardinals and bishops on Monday (Dec. 20) to ask them to reflect on the church's responsibility in the child sex abuse scandals.
>
> Benedict qualified his mea culpa by stating that the scandal (in which priests who sexually abused children were often ignored or protected by the Catholic Church) was partly justified by the broader social context. Benedict said that while the church accepted some responsibility, he could not be silent about "the context of these times. ... There is a market in child pornography that seems in some way to be considered more and more normal by society."

35

Benedict claimed that as recently as the 1970s, "pedophilia was theorized as something fully in conformity with man and even with children." In this climate, the Catholic Church's actions were merely reflecting the moral relativism of the times: "It was maintained — even within the realm of Catholic theology — that there is no such thing as evil in itself or good in itself," Benedict said. That is, church leaders weren't sure if child sexual abuse was wrong, since secular society seemed to accept it.

The pope's statement is actually a logical fallacy with the Latin name of "tu quoque," roughly translated as "you, also," or "you're another." It's a version of a defense heard on schoolyards around the world when a child is caught doing something bad: "Well, he did it too!" This "everyone's doing it" fallacy is often invoked by tax evaders and speeders. One person's illegal or immoral act cannot be used to justify the same act by another person; it just doesn't work that way.

Pope Benedict is simply wrong when he claims that child sexual abuse and pornography were socially acceptable in the 1970s and 1980s, when the bulk of sexual abuse occurred. Even if it were true, there's little reason to think that pedophile priests would be especially susceptible to perceived secular moral decay. The Pope's acknowledgment, that Catholic priests do not have the wisdom nor the moral compass to realize that raping children is wrong or harmful, is a remarkable admission, and hardly comforting.[58]

Do not miss Benjamin Radford's perceptive interpretation of Pope Benedict's statement: "That is, church leaders weren't sure if child sexual abuse was wrong, since secular society seemed to accept it."[59] The essence of what Pope Benedict revealed in his statement is that the Roman Catholic priests raped children, because they did not think it was wrong.

Pope Benedict tried to blame the rape of children on the fact that the priests were acting in accordance with the societal moral norm in doing so. Since we know that it is a fiction that the societal norm was that it was okay to rape children, why would the pope say it was the societal norm? Because, he was trying to justify the unjustifiable. In the process, Pope Benedict revealed that hidden within the recesses of the reprobate consciences of the priests, bishops, cardinals, and popes is their belief that it is not wrong to rape children. The priests acted upon that belief, and the pope has justified their behavior upon that belief. The steps taken by the papacy to protect pedophile priests can only be explained by the fact that the papacy does not think it is wrong to rape children. Pope Benedict's statement is a tacit admission of that fact. The pope is truly the man of sin.

By framing the issue as a retrospective on the 1970's, Pope Benedict was subtly trying to portray the priestly rape of children as something that is in the past. In fact, it has continued unabated to present day, and Pope Benedict knew that. The only thing the Vatican is doing about it, is to institute steps to keep the evidence from becoming known and protect the priests from prosecution.

Pope Benedict's attempt to justify the pederasty of his priests goes hand-in-hand with the policies and procedures that have been instituted by the papacy to impede and obstruct justice at every turn. The case of Archbishop Jozef Wesolowski illustrates the institutionalized obstruction of justice by the papacy

Archbishop Jozef Wesolowski is being investigated by the Dominican Republic with criminal sexual abuse of minors. Archbishop Wesolowski was the Vatican Nuncio to the Dominican Republic. A nuncio is the representative of the pope, who acts as his ambassador. In his capacity as nuncio, Wesolowski is in direct and regular communication with the pope.

Cardinal Nicolas de Jesus Lopez, who is the Archbishop of Santo Domingo, informed Pope Francis in July 2013 about the investigation into allegations that Archbishop Wesolowski had sexually abused teenage boys in the Dominican Republic. Within a month of being informed of the investigation, Pope Francis recalled Wesolowski to the Vatican. Pope Francis did this in order to protect Wesolowski from being prosecuted for his pederastic crimes. The Polish government is also investigating Wesolowski for criminal pederasty. The Polish government sent a formal request to the Vatican to extradite Wesolowski to Poland.[60] The Associated Press reported the Vatican's terse rejection of the request:

> The Vatican has told Polish prosecutors that its former ambassador to the Dominican Republic, under investigation for alleged sex abuse, is covered by diplomatic immunity and that the Vatican doesn't extradite its citizens, Polish officials said in the latest development in an embarrassing case for the Holy See.[61]

In February 2014, the United Nations issued a scathing report against the systematic criminal conduct of the Vatican in aiding and abetting the worldwide rape and molestation of tens of thousands of children by Roman Catholic priests. The Associate Press reported:

> The Vatican "systematically" adopted policies that allowed priests to rape and molest tens of thousands of children over decades, a UN human rights committee said Wednesday, urging the Holy See to open its files on pedophiles and bishops who concealed their crimes....
>
> In its report, the committee blasted the "code of silence" that has long been used to keep victims quiet, saying the Holy See had "systematically placed preservation of the reputation of the church and the alleged offender over the protection of child victims." It called on the Holy See to provide compensation to victims and hold accountable not just the abusers, but also those who covered up their crimes.
>
> "The committee is gravely concerned that the Holy See has not acknowledged the extent of the crimes committed, has not taken the necessary measures to address cases of child sexual abuse and to protect children, and has adopted policies and practices which have led to the continuation of the abuse by, and the

impunity of, the perpetrators," the report said. ... No Catholic bishop has ever been sanctioned by the Vatican for sheltering an abusive priest.[62]

Keep in mind that it is the UN that is criticizing the Vatican. You would think that someone who lives in a glass house should not throw stones. Henry Makow describes the moral corruption of just one of the UN agencies:

> With disasters around the world—wars, earthquakes, epidemics, famines-- one would assume that the UN had its hands full. Instead, the UN gives priority to promoting abortion, homosexuality and birth control.
>
> The UN agency, UN Fund for Population Activities (UNFPA) is the paramount agency at the UN pushing sexual issues. Without exaggeration, the UNFPA is downright sinister. In 2008, UNPPA spent $165.1 million on "reproductive health" (i.e. abortion.)
>
> In December, 2012, UNFPA hosted a "Global Youth Forum" in Bali. The final declaration featured a call for abortion-on-demand, "gay, lesbian and transgender rights," and legalized prostitution.
>
> When UNFPA presented these results to the UN General Assembly, which is more representative of the popular will, the latter barely even acknowledged the document. In fact, UN diplomats refused to even officially "take note" of the document. They knew it was a set up by UNFPA.
>
> Delegates to the UN General Assembly have become weary of the UNFPA's harsh manipulation and insistence that abortion and sexual rights be introduced into countries which have no wish to go in this direction. Yet UNFPA continues relentlessly in pursuit of these issues.[63]

Even a morally corrupt organization like the UN is upset by the sexual predation of Catholic priests and the system erected by the papacy to protect the pederastic priests. A 1985 letter by Cardinal Joseph Ratzinger (later to become Pope Benedict XVI) is the smoking gun proving a scheme to protect pedophile priests. The Telegraph reports:

> The 1985 letter typed in Latin and signed by the then Cardinal Joseph Ratzinger [later to become Pope Benedict XVI] said any decision to remove Stephen Kiesle, a San Francisco priest, from the priesthood must take into account the "good of the universal church."
>
> The letter, obtained by the Associated Press news agency, could provide the first direct evidence to undermine the Vatican's insistence that the Pope was never involved in blocking the removal of paedophile priests during his two decades as head of the Catholic Church's Congregation for the Doctrine of the Faith, the department that deals with sex abuse cases.[64]

The Ratzinger letter is the tip of the iceberg. The papacy has established secret procedures that have been used for years to protect priests, sweep allegations of sexual abuse under the rug and dissuade sex abuse victims from pursuing their complaints with the police. CBS News Correspondent Vince Gonzales has uncovered official Catholic Church instructions stored in secret Vatican archives for over 40 years, which document that the Roman Catholic Church, at the highest levels of authority, has engaged in a systematic and pervasive cover-up of criminal sexual conduct by its priests.[65] On March 16, 1962 the Vatican sent secret instructions under seal stamped "CONFIDENTIAL" from the Cardinal Secretary of *The Supreme and Holy Congregation For the Holy Office*, Alfredo Cardinal Ottaviani, and personally approved by Pope John XXIII, to "ALL PATRIARCHS, ARCHBISHOPS, BISHOPS, AND OTHER DIOCESAN ORDINARIES 'EVEN OF THE ORIENTAL RITE.'"

The instructions, which were ordered to be "observed in the minutest detail," required all those in the Catholic Church who have any knowledge of a matter of criminal sexual conduct by a priest to be constrained to "perpetual silence" from ever revealing the crimes to anyone.[66] The instructions stated that the criminal sexual conduct of the priests is considered a "secret of the Holy Office."[67] The penalty for revealing such matters is "excommunication *latae sententiae ipso facto.*"[68] The clear intent of the instructions was to gag those with authoritative inside knowledge of the sexual crimes of the priests and shield those priests from criminal prosecution.

The secret instructions expressly mention solicitation and the "worst crime" which is described in Title V of the instructions as "any obscene external deed, gravely sinful, in any [sic] perpetrated by a cleric or attempted with a person of his own sex."[69] The "worst crime" also includes "any obscene, external act, gravely sinful, perpetrated in any way by a cleric or attempted by him with youths of either sex or with brute animals (bestiality)."[70] Those who take part in the official Catholic Church proceedings investigating the sexual crimes of the priests are bound by a solemn oath never to reveal anything about the criminal sexual conduct of a priest that surfaces during the investigation. Every person taking part in the investigation is bound by oath not to: "even for the most urgent and most serious cause, even for the purpose of a greater good, commit anything against this fidelity to the secret unless a particular faculty of dispensation has been expressly given to [him] by the Supreme Pontiff."[71] The fact that only the pope can allow an exception is proof that the pope is the authority behind the coverup. The coverup is complete with the requirement that "[t]he oath of keeping the secret must be given in these cases also by the accusers or those denouncing the priest and the witnesses."[72]

The Vatican instructions set out procedural protections that slant the investigation of allegations of clerical misconduct in the priests' favor. For example, the accuser must bring charges against the priest "within a month" of the alleged crime.[73] Furthermore, while witnesses must testify under oath,[74] the instructions state that: "In every way the judge is to remember that it is never right for him to bind the accused [priest] by an oath to tell the truth (Cfr. Cannon 1744)."[75] The above instructions from the Holy Office under the official seal of the Vatican proves that the Roman Catholic Church is actively engaging in a criminal conspiracy to aid and abet their priests in concealing their criminal sexual conduct in order to avoid criminal prosecution. Larry Drivon, a lawyer who represents victims of sexual abuse by priests, accurately characterized the instructions as "an instruction manual on how to deceive and how to protect pedophiles, and exactly how to avoid the truth coming out."[76] Drivon has concluded that the Vatican's conduct constitutes "racketeering."

The Catholic Church will do anything to conceal the criminality of its predatory priests, even to the point of obstructing justice by destroying evidence of the criminal sexual conduct of its priests. The Washington Post reported: "In a controversial 1990 speech before the Midwest Canon Law Society, Cleveland Auxiliary Bishop A. James Quinn advised church leaders to purge these archives, destroying all 'unsigned letters alleging misconduct.' The most explosive of the reports, Quinn advised, should be handed to the papal nunciature in the United States, which has diplomatic immunity. 'Standard personnel files,' Quinn said, 'should contain no documentation relating to possible criminal behavior.'"[77]

Make no mistake about it, the behavior of the Roman Catholic Church in transferring confirmed criminal sexual pedophile priests to new unsuspecting churches, knowing full well that they would continue their criminal abominations against other children, is criminal. The pervasive and continual pattern of such aiding and abetting of criminal pedophiles compounded by extraordinary efforts to conceal records and other evidence of their criminality can only be properly described as organized crime. "A well-known Minnesota plaintiffs attorney, Jeffrey Anderson, recently filed three civil racketeering lawsuits, arguing that the Catholic Church acts like an ecclesiastical crime family. The bishops, in his telling, cover up for pedophile priests by moving them from state to state to avoid detection. He named a star defendant in one case: the Holy See. 'They've used papal immunity to conceal documents, and that evidence leads us to the Vatican,' Anderson said. 'If they're going to act like mobsters, we'll go after them like the mafia.'"[78]

The Catholic Church has created an environment that is conducive to sexual deviance. The devilish doctrine of forbidding Catholic priests to marry is directly contrary to God's plan for the leadership of his church. As the following passages prove, God's plan for his church is that an elder be faithful to his word and be the husband of one wife.

For this cause left I thee in Crete, that thou shouldest set in order the things that are wanting, and ordain elders in every city, as I had appointed thee: If any be blameless, **the husband of one wife**, having faithful children not accused of riot or unruly. For a bishop must be blameless, as the steward of God. (Titus 1:5-7)

This is a true saying, If a man desire the office of a bishop, he desireth a good work. A bishop then must be blameless, **the husband of one wife**, vigilant, sober, of good behaviour, given to hospitality, apt to teach. (1 Timothy 3:1-2)

It may be preferable in many circumstances for a person to remain unmarried. God, however, knows that many cannot remain single without burning with the passion of the flesh. He, therefore, recommends that people who are single and find themselves burning with the temptations of the flesh get married. "[T]o avoid fornication, let every man have his own wife, and let every woman have her own husband." (1 Corinthians 7:2) See also, 1 Corinthians 7:8-9. When, however, men and women remain single because of some extra-biblical restriction, it is bound to result in sinful acts born out of the lust of the flesh.

God describes forbidding to marry as a doctrine of devils. 1 Timothy 4:1-3. The Catholic doctrine that requires priests to remain unmarried has been the cause of countless acts of immorality. There were 6,800 registered prostitutes in Rome in 1490 to service, for the most part, the clerics of Rome. Keep in mind, that was in a city with a population of only 90,000, and the figure does not include clandestine prostitutes.[79] Many Popes in fact were the illegitimate offspring of purportedly celibate Popes. For example, Pope Sylverius (536-537) was fathered by Pope Hormisdas (514-523), and Pope John XI (931-935) was fathered by Pope Sergius III (904-911).[80]

The sexual immorality continues today on a scale that is unimaginable. In 1994 former Jesuit priest Terence German filed a 120 million dollar lawsuit against the Catholic Church, Pope John Paul II, and Cardinal John O'Connor alleging that they had turned a blind eye to the "pervasive sexual and financial misconduct" of other priests.[81] The Catholic Church has engaged in a concerted coverup of the widespread pedophilia within the ranks of the Roman Catholic priesthood. The church knowingly transfers confirmed pedophile priests from one diocese to another, exposing the unsuspecting youngsters of each new diocese to the predatory sexual lusts of the priests.

For example, in Santa Fe, New Mexico victims have filed 50 lawsuits against the Catholic Archdiocese alleging that more than 45 priests had sexually abused 200 people over a 30 year period.[82] The Franciscan boys' seminary in Santa Barbara, California was closed down because the majority of the priests were involved sexually with their students.[83]

In Dallas eleven former altar boys won a 119 million dollar judgment against the Roman Catholic Church. The victorious plaintiffs later agreed to settle the case for 23.4 million dollars rather than be subjected to dilatory appellate tactics of the Catholic Church. The evidence revealed that the altar boys were the objects of the predatory sexual desires of Catholic Priest Rudolph Kos. Kos is now serving a life sentence for sexual assault.[84]

James R. Porter, a Catholic priest was removed from his priestly duties on eight separate occasions between 1960 and 1974 because he had sexually assaulted children. Each time he was removed, the Bishop and other high Catholic officials permitted him to return to his priestly duties in another unsuspecting parish. Each time he returned to his duties he resumed his pedophilia. More than 100 victims of Porter's sexual deviance have thus far come forward. He was indicted on 32 counts of sexual abuse. Porter admitted in a 1973 letter to Pope Paul VI to having homosexual involvement with parish children in five different states. While the Catholic Church provided Porter with counseling and care, there was no outreach at all to the victims of his sexual lusts.[85]

Catholic Priest Brendan Smyth was jailed in June 1994 after admitting to 17 counts of indecently assaulting young boys and girls from 1964 to 1988. His pedophilia began in the 1940's. He was transferred from diocese to diocese after each revelation. He engaged in his sexual misconduct in Wales in the 1950's, in Ireland in the 1960's and 70's, in the United States in the 1980's, and again in Northern Ireland in the 1990's. Smyth's superiors in the Norbertine Order of priests admitted that they knew for almost thirty years about Smyth's sexual assault on children, and yet they took no action other than to transfer him, thus allowing him to continue his pattern of child molestation.[86]

Even after being convicted of felony sex crimes many priests are not defrocked by Rome. For example, Gordon MacRae, Leo Shea, and Roger Fortier were all convicted of sexual crimes, but were merely placed on administrative suspension.[87] Shea and MacRea were convicted in 1994, Fortier was convicted in 1998. Yet they remain Catholic priests. The suspensions only prevent the priests from performing Catholic sacraments during the term of suspension.

Boston Cardinal Bernard Law admitted that he knowingly shuttled Catholic priest John Geoghan from parish to parish for almost 10 years between 1984 and 1993 after each new allegation that Geoghan had molested young parish boys, some as young as four years old.[88] That allowed Geoghan to continue his predatory molestation of over 130 young boys, many of whom have since sued Cardinal Law and the Boston Archdiocese.

The sad truth is that Geoghan is just the tip of the iceberg. The Boston Catholic archdiocese was compelled to release the names of 80 priests in Boston who had been accused of child molestation over the past 40 years. That list of 80 priests is by no means complete. For example, several men who were molested as young alter boys, came forward when they noticed that the list did not name Joseph Birmingham who was shuttled around to 6 different parishes as he committed serial pedophilia at each new unsuspecting parish. Birmingham died in 1989. One of the former altar boys, Thomas Blanchete, now an adult, told Fox 25 News (Boston) that he told Cardinal Law at Birmingham's funeral in 1989 about Birmingham molesting him and his brothers. To Blanchete's amazement, Cardinal Law invoked the power of confession never to speak of the matter again in an attempt to silence Blanchete.[89]

According to the Attorney General of Massachusetts, Tom

Reilly, the abuse by the priests in Boston went back 60 years and involved more than 250 priests.[90] On July 24, 2003, Reilly unveiled a 76 page report based on Catholic Church records. Reilly stated that the church made "deliberate, intentional choices to protect the church and its reputation at the expense of children. In effect they sacrificed the children for many, many years."[91] Reilly stated that a "culture of secrecy and an institutional acceptance" of clerical sexual abuse prevailed in the Boston Archdiocese.

Reilly stated that "the church authorities failed to report the abuse to law enforcement or child protection authorities"[92] Instead, the church quietly settled hundreds of cases with victims who reported their cases to church officials. In a handful of cases where the victims went directly to law enforcement authorities, the priests were prosecuted. By quietly settling most of the cases, however, the church was able to present a facade that the priests being prosecuted were an aberrant few, when in fact there were hundreds of pedophile priests actively preying on innocent children; the church knew it and protected the offenders. Reilly further stated that the church hierarchy aggressively lobbied against attempts to broaden laws to require self reporting by clergy.

Cardinal Law was forced to resign as Archbishop of Boston. Pope John Paul II then assigned him to the post of Archpriest of St. Mary Major Basilica in Rome. Cardinal Law retained his authority as a Cardinal within the Roman Catholic Church and was thus able to take part in the voting for two new popes, retired Pope Benedict XVI and Pope Francis I. Incidently, Cardinal Ratzinger (retired Pope Benedict XVI) was the Cardinal in charge of the Vatican's Congregation for the Doctrine of the Faith and was instrumental in protecting the pedophile priest Marcial Maciel, founder and head of the Legion of Christ.

The best indication that Rome approved of Cardinal Law's pattern of protecting pedophile priests was that he was chosen for the honor of saying one of the memorial Masses at St. Peter's Basilica during the *Novemdiales,* which is a series of rites over nine days in memory of the deceased Pope John Paul II. Officials from the Survivors Network, an organization that represents hundreds of victims of pedophile priests, traveled to the Vatican to protest Cardinal Law's prominent position in the memorial for the deceased pope. As Barbara Blaine, the president of the Survivors Network, was speaking to the media in Vatican City, two police officers approached and physically pushed her and the media about eight feet outside Vatican territory and back into Italy. Within an hour Cardinal Law and a procession of priests and cardinals in white and red vestments marched down the main aisle of the massive St. Peter's Basilica to say the memorial Mass.[93] The scene represented what the Catholic Church is all about: pedophile priests in all their regalia in positions of honor within the church, while their victims are cast aside to be neglected and ignored.

How many children were molested by priests in Boston? Attorney General Reilly estimated that the number "likely exceeds 1,000."[94] David Clohessy, Chairmen of the Survivors Network of Those Abused by Priests, stated that while the figures obtained from the Catholic records were shocking, they were, without doubt, partial figures.[95] The findings of experts who have studied child molestation seem to support Clohessy's conclusion. The recidivism among child molesters is very high. An Emory University Study conducted by a leading child abuse researcher, Dr. Gene Abel, found that the average child molester claims 380 victims in a lifetime.[96]

Assuming Dr. Abel's conclusion is accurate, that would mean that the 250 pedophile priests who have been shuttled through the Boston Archdiocese potentially could abuse a total of over 95,000 children during their lifetimes. One should be mindful that only a very small percentage of child molestation victims ever report their victimization, which in part explains why the total figures announced by the Attorney General were not much higher. Another explanation is that the figures cited by Dr. Abel are lifetime figures, and often priests are shuttled from one parish to another once they are caught, so a priest likely would not have committed all of their molestations of children while in Boston.

Finally, the figures used by the Attorney General were supplied by the Boston Archdiocese itself, which has a vested interest in mitigating the scale of the child abuse by its priests. As large as these numbers are, one should be not forget that this is just one archdiocese. Such abuse by priests has been taking place on this scale for centuries on a worldwide basis. The total number of victims of priestly predation is staggering. The Roman Catholic Archdiocese of Boston initially offered 55 million dollars to settle the hundreds of pending civil suits stemming from the sexual abuse by priests.[97] Ultimately, on or about September 2003, the Boston Archdiocese agreed to pay $85 million to settle the lawsuits brought by over 500 plaintiffs. The Huffington Post reported that "[i]n 2007, the Los Angeles archdiocese, which serves 4 million Catholics, reached a $660 million civil settlement with more than 500 victims of child molestation, the biggest agreement of its kind in the United States."[98]

The Roman Catholic religious order known as the Christian Brothers of Ireland in Canada had systematically used their orphanages and schools across that country to molest, abuse, and physically torture children in their care. The case was so appalling that, in 1996, a court in Ontario directed the religious order to cease its operations throughout Canada and sell off every scrap of property it owned to pay compensation to the victims of these heinous acts. That is not the end of the story. Unfortunately, the court picked the Chicago accounting firm of Arthur Andersen (of WorldCom and Enron infamy) to wind up the affairs of the religious order and liquidate the property. So far, Andersen has consumed all $7 million (Canadian) of assets it has recovered, spending some of it on its own fees and much of the rest on fees to lawyers Andersen hired. There are 43 million dollars in assets yet to be sold. However, Arthur Andersen is in arrears on its legal bills, and some of that money will no doubt disappear into the lawyers' and Andersen's pockets. The victims were molested by the Catholic priests and then robbed by shyster accountants. The news of the molestation by the Christian Brothers of Ireland was completely ignored by the major media outlets. It was left to Terry Roberts a reporter for *The Telegram*, a local newspaper in St. John, to report the story.

The world famous Boys Town Catholic orphanage just outside Omaha, Nebraska is a hotbed of pederasty. State Senator John W. DeCamp in his book, *The Franklin Cover-up,* revealed that his investigation of the failed Franklin Savings and Loan uncovered evidence that young boys were taken from Boys Town and transported throughout the country to sodomite drug parties.[99] The only concern of the Roman Catholic Church is to prevent any revelations that might harm its reputation. Senator DeCamp explained one case told to him by the Executive Director of Boys Town, Monsignor Robert Hupp, where a young child was sexually abused and murdered by a Catholic priest. This information was revealed to the Roman Catholic Archbishop of

Omaha, whose response was to ship the guilty priest out of state for "alcohol treatment." No thought was given to prosecuting the priest. Monsignor Hupp, however, was removed from his post as head of Boys Town, for the audacity of revealing the sins of a fellow priest to Senator DeCamp.[100]

Cathy O'Brien, in her book *Trance-Formation of America*, alleged that Boys Town along with the Roman Catholic hierarchy was part of a national syndicate that included elements from the federal government that supplied young children to rich and powerful pederasts throughout the world. She alleged that the syndicate used trauma based mind control to induce multiple personalities and amnesia in their victims. Many of the sexual activities in which Cathy O'Brien took part happened at the exclusive Bohemian Grove. She alleged that many of the world's government and business leaders would gather at the Bohemian Grove periodically and engage in all manner of deviant sexual conduct. Their aberrance was surreptitiously filmed apparently for the purpose of later blackmailing the politically powerful deviants.

Canon lawyer Thomas Doyle, coauthor of the Doyle-Moulton Peterson report on abuse in the clergy, estimated that in 1990 approximately 3,000 of the 50,000 Catholic priests in the United States were sexually involved with children. Richard Sipes, a former Catholic priest who counsels victims of abuse, confirms the estimate of Doyle that there are 3,000 pedophile Catholic priests in the U.S.[101] It has been estimated that 12,000 priests are sexually involved with adult women, and 6,000 priests are engaged in sexual activity with men in the U.S. alone.[102] Approximately 400 priests either confessed to or were convicted of sexually abusing minors in the 10 years between 1982 and 1992.[103] Catholic priest Andrew Greeley, in a 1993 essay in America Magazine, estimated that 2,500 priests had abused 100,000 victims in the United States alone. Thus far, the Roman Catholic Church has paid out an estimated one billion dollars in out of court settlements involving sexual misconduct by Catholic priests in the United States alone, and the fornication continues today.[104] Catholic officials have admitted that it has been their practice to reassign sexual offender priests to different parishes after the priests receive child sexual abuse psychological counseling.[105] There has been a recommendation by the National Conference of Bishops that the policy of reassignment of pedophile priests to new parishes be changed. It is not known if that recommendation has been implemented; one thing is certain is that any action taken by the church hierarchy will be just window dressing.

As a result of the public outcry over the pederasty in the Catholic priesthood, in 2002 the U.S. Catholic Bishops commissioned the John Jay College of Criminal Justice to survey the Catholic Bishops to find out the degree of the problem. On February 27, 2004, their report was issued. The report found that more than 10,600 children were molested by 4,392 Catholic priests between 1950 and 2002.[106] That means that 4 % of the 109,694 Catholic priests serving during that 52 year period had molested children.[107] The report acknowledged that because the figures were based upon voluntary reporting by the Catholic bishops, the figures were almost certainly an undercount of the true degree of the abuse.[108] Combine the voluntary nature of the reporting with the fact that the figures only take into account formal complaints, and one can safely infer that the undercount is significant.

Of the 10,600 reported cases, 6,700 were investigated and substantiated, 3,300 were not investigated because the accused priest had died, and approximately 1,000 of the claims were not substantiated.[109] The 145 page report stated that the culture in the Catholic seminaries, where the priests are trained, tolerated moral laxity and had a sodomite subculture.[110] The report further stated that the failure by the Catholic hierarchy to discipline sexually active priests created an environment that made clerics reluctant to report the sexual abuse of children.[111] The report revealed that 5.8 % of the abused children were under 7 years old, 16 % were 8 to 10 years old, 50.9 % of the children were between 11 and 14 years old, and 27.3 % were between ages 15 and 17.[112] The report revealed that 81 % of the victims were boys, and 19 % were girls.[113] The known costs to settle the lawsuits generated by the priestly abuse was reported to be approximately 572 million dollars.[114] As large as that figure is, it does not give an accurate picture of the damages paid out by the Catholic church. Many dioceses did not report figures and the total given in the report does not include the 85 million dollar settlement by the Boston Archdiocese, nor does it include the many hundreds of pending claims. A more complete accounting of the costs resulted in an approximate figure of a billion dollars.[115]

The most notable aspect of the bishops' report is what it does not say. The report does not identify a single priest nor the specific parishes that were the locations of the clerical abuse. Why is that critical information missing? Because the Catholic institution knows that to reveal the name of even a single priest would cause all those who were abused by that priest, but who have yet not reported the abuse, to come forward. That is what has happened in Boston and other places.

For example, when John Geoghan's name was publicized as a child molesting Catholic priest in Boston, the victims came out of the woodwork. Approximately 130 victims of Geoghan's child molesting spanning 10 years in Boston came forward. As explained earlier, Dr. Gene Abel, a leading expert on child abuse, determined in his research that the average child molester claims 380 victims in a lifetime.[116] Given that there were 4,392 priest involved in the reported molestations, there could be as many as 1,668,960 victims of child molestation by Catholic priests in the United States.

By only giving the raw numbers of official reports of molestation in the bishops' report, the Catholic church can conceal the true degree of the abuse. The Catholic church can then use its statistics to suggest that on the average each of the 4,392 pedophile priests only abused approximately 2 children over a 52 year period, for a total of 10,600 victims. When in fact, the reported 10,600 victims are just the tip of the pederastic iceberg. The purpose of the bishops' report was not to reveal but rather to conceal. The bishops' report is a smokescreen.

The papal response in covering up this epidemic of clerical abuse speaks loudly that the pope condones such conduct. The most glaring example of the pope's moral corruption is his handling of the pedophilia allegations against Catholic priest Marcial Maciel (1920-2008), founder and head of the Legion of Christ. Maciel founded the Legion of Christ in Mexico in 1941; he established seminaries in Spain and Rome.[117] The Legion of Christ recruits boys as young as 10 years old to leave their families and follow a course of study in prep schools in Latin America, Europe and the United States to become Catholic priests.[118] In 1978, the Legion's American leader, Juan Vaca, wrote a letter that was sent directly to the Pope John Paul II via diplomatic pouch by officials in the Rockville, N.Y., diocese.[119] The letter detailed a history of sexual activity he had with Maciel, beginning when Vaca was a teenage seminarian and continuing into his 20s. He also accused Maciel of having had sexual relations with other Legion of Christ students. When Vaca left the Catholic priesthood in 1989, he wrote a second letter to the pope repeating his charges.[120] "Vaca also told ABC NEWS how he was instructed to bring other boys from their bedrooms to Maciel's room. Vaca said Maciel had different boys visit his rooms on different nights. 'In some instances, two were together with him - myself and another one,' he said. Vaca said Maciel rewarded him with special privileges, such as a private meeting with Pope Pius XII, who served as pope from 1939 to 1958. Maciel always assured Vaca he was doing nothing wrong. When Vaca admitted concerns of committing a sin, Vaca said Macial absolved him from his sin 'in the name of the Father and of the Son and of the Holy Spirit.'"[121]

Vaca is not alone in his charges. A Florida priest, who also left the Legion of Christ, sent a similar letter to the pope.[122] "In 1997, nine priests, former priests and former seminarians accused Maciel of molesting them when they were as young as 10. They told the Hartford Courant that since 1978, they had tried and failed to get Rome to investigate."[123] ABC News revealed the surprising response of Pope John Paul II to such credible charges brought against Macial. "In 1997, they went public, telling their story to *The Hartford Courant*, a newspaper in Connecticut. *Courant* reporters Jerry Renner and Jason Berry, who wrote the story, repeated the allegations to the Vatican, yet received no response from the Vatican. However, later that year, the pope took a step that surprised them. Maciel was appointed to represent the pope at a meeting of Latin American bishops, which Renner and Berry took as a clear signal the Vatican had ignored the allegations."[124]

The signal being sent by the pope is not that he has ignored the allegations, rather the signal is that the pope condones pedophilia. Not only does the pope condone pedophilia, it is clearly part and parcel of the Catholic priestcraft. As reported by ABC News: "Then, four years ago, some of the men tried a last ditch effort, taking the unusual step of filing a lawsuit in the Vatican's secretive court, seeking Macial's excommunication. Once again they laid out their evidence, but it was another futile effort - an effort the men say was blocked by one of the most powerful cardinals in the Vatican. The accusers say Vatican-based Cardinal Joseph Ratzinger [later Pope Benedict XVI], who heads the Vatican office [Congregation for the Doctrine of the Faith] to safeguard the faith and the morals of the church, quietly made the lawsuit go away and shelved it. There was no investigation and the accusers weren't asked a single question or asked for a statement."[125] The most telling evidence that pedophilia is condoned by the Vatican is that Ratzinger, who so effectively swept the allegations against Macial under the proverbial rug, was appointed by Pope Paul II to investigate a sex abuse scandal involving scores of Catholic priests throughout the United States.

Maciel also led a secret life with a family, where he fathered several children. How did Maciel explain his long absences from the family? His son, Raul Gonzalez Lara, told ABC News Nightline "My dad told my mom that he was a CIA agent."[126] The family had no idea that he was a Catholic priest. His secret family discovered that he was a Catholic priest when they saw him wearing priest garb on the cover of an international publication announcing the allegations of pedophilia against him. His son, Raul Gonzalez Lara, has alleged that Maciel sexually molested him.[127] The molestation began when he was seven years old. Maciel died in 2008, and in 2010 Gonzalez Lara filed suit against the Legion of Christ.

How did the Legion of Christ respond to the lawsuit? They filed a counterclaim against Gonzalez Lara alleging that "Raul acted illicitly and/or against good customs in violation of Articles 7.145 of the Civil Code of the State of Mexico and 7.149 of the Civil Code of the State of Mexico when he willfully and knowingly used extortionate means to attempt to obtain $26 million from the Legionaries of Christ by threatening to cause embarrassment, hatred, ridicule and contempt through public allegations of sexual abuse."[128] Connecticut attorney Joel Faxon, who represents Gonzales Lara, said: "We know that the counterclaim is a spurious and ineffective effort by the Legion to intimidate and threaten the plaintiff."[129]

The 2010 lawsuit by Gonzales Lara against the Legion of Christ was filed in Connecticut, which is the American headquarters for the Legion of Christ. Yet the counterclaim from the Legion of Christ, filed in 2011, cites a violation of foreign law, which is entirely irrelevant to the merits of the Connecticut case. The counterclaim alleges extortion in violation of Mexican law (not Connecticut law) which is based upon the threatened publication of sexual abuse by Maciel. How could a matter that has become known throughout the world ever the basis of an extortion attempt? It makes no sense. The claim by the Legion of Christ is that Gonzalez Lara engaged in extortion by "threatening to cause embarrassment, hatred, ridicule and contempt through public allegations of sexual abuse." The Legion of Christ had already been embarrassed and ridiculed by the fact that its founder Maciel had been publicly exposed for having been the perpetrator of a long series of sexual crimes. Indeed, the notoriety of Maciel's criminal sexual conduct became so obvious to all that even his most staunch defender, the Vatican, finally had to publicly admit in 2010 that Maciel engaged in "serious and objectively immoral behaviour."[130] By the time Gonzalez met with the Legion of Christ officials to request payment of a trust fund that Maciel promised him, the damage to Maciel's and the Legion of Christ's reputation had already been done.

The response of the Legion of Christ to Gonzalez Lara's lawsuit got even weirder. In 2013, the Legion of Christ had 33 year-old Gonzalez Lara arrested in Mexico on the very same allegations of extortion cited in their counterclaim. Official corruption is rampant in Mexico, and the Legion of Christ, as with all Catholic institutions, are expert at using corrupt government institutions to their benefit. American journalist David Lida, author of *First Stop in the New World*, a book on Mexico City, stated that "given that most Mexicans don't trust official institutions, it's not surprising that people are voicing suspicions that the charges were trumped up in an attempt to discredit Gonzalez Lara and to salvage the scant remains of Maciel's reputation."[131]

Let us review the Vatican response to the Maciel pedophilia allegations. Pope John Paul II is personally notified in 1978 through diplomatic pouch by the head of the Legion of Christ order in the United States that he was molested as a child by Catholic priest, Marcial Maciel. The pope takes no action. The pope is notified again in 1989 by the same priest. Still, the pope takes no action. In 1997 nine other priests notify the Vatican that Maciel had also molested them and other boys as young as 10 years old. The pope responds by appointing the pedophile priest, Marcial Maciel, to be his official representative at a meeting of Latin American bishops. The victimized priests are so frustrated that in 1998 they seek a hearing in the Vatican to have Maciel excommunicated. Cardinal Joseph Ratzinger, who heads the Congregation for the Doctrine of the Faith, quietly blocks the legal action. There was no investigation; the accusers weren't even questioned. Then in 2002, when evidence of widespread pedophilia by

Catholic priests explodes in the U.S. media, the pope issues a statement condemning pedophilia among Catholic priests. However, he appoints Cardinal Ratzinger, who so effectively suppressed any hearing into the Maciel pedophilia, to head up the official investigation. The implications are clear. The pope and the Vatican verbally condemn pedopilia, but their actions demonstrate that they in fact condone pedophilia and are hell-bent on sweeping it under the rug.

According to the Holy See's chief exorcist, the worldwide sex scandal perpetrated by the Vatican is evidence that "the Devil is at work inside the Vatican."[132] Richard Owen, a reporter for The Times, reported:

> Father Gabriele Amorth, 85, who has been the Vatican's chief exorcist for 25 years and says he has dealt with 70,000 cases of demonic possession, said that the consequences of satanic infiltration included power struggles at the Vatican as well as "cardinals who do not believe in Jesus, and bishops who are linked to the Demon."
>
> He added: "When one speaks of 'the smoke of Satan' [a phrase coined by Pope Paul VI in 1972] in the holy rooms, it is all true – including these latest stories of violence and paedophilia."
>
> He claimed that another example of satanic behaviour was the Vatican "cover-up" over the deaths in 1998 of Alois Estermann, the then commander of the Swiss Guard, his wife and Corporal Cedric Tornay, a Swiss Guard, who were all found shot dead. "They covered up everything immediately," he said. "Here one sees the rot."
>
> A remarkably swift Vatican investigation concluded that Corporal Tornay had shot the commander and his wife and then turned his gun on himself after being passed over for a medal. However Tornay's relatives have challenged this. There have been unconfirmed reports of a homosexual background to the tragedy and

the involvement of a fourth person who was never identified.[133]

We don't need a Vatican official to instruct us on the presence of Satan in the Vatican. Satan's presence is clear. The Holy Bible tells us "Beware of false prophets, which come to you in sheep's clothing, but inwardly they are ravening wolves. Ye shall know them by their fruits." Matthew 7:15-16. The horrible pederastic acts of the ravenous priests is the sour fruit of the institutionalized witchcraft of the Roman Catholic Church. The pervasive abominable acts of the priests prove that the Catholic tree is corrupt to its very root. It cannot bring forth good fruit, because there is no good in it. It is good only for destruction, which God has planned for it.

> A corrupt tree bringeth forth evil fruit. A good tree cannot bring forth evil fruit, neither can a corrupt tree bring forth good fruit. Every tree that bringeth not forth good fruit is hewn down, and cast into the fire. Wherefore by their fruits ye shall know them. Matthew 7:17-20.

Those ungodly Roman priests are brute beasts being led by their lusts into destruction. The priests should heed the warnings of God. God destroyed Sodom and Gomorrha as a warning to those who would follow the ungodly example of the inhabitants of those two abominable cities:

> **[T]urning the cities of Sodom and Gomorrha into ashes condemned them with an overthrow, making them an ensample unto those that after should live ungodly**; And delivered just Lot, vexed with the filthy conversation of the wicked: (For that righteous man dwelling among them, in seeing and hearing, vexed his righteous soul from day to day with their unlawful deeds;) The Lord knoweth how to deliver the godly out of temptations, and **to reserve the unjust unto the day of judgment to be punished: But chiefly them that walk after the flesh in the lust of uncleanness,** and despise government. **Presumptuous are they, selfwilled,** they are not afraid to speak evil of dignities.

Whereas angels, which are greater in power and might, bring not railing accusation against them before the Lord. But these, **as natural brute beasts, made to be taken and destroyed**, speak evil of the things that they understand not; and shall utterly perish in their own corruption;   And shall receive the reward of unrighteousness, as they that count it pleasure to riot in the day time. Spots they are and blemishes, sporting themselves with their own deceivings while they feast with you; **Having eyes full of adultery, and that cannot cease from sin; beguiling unstable souls: an heart they have exercised with covetous practices; cursed children:**   Which have forsaken the right way, and are gone astray, following the way of Balaam the son of Bosor, who loved the wages of unrighteousness; But was rebuked for his iniquity: the dumb ass speaking with man's voice forbad the madness of the prophet.   These are wells without water, clouds that are carried with a tempest; to whom the mist of darkness is reserved for ever. **For when they speak great swelling words of vanity, they allure through the lusts of the flesh, through much wantonness, those that were clean escaped from them who live in error. While they promise them liberty, they themselves are the servants of corruption: for of whom a man is overcome, of the same is he brought in bondage.** For if after they have escaped the pollutions of the world through the knowledge of the Lord and Saviour Jesus Christ, they are again entangled therein, and overcome, the latter end is worse with them than the beginning. For it had been better for them not to have known the way of righteousness, than, after they have known it, to turn from the holy commandment delivered unto them. But it is happened unto them according to the true proverb, **The dog is turned to his own vomit again; and the sow that was washed to her wallowing in the mire**. (2 Peter 2:6-22), *see also* Jude 1:7-16.

The pope can falsely portray himself as trying to address the pederasty while at the same time aiding and abetting their flight from prosecution because the Catholic moral teachings permit such false denials and coverups. Lesson 17, "The Love and Service of Man," from *The Catholic Religion* published by the Catholic Enquiry Center contains the following Catholic moral guidance:

> It is lawful sometimes to conceal the truth or part of it. There are occasions when it would be harmful to oneself or others to tell the whole truth. It is not sinful to make ambiguous statements to make mental reservations on certain issues as when a person is bound by secrecy, or is questioned by one who has no right to certain information.[134]

God, on the other hand, has a stricter standard for honesty.

> These six *things* doth the LORD hate: yea, seven *are* an abomination unto him: A proud look, **a lying tongue**, and hands that shed innocent blood, An heart that deviseth wicked imaginations, feet that be swift in running to mischief, **A false witness *that* speaketh lies**, and he that soweth discord among brethren. (Proverbs 6:16-19)

> **Lying lips *are* abomination to the LORD**: but they that deal truly *are* his delight. (Proverbs 12:22)

> But the fearful, and unbelieving, and the abominable, and murderers, and whoremongers, and sorcerers, and idolaters, and **all liars, shall have their part in the lake which burneth with fire and brimstone: which is the second death**. (Revelation 21:8)

The abominable pederasty within the Roman church is evidence that it is the mysterious "BABYLON THE GREAT, THE MOTHER OF HARLOTS AND ABOMINATIONS OF THE EARTH." Revelation 17:5.

One might ask, how can people remain in such a church, when the prelates are so manifestly evil? In Michael Malone's The Book of

Obedience, he quotes a Catholic saint (Catherine of Siena), who explains the Roman Catholic view of obedience. This will give the reader some sense of how the Catholic "faithful" are conditioned to submit to the reprobate priests of the Catholic Church.

> Even if the Pope were Satan incarnate, we ought not to raise up our heads against him, but calmly lie down to rest on his bosom. He who rebels against our Father is condemned to death, for that which we do to him we do to Christ: we honor Christ if we honor the Pope; we dishonor Christ if we dishonor the Pope. I know very well that many defend themselves by boasting: 'They are so corrupt, and work all manner of evil!' But God has commanded that, even if the priests, the pastors, and Christ-on-earth [the pope] were incarnate devils, we be obedient and subject to them, not for their sakes, but for the sake of God, and out of obedience to Him.[135]

5 Satanic Ritual Abuse by Catholic Priests

There is a reason that pederasty is so prevalent among Catholic priests. Unnatural celibacy drives them to it. There is an unseen spiritual force that works on the priests. The bible states that forbidding to marry is a doctrine of devils. 1 Timothy 4:1-3. The pedophilia by the priests of Rome finds its source in demonic influence. The occult Luciferianism of the Catholic Church, has a very real subliminal effect on its practitioners, the priests. The Roman theology is an esoteric phallic theology, wherein the priests are driven by the devil to those abominable acts.

God explains in Romans 1:18-32 the process of religious degeneration wherein vile affections, like sodomy, are the direct consequence of idolatry. The Catholic priests have "changed the glory of the uncorruptible God into an image made like to corruptible man" (Romans 1:23), and teach others to worship graven images. All idols are demonic. 1 Corinthians 10:19-20. As a consequence of idol worship, "God also gave them up to uncleanness through the lusts of their own hearts, to dishonour their own bodies between themselves." Romans 1:24. God did this because they "changed the truth of God into a lie, and worshipped and served the creature more than the Creator." Romans 1:25. In Romans 1:26, God states that it is "for this cause" that he gave them up completely to vile affections. The cause God references in Romans 1:26 is idolatry, the resulting vile affections are the sins of Sodom, which God explains in Romans 1:26-27. The Catholic priests are possessed by the devil, through their idolatrous religion, and being possessed by the devil, they are driven to lust for the sin of sodomy; "the men, leaving the natural use of the woman, burned in their lust one toward another; men with men working that which is unseemly." Romans 1:27. God has given the Catholic priests over to a reprobate mind. Romans 1:28. The Catholic priests are possessed by devils who fill them with all unrighteousness, fornication, and wickedness. Romans 1:29.

Indeed, the sexual exploitation of the children by Catholic priests is part and parcel of secret satanic ritual abuse. In 1996, William Kennedy had a conversation with the famous Jesuit priest, Malachi Martin, who told Kennedy that his sources in the Vatican revealed to him that Cardinal Bernard Law was deeply involved in a ring of pedophile priests, many of whom were involved in satanic ritual abuse of their victims.

> Martin told me that he had solid information that Boston's prelate, Cardinal Bernard Law, was complicit in the operation of a ring of pedophile priests, some of whom were practicing Satanists. In the course of the next twenty minutes Martin outlined the evidence he had obtained concerning Law and other prelates in the American Catholic Church. He said that some of his sources in the Vatican reported that a major cover-up was afoot in Boston involving the Church, which was paying off former victims for their silence and using forms of intimidation to quell others who suffered under these vile priests. He told me of letters he received from victims in Boston, some of whom had suffered under the nefarious activities of a group of Devil-worshiping Catholic priests.[136]

At the time, Kennedy investigated the matter but could not substantiate Martin's allegations. Martin explained to him that he could not find any evidence of the satanic ritual abuse, because the Vatican was engaging in extraordinary efforts to cover up its crimes. Martin told him that the child molestation was so pervasive that the Catholic Church could not keep a lid on it, and it would soon break loose in the news. It was not until after Martin had died that Kennedy discovered the truth of Martin's allegations. In 2004, the Boston diocese child molestation case broke open and became front page news in the Boston Globe. Kennedy investigated the allegations and concluded that "there are priests of the Church of Rome who have brought together elements of Satanism and Catholicism in the rape of women and children."[137] Kennedy states:

> A few [victims of sexual abuse by priests] began telling me of their experiences, which fit the picture Martin had outlined. One man told me about being abused in a Catholic boy's home in what he called "the black room," a ritual chamber used by priests to rape young boys. Another man who also lived at this home told me about certain devilish practices that occurred in the black room. After reading Irish journalist Alison O'Connor's book *A Message from Heaven* (2000) about the priest crisis in Ireland, I learned that a certain Irish priest also used what his victims (who referred to themselves as "survivors") called "the devil's room" to molest children.
>
> There seemed to be a network of these ad hoc ritual chambers used by Catholic priests all over the world. This was all very hard to assimilate.
>
> As more and more reports of sexually abusive priests came out in the popular press, more and more cases of what can only be described as satanic ritual abuse emerged in the popular media. The complicity of the Church hierarchy made it a full-blown cabal, and the cases of ritual abuse revealed that this conspiracy was satanic in nature.

The discovery of satanic ritual abuse by Roman Catholic priests must be taken in context. Prior to the story breaking in the Boston Globe, there had been a series of notorious cases throughout the country of satanic ritual abuse that were proven to be hoaxes. William Kennedy analyzed those false claims of satanic ritual abuse and opined that they were orchestrated to act as smokescreens to conceal the very real satanic ritual abuse of Roman Catholic clerics. He discovered that there seemed always to be some organization affiliated with the Catholic Church at the forefront fanning the flames of hysteria over false claims of satanic ritual abuse. When the charges were later proven to be false, it had the effect of causing the media and civil authorities to ignore the real claims of satanic ritual abuse by Roman Catholic priests. Kennedy stated: "The Satanic Panic of the 1980s may in fact have been an elaborate ruse, acting as a smoke screen to cover the truly Luciferian activity engaged in by Catholic clergymen and their Vatican protectors."[138]

This same strategy can be seen in action in many notorious sex trafficking investigations. One recent example is Somaly Mam, the celebrated Cambodian advocate against worldwide sex trafficking. Mam became one of the most compelling activists for victims of sex trafficking. Her cause was joined by a who's who of famous people, including Hillary Rodham Clinton, Queen Sofia of Spain, and the pope. In 2009, Mam was listed as one of Time magazine's 100 Most Influential People. She was the namesake for the Somaly Mam Foundation. However, it turns out she was an impostor.[139] It has been discovered that Mam's story of being a sex trafficking victim is false.[140] It was further determined that some of the girls whom she presented to the media and talk shows, such as the Opra Winfrey Show, as victims of sex trafficking were also impostors who told fictional stories.[141] Mam's hoax was exposed in an investigative report that was the cover story for the May 30, 2014, Newsweek magazine.

According to the 2005 U.S. Department of State Trafficking in Persons Report, "[e]ach year more than a million children are exploited in the global commercial sex trade."[142] Worldwide sex trafficking is very real. There was no need to for Somaly Mam to present false victims with fabricated stories. There are more than a million children added to the list of very real victims each year. What possible motive would there be to perpetrate such fraud? The only explanation is that the rise and fall of Somaly Mam was planned in advance. It was done to discredit the real claims of sex trafficking and call into question the credibility of victims who escape their bonds to reveal to the world the abominable subculture of sex trafficking. There are very powerful interests involved in worldwide sex trafficking. Mam has served to undermine the efforts to investigate and prosecute sex trafficking crimes and rescue its victims. The Somaly Mam Foundation lives on, but effective May 28, 2014, Somaly Mam has resigned from the foundation, and the foundation has severed ties with her. How effective can a foundation be that is named after an impostor and whose namesake no longer has any affiliation with it? Such an organization cannot continue very long. Its mission to end human trafficking will itself be terminated. That seems to have been the objective from the start.

The strategy of creating false claims of satanic ritual abuse for the purpose of discrediting them seems to have accomplished the purpose of steering investigations away from evidence of satanic ritual abuse. Prosecutors and police seem to always try to downplay the ritual aspects of criminal cases involving Catholic priests. The 2006 conviction of Catholic priest Gerald Robinson is a recent example of that phenomenon. Robinson was convicted of the ritual murder of a Catholic nun, Sister Margaret Ann Pahl. The victim was stabbed over 30 times in the church sacristy, with many of the stab wounds in the shape of an upside-down cross, as though there was a cross laid on top of her with the stab wounds done in an outline of the cross. The ritual aspects of the murder were played down by the prosecutor, who made the following statement in his closing argument that "the murder was not a satanic or ritualized killing."[143] As Queen Gertrude said in Hamlet: he "doth protest too much, methinks." If what the prosecutor said was true, it was completely unnecessary to say so. Such a statement would only be necessary if there was evidence of ritual murder that he was trying to gloss over. After the guilty verdict was announced, though, the prosecutor admitted that the case was said by experts to be a "classic textbook satanic cult killing."[144]

A woman recognized Robinson when she saw news accounts of the murder. She remembered him as one of many persons who sexually abused her during satanic rituals performed from 1968 to 1975. Mark Reiter reported for the *Toledo Blade*:

> The woman said the abuse included chanting of Satanic verses, cutting her with a knife as a sacrifice to Satan, drawing an upside-down cross on her abdomen, and forcing her to drink the blood of sacrificed animals, such as a rabbit. She said the men dressed in nun's clothing and performed the rituals while she was on a table. They restrained her if she tried to leave. In addition to being raped and molested, the woman also alleges that she was forced to perform sexual acts on the men. She said the abuse escalated dramatically as

the sessions continued, to the point of including putting lighted matches to her feet and the corner of her eyes. She said the abuse took place in the basement of the church until 1972 when it was moved to an undisclosed wooded area. The lawsuit contends that Father Robinson and Mr. Mazuchowski "had a close relationship with Survivor Doe's mother, who also participated in the ceremonies in the woods and was becoming high priestess of Satan."[145]

She was not the only victim. She was one of four victims who came forward to allege satanic ritual abuse by Catholic priests in the Toledo, Ohio area. Michael D. Sallah and Mitch Weiss reported for the Toledo Blade:

Four women told detectives about being abused between the late 1960s and 1986 during cult-like ceremonies involving altars and men dressed in robes, the accusers told The Blade. "I've had nightmares about this since I was a child," said one woman, who asked not to be named. "I didn't think anyone would believe me."[146]

The *Toledo Blade* newspaper reported that a 41-year-old woman appeared before a church review board in June, 2003 to ask them to pay for her $50,000 in counseling costs she incurred as a result of satanic ritual abuse suffered at the hands of Catholic priests.

She claimed they gathered in church basements and rectories in "cult-like ceremonies" where children were molested and ordered to watch other youngsters being abused. She named four clerics, including Chet Warren, a former Oblates of St. Francis de Sales priest ousted from his order in 1993 after five other women accused him of sexual misconduct. She claimed Father Warren had orchestrated her repeated abuse, including arranging one encounter with the man now facing murder charges: Father Robinson.[147]

None of the victims knew each other, but each of their stories matched. What was the response of the Roman Catholic Church? On the very day scheduled for the interview of former Catholic priest Chet Warren, the review board ended the investigation and closed the case. The Catholic review board used the age-old trick of making an unreasonable demand as an excuse to end the investigation. The review board demanded that the victim be subjected to a psychological examination. When she refused, that gave them the excuse they needed to shut down the investigation.

> In an interview with The Blade, in which she asked not to be identified, the woman said she was upset at the church's request. "My question back to them was why don't they tell the priest who abused me to undergo psychiatric tests," she said. "Do hospitals ask rape victims to have psychiatric evaluations?" She said she allowed church investigators to talk to her therapist and family members. "I tried to comply with everything they asked."[148]

The Catholic Church simply was not going to investigate the matter, because they knew full well that it would uncover evidence that the widespread abuse of children is part of a pattern of satanic ritual abuse by priests in the Roman Church.

Kennedy's investigation of the sexual abuse by Catholic priests revealed evidence of satanic ritual abuse that seems never to be discussed by the media or the civil authorities. Kennedy tells of Roman Catholic priest, Shaun Fortune, who molested scores of young boys over several decades. The Catholic hierarchy knew that Fortune was accused of molesting boys as a Boy Scout leader when he was studying for the priesthood.[149] The Boy Scouts banned him from their organization and any Boy Scout events, but the Catholic Church had a completely different response. The Catholic hierarchy didn't seem to care that Fortune was a child molester; they ordained him as a Catholic priest anyway.

It was, therefore, not a surprise when, after Fortune was ordained, complaints of child molestation flooded in from North Belfast. The Catholic Church responded by transferring Fortune to the Church of St. Aidan near Fethard. Not surprisingly, he continued his molestation of young boys at his new parish. There were allegations that Fortune was the perpetrator of satanic ritual abuse of children. There was a room in a Catholic retreat house that some of the victims referred to as "The Devils Room."[150]

When complaints were made to Bishop Donald Herlihy and his successor, Bishop Brendan Comiskey, no action was taken against Fortune. Instead, Bishop Comiskey went on record several times praising the work of Fortune. The furor reached a fever pitch, which caused Bishop Comiskey to reassign Fortune. Kennedy states that "although Comiskey was aware of Fortune's sexual misconduct with children, his money-making schemes, and his practice of satanic sorcery, the bishop reassigned him in 1989 to Ballymurn, a parish far from his last parish."[151] This time, Fortune engaged the services of a sodomite lover and was found in possession of child pornography. The media caught wind of Fortune's behavior and investigated. BBC News producer Sarah MacDonald concluded that "the bishop and papal nuncio kept telling the victims that the matter was being investigated and addressed by the Vatican when in reality absolutely nothing had been done to halt Fortune's sex rampage. If anything, the Vatican's lack of action seemed to encourage Fortune."[152] Fortune's sexual abuse of young boys is believed to be the cause of the suicide deaths of four children in Fethard.

Roman Catholic priest Paul R. Shanley was associated with the Process Church of the Final Judgement, which was a satanic cult that engaged in all manor of occult practices, including sexual rites. The Process Church was closely associated with L. Ron Hubbard's Scientology and had strong ties to the infamous cult murderer Charles Manson.[153] It incorporated ceremonies of Freemasonry and the Knights Templar. It was an offshoot of the Order Templar Orientis, whose onetime leader was Aleistar Crowley. Crowley was a avowed worshiper of Satan who was so evil that he was called "The Beast."

Shanley would take part in ritual abuse of boys in the "Black Room" at the Alpha Omega House, a counseling center for troubled youth that was run by Bernard Lane, who graduated in the same 1960 St. John seminary class as Shanley.[154] Alpha Omega House was a joint project between the Roman Catholic Archdiocese of Boston and the Massachusetts Department of Youth Services. Lane was another of the pedophile Catholic priests who was shuttled from one unsuspecting parish to another and allowed to abuse young boys at each new location until he was found out and moved again by the Cardinal. The "Black Room," as the name suggests, was painted completely black and contained an inverted cross and a face-down crucifix, both of which are common features of satanic ceremonies. Young boys, ranging in age from pre-pubescent to 17 years-old, were taken to the room and forced to have sex with Lane, Shanley, and other priests.[155] The sexual activities were performed under the guise of "therapy" and "spiritual guidance." It didn't seem to matter who from the Catholic Church was in charge of the Alpha Omega House. Lane was later replaced by Catholic priest C. Melvin Surette, who was also accused of molesting children at the Alpha Omega House.[156]

William Kennedy opined that Alpha Omega House was an off-shoot of the Process Church. Both had ceremonial chambers, with the Alpha Omega House having the "Black Room," and the Process church having the "Alpha Room." The Process church also called their public rituals Alpha, and Omega was the title given to the highest rank in the church.[157]

Shanley was a child rapist and outspoken advocate of pedophilia. He was able to blackmail Cardinal Medeiros, who thus gave Shanley a free hand to sexually exploit children in the greater Boston area. After Medeiros died in 1984, he was replaced by Cardinal Bernard Law, who continued to allow Shanley and more than 100 other pedophile priests to prey on young children.

Catholic priest Shanley was emboldened by the fact that the Catholic hierarchy would do nothing to stop his rape of children. He became a gay rights activist and began attending gay rights rallies. Shanley gave a speech in 1977 in Rochester, New York at the Men and Boys Conference where he stated that he "could think of no sexual act that caused sexual damage to children — including incest and bestiality" and that "it is the child who seduces the adult in pedophile relationships."[158]

Shanley's speech reveals the dirty secret of gay rights: their ultimate objective is freedom to engage in pederasty without any legal impediment. Shanley's repugnant speech at the Men and Boys conference on the merits of sex between adult males and boys of any age, prompted the conference organizer, Tom Reeves, to establish the North American Man-Boy Love Association (NAMBLA).[159] The objective of NAMBLA is to legalize sex between adults and children. The host of the television show *America's Most Wanted*, John Walsh, whose 6 year-old son, Adam, was kidnapped and murdered in 1981, testified against NAMBLA. The organization responded by threatening to kill Walsh's young daughter, Megan.[160] Walsh was forced to move three different times in one year due to the threats to him and his family.

Wisconsin Catholic priest Alfred Kunz worked closely with Jesuit priest Malachi Martin investigating satanic ritual abuse by pedophile priests within the Catholic Church. His investigation into satanic ritual abuse was made almost impossible by the gag orders attached to monetary settlements, which closed off information from victims and the routine transfer of pedophile priests to new perishes, without any information about the location of the newly assigned parish.[161] Apparently, Kunz was getting too close to the truth of satanic ritual abuse. On March 4, 1998, he was found murdered, with his throat slashed from ear to ear.

Kennedy opined that the killing of Kunz bore the characteristics of a satanic cult murder of someone the cultists viewed as having inside information. Kennedy explains:

> In various secret societies, rituals involve certain oaths and penalties for anyone who exposes the operation of the cult, including outsiders. The most common of these penalties involves the betrayer having his throat slit. Such fraternal organizations maintain their power over members through ritual programming and do not tolerate security breaches. Examples of this can be found in Illustrations of Freemasonry, by Captain William Morgan, a book which exposed many of this fraternity's secret inner workings. Its author was likewise murdered and found with his throat slit, his body floating in a river.[162]

Kuntz, was a Catholic priest, who was seeking to expose the Luciferian influence within the Catholic clergy. According to their satanic ethic, because Kuntz was viewed as one of the insiders in the Catholic clergy, he was deserving of having his throat slit. Kennedy spoke with Malachi Martin about the murder of Kunz:

> In an interview six weeks after Kunz's murder, Martin swore he had inside information that the killing was the "signature" work of 'Luciferians.' ... "What Luciferians resent is interference with someone they regard as theirs. ... We are all convinced beyond anything that he was killed in hatred of the faith as punishment and as an example for the rest of us."[163]

By 1990, Shanleys' Catholic Church personnel file was bulging with multiple allegations of child abuse. Despite that fact, Catholic priest Robert Banks, a top deputy to Cardinal Bernard Law, sent the San Bernardino Roman Catholic diocese a letter vouching for him. Banks wrote: "I can assure you that Father Shanley has no problem that would be a concern to your diocese."[164]

Once in California, Shanley, along with another pedophile priest from Boston, John J. White, purchased a hotel that catered exclusively to sodomites. It has not been established where the two priests got the money to buy a hotel. The "clothing optional" hotel was considered a must place for sodomites, who engaged in open sex by the pool. Shanley would bring in young underage boys, whom he would pimp out to his guests, who came from all over the world for illicit sex with boys brought there by Shanley.

When it looked like Shanley's hotel pimping activities in California might become known, Shanley was transferred by the Catholic Church to New York. Upon his arrival in New York, Shanley was appointed the acting director of Leo House, which was a guest house run by the Catholic Church for students and clergy. William Kennedy determined that "Leo House turned out to be another front for gay sex and man-boy love."[165]

With full knowledge of Shanley's criminal pederasty, Cardinal Law granted Shanley retirement in 1996 from the Catholic priesthood, with full pay and health benefits. Cardinal Law said this about Shanley in his farewell letter: "for 30 years in assigned ministry you brought

God's Word and His Love to His people and I know that that [sic] continues to be your goal despite some difficult limitations."[166] The civil authorities had a different opinion of Shanley's career. In February 2005, Shanley was found guilty of rape of a male minor. He received a sentence of 12 to 15 years in prison. On January 10, 2010, the Supreme Court of Massachusetts unanimously affirmed Shanley's conviction.

Kennedy revealed the satanic ritual abuse perpetrated by Catholic priest Robert Meffan. Meffan was involved in sexual rituals with young girls he recruited to be nuns. He engaged in arcane occult rituals where the girls would have sex with him as a form of religious worship. He convinced the young girls that he was Christ and that they were brides of Christ, and in that role should have sex with him. His theology paralleled that of Satanist Aleister Crowley.[167]

> It is anyone's guess how or where Robert Meffan learned about sex magic, but it is clear he practiced it within the confines of the Sisters of Saint Joseph nunnery. Like Crowley, Meffan considered himself an incarnation of Jesus Christ. Like Crowley, he recruited young, emotionally disturbed women. Like Crowley, he offered these girls unique mystical experiences for participating in occult ceremonies. Like Crowley, Meffan employed visualization and sex rituals (one may recall that Meffan told the girls to think of themselves as "brides of Christ having sex with Jesus in Heaven") to confirm his own divinity in his own mind.[168]

Kennedy wonders where Meffan learned about sex magic. The answer is that he learned it in the Catholic seminary. Meffan's satanic ritual sex practice is based upon the very foundations of Catholic theology. The official doctrine of the Catholic Church is that the priest is *alter-Christos* (another Christ). The following doctrine is given on a Roman Catholic website at www.catholic.com: "The Church teaches that the priest ministers *in persona Christi*, in the person of Christ."[169] This doctrine is confirmed in § 1581 of the Catholic Catechism, which states that the sacrament of Holy Orders "configures the recipient to Christ by a special grace of the Holy Spirit, so that he may serve as Christ's instrument for his Church. By ordination one is enabled to act as a representative of Christ, Head of the Church, in his triple office of priest, prophet, and king."

The Catholic priest acts as the very person of Christ once he is ordained by receiving Holy Orders. It is the official doctrine that no matter how evil is the Catholic priest, he remains in true character, *alter-Christos* (another Christ). The Catholic Catechism at § 1584 states unequivocally:

> Since it is ultimately Christ who acts and effects salvation through the ordained minister, the unworthiness of the latter does not prevent Christ from acting. St. Augustine states this forcefully: As for the proud minister, he is to be ranked with the devil. Christ's gift is not thereby profaned: what flows through him keeps its purity, and what passes through him remains dear and reaches the fertile earth.... the spiritual power of the sacrament [of Holy Orders] is indeed comparable to light: those to be enlightened receive it in its purity, and if it should pass through defiled beings, it is not itself defiled.

An authorized Catholic order known as *Opus Sanctorum Angelorum* described by the Vatican as "a public association of the Church in conformity with traditional doctrine and with the directives of the Holy See,"[170] summarized the official Catholic doctrine that the Jesus Christ is present in the person of the Catholic priest:

> Christ remains among us, however, in more ways than in His substantial presence in the Eucharist. As the Second Vatican Council teaches following the long tradition of the Church, **Christ is also really present among us "in the person of His minister"** (Sacrosanctum Concilium, 7). **The priest makes Christ present because he acts in persona Christi** at every liturgical celebration. In persona Christi, as Pope John Paul II teaches, "means more than offering 'in the name of' or 'in the place of' Christ. In persona means in specific sacramental identification with the eternal High Priest Who is the author and principal subject of

this sacrifice of His, a sacrifice in which, in truth, nobody can take His place" (Dominicae Cenae, 8). **When, therefore, the priest says, "This is My body...This is My blood", it is Christ Himself Who speaks and offers Himself to the Father.** When the priest absolves us from our sins, he does not say "Christ absolves you from your sins". Rather, he says, "Ego te absolvo... I absolve you", that is, Christ acting in me absolves you from your sins. On the altar, in the confessional, praying the divine office: **Christ is there, really present, in the person of His minister.**[171] (emphasis added)

That deification of the priest is confirmed by Pope Paul VI's 1963 Constitution on the Sacred Liturgy (*Sacrosanctum Concilium*):

To accomplish so great a work, Christ is always present in His Church, especially in her liturgical celebrations. **He is present in the sacrifice of the Mass, not only in the person of His minister,** "the same now offering, through the ministry of priests, who formerly offered himself on the cross", but especially under the Eucharistic species. ... From this it follows that every liturgical celebration, because it is an action of **Christ the priest** and of His Body which is the Church.[172] (emphasis added)

In occult writings, there are often two ways to read a passage; one for the initiates and another for the uninitiated. In the above passage, the term "Christ the priest" could be read as a series, where it is meant to list Christ and then the priest. However, such a reading would require a comma after "Christ." The explanation given to the uninitiated is that the missing comma was a mistake. However, when you read the document for what it actually says, it is clearly expressing the idea that the priest is Christ. Hence, the esoteric and correct reading is "Christ the priest." Although he doesn't use the term "Christ the priest," the doctrinal meaning of "Christ the priest" is reiterated by Pope John Paul II in his encyclical letter *Dominicae Cenae*:

The priest offers the holy Sacrifice in persona Christi;

this means more than offering "in the name of" or "in place of" Christ. In persona means in specific sacramental identification with "the eternal High Priest" who is the author and principal subject of this sacrifice of His, a sacrifice in which, in truth, nobody can take His place.[173] (emphasis added)

Jesus stated that "many shall come in my name, saying, I am Christ; and shall deceive many." (Matthew 24:5) Prophecies often have dual fulfilment, and that is one of them. The many popes are the prophesied "many" who will come in Christ's name and say "I am Christ." So also the many priests are the prophesied "many" who shall come in Christ's name and say "I am Christ." The many popes and priests are closely related as one cannot become pope without first being a priest. The issue was of great concern to Jesus, as he repeatedly mentioned it. He warned people not to be deceived and follow after the "many" who would claim to be Christ. "And he said, Take heed that ye be not deceived: for many shall come in my name, saying, I am Christ; and the time draweth near: go ye not therefore after them." (Luke 21:8)

Furthermore, nuns are in fact inculcated with the belief that they are brides of Christ. The doctrine of the priests being "*in persona Christi*" combined with the doctrine of the nuns being "brides of Christ," act as potent ingredients for licentiousness. Those explosive ingredients for sin find their flash point in the nun's vow of obedience to the priests. The rampant sexual abuse of nuns by priests finds its cause in the vile doctrines of the Catholic Church. Meffan's satanic ritual abuse theology is explained completely by Roman Catholic doctrine. Indeed, Maria Monk reveals that upon taking the black veil as a cloistered nun she was informed by the mother superior that she must take an oath of obedience to the priests, which included obeying their command to have sexual intercourse with her. The mother superior persuaded Maria Monk that she should view such licentiousness as a virtue, that such conduct was doing a service to God. The mother superior stated that the nuns should deny nothing to the priest, because of the great sacrifices made by the priests on behalf of the world. She stated that the priests should be looked upon as their saviors, because they have the power to forgive their sins. Later that very day, Maria Monk was gang-raped by several priests, which seemed to be part of her initiation ritual into the cloistered nunnery.[174]

It is notable that Satanist Aleister Crowley, just as do Catholic priests, believed that he was Christ. Here we have a Satanist and Catholic priests sharing the same delusive megalomania. The parallelism reveals the Catholic theology as being essentially satanic.

The pattern of the Vatican is to continue to support and defend priests during and after their having raped children. For example, Bishop Robert Banks urged prosecutor to be lenient with Catholic priest Eugene O'Sullivan, who pleaded guilty to raping a young alter boy. The shameful thing is that when Banks requested leniency for O'Sullivan, Banks knew that there were yet other victims that O'Sullivan had raped.[175] After Catholic priest John R. Hanlon was indicted on rape charges in 1992, Bishop Alfred C. Hughes concealed from law enforcement officials evidence that he had about a second victim of Hanlon.[176]

An often ignored aspect of pedophile priests is the evidence of satanic ritual abuse. The evidence of evil spiritual influence is present, but it is simply not reported. To pull that string will unravel the cover that conceals the Luciferian theology of Roman Catholicism. It seems that there is a concerted effort by the media and civil authorities to ignore any evidence of satanic rituals being a part of the pedophilia practiced by the pederastic Catholic priests. Kennedy opines that the Roman Church made two major concession during Vatican II. The first concession was to allow overt membership by Catholics in Masonic orders. The second concession was the secret protection of the very powerful cliche of Satan worshiping pederasts in the Roman Catholic Church that Malachi Martin called "Lucifer's Lodge." The child molestation by the Catholic clergy is part and parcel of satanic ritual abuse.

> Malachi Martin called "Lucifer's Lodge" — the cult of Luciferian and Satanist priests who operated covertly in the Church with the protection of Catholic prelates. Satanist Catholic priests like Sean Fortune and Bernard J. Lane were practicing a form of Luciferian religion even though they did not seek to be worshiped as Christ. Indeed, they performed what Martin referred to as "the culmination of the Fallen Angel's rites" — i.e., the rape of male children. In this diabolical

scenario the child becomes a substitute for Christ. The Satanist priest destroys the innocence of his victim as an attack upon the innocence of Christ. In this sense the male child victim becomes a proxy for the symbolic destruction of God — a clearly Luciferian practice. Luciferian and Satanist priests are merely different sides of the same diabolic coin, with the Satanists practicing what is considered by this cult to be a somewhat higher form of Devil worship.[177]

William Kennedy cites the March 16, 1962, secret instructions under seal and personally approved by Pope John XXIII, as evidence of the official papal accommodation and protection of the significant Luciferian pedophile element in the Roman Catholic Church. The secret instructions from the pope were never meant to be revealed publicly. The secret instructions set out procedural protections that slant the investigation of allegations of clerical misconduct in the priests' favor and served to conceal the revelation of satanic ritual abuse by priests. The instructions, which were ordered to be "observed in the minutest detail," required all those in the Catholic Church who have any knowledge of a matter of criminal sexual conduct by a priest to be constrained to "perpetual silence" from ever revealing the crimes to anyone.[178] The secret instructions stated that the criminal sexual conduct of the priests is considered a "secret of the Holy Office."[179] Larry Drivon, a lawyer who represents victims of sexual abuse by priests, accurately characterized the instructions as a form of racketeering. He stated that the instructions from the pope served over the years as "an instruction manual on how to deceive and how to protect pedophiles, and exactly how to avoid the truth coming out."[180]

Catholic priests are raping young children as part of their occult worship of the fallen angel, Lucifer. Devil possession is the result of satanic ceremonies. The devil possessed priests are driven by Satan to engage in abominable sexual deviancy. Because of that, the pederasty by the Catholic clergy will never end. The Vatican knows that it cannot stop the pedophilia by devil possessed priests and it has no intention of doing so. It is the very nature of beast. That is why virtually all of its efforts are focused on concealment. It must conceal the evidence of its satanic ritual abuse of children at all costs.

6 Speaking Lies in Hypocrisy

Some try to defend the pope against being the man of sin of 2 Thessalonians 2:3 by pointing to the charitable works of the Catholic Church. A closer look at those charities, however, reveals that they are fronts designed to conceal the dark plans of the man of sin. The Vatican is truly the habitation of seducing spirits "speaking lies in hypocrisy." See 1 Timothy 4:1-3.

The papacy presents a public facade of righteousness. That pubic facade, however, is a smokescreen that conceals an anti-Christian agenda. The papacy is the progeny of the hypocritical scribes and Pharisees, condemned by Jesus. Matthew 23:13-15. The Roman Catholic Church funds organizations that work to undermine biblical standards, all the while claiming to uphold those very standards.

For example, the Catholic Campaign for Human Development (CCHD) gives millions of dollars in grants to numerous radical left organizations. CCHD was founded in 1970 as the Catholic bishops' anti-poverty program. In 1997 CCHD funded the following organizations, all of which endorsed the National Organization for Women's (NOW) 1996 "Fight for the Right" [to abortion] march in San Francisco: Association of Community Organizations for Reform Now (ACORN) ($310,000 grant from CCHD), Asian Immigrant Women Advocates ($20,000 grant from CCHD), the Center for Third World Organizing (CTWO) ($25,000 grant from CCHD), the Chinese Progressive Association ($30,000 grant from CCHD), and the Santa Clara Center for Occupational Safety and Health ($30,000 grant from

CCHD).[181] ACORN was a co-sponsor of the February 1996 conference of the Feminist Majority Foundation which advocates abortion rights. The CTWO advocates homosexual marriage laws. CTWO in turn sponsors WAGE (Winning Action for Gender Equality), which is harshly critical of those such as Christians who support the traditional nuclear family and Christian values.

CCHD funds many radical left and communist front organizations indirectly by funding coalitions of allegedly charitable groups.[182] For example, in 1997 CCHD awarded a grant to Greater Birmingham Ministries, which in turn sponsored another coalition, Alabama Arise. Members of Alabama Arise included the AFL-CIO and the American Civil Liberties Union (ACLU).[183] CCHD also awarded a grant to the Philadelphia Unemployment Project Coalition for JOBS; that coalition included AFSCME locals, the Pennsylvania AFL-CIO, the state chapter of NOW, and the Woman's Law Project (WLP).[184] NOW is an aggressive proponent of abortion and special sodomite rights. NOW supports partial birth abortions and opposes any restriction on abortion, including parental notification. The WLP is a legal services provider in Philadelphia that advocates lesbian and homosexual parenting rights and abortion rights. AFSME and the AFL-CIO both contribute to groups that advocate abortion rights and homosexual "marriage." The ACLU is the leading opponent of religious freedom in schools and opposes restrictions on abortions.

Some might argue that the Catholic bishops just made some errors. The evidence, however, suggests that the leftist anti-American slant to the CCHD grants is knowing and purposeful. For the past ten years the Capital Research Center has publicized to all who would listen the radical left slant to the CCHD grants, but the CCHD has done little to nothing to curtail the support of the radical anti-Christian left.[185]

The CCHD responded in 1998 to criticism by proposing changes to its guidelines. The new guidelines were adopted, and they specifically forbade the CCHD from awarding grants to organizations which "promote or support abortion, euthanasia, the death penalty, or any other affront to human life and dignity."[186] Apparently the new guidelines were merely lip service, designed to appease conservative Catholics. There, in fact, has been no significant change in the grants by the CCHD. The CCHD is still funneling money to radical left, communist, and pro abortion organizations.

For Example, not only did the CCHD not cut off its funding of ACORN in 1999-2000, they increased the funding for 17 state and local chapters of ACORN by 18%, to a total of $517,000.[187] The CCHD also continued to fund the Philadelphia Unemployment Project during 1999-2000. The project's "Jobs Campaign" coalition includes a branch of ACORN, AFSCME locals, the Pennsylvania and Philadelphia AFL-CIO, the state chapter of NOW, and the Women's Law Project, all of which support abortion rights.[188] In addition, the CCHD continues its perennial financial support to affiliates of the Industrial Areas Foundation (IAF). IAF was founded by Saul Alinsky, who was author of *Rules for Radicals*, which is a bible for left-wing political protest groups.[189] The CCHD is carrying out the official, but covert, un-American and anti-Christian policies of the Roman Catholic Church. Suzanne Belongia, CCHD director in Winona, Minnesota, in an attempt to defend CCHD pointed out that Pope John Paul II, officially endorsed CCHD when he visited Washington, D.C., early in his pontificate.[190]

The information about the CCHD grants gives us a little peak at the wolf under the sheep's clothing. Politician Huey Long once said, "if you have a reputation as an early riser, you can sleep until noon."[191] Publicly the Catholic Church is against abortion and for traditional family values; while behind the scenes the Roman church is financially supporting pro abortion and anti-Christian groups. The CCHD reveals the Roman Catholic Church as the consummate Machiavellian political organization.

A hypocrite is a person who pretends to have religious beliefs or morals that are the opposite of his behavior. The Roman Catholic hierarchy are the same as the hypocrites that Jesus criticized.

> Ye hypocrites, well did Esaias prophesy of you, saying, This people draweth nigh unto me with their mouth, and honoureth me with their lips; but their heart is far from me. But in vain they do worship me, teaching for doctrines the commandments of men. (Matthew 15:7-9)

7 Changing the Times and the Laws

Ian Paisley further identifies the pope as the man of sin, because he trades in sin. That means that the pope justifies and encourages that which God has stated is a sin. For example, God clearly states in the second commandment that we are not to make graven images of that which is in heaven or that which is in the earth, or that which is in the water under the earth, and that we are not to bow down or serve those images. Exodus 20:4-5. However, the Catholic Church instructs its members to venerate graven images of Jesus, Mary, and the saints. The Catechism of the Catholic Church states:

> Basing itself on the mystery of the incarnate Word, the seventh ecumenical council at Nicaea justified against the iconoclasts the veneration of icons - of Christ, but also of the mother of God, the angels, and all the saints. By becoming incarnate, the Son of God introduced a new economy of images.[192]

What does God think about this veneration of graven images? The following are the first two of the Ten Commandments.

> And God spake all these words, saying, I am the LORD thy God, which have brought thee out of the land of Egypt, out of the house of bondage. **Thou shalt have**

no other gods before me. Thou shalt not make unto thee any graven image, or any likeness of any thing that is in heaven above, or that is in the earth beneath, or that is in the water under the earth: Thou shalt not bow down thyself to them, nor serve them: for I the LORD thy God am a jealous God, visiting the iniquity of the fathers upon the children unto the third and fourth generation of them that hate me; And shewing mercy unto thousands of them that love me, and keep my commandments. (Exodus 20:1-6)

Lucius Ferraris, a Franciscan Monk, in his authoritative work, Prompta Bibliotheca Canonica, states: "The Pope is of so great authority and power, that he is able to modify, declare, or interpret even divine laws."[193] Indeed, Pope Nicholas I stated: "Wherefore, no marvel if it be in my power to dispense with all things, yea, with the precepts of Christ."[194]

The audacious pope has in fact thought to change the very laws of God. The Roman church teaches that by coming to earth as a man, Christ instituted a new era of images. That is a deception by the papacy. God commanded Christians in the New Testament time and again to keep away from idols.

Little children, **keep yourselves from idols**. Amen. (1 John 5:21)

But that we write unto them, that they **abstain from pollutions of idols**, and from fornication, and from things strangled, and from blood. (Acts 15:20)

Wherefore, my dearly beloved, **flee from idolatry**. (1 Corinthians 10:14)

And **what agreement hath the temple of God with idols**? for ye are the temple of the living God; as God hath said, I will dwell in them, and walk in them; and I will be their God, and they shall be my people. (2 Corinthians 6:16)

> Now the works of the flesh are manifest, which are these; Adultery, fornication, uncleanness, lasciviousness, **Idolatry**, witchcraft, hatred, variance, emulations, wrath, strife, seditions, heresies, (Galatians 5:19-20)

The Catholic Church at the Council of Trent instructs that its members are to honor relics and pray to the saints. The council condemned anyone who teaches a contrary doctrine.

> The holy Synod enjoins on all bishops, and others who sustain the office and charge of teaching, that, agreeably to the usage of the Catholic and Apostolic Church, received from the primitive times of the Christian religion, and agreeably to the consent of the holy Fathers, and to the decrees of sacred Councils, they especially **instruct the faithful diligently concerning the intercession and invocation of saints; the honour (paid) to relics; and the legitimate use of images**: teaching them, that the saints, who reign together with Christ, offer up their own prayers to God for men; that **it is good and useful suppliantly to invoke them**, and to have recourse to their prayers, aid, (and) help for obtaining benefits from God, through His Son, Jesus Christ our Lord, who is our alone Redeemer and Saviour; but that they think impiously, who deny that the saints, who enjoy eternal happiness in heaven, are to be invocated; or who assert either that they do not pray for men; or, that the invocation of them to pray for each of us even in particular, is idolatry; or, that it is repugnant to the word of God; and is opposed to the honour of the one mediator of God and men, Christ Jesus; or, that it is foolish to supplicate, vocally, or mentally, those who reign in heaven. Also, that the holy bodies of holy martyrs, and of others now living with Christ,--which bodies were the living members of Christ, and the temple of the Holy Ghost, and which are by Him to be raised unto eternal life, and to be glorified,--are to be venerated by the faithful; through which (bodies) many benefits are

> bestowed by God on men; so that **they who affirm that veneration and honour are not due to the relics of saints; or, that these, and other sacred monuments, are uselessly honoured by the faithful; and that the places dedicated to the memories of the saints are in vain visited with the view of obtaining their aid; are wholly to be condemned, as the Church has already long since condemned, and now also condemns them. Moreover, that the images of Christ, of the Virgin Mother of God, and of the other saints, are to be had and retained particularly in temples, and that due honour and veneration are to be given them.**[195] (emphasis added)

God does not want us to make, bow down to, or worship graven images because he is a jealous God who will not share his glory with anyone or anything.

> **I am the LORD: that is my name: and my glory will I not give to another, neither my praise to graven images.** (Isaiah 42:8)

Why does God want to prohibit even the making of graven images? Because behind every idol is a devil. See 1 Corinthians 10:19-20. The Catholic idolatry is a mysterious worship of Satan. That is another reason why God calls the great harlot church "Mystery." The Vatican hierarchy also worships Satan directly. As the book of Revelation points out, the Vatican has become the habitation of devils and every foul spirit. Revelation 18:2. Former Catholic Archbishop Emmanuel Milingo revealed before the Fatima 2000 International Congress on World Peace in Rome on November 18-23, 1996 that Satan worship is practiced within the very walls of the Vatican.[196] Archbishop Milingo cited Pope Paul VI as agreeing with his observations: "Paul VI said that the smoke of Satan had entered into the Vatican."[197]

Former Jesuit Malachi Martin, a well respected scholar of considerable renown who was considered an expert on the Vatican, wrote a novel titled *Windswept House*. He stated that he had to write the book as a novel but that the novel is 85 % based on fact. One of the startling revelations in his book is that there are sodomites and Satanists among the cardinals of Rome. He also recounted the actual occurrence of a satanic "Black Mass" in which members of the Vatican hierarchy participated.[198] Martin had this to say about Archbishop Milingo's allegations:

> Archbishop Milingo is a good Bishop and his contention that there are satanists in Rome is completely correct, Anybody who is acquainted with the state of affairs in the Vatican in the last 35 years is well aware that the prince of darkness has had and still has his surrogates in Rome.[199]

A troubling aspect of these revelations is that they went completely unreported by the newspapers and large circulation magazines in the United States. That should be some indication of the control the Vatican has over the press in the United States. The A.P. Vatican bureau reporter, Dan Walkin, when asked about the lack of coverage of such sensational news, had no acceptable explanation for not covering the story.[200]

The Catholic Church claims that the veneration of idols practiced by Catholics is not the same as the worship of images prohibited in the Ten Commandments. The Second Commandment is very specific as to what conduct toward graven images is prohibited. **"[t]hou shalt not make unto thee any graven image, or any likeness of any thing that is in heaven above, or that is in the earth beneath, or that is in the water under the earth: Thou shalt not bow down thyself to them, nor serve them."** Whether one calls it worship or veneration, bowing down to a graven image is prohibited.

Knowing that their doctrine of venerating graven images is directly prohibited by God in his Ten Commandments, it was necessary for the Catholic church in their official catechism to change the first commandment and to completely remove the second commandment. The Catholic Ten Commandments, which is titled by the Vatican: "A Traditional Catechetical Formula,"[201] simply states the following in place of the first two commandments: "1. I am the Lord your God: you shall not have **strange gods** before me."[202] The Catholic second commandment is actually the third commandment as given by God as it appears in Exodus, chapter 20. The Catholic second commandment reads: "2. You shall not take the name of the LORD your God in vain."[203]

Notice that the prohibition against making graven images and bowing to them or serving them is deleted in the Catholic Ten Commandments. In addition, the Romish church allows the worship of other gods as long as they are not strange gods. So it is permissible to have Mary and all the saints as other gods, because they are not "strange gods" according to Catholic doctrine. God's first commandment, however, states that "I am the LORD thy God, which have brought thee out of the land of Egypt, out of the house of bondage. Thou shalt have **no other gods** before me." They have changed the commandments of God in order to set up their own religion in direct opposition to God's true commands.

In the Catholic Catechism, the second commandment is completely deleted. This leaves the Catholic Church in a quandary; they only have nine commandments in their catechism. Not to worry, the Catholic Church simply splits the last commandment into two commandments to make up for the missing commandment in the Catholic Catechism. So the single commandment against coveting is changed into two commandments against coveting thy neighbor's goods and coveting thy neighbor's wife.[204]

This ineffective attempt to change God's commandments is a fulfillment of the prophecy in Daniel regarding the beast, the antichrist. Daniel prophesied that the beast would "think to change times and laws."

> And the ten horns out of this kingdom are ten kings that shall arise: and another shall rise after them; and he shall be diverse from the first, and he shall subdue three kings. **And he shall speak great words against the most High, and shall wear out the saints of the most High, and think to change times and laws**: and they shall be given into his hand until a time and times and the dividing of time. (Daniel 7:24-25)

In Revelation, there is a great red dragon who "stood before the woman which was ready to be delivered, for to devour her child as soon as it was born." Revelation 12:4. Who is this great red dragon? It is none other than "that old serpent, called the Devil, and Satan, which deceiveth the whole world." Revelation 12:9. The child that the great red dragon was ready to devour was Jesus. Who was the agent of the devil that tried to kill Jesus? Herod, King of Israel.

> Then Herod, when he saw that he was mocked of the wise men, was exceeding wroth, and sent forth, and slew all the children that were in Bethlehem, and in all the coasts thereof, from two years old and under, according to the time which he had diligently enquired of the wise men. (Matthew 2:16)

The dragon was then cast out of heaven to the earth and "when the dragon saw that he was cast unto the earth, he persecuted the woman which brought forth the man child." Revelation 12:13. The woman was then protected by God. The dragon then made war with her seed. Who is her seed? They are the children of God who "have the testimony of Jesus Christ." Revelation 12:17.

> And to the woman were given two wings of a great eagle, that she might fly into the wilderness, into her place, where she is nourished for a time, and times, and half a time, from the face of the serpent. And the serpent cast out of his mouth water as a flood after the woman, that he might cause her to be carried away of the flood. And the earth helped the woman, and the earth opened her mouth, and swallowed up the flood which the dragon cast out of his mouth. **And the dragon was wroth with the woman, and went to make war with the remnant of her seed, which keep the commandments of God, and have the testimony of Jesus Christ. And I stood upon the sand of the sea, and saw a beast rise up out of the sea, having seven heads and ten horns, and upon his horns ten crowns, and upon his heads the name of blasphemy.** And the beast which I saw was like unto a leopard, and his feet were as the feet of a bear, and his mouth as the mouth of a lion: and the dragon gave him his power, and his seat, and great authority. (Revelation 12:14-

13:2)

Notice that after the dragon was cast to the earth, a great beast was seen rising out of the sea. This sea beast has the same "seven heads and ten horns, and seven crowns upon his heads" as the dragon who was in heaven ready to devour the newborn child in Revelation 12:3. This is clearly the earthly manifestation of the dragon, who is the devil. The description suggests that it is a continuation of the heathen governments of the earth. In Daniel, chapters 7-8 we read that the leopard, the bear, and the lion were symbolic of three successive kings. Daniel refers to a fourth kingdom that would be diverse from the rest. That kingdom will have ten horns. Another single horn shall arise after the ten horns; he will be diverse from the ten horns, subdue three kings, and "shall speak great words against the most High, and shall wear out the saints of the most High, and **think to change times and laws**: and they shall be given into his hand until a time and times and the dividing of time." Daniel 7:25.

The key to identifying the horn of Daniel is to find an institution that has changed God's laws and times. As we have seen, the Roman Catholic Church has changed God's laws by deleting the second of the Ten Commandment and then dividing the last commandment into two commandments to make up for the missing commandment.

The Catholic Church has also changed the times. It claims that the Lord's day is the first day of the week (Sunday) because Jesus purportedly rose from the dead on Sunday and that consequently Sunday replaces the seventh day (Saturday) as the day of rest.[205] The only reference in the Bible to the "Lord's day" is found in Revelation 1:10 and is probably a reference to the sabbath of the seventh day of the week (Saturday).

We are justified not by keeping the sabbath or any other ordinance, but by faith in Jesus Christ. Jesus nailed the Old Testament law to the cross. He fulfilled the requirements of the law on our behalf. We are no longer obligated to the law, including the sabbath requirements. "Let no man therefore judge you in meat, or in drink, or in respect of an holyday, or of the new moon, or of the **sabbath days**: Which are a shadow of things to come; but the body is of Christ." (Colossians 2:16-17) God did away with the requirements of the law under the New Testament. "In that he saith, A new covenant, he hath made the first old. Now that which decayeth and waxeth old is ready to vanish away." (Hebrews 8:13) We keep the new law out of love for God. Our obedience to his new law is evidence of our faith.

> **A new commandment I give unto you, That ye love one another**; as I have loved you, that ye also love one another. By this shall all men know that ye are my disciples, if ye have love one to another. (John 13:34-35)

The Catholic Church, on the other hand, requires that "[o]n Sundays and other holy days of obligation, the faithful are to refrain from engaging in work or activities that hinder the worship owed to God."[206] As a result of the Roman Catholic Church's twisting of the Holy Scripture, they have changed the sabbath day, or day of rest, from the last day of the week (Saturday) to the first day of the week (Sunday). God did not establish the first day of the week (Sunday) as the sabbath, but rather he established that "the seventh day is the sabbath of the Lord thy God." Exodus 20:10. The Roman Catholic Church's changing of the day of rest from the seventh day to the first day of the week, along with their deletion of the second commandment, is a fulfillment of the prophecy in Daniel that the horn would "think to change times and laws." Daniel 7:25.

Christian theologians understood that there was no authority for the change of the Sabbath from the last day of the week to the first day of the week. Isaac Williams stated: "Where are we told in the Scriptures that we are to keep the first day at all? We are commanded to keep the seventh, but we are nowhere commanded to keep the first day."[207] Lionel Beere stated: "Many people think that Sunday is the Sabbath, but neither in the New Testament nor in the early church, is there anything to suggest that we have any right to transfer the observance of the seventh day of the week to the first."[208] The Manual of Christian Doctrine states: "Is there any command in the New Testament to change the day of the weekly rest from Saturday to Sunday? None."[209] What is the historical reason for the change? It is born of the heathen worship of the sun.

In the year 321 A.D., Constantine decreed, "On the venerable day of the Sun let the magistrates and people residing in cities rest, and let all workshops be closed."[210] The Catholic church followed Constantine's edict and even used the verbiage used by Constantine describing the day as the "day of the sun." Section 2174 of the Catechism of the Catholic Church states: "We all gather on the day of the sun, for it is the first day [after the Jewish sabbath, but also the first day] when God, separating matter from darkness, made the world; and on this same day Jesus Christ our Savior rose from the dead."[211] (brackets in original)

The use of the term "day of the sun" in the Catechism of the Catholic Church is notable because it is an acknowledgment of the heathen origin for the change in the Sabbath to Sunday. In Rome, before and during Constantine's reign, the people practiced sun-worship (Mithraism). Mithraism was the official religion of the Roman Empire. It had its own day of worship, from which we now have the name Sunday. December 25th was celebrated as the birth of the sun god, Mithras. December 25th was simply changed by the Catholic Church to become the day upon which the birth of the Catholic version of Jesus was celebrated. The Catholic Jesus is a different Jesus about whom the Apostle Paul warned in 2 Corinthians 11:4. We have a direct link between the Roman Catholic Jesus and the sun god Mithras. The Catholic religion is the esoteric sun god worship. Dr. Gilbert Murray, M.A., D.Litt., LLD, FBA, Professor of Greek at Oxford University summarizes the history of Sunday worship:

> Now since Mithras was the sun, the Unconquered, and the sun was the Royal Star, the religion looked for a king whom it could serve as a representative of Mithras upon earth. The Roman Emperor seemed to be clearly indicated as the true king. In sharp contrast to Christianity, Mithraism recognized Caesar as the bearer of divine grace. It had so much acceptance that it was able to impose on the Christian world its own sun-day in place of the Sabbath; its sun's birthday, the 25th of December, as the birthday of Jesus.[212]

The Papacy justified the changing of the sabbath from the last day of the week to the first day based upon the fiction that Jesus rose from the dead on Sunday. The Catholic dogma that Jesus was crucified on Friday and resurrected on Sunday is wrong. Jesus was crucified on Passover, which was the 4th day of the week, Wednesday (Matthew 26:2; John 13:1, 18:28, 39; Luke 22-23). That is why the day Jesus Christ was crucified is referred to as the "preparation of the Passover" and not the preparation "for" the Passover. The Passover was the preparation day for the unleavened bread sabbath that always follows the Passover.

> And it was the **preparation of the Passover**, and about the sixth hour: and he saith unto the Jews, Behold your King! (John 19:14)

The day Jesus was crucified was the preparation day before the sabbath (Mark 15:42), which is why many believe it was the sixth day of the week, Friday. What many do not realize is that there were many other Sabbaths throughout the year in addition to the weekly sabbath. That would mean that there would be many occasions when there would be two sabbath days during some weeks. The week of Jesus' crucifixion was one of those weeks with two Sabbaths. How can one know that there were two Sabbaths? Because the Bible states that Christ was crucified the day before the "high sabbath," and not the day before the weekly sabbath.

> The Jews therefore, **because it was the preparation, that the bodies should not remain upon the cross on the sabbath day, (for that sabbath day was an high day**,) besought Pilate that their legs might be broken, and that they might be taken away. (John 19:31)

The next day after Jesus' crucifixion was a high sabbath, it was the first day of the seven day feast of unleavened bread and the 5th day of the week, Thursday (John 19:31). The fourteenth day of the first month is the Passover (Leviticus 23:4-5, Exodus 12:17-18). Passover is immediately followed by the seven days of unleavened bread (Leviticus 23:6-7, Exodus 12:15-16). A Sabbath day is a day of rest. God ordained that the Fifteenth day of the first month (the day after Passover) was to be a day of rest, that is a sabbath day (Leviticus 23:6-7).

The order of the preparation and purchase of the spices by the women to anoint Jesus's body is evidence that there were two sabbath days during the week of Christ's crucifixion. The women prepared the spices the day before the sabbath but did not buy them until after the sabbath. The preparation of the spices before they were purchased is not possible. The solution to the seeming impossibility is that there were two sabbaths. The spices were not prepared before they were purchased.

The women are described as preparing the spices before the weekly sabbath and purchasing them after the unleavened bread sabbath. The day after the yearly Passover sabbath was the 6th day of the week (Friday). On that day (Friday), the women bought the spices (Mark 16:1) and prepared the spices for Jesus' body (Luke 23:56). The women prepared the spices and ointments before the weekly sabbath (Luke 23:53-24:3), they bought the spices after the Passover sabbath (Mark 16:1-6). The women bought the spices and prepared the spices on the same day, Friday, which was described alternatively as the day after the Passover sabbath (Mark 16:1-6) and the day before the weekly sabbath (Luke 23:53-24:3).

Those passages point to a Wednesday crucifixion with the unleavened bread sabbath the next day, Thursday, and Christ rising from the dead exactly 3 days and 3 nights, 72 hours, later on the weekly sabbath, Saturday. The women would have both purchased the spices and prepared them on Friday, which would have been before the weekly sabbath on Saturday and after the unleavened bread sabbath, which was on Thursday. The tomb was found empty on the first day of the week, he did not rise from the dead on that day.

The women rested on the 7th day, Saturday, which was the weekly sabbath (Luke 23:56). Early the first day of the week, Sunday, they came to the tomb to find it empty and saw an angel who announced that Jesus had already risen (Mark 16:1-6). Just as Jesus prophesied, he rose from the dead precisely 3 days and 3 nights after his burial (Matthew 12:40, 20:19). While the tomb was found empty on the first day of the week, Sunday, he rose from the dead on the evening of the 7th day, Saturday.

To hold that Jesus was crucified and was buried on the 6th day of the week (Friday) and rose from the dead on the First day of the week (Sunday) would be to say Jesus was wrong about his prophecy, because he prophesied that he would be in the tomb 3 days and 3 nights. "For as Jonas was three days and three nights in the whale's belly; so shall the Son of man be **three days and three nights** in the heart of the earth." (Matthew 12:40) The span between the evening of Friday and the early morning of Sunday is not 3 days and 3 nights. However, a Wednesday burial with a Saturday resurrection is exactly 3 days and 3 nights.

Yet another fulfillment of Daniel's prophecy that the antichrist would "think to change times." Daniel 7:25. In 1582, Pope Gregory XIII decreed a change in the calendar. He dropped 10 days from the calendar in October 1582 and ruled that the new year would begin on January 1st, rather than March 25th. It had been the custom since 45 B.C. under the Julian calendar (named after Julius Caesar, who instituted the calendar) to start the new year on March 25th, which was the beginning of the first of the four seasons.

Catholic countries in Europe immediately adopted the new calendar of Pope Gregory XIII. Many Protestant countries, however, resisted the calendar change and continued to follow the Julian calendar until the 1700's. It was not until 1752 that Protestant Britain adopted the Gregorian calendar throughout its empire, including its American colonies.[213] Virtually all countries in the world today use the Gregorian calendar instituted by the decree of Pope Gregory XIII.

8 Many Shall Say "I Am Christ"

The papal claim to be vicar of Christ, means exactly what the title implies. The papacy is in place of Christ in every aspect of Christ's position and authority. The popes' essential claim is that they are Christ on earth, with all the authority of God Almighty. Cardinal Giuseppe Melchior Sarto (later to elevated to Pope Pius X) said unequivocally that the pope of Rome "is Jesus Christ Himself" and all must obey his every command without delay, because the command of he pope is the command of God Almighty. On or about November 25, 1894, Cardinal Sarto (later Pope Pius X) stated:

> **The Pope is not simply the representative of Jesus Christ. On the contrary, he is Jesus Christ Himself, under the veil of the flesh,** and who by means of a being common to humanity continues His ministry amongst men ... Does the Pope speak? It is Jesus Christ Who is speaking. Does he teach? It is Jesus Christ Who teaches. Does he confer grace or pronounce an anathema? It is Jesus Christ Himself Who is pronouncing the anathema and conferring the grace. Hence consequently, **when one speaks of the Pope, it is not necessary to examine, but to obey**: there must be no limiting the bounds of the command, in order to suit the purpose of the individual whose obedience is demanded: there must be no cavilling at the declared

will of the Pope, and so invest it with quite another than that which he has put upon it: no preconceived opinions must be brought to bear upon it: **no rights must be set up against the rights of the Holy Father** to teach and command; his decisions are not to be criticized, or his ordinances disputed. Therefore by Divine ordination, all, no matter how august the person may be — whether he wear a crown or be invested with the purple, or be clothed in the sacred vestments: **all must be subject to Him** Who has had all things put under Him.[214] (emphasis added)

When Cardinal Sarto's homily was publicized worldwide, it created a furor of indignation among Protestants. In 1896, Cardinal Sarto tried to calm the furor in a correspondence to a priest by clarifying what he said. Notice, in the clarification quoted below, that Cardinal Sarto very cleverly does not expressly deny having made the above statement. Sarto's response falls into a category of responses commonly described in the political world as a "non-denial, denial." Cardinal Sarto's letter stated:

I have read all the Homilies I have made since my coming here in Venice, and only in the sermon for the Anniversary of the election of the Holy Father I said these exact words: "The Pope represents Jesus Christ Himself, and therefore is a loving father. The life of the Pope is a holocaust of love for the human family. His word is love. Love, his weapons; love, the answer he gives to all those who hate him; love, his flag—i.e., the Cross, which signed the greatest triumph on earth and in heaven . . . &c." A father of the Company of Jesus also wrote me interesting me to state the very words I have read for refuting the Protestant newspaper, and I could not but give him the answer I give you, whilst I sign myself, with esteem and affection, Yours obligedly and affectionately in Jesus Christ, JOSEPH, Cardinal Sarto, Patriarch.[215]

What is interesting about Sarto's letter is that he did not expressly deny the words attributed to him. His clarification was presented as a denial, but close reading of his words reveals his statement to be a cleverly crafted response giving the impression of a denial, without actually denying anything. He tells his reader what he alleges he said, but he nowhere denies having said that the pope "is Jesus Christ Himself, under the veil of the flesh," and that "all must be subject to him."

Deception seems to be a well practiced art among the Catholic clergy. That being the case, why would Cardinal Sarto not just deny making the statement? Because, he made the statement in a church full of witnesses, who heard it and memorialized it. A flat denial would have been easily refuted, and he would be exposed as liar. More importantly, his statement that the pope "is Jesus Christ Himself, under the veil of the flesh," and that "all must be subject to him," is in fact Roman Catholic doctrine. If he denied having made the statement, the denial would be interpreted (properly so) as a denial of the underlying Catholic doctrine. He simply could not deny it. Instead, he engaged in Jesuitical prevarication, using subtle phrasing, to give the impression he denied making the statement, without actually denying anything.

Another interesting thing about Cardinal Sarto's "non-denial, denial" is that he refers to a homily given on the anniversary of the elevation of the sitting pope, Pope Leo XIII. Pope Leo XIII was elected pope on February 20, 1878. That would put the date for the cover-homily Cardinal Sarto alleges he gave as being on or about February 20, 1895. The problem with his assertion is that homily he cites was given two months after his blasphemous words spoken on November 25, 1894, were first published in Protestant periodicals in December 1894. It is impossible that his alleged cover-homily of February 20, 1895, explains his blasphemous words quoted above, because his alleged cover-homily had not yet been delivered when his blasphemous words were first published to the world in December 1894.

Some take the view that the "man of sin" described by Paul in 2 Thessalonians is going to be a future individual antichrist. They interpret "man of sin" to be a singular "man." That interpretation is contrary to the prophecy of Jesus that "many shall come in my name, saying, I am Christ; and shall deceive many." (Matthew 24:5) There is further significant biblical authority refuting the error of a single future antichrist. Steve Wohlberg explains the error of the interpretation of a single future antichrist:

>Paul called the Antichrist, "the man of sin ... the son of perdition" (2 Thess. 2:3). It is primarily because of this verse that millions have come to believe that there will be only one super-sinister Mr. Sin who will rise to power after the Rapture. Is it true? Will there be only one man - the Antichrist? Is this what Paul really meant?
>
>First of all, in the little book of 1 John, the Bible plainly says there are "many antichrists" (1 John 2:18) and a "spirit of antichrist" (1 John 4:3). John also wrote that any person who denies the true doctrine of Jesus Christ is "a deceiver and an antichrist" (2 John 7,9). Thus, so far, the idea of there being only "one" antichrist fails the biblical test.
>
>There are other equally inspired statements in the Bible which parallel Paul's expression, "the man of sin." Prophecy also refers to this same Antichrist as the "little horn" (Daniel 7:8), the "beast" (Revelation 13:1), "the mystery of iniquity" (2 Thessalonians 2:7), and "that Wicked" (2 Thess. 2:8). Do all of these expressions refer to one evil person who will rise to power after the Rapture? You are about to see that they do not.
>
>Most agree that Daniel's "little horn," Revelation's mysterious "beast," and Paul's "man of sin," all refer to the same thing. Daniel 7 describes four beasts - a lion, a bear, a leopard, and a dragon-like beast with ten horns (Daniel 7:3-7). Then comes the "little horn" out of the head of the fourth beast (Daniel 7:8). This little horn has "eyes like the eyes of a man," "a mouth speaking great things," and "makes war on the saints" (Daniel 7:8, 21). This is exactly what "the beast" has and does in Revelation 13:5,7. Thus the "little horn" is the same as "the beast." But what many fail to discern is that in Daniel 7, a beast is clearly defined as a

kingdom, not a man. The Holy Word says, "...the fourth beast shall be the fourth kingdom upon the earth" (Daniel 7:23).

The Bible doesn't say the "little horn" is a man, but rather that it would have "eyes like the eyes of a man" (Daniel 7:8). When Paul used the expression, "the man of sin," in 2 Thessalonians 2:3, he was simply referring to the "little horn" with its "eyes like the eyes of a man." Yet that same horn is called a "beast" in Revelation 13:1, and the Bible clearly tells us that a beast represents a great kingdom (Daniel 7:23).

A careful study of 2 Thessalonians 2 reveals the impossibility of "the man of sin," also called "the mystery of iniquity," and "that Wicked," as only applying to one man. First, "the mystery of iniquity," although under restraint, was "already at work" in Paul's time (verse 7). Second, it would continue all the way until the visible return of Jesus Christ at the end of the world (verse 8). Thus it cannot refer to only one man, for that man would have to be almost 2,000 years old!

Did Paul ever use the expression "the man" in any of his other writings in such a way that it does not refer to only one man? Yes. Paul wrote, "All Scripture is given by inspiration of God, and is profitable for doctrine, for reproof, for correction, for instruction in righteousness: That the man of God may be perfect, thoroughly furnished unto all good works." 2 Timothy 3:16, 17. Here "the man of God" does not refer to only one Holy Man, but rather to a succession of godly men throughout history who follow the Scriptures. Paul also used the phrase, "the minister of God" (Romans 13:4) to refer to all civil officers throughout history who restrain evil. Thus, Paul's mysterious phrase, "the man of sin," which is the same as the "little horn," and the "beast," may properly refer to an actual "kingdom" with "eyes like the eyes of a man," that is, to a kingdom centered in a historical succession of supremely exalted men who, according to the Scriptures, are part of "the mystery of iniquity."[216]

9 Signs and Lying Wonders

We find in Paul's description of the antirchrist that his coming "is after the working of Satan with all power and signs and lying wonders, And with all deceivableness of unrighteousness."

> Let no man deceive you by any means: for that day shall not come, except there come a falling away first, and that **man of sin** be revealed, **the son of perdition**; Who opposeth and exalteth himself above all that is called God, or that is worshipped; so that he as God sitteth in the temple of God, shewing himself that he is God. Remember ye not, that, when I was yet with you, I told you these things? And now ye know what withholdeth that he might be revealed in his time. For the mystery of iniquity doth already work: only he who now letteth will let, until he be taken out of the way. And then shall that Wicked be revealed, whom the Lord shall consume with the spirit of his mouth, and shall destroy with the brightness of his coming: Even him, **whose coming is after the working of Satan with all power and signs and lying wonders, And with all deceivableness of unrighteousness** in them that perish; because they received not the love of the truth, that they might be saved. And for this cause God shall send them strong delusion, that they should believe a lie: That they all might be damned who believed not the truth, but had pleasure in unrighteousness. (2 Thessalonians 2:3-12)

Christ entered his ministry in the world with miracles and wonders. Christ forgave sin, cured the ill, raised the dead, walked on water and calmed the seas. The antichrist seeks to imitate Christ. However, the antichrist must resort to "signs and <u>lying</u> wonders." There is hardly a miracle of Christ that the papacy has not claimed also as a sign of its spiritual authority. The claimed miracles can often be exposed as lying subterfuges. That has not stopped the papacy from claiming to be able to perform spiritual miracles that are within the province of God. Indeed, the Roman Church has set up an edifice of sacraments in which to wrap its phoney miraculous powers. One sacrament is the miracle to regenerate the soul through infant baptism. Another miracle is to call Jesus down from heaven and enter a piece of bread to act as an unbloody sacrifice during the Mass. Yet another miracle transforms a man into *alter-Christos* (another Christ) upon becoming a Catholic priest, who then in the person of Christ claims the miracle of forgiving sins. Wylie explains:

> The *Spiritual* performances of the Church of Rome are emphatically "lying wonders." Baptismal regeneration is a lying wonder, sacramental grace is a lying wonder, priestly power is a lying wonder, the absolution of the Confessional is a lying wonder, transubstantiation is the biggest wonder and the greatest lie of all, and extreme unction is a last and fatal lie. There is no reality behind any of these things, and they are the more to be deplored that they have immediate reference to the eternal world, and that millions take their departure to the world fully confiding in these lies for salvation.
>
> Let us mark the parallelism. It is at once a parallel and a contrast. The Gospel came amid the effulgence of real miracles which were wrought by God, and were a Divine attestation to the Messiahship of His Son. Popery came amid the murky and delusive glare of false miracles, which were wrought by Satan, and which were his sign manual, bearing witness to all that the system in behalf of which they were done was the "Mystery of Iniquity."[217]

The Roman Catholic priests claim that when consecrating the bread and wine during Mass they are the lord Jesus Christ.

> **The priest is also one and the same, Christ the Lord**; for the ministers who offer Sacrifice, consecrate the holy mysteries, **not in their own person, but in that of Christ** . . . and thus **acting in the Person of Christ the Lord**, he changes the substance of the bread and wine into the true substance of His body and blood. *CATECHISM OF THE COUNCIL OF TRENT.*[218]

The greatest miracle performed by Jesus is the forgiveness of sins. It is a miracle that is solely within the province of God Almighty. When they brought a person sick of the palsy to Jesus, he performed the greater miracle of forgiving the man's sins. Jesus made the point that forgiving sins is the greatest of miracles by asking the rhetorical question "whether is easier, to say, Thy sins be forgiven thee; or to say, Arise, and walk?" Jesus then told the man to arise, and the man was healed. Jesus healed the man to prove that he was God and thus had the authority to forgive sins.

> And, behold, they brought to him a man sick of the palsy, lying on a bed: and Jesus seeing their faith said unto the sick of the palsy; Son, be of good cheer; thy sins be forgiven thee. And, behold, certain of the scribes said within themselves, This man blasphemeth. And Jesus knowing their thoughts said, Wherefore think ye evil in your hearts? For whether is easier, to say, Thy sins be forgiven thee; or to say, Arise, and walk? But that ye may know that the Son of man hath power on earth to forgive sins, (then saith he to the sick of the palsy,) Arise, take up thy bed, and go unto thine house. And he arose, and departed to his house. (Matthew 9:2-7)

The pope and his minion priests do not have the authority to forgive sins. Their purported miracle of forgiving sin by the Catholic priest is a "lying wonder."

Since the Catholic Church claims that the priests are another

Christ and another Lord, it should be no surprise that the Catholic Church claims that its priests have the same authority as the Lord to forgive sins. The priests hear confessions from a people seeking absolution for their sins.

> **Indeed bishops and priests, by virtue of the sacrament of Holy Orders, have the power to forgive sins.** CATECHISM OF THE CATHOLIC CHURCH, § 1461, 1994.

Even the Jewish scribes understood that only God has the authority to forgive sins because sin is the violation of God's law. *See e.g.,* Exodus 32:33, Numbers 32:33, Deuteronomy 9:16, Joshua 7:20, 2 Samuel 12:13, Psalm 41:4, Jeremiah 3:25, Jeremiah 50:14, and Luke 15:21. The difference between the forgiveness of sin by Jesus and the forgiveness of sin by the Roman Catholic priest is that Jesus is God and thus has the authority to forgive sin (which the Jews did not understand) but the Catholic priests are pretenders and have no authority to forgive sins.

> When Jesus saw their faith, he said unto the sick of the palsy, Son, thy sins be forgiven thee. But there were certain of the scribes sitting there, and reasoning in their hearts, **Why doth this man thus speak blasphemies? who can forgive sins but God only?** And immediately when Jesus perceived in his spirit that they so reasoned within themselves, he said unto them, Why reason ye these things in your hearts? Whether is it easier to say to the sick of the palsy, Thy sins be forgiven thee; or to say, Arise, and take up thy bed, and walk? But **that ye may know that the Son of man hath power on earth to forgive sins, (he saith to the sick of the palsy,) I say unto thee, Arise, and take up thy bed, and go thy way into thine house.** And immediately he arose, took up the bed, and went forth before them all; insomuch that they were all amazed, and glorified God, saying, We never saw it on this fashion. (Mark 2:5-12)

The confessional has been the sight of countless seductions of women and young girls by priests.[219] In 1837, Rosamond Culbertson revealed her first-hand knowledge of how the priests use the confessional to seduce and ravish young women. Rosamond Culbertson gave an example she witnessed of a young 14 year old girl named Mariettee, who confessed to a Catholic priest, Manuel Canto. The priest told Culbertson that Mariettee confessed to him that she had stolen two shillings from her mother. Canto told Mariettee that he would not forgive her sin unless she would consent to all his wishes. If she did not obey him, Canto told her that he would be a witness against her and send her to hell. Having sown the fear of eternal damnation in Mariettee's heart, the beastly priest Canto used that trepidation to persuade Mariettee to come to his private abode. Culbertson was present in the house when Mariette arrived. Priest Canto then executed his plan and violated Mariettee.[220] Such was the common practice among the Catholic priests of Cuba and indeed all countries where the Catholic church has hegemony.

In 1892, a former Catholic nun in England, Margaret Shepard, explained the general state of moral degeneracy of the Catholic priests, who use the confessional to seduce women and, when required, arrange a abortions to conceal their sin.

> I presume many of my readers will feel shocked when I say that a Roman Catholic priest, as a general rule, will try to have a liaison with a married woman in preference to one unmarried, that in the event of any offspring no scandal will take place. When, however, it is the case of an unmarried woman, priests, who are perfect adepts at malpractice, will see that the girl is supplied with the needful medicine, and where necessary will himself perform an operation for the purpose of hiding the evidence.[221]

The seduction in the confessional is made possible in part by the indoctrination of all penitents that the priest is in the place of Jesus Christ and should be obeyed as though he were God Almighty. For example, Pope Paul VI stated:

> Obey blindly, that is, without asking reasons. Be careful, then, never to examine the directions of your

confessor....In a word, keep before your eyes this great rule, that in obeying your confessor you obey God. Force yourself then, to obey him in spite of all fears. And be persuaded that if you are not obedient to him it will be impossible for you to go on well; but if you obey him you are secure. But you say, if I am damned in consequence of obeying my confessor, who will rescue me from hell? What you say is impossible.[222]

Paul marks the coming antichrist not only with "the working of Satan with all power and signs and lying wonders," but also "with all deceivableness of unrighteousness." Wylie explains the meaning of those words and how they accurately describe the papacy:

> Let us mark the phrase. It is a very remarkable one. It is used in no other place; it is employed to describe no other system; it describes the great apostacy, and it alone. It is not simply "deceivableness," nor is it simply "unrighteousness" -it is the "deceivableness of unrighteousness;" nay, it is the "all-deceivableness of unrighteousness."
>
> Craft and deceivableness were no unknown things before the Papacy entered the world. Priests and statesmen have, in every age, dealt largely in deceivableness. But the deceivableness peculiar to herself -it is the deceivableness of unrighteousness. Not only is it a craft more subtle and more defined than any with which man operated in former ages: it is a craft of a new order. It is a system of unrighteousness so set forth as to seem that system of righteousness which God has revealed for the salvation of the world, and by consequence accepted as such by all who, not taught of the Holy Ghost, are deceived and destroyed by it.[223]

The papacy is a dark clouded mirror that reflects the gospel of righteousness but in a way that distorts it, resulting in a false gospel of unrighteousness. Wylie perceptively details the distortion:

> Paganism was a system of deceivableness. It was the

worship of a false god, under the pretence of being the worship of the true God. But popery is a deceivableness on a scale far beyond that of paganism. The one was a counterfeit of the religion of the Gospel. Popery has a god of its own - him, even, whom the canon law calls the "Lord our God." It has a saviour of its own - the Church, to wit. It has a sacrifice of it own - the Mass. It has a mediator of its own - the Priesthood. It has a sanctifier of its own - the Sacrament. It has a justification of its own - that even of infused righteousness. It has a pardon of its own - the pardon of the Confessional; and it has in the heavens an infallible, all-prevailing advocate unknown to the Gospel - the "Mother of God." It thus presents to the world a spiritual and saving apparatus for the salvation of men, and yet it neither sanctifies nor saves anyone. It looks like a church; it professes to have all that a church ought to have; and yet, it is not a church. It is a grand deception -"the all-deceivableness of unrighteousness."[224]

The papacy is built upon a foundation of deception where evil is celebrated as good. Wylie explains:

This vast deceivableness is one of the main sources of the strength of the so-called Church of Rome. She has the art of enlisting all the claims of virtue, and all the sanctions of law, on the side of that by which virtue is outraged and law violated. Where her purpose is the most cruel, her speech is ever the most bland. Where her motive is the most villainous, her profession is ever the most plausible. She always gives the holiest name to the most unholy deed. When she burns a heretic she calls it an *auto-da-fe* -an act of faith. When she ravages a province with fire and sword, she styles it a crusade -that is, an evangelistic expedition. Her torture chamber is styled the "Holy Office." And when she deposes monarchs, stripping them of crown and kingdom, and compelling them, as she did Henry IV of Germany, to stand with naked feet at her gates amid the drifts of winter, it is with the make-believe of a kind father administering salutary chastisement to an erring son. In short, she not only transforms herself into an angel of light, but vice itself she transforms into virtue, decking blackest crime in the white robe of innocence, and arraying foulest iniquity with the resplendent airs of holiness.

What are the sacraments by which she professes to replenish men with grace? What are the Masses by which she professes to impart Christ and his salvation to them? What are the crucifixes, rosaries, and amulets, by which she fortifies men against the assaults of Satan and evil spirits? What are the indulgences by which she shortens the sufferings of souls in purgatory? What are the pardons with which she sends men away into the other world? What are the vows of poverty under which she cherishes a pride the most arrogant, and an avariciousness the most insatiable? What are the vows of celibacy under which she veils an unbridled lewdness? What are the dispensations by she releases men from the obligations of the moral law, and professes to annul oaths, promises, and covenants? Above all, what are her logic and system of ethics by which, as in the hands of Ligouri, she makes vice and virtue falsehood and truth change sides, and shows how one, if he but direct aright his intention, can commit the most monstrous crime and yet contract not a particle of guilt? What are these things, we ask, save the "deceivableness of unrighteousness?" for surely the utmost limits of deception have here been reached, and the Deceiver himself can go no farther. He has produced his masterpiece.[225]

God has placed a curse upon any religion that calls evil good and good evil. "Woe unto them that call evil good, and good evil; that put darkness for light, and light for darkness; that put bitter for sweet, and sweet for bitter!" (Isaiah 5:20)

10 Whosoever Sins Ye Remit, They Are Remitted

The official doctrine of the Catholic Church is that "bishops and priests, by virtue of the sacrament of Holy Orders, have the power to forgive sins."[226] The Catholic Church cites the verses in John 20:22-23 among its foundational authorities for the practice of the sacrament of confession, whereby they allege that the Catholic priest has the authority during auricular confession to forgive sins.[227] The Vatican principally relies upon the passage at verse 23: "Whose soever sins ye remit, they are remitted unto them; and whose soever sins ye retain, they are retained." The passage must be read in context to understand what it means:

> Then said Jesus to them again, Peace be unto you: as my Father hath sent me, even so send I you. And when he had said this, he breathed on them, and saith unto them, Receive ye the Holy Ghost: Whose soever sins ye remit, they are remitted unto them; and whose soever sins ye retain, they are retained. (John 20:21-23)

The passage clearly addresses the retention and remission of sins. Remission means "to cancel or free someone from (a punishment, debt, etc.)"[228] There is no question that Jesus' disciples were given the authority to remit sins and retain sins. However, the Catholic Church has removed the passage from its context and perverted its meaning.

The Catholic Church alleges that John 20:22-23 gave the apostles unique authority to forgive sins; and that unique authority has been passed down to the Catholic priests as successors to the apostles through the Catholic popes, cardinals, and bishops. The Vatican alleges that the exercise of the unique authority to forgive sins can only take place during a sacramental rite of the Catholic Church, known as "reconciliation" (a/k/a confession). The Catholic claim is that during the sacrament of confession, the Catholic priest has the exclusive authority, handed down to them as successors of the apostles, to forgive sins that are confessed directly to them.

When we read the context of the passage in John 20:21-23 we see that the authority given to the disciples was in accordance with the commission given by Jesus Christ. He stated "as my Father hath sent me, even so I send you." In order to understand the commission to remit and retain sins, we must look to what the Father commissioned Jesus to do, because Jesus stated that the commission to the disciples from Jesus was "as" the commission to Jesus from the Father. What did the Father send Jesus to do? He sent Jesus to be crucified; Jesus explained: "Now is my soul troubled; and what shall I say? Father, save me from this hour: but for this cause came I unto this hour." (John 12:27) Jesus explained at the last supper that he was sent by the Father so shed his blood on the cross for the remission of sins. "For this is my blood of the new testament, which is shed for many for the remission of sins." (Matthew 26:28) The remission of sins were made possible by the crucifixion of Jesus, which was a propitiation for the sins of his elect. "Whom God hath set forth to be a propitiation through faith in his blood, to declare his righteousness for the remission of sins that are past, through the forbearance of God." (Romans 3:25)

How is one to receive the blessing of that propitiation? One must believe in Jesus Christ. "That if thou shalt confess with thy mouth the Lord Jesus, and shalt believe in thine heart that God hath raised him from the dead, thou shalt be saved." Romans 10:9. If one does not believe in Jesus Christ, one's sins are retained. "I said therefore unto you, that ye shall die in your sins: for if ye believe not that I am he, ye shall die in your sins." (John 8:24)

We know, therefore, according to the gospel, that the retention and remission of sins is based entirely on whether a person believes or does not believe in Jesus Christ. There is no other basis upon which a person is saved or damned. Auricular confession is not mentioned anywhere in the gospel as the basis for the remission of sins. The gospel states clearly that it is only by faith in Jesus Christ that sins are forgiven.

The forgiveness of sins does not come via auricular confession to a priest but rather by faith in Jesus Christ. How is one to believe in Jesus Christ? The bible tells us that "faith cometh by hearing, and hearing by the word of God." (Romans 10:17) That means that the commission given to the apostles to retain and remit sins was entirely based upon their preaching the gospel of Jesus Christ.

When Jesus stated in John 20:21 "as my Father hath sent me, even so send I you," he was referring to his commission sending them to all the world to preach the gospel. *See* Mark 16:15-16. When Jesus followed that statement by saying that "whose soever sins ye remit, they are remitted unto them; and whose soever sins ye retain, they are retained," he was referring to the effect of the disciples' preaching of the gospel. Jesus commanded his disciples to preach the gospel to all the world, because faith in Jesus Christ only comes by hearing the gospel. If one believes in Jesus Christ his sins are remitted and he is saved. If a person does not believe in Jesus Christ, his sins are retained and he is damned. "And he said unto them, Go ye into all the world, and preach the gospel to every creature. He that believeth and is baptized shall be saved; but he that believeth not shall be damned." (Mark 16:15-16)

The gospel is preached in order to facilitate the forgiveness of sins. "Be it known unto you therefore, men and brethren, that through this man is preached unto you the forgiveness of sins: And by him all that believe are justified from all things." (Acts 13:38-39) All those who believe in Jesus Christ are disciples of Christ. All disciples have been commissioned to preach the gospel. The gospel is the means by which one believes in Jesus Christ, and that faith is, in turn, the means for the remission of sins.

> And he commanded us to preach unto the people, and to testify that it is he which was ordained of God to be the Judge of quick and dead. To him give all the prophets witness, that through his name whosoever believeth in him shall receive remission of sins. Acts

10:42-43

Consequently, all believers, through the commission to preach the gospel, have been given the authority to remit and retain sins. Indeed, the letter to the Romans states that whoever calls on the name of the Lord Jesus will be saved from their sins, but that one cannot call on the name of the Lord unless one hears the gospel:

> For whosoever shall call upon the name of the Lord shall be saved. How then shall they call on him in whom they have not believed? and how shall they believe in him of whom they have not heard? and how shall they hear without a preacher? And how shall they preach, except they be sent? as it is written, How beautiful are the feet of them that preach the gospel of peace, and bring glad tidings of good things! (Romans 10:13-15)

Remission of sins is entirely by the grace of God. Faith is the means that God has instituted for the forgiveness of sins. Without faith there is no remission of sins. Salvation from sin is only by grace through faith. "For by grace are ye saved through faith; and that not of yourselves: it is the gift of God: Not of works, lest any man should boast." (Ephesians 2:8-9)

Whenever Jesus forgave sins during his ministry, it was always based upon his sovereign grace through faith. For example, in Luke, when Jesus forgave the woman who washed his feet with her hair and her tears, he did so based upon her faith. "And he said unto her, Thy sins are forgiven. And they that sat at meat with him began to say within themselves, Who is this that forgiveth sins also? And he said to the woman, **Thy faith hath saved thee; go in peace.**" (Luke 7:48-50)

When Jesus forgave the sins of the man who was paralyzed by the palsy, he did so based upon the demonstrated faith of the man. "And, behold, they brought to him a man sick of the palsy, lying on a bed: and **Jesus seeing their faith said unto the sick of the palsy; Son, be of good cheer; thy sins be forgiven thee.**" (Matthew 9:2) See also, Mark 2:5; Luke 5:20.

When Jesus told his disciples that he was giving them the keys to heaven and they had the power to bind and loose, he was referring to their commission to preach the gospel. Faith in Jesus is the means by which men are to be loosed from their sins. Rejection of Jesus leaves the person bound to their sins. "And I will give unto thee the keys of the kingdom of heaven: and whatsoever thou shalt bind on earth shall be bound in heaven: and whatsoever thou shalt loose on earth shall be loosed in heaven." (Matthew 16:19) See also Matthew 18:18.

People must believe in Jesus unto salvation before they die or they will remain bound to their sins and be damned to hell. If they turn from sin in repentance and toward Christ in faith, they will be loosed from their sins and enter heaven after their death. They are loosed from their sin on earth and that loosing is effectual in heaven as well. Those who reject Jesus Christ, remain bound to sin, and that binding keeps them out of the book of life. See Revelation 20:11-15. The saving faith, resulting in forgiveness of sins, must be granted to a person by God while he is alive on earth. There is no forgiveness of sin after death. In Luke 16:22-26, Jesus explained how a rich man was in hell and pleaded to cross over to heaven. Jesus explained that there was a great gulf between heaven and hell, and the rich man could not ever cross over it. What was bound on earth (his sins) was bound in heaven. In that episode, Lazarus was seen in heaven. Lazarus was saved from his sins before he died and now being in heaven could not ever cross over the great gulf and enter hell. What was loosed on earth (his sins) was loosed in heaven.

The remission and retention of sins is entirely based upon the faith of those who hear the gospel. How is it possible to have such faith? That faith is a gift of God that comes down from heaven. "For by grace are ye saved through faith; and that not of yourselves: it is the gift of God." (Ephesians 2:8) Indeed, Jesus is both the author and finisher of our faith. Hebrews 12:2. The faith necessary for salvation is given by God based entirely on his grace, which he determined in heaven before even the creation of the world.

> Blessed be the God and Father of our Lord Jesus Christ, who hath **blessed us with all spiritual blessings in heavenly places in Christ: According as he hath chosen us in him before the foundation of**

the world, that we should be holy and without blame before him in love: Having predestinated us unto the adoption of children by Jesus Christ to himself, according to the good pleasure of his will. (Ephesians 1:3-5)

The effective call of the gospel is based upon the love of God for his elect. No man can come to Jesus unless it was preordained in heaven and God the Father draws his chosen to Jesus.

No man can come to me, except the Father which hath sent me draw him: and I will raise him up at the last day. It is written in the prophets, And they shall be all taught of God. Every man therefore that hath heard, and hath learned of the Father, cometh unto me." (John 6:44-45)

The calling of the Lord is according to his will and pleasure. He shows mercy to his elect, whom he loves so much that he came and died on the cross as a propitiation for theirs sins. The salvation of his beloved elect was preordained in heaven.

And we know that all things work together for good to them that love God, to them who are the called according to his purpose. For whom he did foreknow, he also did predestinate to be conformed to the image of his Son, that he might be the firstborn among many brethren. Moreover whom he did predestinate, them he also called: and whom he called, them he also justified: and whom he justified, them he also glorified. (Romans 8:28-30)

The saving faith is a provision that comes from God in heaven. Indeed, without Jesus regenerating the soul, all would be bound to sin and damned to hell. "For the Son of man is come to save that which was lost." (Matthew 18:11) Jesus made the point that he did not come to earth to condemn, but to save, because all in the world are condemned already.

For God so loved the world, that he gave his only

begotten Son, that whosoever believeth in him should not perish, but have everlasting life. **For God sent not his Son into the world to condemn the world; but that the world through him might be saved. He that believeth on him is not condemned: but he that believeth not is condemned already, because he hath not believed in the name of the only begotten Son of God.**" (John 3:16-18)

The Catholic dogma adds the confessional to faith. Catholics believe in a false Jesus, who did not fully atone for their sins on the cross. Therefore, it is necessary that the Catholic "faithful" go to the Catholic version of Christ, in the form of a priest, and have their sins forgiven, based upon penance, as instructed by the priest. The penance is a work that is added to faith in the false Catholic Jesus.

Under the true gospel, all sins of the elect believer, both past and present, are atoned for by Jesus on the cross. "For Christ also hath once suffered for sins, the just for the unjust, that he might bring us to God." (1 Peter 3:18) If any works are added to the atonement of Jesus on the cross, that is clear evidence in the lack of faith in the true Jesus and his effectual atonement. Good works are a manifestation of salvation, they do not earn salvation. We are saved by the grace of God alone through faith in Jesus Christ alone. Our salvation "is not of works." Ephesians 2:9. The gospel is clear that salvation is all by the grace of God. If you add works to grace, it ceases to be grace. "And if by grace, then is it no more of works: otherwise grace is no more grace. But if it be of works, then is it no more grace: otherwise work is no more work." (Romans 11:6)

One should look to Father in heaven through faith in Jesus Christ for the remission of sin and not to the Catholic "father" on earth in the confessional. Jesus admonished against looking for spiritual leadership from those who demand to be called "father," thus indicating that they are taking the place of God on earth, as do the Catholic priests. "And call no man your father upon the earth: for one is your Father, which is in heaven." (Matthew 23:9)

11 Doctrines of Devils

Once a Roman Catholic receives the sacrament of "Holy Orders" he becomes a Catholic priest, and is thereafter prohibited from getting married.[229] In addition, during Lent Catholics are forbidden to eat meat on Friday.[230] God has expressly identified those two practices as "doctrines of devils."

> Now the Spirit speaketh expressly, that in the latter times some shall depart from the faith, giving heed to **seducing spirits, and doctrines of devils**; Speaking lies in hypocrisy; having their conscience seared with a hot iron; **Forbidding to marry, and commanding to abstain from meats**, which God hath created to be received with thanksgiving of them which believe and know the truth. For every creature of God is good, and nothing to be refused, if it be received with thanksgiving: For it is sanctified by the word of God and prayer. (1 Timothy 4:1-5)

One should be mindful that the Devil can appear as an angel of light, and the ministers of the Devil can transform themselves to appear as ministers of righteousness.

> For such are false apostles, deceitful workers, transforming themselves into the apostles of Christ. And no marvel; **for Satan himself is transformed into**

> an angel of light. **Therefore it is no great thing if his ministers also be transformed as the ministers of righteousness**; whose end shall be according to their works. (2 Corinthians 11:13-15)

It, therefore, would not be surprising if the devil decided to appear as an apparition of the Virgin Mary. In 1846, the year Pope Pius IX was elected pope, a devil masquerading as the Virgin Mary appeared to two children at La Salette in France. That apparition provided a secret message to the pope. The contents of the message were never made public, but in writing down the secret message one of the children asked how to spell the words "infallibility" and "antichrist."[231] What could the secret message have been? Those who know, aren't talking. We do know, however, that on December 8, 1854 Pope Pius IX issued his Papal Bull, Ineffabilis Deus, officially declaring that Mary was immaculately conceived and remained without sin. Only a devil could come up with such an ungodly and diabolical teaching. However, it was not a new doctrine; it had long been discussed secretly within the Roman Catholic Church.

The Roman Catholic Church is spiritual Babylon. It is not the Church of Jesus Christ, it is the church of Satan. It is the habitation of devils.

> And he cried mightily with a strong voice, saying, **Babylon the great is fallen, is fallen, and is become the habitation of devils, and the hold of every foul spirit**, and a cage of every unclean and hateful bird. (Revelation 18:2)

Just as the religious leaders did at and before the first coming of Jesus Christ, so today the religious leaders have set up a system of man made, devil inspired rules that are in direct conflict with the teaching of God. They pretend to be Christians but in fact are wicked and evil servants of Satan, deceiving and being deceived. Jesus warned us about them.

> Beware of **false prophets, which come to you in sheep's clothing, but inwardly they are ravening wolves.** (Matthew 7:15)

12 Putting Christ to an Open Shame

Wylie identifies the principal lying wonder of the papacy as the doctrine of transubstantiation. There can be no doubt that the abominable subterfuge of transubstantiation is the cornerstone of Catholic theology. It is truly a wonder of wonders that the Catholic priest can claim the authority to order the Lord God Almighty Jesus Christ from heaven and enter into and become a piece of bread. That is not hyperbole; that is the official Catholic doctrine. In 1915, Roman Catholic Priest David S. Phelan arrogantly explained his power over Jesus Christ during the blasphemous Catholic Mass:

> I never invite an angel down from heaven to hear Mass here. The is not the place for angels. The only person in heaven I ever ask to come down here is Jesus Christ, and Him I command to come down. He has to come when I bid him. I took bread in my fingers this morning and said: 'This is the body and blood of Jesus Christ', and He had to come down. This is one of the things He must do. He must come down every time I say Mass at my bidding. ... I do it in obedience, reverence, homage, and adoration, but I do it, and when I do it, Christ must obey."[232]

The Judaic/Babylonian liturgy of the Eucharist in the Roman Catholic Church involves a witchcraft ceremony, during which a piece of bread (the host) and some wine is purported to be transformed into

Jesus Christ. It is the official teaching of the church that the host and wine both become the body, blood, soul, and divinity of the Lord God Jesus Christ. The Catholic Church teaches that the appearance of bread and wine remain, but that they have been transubstantiated into the actual Lord God Almighty Jesus Christ.

> **In the most blessed sacrament of the Eucharist 'the body and blood, together with the soul and divinity, of our Lord Jesus Christ and, therefore, *the whole Christ is truly, really, and substantially* contained.'** CATECHISM OF THE CATHOLIC CHURCH, § 1374, 1994 (italics in original, bold emphasis added).

The Catholic Church is saying, in no uncertain terms, that Jesus Christ himself, God Almighty, is present during the Catholic Mass in the outward form of bread and wine.

> By the consecration the transubstantiation of the bread and wine into the Body and Blood of Christ is brought about. Under the consecrated species of bread and wine **Christ himself, living and glorious, is present in a true, real, and substantial manner: his Body and his Blood, with his soul and his divinity.** CATECHISM OF THE CATHOLIC CHURCH, § 1413, 1994 (emphasis added).

> **Here the pastor should explain that in this Sacrament are contained not only the true body of Christ and all the constituents of a true body, such as bones and sinews, but also Christ whole and entire. He should point out that the word *Christ* designates the God-man, that is to say, one Person in whom are united the divine and human natures; that the Holy Eucharist, therefore, contains both, and humanity whole and entire, consisting of the soul, all the parts of the body and the blood, all of which must be believed to be in this Sacrament. In heaven the whole humanity is united to the Divinity in one hypostasis, or Person; hence it would be impious, to suppose that the body of Christ, which**

is contained in the Sacrament, is separated from His Divinity. THE CATECHISM OF THE COUNCIL OF TRENT (emphasis added).[233]

The Catholic doctrine is that during communion Catholics are actually eating God Almighty when they consume the Eucharistic host. Anyone who disagrees with that doctrine is under a papal curse. "If anyone say that Christ, given in the Eucharist, is eaten spiritually only, and not also sacramentally and really, let him be anathema." COUNCIL OF TRENT, ON THE MOST HOLY SACRAMENT OF THE EUCHARIST, Canon VIII.

The Catholic doctrine of transubstantiation is actually ceremonial witchcraft. William Schnoebelen was a former satanic priest, master Mason, alleged member of the Iluminati, and a Catholic priest in the Old Roman Catholic Church (O.R.C.C.). The O.R.C.C. is a splinter group from the Vatican which has valid holy orders, has celebrated Mass for centuries, and allows for a married priesthood.[234] Schnoebelen stated that the Catholic liturgy of the Mass is basically an occult magic ritual. It is, therefore, easy for Satanists to tweak it slightly in order to make it into the consummate black magic ritual.[235] Schnoebelen degenerated in his climb up the satanic hierarchy to the point where he became a Nosferatic priest.[236] A Nosferatic priest is a Vampire. *Nosferatu* is the Romanian word for the "undead" or vampire. Since all members of the Nosferatic priesthood must first be priests of the Catholic or Eastern Orthodox Rite, they believe that they have the power to produce the full nine pints of the blood of Jesus contained in the chalice of wine through the magic of transubstantiation. When real human blood was not available to him, he satisfied his demonic need for human blood through the liturgy of the Catholic Mass.[237]

Because the Catholic Church teaches that the Eucharist is God in the form of bread and wine, it requires that all worship the Eucharist as God. "Because Christ himself is present in the sacrament of the altar, he is to be honored with the worship of adoration." CATECHISM OF THE CATHOLIC CHURCH, § 1418, 1994. The Roman Catholic Church teaches that all should worship the bread as though it is God.

> Wherefore, there is no room left to doubt that all the faithful of Christ may, according to the custom ever

received in the Catholic Church, render in veneration the worship of *latria*, which is due to the true God, to this most holy Sacrament. COUNCIL OF TRENT, DECREE CONCERNING THE MOST HOLY SACRAMENT OF THE EUCHARIST, Session XIII, Chapter V, October 11, 1551.

The Roman Catholic Church places a curse on anyone who says that the Eucharistic Host should not be worshiped.

If anyone saith, in the Holy Sacrament of the Eucharist, Christ, the only-begotten son of God, is not to be adored with the worship, even external, of latria; and is, consequently, neither to be venerated with a special festive solemnity, nor to be solemnly borne about in processions, according to the laudable and universal right and custom of Holy church; or is not to be proposed publicly to the people to be adored, and that the adorers thereof are idolaters; let him be anathema. COUNCIL OF TRENT, ON THE MOST HOLY SACRAMENT OF THE EUCHARIST, Canon VI.

The Catholic Church teaches that wine and bread have been turned into the body and blood of Christ, and that when one is consuming the bread and wine it is only the form of bread and wine, it is actually the body, blood, soul, and divinity of Christ. The Catholic Church teaches that the wine is actually Christ's blood but only appears to be wine, and the bread is actually Christ's flesh but only appears to be bread. The Catholic doctrine of transubstantiation is a sin. In the following passages God has made it clear that people are to abstain from drinking *any manner* of blood. Presumably, any manner of blood includes transubstantiated blood.

Moreover ye shall **eat no manner of blood, whether it be of fowl or of beast, in any of your dwellings**. Whatsoever soul it be that eateth any manner of blood, even that soul shall be cut off from his people. (Leviticus 7:26-27)

And whatsoever man there be of the house of Israel, or

of the strangers that sojourn among you, that eateth **any manner of blood; I will even set my face against that soul that eateth blood,** and will cut him off from among his people. (Leviticus 17:10)

[A]bstain from meats offered to idols, and from blood, and from things strangled, and from fornication: from which if ye keep yourselves, ye shall do well. Fare ye well. (Acts 15:29)

The Catholic church quotes the following passage, purporting it to support its claim that during the Catholic Mass bread is turned into God.

And he took bread, and gave thanks, and brake it, and gave unto them, saying, This is my body which is given for you: **this do in remembrance of me.** (Luke 22:19)

That passage in Luke does not support the proposition that bread is thereafter to be turned into God. Before Christ came to earth, God required ceremonial sacrifices from the Jews. Those sacrifices were done in order to bring to mind the coming Messiah. The Jews looked forward to Christ, the sacrificial lamb of God. The Old Testament sacrifices themselves did not atone for the sins. Jesus was the atonement. Salvation from sins came then, as now, by the grace of God through faith in God and his Messiah, Jesus. The memorial instituted by Christ during the last supper was for us to look back to the sacrifice of Christ, just as the Jews used to look forward toward Christ's coming. We are to do it in remembrance of him and his sacrifice for us.

For the law having a shadow of good things to come, and not the very image of the things, can never with those sacrifices which they offered year by year continually make the comers thereunto perfect. For then would they not have ceased to be offered? because that the worshippers once purged should have had no more conscience of sins. **But in those sacrifices there is a remembrance again made of sins every year. For it is not possible that the blood of bulls and of goats should take away sins.** (Hebrews 10:1-4)

Jesus never intended that the breaking of bread be any more than a memorial to bring remembrance of him and his sacrifice on the cross.

> And when he had given thanks, he brake it, and said, Take, eat: this is my body, which is broken for you: **this do in remembrance of me.** After the same manner also he took the cup, when he had supped, saying, This cup is the new testament in my blood: **this do ye, as oft as ye drink it, in remembrance of me. For as often as ye eat this bread, and drink this cup, ye do shew the Lord's death till he come.** (1 Corinthians 11:24-26)

Jesus was using a metaphor, when he said "this is my body" and "this is my blood." He had also called himself the "lamb of God" and "the bread of life." These phrases were intended to be figurative expressions. We don't think of Christ as a literal lamb; why does the Romish church interpret the Jesus' words at the last supper literally?

The Roman church often cites Matthew 26:26-28 in support of its claim that the priest, during the Catholic Mass, changes bread and wine into the blood and body of Jesus.

> And as they were eating, Jesus took bread, and blessed it, and brake it, and gave it to the disciples, and said, Take, eat; this is my body. And he took the cup, and gave thanks, and gave it to them, saying, Drink ye all of it; For this is my blood of the new testament, which is shed for many for the remission of sins. (Matthew 26:26-28)

Jesus was eating the Passover meal with his disciples. The Passover was intended to be a memorial that was to celebrate God having freed the Jews from Egyptian slavery. The fourteenth day of the first month is the Passover (Leviticus 23:4-5, Exodus 12:17-18). Passover is immediately followed by the seven days of unleavened bread (Leviticus 23:6-7, Exodus 12:15-16). At the last supper Jesus was making reference to the fact that the unleavened bread that was eaten during Passover not only looked back to the spotless lamb of Passover, but also looked forward to him as the Christ, who would die as the Passover lamb for the sins of the world. 1 Peter 1:18-19. Just as the Passover memorial looked back to the Passover lamb, so also would this new Passover last supper harken back to the Passover lamb of God, Jesus Christ, who was crucified for our sins. Just as the unleavened bread eaten on Passover was not the actual lamb, but only a memorial, so also the unleavened bread and wine celebrating the last supper are not the actual body and blood of Jesus; they are only memorials.

The Catholic church teaches that Jesus actually turned the fruit of the vine into blood. By taking verses 26-28 of Matthew chapter 26 out of context the Catholic church has been able to deceive the whole world. All one need do to see that Jesus did not actually change the fruit of the vine in the cup into his blood is to put verses 26-28 back in context by reading the next verse, verse 29. "But I say unto you, I will not drink henceforth of **this fruit of the vine**, until that day when I drink it new with you in my Father's kingdom." (Matthew 26:29) Notice, in that very verse (verse 29) following his statement that "this is my blood" Jesus states plainly that what was in the cup was still the "fruit of the vine." It had not been changed into his blood. Verse 29 reveals that his statement that "this is my blood" was simply a metaphor. That is why the Catholic church does not want the common people to read the Bible. Once the people see the passages in context, they understand the deceptive sophistry of the Catholic church.

The passage found in the Holy Bible at John 6:27-66 explains clearly what Jesus meant when he said "this is my body" and "this is my blood." In that Bible passage Jesus starts out by telling his disciples "labour not for the meat which perisheth, but for that meat which endureth unto everlasting life." That meat is a Spiritual meat. Jesus points out that to eat his flesh and drink his blood is spiritual language that represents believing on him. Only those, however, that are chosen by God for eternal life can understand these truths. Read the passage carefully; you will understand that eating Jesus' flesh and drinking his blood are metaphors for believing in him. Jesus makes the point clear four different times in that passage (verses 29, 35, 40, and 47). One can only understand this spiritual truth if one has the Holy Spirit to guide him. It is foolishness to the unsaved. The unsaved read the passage and are easily persuaded by the Catholic church that Jesus is talking about literally eating his flesh and drinking his blood.

Labour not for the meat which perisheth, but for that meat which endureth unto everlasting life, which the Son of man shall give unto you: for him hath God the Father sealed. Then said they unto him, What shall we do, that we might work the works of God? Jesus answered and said unto them, **This is the work of God, that ye believe on him whom he hath sent.** They said therefore unto him, What sign shewest thou then, that we may see, and believe thee? what dost thou work? Our fathers did eat manna in the desert; as it is written, He gave them bread from heaven to eat. Then Jesus said unto them, Verily, verily, I say unto you, Moses gave you not that bread from heaven; but **my Father giveth you the true bread from heaven. For the bread of God is he which cometh down from heaven, and giveth life unto the world.** Then said they unto him, Lord, evermore give us this bread. **And Jesus said unto them, I am the bread of life: he that cometh to me shall never hunger; and he that believeth on me shall never thirst.** But I said unto you, That ye also have seen me, and believe not. All that the Father giveth me shall come to me; and him that cometh to me I will in no wise cast out. For I came down from heaven, not to do mine own will, but the will of him that sent me. And this is the Father's will which hath sent me, that of all which he hath given me I should lose nothing, but should raise it up again at the last day. **And this is the will of him that sent me, that every one which seeth the Son, and believeth on him, may have everlasting life: and I will raise him up at the last day.** The Jews then murmured at him, because he said, I am the bread which came down from heaven. And they said, Is not this Jesus, the son of Joseph, whose father and mother we know? how is it then that he saith, I came down from heaven? Jesus therefore answered and said unto them, Murmur not among yourselves. No man can come to me, except the Father which hath sent me draw him: and I will raise him up at the last day. It is written in the prophets, And they shall be all taught of God. Every man therefore that hath heard, and hath learned of the Father, cometh unto me. Not that any man hath seen the Father, save he which is of God, he hath seen the Father. **Verily, verily, I say unto you, He that believeth on me hath everlasting life. I am that bread of life.** Your fathers did eat manna in the wilderness, and are dead. **This is the bread which cometh down from heaven, that a man may eat thereof, and not die. I am the living bread which came down from heaven: if any man eat of this bread, he shall live for ever: and the bread that I will give is my flesh, which I will give for the life of the world.** The Jews therefore strove among themselves, saying, How can this man give us his flesh to eat? Then Jesus said unto them, Verily, verily, I say unto you, Except ye eat the flesh of the Son of man, and drink his blood, ye have no life in you. Whoso eateth my flesh, and drinketh my blood, hath eternal life; and I will raise him up at the last day. For my flesh is meat indeed, and my blood is drink indeed. He that eateth my flesh, and drinketh my blood, dwelleth in me, and I in him. As the living Father hath sent me, and I live by the Father: so he that eateth me, even he shall live by me. This is that bread which came down from heaven: not as your fathers did eat manna, and are dead: he that eateth of this bread shall live for ever. These things said he in the synagogue, as he taught in Capernaum. Many therefore of his disciples, when they had heard this, said, This is an hard saying; who can hear it? When Jesus knew in himself that his disciples murmured at it, he said unto them, Doth this offend you? What and if ye shall see the Son of man ascend up where he was before? It is the spirit that quickeneth; the flesh profiteth nothing: the words that I speak unto you, they are spirit, and they are life. But there are some of you that believe not. For Jesus knew from the beginning who they were that believed not, and who should betray him. And he said, Therefore said I unto you, that **no man can come unto me, except it were given unto him of my Father**. From that time many of his disciples went back, and walked no more with him. (John 6:27-66)

The Catholic church teaches that the bread and wine is to be worshiped with the same veneration that one would feel if one were worshiping God. That worship is due to the bread and wine because the Romish church teaches that the consecrated bread and wine are in fact God in the form of bread and wine.

> [I]n the modern Roman Rite the public worship of the Eucharist is envisaged as a normal part of the liturgical life of diocesan, parish and religious communities.[238]

> With a delicate and jealous attention the Church has regulated Eucharistic worship to its minutest details. . . . [E]verything is important, significant, and divine when there is a question of the Real Presence of Jesus Christ.[239]

> Wherefore, there is no room left to doubt that all the faithful of Christ may, according to the custom ever received in the Catholic Church, **render in veneration the worship of *latria*, which is due to the true God, to this most holy Sacrament.** For not therefore is it the less to be adored on this account, that it was instituted by Christ the Lord in order to be present therein, of Whom the Eternal Father, when introducing Him into the world, says: 'and let all the angels of God adore Him;' Whom the Magi falling down, adored; Who, in fine, as the Scripture testifies, was adored by the Apostles in Galilee. *THE COUNCIL OF TRENT, DECREE CONCERNING THE MOST HOLY SACRAMENT OF THE EUCHARIST, On the Cult and Veneration to be Shown to This Most Holy Sacrament,* October 11, 1554.

> ***Worship of the Eucharist.*** In the liturgy of the Mass we express our faith in the **real presence of Christ under the species of bread and wine** by, among other ways, **genuflecting or bowing deeply as a sign of**

> **adoration** of the Lord. The Catholic Church has always offered and still offers to the sacrament of the Eucharist the cult of **adoration,** not only during Mass, but also outside of it, reserving the consecrated hosts with the utmost care, exposing them to the **solemn veneration** of the faithful, and carrying them in procession." *CATECHISM OF THE CATHOLIC CHURCH*, § 1378, 1994 (italics in original, bold type added).

God, however, has an objection to this Catholic worship of idols.

> And God spake all these words, saying, I am the LORD thy God, which have brought thee out of the land of Egypt, out of the house of bondage. **Thou shalt have no other gods before me. Thou shalt not make unto thee any graven image, or any likeness of any thing that is in heaven above, or that is in the earth beneath, or that is in the water under the earth: Thou shalt not bow down thyself to them, nor serve them**: for I the LORD thy God am a jealous God, visiting the iniquity of the fathers upon the children unto the third and fourth generation of them that hate me; And shewing mercy unto thousands of them that love me, and keep my commandments. (Exodus 20:1-6)

The Catholic Church takes the bible passage found at 1 Corinthians 11:29 out of context to support their position that the wine and bread are miraculously turned into the Lord Jesus during the Catholic Mass. The passage reads: "For he that eateth and drinketh unworthily, eateth and drinketh damnation to himself, not discerning the Lord's body."

Looking at the passages that precede and follow 1 Corinthians 11:29 we see that Paul was speaking of fellowship within the body of Christ. It is apparent when reading the passage in context that Paul was calling the church of Christ the "Lord's body." He was admonishing the church not to be divided and not to be inconsiderate of one another. He wanted them to understand that when they join to eat the Lord's supper they are members of the "Lord's body" that have joined in a memorial to Christ's death. Apparently, some were coming together for the Lord's supper to have a meal and not for fellowship in remembrance of the crucifixion of Christ. They were not being charitable; they were eating while others of the church went hungry. They were not discerning that God's church is the "Lord's body." The context of the passage proves that the reference in the passage to "the Lord's body" is not describing the bread and wine being consumed but rather the believers that are consuming the bread and wine.

> Now in this that I declare unto you I praise you not, that ye come together not for the better, but for the worse. For first of all, when ye come together in the church, I hear that there be divisions among you; and I partly believe it. For there must be also heresies among you, that they which are approved may be made manifest among you. When ye come together therefore into one place, this is not to eat the Lord's supper. For in eating every one taketh before other his own supper: and one is hungry, and another is drunken. What? have ye not houses to eat and to drink in? or despise ye the church of God, and shame them that have not? What shall I say to you? shall I praise you in this? I praise you not. For I have received of the Lord that which also I delivered unto you, That the Lord Jesus the same night in which he was betrayed took bread: And when he had given thanks, he brake it, and said, Take, eat: this is my body, which is broken for you: **this do in remembrance of me.** After the same manner also he took the cup, when he had supped, saying, This cup is the new testament in my blood: **this do ye, as oft as ye drink it, in remembrance of me. For as often as ye eat this bread, and drink this cup, ye do shew the Lord's death till he come**. Wherefore whosoever shall eat this bread, and drink this cup of the Lord, unworthily, shall be guilty of the body and blood of the Lord. But let a man examine himself, and so let him eat of that bread, and drink of that cup. **For he that eateth and drinketh unworthily, eateth and**

drinketh damnation to himself, not discerning the Lord's body. For this cause many are weak and sickly among you, and many sleep. For if we would judge ourselves, we should not be judged. But when we are judged, we are chastened of the Lord, that we should not be condemned with the world. Wherefore, my brethren, when ye come together to eat, tarry one for another. And if any man hunger, let him eat at home; that ye come not together unto condemnation. And the rest will I set in order when I come. Now concerning spiritual gifts, brethren, I would not have you ignorant. Ye know that ye were Gentiles, carried away unto these dumb idols, even as ye were led. Wherefore I give you to understand, that no man speaking by the Spirit of God calleth Jesus accursed: and that no man can say that Jesus is the Lord, but by the Holy Ghost. Now there are diversities of gifts, but the same Spirit. And there are differences of administrations, but the same Lord. And there are diversities of operations, but it is the same God which worketh all in all. But the manifestation of the Spirit is given to every man to profit withal. For to one is given by the Spirit the word of wisdom; to another the word of knowledge by the same Spirit; To another faith by the same Spirit; to another the gifts of healing by the same Spirit; To another the working of miracles; to another prophecy; to another discerning of spirits; to another divers kinds of tongues; to another the interpretation of tongues: **But all these worketh that one and the selfsame Spirit, dividing to every man severally as he will. For as the body is one, and hath many members, and all the members of that one body, being many, are one body: so also is Christ. For by one Spirit are we all baptized into one body,** whether we be Jews or Gentiles, whether we be bond or free; and have been all made to drink into one Spirit. **For the body is not one member, but many.** If the foot shall say, Because I am not the hand, I am not of the body; is it therefore not of the **body?** And if the ear shall say, Because I am not the eye, I am not of the **body**; is it therefore not of the **body**? If the whole **body** were an eye, where were the hearing? If the whole were hearing, where were the smelling? But now hath God set the members every one of them in the **body**, as it hath pleased him. And if they were all one member, where were the body? But now are they **many members, yet but one body**. And the eye cannot say unto the hand, I have no need of thee: nor again the head to the feet, I have no need of you. Nay, much more those members of the body, which seem to be more feeble, are necessary: And those members of the body, which we think to be less honourable, upon these we bestow more abundant honour; and our uncomely parts have more abundant comeliness. For our comely parts have no need: but God hath tempered the body together, having given more abundant honour to that part which lacked: **That there should be no schism in the body; but that the members should have the same care one for another. And whether one member suffer, all the members suffer with it; or one member be honoured, all the members rejoice with it. Now ye are the body of Christ, and members in particular.** And God hath set some in the church, first apostles, secondarily prophets, thirdly teachers, after that miracles, then gifts of healings, helps, governments, diversities of tongues. Are all apostles? are all prophets? are all teachers? are all workers of miracles? Have all the gifts of healing? do all speak with tongues? do all interpret? But covet earnestly the best gifts: and yet shew I unto you a more excellent way. (1 Corinthians 11:17-12:31)

The following passage describes the Christian believers as "one bread, and one body."

Wherefore, my dearly beloved, flee from idolatry. I speak as to wise men; judge ye what I say. The cup of blessing which we bless, is it not the **communion** of the blood of Christ? The bread which we break, is it not the **communion** of the body of Christ? **For we**

being many are one bread, and one body: for we are all partakers of that one bread. (1 Corinthians 10:14-17)

The wine and bread that are consumed are a way of sharing and communicating within the church in order to commemorate Christ's suffering and death. The bread and wine are not only a commemoration of the crucifixion of Jesus but also our joining with him in that crucifixion. That is what is meant by the communion of the blood and body of Christ. The "Lord's body" is his church. The passage states that we are all partakers of that one bread. That means that by faith in Jesus our sinful flesh was crucified with Christ on the cross and that we are to no longer live after the flesh but after the Spirit. The following Bible passages testify that our sinful flesh was crucified with Christ, and we are therefore freed from the slavery of sin and can follow the Spirit of the Lord, who is in us; just as Jesus rose from the dead, so all believers will also rise from the dead.

I am crucified with Christ: nevertheless I live; yet not I, but Christ liveth in me: and the life which I now live in the flesh I live by the faith of the Son of God, who loved me, and gave himself for me. (Galatians 2:20)

And they that are Christ's have crucified the flesh with the affections and lusts. If we live in the Spirit, let us also walk in the Spirit. (Galatians 5:24-25)

Always bearing about in the body the dying of the Lord Jesus, that the life also of Jesus might be made manifest in our body. For we which live are alway delivered unto death for Jesus' sake, that the life also of Jesus might be made manifest in our mortal flesh. So then death worketh in us, but life in you. (2 Corinthians 4:10-12)

Know ye not, that so many of us as were baptized into Jesus Christ were baptized into his death? Therefore we are buried with him by baptism into death: that like as Christ was raised up from the dead by the glory of

> the Father, even so we also should walk in newness of life. For if we have been planted together in the likeness of his death, we shall be also in the likeness of his resurrection: **Knowing this, that our old man is crucified with him, that the body of sin might be destroyed, that henceforth we should not serve sin. For he that is dead is freed from sin. Now if we be dead with Christ, we believe that we shall also live with him: Knowing that Christ being raised from the dead dieth no more; death hath no more dominion over him. For in that he died, he died unto sin once: but in that he liveth, he liveth unto God. Likewise reckon ye also yourselves to be dead indeed unto sin, but alive unto God through Jesus Christ our Lord.** (Romans 6:3-11)

Before Jesus was crucified he prayed for his disciples to God the Father. During that prayer, he prayed that all who believe in him become one, just as Jesus and his Father are one.

> I pray for them: I pray not for the world, but for them which thou hast given me; for they are thine. And all mine are thine, and thine are mine; and I am glorified in them. And now I am no more in the world, but these are in the world, and I come to thee. Holy Father, keep through thine own name those whom thou hast given me, **that they may be one, as we are.** (John 17:9-11)

In that prayer Jesus expressed his will that all those that believe in him should not only be one with each other but also one with him and his Father.

> Neither pray I for these alone, but for them also which shall believe on me through their word; **That they all may be one; as thou, Father, art in me, and I in thee, that they also may be one in us**: that the world may believe that thou hast sent me. And the glory which thou gavest me I have given them; **that they may be one, even as we are one: I in them, and thou in me, that they may be made perfect in one**; and

that the world may know that thou hast sent me, and hast loved them, as thou hast loved me. Father, I will that they also, whom thou hast given me, be with me where I am; that they may behold my glory, which thou hast given me: for thou lovedst me before the foundation of the world. O righteous Father, the world hath not known thee: but I have known thee, and these have known that thou hast sent me. And I have declared unto them thy name, and will declare it: **that the love wherewith thou hast loved me may be in them, and I in them.** (John 17:20-26)

All Jesus' prayers were answered. Jesus stated: **"I am in my Father, and ye in me, and I in you."** (John 14:20) The indwelling of the Holy Ghost that creates a spiritual temple of the Lord is a recurring theme of the gospel. All members of Christ's church are joined together to form one body in Christ!

One God and Father of all, who is above all, and through all, and in you all. (Ephesians 4:6)

For as we have many members in one body, and all members have not the same office: **So we, being many, are one body in Christ, and every one members one of another.** (Romans 12:4-5)

All those who believe in Jesus are members of his church and are one with Jesus and his Father. Jesus Christ is the head of the church; the church is his body.

And he is the head of the body, the church: who is the beginning, the firstborn from the dead; that in all things he might have the preeminence. (Colossians 1:18)

And hath put all things under his feet, and gave him *to be* the head over all things to the church, Which is his body, the fulness of him that filleth all in all. (Ephesians 1:22-23)

For no man ever yet hated his own flesh; but nourisheth and cherisheth it, even as the Lord the church: **For we are members of his body, of his flesh, and of his bones.** (Ephesians 5:29-30)

Who now rejoice in my sufferings for you, and fill up that which is behind of the afflictions of Christ in my flesh **for his body's sake, which is the church**: Whereof I am made a minister, according to the dispensation of God which is given to me for you, to fulfil the word of God; Even the mystery which hath been hid from ages and from generations, but now is made manifest to his saints: To whom God would make known what is the riches of the glory of this mystery among the Gentiles; which is **Christ in you, the hope of glory**: (Colossians 1:24-27)

There is one church body; it is a spiritual body that is joined together by the Holy Spirit.

Endeavouring to keep the unity of the Spirit in the bond of peace. **There is one body, and one Spirit, even as ye are called in one hope of your calling**; (Ephesians 4:3-4)

Believers are the temple of God, because the Holy Spirit indwells those who are chosen by God to believe in Jesus.

What? know ye not that **your body is the temple of the Holy Ghost** which is in you, which ye have of God, and ye are not your own? (1 Corinthians 6:19)

Know ye not that **ye are the temple of God**, and that the Spirit of God dwelleth in you? If any man defile the temple of God, him shall God destroy; for the temple of God is holy, which temple ye are. (1 Corinthians 3:16-17)

The Catholic Church minds the things of the flesh; it has twisted spiritual truths into carnal lies. Their misapplication of the

Bible passage at 1 Corinthians 11:29 is just one example of their taking of Bible passages out of context and misrepresenting them to support their unbiblical doctrines. God's church is not a physical building that is joined by brick and mortar, it is a spiritual building; it is the "Lord's body," with its members joined by the Holy Spirit. The Lord's supper is a memorial for the Lord's body.

> **For they that are after the flesh do mind the things of the flesh; but they that are after the Spirit the things of the Spirit.** For to be carnally minded is death; but to be spiritually minded is life and peace. Because the carnal mind is enmity against God: for it is not subject to the law of God, neither indeed can be. So then they that are in the flesh cannot please God. But ye are not in the flesh, but in the Spirit, if so be that **the Spirit of God dwell in you.** Now if any man have not the Spirit of Christ, he is none of his. And if Christ be in you, the body is dead because of sin; but the Spirit is life because of righteousness. But **if the Spirit of him that raised up Jesus from the dead dwell in you, he that raised up Christ from the dead shall also quicken your mortal bodies by his Spirit that dwelleth in you.** (Romans 8:5-11)

The Catholic church has ruled that the unbloody sacrifice of the Eucharist at Mass is as effective a propitiation for sin as the actual crucifixion of Jesus Christ. A propitiation for sin is a sacrifice to appease God. That is to satisfy God and render favorable the object of his prior disfavor. God, however, was satisfied with Christ's sacrifice. When Jesus said "it is finished" he meant what he said, "it is finished." John 19:30. To believe that it is necessary to have a continual sacrifice is to not believe in the Jesus of the Bible. The Jesus that the Romish church teaches is a different Jesus, an ineffectual Jesus. The *Catechism of the Catholic Church* states:

> **In the divine sacrifice which is celebrated in the Mass, the same Christ who offered himself once on a bloody manner on the alter of the cross is contained and is offered in an unbloody manner.**[240]

> As often as the sacrifice of the Cross by which **'Christ our Pasch has been sacrificed' is celebrated on the altar, the work of our redemption is carried out.**[241]

The Catechism of the Council of Trent states:

> We therefore confess that the Sacrifice of the Mass is and ought to be considered one and the same Sacrifice as that of the cross, for the victim is one and the same, namely, Christ our Lord, who offered Himself once only, a bloody sacrifice on the altar of the cross. The bloody and unbloody victim are not two, but one victim only, whose sacrifice is **daily renewed** in the Eucharist, in obedience to the command of our Lord: *Do this for a commemoration of me.*[242]

> [T]he sacred and holy Sacrifice of the Mass is not a Sacrifice of praise and thanksgiving only, or a mere commemoration of the Sacrifice performed on the cross but also truly a **propitiatory** Sacrifice.[243]

The Holy Bible, on the other hand, states that the one sacrifice of Jesus was sufficient for all his elect, for all time.

> So Christ was **once offered** to bear the sins of many; and unto them that look for him shall he appear the second time without sin unto salvation. (Hebrews 9:28)

> By the which will we are sanctified through the offering of the body of Jesus Christ **once for all**. And every priest standeth daily ministering and offering oftentimes the same sacrifices, which can never take away sins: But this man, after he had **offered one sacrifice for sins for ever**, sat down on the right hand of God; From henceforth expecting till his enemies be made his footstool. For **by one offering he hath perfected for ever them that are sanctified.** (Hebrews 10:10-14)

Christ made his one sacrifice on the cross whereby those that believe in him are made perfect, consequently there will be no more offering of any kind for sin, period.

> But this man, after he had offered one sacrifice for sins for ever, sat down on the right hand of God; From henceforth expecting till his enemies be made his footstool. For **by one offering he hath perfected for ever them that are sanctified**. Whereof the Holy Ghost also is a witness to us: for after that he had said before, This is the covenant that I will make with them after those days, saith the Lord, I will put my laws into their hearts, and in their minds will I write them; And their sins and iniquities will I remember no more. **Now where remission of these is, there is no more offering for sin**. (Hebrews 10:12-18)

This unbloody re-crucifixion of Christ during the Catholic Mass is a re-enactment of the humiliation suffered by Christ on the cross. This re-enactment is not only unnecessary, it is a blasphemy. The bible states that we are to look to Jesus in faith, not in ceremony. Jesus despised the shame of the cross. "Looking unto Jesus the author and finisher of our faith; who for the joy that was set before him **endured the cross, despising the shame**, and is set down at the right hand of the throne of God." (Hebrews 12:2)

Jesus was crucified once for all time. The Catholic Mass is a demonstration that the Catholic Church does not believe in the sufficiency of Jesus' sacrifice on the cross. They require that he be crucified over and over again, day after day, week after week, month after month, year after year. The Catholic Mass is more than an affront to Christ; it is a ceremonial attack on Christ. It is an antichrist ceremony, whereby the Roman church puts Christ to an open shame by crucifying him anew. The bible states that it is a terrible sin to crucify Jesus again, because it once again puts him to an open shame. "If they shall fall away, to renew them again unto repentance; seeing **they crucify to themselves the Son of God afresh, and put him to an open shame**." (Hebrews 6:6)

13 The Dark Secret of the Catholic Liturgy

As blasphemous as is the exoteric meaning of the Catholic Eucharistic Mass, there is yet a still an even more abominable esoteric meaning behind the ceremony.

The Jewish book of mysticism, the Kabbalah, is the key to the esoteric meaning of the Catholic liturgy. The Catholic celebration of the Eucharist is actually a witchcraft ceremony involving a pantheon of gods and goddesses, born of the Babylonian theosophy brought into the Catholic Church by the Jews.

The Catholic Encyclopedia reveals that the Jewish liturgy is the source for the Eucharistic liturgy of the Catholic Church.[244] Athol Bloomer explains that the Jewish cabalistic concept of the *Shekinah* presence of God is the source for the Catholic mystical concept of the presence of God in the Eucharist.

Bloomer's theological statement was confirmed by Cardinal Ratzinger. Before becoming Pope Benedict XVI, Cardinal Ratzinger was Prefect for the Vatican Office of the Congregation for the Doctrine of the Faith, and was viewed as being the preeminent Catholic theologian of his time. Cardinal Ratzinger explained how the attendant worship of the host during the Catholic liturgy is based upon the Eucharist being *Shekinah*:

It is the tent of God, his throne. **Here he is among us. His presence (Shekinah) really does now dwell among us** - in the humblest parish church no less than in the grandest cathedral. Even though the definitive Temple will only come to be when the world has become the New Jerusalem, still what the Temple in Jerusalem pointed to is here present in a supreme way. The New Jerusalem is anticipated in the humble species of bread.

So let no one say, "The Eucharist is for eating, not looking at." It is not "ordinary bread", as the most ancient traditions constantly emphasize. Eating it - as we have just said - is a spiritual process, involving the whole man. "Eating" it means worshipping it. Eating it means letting it come into me, so that my "I" is transformed and opens up into the great "we," so that we become "one" in him (cf. Gal 3:16). Thus adoration is not opposed to Communion, nor is it merely added to it. No, Communion only reaches its true depths when it is supported and surrounded by adoration.[245] (emphasis added, parenthetical in original)

Athol Bloomer is a Jew who converted to Catholicism and is now a Catholic lay missionary with the Missionary Society of Our Lady of the Blessed Sacrament. His theological articles explaining the influence of the Jewish Kabbalah on the Catholic liturgy are posted on the website of the *Association of Hebrew Catholics*. The *Association of Hebrew Catholics*, proudly proclaims on their website that they have received the official endorsement of Pope John Paul II, Archbishop Raymond Burke, and Bishop Carl Mengeling. Bishop Mengeling specifically approved the theology of the *Association of Hebrew Catholics*, saying that the association was "faithful to the magisterium"[246] of the Catholic Church.

The magisterium of the Catholic Church mentioned by Bishop Mengeling in his letter is the authority vested in the papacy (in communion with the bishops and cardinals) to set down what is the authentic doctrine of the Catholic Church. The Catholic magisterium adds tradition to the bible. Indeed, § 97 of *The Catechism of the*

Catholic Church redefines the word of God to include the Catholic traditions: "Sacred Tradition and Sacred Scripture make up a single sacred deposit of the Word of God."[247] By this method, they have made "the word of God of none effect through [their] tradition." Mark 7:13.

One scheme used by Jews to alter church doctrines to align with their own is to get the church to buy into the unbiblical terms used in Jewish tradition. *Shekinah* is an example of that scheme. The word *Shekinah* appears nowhere in either the Old or New Testaments. *Shekinah* is a wholly Jewish concept that was born of their Kabbalah; it is also found in the Jewish Talmud and Targums.

Shekinah was inculcated into the Catholic theology from Judaism. There is an esoteric meaning to *Shekinah* that is only understood by those initiated into occult Babylonian theology. Michael Hoffman in his book *Judaism Discovered* reveals that **Shekinah is a Babylonian female goddess**. *Shekinah* is supposed to represent the benevolent spirit to balance out the malevolent spirit of Lilith. Hoffman explains the secret doctrine of the dual spirits is that they are actually one and the same spirit.[248] "The bogus claim that Lilith and *Shekinah* are two distinct entities representing separate forces of black magic and white magic is strictly for the *peti yaamin lekhol davar* ['The fool who will believe anything.']"[249]

Hoffman further explains: "The nucleus of Orthodox Judaism at its deepest, most esoteric level is the sexual propitiation of the myrionymous ['many named'] goddess, Isis-Hecate-Demeter-Ishtar-Shekhinah-Lilith. The consummation of the spiritual and sexual union of the female goddess *Shekhinah* with her male consort (*Sefirah Tiferet*), the 'Holy One,' into one androgynous being (the *mysterium coniunctionis* of alchemy), is one of the charter objectives of Kabbalistic Judaism, and this mirrors uncannily the theology of the sorcerers of ancient Egypt and Babylon, whose ritual working was dedicated to the magical union of the goddess and the god."

The Catholic Mass is derived from the Jewish liturgy, which at its core, an esoteric ceremony involving the magical union of god and goddess. Recall that during the Catholic liturgy, the consecrated bread and wine are claimed to become the very body, blood, soul, and divinity of Christ. There is an occult doctrine flowing from the Jewish Kabbalah, which is not shared with the uninitiated, that the transubstantiation of the Eucharist during Catholic Mass is an esoteric magical union of the female goddess, *Shekinah*, and a male god, *Tif'eret*.

Bloomer explains that there is a sefirotic code in the Kabbalah that is the foundation for the true, but hidden, meaning behind the Catholic Mass. Bloomer explains that the god of the Kabbalah, who is called *Ein Sof,* is made up of ten attributes (*sefirot*). Each *sefirah* (singular of *sefirot*) is not only designated as a particular trait of *Ein Sof* but is also an anthropomorphic part of that one god. In addition, each *sefirah* is a god or goddess in its own right.

The Kabbalah infuses orthodox Judaism with a powerful undercurrent of phallic worship and practice, including sex magic.[250] The sex magic is an offshoot of the secret doctrine in Judaism, which is a common doctrine found in secret societies, that the mystic can find redemption through an "heroic" willingness to do evil.[251] The secret rabbinic doctrine is that evil can be redeemed by embracing it; there is a spiritual good in doing evil.[252] That explains why Jesus said to the Jews: "Ye are of your father the devil, and the lusts of your father ye will do."John 8:44.

Jewish scholars readily acknowledge that there are parallels between the Cabalistic concept of god and the concept of god found in Buddhism, Hinduism, and so-called Gnosticism.[253] That is not surprising, since they all flow from the same mystical waters of Babylon.

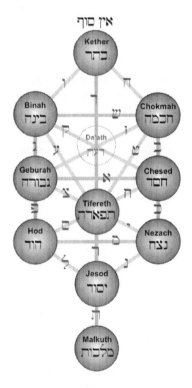

The Ten *Sefirot* of *Ein Sof*

140

Bloomer reveals that these Cabalistic *sefirot* each correlate to some aspect of the Catholic religion. For example, the *Shekinah* (a/k/a *Malkuth*) is not only the Eucharistic host, but it also represents the church community. During the Catholic Mass, the Eucharist (*Shekinah*) is the bride who is being united with *Tif'eret* through *Yesod* (a/k/a *Jesod*), which is the phallus of *Ein Sof*. Bloomer states that "the Sabbath Eve is seen as the weekly celebration of the Sacred Wedding."[254]

The Jewish weekly Sabbath Eve correlates directly with the weekly Catholic Mass. Bloomer explains:

> In the New Covenant the Sabbath meal along with all the festival meals is transformed into the Mass as the Wedding Feast of the Eucharistic King. Thus the Jewish Sabbath Meal is a type of the Mass and Eucharist. All the festival meals of Judaism including the Passover have their roots in the weekly Sabbath Evening Meal. These meals all find their fulfillment or culmination in the meal of the Eucharistic Sacrifice, which we call the Holy Mass."[255]

Bloomer confirms *The Catholic Encyclopedia's* statement that the Catholic Mass is actually the culmination of the Jewish Sabbath celebration. The esoteric meaning behind the Catholic Mass, which is hidden from the gentiles, but is understood by Jews, is that it is a mystical/sexual union between the god, *Tif'eret* (a/k/a *Tiphereth*), and the goddess, *Shekinah*, through the divine phallus, *Yesod*.[256] This is exactly what Michael Hoffman meant when he explained that the charter objective of Cabalistic Judaism is the consummation of the spiritual and sexual union of the female goddess, *Shekinah*, with her male consort, *Tif'eret*, into one androgynous god.

Bloomer states that "an understanding of the Eucharist as the *Shekinah* Presence dwelling in the tabernacles of the Church is helped with a knowledge of the Jewish mystical traditions called Kabbalah."[257] Bloomer is understating the importance of the Kabbalah to understanding the esoteric meaning of the Catholic Mass. In fact, for the initiates, the Kabbalah not only helps, but is indispensable to understanding what is truly going on during the Catholic Mass.

Bloomer states that the words used in the bible have hidden mystical meanings that are not expressed in the text itself, and therefore one must resort to a tradition found somewhere other than the bible to unlock their alleged true meanings. The method of interpreting the bible through traditions memorialized in external texts is the method used by all religious charlatans to undermine God's word. Jesus explained the deception accomplished by such a practice when he told the Jewish Pharisees and scribes: "Full well ye reject the commandment of God, that ye may keep your own tradition. ... Making the word of God of none effect through your tradition." Mark 7:9, 13. Bloomer states that "the Jewish mystical tradition as recorded in the Zohar (an important work of Kabbalah written by Moses de Leon), relates that all Scripture has a hidden mystical meaning as well as the literal historical meaning. The earthly meaning is only a shadow of the true heavenly or mystical reality."[258]

Bloomer is wrong. The true meaning of the bible is not revealed in the Kabbalah, but rather by the Holy Spirit. "Howbeit when he, the Spirit of truth, is come, he will guide you into all truth: for he shall not speak of himself; but whatsoever he shall hear, that shall he speak: and he will shew you things to come." John 16:13. Indeed, without the guidance of the Holy Spirit, it is impossible to understand the Holy Scriptures. "[T]he natural man receiveth not the things of the Spirit of God: for they are foolishness unto him: neither can he know them, because they are spiritually discerned." 1 Corinthians 2:14.

The mystical writings of the Kabbalah twist and corrupt the true meaning of the bible. For example, Bloomer states that the *Sheckinah*, which is the Catholic Eucharist, is feminine, which it turn means that the Catholic Jesus has a feminine gender.

> The Shekinah is often refered to in the feminine form because in the Jewish traditions the Holy Spirit and wisdom are at times referred to in the feminine gender. Understanding (Binah) which is closely linked to Wisdom (Hokmah) is also referred to in feminine terminology. Yeshuah also gives himself feminine imagery when he describes himself as a mother hen who gathers her chicks under her wings – this is a direct allusion to the concept of the 'wings of

Shekinah' found in Rabbinic literature.[259]

Bloomer reveals the entry point of the secret doctrine of the Catholic Mass. He states that "[i]t is through Malkut/Shekinah that one enters the heavenly realm or palaces of the Divine Sefirot (or Attributes of the Divinity)."[260] According to Bloomer, one enters the heavenly realm through the Eucharist, which is *Shekinah*. This is the point at which the secret doctrine is revealed in all its evil splendor. The means of entering the heavenly realm is through *Yesod*. *Yesod* is the phallus of the heathen god called *Ein Sof*, who is the Catholic version of God the Father.

> Netzach [a/k/a Nezach] and Hod are seen as the right and left legs of God and are considered the source of prophecy. **Yesod [a/k/a Jesod] is the foundation of the world and the axus mundi or cosmic pillar as the phallus of the divine Body.** Yesod is also called Tsaddik (righteous) and is thus associated with the title of Tsaddik given to the Messiah. Proverbs 10:25 states: " The Righteous One (Tsaddik) is the foundation (Yesod) of the world". **The light and power of the Sefirot are channelled through Yesod to the last Sefirah (the 10th) of Malkut/Shekinah. Tif'eret [a/k/a Tiphereth] and Shekinah [a/k/a Malchuth] are united by Yesod.** Shekinah is seen as the Bride and in this context can be associated with the Church (Community) as the Bride of the Messiah. Kabbalah sees that the human marriage symbolises the Heavenly or Divine Marriage. As we have seen above the Sabbath Eve is seen as the weekly celebration of the Sacred Wedding.[261] (emphasis added)

Bloomer describes the Catholic liturgy as a union of *Tif'eret* with *Shekinah* (a/k/a *Malkut* or *Malchuth*) through the phallus, called *Yesod* (a/k/a *Jesod*). *Tif'eret*, *Yesod*, and *Shekinah* are each separate gods and goddesses who are joined together with seven other gods and goddesses (for a total of ten) in a single deity called *Ein Sof* (the Catholic version of God the Father). This is the occult doctrine of the Catholic Mass.

This esoteric sexual blasphemy of the Catholic Mass flows from the Babylonian phallic religion that was adopted by the Jews and inculcated by them into the Catholic Church. Dan Cohn-Sherbok and Lavinia Cohn-Sherbok explain the development of the esoteric sexual meanings concealed within the orthodox Jewish liturgy:

> Likewise, Phallic symbolism was employed in speculations about the ninth *Sefirah, Yesod*, from which all the higher *Sefirot* flowed into the *Shekinah* as the life force of the cosmos. In later centuries erotic terminology was used in the Hasidic works to describe movement in prayer which was depicted as copulation with the *Shekhinah*.[262]

The movement in prayer mentioned by Dan and Lavinia Cohn-Sherbok is called *shuckling* (a/k/a *shokeling* or *shoklen*). It is also called *davening*, which is simply a Yiddish word for prayer. The *shuckling* by Jews simulates the movement of copulation in sexual union with *Shekhinah*. *Shuckling* is symptomatic of the fact that Judaism is a phallic religion, which is has liturgical practices and prayers with occult sexual meanings. Baal Shem Tov is considered the founder of Hasidic Judaism and a highly respected authority on Jewish theology. Baal Shem Tov stated that "Prayer is mating with the Shechinah."[263] The mating during prayer is manifested in swaying back and forth. Rabbi Eli Malon explains: "By 'prayer,' he [Baal Shem Tov] meant the literal swaying back and forth, suggestive of intercourse, that is customary of traditional Jewish prayer."[264] The swaying is understood by Jews to signify copulation with the goddess Shekinah.[265] Former Jew, Nathaniel Kapner (a/k/a Brother Nathaniel), confirms the hidden meaning of the swaying by the Jews:

> Watch closely how the rabbis thrust their pelvises and penises back and forth in a prescribed prayer movement called "davening" in which the Jew copulates with the 'Shekinah' in order to give birth to an erotic union with the 'Ein Soph,' the Kabbalistic masculine emanation of their false god.[266]

The occult sexual meaning behind *shuckling* is generally known among Jews, but is kept hidden from Gentiles. In 2013, Rabbi Michael

Leo Samuel openly discussed in an article addressed to a Jewish audience in the *San Diego Jewish Herald*, the *shuckling* of Hasidic Jews in front of a Victoria's Secret lingerie store. He wondered if the Hasidic Jews needed a visual aid for their *davening*. Samuel paraphrased the writings of Baal Shem Tov regarding the meaning of the swaying during Jewish prayer:

> Prayer is zivug (coupling) with the Shechinah. Just as there is motion at the beginning of coupling, so, too, one must move (sway) at the beginning of prayer. Thereafter one can stand still, without motion, attached to the Shechinah with great deveikut (cleaving to God) As a result of your swaying, you can attain great bestirment. For you think to yourself: "Why do I move myself? Presumably it is because the Shechinah surely stands before me." This will effect in you a state of great hitlahavut (enthusiasm; rapture).[267] (parentheticals in original)

It seemed that Rabbi Samuel was upset that the Jews were *shuckling* in front of a Victoria's Secret lingerie store, because it revealed too much about the occult meaning of the Jewish religion to the world. Rabbi Samuel stated: "With respect to the Hassidic Jews praying in front of the Victoria's Secret lingerie store, they really believe that the world is not observing. They behave like a young child who covers his ears and screams, thinking that nobody around him can hear him."[268]

As is the case with the clerics of all phallic religions, there is rampant pederasty among Jewish clerics. Rabbinic pederasty is documented in this author's book, *Solving the Mystery of BABYLON THE GREAT*. The reason why the great harlot of Babylon described in Revelation 17:5 has "MYSTERY" written across her forehead is because this ostensibly gentile church of Rome actually practices the Cabalistic Jewish religion of the Pharisees, which is derived from the occult sorceries of Babylon. This truth is concealed from the uninitiated Catholics. It is truly a "MYSTERY" to them. This Babylonian Judaism is the same Judaism that Christ criticized when he stated: "Ye are of your father the devil, and the lusts of your father ye will do." (John 8:44) That Judaic/Babylonian occult foundations of Catholic doctrine is explained in more detail in this author's aforementioned book.

Bloomer reveals:

> This heavenly or mystical understanding of the *Sefirot* opens up a fuller understanding of the unity of the Godhead with the Church and with each member of the Church. It is only through the Eucharist that this mystery of unity can be found. The Eucharist is the way to the mystical union or marriage of the soul with the Heavenly Bridegroom.[269]

The uninitiated members of the Catholic church think the bridegroom is Jesus, however, the Jesus of the Catholic church is not the same Jesus in the bible; the Catholic Jesus who is the bridegroom is actually the heathen god *Tif'eret* who is joined with the *Shekinah* (Eucharist) through the phallus (*Yesod*) of a heathen god (*Ein Sof*) to consummate the marriage. The consummation causes the transubstantiation of the Eucharist into the full trinity of heathen gods being present in the Eucharistic host. Bloomer reveals that "the Trinity is encompassed within the Sacred Host. The Trinity dwells not so much in the heights but in the depths of the Sacred Host of the Altar — which is the Sacred Heart."[270] The Catholic Trinity in the Eucharist refers to the heathen gods and goddesses Isis, Horus, and Seb. Indeed, that is the esoteric meaning of the initials IHS that appear on the host. This brings us back to Hoffman's conclusion that the charter objective of Kabbalistic Judaism is the sexual union of the female goddess *Shekhinah* with her male consort *Tif'eret* into one androgynous deity. The Catholic liturgy is a parallel variation, where the product of the union of *Tif'eret* and *Shekhinah* through the phallic god, *Yesod*, is the heathen trinity of Isis, Horus, and Seb.

The Trinity that is understood by the initiates of the mystery religions is not God the Father, God the Son, and God the Holy Spirit of the bible. The Trinity of he mystery religions has manifold meanings. One meaning is found in the Trinity of heathen gods, Isis, Horus, and Seb, in the Catholic Eucharist. Another form of Trinity is found in the triads of the Kabbalah. Bloomer explains the Trinity found in the Kabbalah, and in so doing reveals that it is not one true God of the Bible. The Catholic Trinity is integral to the Jewish god *Ein Sof*. Each of the separate Triads of *Ein Sof* consists of one of the individual members of the Catholic Trinity, with each triad itself consisting at the same time of the three persons of the Catholic Trinity. This heathen Trinity is not the Godhead of the bible as described in 1 John 5:7. Bloomer explains:

> On one level each Sefirah in each Triad can represent a person of the Holy Trinity. Also each of the three Triads can also represent one of the persons of the Trinity. The Head Triad with the Father, the middle Triad with the Son and the Lower Triad with the Holy Spirit. In the Head Triad Keter [a/k/a Kether] represents the Father, Hokmah [a/k/a Chokman] the son and Binah the Holy Spirit. Within the Middle Triad Din [a/k/a Geburah] represents the Father, Hesed [a/k/a Chesed] the Holy Spirit and Tif'eret [a/k/a/ Tiphereth] (Rachamim) with the Son. In the Lower triad Hod represents the Father, Netzach [a/k/a Nezach] the Holy Spirit and Yesod the Son. The dynamic of reaction within the family of the Godhead is animated by Hesed. Hesed is the blood of the Divine Body.[271]

It is likely that the very idea of a Trinity flows from the Cabalistic idea of three Triads making up the god of Judaism. Many Christians would be surprised to know that God is never described in the bible as a Trinity, but is in fact always described as a unity; that is one God. Jesus Christ, God the Father, and the Holy Spirit are all one God."Hear, O Israel: The LORD our **God is one** LORD." (Deuteronomy 6:4) "And Jesus answered him, The first of all the commandments is, Hear, O Israel; The Lord our **God is one** Lord." (Mark 12:29) "But to us there is but **one God**, the Father, of whom are all things, and we in him; and one Lord Jesus Christ, by whom are all things, and we by him." (1 Corinthians 8:6) "For there is **one God**, and one mediator between God and men, the man Christ Jesus;" (1 Timothy 2:5) "For there are three that bear record in heaven, the Father, the Word, and the Holy Ghost: and **these three are one**." (1 John 5:7) "**I and my Father are one.**" (John 10:30)

Bloomer reveals that *Tif'eret* was also known as the sun in the Jewish Kabbalah.[272] He states that the *sefirah Yesod* is associated with

Osiris.[273] Osiris is an Egyptian sun god.[274] He was both the son of Ra and the son of Seb.[275] Osiris and Tammuz are one and the same heathen god.[276] Tammuz was likely the Babylonian origin for the Egyptian god Osiris. Ezekiel reveals the worship of Tammuz by the Jews: "Then he brought me to the door of the gate of the LORD'S house which was toward the north; and, behold, there sat women weeping for Tammuz." (Ezekiel 8:14)

Seb is also known as Geb.[277] In Egyptian heathen theology Osiris is both the father and son of Horus.[278] Isis was both Osiris' sister and his wife.[279] Some time after Osiris' death, Isis was able to revive him long enough to conceive Horus.[280] Isis was a moon-goddess; the Romans called her Diana.

Bloomer states that "Miriam ha Kadosha (Holy Mary) is the spouse of the Holy Spirit (or Binah) and Mother of the Eucharistic Lord (the *Shekinah*)." Bloomer equates Mary with Miriam ha Kadosha, who in the Zohar 1:34a is called 'Moon of Israel.'[281] Miriam ha Kadosha seems to be the Jewish corollary to the ancient moon goddess, whom the Romans called Diana and the Greeks called Artemis. Bloomer equates Mary with Miriam ha Kadosha and therefore also Diana and Artemis. Miriam ha Kadosha has a regal status in the Jewish pantheon of goddesses. She is equated with the Jewish warrior queen of heaven, Matronita. Bloomer writes the following in a posting under the name Aharon Yosef: "Matronita is a term appropriate to Miriam ha Kedosha who is both married matron and innocent Virgin. Matronita is in this section of Zohar is called the Shekhinah. The concepts of Shekhinah and Matronita are both symbolised by the Moon."[282] Michael Hoffman states: "Worship of the *Shekinah* in the form of the moon goddess is a formal rite in Orthodox Judaism."[283]

There is a corollary between the moon godesses from the different cultures: Diana (Roman), Artemis (Greek), Matronita (Jew), *Shekinah* (Jew), Miriam ha Kadosha (Jew), Mary (Catholic), Eucharist (Catholic). The symbolism of the Eucharist represents many different goddesses and gods. The Eucharist is not only a representation of the moon goddess, but also the sun god. In fact, the esoteric meaning of the Eucharist includes a Trinity of gods and goddesses within the Eucharistic host.

The Eucharistic host actually carries the initials of the heathen Trinity of gods that it symbolizes. The host carries the Symbol IHS, as depicted in the picture in subsequent pages,[284] which refers to Isis, Horus, and Seb. Alexander Hislop explains:

> In regard to the Pagan character of the "unbloody sacrifice" of the Mass, we have seen not little already. But there is something yet to be considered, in which the working of the mystery of iniquity will still further appear. There are letters on the wafer that are worth reading. These letters are I. H. S. What mean these mystical letters? To a Christian these letters are represented as signifying, "*Iesus Hominum Salvator*," "Jesus the Saviour of men." But let a Roman worshipper of Isis (for in the age of the emperors there were innumerable worshippers of Isis in Rome) cast his eyes upon them, and how will he read them? He will read them, of course, according to his own well known system of idolatry: "Isis, Horus, Seb," that is, "The Mother, the Child, and the Father of the gods,"--in other words, "The Egyptian Trinity." Can the reader imagine that this double sense is accidental? Surely not. The very same spirit that converted the festival of the Pagan Oannes into the feast of the Christian Joannes, retaining at the same time all its ancient Paganism, has skilfully planned the initials I. H. S. to pay the semblance of a tribute to Christianity, while Paganism in reality has all the substance of the homage bestowed upon it.[285]

Indeed, under the occult doctrine of the Catholic Church, IHS does not refer to Jesus, because during the Catholic liturgy, the Catholic Jesus is the bridegroom (a/k/a *Tif'eret*) and not the Eucharist. The Catholic Jesus (*Tif'eret*) is joined with the *Shekinah* (Eucharist) through the phallus (*Yesod*) of a heathen god (*Ein Sof*) to consummate the marriage during the liturgy. The IHS signifies the three gods and goddesses who are the progeny of the blasphemous union.

There is nothing in the bible at all regarding the shape of the bread to be used as a memorial as Jesus commanded during the last supper. Given that fact, why does the Catholic Church use a round wafer as a Eucharist during the Catholic Mass? The answer comes from heathen antiquity. Hislop discovered:

> The importance, however, which Rome attaches to the roundness of the wafer, must have a reason; and that reason will be found, if we look at the altars of Egypt. "The thin, round cake," says Wilkinson, "occurs on all altars." Almost every jot or tittle in the Egyptian worship had a symbolical meaning. **The round disk, so frequent in the sacred emblems of Egypt, symbolised the sun.** Now, when Osiris, the sun-divinity, became incarnate, and was born, it was not merely that he should give his life as a sacrifice for men, but that he might also be the life and nourishment of the souls of men.[286]

Not only was the sun worshiped in Egypt, but it was also worshiped by the Jews, who worshiped the sun god, Baal. Ezekiel reveals the heathen worship of the sun by the Jews: "And he brought me into the inner court of the LORD'S house, and, behold, at the door of the temple of the LORD, between the porch and the altar, were about five and twenty men, with their backs toward the temple of the LORD, and their faces toward the east; and they worshipped the sun toward the east." (Ezekiel 8:16)

Hislop explains that "the 'round' wafer, whose 'roundness' is so important an element in the Romish Mystery, what can be the meaning of it, but just to show to those who have eyes to see, that the 'Wafer' itself is only another symbol of Baal, or the Sun."[287] The Eucharist represents the heathen sun god. Further proof of this is the fact that the monstrance used to contain the Eucharistic host always forms rays of the sun emanating from the Eucharist. All one need do is read the history of the Jews in the bible to find the source for this sun god worship. "And they forsook the LORD, and served Baal and Ashtaroth." (Judges 2:13) The Catholic Mass is a continuation of the apostasy of the Jews in their worship of the sun god, Baal, in the form of the Eucharist. *Tif'eret* is the sefirah god that was also known as the sun in the Jewish Kabbalah.[288] *Tif'eret* would seem to be the very same heathen sun god, Baal, who was worshiped by the ancient Jews.

It is notable that the circular disk Eucharist is purported by the Catholic Church to be the very body of Christ. The consumption of the Eucharist is the consumption of the flesh of Jesus in the form of bread. As we have seen, the esoteric doctrine is that the cake wafer is actually a symbol of the sun god, Baal. The Jews would offer their children as sacrifices to be burned alive as sacrifices to Baal. See Jeremiah 19:5. The priest of Baal would then eat the flesh of the children.[289] "Cahna-Bal" means "priest of Baal."[290] Cahna-Bal is the origin of the word "cannibal" which means one who eats human flesh.[291] The consumption of the Eucharist purports to be the consumption of the actual flesh and blood of Jesus in the outward form bread. The hidden mystery is that the consumption of the Eucharist is an unbloody re-enactment of the ritual flesh eating by the priests of Baal.

In addition to the macabre cannibalism of Baal worship, the hidden mysteries of the Eucharist also includes mystical/sexual meanings. The transubstantiation of the host into the Eucharist during Catholic Mass is a magical union of the female goddess *Shekinah* and a male god, *Tif'eret*, through the heathen god *Yesod*. *Yesod* is also the phallus of a heathen god (*Ein Sof*) that the Cabalists equate with the God the Father, but who in fact is Satan. There are many esoteric meanings behind the Catholic celebration of the Eucharist. In the end, an entire trinity of gods and goddesses are present in the Eucharistic host which bears the inscription of those gods: IHS, which stands for Isis, Horus, and Seb.

Another Cabalistic meaning behind the Eucharist revealed by Bloomer is that the goddess Mary, who is the "Queen of Heaven," is the spouse of *Binah*. *Binah* in the Kabbalah correlates to the Holy Spirit in Catholic theology. *Binah* is a goddess who is considered the "divine womb." The goddess Mary is considered the daughter of *Keter* (a/k/a *Kether*) and the mother of *Hokmah* (a/k/a *Chokmah*). *Keter* in Kabbalah correlates to the Father in Catholic theology and *Hokmah* is the Son. *Shekinah* (Eucharist) is a heathen goddess bride born from *Binah*.

The Jesus of the Catholic Church is not the Jesus of the bible. The true Jesus is blasphemed in the Kabbalah. "According to the most important Kabbalistic text, the Zohar, Jesus is a 'dead dog' who resides amid the filth and vermin."[292] The secret doctrine of the Catholic Mass, which is born of the Kabbalah, is that the Jesus of the Eucharistic Mass is an androgynous god/goddess in the form of bread, who is magically made present through transubstantiation, which esoterically is a mystical sex rite.

This secret doctrine of the Mass was woven carefully by the Jews from the Kabbalah into the Catholic church. As with all secret doctrines, at first it was done through stealth. Later it was done with much more freedom by authorization of Pope Sixtus IV, who ordered that the Cabalistic writings be translated into Latin so that the divinity students could learn the secrets hidden therein. Those clergy became bishops, archbishops, cardinals, and popes who steered the Catholic ship into the heathen abyss of Jewish rebellion against God.

Below is a typical Eucharistic host that is used by Catholic priests during Catholic Mass. That particular Eucharistic Host was baked by the Benedictine Sisters, which is a Catholic order of nuns.[293] Notice that it has IHS, signifying Isis, Horus, and Seb, prominently embossed on the bread.

Hislop states that the exoteric meaning of IHS is "'*Iesus Hominum Salvator*,' 'Jesus the Saviour of men.'"[294] The Catholic Church, however, states that Hislop is wrong. Catholic Priest Ryan Erlenbush explains: "It is popular legend that the IHS stands for the Latin phrase *Iesus Hominum Salvator*, "Jesus the Savior of (all) Men". While this is a fine devotion, it is not historically accurate."[295] *The Catholic Encyclopedia* confirms Erlenbush's position: "IHS was sometimes wrongly understood as '*Jesus Hominum* (or *Hierosolymae*) *Salvator*', i.e. Jesus, the Saviour of men (or of Jerusalem=*Hierosolyma*)."[296]

Eucharistic Host With Embossed Letters IHS, Signifying Isis, Horus, and Seb

That tells us what the Roman Catholic Church states that IHS does not mean, but what does the Catholic Church say it means? The public exoteric meaning for IHS as expressed in *The Catholic Encyclopedia* (carrying the official imprimatur of John Cardinal Farley, Archbishop of New York) is that the letters represent "a monogram of the name of Jesus Christ."[297] The explanation given in the encyclopedia is that Jesus' name was represented by "IC and XC or IHS and XPS for *Iesous Christos*."[298] That explanation, however, is unhelpful. It does not explain where the letters IHS come from. That section of the encyclopedia then explains how through the ages, IHS has been used by certain religious orders but does not explain its derivation. The encyclopedia simply states that IHS was used. It purports to be an explanation, but it explains nothing.

In another section of *The Catholic Encyclopedia,* under the same imprimatur of John Cardinal Farley, it states: "In the Middle Ages the Name of Jesus was written: IHESUS; the monogram [IHS] contains the first and last letter of the Holy Name."[299] The problem with that explanation is that it is based upon a misspelling of Jesus' name. In fact, that point is made in another section of *The Catholic Encyclopedia*, where it states: "Eventually the right meaning was lost, and erroneous interpretation of IHS led to the faulty orthography 'Jhesus.'"[300] The modern Latin "J" is equivalent to the ancient Latin "I" in the Latin alphabet. "IHESUS" contains all uppercase letters and is intended by the Catholic Church as equivalent to "Jhesus." The problem is that Jesus has never been spelled anywhere in the Holy Scriptures with all uppercase letters.

The Catholic authorities cannot seem to get their exoteric explanation straight. In one section of *The Catholic Encyclopedia* it states that "Jhesus" is erroneous, yet in another section of that same encyclopedia, it cites that same misspelling "IHESUS" as the basis for IHS.

It is clear that "Jhesus" and "IHESUS" are both misspellings of Jesus. "Jhesus" ("IHESUS") is a combination of Greek and Latin letters, which makes no sense. The "h" ("H") is a redundant letter; it duplicates the Latin "e" ("E"). All of the other letters in Jhesus (IHESUS) are Latin except for the Greek letter "h" ("H").

What is the exoteric explanation for IHS? Catholic Priest Ryan Erlenbush presents the standard Catholic exoteric explanation for IHS:

> The insignia 'IHS' comes from the Latinized version of the Greek Ιησους . . . taking the first three letters in capitals IHS(ous). . . This is the true meaning of IHS, it is the first three letters of the Greek spelling of the Holy Name of Jesus. The insignia is nothing more (and nothing less) than the symbol of the Holy Name.[301]

A letter-by-letter analysis of Erlenbush's standard Catholic explanation proves that it is a fraud. The first letter in Greek "I" is iota and carries the consonant "J" sound for the English, Latin, and Greek in the context of Jesus' name. In ancient Latin, there was no letter "J" and so it seems that the transliteration of the Greek "I" to Latin "I" makes sense. "I" is the same letter in both Greek and Latin.

The long "e" sound in Greek was represented by the letter η (eta), and so the Greek spelling of Jesus' name would appear in Greek as Ιησοῦς. That would tend to offer an explanation for the "I" and the "h" as the first two letters of Jesus' name in the Greek alphabet. However, it makes no sense to represent Jesus' name as IHS in the Greek alphabet, since the second letter of his name is a lowercase Greek letter (eta) which appears as a lower case "h" (η) and not as an uppercase letter "H." Further, if IHS is supposed to be a Latinized monogram for the first three letters of Jesus' name, the second letter should be an "E" not an "H," because the Greek eta (η) is translated to "E" in Latin (and English), not "H."

The third Greek letter in Jesus name is sigma, which looks like a small letter "o" with a tail at the top (σ). The lowercase sigma has a different appearance when it is the last letter in a word (ς), as in Jesus' name, Ιησοῦς. The Greek uppercase letter for sigma, however, is always the same (Σ). Sigma has the "s" sound in English, Latin, and Greek. However, the "S" in IHS is not the Greek uppercase sigma (Σ), it is the Latin (and English) uppercase letter "S." The Greek uppercase sigma (Σ) is unique and does not look like a Latin uppercase letter "S."

This is where the Catholic exoteric explanation falls apart. If the letters are supposed to be Latinized Greek letters, why leave the second letter in its original Greek and not translate it into Latin? The second letter is changed from a Greek small eta (η) to a Greek capital eta (H), but it is not translated into Latin, which if done so would make it an "E." The third letter was translated from the Greek small sigma (σ) to the Latin capital "S," but that was not done with the second Greek letter eta (η). The second letter was capitalized, but it remained a Greek letter. Each letter is treated differently in order to create the contrivance of IHS.

If IHS is a Latinized monogram for the first three letters of Jesus' name, as claimed by Erlenbush, then it should be written IES and not IHS. It makes no sense to mix Greek and Latin letters in a monogram. Even if one accepts that the "I" and the "S" are Latinized Greek letters, it makes no sense not to Latinize the Greek eta (η) from a Greek "H" to a Latin "E." The monogram is a mixture of Latin and Greek letters. IHS contains a Latin "I," a Greek "H," and a Latin "S." That simply makes no sense.

Finally, it is absurd to represent Jesus' name with a monogram for his first three letters. That was never a practice of the Christian Church. Monograms traditionally represented the first letters of a person's given name (often including a middle name) and the surname; it was generally not a practice to represent a person in a monogram by the first three letters of his given name. Ron Byerly draws the obvious conclusion that "[o]ne wouldn't write 'PET' for Peter, or 'MOS' for Moses, or 'JAM' for James. So why IHS for Jesus."[302] The Roman Catholic exoteric explanation for IHS is thus revealed as a deception that conceals its true esoteric meaning.

The difficulty in coming up with a good exoteric explanation for IHS is not lost on the Catholic Church. That has made it necessary for *The Catholic Encyclopedia* to come up with several competing explanations for the initials, none of which are definitive. As explained above, one of the exoteric explanations has been contradicted in another section of the encyclopedia. How can the Catholic Church be so uncertain about what the initials on its Eucharistic Host mean? Obviously, the several competing public explanations are intended as smokescreens to conceal the true esoteric meaning. The true meaning of IHS was revealed by Hislop. IHS represent the heathen gods Isis (mother god), Horus (son god), and Seb (father god).

155

The source document (the Kabbalah) for the Catholic Jesus offers a god/goddess combination in his place under the guise of the bread in the Eucharist. The Catholic Church kept the name Jesus, but the Jesus of the Eucharist is not the Jesus of the bible. The very thing that Paul warned the Corinthians about has happened: "For if he that cometh preacheth **another Jesus**, whom we have not preached, or if ye receive **another spirit**, which ye have not received, or **another gospel**, which ye have not accepted, ye might well bear with him." (2 Corinthians 11:4). The members of the Catholic Church have gone after another spirit, another gospel, and **another Jesus**.

The adoration of the Eucharist mentioned by Bloomer is plain and simple idolatry born from the Jewish Kabbalah. The Catholic church is following the mystical teachings of the Kabbalah when it admonishes its members to worship the Eucharist. The Catholic worship of the bread and wine is the same thing that the rebellious Jews did when they made the golden calf after they were brought out of the land of Egypt. Exodus 32:3-4.

14 The Antichrist Guarantees Heaven for the Jews

The Judaic/Babylonian origin of the Papacy is not only manifested in Catholic liturgy, it can also be seen in Catholic doctrine. Once a Jew is saved he becomes a Christian; he will no longer follow Judaism. According to the Catholic Church, however, conversion is unnecessary because the Jews have a "sonship" based upon an "irrevocable" calling of God, simply by virtue of being of the Jewish "race."

According to the official teachings of the Catholic Church Jews go to heaven even though they are outside the Catholic Church, and even though all Jews have rejected Christ. In fact, the Catholic Catechism states that the Jewish race itself is Christ. That is exactly what the Talmud says. The religion of Judaism establishes that the Jews themselves are their own Christ.[303] The Catholic Church accepts that doctrine and has made it part of its official catechism. The *Catechism of the Catholic Church § 839* states:

> *The relationship of the Church with the Jewish People.* When she delves into her own mystery, the Church, the People of God in the New Covenant, discovers her link with the Jewish People, "the first to hear the Word of God." The Jewish faith, unlike other non-Christian religions, is already a response to God's revelation in the Old Covenant. **To the Jews "belong the sonship,**

the glory, the covenants, the giving of the law, the worship, and the promises; to them belong the patriarchs, and of **their race, according to the flesh, is the Christ,"** **"for the gifts and the call of God are irrevocable."**[304]

In fact, the official teaching of the Catholic Church is that "Israel is the priestly people of God, called by the name of the LORD, and the first to hear the word of God, the people of elder brethren in the faith of Abraham."[305] The Catholic Church officially views Jews as elder brethren of the faith of Abraham. The faith of Abraham signifies saving faith. According to the Catholic Church, Jews are saved by their fleshly lineage as Jews, without regard to whether they have faith in Jesus.

What does Jesus say about the Jews? Jesus told them:"Ye are of your father the devil, and the lusts of your father ye will do."John 8:44. Why would Jesus say such a thing? Because the Jews supplanted the laws of God in the Old Testament with their oral traditions, just as has the Catholic Church. The Jews have a long history of rejecting the commands of God. Jesus said to the scribes and Pharisees: "And he said unto them, Full well ye reject the commandment of God, that ye may keep your own tradition. . . . Making the word of God of none effect through your tradition, which ye have delivered: and many such like things do ye." (Mark 7:9,13)

There is a clear parallel between the traditions of the scribes and pharisees of old and those of the Roman Papacy. The Roman Catholic Church follows the practice of the Jews and calls the combination of man's tradition and God's word "the Word of God." To a Protestant Christian the word of God means the Holy Bible. However, to the Roman Catholic, it means the Holy Bible plus their traditions.

Sacred Tradition and Sacred Scripture make up a single sacred deposit of the Word of God. *CATECHISM OF THE CATHOLIC CHURCH*, § 97, 1994.

[T]he church, to whom the transmission and interpretation of Revelation is entrusted, **does not**

> derive her certainty about all revealed truths from the holy Scriptures alone. Both Scripture and Tradition must be accepted and honored with equal sentiments of devotion and reverence. *Id.* at § 82 (emphasis added).

The papacy has used the same method for which Jesus reprimanded the Jews in Mark 7:9-13. The Romish church has mixed its tradition with the holy scriptures and by that mixture have created a hybrid religion that uses exoteric Christian language as a cover for an esoteric Babylonian religion. All it takes is a little leaven of heathen doctrine to leaven and entirely corrupt the pure doctrine of Jesus Christ. Galatians 5:9.

To what traditions was Jesus referring when he upbraided the Pharisees for using them to transgress and replace the laws of God? Can we find out about those traditions today? Yes; the Talmud is a codification of the traditions of the scribes and Pharisees to which Jesus spoke. Michael Rodkinson (M. Levi Frumkin), who wrote the first English translation of the Babylonian Talmud, states the following in his book *The History of the Talmud*:

> Is the literature that Jesus was familiar with in his early years yet in existence in the world? Is it possible for us to get at it? To such inquiries the learned class of Jewish rabbis answer by holding up the Talmud. **The Talmud then, is the written form of that which, in the time of Jesus, was called the Traditions of the Elders,** and to which he makes frequent allusions.[306] (emphasis added)

So we see that the traditions of the Jews are memorialized in the Talmud. During the time of Christ, the Talmud existed only in oral form, which Jesus referred to as the traditions of the scribes and Pharisees. This early oral tradition is called the Mishnah. It was only after Christ's crucifixion that the Mishnah was reduced to writing. The rabbis later added rabbinical commentaries to the Mishnah, which are called the Gemara.[307] Together these comprise the Talmud, which is now a collection of books.

There are today two basic Talmudic texts, the Babylonian Talmud and the Jerusalem Talmud. The Babylonian Talmud is regarded as the authoritative version and takes precedence over the Jerusalem Talmud.[308] The Babylonian Talmud is based on the mystical religious practices of the Babylonians which were assimilated by the Jewish Rabbis during their Babylonian captivity around 600 B.C. The Rabbis then used these occult traditions in place of the word of God. In rabbinic Judaism, the Talmud has primacy and authority over God's word in the Old Testament.[309]

According to the Babylonian Talmud, Tractate 'Abodah Zarah, Folio 17a, Christians are allied with hell. Tractate Sanhedrin, Folio 106a curses Jesus. In Tractate Gittin, Folio 57a, Jesus is described as being tormented in boiling hot semen. In Tractate Gittin, Folio 57b, Jesus has been sent to hell, where he is being punished by boiling excrement for mocking the Rabbis. In Tractate Sanhedrin, Folios 90a and 100b, it states that those who read the gospels are doomed to hell. In Tractate Shabbath, Folio 116a, it states that the New Testament is blank paper and is to be burned. The hatred by Jews against Christ, Christians, and the gospel is so intense that Jews are taught to utter a curse when passing a Christian Church, calling on their heathen god (Hashem) to "destroy this house of the proud."[310]

Rabbi ben Yohai, who believed he was beyond the jurisdiction of God, did not think gentiles were even worthy to live. His views regarding gentiles were that "even the best of gentiles should all be killed."[311] Rabbi ben Yohai is not a rabbi on the fringes of Judaism; he is in fact one of the most revered of rabbis in Judaism; his grave is a shrine in Israel. He authored the Zohar, which is the principle work of the Kabbalah.

The Jews recite *Amidah*, which is a set of eighteen (by some accounts nineteen) weekly Jewish prayers. The twelfth prayer is called *Birkat ha-minim*. The *Birkat ha-minim* is actually a hateful curse against heretics and enemies of the Jews, particularly Christians. The curse was first introduced in the *Amidah* in the first century at Jabneh by Samuel ha Katan, at the request of Rabban Gamaliel II in order to drive followers of Jesus Christ from the synagogues.

The common Jews are as much victims of the Jewish hierarchy

as are the gentiles and Christians. The common Jews are being spiritually brainwashed to the bidding of their rabbis. Jesus explained the process: "Woe unto you, scribes and Pharisees, hypocrites! for ye compass sea and land to make one proselyte, and when he is made, ye make him twofold more the child of hell than yourselves." (Matthew 23:15)

The Papacy has the most learned Catholic theologians from which to obtain authoritative information on Jewish doctrine. The Vatican knows full well that the Jews hate Christ and Christians. Once it is understood, that the papacy is the antichrist, it is perfectly understandable that the pope would fully accept Jews as spiritual brothers against their common enemy, Lord God Jesus Christ. "Can two walk together, except they be agreed?" (Amos 3:3)

The Catholic view that Jews are heirs to the promise due to their blood lineage to Abraham is a false theology that is unsupported by scripture. In Galatians 3:16, God stated: "Now to Abraham and his seed were the promises made. He saith not, And to seeds, as of many; but as of one, And to thy seed, which is Christ." Jesus Christ is the seed that is the source of the blessing. All who believe in Jesus Christ, are the recipients of the promises as the spiritual children of God. All who believe in Jesus Christ are Abraham's spiritual seed, and heirs according to the promise of the coming Christ given to Abraham. "And if ye be Christ's, then are ye Abraham's seed, and heirs according to the promise." Galatians 3:29.

God's promised blessings were not intended to flow through the blood line of Abraham; God's promised blessings were to flow to those who have the faith of Abraham. The "seed" of Abraham who inherit the blessings from God are those that have the faith of Abraham, not those that have the flesh of Abraham. (Galatians 3:16, 26, 29)

> Not as though the word of God hath taken none effect. For they are not all Israel, which are of Israel: Neither, because they are the seed of Abraham, are they all children: but, In Isaac shall thy seed be called. That is, They which are the children of the flesh, these are not the children of God: but the children of the promise are counted for the seed. (Romans 9:6-8)

Christ has broken down forever any distinction between Jew and Gentile in his kingdom.

> For the scripture saith, Whosoever believeth on him shall not be ashamed. For there is no difference between the Jew and the Greek: for the same Lord over all is rich unto all that call upon him. For whosoever shall call upon the name of the Lord shall be saved. (Romans 10:11-13)

The children of the flesh are not the elect of God; God's elect are the children of the promised Christ; they are spiritual children, born by God's grace through faith in Jesus Christ. Romans 9:6-8. "For ye are all the children of God by faith in Christ Jesus." (Galatians 3:26) The promises to Abraham were to be fulfilled on behalf of spiritual Israel, which is the church.

Abraham was the father of Isaac, who in turn was the father of Jacob; Jacob (also known as Israel) had 12 sons that were the progenitors of the 12 tribes of Israel. Abraham was also the father of Ishmael, but because Ishmael was the son of Abraham's bondwoman, the bondwoman and Ishmael were cast out. Genesis 21:10-14. Through Isaac, who was the son of Abraham's wife, Sarah, were to flow the promises of God to Abraham. Genesis 21:12. However, Isaac had two sons, Jacob and Esau. The promise given to Abraham flowed not to Esau, but to Jacob. In fact, God states in Romans 9:13: "As it is written, Jacob have I loved, but Esau have I hated." See also Malachi 1:1-3. God elected Jacob (Israel) as the person through whom his promises would flow.

In each of Abraham's generations the blessing to Abraham flowed according to the election of God. No blessing was obtained that was sought through blood or effort. For example, the bondwoman (Hagar) conceived and gave birth to Abram's first son (Ishmael). God later renamed Abram, Abraham. Genesis 17:5. However, Ishmael was not the seed through which the promises would flow. Ishmael was born because Abraham's wife, Sarai, decided that she would help God with his promise that Abram (Abraham) would be the father of many. Sarai was later renamed Sarah by God. Genesis 17:15. Sarai arranged for Hagar to conceive a child by Abram (Abraham). Genesis 16:1-4.

However, Ishmael was not a child of the promise. God worked a miracle and had Sarah bear a child of Abraham, even though she was at that time beyond child bearing age (Sarah was 90 years old and Abraham was 100 years old). Genesis 17:17. That child born of the promise was Isaac. It was the bloodline of Isaac through which the promised seed, who is Christ, would be born. Genesis 17:19-21, 21:3; Hebrews 11:18; Galatians 4:28.

God told Abraham: "And God said, Sarah thy wife shall bear thee a son indeed; and thou shalt call his name Isaac: and I will establish my covenant with him for an everlasting covenant, and with his seed after him." Genesis 17:19. God reveals the spiritual truth of Geneis 17:19 in Galatians 4:28, where Paul states: "Now we, brethren, as Isaac was, are the children of promise." As Isaac was Abraham's physical seed, so also Christians are the spiritual seed of Abraham, through whom the everlasting covenant flowed. Isaac's miraculous physical birth is an allegory for the miraculous spiritual birth of those who are of the faith of Abraham. Christians are miraculously born again by the grace of God through faith in Jesus Christ. John 3:3. "Even as Abraham believed God, and it was accounted to him for righteousness. Know ye therefore that they which are of faith, the same are the children of Abraham." Galatians 3:6-7. The physical seed of Abraham are not the objects of the promise, it is only the spiritual seed that is born by the Grace of God through faith in Jesus Christ. "That which is born of the flesh is flesh; and that which is born of the Spirit is spirit." John 3:6.

Fleshly Israel rebelled against God and therefore has been cut off from the tree of life. God has saved a remnant of fleshly Israel to be grafted back into the tree of life, but their ingrafting is upon the same grounds as everyone else, by the grace of God through faith in Jesus Christ.

There is one covenant that is fulfilled in Christ. Salvation is by the grace of God alone through faith in Jesus Christ alone for both Jew and Gentile. "For by grace are ye saved through faith; and that not of yourselves: it is the gift of God: Not of works, lest any man should boast." (Ephesians 2:8-9)

A Jew who is truly saved and believes in the Jesus of the bible will not go back and follow his heathen Judaic superstitions and neither will a saved Catholic return to the Catholic Church. "And a stranger will they not follow, but will flee from him: for they know not the voice of strangers." John 10:5. The salvation of Jews is not by virtue of their status as Jews, but rather the salvation of Jews, as with the salvation of Gentiles, is totally based upon God's election by his sovereign grace through faith in Jesus alone.

Paul later makes it clear that his desire for his kinsmen according to the flesh is not that all fleshly Israel are a part of God's plan for the Jews. Paul reveals that the seed of Abraham referenced in the bible is not a reference to the flesh of Abraham; the biblical seed of Abraham are those who have the promised faith of Abraham. They are a unique people made up of both Jews and Gentiles. Paul explains that point a few verses later in Romans 9:6-8:

> Not as though the word of God hath taken none effect. For they are not all Israel, which are of Israel: Neither, because they are the seed of Abraham, are they all children: but, In Isaac shall thy seed be called. That is, They which are the children of the flesh, these are not the children of God: but the children of the promise are counted for the seed. Romans 9:6-8.

Paul emphatically states that the children of the flesh of Abraham "are not the children of God." It could not be clearer. The Jews of the flesh are not the seed of Abraham to whom the promises flow. The promises flow to the Jews and Gentiles who are elected by God for salvation.

> And that he might make known the riches of his glory on the vessels of mercy, which he had afore prepared unto glory, Even us, whom he hath called, not of the Jews only, but also of the Gentiles? As he saith also in Osee, I will call them my people, which were not my people; and her beloved, which was not beloved. And it shall come to pass, that in the place where it was said unto them, Ye are not my people; there shall they be called the children of the living God. Romans 9:23-26.

The New Testament is a codicil to the Old Testament. The

codicil gives further revelation about God's plan for his people. God's people are his elect who are made up of both Jew and Gentile.

> For the scripture saith, Whosoever believeth on him shall not be ashamed. For there is no difference between the Jew and the Greek: for the same Lord over all is rich unto all that call upon him. Romans 10:11-12.

15 The Antichrist is Caught Worshiping Lucifer

While Latin is a root language, Latin is also a dead language. It is a language used in witchcraft and has historically been chanted during Roman Catholic Masses and other Catholic ceremonies. The Latin chanting during Catholic Masses was for the most part discontinued after the Vatican II reforms. However, the Latin chanting is being renewed in modern day Catholic Masses. Latin is an unknown tongue for most people. God has admonished that no one in a church should speak in an unknown tongue unless there is someone there to interpret what is being said.

> If any man speak in an unknown tongue, let it be by two, or at the most by three, and that by course; and let one interpret. But if there be no interpreter, let him keep silence in the church; and let him speak to himself, and to God. (1 Corinthians 14:27-28)

The reason God does not want church services to include unknown tongue is that the service can be turned into a blasphemous worship of Satan without the congregation being aware of it. For example, in 2012, Pope Benedict XVI presided as celebrant over an Easter Mass where a Catholic deacon chanted a Latin passage called the *Exsultet* (a/k/a *Exultet*). The pertinent part of his Latin chant is as follows:

> Flammas eius **Lucifer** matutinus inveniat: ille, inquam, **Lucifer**, qui nescit occasum, **Christus Fillus tuus**, qui, regressus ab inferis, humano generi serenus illuxit, et vivit et regnat, in saecula, saeculorum.[312] (emphasis added)

The Easter Mass was broadcast over Vatican television. The Vatican commentator, summarized the meaning of the chant in English as follows:

> The deacon is chanting: "Oh truly blessed night worthy alone to know the time and hour when Christ rose from the underworld with this holy building shaped with joy," he chanted, "in the awesome glory of this holy night."[313]

The first problem with the interpretation by the commentator is that the Vatican provided an interpreter for the television audience, but there was no interpreter for the church audience. The second problem with the interpretation is that the Vatican interpreter gave an abbreviated summary of the chant which was incomplete. His resulting interpretation of what the deacon chanted was therefore misleading. The interpreter glossed over and concealed the true meaning of the deacon's chant. The actual English translation of the pertinent section of the deacon's chant is as follows:

> Flaming **Lucifer** finds mankind, I say: Oh **Lucifer**, who will never be defeated, **Christ is your son** who came back from hell, shed his peaceful light and is alive and reigns in the world without end.[314] (emphasis added)

This same *Exsultet* chant was repeated in an Easter Mass in 2013, where the celebrant was the newly installed Pope Francis I.[315]

Dear reader, understand that God warned that there is a false Jesus. "For if he that cometh preacheth **another Jesus**, whom we have not preached, or if ye receive another spirit, which ye have not received, or another gospel, which ye have not accepted, ye might well bear with him." (2 Corinthians 11:4)

Just because the Catholic Church uses the name Christ does not mean that he is the Jesus Christ of the Holy Bible. The Catholic Church has a different Jesus, a different gospel, and a different spirit, of which Paul warned in 2 Corinthians 11:4. Revealingly, the Catholic Encyclopedia states that Lucifer is actually a metaphorical reference to Jesus. The Catholic Encyclopedia cites the *Exultet* as authority for its position that Lucifer is Jesus:

> The name **Lucifer** originally denotes the planet Venus, emphasizing its brilliance. The Vulgate employs the word also for "the light of the morning" (Job 11:17), "the signs of the zodiac" (Job 38:32), and "the aurora" (Psalm 109:3). Metaphorically, the word is applied to the King of Babylon (Isaiah 14:12) as preeminent among the princes of his time; to the high priest Simon son of Onias (Ecclesiasticus 50:6), for his surpassing virtue, to the glory of heaven (Apocalypse 2:28), by reason of its excellency; finally to **Jesus Christ** himself (2 Peter 1:19; Apocalypse 22:16; the **"Exultet"** of Holy Saturday) the true light of our spiritual life.[316]

The Jesus Christ of the bible is the Almighty Lord God who created all things and came down from heaven to earth and died on the cross as a propitiation for the sins of his elect. Jesus Christ then rose from the dead and ascended into heaven where he rules at the right hand of God the Father as King of kings and Lord of lords.

The Easter *Exsultet* chant reveals that the Christ of the Roman Catholic Church is not the Christ of the bible, but is rather the son of Lucifer who comes up from hell and reigns in the world. Lucifer was Satan's name before he was cast out of heaven. Isaiah 14:12. According to the Catholic Church, Lucifer will never be defeated. God says otherwise. Indeed, the fiery end of the antichrist, his false prophet, and the devil is preordained by God.

> And the devil that deceived them was cast into the lake of fire and brimstone, where the beast and the false prophet are, and shall be tormented day and night for ever and ever. (Revelation 20:10)

In witchcraft all chants have two meanings. The double meaning offers the practitioners of witchcraft a ready defense against the charge of witchcraft. There is the false exoteric meaning, which acts as a deceptive cover for the true esoteric meaning of the chant.

Sure enough, Catholic theologians have come to the defense of the Roman Church by pointing people to the false publically proclaimed meaning in order to explain away the discovered esoteric meaning. The publicly proclaimed exoteric meaning is that Lucifer in Latin should be translated as "morning star" in English. Their claim is that the chant is not referring to Lucifer, the fallen angel, but rather to Jesus, who is the "morning star." Indeed, Jesus is the morning star. The bible attests to that fact. "I Jesus have sent mine angel to testify unto you these things in the churches. I am the root and the offspring of David, and the bright and **morning star**." (Revelation 22:16) However, the claim that the word Lucifer means morning star is a diabolical and blasphemous deception.

The claim that Lucifer should be translated as "morning star" and is a reference to Christ is a manifestly false contrivance. The falsity of it can be seen by simply looking at the context of the chant. The chant makes no sense if the word Lucifer is supposed to refer to Christ. That is because in the chant Christ is the son of Lucifer. If Lucifer is supposed to be Christ, that would make Christ the son of Christ. That makes no sense. The exoteric meaning just does not hold up under scrutiny. It is clearly a cover for the true meaning that the chant is a praise and worship of Lucifer.

Furthermore, the argument that Lucifer should be translated "morning star" is part of an age-old deception. In Isaiah there is a passage about Lucifer that refers to him as "Lucifer, son of the morning." Isaiah 14:12. The Roman Catholic Church and its accomplices have flooded the market with corrupted bible versions that have changed key passages in the bible. God's word in the English language is found in the Authorized (King James) Version of the Holy Bible (AV or KJV). One example of a corrupt bible version is the New International Version (NIV). In Isaiah 14:12 there is a description of the fall of Lucifer. The NIV changed the subject of the passage at Isaiah 14:12 from "Lucifer" to the "morning star."

AV	**NIV**
How art thou fallen from heaven, O **Lucifer**, son of the morning! how art thou cut down to the ground, which didst weaken the nations! For thou hast said in thine heart, I will ascend into heaven, I will exalt my throne above the stars of God: I will sit also upon the mount of the congregation, in the sides of the north: I will ascend above the heights of the clouds; I will be like the most High. Yet thou shalt be brought down to hell, to the sides of the pit. (Isaiah 14:12-15 AV)	How you have fallen from heaven, O **morning star**, son of the dawn! You have been cast down to the earth, you who once laid low the nations! You said in your heart, "I will ascend to heaven, I will raise my throne above the stars of God: I will sit enthroned on the mount of assembly, in the utmost heights of the sacred mountain. I will ascend above the tops of the clouds; I will make myself like the most High." But you are brought down to the grave, to the depths of the pit. (Isaiah 14:12-15 NIV)

The rendering of morning star in Isaiah 14:12 is more than a mere mistranslation; it is a blasphemous deception. What is the significance of that change from "Lucifer" to "morning star"? That change blasphemes Jesus and the Holy Spirit. That is because in Revelation 22:16, Jesus calls himself the "morning star." "I Jesus have sent mine angel to testify unto you these things in the churches. I am the root and the offspring of David, and the bright and **morning star**." (Revelation 22:16)

Do you see what Satan's minions have done? Jesus is the "morning star" in the NIV Isaiah passage. Satan has taken a passage that refers to Lucifer's destruction and has twisted it in the NIV to describe the destruction of the "morning star." In the NIV, the "morning star" is "brought down to the grave, to the depths of the pit." The "morning star" is Jesus Christ.

The authors of the NIV have committed the unpardonable sin

by changing Isaiah chapter 14 in the NIV to blasphemously attribute to the Lord Jesus the judgment that will befall Lucifer. In their NIV counterfeit bible, Isaiah chapter 14 has been changed to prophesy that it is the Lord Jesus (morning star) who is cast into hell, and not Lucifer. To equate the Lord Jesus with Lucifer is to blaspheme the Holy Spirit. Jesus responded to the Pharisees who stated that Jesus used the power of Beelzebub (Satan) to cast out devils in pertinent part as follows:

> Wherefore I say unto you, All manner of sin and blasphemy shall be forgiven unto men: but the blasphemy against the Holy Ghost shall not be forgiven unto men. And whosoever speaketh a word against the Son of man, it shall be forgiven him: but whosoever speaketh against the Holy Ghost, it shall not be forgiven him, neither in this world, neither in the world to come. (Matthew 12:31-32 AV)

To attribute to God he characteristics of the devil is considered blaspheming the Holy Ghost; that is an unpardonable sin. The publishers of the NIV knew exactly what they were doing. That is evidenced by the fact that the NIV Study Bible cross references in a footnote their use of "morning star" in Isaiah 14:12 with the "morning star" in Revelation 2:28. Revelation 2:28 refers to the blessings to him that overcomes the world and keeps God's works to the end: "And I will give him the **morning star**." (Revelation 2:28 AV) The NIV then cross references the term "morning star" in Revelation 2:28 with "morning star" in Revelation 22:16, where Jesus clearly states that he is the "morning star."

The publishers of the NIV thus correlated the use of "morning star" in all three passages. The cross references are clear evidence that the editors knew that changing the destruction of Lucifer to the destruction of the "morning star" in Isaiah 14 meant that it was Jesus Christ who was being destroyed in the NIV Isaiah 14 passage.

The NIV is based upon corrupted texts that were provided by the Roman Catholic Church. The two primary manuscripts that form the basis for the NIV, and indeed all modern English bibles, except for the Authorized (King James) Version, are the *Sinaiticus* and the *Vaticanus*.

The manuscript *Sinaiticus*, which is often referred to by the first letter of the Hebrew alphabet, *Aleph*, is written in book form (codex) on velum.[317] It contains many spurious books such as the Shepherd of Hermes, the Didache, and the Epistle of Barnabas.[318] *Sinaiticus* was discovered in a waste basket in St. Catherine's monastery on Mount Sinai in February of 1859.[319] *Sinaiticus* is covered with alterations that are systematically spread over every page and were made by at least ten different revisors.[320] The alterations are obvious to anyone who examines the manuscript.[321] Most of the revisions to the text were made in the sixth or seventh century.[322]

The manuscript *Vaticanus*, often referred to by the letter "B," originated in the Vatican library, hence the name.[323] *Vaticanus* was first revealed in 1841; where the transcript had been prior to that date is unclear.[324] One thing this is clear is that the manuscript omits many portions of scripture which explain vital Christian doctrines. *Vaticanus* omits Genesis 1:1 through Genesis 46:28; Psalms 106 through 138; Matthew 16:2,3; Romans 16:24; the Pauline Epistles; Revelation; and everything in Hebrews after 9:14.[325]

It should not be surprising that the Vatican would produce a manuscript that omits the portion of the book of Hebrews which exposes the Mass as completely ineffectual and deletes Revelation chapter 17, which reveals Rome as the seat of "MYSTERY, BABYLON THE GREAT, THE MOTHER OF HARLOTS AND ABOMINATIONS OF THE EARTH." It is notable that the two primary manuscripts used by the new bible versions were found in the care and custody of the Roman Catholic Church.

The *Vaticanus* and *Sinaiticus* manuscripts, which make up less than one percent of the existing ancient manuscripts, differ significantly from the Received Text that is the basis for the Authorized (King James) Version. *Vaticanus* omits at least 2,877 words; it adds 536 words; it substitutes 935 words; it transposes 2,098 words; and it modifies 1,132 words; making a total of 7,578 verbal divergences from the Received Text. *Sinaiticus* is an even worse corruption, having almost 9,000 divergences from the Received Text.[326]

The combined effect of having a corrupted text and then having that text interpreted using a free-form translation method known as dynamic equivalence has been that the NIV has 64,098 fewer words than the King James Bible.[327] That is a 10% loss in the bible. That means that an NIV bible would have 170 fewer pages than a typical 1,700 page King James Bible.[328] Let's read what God thinks about such deletions of his holy words. "And if any man shall take away from the words of the book of this prophecy, God shall take away his part out of the book of life, and out of the holy city, and from the things which are written in this book." Revelation 22:19. God takes the misuse of his name very seriously (Exodus 20:7), but it is even more serious to tamper with God's word. [T]hou hast magnified thy word above all thy name. (Psalms 138:2)

The Catholic Publication of corrupt counterfeit bibles is not surprising. It is different in kind, but not different in effect from nullifying God's word through Catholic traditions.

The New International Version (NIV) is the most popular of the new bible versions. Reportedly, the NIV represents 45 % of all bibles sold.[329] Dr. Virginia Mollenkott, the textual style editor for the NIV, is an admitted lesbian.[330] The Chairman of the NIV Old Testament Committee, Dr. Woudstra, was considered to be sympathetic to the interests and practices of sodomites. The NIV chief editor vaunted the fact that the NIV showed that it is a great error to believe that in order to be born again one has to have faith in Jesus as Savior.[331]

Rupert Murdoch owns the exclusive rights to the NIV.[332] The NIV is published by Zondervan, which is owned by Murdoch's News Corporation.[333] Murdoch's News Corporation also owns Harper Collins, the publisher of Anton LaVey's Satanic Bible. LaVey is the founder of The Church Of Satan. He is reputed to have been a Jew, whose real name was Howard Levey. Both the Satanic Bible and the NIV Bible are featured on the Harper Collins sales website.[334] "Can two walk together, except they be agreed?" (Amos 3:3 AV) LaVey's book is an exoteric Satanic Bible, whereas the NIV is an esoteric Satanic Bible.

Time magazine called Murdoch one of the four most powerful people in the world, and for good reason; he has a media empire that includes Twentieth Century Fox, Fox Television, cable television providers, satellites, and newspapers and television stations throughout

America, Europe, and Asia.[335] The pope bestowed upon Murdoch the title of "Knight Commander of St. Gregory" for promoting the interests of the Roman Catholic Church.[336]

There is both a Catholic version and a Protestant version of the NIV. The notable difference between the two is the Catholic version contains the apocryphal books that are considered part of the biblical cannon by the Vatican. The apocryphal books are rejected and considered non-cannonical by Protestant Christians.

Defenders of the new bibles claim that the essential doctrines of the Christian Faith are expressed in the new bibles, even though they have been deleted or changed in many passages. James H. Son, author of *The New Athenians*, likened the logic of that argument to removing a stop sign from a busy street intersection and then justifying the removal because the other traffic signals in the city were left intact. Even though the sign only contained one word, that word is of critical importance to those who arrive at the intersection, just as each word in the Holy Bible is of critical importance to those who are reading it.

God has made the point in the Holy Bible that **every word** of God is important. "And Jesus answered him, saying, It is written, That man shall not live by bread alone, **but by every word of God**." (Luke 4:4 AV) Incidently, the doctrine of Luke 4:4 is missing in the new bible versions. The NASB, which is another corrupt bible version based upon the *Vaticanus* and *Sinaiticus* manuscripts, leaves out the last clause and simply states: "And Jesus answered him, 'it is written, MAN SHALL NOT LIVE ON BREAD ALONE.'" (Luke 4:4 NASB) The new versions leave the reader in ignorance as to what it is other than bread by which man lives.

> And he humbled thee, and suffered thee to hunger, and fed thee with manna, which thou knewest not, neither did thy fathers know; that he might make thee know that man doth not live by bread only, but **by every word that proceedeth out of the mouth of the LORD doth man live**. (Deuteronomy 8:3 AV)
>
> **Every word of God is pure**: he is a shield unto them that put their trust in him. (Proverbs 30:5 AV)

Look at the passage in Galatians 3:16, wherein God points out the importance of every one of his words. In that passage God explains the importance of the distinction between the singular word "seed" and the plural word "seeds."

> Now to Abraham and his **seed** were the promises made. **He saith not, And to seeds**, as of many; but as of one, And to thy seed, which is Christ. (Galatians 3:16 AV)

If one looks at the AV passages that refer to the promises made to Abraham, one sees that in fact God refers to Abraham's "seed," singular. In the NIV, however, the passages that prophesy the blessings that were to flow from Abraham's seed, Jesus Christ, are changed and obscured. If one were to try to find the passages referred to in Galatians 3:16 in the NIV one would not be able to do so, because the NIV does not use the word chosen by God but has substituted words chosen by man as inspired by Satan.

AV	NIV
And in thy **seed** shall all the nations of the earth be blessed; because thou hast obeyed my voice. (Genesis 22:18 AV)	[A]nd through your **offspring** all nations on earth will be blessed, because you have obeyed me. (Genesis 22:18 NIV)
And I will establish my covenant between me and thee and thy **seed** after thee in their generations for an everlasting covenant, to be a God unto thee, and to thy **seed** after thee. (Genesis 17:7 AV)	I will establish my covenant as an everlasting covenant between me and you and your **descendants** after you for the generations to come, to be your God and the God of your **descendants** after you. (Genesis 17:7 NIV)

It is important for God's heirs to know who they are. His heirs are those who have the faith of Abraham, not those that have the flesh of Abraham.

> Even as Abraham believed God, and it was accounted

> to him for righteousness. Know ye therefore that they which are of faith, the same are the children of Abraham. And the scripture, foreseeing that God would justify the heathen through faith, preached before the gospel unto Abraham, saying, In thee shall all nations be blessed. **So then they which be of faith are blessed with faithful Abraham.** (Galatians 3:6-9 AV)

This point is understood by the passage in Galatians 3:16 that explains what is meant by the precise word "seed" used in the Old Testament. **"And if ye be Christ's, then are ye Abraham's seed, and heirs according to the promise."** (Galatians 3:29 AV)

Without the precise word "seed" the meaning of the will of God can be misinterpreted to support false doctrines like the pretribulation rapture fraud, which makes Christ's church a mere parenthesis in history. Under the pretribulation rapture corruption, fleshly Israel is to inherit the promises of God, contrary to God's express intent that it is those who are chosen and justified by his sovereign grace who are his heirs and not those who are born of the flesh of Abraham. **"That being justified by his grace, we should be made heirs according to the hope of eternal life."** (Titus 3:7 AV)

> Not as though the word of God hath taken none effect. For they are not all Israel, which are of Israel: Neither, because they are the seed of Abraham, are they all children: but, In Isaac shall thy seed be called. That is, **They which are the children of the flesh, these are not the children of God: but the children of the promise are counted for the seed."** (Romans 9:6-8 AV)

That is one example of a false doctrine that is supported by the change of just one word. There are other false doctrines that have sprung from other corrupt changes to God's word in the new bible versions.

There are many other passages where the doctrines of God have been completely reversed. In the KJV (AV) the ways of the wicked are always "grievous." Psalms 10:4-5. The devil cannot have that, so Psalms 10:4-5 in his NKJV states the ways of the wicked are always "prospering." The wicked "were forgotten" in Ecclesiastes 8:10 of God's word in the KJV, but in the NIV Ecclesiastes 8:10 passage the wicked "receive praise."

As explained in detail in this author's book, *Solving the Mystery of BABYLON THE GREAT*, the Catholic dogma is imbued with Zionism. It is not surprising, therefore, to find that in Hosea 10:1, Israel is a "spreading vine" in the NIV. Hosea 10:1 in the NASB depicts Israel is a "luxuriant vine." God, however, states that "Israel is an empty vine" in his KJV Holy Bible at Hosea 10:1.

God states that "the words of a talebearer are as wounds." Proverbs 26:22. However, the NIV change agents contradict God by saying in Proverbs 26:22 of their NIV that "the words of a gossip are like choice morsels." In Proverbs 25:23 God states that "the north wind driveth away rain." The NASB, however, states in their Proverbs 25:23 that "the north wind brings forth rain." These are just a few of the many doctrinal changes. The new bible versions are truly different bibles with a different gospel.

Indeed, the papacy is not finished with its rewrite of the bible to further its Zionist ends. In *The Document of the Vatican Commission for Religious Relations with Judaism § 4*, it states: **"We propose, in the future, to remove from the Gospel of St. John the term, 'the Jews' where it is used in a negative sense, and to translate it, 'the enemies of Christ.'"**[337]

At a speech at Hebrew University in Jerusalem, Roman Catholic Cardinal Joseph Bernadine stated:

> [T]here is need for... theological reflection, especially with what many consider to be the problematic New Testament's texts ... Retranslation ... and reinterpretation certainly need to be included among the goals we pursue in the effort to eradicate anti-semitism.
>
> [T]he gospel of John ... is generally considered

> among the most problematic of all New Testament books in its outlook towards Jews and Judaism . . . this teaching of John about the Jews, which resulted from the historical conflict between the church and synagogue in the latter part of the first century C.E., can no longer be taught as authentic doctrine or used as catechesis by contemporary Christianity . . . Christians today must see that such teachings . . . can no longer be regarded as definitive teachings in light of our improved understanding.[338]

The brazenness of Cardinal Bernadine is amazing. He is saying that "the teaching of John about the Jews ... can no longer be taught as authentic doctrine." John was merely the vessel used by the Holy Spirit through which God spoke. "All scripture is given by inspiration of God, and is profitable for doctrine, for reproof, for correction, for instruction in righteousness." (2 Timothy 3:16) Cardinal Bernadine disagrees with God and states that God's word is not profitable for doctrine. Cardinal Bernadine actually thinks that he has the authority to overrule God Almighty. That is the character of all of the prelates of Rome. They are arrogant liars. "Let God be true, but every man a liar." (Romans 3:4)

The promoters of the new bible versions claim that they are merely updating the archaic English in the King James Bible. They are being disingenuous. The Holy Bible is a legal document. The English of the King James Bible is not archaic, it is precise. The precise language used has eternal importance. Thee, thou, thy, and thine are singular pronouns. Thou is the subjective second person singular, thee is the objective second person singular, and thy and thine are possessive second person singular. Ye is a subjective second person plural pronoun. In the King James text the precision of the language puts the reader in the midst of the narrative. The reader is able to tell whether the person is the object of the action or the subject causing the action. The reader can also tell if the subject or object is a group or an individual. The new versions use either the pronouns "you" or "your" for all of the narratives and the reader is not able to know anything about the setting of the narrative. All one need do is read Galatians 3:16 to know that singularity and plurality are important to God.

The writers of the Authorized (King James)Version (AV or

KJV) did not use the more precise pronouns for the reason that their use was the customary language of the 16th century; they purposely used those words because they wanted to accurately and faithfully translate God's word into English. To prove the point, all one need do is read the dedicatory at the beginning of the Holy Bible (AV); the dedicatory was written at the completion of the AV Holy Bible in 1611 A.D., not once was thee, thou, thy, thine, or ye used in the dedicatory.

Clearly, Lucifer is distinct from the Lord God Jesus Christ. The Vatican certainly knows that, and so do the heathens, whose footsteps the Vatican is following in its worship of Lucifer. For example, Albert Pike, the theological pontiff of Masonry, made a clear distinction between JEHOVAH and Lucifer. Pike clearly knew that God is distinct from Lucifer. Pike clearly stated that he worships Lucifer instead of God. Pike wrote that "[i]t is certain that its true pronunciation is not represented by the word Jehovah; and therefore that *that* is not the true name of Deity, nor the Ineffable Word."[339] God's word, however, states clearly that JEHOVAH is God's name. "That men may know that thou, whose name alone is JEHOVAH, art the most high over all the earth." (Psalms 83:18)

If the Masons do not recognize JEHOVAH as God, who is their god? The god of the Masons is Lucifer, which was Satan's name before he rebelled against God and was cast out of heaven. Albert Pike said that "[t]he doctrine of Satanism is heresy; and the true and pure philosophic religion is the belief in Lucifer, the equal of Adonay; but Lucifer, God of Light and God of Good is struggling for humanity against Adonay, the God of Darkness and Evil."[340] Adonay is the Old Testament Hebrew word for God. Pike not only acknowledges that Lucifer is the god of Freemasonry, but he also blasphemes God by calling God "the God of Darkness and Evil."

Just as Pike understood and made a clear distinction between God and Lucifer, so too has the Vatican. The dissembling claim that Lucifer is intended by the papacy to mean Jesus Christ in their Easter *Exsultet* chant cannot survive the mildest scrutiny. The Vatican has made its choice between God and Lucifer and the chant in praise of Lucifer tells the world that they worship Lucifer. That makes the papacy the enemy of God.

He that is not with me is against me; and he that gathereth not with me scattereth abroad. Wherefore I say unto you, All manner of sin and blasphemy shall be forgiven unto men: but the blasphemy against the Holy Ghost shall not be forgiven unto men. (Matthew 12:30-31)

All occult religions worship Lucifer (i.e., Satan). That fact is kept secret from the uninitiated followers of those heathen religions. A close study will reveal the true nature of a religion. The Roman Catholic *Exsultet* is just one piece of evidence that the Roman Catholic religion is the occult worship of Lucifer.

16 A Hellish Stopover on the Way to Heaven

Further evidence that the Roman church does not consider the one sacrifice of Jesus Christ on the cross was sufficient is its doctrine of *purgatory*. The Romish church teaches that the sacrifice of Jesus Christ on the cross did not satisfy God. It claims that God requires additional punishment of the believer in order to expiate the sins. This expiation can be done on earth through penance. If, however, the sin is not punished on earth the sin must be punished after death in a place called Purgatory. Purgatory is a place where sins are purportedly purged and after the sins are purged the poor tormented one is then finally granted entrance into heaven.[341] The official *Catechism of the Catholic Church* states:

> All who die in God's grace and friendship, but are imperfectly purified, are indeed assured of their eternal salvation; but after death they undergo purification, so to achieve the holiness necessary to enter the joy of heaven. The church gives the name *Purgatory* to this final purification of the elect, which is entirely different from the punishment of the damned.[342]

The bible is clear that there is no purgatory. In John 3:36 Jesus states that there are only two possibilities. "He that believeth on the Son hath everlasting life: and he that believeth not the Son shall not see life; but the wrath of God abideth on him." (John 3:36) In Matthew 25:46 Jesus explains that at the judgment seat of Christ those who manifest the true faith of Jesus Christ will receive life eternal, whereas those who lack the true faith will suffer everlasting punishment for their sins. There is no middle ground, between the two. There is heaven and hell. There is no purgatory. In Luke 16:26 Jesus stated emphatically in the story of Lazarus that "there is a great gulf fixed" between heaven and hell there can be no passing back and forth.

All who do not adhere to the doctrine of purgatory are under an official curse from the Roman Catholic Church, which is memorialized by *The Council of Trent*:

> If anyone saith that, after the grace of justification has been received, to every penitent sinner the guilt is remitted, and the debt of the eternal punishment is blotted out in such a way that there remains not any debt of temporal punishment to be discharged either in this world, or in the next in **Purgatory**, before the entrance to the Kingdom of Heaven can be opened (to him); let him be anathema.[343]

Purgatory is a money maker for the Catholic Church. Under that abominable doctrine, people are compelled to give to the Catholic Church in order to pay the penalty for sins purportedly not atoned for by Christ's sacrifice. These alms and penance are not just given for one's own sins but also for the sins of others who have already died as a way of getting them out of Purgatory.

> From the beginning the Church has honored the memory of the dead and offered prayers in suffrage for them, above all the Eucharistic sacrifice, so that thus purified they may attain the beatific vision of God. The church also commends almsgiving, indulgences, and works of penance undertaken on behalf of the dead. CATECHISM OF THE CATHOLIC CHURCH, § 1032 (1994).

There is absolutely no authority in the Bible for such a place as purgatory. In fact, the doctrine of purgatory is directly contrary to the

Gospel of Christ. The Gospel is that we are saved from the wrath of God by the grace of God through faith in Jesus Christ.

> And to wait for his Son from heaven, whom he raised from the dead, even Jesus, which **delivered us from the wrath to come.** (1 Thessalonians 1:10)

Those who are saved by grace through faith in Jesus Christ will not suffer any wrath in hell or a fictional purgatory.

> For **God hath not appointed us to wrath**, but to obtain salvation by our Lord Jesus Christ, (1 Thessalonians 5:9)

> Much more then, being now justified by his blood, **we shall be saved from wrath** through him. (Romans 5:9)

> Verily, verily, I say unto you, **He that heareth my word, and believeth on him that sent me, hath everlasting life, and shall not come into condemnation; but is passed from death unto life.** (John 5:24)

There is only Heaven and Hell that awaits those who die. There is a great gulf between Heaven and Hell. Once a person is in Hell, he cannot ever enter Heaven. Luke 16:22-26. There is everlasting fire and eternal life; there is no halfway purgatory between heaven and hell.

> Then shall he say also unto them on the left hand, Depart from me, ye cursed, into **everlasting fire**, prepared for the devil and his angels . . . And these shall go away into everlasting punishment: but the righteous into **life eternal.** (Matthew 25:41, 46)

> He that believeth on the Son hath **everlasting life**: and **he that believeth not the Son shall not see life; but the wrath of God abideth on him.** (John 3:36)

> Verily, verily, I say unto you, He that believeth on me

hath **everlasting life**. (John 6:47)

But now being made free from sin, and become servants to God, ye have your fruit unto holiness, and the end **everlasting life**. (Romans 6:22)

Since Jesus has atoned for our sins there is nothing more for us to do. If we believe in Christ, our sins are forgiven and we are justified before God. God has promised that if we believe he will remember our sins no more. We are not justified because of what we have done but because of what Jesus has done for us. God does not want penance from us, he wants repentance.

Above when he said, Sacrifice and offering and burnt offerings and offering for sin thou wouldest not, neither hadst pleasure therein; which are offered by the law; Then said he, Lo, I come to do thy will, O God. He taketh away the first, that he may establish the second. By the which will **we are sanctified through the offering of the body of Jesus Christ once for all**. And every priest standeth daily ministering and offering oftentimes the same sacrifices, which can never take away sins: But this man, after he had offered one sacrifice for sins for ever, sat down on the right hand of God; From henceforth expecting till his enemies be made his footstool. **For by one offering he hath perfected for ever them that are sanctified**. Whereof the Holy Ghost also is a witness to us: for after that he had said before, This is the covenant that I will make with them after those days, saith the Lord, I will put my laws into their hearts, and in their minds will I write them; **And their sins and iniquities will I remember no more. Now where remission of these is, there is no more offering for sin**. (Hebrews 10:8-18)

17 Charging Admission to Enter Heaven

The Bible teaches that "the love of money is the root of all evil." 1 Timothy 6:10. The Roman church loves money. The Roman Catholic Church is the single richest organization in the world.[344] The wealth of the Catholic Church has been amassed over many centuries. At the time of the Mexican Revolution, the Catholic Church owned between one third to one half of all the land in Mexico.[345]

D. Antonio Gavin was a Catholic priest in Spain in the 1600's. He was forced to flee from Spain during the Spanish Inquisition to the safety of England. There he wrote a book titled *A Master Key to Popery*, which exposed just a small portion of the Vatican wealth. For example, the Cathedral of St. Salvator, in the small city of Zaragoza, contained ten thousand troy ounces of silver, 84 chalices, 20 of which were made of solid gold. The *custodia* used to carry the Host in procession was made of five hundred troy pounds of solid gold and was set with diamonds, emeralds and other precious stones. The *custodia* was so valuable that several goldsmiths tried but were unable to estimate its value.[346]

Our Lady of the Pillar, another church in Zaragova, had a crown on the image of the Virgin Mary that weighed twenty five troy pounds and was set all over with so many diamonds that no gold could be seen on it. People seeing the crown thought it was made entirely of diamonds. The idol of Mary also had 6 other pure solid gold crowns set with diamonds and emeralds. The image of Mary had 365 necklaces of pearls and diamonds (one for each day of the year), and innumerable crafted roses of diamonds and other precious stones. There were so many diamond roses, in fact, that a different set of roses could adorn the idol each day for three years straight. The graven image had a different skirt for each day of the year; the skirts were embroidered in gold, diamonds, and other precious stones. That was not the only image in the church, another five foot image was made entirely of silver and adorned with precious stones with a diamond studded crown of pure gold.[347]

When the General of the English forces, the "Right Honorable Lord Stanhope," was shown the treasures at the cathedral of St. Salvator he exclaimed that if all the kings of Europe gathered together all of their treasuries they could not buy half of the riches in the cathedral.[348] That was just one cathedral, in one small city in Spain, 300 years ago.

The Vatican wealth continues to compound. Avro Manhattan, the world's foremost authority on Vatican politics, revealed in his book, *The Vatican Billions*, that as of 1983 the Jesuit order of priests had tax free annual income from the United States alone of no less than $250 million.[349] Manhattan determined that the Jesuits held a 51% ownership interest in the Bank of America (which in 1998 merged with Nationsbank to form Bank America), and that they are also major stockholders in companies that have strategic military significance to the U.S., such as Boeing and Lockeed.[350] Those holdings represent only a portion of the Jesuit wealth. The Jesuit wealth, in turn, is only a small portion of the vast Vatican wealth. There are hundreds of other orders of Catholic priests including 125 orders of monks and 414 orders of nuns operating in the United States.[351] One order of nuns, the Little Sisters of the Poor, have assets valued conservatively in excess of one billion dollars.[352]

"In a statement published in connection with a bond prospectus, the Boston archdiocese listed its assets at Six Hundred and Thirty-five Million ($635,891,004), which is 9.9 times its liabilities. This leaves a net worth of Five Hundred and Seventy-one million dollars

($571,704,953). It is not difficult to discover the truly astonishing wealth of the church, once we add the riches of the twenty-eight archdioceses and 122 dioceses of the U.S.A., some of which are even wealthier than that of Boston."[353] The Catholic Church's wealth just in the United States alone has been conservatively estimated at over $100 billion.[354]

The above figures are as of 1983. No doubt the amounts have increased exponentially since 1983 in view of the fact that the church pays no real estate taxes, income taxes, inheritance taxes, sales taxes, or gift taxes.[355] The Catholic Church has accumulated such vast wealth that as of 1965 it owned 25 percent of all privately owned real estate in the United States.[356] The Catholic Church is a recipient of hundreds of millions of dollars in federal and state grants for construction of hospitals and other buildings and projects.[357] Nino Lo Bello, former Rome correspondent for *Business Week*, calls the Vatican "the tycoon on the Tiber." His research indicates that the Vatican owns one third of Rome's real estate and is the largest holder of stocks and bonds in the entire world.[358]

The Roman cult, however, is not satisfied with its immense wealth, it wants more. In fact Pope Innocent II claimed ownership of the entire universe as the "TEMPORAL SOVEREIGN OF THE UNIVERSE."[359] Even today the Pope wears a triple crown because he claims to rule as king over heaven, hell, and earth.

Vatican doctrines are set up to extract the most money possible from its flock. This fleecing of the flock started from the beginning and continues today. Before she was saved by the grace of God to the true faith of Jesus Christ, Rosamond Culbertson, was kept for five years as the concubine of a Catholic priest named Manuel Canto in Cuba in the 1830's. She was often present to see and hear the depravity of the Catholic priests as they acted and spoke freely while drunk in her presence. The priests were always scheming to use some trick to get money or other property from their deceived flock. Culbertson wrote a book that recounted many examples of the pecuniary conniving of the Catholic priests.[360]

One of the doctrines used to make the harlot of Rome rich is the doctrine of indulgences. Under Catholic doctrine an indulgence is the removal of the temporal punishment for sins. The Catholic Church teaches that the sin has been forgiven through the Catholic sacraments but that a person must be punished for that sin either on earth or after death for an unspecified time in purgatory. That punishment, however, can be remitted through an indulgence granted by the Catholic Church.[361] An indulgence can be of the entire punishment (plenary indulgence) or only a part of the punishment (partial indulgence).[362] A Catholic church member can also obtain an indulgence from the church on behalf of another person whether the recipient of the indulgence is living or dead.

> It has likewise defined, that, if those truly penitent have departed in the love of God, before they have made satisfaction by worthy fruits of penance for sins of commission and omission, the souls of these are cleansed after death by purgatorial punishments; and so that they may be relieved from punishments of this kind, namely, the sacrifices of Masses, prayers, and almsgiving, and other works of piety, which are customarily performed by the faithful for other faithful according to the institutions of the Church. COUNCIL OF FLORENCE, 1439.[363]

In the middle ages the Romish church was quite brazen and would actually sell indulgences outright.[364] The Romish church is still selling indulgences, it is just not as direct about it as it once was. To whom do they think the alms are going to be payed? The Catholic Church, of course. Who is going to say the Masses? The Catholic Priest, of course. In other words in order to get a loved one out of the torments of Purgatory it is necessary to pay money. There are two types of Masses in the Catholic Church, High Mass and Low Mass. High Masses are more expensive than Low Masses. "Any priest who celebrates Mass may receive an offering or 'Mass stipend' to apply that Mass for a specific intention. This approved custom of the Church is regulated by the Code of Canon Law and provincial and diocesan laws."[365] The Irish have a saying: high money, High Mass; low money; Low Mass; no money, NO MASS![366]

The Gospel clearly states that neither salvation nor any gift of God can be purchased with gold, silver, or anything else. Salvation has already been purchased with the precious blood of Christ.

> **Forasmuch as ye know that ye were not redeemed with corruptible things, as silver and gold, from your vain conversation received by tradition from your fathers; But with the precious blood of Christ**, as of a lamb without blemish and without spot: Who verily was foreordained before the foundation of the world, but was manifest in these last times for you, Who by him do believe in God, that raised him up from the dead, and gave him glory; that your faith and hope might be in God. (1 Peter 1:18-21)

And when Simon saw that through laying on of the apostles' hands the Holy Ghost was given, he offered them money, Saying, Give me also this power, that on whomsoever I lay hands, he may receive the Holy Ghost. But Peter said unto him, **Thy money perish with thee, because thou hast thought that the gift of God may be purchased with money.** (Acts 8:18-20)

18 Fire from Heaven

John describes a beast that "doeth great wonders, so that he maketh fire come down from heaven on the earth in the sight of men." (Revelation 13:13) The fulminations by the organization of the papacy are so much fire called down from heaven. Wylie explains:

> The prophecy [of Revelation 13:13] found a striking fulfilment in the papal interdicts and excommunications so frequent in the Middle Ages, and not unknown in even our own day. These ebullitions of pontifical vengeance, it was pretended, were fire out of heaven: the fire of the wrath of God which the Pope had power to evoke, therewith to burn up his enemies. The blinded nations believed that in the voice of the Pope they heard the voice of God, and that the fulminations of the Vatican were the thunderings and lightnings of Divine wrath. ... To the mightiest sovereign even the papal excommunication was a dreadful affair. He shook and trembled on his throne for his army could give him no protection; it was well, indeed, if both soldiers and subjects did not unite in carrying out the papal behest by driving him from his kingdom, if some fanatic monk, by the more quick despatch of the dagger, did not save them the trouble. European history furnishes a list of more than

> sixty-four emperors and kings deposed by the Popes. In the number is Henry II of England, deposed by Alexander III; King John, by Innocent III.; Richard and Edward, by Boniface IX, Henry VIII., by Clement VII, and again by Paul III.; Elizabeth, by Pius V. Even King Robert the Bruce had this terrible curse launched against him, but thanks to the Culdee element still strong in Scotland, King Robert and his subjects held the Pope's fulmination but a brutum fulmen, and so it did not harm them. Almost all the bulls against crowned heads have contained clauses stripping them of their territories, and empowering their neighbour kings to invade and seize them; and influenced partly by a desire to serve the Pope, and partly by the greed of what was not their own, they have not been slow to act on the papal permission. ... The Romanists themselves have chosen the very figure of the Apocalypse, "fire from heaven," to designate the Papal excommunications and anathemas. Thus Gregory VII spoke of the Emperor Henry IV when excommunicated as "struck with thunder." (Afflatum fulmino -Danburg, 587.)[367]

Wylie explains that when the pope was through subduing kings he next focused on sending his fire from heaven against "heretics;" the most notable curse against "heretics" is found in the *Bullum Coenae Domini.*"

> In Rome's Great Book of Curses one of the most notable is the "Bullum Coenae Domini." It is truly an utterance from the "mouth speaking great things." Framed since the Reformation, it curses all the various sections of the protestant Church, giving special prominence to Calvinists and Zuinglians. Its scope is wide indeed. The world and its inhabitants, so far as they were known to the framers of this bull, are compendiously cursed in it. Its thunders are heard re-echoing far beyond the limits if Christendom, and its lightnings are seen to strike the pirates of barbarous seas, as well as the Calvinists of Great Britain.

This bull was wont to be promulgated annually by the Pope in person, attended by a magnificent array of cardinals and priests. The ceremony took place in Maunday Thursday, the Thursday before Easter, and was accompanied by numerous solemnities, fitted to strike the spectators with awe. It was read from the lofty vestibule of the Church of the Lateran, amid the firing of cannon, the ringing of bells, the blaring of trumpets, and the blazing of torches. When the curses of the bull had been thundered forth, the torches were extinguished and flung into the great piazza beneath, to signify the outer darkness into which all heretics shall finally be hurled. Pope Ganganelli in 1770 forbade the public reading of the bull Coenae Domini, but the practice was soon revived, and is still continued at Rome, though not in the same public fashion. But the discontinuance of its open promulgation matters nothing; it is unrepealed; all heretics are, *ipso facto*, under its ban, and the establishment of the papal Hierarchy gives it to all Romanists the force of law in the united Kingdom.[368]

Read the following excerpt from the Papal Bull *In Coenae* (a/k/a *Coena*) *Domini*; it is clearly fire called down from heaven on the earth in the sight of men.

As the members of one body under Christ their Head, and his Vicar on earth, the Roman Pontiff, the successor of St. Peter, from whom the unity of the whole Church flows; and that thus, with the help of Divine grace, they may so enjoy quietness in this life, as that hereafter also they may attain unto to the enjoyment of blessedness. ... We, therefore ... Excommunicate and Anathematize, on behalf of God Almighty, Father, Son, and Holy Ghost, and by the authority of the Blessed Apostles Peter and Paul, and Our own, all Hussites, Wickliffites, Lutherans, Zwinglians, Calvinists, Huguenots, Anabaptists, Trinitarians, and all apostates from the Christian faith, and, all and singular, *all other Heretics, by whatever name they may be called and whatever sect they may be*; and all that believe, harbour, or abet them, and generally all their protectors; and further, those who, without Our authority and that of the Apostolic See, knowingly, for any cause whatever, publicly or secretly, upon whatever plea or pretext, *read or keep, print or defend, their books containing heresy or treating of religion*; likewise schismatics, and those who *pertinaciously withdraw themselves, or desert, from obedience to Us and to the Roman Pontiff for the time being.*[369] (italics in original)

Notice the context of *In Coenae Domini*. The context suggests an authorship by someone other than the pope. That is significant, because when Revelations 13 is read in context we see that there is a second beast that makes his appearance. While the fire sent down was in the sight of men and on behalf of the antichrist, it was sent down by a second beast. This second beast has been described as the "false prophet" in Revelation 16:13, 19:20, and 20:10.

> And I beheld another beast coming up out of the earth; and he had two horns like a lamb, and he spake as a dragon. And he exerciseth all the power of the first beast before him, and causeth the earth and them which dwell therein to worship the first beast, whose deadly wound was healed. And he doeth great wonders, so that he maketh fire come down from heaven on the earth in the sight of men, And deceiveth them that dwell on the earth by the means of those miracles which he had power to do in the sight of the beast; saying to them that dwell on the earth, that they should make an image to the beast, which had the wound by a sword, and did live. (Revelation 13:11-14)

As explained later in this book, the false prophet can be none other than the Jesuits.

19 Raping the Church

Arthur Pink was described by his biographer, Iain Murray, as one of the most influential evangelical authors in the second half of the twentieth century. Arthur Pink stated that the pope could not be the antichrist, because Pink claimed that according to his interpretation of 2 Thessalonians 2 the church must be raptured out of the world before the antichrist is revealed. Pink seems to have later disavowed the premillennial rapture doctrine (calling all such dispensationalism a "pernicious error").[370] Pink, for a time, though, had fallen for the rapture deception that conceals the presence of the papal antichrist. His early writing below from his book, *The Antichrist*, is representative of those who adhere to the rapture error.

> The Antichrist cannot be revealed until the mystic Body of Christ and the Holy Spirit have been removed from the earth. This is made clear by what we read in 2 Thess. 2. In verse three of that chapter the apostle refers to the revelation of the Man of Sin. In verse four he describes his awful impiety. In verse five he reminds the Thessalonians how that he had taught them these things by word of mouth when he was with them. And then, in verse six he declares "And now ye know what withholdeth that he might be revealed in his time". And again he said, "For the mystery of iniquity doth already work: only He who now letteth (hindereth) will let until He be taken out of the way". There are two agencies,

then, which are hindering, or preventing the manifestation of the Antichrist, until "his time" shall have come. The former agency is covered by the pronoun "what", the latter by the word "He". The former, we are satisfied, is the mystical Body of Christ; the latter being the Holy Spirit of God. At the Rapture both shall be "taken out of the way", and then shall the Man of Sin be revealed. If, then, the Antichrist cannot appear before the Rapture of the saints and the taking away of the Holy Spirit, then, here is proof positive that the Antichrist *has not yet appeared.*[371]

The term "rapture" is not found anywhere in the Holy Scriptures. It is in fact a derivation of the Latin *Raptus. Raptus* is a word that can be found in some of the passages in the Latin translation of the bible, which is known as the Latin Vulgate. *Raptus* is a mistranslation of the Greek word *harpazo,* which literally means "caught up." *See* 2 Corinthians 12:4 in the Latin Vulgate.

Many people believe that rapture is synonymous with resurrection, but that is not true. While rapture does include the idea of being taken away, it is very different from the resurrection promised by Jesus. Rapture means "the act of seizing and carrying off as prey or plunder . . . the act of carrying off a woman . . . rape."[372] The root word for rapture is rapt which means "Rape (abduction or ravishing) . . . . The act or power of carrying forcibly away."[373] Ravish means "[t]o seize and carry away by violence. . . . To have carnal knowledge with a woman by force and against her consent."[374] Both rapture and rape share the same Latin root word, *raptus.*[375] *Raptus* means "a carrying off, abduction, rape."[376]

The Holy Scripture describes the church as the chaste bride of Christ who is with Christ at the wedding supper of the Lamb. (Revelation 19:7; 22:17; Matthew 22:1-14; 2 Corinthians 11:2; Ephesians 5:25-33) The wedding supper of the Lamb will take place at the resurrection of the saints when this world ends.

By using the term rapture, these "scholars" are blasphemously describing that holy and glorious resurrection of the church as a rape! This church rape doctrine that has infected the modern Protestant churches can be traced to its historic genesis in the Jesuits: Cardinal Robert Bellarmine, Emanuel de Lacunza, and Francisco Ribera. For more information on the historical background of the rapture deception, read this author's book: *Solving the Mystery of BABYLON THE GREAT*.

Let us, like the noble Bereans, check the pretribulation rapture teachings against the scriptures. *See* Acts 17:11. Those that hold to the pretribulation rapture teaching cite 2 Thessalonians 2:1-12 in support of their doctrine.[377]

> Now we beseech you, brethren, by the coming of our Lord Jesus Christ, and by our gathering together unto him, That ye be not soon shaken in mind, or be troubled, neither by spirit, nor by word, nor by letter as from us, as that the day of Christ is at hand. Let no man deceive you by any means: for that day shall not come, except there come a falling away first, and that man of sin be revealed, the son of perdition; Who opposeth and exalteth himself above all that is called God, or that is worshipped; so that he as God sitteth in the temple of God, shewing himself that he is God. Remember ye not, that, when I was yet with you, I told you these things? And now ye know what withholdeth that he might be revealed in his time. For the mystery of iniquity doth already work: only he who now letteth will let, until he be taken out of the way. And then shall that Wicked be revealed, whom the Lord shall consume with the spirit of his mouth, and shall destroy with the brightness of his coming: Even him, whose coming is after the working of Satan with all power and signs and lying wonders, And with all deceivableness of unrighteousness in them that perish; because they received not the love of the truth, that they might be saved. And for this cause God shall send them strong delusion, that they should believe a lie: That they all might be damned who believed not the truth, but had pleasure in unrighteousness. (2 Thessalonians 2:1-12)

If one looks at those passages it is clear that they refer to the resurrection of believers at the end of the world. Looking at verse one we see that the topic that is being addressed by the Apostle Paul is "the coming of our Lord Jesus Christ" and "our gathering together unto him." The apostle Paul was telling the Thessalonians that "that day" would not come until there is a falling away first. Notice that Paul refers to "that day," which indicates that the coming of our Lord and our gathering together unto him are to happen contemporaneously. The first thing that happens is the falling away. Then, the man of sin, the son of perdition is revealed. Verse four indicates that this man of sin will exalt himself above God. Clearly, this is a reference to the antichrist. So we know that the antichrist will be revealed before the coming of Jesus Christ and the resurrection of the Saints. The pretribulation rapturists reverse this sequence and hold that Jesus will return secretly and rapture the saints, and then after the rapture the antichrist will be revealed.

The pretribulation rapturists hold that the person in verse seven who lets (restrains) the antichrist is the Holy Spirit who resides in the body of believers. They teach that when the rapture takes place the Holy Spirit will be taken out of the world and the antichrist will then the revealed.[378] If you look at those passages in 2 Thessalonians 2 the apostle Paul was telling the Thessalonians that "that day" would not come until there is a falling away first. Then, the man of sin, the son of perdition is revealed. Verse four indicates that this man of sin will exalt himself above God. Clearly, this is a reference to the antichrist. So we know that the antichrist will be revealed before the coming of Jesus Christ and the resurrection of the Saints.

If, however, he that letteth is the Holy Spirit that means that verse 3 contradicts verses 6-8. If the Holy Spirit is he that letteth, preventing the antichrist from being revealed and his being taken out of the way is the resurrection (rapture) of the saints and it happens first "then" the antichrist is revealed, that is the reverse of the sequence in verse 3. Verse 3 states that the resurrection shall not come except there be a falling away first and the man of sin is revealed. In fact, he that letteth is the Roman Emperor, who was replaced by the pope as Pontiffex Maximus (Supreme Pontiff), the ruler of all religions. The pope is the antichrist.

Furthermore, the position that the Holy Spirit will be removed from the earth through the rapture of the saints contradicts the promise that Jesus made. Jesus stated in Matthew 28:20 that he would be with us always even unto the end of the world. Jesus is with us through the Holy Spirit. We know from 1 John's 5:7 that "there are three that bear record in heaven, the father, the Word, and the Holy Ghost: and these three are one." (1 John 5:7) So we see that Jesus and the Holy Spirit are one. If you remove the Holy Spirit from the world then Jesus is removed and he cannot then be with us unto the end of the world.

Jesus makes it even clearer in the Gospel of Matthew that the Holy Spirit will abide with us forever: "And I will pray the Father, and he shall give you another Comforter, that **he may abide with you for ever.**" (John 14:16) Who is the comforter that Jesus was referring to? In John 14:26 Jesus states that the comforter is the Holy Spirit. If the Holy Spirit is removed from the world through the rapture, and the rapture is followed by a seven year tribulation period, how could Jesus keep his promise that the Holy Spirit will be with us forever? The answer is simple; there will not be a pretribulation rapture, there will be a resurrection, and that resurrection will be at the end of the world when Christ returns. The pretribulation rapture is not supported by Scripture and in fact is contrary to Scripture.

One of the tenets of the pretribulation rapture teaching is that once the believers in Christ are raptured out of the world there will only be unbelievers left behind. The unbelievers will then go through the seven year period of tribulation during which the antichrist will make his appearance.[379] The problem with that sequence is that it is contrary to the sequence of events as explained by Jesus.

> Another parable put he forth unto them, saying, The kingdom of heaven is likened unto a man which sowed good seed in his field: But while men slept, his enemy came and sowed tares among the wheat, and went his way. But when the blade was sprung up, and brought forth fruit, then appeared the tares also. So the servants of the householder came and said unto him, Sir, didst not thou sow good seed in thy field? from whence then hath it tares? He said unto them, An enemy hath done this. The servants said unto him, Wilt thou then that we go and gather them up? But he said, Nay; lest while ye gather up the tares, ye root up also the wheat with them. **Let both grow together until the harvest: and**

> **in the time of harvest I will say to the reapers, Gather ye together first the tares, and bind them in bundles to burn them: but gather the wheat into my barn**. (Matthew 13:24-30) (emphasis added)

Jesus states in his parable in *Matthew* 13:24-30 that the kingdom of heaven is like a man who sows good seed this field but an enemy sows tares. The man allows the tares and the wheat to grow up together until the harvest. It is not until the harvest that the tares and the wheat are gathered. The wheat is not gathered some time before the tares. The tares are gathered "first" and burned, then the wheat is gathered into the barn. We see from the parable that the tares are gathered first and then the wheat, just the reverse of the pretribulation rapture teaching. One might say "that is just a parable, you can make that mean anything you wish." Jesus himself, however, explained later in *Matthew* the meaning of that parable.

> Then Jesus sent the multitude away, and went into the house: and his disciples came unto him, saying, Declare unto us the parable of the tares of the field. He answered and said unto them, He that soweth the good seed is the Son of man; The field is the world; the good seed are the children of the kingdom; but the tares are the children of the wicked one; The enemy that sowed them is the devil; the harvest is the end of the world; and the reapers are the angels. As therefore the tares are gathered and burned in the fire; so shall it be in the end of this world. The Son of man shall send forth his angels, and they shall gather out of his kingdom all things that offend, and them which do iniquity; And shall cast them into a furnace of fire: there shall be wailing and gnashing of teeth. Then shall the righteous shine forth as the sun in the kingdom of their Father. Who hath ears to hear, let him hear. (Matthew 13:36-43)

Notice that Jesus states that both the tares and the wheat are to be left alone to grow up together until the end of the world. He does not say that the wheat should be plucked out ahead of time and the tares will be left behind. He states that he will wait until the end of the world and then his angels will "first" gather out of the field the tares (the children of the wicked one) and they will be bound and cast into a furnace of fire where there shall be wailing and gnashing of teeth. It is after the gathering of the tares that the children of God are gathered together. They are gathered at the end of the world not during some rapture years earlier.

The pretribulation rapturists will cite Revelation 20:5-6 to support their argument that their will be a rapture and then some time later a second resurrection. Revelation 20:5-6 does mention a first resurrection, which suggests that there is a second resurrection. Indeed, there is a second resurrection, but that is not a physical resurrection as some have supposed, it is a spiritual resurrection. The pretribulation rapturists ignore Revelation 20:4, where John says: "And I saw thrones, and they sat upon them, and judgment was given unto them: **and I saw the souls** of them that were beheaded for the witness of Jesus, and for the word of God." Notice he saw the "souls" of the saved, he did not see their bodies. They had been spiritually resurrected (the first resurrection) but not yet bodily resurrected. Before one is born again, he is dead in trespasses and sins. The Holy Spirit quickens the believer and he is made alive, he is spiritually resurrected from the dead. The spiritual rebirth by the grace of God through faith in Jesus Christ is the first resurrection mentioned in Revelation 20:4-6.

> **And you hath he quickened, who were dead in trespasses and sins**. (Ephesians 2:1)

> Even when we were dead in sins, hath quickened us together with Christ, (by grace ye are saved;) **And hath raised us up together, and made us sit together in heavenly places in Christ Jesus**: (Ephesians 2:5-6)

> **If ye then be risen with Christ, seek those things which are above**, where Christ sitteth on the right hand of God. (Colossians 3:1)

The second resurrection is the resurrection of the bodies of the believers at the coming of the Lord Jesus Christ.

20 Dethroning Caesar

If the church is not that which "letteth" in 2 Thessalonians 2, who or what is it? He who letteth was the Caesar of Rome. Wylie explains that Paul did not name the Roman Caesar because of concern that expressly saying that Caesar's power and station would end before the antichrist could come to power would bring the displeasure of the Roman authorities down on the Christian church.

> The apostle begins at the lowest stage of the vast ascent. "And now ye know what withholdeth that he might be revealed in his time. For the mystery of iniquity doth already work: only He who now letteth will let, until he be taken out of the way; and them shall that wicked be revealed." (2 Thess. 2: 6-8) The time for the revelation or apocalypse of Antichrist –for Antichrist was to have his apocalypse even as Christ had his – was not yet come. The "mystery of iniquity" was already working – working in the region of principles and influences, and working in the region of seducing spirits; but meanwhile, there existed a great "let," or obstruction to his open revelation. Paul hints very plainly that the Thessalonian Christians knew what that obstruction was, and therefore he did not name it. He had visited them sometime before, and talked freely with them about the coming apostasy, and

had mentioned the "let" which must first be removed before the apostasy could be free to develop itself. That obstruction was the Roman Empire. When present, talking freely with them on the subject, Paul could say so in express terms; but it might be dangerous to name the Roman Empire in an epistle to be read openly, and go the round of the churches. That might draw down on the Christians the displeasure of the Roman authorities. The apostle knew the hindrance in Antichrist's path, having learned it, doubtless, by the study of Daniel, and the revelation of the spirit. It was known, moreover, to the early fathers, who all turned their eyes to Rome as the fated spot where the "lawless one" was first to show himself; but they spoke of him with bated breath, and in circumlocutionary phrase.

While the Roman Empire stood it was impossible that Antichrist should appear. Caesar was Pontifex Maximus; and while he held possession, there could not be two High Priests occupying the same capital, sharing the same throne, and sacrificing at the same altars. The first and lesser Pontifex Maximus must be removed before the second and greater could stand up. This was to happen in no long time. God would remove the "let," by bringing the Goths into Italy, overturning the empire, and making vacant the throne of Caesar. Then Antichrist would climb up to the empty seat. "God chased the Caesars from Rome," says De Maistre, "that he might give it to the Popes."

Let us mark next that it had been decreed of both Christ and Antichrist, that they should occupy thrones –no meaner seat than a royal one must either of them have. Christ was to sit on the throne of David, and Antichrist was to sit on the throne of Caesar. [380]

21 Sitting as God in the Temple of God

Isaiah's prophecy reveals the innermost evil thoughts of Satan. Satan desires to be like the most high God. He seeks to rule as God and be worshiped in the heavenly congregation. His doom, however, is sealed; he will serve an eternal sentence in hell.

> **For thou hast said in thine heart, I will ascend into heaven, I will exalt my throne above the stars of God: I will sit also upon the mount of the congregation, in the sides of the north: I will ascend above the heights of the clouds; I will be like the most High**. Yet thou shalt be brought down to hell, to the sides of the pit. (Isaiah 14:13-14)

Satan's plans were thwarted by God when God threw him out of heaven and to the earth. Satan now seeks to make war against God and his elect.

> And **there appeared another wonder in heaven; and behold a great red dragon**, having seven heads and ten horns, and seven crowns upon his heads. And his tail drew the third part of the stars of heaven, and did cast them to the earth: and the dragon stood before the woman which was ready to be delivered, for to devour her child as soon as it was born. And she brought forth

a man child, who was to rule all nations with a rod of iron: and her child was caught up unto God, and to his throne. And the woman fled into the wilderness, where she hath a place prepared of God, that they should feed her there a thousand two hundred and threescore days. **And there was war in heaven: Michael and his angels fought against the dragon; and the dragon fought and his angels, And prevailed not; neither was their place found any more in heaven. And the great dragon was cast out, that old serpent, called the Devil, and Satan, which deceiveth the whole world: he was cast out into the earth, and his angels were cast out with him.** And I heard a loud voice saying in heaven, Now is come salvation, and strength, and the kingdom of our God, and the power of his Christ: for the accuser of our brethren is cast down, which accused them before our God day and night. And they overcame him by the blood of the Lamb, and by the word of their testimony; and they loved not their lives unto the death. Therefore rejoice, ye heavens, and ye that dwell in them. **Woe to the inhabiters of the earth and of the sea! for the devil is come down unto you, having great wrath, because he knoweth that he hath but a short time. And when the dragon saw that he was cast unto the earth, he persecuted the woman which brought forth the man child.** And to the woman were given two wings of a great eagle, that she might fly into the wilderness, into her place, where she is nourished for a time, and times, and half a time, from the face of the serpent. And the serpent cast out of his mouth water as a flood after the woman, that he might cause her to be carried away of the flood. And the earth helped the woman, and the earth opened her mouth, and swallowed up the flood which the dragon cast out of his mouth. **And the dragon was wroth with the woman, and went to make war with the remnant of her seed, which keep the commandments of God, and have the testimony of Jesus Christ.** (Revelation 12:3-17)

When his rebellion against God in heaven failed he decided that he would try to set up his throne on earth from which he could fight his evil spiritual war against God and his elect.

The Vatican College of Cardinals is the Roman Catholic version of the Jewish Sanhedrin. The College of Cardinals, like the Sanhedrin, has traditionally had 71 members. However, that number has been expanded in modern times. The members of the College of Cardinals are called cardinals for a reason. Cardinal means "**chief**, principal, preeminent, or fundamental."[381] The Catholic Cardinals fill the office of the Jewish "**chief**" Priests who, along with the scribes and elders, were members of the Sanhedrin. The Sanhedrin selected the High Priest[382] who was the head of the Sanhedrin, just as the cardinals select a Pope who is the head of the College of Cardinals. The seventy-first member of the Sahehdrin is the High Priest.[383] The Catholic corollary to the High Priest is the pope, who as head has traditionally been the seventy-first member of the College of Cardinals.[384]

In addition to his other priestly responsibilities, the high priest's principal duty was to perform the service on the Day of Atonement. On the Day of Atonement he entered the holy of holies in the Jewish Temple to make expiation for the people by sprinkling blood of the animal sacrifice on the mercy seat.[385] Hebrews 9:7.

Recall that it was the Jewish High Priest who had Jesus arrested and condemned to death.

> But he held his peace, and answered nothing. Again the high priest asked him, and said unto him, Art thou the Christ, the Son of the Blessed? And Jesus said, I am: and ye shall see the Son of man sitting on the right hand of power, and coming in the clouds of heaven. **Then the high priest rent his clothes, and saith, What need we any further witnesses? Ye have heard the blasphemy: what think ye? And they all condemned him to be guilty of death.** And some began to spit on him, and to cover his face, and to buffet him, and to say unto him, Prophesy: and the servants did strike him with the palms of their hands. (Mark 14:61-65)

With the destruction of the temple on or about 70 A.D. there was no more need for an earthly high priest; no temple, no high priest. There has not been a temple high priest since the destruction of the temple. The temple was destroyed by God using the Roman army, because there was no need for the symbolic animal blood atonement, since Christ, who was the real lamb of God, is the actual atonement sacrificed once for all time. Hebrews 9:8-9. There is no more need for continual animal sacrifices and thus no need for an earthly High Priest.

> But Christ being come an high priest of good things to come, by a greater and more perfect tabernacle, not made with hands, that is to say, not of this building; Neither by the blood of goats and calves, but by his own blood he entered in once into the holy place, having obtained eternal redemption for us. (Hebrews 9:11-12)

Jesus is now our High Priest in the holy of holies in heaven. Hebrews 4:14.

> **For Christ is not entered into the holy places made with hands, which are the figures of the true; but into heaven itself, now to appear in the presence of God for us**: Nor yet that he should offer himself often, as the high priest entereth into the holy place every year with blood of others; For then must he often have suffered since the foundation of the world: but now once in the end of the world hath **he appeared to put away sin by the sacrifice of himself**. And as it is appointed unto men once to die, but after this the judgment: So **Christ was once offered to bear the sins of many**; and unto them that look for him shall he appear the second time without sin unto salvation. (Hebrews 9:24-28)

Just as Satan did when he deceived Eve he is now promising his followers that they can be as God. The Holy Bible warns of one who will sit in God's temple claiming the authority of God. That is just what the Pope is doing by calling himself the head of the Catholic church. Catholic church means universal church.[386] God, not the pope, is the head of the universal church.

> Now we beseech you, brethren, by the coming of our Lord Jesus Christ, and by our gathering together unto him, That ye be not soon shaken in mind, or be troubled, neither by spirit, nor by word, nor by letter as from us, as that the day of Christ is at hand. Let no man deceive you by any means: for that day shall not come, except there come a falling away first, and that **man of sin be revealed, the son of perdition; Who opposeth and exalteth himself above all that is called God, or that is worshipped; so that he as God sitteth in the temple of God, shewing himself that he is God.** (2 Thessalonians 2:1-4)

Arthur Pink taught that the pope of Rome could not be the antichrist. While I make no judgement about Pink's other writings, he is wrong regarding the identity of the antichrist. Pink based his opinion, in part, on his view that the antichrist is prophesied in 2 Thessalonians 2:4 to sit in the temple of God and claim to be God. Pink opined that because the pope has never sat in the temple in Jerusalem, he could not be the antichrist. Pink stated:

> In 2 Thess. 2:4 we learn that the Man of Sin shall sit "in the Temple of God", and St. Peter's at Rome cannot possibly be called that. The "Temple" in which the Antichrist shall sit will be the rebuilt temple of the Jews, and that will be located not in Italy but in Jerusalem.[387]

Pink has misinterpreted the meaning of "Temple of God" in 2 Thessalonians 2:4. In order to conceal the fact that the pope fulfills the prophecy in 2 Thessalonians 2:1-4 of the antichrist sitting in the Temple of God, the pope had his minions, the Jesuits (Cardinal Robert Bellarmine, Emanuel de Lacunza, and Francisco Ribera) promote the millennium temple fable so that the deceived will be looking for the antichrist in the distant future and not see the papal antichrist right beneath their noses. Those that accept this millennium temple myth, however, have rejected righteousness by faith in Jesus Christ and instead teach a rebuilding of the physical temple, where righteousness will be by the law.

This Zionist/Catholic millennium doctrine is a rejection of Christ, the Chief cornerstone of the spiritual temple of God. The rebuilding of the physical temple with physical stone is a rejection of the rock of salvation, Jesus Christ. "But Israel, which followed after the law of righteousness, hath not attained to the law of righteousness. Wherefore? Because **they sought it not by faith, but as it were by the works of the law. For they stumbled at that stumblingstone**; As it is written, Behold, I lay in Sion a stumblingstone and rock of offence: and whosoever believeth on him shall not be ashamed." (Romans 9:31-33) Jesus Christ is the stone that has been rejected by the builders of this false religion; to them he is a rock of offense upon whom they will stumble to their ultimate demise. "For if they which are of the law be heirs, faith is made void, and the promise made of none effect." (Romans 4:14) Jesus is the rock of salvation. Psalms 62:6; 89:26; 95:1. Christians are spiritual stones that are incorporated into Jesus Christ to make a holy temple of the Lord. "Ye also, as lively stones, are built up a spiritual house, an holy priesthood, to offer up spiritual sacrifices, acceptable to God by Jesus Christ." (1 Peter 2:5)

The pope is a usurper, who is against Christ and claims to take the place of Christ in his temple (the church). What is the temple of God in which the antichrist sits claiming to be God? It is not a reference to a physical temple in Jerusalem. Wylie explains:

> Let us mark first where Antichrist is said to sit. "He sitteth in the temple of god."This temple cannot be that of the Jews on Mount Moriah, for the apostle is speaking of anact which was to be done by One who was not to appear till after the fall of the Roman Empire; but long before the empire fell the temple of the Jews was laid in ashes. (In the "Acts" the Jewish temple is spoken of twenty five times. In all these passages the word used is *ieron* (hieron), never *vaos* (naos). The term here used by the apostle is *vaos*. Christian Church," as also Chrysostem, Augustine, and Thomas Aquinas.) The name *temple* is carried over to the Christian Church, and in places innumerable in the New Testament, it is used to denote, sometimes an

individual believer, and sometimes the whole body of professing Christians. Writing to the Corinthian Christians Paul says, "Know ye not that ye are the *temple of God.*"(1 Cor. iii. 16) And again collectively, "Jesus Christ the chief corner stone; in whom all the building, fitly framed together, groweth unto an *holy temple* in the *Lord.*" (Eph. ii. 20.) We conclude that the temple in which Antichrist is here seen to sit is the Christian Church. This interpretation preserves the unity of Paul's Prophecy. Antichrist or "man of sin" was to be the outcome and head of the apostacy; but the apostacy was to spring up in the Christian Church, for "the falling away" was to be, and only could be, a falling away from the Christian faith. Antichrist therefore could "sit," that is, establish himself and exercise jurisdiction, nowhere but in the professedly Christian Church. As a Vice-Christ it behooved all his visible characteristics and all his environments to be professedly Christian and ecclesiastical.

This effectually disposes of all those theories of Antichrist which would find him in some powerful atheistic confederacy, or in some masterful, political chief, or other embodiment of monstrous iniquity and tyranny yet to arise, and which, during a brief but terrible career, should desolate the world. Such a power could in no sense be said to sit in the temple of God. It would be a power outside the temple; and so far from aspiring to office and dignity in the "temple" -that is, in the church -such a power must needs, from its instincts and character, make war on the church, under the banner of open hostility, and with the cry of: Raze it, raze it."[388]

Indeed, the scriptures testify that each saved Christian individually and all saved Christians corporately make up the temple of God.

> Know ye not that **ye are the temple of God**, and that the Spirit of God dwelleth in you? If any man defile

the temple of God, him shall God destroy; for **the temple of God is holy, which temple ye are**. (1 Corinthians 3:16-17)

What? know ye not that **your body is the temple of the Holy Ghost** which is in you, which ye have of God, and ye are not your own? For ye are bought with a price: therefore glorify God in your body, and in your spirit, which are God's. (1 Corinthians 6:19-20)

In whom all the **building fitly framed together groweth unto an holy temple in the Lord**: (Ephesians 2:21)

Wylie describes how the pope claims the authority of God Almighty as he reigns from his perch in the Vatican.

Sitting in the Temple of God, that is, speaking *ex cathedra* as Vice-Christ, the Pope has, in the most unequivocal manner, claimed to be God. To this daring pitch of ambition and blasphemy has he carried the parallelism or imitation. The true Christ is God, therefore the Vice-Christ must claim to be God also. In the canon law the pope is called God. (Decretum Gregorii XIII. Destinc 96, Can 7.) Again he is called "Lord and God" (Decretales Gregorii IX., Tit. 7.) And again Innocent says in the decretals, speaking of the Pope, "God because he is God's vicar." The cannon law and the decretals are called by Romanist writers the pope's oracle, they are a true expression of the pontifical mind. To the same effect the papal casuists say, "As Christ was God, he too was to be looked on as God." The Sacrum Ceremoniale has the phrase, "The apostolic Chair is the seat of God." "The Roman Pontiff" says the Decretum of Gregory, "not as mere man, but as true God, reigns in the earth." (Daubuz, 581.) Not to multiply instances in which the Pope calls himself God, or accepts the title from others, we close by referring to a recent illustration. Sir Culling E. Smith, in a tour in Italy, found a book published in

1794, with the title: -"History of the Ancient Republic of Amalfi, dedicated to the Vice-god Benedict XIII. With permission of superiors." (Decret. Greg. I. 7, 3.) So does the Pope bear testimony to himself. A greater than he said, "If I bear witness of Myself My witness is not true."

He has sought to support his claim to this great title by great deeds. Whatever God does the Pope professes to do also. Does God require that to him every knee shall bow? So, too, the Pope; he requires to be worshipped with prostration and kissing. Does god reveal Himself as the only holy?" So, too, the Pope. He claims to be styled "his holiness." Is God the "only wise?" So, too, is the Pope: he claims to be "inerrable." Did God plant His throne on the summit of Sinai, and thence promulgate those ten commandments which are the world's law? So, too, the Pope: he has planted [his] seat on the seven hills in the character of the world's supreme lawgiver and judge, and he claims an equal authority an infallibility for all that he is please to promulgate *ex cathedra* as Jehovah claims for the precepts of the decalogue. Is it God's prerogative to pardon sin? The Pope assumes the same great prerogative. He pardons the sins of the living and the dead. Is it god's prerogative to assign to men their eternal destiny? This, too, does the Pope. He pretends to hold the keys that open and shut purgatory, and while he reserves to his followers a sure passport to the realms of paradise, he consigns all outside his church to eternal woe. In fine, does God sit between the Cherubim and receive the homage of His people in His sanctuary? The Pope, seated on the high altar of St Peter's while incense is burned before him, and the knee is bent to him, is invoked as the Lord our God. Romanists are accustomed to call the altar the throne of God, inasmuch as thereon they place the host. The use the Pope finds for it on these occasions, is the not very dignified one of a footstool. "He as God sitteth in the temple of God showing himself that he is God."[389]

The Roman Catholic organization purports to be the universal church of God with the pope as the head of that church. But how can that Romish organization be God's church when it is chock full of idols?

> **And what agreement hath the temple of God with idols?** for ye are the temple of the living God; as God hath said, I will dwell in them, and walk in them; and I will be their God, and they shall be my people. (2 Corinthians 6:16)

> For if any man see thee which hast knowledge sit at meat in the **idol's temple**, shall not the conscience of him which is weak be emboldened to eat those things which are offered to idols; (1 Corinthians 8:10)

The leader of the Roman Catholic organization, the pope, has claimed that not only is he the leader of the Roman Catholics but also claims that he is the head of the true church of God including Protestant Christians whom he refers to as "separated brethren." He boldly claims that entrance into Heaven is dependant on submission to his authority.

> **We declare, state and define that it is absolutely necessary for the salvation of all human beings that they submit to the Roman Pontiff.** *Bull Unum Sanctum,* Pope Boniface VIII, 1302.

Such a doctrine reveals the Pope as the antichrist. He is implying by that statement that he holds the position and authority of God Almighty. Further on you will read where the Pope expressly claims the authority of God. Jesus, however, made it clear that he, being God, was the only way to heaven.

> Jesus saith unto him, **I am the way, the truth, and the life: no man cometh unto the Father, but by me.** (John 14:6)

> This is the stone which was set at nought of you builders, which is become the head of the corner. **Neither is there salvation in any other: for there is**

> **none other name under heaven given among men, whereby we must be saved.** (Acts 4:11-12)

The pope claims power over the governments of the earth. During the coronation ceremony the Pope is crowned with these words: "Take thou the tiara adorned with the triple crown, and know that thou art the father of princes and kings and the governor of the world"[390]

The pope does not limit his power to political matters. He also claims plenary power over spiritual matters. The pope claims to sit in place of Almighty God, with equal authority and infallibility of the Lord Jesus Christ.[391] Pope Boniface VIII stated that all must submit to the authority of the pope or be damned to hell.

> The Roman Pontiff judges all man, but is judged by no one. We declare, assert, define and pronounce: to be subject to the Roman Pontiff is to every human creature altogether necessary for salvation.[392] *Bull Unum Sanctum*, November 18, 1302.

Pope Nicholas I, who reigned as pope from 858 to 867 A.D., stated:

> I am all in all and above all, so that God Himself, and I, the Vicar of God, hath both one consistory, and I am able to do almost all that God can do . . . Wherefore, if those things that I do be said not to be done of man, but of God. **What can you make me but God?** Again, if prelates of the Church be called and counted of Constantine for gods, I then, being above all prelates, seem by this reason to be above all gods. **Wherefore, no marvel if it be in my power to dispense with all things, yea, with the precepts of Christ.**[393] (emphasis added)

Pope Nicholas claimed the power over God even to dispense with the precepts of Christ. To claim the power to dispense with the precepts of God is fulfilment of the prophesy in 2 Thessalonians 2:4 that the antichrist not only sits in the temple of God, claiming to be God, but he also **"opposeth and exalteth himself above all that is called God,**

or that is worshipped." 2 Thessalonians 2:4.

Lest there be any doubt, Pope Innocent III confirms the blasphemy of Nicholas and the prophecy of 2 Thessalonians 2:4 by stating: "We may according to the fullness of our power, dispose of the law and dispense above the law. Those whom the Pope of Rome doth separate, it is not a man that separates them but God. For the Pope holdeth place on earth, not simply of a man but of the true God."[394]

Indeed, the pope has such exalted power, that even his subordinate priests have authority over God. Roman Catholic Priest David S. Phelan explained the power of all Catholic priests over Lord God Jesus Christ during the blasphemous Catholic Mass. Phelan stated that he had the power and authority to command Jesus to come down from heaven during the Mass. Phelan said that "He has to come when I bid him. ... He must come down every time I say Mass at my bidding. ... and when I do it, Christ must obey."[395] Who can deny that such a "lying wonder" is "after the working of Satan," in fulfilment of the prophecy of the antichrist in 2 Thessalonians 2:9.

Within the very *Bull Unum Sanctum,* Pope Boniface VIII states unequivocally that he holds the station of God on earth: "Therefore, of the one and only Church there is one body and one head, not two heads like a monster; that is, Christ and the Vicar of Christ, Peter and the successor of Peter."[396] The pope is clearly expressing his station as that of the head of the church, which we know can only be headed by Lord God Almighty Jesus Christ. Indeed the bible makes clear that all things are under the authority of Jesus Christ, who rules from heaven at the right hand of God the Father.

> Which he wrought in Christ, when he raised him from the dead, and set him at his own right hand in the heavenly places, Far above all principality, and power, and might, and dominion, and every name that is named, not only in this world, but also in that which is to come: And hath put all things under his feet, and gave him to be the head over all things to the church, Which is his body, the fulness of him that filleth all in all. (Ephesians 1:20-23)

The pope has usurped the Lord God Jesus Christ and claims to be the head of the church, indeed, the head of all authority as "God Almighty" on earth. Pope Pius V proclaimed that "[t]he Pope and God are the same, so he has all power in Heaven and earth."[397] Pope Leo XIII, in his purportedly infallible 1894 encyclical, *Praeclara Gratulationis Publicae*, stated unequivocally: "**[W]e hold upon this earth the place of God Almighty.**"[398] (emphasis added). Please note that more than 1,000 years span between Pope Innocent I's statement: **"What can you make me but God?"**[399] and *Praeclara Gratulationis Publicae* of Pope Leo XIII. Clearly, the papacy holding the seat and authority of God Almighty on earth is the established official doctrine of the Roman Catholic Church.

In 1512 Christopher Marcellus said this to Pope Julius II during the Fifth Lateran Council: "Take care that we lose not that salvation, that life and breath which thou hast given us, for thou art our shepherd, thou art our physician, thou art our governor, thou art our husbandman, **thou art finally another God on earth.**"[400] (emphasis added)

The *Gloss of Extravagantes* of Pope John XXII contains the following words describing the pope: *Dominum Deum Nostrum Papam*, which translated into English mean **"our Lord God the Pope.**"[401] (emphasis added)

The view of the Roman Catholic Church remains that the pope is considered God on earth. Indeed, as recently as 1996, Pope John Paul II referring to the obedience of the so-called saints of the Catholic Church to the pope stated:

> Against this background of love towards Holy Church, "the pillar and bulwark of the truth" (1 Tim 3:15), we readily understand the devotion of Saint Francis of Assisi for **"the Lord Pope,"** the daughterly outspokenness of Saint Catherine of Siena towards the one whom she called **"sweet Christ on earth."**[402] (emphasis added)

There can be no doubt that the official teachings of the papacy is that the pope has "primacy over the whole world."

> [T]he Roman pontiff possess **primacy over the whole world**; and that the Roman pontiff is the successor of Blessed Peter, Prince of the Apostles, and is true **Vicar** of Christ, and Head of the whole Church, and **Father** and Teacher of all Christians; and that full power was given to him in Blessed Peter by Jesus Christ our Lord, to **rule**, feed and govern the universal Church. . . . **This is the teaching of Catholic truth, from which no one can deviate without loss of faith and of salvation**. And since, by the define right of Apostolic primacy, one Roman pontiff is placed over the universal Church, We further teach and declare that he is the **supreme judge** of the faithful . . . none may reopen the judgment of the Apostolic See, than whose authority there is no greater. *The Vatican Council*, Session IV, chapter III, July 18, 1870 (emphasis added).

The official Vatican doctrine is that the pope has authority over all kings and governments in the world.

> **[R]oyal power derives from the Pontifical authority**.[403] *Pope Innocent III.*

> **[T]emporal power should be subject to the spiritual**.[404] *Pope Boniface VII.*

The pope claims primacy over the whole world, but when the disciples asked Jesus who is the greatest in the Kingdom of heaven, Jesus did not say "Peter." He said whoever humbles himself as a little child shall be the greatest. *See* Matthew 18:1-4. Christ is the head of the church, not Peter or his alleged successor, the pope. *See* Ephesians 5:23.

22 Blessing Bloody Murder

The emperor of Rome was considered the Supreme Pontiff (*Pontifex Maximus*), [405] which was the high priest of the pagan religions of Rome.[406] He was also worshiped as a god.[407] The pope of Rome is the successor to the Roman emperors. The pope carries the same title as the Roman emperors, Supreme Pontiff. The pope also purports to hold the office of God on Earth. He claims that one must submit to him in order to gain entrance into heaven. All who dare to challenge his authority are cursed by him and persecuted. The Catholic church persecuted Christians throughout the inquisition because they refused to submit to the pope.

Although the persecution of Christians had been taking place unabated since the first century, in 1179 Pope Alexander III and the Lateran Council urged the use of force and established incentives for violence against Christians such as two years' remission of penance for those who murdered a "heretic." In 1231 Pope Gregory IX formally established the papal inquisitional tribunal (*inquisitio haereticae pravitatis*). In 1252, Pope Innocent IV expressly authorized the use of torture, which by then had already been the established practice of the Catholic Church for centuries.[408] The enemies of the Roman Catholic Church were called "heretics." These so called "heretics" were often tortured, mutilated, and burned at the stake.[409] Their goods were confiscated, condemning their descendants to a life of penury.[410] Thomas Aquinas (1226-1274), a Catholic saint wrote: "It is more wicked to corrupt the faith on which depends the life of the soul than to debase the coinage which provides merely for temporal life; wherefore if coiners and other malefactors are justly doomed to death, much more may heretics be justly slain once they are convicted."[411]

During the inquisition tens of millions of people were killed as enemies of the Catholic Church. In one day alone (August 24, 1572) between 50,000[412] and 100,000[413] Huguenots (French Protestants) were massacred in Paris during the St. Bartholomew Day Massacre. Pope Gregory XIII received the news with great rejoicing and, in grand procession, went to the Church of St. Louis to give thanks. He ordered the papal mint to strike medals in commemoration of the massacre. The obverse side of the medal depicts Pope Gregory XIII and on the reverse side is an avenging angel with a cross in one hand and a sword in the other, before whom a band of Huguenots, with horror on their faces, are fleeing. The inscription *UGONOTTORUM - STRAGES - 1572*, which is a Latin metonym that means the "The Slaughter of the Huguenots - 1572." appeared on the coin.[414]

Joseph Jenkins, who is a Catholic priest and the pastor of Holy Family Church, Mitchellville, Maryland, in the Catholic Archdiocese of Washington, D.C., disputes that there was celebration by the pope of the St. Bartholomew Day slaughter of the Huguenots. Jenkins claims that "all the ado is made by a lie" and instead that "when the full bloody details became available, the Pope wept and prayed for the poor people murdered."[415]

Jenkins claims that it is a lie that medals were struck by the pope in commemoration of the slaughter. Perhaps the production of the medal in question will resolve the matter. The picture below is of the very medal struck by Pope Gregory XIII in celebration of the slaughter of the Huguenots.

The Christian's Monthly Magazine reported that the papacy continued to glory in the St. Bartholomew Day massacre of the Huguenots for hundreds of years thereafter. In fact, as late as 1844, that very medal could still be purchased from the Vatican mint.[416] As proof of that fact, the author of the article in *The Christian's Monthly Magazine* purchased a St. Bartholomew Day Massacre medal when he was at the Vatican.

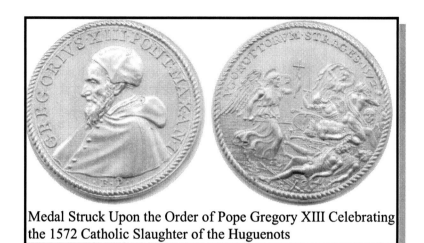

Medal Struck Upon the Order of Pope Gregory XIII Celebrating the 1572 Catholic Slaughter of the Huguenots

Indeed, Pope Gregory was so pleased with his handy-work that he commissioned a special mural by painter Giorgio Vasari to celebrate the slaughter of the Huguenots.[417] Jenkins has this to say about the mural:

> As for whether or not there is a picture in the Vatican detailing the event, I cannot say. However, given the inaccuracy of so many other details by the anti-Catholic critic, I would seriously doubt it. If there is one, it could just as well be there as a piece of art that reminds us all of man's inhumanity to man. The vicars who represent the Prince of Peace, do not relish such violence against the Gospel of Life.[418]

Jenkins is claiming ignorance of the existence of the mural. He claims that if such a mural exists, it would not be to relish the spectacle of the massacre but only for the purpose of the Vatican artfully reminding us of the man's inhumanity to man. Jenkins would have a point if the mural was painted by the families of the Huguenot victims. However, it was commissioned by the principal authority who ordered the massacre. Jenkins' claim is like the claim of a murderer who is caught with a photo in his possession which he took of the bloody and dead murder victim arguing that he took the picture not to relish the murder but only to remind others of man's inhumanity to man, because he is a peaceful man who does not relish such violence.

Vatican Mural Celebrating the Catholic Slaughter of French Protestants in 1572

The Vatican mural certainly exists, and Jenkins, being a Catholic priest, knows or should know that. Riley Fraas, pastor of Hope Congregational Church in Bethune, Colorado, has personally seen the mural, which is to this day still proudly displayed at the Vatican. The mural is depicted on this page. It is still proudly displayed in the Vatican, for the very reason that the pope in fact continues to relish "such violence against the Gospel of Life." The continuing proud display in the Vatican of the mural depicting the massacre of Christians by Catholics is certain evidence that the bloodthirsty hatred of the papacy toward Christ and his followers has not abated.

Jenkins may deny the culpability of the papacy in the St. Bartholomew Day massacre of the Huguenots, but the pope does not. While in Paris to celebrate the 12th World Youth Day on August 23rd, 1997, the eve of the anniversary of the St. Bartholomew Day massacre, Pope John Paul II made a brief apology for the acts of French Catholics 425 years ago, by admitting that "Christians did things which the Gospel condemns."[419] Note that the apology pinned the blame on the French Catholics, as though they were rogue elements outside the control of the Vatican. In fact, they were the very agents of the Vatican carrying out its wishes. Indeed, the pope would never apologize for the acts of the papacy, because the pope is considered infallible and his doctrinal edicts are considered without error.

Of course, the pope's apology is a ruse designed to curry favor and deceive the masses into believing that the papacy has changed. The devil is a liar and his antichrist is a liar; the sincerity of the pope's apology cannot be believed. The continued unrepentant display in the Vatican by the papacy of the mural depicting the slaughter of the Huguenots is proof that the apology is insincere.

Just as the Jewish religious leaders did with Jesus, the Roman church ordinarily turned Christians over to the secular authorities to carry out the death penalty. In 1542 Pope Paul III established an inquisitional office in the Vatican called the "Holy Roman and Universal Inquisition," in order to fight the spread of Protestantism.[420] In 1908 Pope Pius X dropped the word "inquisition" from the title of the office and it came to be known as simply the "Holy Office."[421] On December 7, 1965 that office was renamed the "Congregation for the Doctrine of the Faith."[422] The title sounds innocuous enough, but there is a long and bloody history attached to that office; in fact, the public burnings of "heretics" were called *autos-da-fe* or "acts of faith."[423] The Congregation for the Doctrine of the Faith still exists in the Catholic church today, holding meetings once a week with the Pope periodically presiding.[424] The office still occupies the Palace of the Inquisition, which is adjacent to the Vatican.[425] One recent Grand Inquisitor was the former archbishop of Munich, Joseph Cardinal Ratzinger.[426] Because of the importance of his position as the chief enforcer of dogma, Ratzinger was viewed at the time by many as the most powerful cardinal in the Catholic Church.[427] Ratzinger was later elected Pope Bendedict XVI.

Lord Acton, an esteemed nineteenth century Roman Catholic historian, is the source for the famous quote about kings and popes: "power tends to corrupt and absolute power corrupts absolutely." He had this further to say: "The papacy contrived murder and massacre on the largest and also on the most cruel and inhuman scale. They [the popes] were not only wholesale assassins but they made the principal of assassination a law of the Christian Church and a condition of salvation.

[The papacy is] the fiend skulking behind the Crucifix."[428]

Some might think that Vatican Council II has changed the direction of the Catholic church, that it is no longer the bloodthirsty harlot of abominations that it once was. Vatican II is in reality a deadly deception. In Vatican II, Protestant Christians who were formerly referred to as "heretics" have now been labeled "separated brethren." The devilish deception becomes apparent when it is realized that Vatican II did not repeal a single papal bull or anathema issued against Christians by past Popes or Vatican councils. In fact, Vatican II reaffirmed the canons and decrees of previous councils, including the Second Council of Nicea, the Council of Florence, and the Council of Trent.[429] The Council of Trent alone accounted for over 100 curses against Christians and Christian beliefs. Christians are still under the countless curses of the Roman Catholic Church, and the "Holy Office" that carried out the many previous inquisitions is still in operation. Just as a leopard cannot change his spots neither can the Vatican change its evil ways. "Can the Ethiopian change his skin, or the leopard his spots? then may ye also do good, that are accustomed to do evil." Jeremiah 13:23. The Catholic Church never changes. The official doctrine of the Catholic Church remains that there is no salvation outside the Roman Catholic Church. In the eyes of the Roman Church Protestant Christians are hell bound, yet they call us "separated brethren." The following quote is from § 846 of the 1994 Catechism of the Catholic Church.

> Basing itself on Scripture and tradition, the Council teaches that the Church, a Pilgrim now on earth, is necessary for salvation: the one Christ is the mediator and the way of salvation; he is present to us in his body which is the Church. He himself explicitly asserted the necessity of faith and Baptism, and thereby affirmed at the same time the necessity of the Church which men enter through Baptism as through a door. **Hence they could not be saved who, knowing that the Catholic Church was founded as necessary by God through Christ, would refuse either to enter it or to remain in it.**[430]

The recent official Vatican statement, *Dominus Iesus*, which was written by the Vatican's chief expert on doctrine, Cardinal Josef Ratzinger (now Pope Benedict XVI), makes it clear that the Catholic Church was being disingenuous when it stated in Vatican Council II that the Vatican considered Protestant Christians "separated brethren." In *Dominus Iesus*, the Catholic Church states that "ecclesial communities" that do not recognize the Eucharist mystery, (that is that Almighty God is fully present in the form of bread and wine) are not truly churches at all.

> Therefore, there exists a single Church of Christ, which subsists in the Catholic Church, governed by the Successor of Peter and by the Bishops in communion with him. The Churches which, while not existing in perfect communion with the Catholic Church, remain united to her by means of the closest bonds, that is, by apostolic succession and a valid Eucharist, are true particular Churches. . . . On the other hand, the **ecclesial communities which have not preserved the valid Episcopate and the genuine and integral substance of the Eucharistic mystery, are not Churches in the proper sense.** DECLARATION "DOMINUS IESUS" ON THE UNICITY AND SALVIFIC UNIVERSALITY OF JESUS CHRIST AND THE CHURCH, *Rome, from the Offices of the Congregation for the Doctrine of the Faith, August 6, 2000* (emphasis added).

Those who will argue that *Dominus Iesus* is just an assertion from one cardinal in Rome, should read the statement of ratification. The purportedly infallible pope with sure knowledge of his alleged apostolic authority confirmed the declaration. "The Sovereign Pontiff John Paul II, at the Audience of June 16, 2000, granted to the undersigned Cardinal Prefect of the Congregation for the Doctrine of the Faith, with sure knowledge and by his apostolic authority, ratified and confirmed this Declaration, adopted in Plenary Session and ordered its publication."

23 Denying that Jesus is the Christ

Another antichrist doctrine is the teaching summarized in the 1994 Catechism of the Catholic Church, §§ 881-882, which contains the official doctrine of the Catholic Church that Peter is the rock upon which God has built his church, and that the Pope as the bishop of Rome is Peter's successor as the vicar of Christ.[431] Wylie explains the distinction between the true church of Christ and the false church of antichrist.

> That "Christ is the Son of God," is the corner-stone of the Gospel church. Out of that root the whole Gospel springs. It is the "rock" on which Christ, addressing Peter, said that He would build His Church. That the "Pope is the Vicar of Christ" is the corner-stone of the papal Church. Out of that root does the whole of popery spring. On that "rock" said Boniface III. in the seventh century, and Gregory VII., with yet greater emphasis in the eleventh, will I build my church.
>
> And let us further mark that both churches rest not on a *doctrine*, but on a *person*. The Church of God rests on a Person, even Christ. No one is saved by simply believing a system of truth. The truth is the light that shows the sinner his way to the Saviour. He is united to Christ by his faith which takes hold of the Saviour, and by the Spirit who comes to dwell in his heart. Thus is

he a member of the Spiritual Body. The Bible, ministers, and ordinances are the channels through which the life of the Head flows into the members of the body. Thus are they built up a spiritual house, a holy temple -"built on the foundation of prophets, and apostles, Jesus Christ Himself the chief cornerstone."[432]

There is only one head of the church. To claim to be the rock of the church is to implicitly deny that Jesus is the rock of the church. To deny that Jesus is the rock is to deny that Jesus is Christ. Denying that Jesus is the Christ is a doctrine specifically identified in 1 John 2:22-23 as a teaching of the antichrist.

Who is a liar but he that denieth that Jesus is the Christ? He is antichrist, that denieth the Father and the Son. Whosoever denieth the Son, the same hath not the Father: (but) he that acknowledgeth the Son hath the Father also. (1 John 2:22-23)

The headship of the church is reserved to Christ alone. "[H]e is the head of the body, the church: who is the beginning, the firstborn from the dead; that in all things he might have the preeminence." (Colossians 1:18) Christ will not share his glory nor his authority nor his station with anyone, Christ has preeminence in all things. "For thou shalt worship no other god: for the LORD, whose name is Jealous, is a jealous God." (Exodus 34:14) The Old Testament prophecies of the coming Christ indicate that the cornerstone of the church is to be a heavenly stone that is cut out without hands, and the church will grow from this stone to become a large spiritual mountain and fill the earth. *See* Daniel 2:34-45. This prophesied rock is Christ. For a man to claim to be the rock of the church is to claim to be Christ, because the Bible makes clear that Christ is the rock, the head of the church. To falsely claim to be Christ, the head of the church, fulfills the prophecies that identify the antichrist.

Let no man deceive you by any means: for that day shall not come, except there come a falling away first, and that man of sin be revealed, the son of perdition; **Who opposeth and exalteth himself above all that is**

> called God, or that is worshipped; so that he as God sitteth in the temple of God, shewing himself that he is God. (2 Thessalonians 2:3-4)

> And the king shall do according to his will; and **he shall exalt himself, and magnify himself above every god, and shall speak marvellous things against the God of gods**, and shall prosper till the indignation be accomplished: for that that is determined shall be done. Neither shall he regard the God of his fathers, nor the desire of women, nor regard any god: for **he shall magnify himself above all.** (Daniel 11:36-37)

In Matthew 16:16 Peter said that Jesus is the Christ, the Son of the living God. Jesus said that upon that rock he would build his church. That passage, which is often cited by the Catholic Church to support their claim that the pope rules God's church, is not supportive of Peter as the rock but rather as Christ being the rock. Jesus asks his disciples "whom say ye that I am?" When Peter answered that he is "the Christ, the Son of the living God." That answer reveals the rock upon which God would build his church, Jesus Christ, and not Peter. That is what Jesus was conveying when he said "upon **this** rock I will build my church."

By the pope saying that Peter is the rock, he is denying Jesus is the rock, the Christ, the Son of the living God. That papal denial of Christ is a fulfillment of the prophecy found in 1 John 2:22-23, which identifies the antichrist as one who will deny that Jesus is the Christ. The pope's claim, essentially, is that Peter is the rock and hence the Christ and that he, as Peter's purported successor, is also Christ. The Bible reveals that the pope is the antichrist!

> When Jesus came into the coasts of Caesarea Philippi, he asked his disciples, saying, **Whom do men say that I the Son of man am?** And they said, Some say that thou art John the Baptist: some, Elias; and others, Jeremias, or one of the prophets. He saith unto them, But **whom say ye that I am?** And Simon Peter answered and said, **Thou art the Christ, the Son of the living God.** And Jesus answered and said unto

> him, Blessed art thou, Simon Barjona: for flesh and blood hath not revealed it unto thee, but my Father which is in heaven. And I say also unto thee, That thou art Peter, and **upon <u>this</u> rock I will build my church**; and the gates of hell shall not prevail against it. (Matthew 16:13-18)

Christ is the head of the church, not Peter! *See* Ephesians 5:23; Colossians 1:18. If Peter is now the rock of God's church, why would Jesus call Peter Satan within moments of making Peter the foundation of the church? The following passage signifies that those who would have Peter as their rock, have someone who savourest the things of man and not of God.

> But he turned, and said unto Peter, **Get thee behind me, Satan**: thou art an offence unto me: for thou savourest not the things that be of God, but those that be of men. (Matthew 16:23)

The Holy Spirit further signified that the pope is antichrist by having Peter, as the Catholic Church's first purported pope, start his alleged reign by denying Christ 3 times in fulfillment of the prophecy in 1 John 2:22-23. *See* Matthew 26:31-75.

The rock of the Catholic Church is not God. Their rock is only a man trying to take God's place.

> **For their rock is not as our Rock**, even our enemies themselves being judges. For their vine is of the vine of Sodom, and of the fields of Gomorrah: their grapes are grapes of gall, their clusters are bitter: **Their wine is the poison of dragons, and the cruel venom of asps**. (Deuteronomy 32:31-33)

Peter, to whom Jesus was talking, clearly understood what Jesus was saying when he said "upon this rock I will build my church." The rock was Jesus. In the following passages Peter repeatedly refers to Jesus as the stone rejected by the builders becoming the head of the corner. Jesus is the only name under heaven that can save one from the eternal punishment of sin, not Peter and not the pope.

Be it known unto you all, and to all the people of Israel, that by the name of **Jesus Christ of Nazareth**, whom ye crucified, whom God raised from the dead, even by him doth this man stand here before you whole. **This is the stone which was set at nought of you builders, which is become the head of the corner. Neither is there salvation in any other: for there is none other name under heaven given among men, whereby we must be saved.** (Acts 4:10-12)

Wherefore also it is contained in the scripture, **Behold, I lay in Sion a chief corner stone**, elect, precious: and he that believeth on him shall not be confounded. Unto you therefore which believe he is precious: but unto them which be disobedient, the stone which the builders disallowed, the same is made the head of the corner, And **a stone of stumbling, and a rock of offence, even to them which stumble at the word, being disobedient: whereunto also they were appointed.** (1 Peter 2:6-8)

Read through the following passages, and decide for yourself who is the Rock of the Church.

And did all drink the same spiritual drink: for they drank of that spiritual Rock that followed them: and **that Rock was Christ.** (1 Corinthians 10:4)

And are built upon the foundation of the apostles and prophets, **Jesus Christ himself being the chief corner stone.** (Ephesians 2:20)

For other foundation can no man lay than that is laid, which is Jesus Christ. (1 Corinthians 3:11)

My soul, wait thou only upon God; for my expectation is from him. **He only is my rock and my salvation:** he is my defence; I shall not be moved. (Psalms 62:5-6)

He is the Rock, his work is perfect: for all his ways are judgment: a God of truth and without iniquity, just and right is he. (Deuteronomy 32:4)

There is none holy as the LORD: for there is none beside thee: **neither is there any rock like our God**. (1 Samuel 2:2)

And he said, **The LORD is my rock**, and my fortress, and my deliverer; The God of my rock; in him will I trust: he is my shield, and the horn of my salvation, my high tower, and my refuge, my saviour; thou savest me from violence. (2 Samuel 22:2-3)

The LORD is my rock, and my fortress, and my deliverer; my God, my strength, in whom I will trust; my buckler, and the horn of my salvation, and my high tower. (Psalms 18:2)

For who is God save the LORD? or **who is a rock save our God**? (Psalms 18:31)

Unto thee will I cry, **O LORD my rock**; be not silent to me: lest, if thou be silent to me, I become like them that go down into the pit. (Psalms 28:1)

Bow down thine ear to me; deliver me speedily: **be thou my strong rock**, for an house of defence to save me. For **thou art my rock** and my fortress; therefore for thy name's sake lead me, and guide me. (Psalms 31:2-3)

I will say unto **God my rock**, Why hast thou forgotten me? why go I mourning because of the oppression of the enemy? (Psalms 42:9)

From the end of the earth will I cry unto thee, when my heart is overwhelmed: **lead me to the rock that is higher than I**. (Psalms 61:2)

And they remembered that **God was their rock**, and the high God their redeemer. (Psalms 78:35)

He shall cry unto me, **Thou art my father, my God, and the rock of my salvation**. (Psalms 89:26)

But the LORD is my defence; and **my God is the rock of my refuge**. (Psalms 94:22)

O come, let us sing unto the LORD: let us make a joyful noise to **the rock of our salvation**. (Psalms 95:1)

As it is written, Behold, **I lay in Sion a stumblingstone and rock of offence**: and whosoever believeth on him shall not be ashamed. (Romans 9:33)

He is like a man which built an house, and digged deep, and **laid the foundation on a rock**: and when the flood arose, the stream beat vehemently upon that house, and could not shake it: for it was founded upon a rock. (Luke 6:48)

Therefore whosoever heareth these sayings of mine, and doeth them, I will liken him unto a wise man, which **built his house upon a rock**. (Matthew 7:24)

The stone which the builders refused is become the head stone of the corner. (Psalms 118:22)

And he shall be for a sanctuary; but for **a stone of stumbling and for a rock of offence** to both the houses of Israel, for a gin and for a snare to the inhabitants of Jerusalem. (Isaiah 8:14)

Therefore thus saith the Lord GOD, Behold, **I lay in Zion for a foundation a stone, a tried stone, a precious corner stone, a sure foundation**: he that believeth shall not make haste. (Isaiah 28:16)

> Jesus saith unto them, Did ye never read in the scriptures, **The stone which the builders rejected, the same is become the head of the corner**: this is the Lord's doing, and it is marvellous in our eyes? Therefore say I unto you, The kingdom of God shall be taken from you, and given to a nation bringing forth the fruits thereof. And whosoever shall fall on this stone shall be broken: but on whomsoever it shall fall, it will grind him to powder. (Matthew 21:42-44)

The evidence from the Holy Scripture is so clear that even Pope John Paul II has found it necessary to admit that Jesus is the Rock upon which God's Church is built.[433] That is just another of the many contradictory pronouncements of the Roman Catholic Church.

By claiming that Peter is the rock, the pope has denied that Jesus is the rock, which is essentially a denial that Jesus is the Christ. The pope has fulfilled the prophesy in 1 John 2:22-23, which states that the antichrist will deny that Jesus is the Christ. Who then does the pope claim is the Christ? The answer is found when we compare what the Holy Bible says about Christ with what the pope has said. What does it mean when we say that Jesus is Christ? It means that he is the one anointed "God with us." In Matthew 1:23, Jesus is identified as "Emmanuel, which being interpreted is, God with us." The pope, however, claims that he is God with us. **"[W]e hold upon this earth the place of God Almighty."** *Pope Leo XIII* (emphasis added).[434]

Jesus Christ is "an advocate with the Father" for us. 1 John 2:1. In fact he is the "one mediator between God and men." 1 Timothy 2:5. The pope, however, claims the title of Supreme Pontiff. Pontiff means literally bridge builder; it connotes that the pontiff is one who is a bridge or intermediary between God and man. The pope has stated: "To be subject to the Roman Pontiff is to every human creature altogether necessary for salvation." *The Bull Unum Sanctum*, November 18, 1302. In addition, the Catholic Church teaches that Mary and the saints are advocates before the throne of God for us. "[The saints'] . . . intercession is their most exalted service to God's plan. **We can and should ask them to intercede for us and for the whole world.** *CATECHISM OF THE CATHOLIC CHURCH*, § 2683, 1994."

The pope advises people not to bother going to God for forgiveness of their sins. Pope John Paul II stated: "Don't go to God for forgiveness of sins, come to me."[435] The pope seems to be mounting a blasphemous (and futile) *coup d'etat* against God. He advises his penitents to follow him instead of God.

The pope claims the title of Supreme Pontiff, which means supreme bridge-builder (supreme mediator) between man and God. The subordinate priests are lesser pontiffs and also act as mediators. That priestly authority to mediate between man and God is based upon the Catholic doctrine that the Catholic priests claim to act in the place of the Lord Jesus.

> [T]he priest is constituted an interpreter and **mediator between God and man**, which indeed must be regarded as the principal function of the priesthood. *CATECHISM OF THE COUNCIL OF TRENT.*[436]

God says otherwise. There is only one God and only one mediator between God and man, that is Jesus Christ.

> For there is **one God, and one mediator** between God and men, the man **Christ Jesus**; (1 Timothy 2:5)

Jesus Christ is the "author and finisher of our faith." Hebrew 12:2. "For by grace are ye saved through faith; and that not of yourselves: it is the gift of God: Not of works, lest any man should boast." (Ephesians 2:8-9) The pope, however, states that faith comes from man and it must be joined with works, i.e. started and finished by man, not Jesus. The Catholic Church even teaches that works done after death by others are effective for the salvation of the deceased.

> [T]he souls ... are cleansed after death by purgatorial punishments; and so that they may be relieved from punishments of this kind, namely, the sacrifices of Masses, prayers, and almsgiving, and other works of piety, which are customarily performed by the faithful for other faithful according to the institutions of the Church. COUNCIL OF FLORENCE, 1439.[437]

Jesus Christ is the "blessed and only Potentate." 1 Timothy 6:15. Pope Innocent II, however, claimed ownership of the entire universe as the "TEMPORAL SOVEREIGN OF THE UNIVERSE."[438]

Even today the Pope wears a triple crown because he claims to rule as king over Heaven, Hell, and Earth. Jesus Christ is the "great high priest" of God almighty. Hebrews 4:14. The pope claims to be the great high priest. As already mentioned above, the pope claims the title of Supreme Pontiff. He is the successor of the emperors of Rome who were seriatim the Supreme Pontiff (*Pontifex Maximus*),[439] which was the high priest of the pagan religions of Rome.[440] Jesus is higher than the kings of the earth. Psalms 89:27. The pope claims, however, authority over the kings of the earth. "[T]he Roman pontiff possess **primacy over the whole world**." *The Vatican Council*, Session IV, chapter III, July 18, 1870 (emphasis added). Jesus is "Lord of all." Acts 10:36. The pope, though, claims that all must submit to him: "The Roman Pontiff judges all man, but is judged by no one. We declare, assert, define and pronounce: to be subject to the Roman Pontiff is to every human creature altogether necessary for salvation." *The Bull Unum Sanctum*, November 18, 1302 (emphasis added).[441] The pope has claimed every attribute of Christ for himself. He has essentially denied that Jesus is the Christ and laid claim himself to being Christ. The Holy Bible identifies such a one as antichrist. 1 John 2:20-23.

The Bible says that the antichrist will deny the Son and, implicitly, deny the Father. 1 John 2:20-23. The pope makes his identity as the antichrist clear by expressly denying the Father. The pope claims the title "Holy Father." *See Catechism of the Catholic Church*, at § 10. Holy Father is a title that appears only once in all the Holy Scriptures and is reserved for God the Father. John 17:11.

Cardinal Giuseppe Sarto, who later became Pope Pius X, wrote: **"The Pope represents Jesus Christ Himself and is therefore a loving Father."**[442] (emphasis added) Notice how Cardinal Sarto capitalized the word "Father," thus signifying that the pope is considered equivalent to God the Father.

Indeed, since the papacy is founded upon a denial that Jesus is the Christ, it is not surprising to find their dogmatic writings sprinkled with such denials. For example, in 2002, the Vatican published a book by the Pontifical Biblical Commission titled *The Jewish People and Their Sacred Scriptures in the Christian Bible*, with a preface written by Joseph Cardinal Ratzinger (later to become Pope Benedict XVI). The preface by Ratzinger carries the date: "Rome, the feast of the Ascension 2001." The book states:

> It may be asked whether Christians should be blamed for having monopolised the Jewish Bible and reading there what no Jew has found. Should not Christians henceforth read the Bible as Jews do, in order to show proper respect for its Jewish origins?
>
> In answer to the last question, a negative response must be given for hermeneutical reasons. For to read the Bible as Judaism does necessarily involves an implicit acceptance of all its presuppositions, that is, the full acceptance of what Judaism is, in particular, the authority of its writings and rabbinic traditions, which **exclude faith in Jesus as Messiah and Son of God.**
>
> As regards the first question, the situation is different, for **Christians can and ought to admit that the Jewish reading of the Bible is a possible one.**[443] (emphasis added)

The above passage is rather cryptic, which is typical of Vatican dogma. In witchcraft, there are often two meanings, which are contrary to one another, expressed in a single passage. That way, an esoteric message can be given to initiates, while concealing that hidden message behind the camouflaged language carrying the opposite meaning that can be used to deceive the uninitiated. That is the case with the above passage. When the text is parsed, it states on the one hand that Christians should not read the bible as Jews do, because such a reading "exclude[s] faith in Jesus as Messiah and Son of God." On the other hand its states that "Christians can and ought to admit that the Jewish reading of the Bible is a possible one." That possible reading advised by the Vatican's Pontifical Biblical Commission "exclude[s] faith in Jesus as Messiah and Son of God."

The public exoteric meaning of the passage is that Christians

234

should not read the bible as Jews do, because such a reading "exclude[s] faith in Jesus as Messiah and Son of God." The other language in the passage conveys the esoteric meaning that informs their initiates of the true meaning. The true (but esoteric) meaning of the above passage is intended to appease the Jews, who have always read the bible to "exclude faith in Jesus as Messiah and Son of God." The true meaning of the passage is that Christians can and ought to admit that a possible reading of the bible "exclude[s] faith in Jesus as Messiah and Son of God." That instruction by the papacy is a denial that Jesus is the Christ, thus confirming that the papacy is the antichrist in fulfillment of John's prophecy in 1 John 2:22-23.

In addition, the Roman Pontiff could not possibly be a successor to Peter. The Roman church teaches that Peter was the bishop of Rome.[444] There is absolutely no credible evidence to support that claim. In fact it is doubtful that he was ever in Rome. Peter was the apostle to the Jews. *See* Galatians 2:9. Rome was a gentile city. He would have no reason to travel to Rome. Paul, who was an apostle to the gentiles (*see* Romans 11:13), greeted over 25 Christians living in Rome at the end of his letter to the Romans, but he did not greet Peter. *See* Romans 16. If Peter was in fact the Bishop, Paul would certainly have greeted him. He did not greet Peter because Peter was not in Rome. The scriptures, once again, prove the fraud of the papacy; that explains why the Roman Catholic Church want to keep people ignorant of the bible.

24 The Attack of the Moon God

The pope manifests his identity as the antichrist by denying that Jesus is the Christ in sundry ways. For example, according to the official teachings of the Catholic Church, Muslims go to heaven even though they are outside the Catholic Church. The *Catechism of the Catholic Church § 841* states:

> *The Church's relationship with the Muslims.* The plan of salvation also includes those who acknowledge the Creator, in the first place amongst whom are the Muslims; these profess to hold the faith of Abraham, and together with us they adore the one, merciful God, mankind's judge on the last day.[445]

The Vatican position is that Catholics and Muslims worship the same god. T.A. McMahon reveals that "[i]n 1985, Pope John Paul II declared to an enraptured audience of thousands of Muslim youths, 'Christians and Muslims, we have many things in common as believers and as human beings....We believe in the same God, the one and only God, the living God.'"[446]

In the picture below, Pope John Paul II can be seen kissing the Quran. That Quran was given to him during a ceremonial presentation from a Muslim delegation in Iraq "that included the Shiite Imam of Khadum Mosque, the Sunni President of the council that operates the Iraqi Islamic Bank, and a member of the Iraqi Ministry of Religion."[447]

All such ceremonies involving the pope are planned in advance to the last detail. The pope has at his command scores of the world's most educated Catholic theologians to advise him. Pope John Paul II knew the theological significance of kissing the Quran. The kiss was not spontaneous, but was scripted ahead of time. By kissing the Quran, the pope was signifying that he was in agreement and indeed revered the contents of the book. The pope knew exactly what he was doing.

Pope John Paul II Kissing Quran

With that in mind, let us read what the Quran says about Jesus. The Quran is the primary religious text for Muslims. It is believed by Muslims to have been given by revelation from the Angel Gabriel to Muhammad. The Quran at Sura 23:91 states in reference to Jesus that "**no son did Allah beget,**" and again at Sura 17:111: "All the praises and thanks be to **Allah, Who has not begotten a son.**" Allah is the god of Islam. In the Quran at Sura 4:171 it states that Allah did not have a Son. Sura 4:171 adds to the blasphemy by stating that Jesus is a mere messenger of Allah.

> O People of the Scripture, do not commit excess in your religion or say about Allah except the truth. The Messiah, Jesus, the son of Mary, was but a messenger of Allah and His word which He directed to Mary and a soul [created at a command] from Him. So believe in Allah and His messengers. And do not say, "Three"; desist - it is better for you. Indeed, Allah is but one God. Exalted is He above having a son. To Him belongs whatever is in the heavens and whatever is on the earth. And sufficient is Allah as Disposer of affairs. Quran, Sura 4:171

The bible identifies Jesus as the only begotten Son of God. "For God so loved the world, that he gave **his only begotten Son**, that whosoever believeth in him should not perish, but have everlasting life." (John 3:16) "In this was manifested the love of God toward us, because that **God sent his only begotten Son** into the world, that we might live through him." (1 John 4:9) Jesus, the Father, and the Holy Spirit are all one God. "For there are three that bear record in heaven, the Father, the Word, and the Holy Ghost: and these three are one." (1 John 5:7)

The pope, by kissing the Quran, was demonstrating the official Catholic theology, which is in accord with the Muslim theology. Allah, who is the god of Islam, is not the same god as the God of the bible, because the God of he bible includes the only begotten Son of God, Jesus Christ. Allah, on the other hand, "has not begotten a son." The bible makes it clear that "[w]hosoever denieth the Son, the same hath not the Father: (but) he that acknowledgeth the Son hath the Father also." (1 John 2:23) Islam is antithetical to Christianity. The Quran, at Sura 4:157, contradicts the bible and states that Jesus was not crucified. According to Islam, all who follow any religion other than Islam are damned to hell. "And whoever desires other than Islam as religion - never will it be accepted from him, and he, in the Hereafter, will be among the losers." Quran, Sura 3:85. Dr. Nabeel Qureshi, a Muslim convert to Christianity, confirms that Quran, Sura 5:72, states that it is an unforgivable sin in Islam to believe that Jesus is God. Indeed, according to the Quran, Sura 21:98, all who worship Jesus are the "firewood of hell." "Surely you and what you worship besides Allah are the firewood of hell; to it you shall come." Quran, Sura 21:98.

On March 20, 2013, Pope Francis addressed religious leaders and expressed his view that Allah, the god of Islam, to whom Muslims pray, is "the one God." Pope Francis said: "I then greet and cordially thank you all, dear friends belonging to other religious traditions; **first of all the Muslims, who worship the one God, living and merciful, and call upon Him in prayer**, and all of you."[448] Pope Francis knew exactly what he was saying. He was implicitly rejecting Jesus Christ, because the official position of Islam, as stated in their Quran, is that Allah,"the one God," to whom Pope Francis was referring, had no begotten son. That acceptance of Allah is a rejection of Jesus; the rejection of Jesus is a rejection of God the Father. 1 John 2:23. The god of Islam is the same as the god of the papacy. As you read on, you will read proof the god of Islam is Lucifer.

The pope kissing the Quran punctuates the Catholic official theology, which is that Muslims and Catholics worship the same god. *Catechism of the Catholic Church § 841, supra.* That is an implicit rejection that Jesus is the only begotten Son of God. Indeed, the foundational principle of the papacy is that the pope is the successor of Peter, who is portrayed falsely by the papacy to be the rock upon which Christ built his church. That claim is a rejection of the true rock (Jesus Christ) as stated by Peter when he said: "Thou art the Christ, the Son of the living God." (Matthew 16:16) That rejection of Peter's statement identifying Jesus as "the Christ, the Son of the living God" identifies the pope as the antichrist. "Who is a liar but he that denieth that Jesus is the Christ? He is antichrist, that denieth the Father and the Son." (1 John 2:22)

When one understands the theology of Islam, it becomes clearer why the pope, being the antichrist, would openly kiss the Quran. It seems that his act is based upon the view that "my enemy's enemy is my friend." The pope is all too happy to join forces with the Muslim community, because Islam is a religion that openly opposes Jesus Christ. The Islamic apostasy laws are the most notable manifestation of its opposition to biblical Christianity. As will be proven in a later chapter, Islam is the spiritual progeny of the "Mother of Harlots and Abominations of the Earth." Revelation 17:5. The direct and circumstantial evidence points to an alliance between Islam and the Vatican against their common enemy, the Christian church.

The majority of Muslim scholars hold the traditional view that an unrepentant apostate of sound mind is punishable by death or imprisonment.[449] The most notable way to be an apostate under Islamic Sharia law is to convert to another religion. Apostasy by conversion as defined by Islam almost always involves conversion to Christianity.

The majority Islamic view is that conversion to Christianity is punishable by death. The death penalty for conversion to Christianity is the most convincing evidence that Islam is a religion of hate toward Christ. Jesus made it clear that "he that hateth me hateth my Father also." (John 15:23) If Muslims hate Christ and necessarily also the Father, that is the best indication that the god of Islam is not the God of the bible.

Some claim that depicting Islam as punishing people with death for converting to Christianity is not an accurate portrayal of Islam. It is true that there are a minority of Islamic scholars who maintain that it is not a crime to convert from Islam to Christianity.[450] They assert that the Quran expressly states that there should be no compulsion in religion (*e.g.*, Sura 2:256). That view, however, is the minority view among Islamic clerics and scholars. The majority of Islamic scholars rebut such arguments by limiting Sura 2:256 to one who is not a Muslim. The majority argues that Sura 2:256 is inapplicable to one who is already a Muslim, since Islam literally means "submit to Allah's will," and being a Muslim means continued submission. The majority view is that conversion to Christianity is considered rebellion against Allah and therefore punishable by death or imprisonment.

Another claim by the minority liberal Islamic scholars is that the crime and punishment for apostasy comes from an overly strict interpretation of the *ahadith*. *Ahadith* (singular: *hadith*) is a written record of the things that Muhammad did and said. *Ahadith* is a source of religious guidance to Muslims. From the *ahadith*, which is a collection of sayings or reports, Muslims derived what is known as the *sunnah* (tradition), which are the examples or precedent of what Muhammad did, approved, and disapproved. Among those who reject the idea of the death penalty for conversion to Christianity is prominent Islamic scholar, Gamal El-Banna, who has written over 50 books.[451] S. A. Rahman, former Chief Justice of Pakistan, also opines that there is no indication of the death penalty for apostasy in the Quran.[452]

Despite El-Banna's and Rahman's claims, a fair reading of the Quran reveals that it in fact expressly calls for the killing of one who converts from Islam. Sura 4:89 states: "But if they turn back (from Islam), take (hold) of them and kill them wherever you find them." Sura 4:89 is often cited in apostasy trials in Sharia courts as justification for the death penalty.

The liberal interpretation of Islamic law that allows conversion to Christianity remains the minority view. In actual practice in Islamic countries worldwide, people who convert to Christianity are sentenced at least to prison and usually to death. For example, a widow in Egypt and her seven adult children converted to Christianity. In January 2013, she and her seven children were all sentenced to 15 years in prison.[453]

In 2006, a medical worker was facing trial and the death penalty in Afghanistan for converting to Christianity.[454] The case was later dismissed on a technicality when the western media picked up the story and the Afghanistan government came under pressure to reverse the decision. Death remains the penalty for apostasy in Afghanistan, and anyone who converts to Christianity can count on receiving the death penalty in a summary trial, if the government thinks it can do it without it becoming publicized.

In 2010, a trial court in Iran ordered a Christian pastor, Youcef Nadarkhani, 34 year-old father of two young children, to be put to death for leaving Islam and converting to Christianity.[455] His conviction came to light in the western media and it was subsequently reversed by the Iranian Supreme Court.[456] Upon retrial, he was acquitted of apostasy but was convicted of the lesser charge of evangelizing Muslims. He was sentenced to 3 years in prison, but was given credit for the 3 years he had already spent in jail.[457]

The Islamic apostasy laws against conversion to another religion are so strict that even if one has spent his entire life from childhood as a Christian and it is determined that he was born into an Islamic family, the Christian must disavow his Christian faith and become a Muslim or be put to death. Paul Marshal, who is a senior fellow at the Hudson Institute, reported in the June 23, 2014 edition of *The Weekly Standard* about the case of Meriam Ibrahim, who lived her life as a Christian. Meriam was sentenced to death for apostasy, because it was determined that her long-estranged father was a Muslim.

> Meriam Ibrahim ... gave birth in a Sudanese prison just the other day. She was raised a Christian, but after officials learned that her long-absent father was a Muslim, she was sentenced to death for apostasy—for leaving Islam. And since in Sudan a Muslim woman may not be married to a Christian, her marriage to her American husband was declared void, and she was convicted of adultery and sentenced to 100 lashes to be administered before her execution. These punishments will be dropped if she renounces her Christian faith, which she steadfastly refuses to do.[458]

It seems that when the apostasy ruling of an Islamic court comes to light in the western media, the government will find a way to resolve the case short of death. However, in resolving the cases, there is never heard any indication of a fundamental change in the established principle of the death penalty for those who convert to Christianity. In fact, the most learned *fatwas* in Islam confirm the principle of death as a penalty for a person converting to Christianity.

A *fatwa* is a learned opinion on Islamic law. Al-Azhar is an Islamic University in Cairo, Egypt, founded in the year 972. Al-Azhar is considered to be the chief center of Arabic literature and Islamic learning in the world. In 1978, the *Al-Azhar Council of Fatwa*, issued a ruling on a request for opinion in an actual case on the proper punishment for an Egyptian man who converted to Christianity.[459] The council stated, in pertinent part:

> This question was presented by Mr. Ahmed Darwish and brought forward by [name obscured] who is of German nationality.
>
> A man whose religion was Islam and his nationality is Egyptian married a German Christian and the couple agreed that the husband would join the Christian faith and doctrine.
>
> 1) What is the Islamic ruling in relation to this man? What are the punishments prescribed for this act?
>
> 2) Are his children considered Muslim or Christian?
>
> The Answer:
>
> All praise is to Allah, the Lord of the Universe and salutations on the leader of the righteous, our master Muhammed, his family and all of his companions.
>
> Thereafter:
>
> This man has committed apostasy; he must be given a chance to repent and if he does not then he must be

killed according to Sharia.

As far as his children are concerned, as long as they are children they are considered Muslim, but after they reach the age of puberty, then if they remain with Islam they are Muslim, but if they leave Islam and they do not repent they must be killed and Allah knows best.

Seal of Al-Azhar
Head of the Fatwa Council of Al-Azhar.
Abdullah al-Mishadd
23rd September 1978.[460]

Be mindful that such *fatwas* can be used to guide the actions of courts and be enforced by the Islamic states. In Egypt, Article 2 of its Constitution states that "Islam is the religion of the State and Arabic is its official language. The principles of Islamic Sharia are the main source of legislation."[461] Article 1 of the Constitution of Saudi Arabia states that "[t]he Kingdom of Saudi Arabia is a sovereign Arab Islamic state with Islam as its religion."[462] Article 23 of that same constitution states that "[t]he defence of the Islamic religion, society, and country is a duty for each citizen."[463] That is typical of Islamic countries. In Afghanistan, for instance, Chapter 1, Article 2 of the constitution states that "[t]he religion of the state of the Islamic Republic of Afghanistan is the sacred religion of Islam."[464] Article 54 of the Constitution of Afghanistan provides that "[t]he state adopts necessary measures to ensure physical and psychological well being of family, especially of child and mother, upbringing of children and the elimination of traditions contrary to the principles of sacred religion of Islam."[465] Article 149 of the Constitution of Afghanistan provides that the passages regarding the supremacy of Islam contained in the constitution cannot ever be amended. "The principles of adherence to the tenets of the Holy religion of Islam as well as Islamic Republicanism shall not be amended."[466]

The pope kissed the Quran, thus indicating his accord with the doctrines of Islam that conversion from Islam to Christianity is punishable by death. The Islamic apostasy laws prohibiting conversion, of course, only apply against Muslims. However, there is a separate set of religious laws that apply to Muslims and non-Muslims alike. Those laws are called blasphemy laws. Some liberal Islamic legal scholars claim that blasphemy is not a Sharia crime; they argue that evidence of blasphemy should only be used to prove apostasy. That argument seems to be purely academic, because, in practice, most Islamic countries have blasphemy laws, which are separate substantive offenses, and they are enforced. For example: Pakistan Penal Code § 295-C provides in pertinent part the following: "Use of derogatory remarks, etc., in respect of the Holy Prophet: Whoever by words, either spoken or written, or by visible representation or by any imputation, innuendo, or insinuation, directly or indirectly, defiles the sacred name of the Holy Prophet Muhammad (peace be upon him) shall be punished with death, or imprisonment for life, and shall also be liable to fine."[467]

As draconian and oppressive as that statute is, it was not deemed strict enough for the Federal Shariat Court of Pakistan. In 1992, by order of the Federal Shariat Court, 295-C PPC was amended to make death the only possible penalty for blasphemy.[468] That means that under Pakistani law any person who makes a derogatory remark about Muhammad shall be put to death.

Pakistan's first Minister of Minority Religious Affairs, Shahbaz Bhatti, who was Roman Catholic and the only non-Muslim cabinet minister in Pakistan, was assassinated in March 2011, after he lobbied to change blasphemy laws of Pakistan. Tehrik-i-Taliban (which literally means Students of Islam Movement of Pakistan), a militant Muslim group, claimed responsibility for the assassination and justified it by claiming that Bhatti had blasphemed Muhammad by opposing the blasphemy laws. A spokesman for Tehrik-i-Taliban Pakistan stated: "We will continue to target all those who speak against the law which punishes those who insult the prophet. Their fate will be the same."[469] Just two months earlier, in January 2011, Punjab Governor, Salman Taseer, who had also opposed the Pakistan blasphemy laws, was shot dead by one of his bodyguards.[470]

Blasphemy seems to be a catch-all charge in some countries for a whole variety of perceived infractions against Islam. For examples, in 2007, a student journalist, Parwiz Kambakhsh, in Afghanistan was sentenced to death for blasphemy for allegedly distributing an article on the role of woman in Islam. The trial lasted only minutes and the student was not allowed to defend himself. His sentence was commuted to 20 years on appeal. During the appellate hearing, the witness against him retracted his statement, but was ignored.[471]

In August 2005, in Indonesia, a man was sentenced to two years imprisonment for blasphemy for reciting Muslim prayers in a language other than Arabic (Indonesian).[472] In September 2005, three Indonesian women from a Christian Church were sentenced to 3 years imprisonment under the Child Protection Law for allegedly attempting to convert Muslim children to Christianity, even though the family of the children had given permission for the children to attend the Christian youth programs.[473]

The god of Islam is Allah. Many believe that Allah is a transliteration of the word "God" in Arabic. That is not true. The Arabic word for God is "ilah". Allah is a contraction of al-ilah, which means "the god." In the Quran at Sura 20:98, it states: "Your ilah (God) is only Allah."[474] (Muhsin Khan translation; parenthetical in original) The word for "god" in Sura 20:98 is "ilah" and not "Allah." The *Shahadah* is one of the five pillars of Islam, and is recited by all Muslims. The *Shahadah* states: *"ašhadu 'anla ilaha illal-Lah, wa 'ashadu 'anna muhammadan rasulul-Lah."* The literal English translation of the *Shahadah* is "There is no god [ilah] but Allah and Muhammad is the messenger of Allah." Notice that the Arabic word for "god" in the *Shahadah* is "ilah" and not "Allah." Allah is the proper name for the god of Islam, it is not an Arabic translation for the word "god."

Most believe that Allahu Akbar means "God is great." In fact, that is not the correct translation according to Edward William Lane. Edward William Lane was the foremost orientalist, translator and lexicographer of the Arabic Language in the 19th century. He spent 13 years acquiring Arabic source materials and then spent the next 27 years compiling an eight-volume authoritative text on the Arabic Lexicon. His Arab-English Lexicon is viewed at the world's most authoritative lexicon on the proper translation into English of Arabic words.[475] According to Lane, Allahu Akbar literally means, "Allah is Greater." Lane states that the meaning expressed is that Allah is greater than anything else compared to him (i.e., "Allah is the greatest").

Allahu Akbar is an exclamation spoken for many reasons, the

most notable being a battle cry by Muslim warriors. The intent of the battle cry, Allahu Akbar, is to express the idea that the god of Islam is "greater" than the god of the people being attacked. Andrew C. McCarthy of the National Review explains that "[t]his precedent was set by Prophet Muhammad when he attacked the Jews of Khaibar."[476] It continues today to be used as a battle cry against Christians. That is because, Muslims consider their god to be a different (i.e., "greater") god than the God of the Christians. The pope states that the god of the Muslims is the same as the god of the Catholics, which means that the god of the Catholics is not the Christian God of the bible.

Muslims understand that Allahu Akbar means that their god is "greater" and therefore is necessarily not the same as the God of the bible. The use of the term as a cry against the Christian God, Jesus Christ, is stark evidence of that fact. Raymond Ibrahim and Scott Allswang summarize recent occurrences where the cry of "Allahu Akbar" has been a feature of attacks by radical Muslims against Christians.

> Sudan: A Christian compound in Khartoum was stormed by a throng of Muslims "armed with clubs, iron rods, a bulldozer and fire," the day after a Muslim leader called on Muslims to destroy "the infidels' church." Shouting **"Allahu Akbar [God is greater]"** and "No more Christianity from today on—no more church from today on," the jihadis stormed the Bible school bookstore, burning Bibles and threatening to kill anyone resisting them. "What happened could not be imagined—it was terrible," said an eyewitness. "They burned all furniture of the school and the church as well." As usual, "Police at the compound stood back and did nothing to prevent the mob from vandalizing the compound."[477] (bracketed translation in original)
>
> Uganda: Not long after a pastor was attacked with acid and blinded by **"Allahu-Akbar"** screaming Muslims, his friend, another pastor, was shot at by "Islamic extremists," in what is being described as "a new wave of persecution against Christians in Uganda."[478]

Egypt: Muslims "severely sexually harassed" a Christian woman in front of her husband at a bus terminal; when her husband tried to defend her honor, he was violently beaten. Soon afterwards, thousands of Muslims in the region began looting and torching Christian property, screaming **"Allahu Akbar!"** and "cursing the cross." Also, a Muslim ring using sexual coercion to convert Christian girls was exposed.[479]

If Allah is not the same God as in the bible, who is Allah? Before Muhammad, Arabs had a Henotheistic religion. Henotheism is a type of polytheism, where there are many gods, but there is one chief god above the other lesser gods. Allah was the chief of all gods.[480] Allah was well known among the polytheistic Arab tribes. For example, the name of Muhammad's father was "Abd-Allah," which literally means "slave or worshiper of Allah." As explained above, Allah literally means "the god." "Allah" is a contraction of Al Ilah "the God."[481] Allah was originally a title; it was not a proper noun.

When Muhammad displaced the 360 lesser gods and announced that "there is no god but Allah," the tribal Arabs knew "the god" (Allah) to whom Muhammad was referring. The *Encyclopedia of Religion and Ethics* explains how Muhammad's address to the Meccans indicates that the Meccans already knew who Allah was: "The first article of the Muslim creed, therefore–*La ilaha illa-llahu*,–means, only as addressed by him to the Meccans, **'There exists no god except the one whom you already call ALLAH.'**"[482]

Muhammad elevated Allah from the chief deity to the sole deity of the Arabs. Although Muhammad initially announced that Allah was the only god, that did not remain the case. Ibn Ishaq, Mohammed's earliest biographer and virtually every historian and scholar who have studied the matter, agree that an early version of the Quran (formerly at Sura 53:19-22) was revised by Muhammad to allow Muslims to pray to the three daughter goddesses of Allah (Al-Lat, Al-'Uzzá, and Manat).[483] Muhammad later removed those verses and claimed that he was tricked by Satan to include the verses in the Quran, hence they are called the "Satanic Verses." The event is alluded to in the Quran itself at Suras 17:73-74 and 22:51-52.

Islam claims to be a monotheistic religion, with Allah standing alone as the Muslim god. Islam, however, sprang from tribal polytheism, and the Quran contains vestiges of that polytheism. For example, in the Quran there are repeated references made of deities by the use of plural pronouns (e.g., Quran, at Suras 2:52-53, 3:108, 3:44, 3:145, 6:144, 17:1, 37:161-166, and 37:170-182).

Islamic scholars argue that such plural references to other deities are similar in nature to a king or queen using a plural pronoun when rendering a royal edict.[484] However, that explanation actually confirms that the plural pronouns in the Quran refers to a plurality of gods, because when a monarch uses the royal "we" it is intended to either include his court and advisors as being in agreement with the edict, or in other instances it is intended to refer to the entire state, as the monarch is a representative of the state. In either case, the royal "we" is in fact intended to be a reference to a plurality of persons. If the argument is that the we in reference to the god of the Quran is intended to be a royal we, that means it is intended to be a reference to a pantheon of many gods. After examining the context of the use of the plural pronouns in the Quran, Sam Shamoun concluded that such use indicated that Islam was initially intended to be a polytheistic religion.

> The evidence leads us to therefore conclude that the Quran's author(s) believed that Allah exists as a plurality of persons, or that in the earliest strata of Islamic tradition there was a belief that other divine powers existed alongside Allah. It was only later that either the author(s) himself (themselves) or later editors and scholars sought to deny the existence of these other divine beings by changing the text of the Quran. And yet whoever edited the Quran in its final stage didn't do a good job since there are still obvious traces that other divine beings exist which suggests that, at the very least, the first Muslim community believed in the existence of other divine powers.[485]

Muslims reject that the plural reference in the Quran is an allusion to the biblical doctrine that there are three persons in one God, because they have always eschewed that biblical doctrine entirely. That means that the use of the plural pronoun for the many deities in the

Quran is not at all equivalent to the use of the plural pronoun to refer to the one God of the bible in Genesis 1:24. The bible states that "God said, Let us make man in our image, after our likeness." Genesis 1:24. That passage is intended to express the presence of God the Father, God the Son, and God the Holy Spirit. However, all three persons are one God, not three Gods. "The Lord our God is one Lord." Deuteronomy 6:4. However, there are three persons in that one God. "For there are three that bear record in heaven, the Father, the Word, and the Holy Ghost: and these three are one." 1 John 5:7. Muslims utterly reject that God is three persons in one God.

Muhammad was illiterate, and so the Quran, which means "the recitation," was passed down orally from Muhammad to his followers. "The content of the Quran is believed by Muslims to have been transmitted from the Archangel Gabriel to the Prophet Muhammad over the course of twenty-three years (609–32)."[486]

Dr. Robert Morey further explains the origins of Allah:

It should not come as a surprise that the word "Allah" was not something invented by Muhammad or revealed for the first time in the Quran.

The well-known Middle East scholar H.A.R. Gibb has pointed out that the reason that Muhammad never had to explain who Allah was in the Quran is that his listeners had already heard about Allah long before Muhammad was ever born.[487]

Dr. Arthur Jeffery, one of the foremost Western Islamic scholars in modern times and professor of Islamic and Middle East Studies at Columbia University, notes:

"The name Allah, as the Quran itself is witness, was well known in pre-Islamic Arabia. Indeed, both it and its feminine form, Allat, are found not infrequently among the theophorous names in inscriptions from North Africa"[488]

The word "Allah" comes from the compound Arabic

word, al-ilah. Al is the definite article "the" and ilah is an Arabic word for "god." It is not a foreign word. It is not even the Syriac word for God. It is pure Arabic.[489]

Neither is Allah a Hebrew or Greek word for God as found in the Bible. Allah is a purely Arabic term used in reference to an Arabian deity.[490]

Hastings' Encyclopedia of Religion and Ethics states:

"'Allah' is a proper name, applicable only to their [Arabs'] peculiar God."

According to the Encyclopedia of Religion:

"'Allah' is a pre-Islamic name ... corresponding to the Babylonian Bel."[491]

Allah is Bel; Bel is a heathen god mentioned in Isaiah 46:1, Jeremiah 50:2, and 51:44. Morey reveals Islam as a moon cult. Morey describes "Allah" as the moon god, the consort of the sun goddess, and father of a number of female deities, Al-Lat, Al-Uzza, and Manat. That is why the symbol of Islam is the crescent moon.[492] Often among heathen religions, the moon was depicted as a female deity and the sun as a male deity. However, the Arabs followed a variant, where the symbolism of the moon and sun was reversed, with the moon representing the male god, known as Allah.

Important aspects of the theology of the Catholic Church parallels Islam. Both Muslims and Catholics use heathen prayer beads. Furthermore, both Catholics and Muslims regard pilgrimages in order to win the favor of God. Both Catholics and Muslims take pilgrimages to the same sites (e.g., Fatima). Most notably, both Islam and Catholicism require salvation by works.

There are particular similarities between the Islamic and Catholic doctrines regarding the Virgin Mary. The doctrine of the Immaculate Conception of Mary was officially announced as an Article of Faith in the Roman Catholic Church by Pope Pius IX on Dec. 18th, 1854. However, it had long been an esoteric belief within the church hierarchy for many centuries. It was not until 1854 that the pope decided to let its deluded members in on that secret doctrine.

Islam was inculcated with the dogma of the immaculate conception of Mary. Catholic Bishop Fulton Sheen stated that "[t]he Koran, which is the Bible of the Moslems, has many passages concerning the Blessed Virgin. First of all, the Koran believes in her Immaculate Conception, and also, in her Virgin Birth."[493] Incidently, Bishop Sheen, who is now deceased, was a highly regarded theologian within the Catholic community. In fact, in June 2012, Pope Benedict XVI stated that Catholic Bishop Fulton Sheen lived a life of "heroic virtues," which is a major step towards beatification. Bishop Sheen is now considered a "venerable" person within the Catholic pantheon of the dead. According to Bishop Sheen, Islam views both Jesus and Mary as having been virgin born. While the Catholic doctrine of the immaculate conception of Mary suggests that she was virgin born herself, the Catholic Church has not explicitly stated that fact as Catholic doctrine.

Muslim doctrine of the immaculate conception of Mary is primarily found in the *ahadith*, which states that the only children born immaculately, without the touch of Satan, were Mary and Jesus.[494]

George Sale stated that the immaculate conception of Mary was not only in the *ahadith*, but is also found in the Quran itself.[495] George Sale (1697-1736) was a 17th century orientalist and attorney who was the author of a ten volume dictionary and in 1734 translated the Quran into English.

The Muslim adherence to the Catholic doctrine of Mariolotry includes worshiping graven images of Mary. T.A. McMahon explains:

> Most people are aware of the veneration and even worship of Mary found among Roman Catholics, but not many know that much the same deference exists among Muslims. A chapter in the Qur'an is named after Mary ("Surah Maryam"). From the outskirts of Cairo to Bombay to Medjugorje in Bosnia-Herzegovina, hundreds of thousands of the Islamic faith have congregated wherever processions carry her statues and

where her apparitions are said to have appeared. She is esteemed above the most revered women of the Muslim faith, including Muhammad's two favorite wives, Khadija and Aisha, and his daughter Fatima. The hadith teaches that Muhammad selected Mary as his first wife upon entrance into Paradise[496]

The Roman Catholic dogma is that Mary remained a virgin even after the birth of Jesus.[497] This erroneous theological doctrine is refuted by the bible, which states that Jesus had brothers and sisters, obviously born to Mary. See Matthew 12:46; Luke 8:19; Mark 3:31. Islam has adopted the perpetual virginity of Mary myth from the Catholic Church.[498]

Helena Blavatsky is considered by occultists to be one of the foremost experts on witchcraft and the dark arts of the occult. She explained that the Roman Catholic version of the Virgin Mary is actually Venus (a/k/a Isis), the Queen of Heaven, and is also the Catholic "Morning Star."[499] She states that Venus is Lucifer. The worship of the Virgin Mary is the occult worship of Lucifer.

The Catholic Encyclopedia confirms the statement by Blavatsky that Venus is Lucifer. The Catholic Encyclopedia does not, however, state that Mary is Venus; it, instead, states that Lucifer denotes Venus and Lucifer is another metaphorical name for Jesus.[500] The passage in the Catholic Encyclopedia that states that Lucifer is a metaphorical name for Jesus is the authoritative position of the Roman Catholic Church and is accompanied by the Nihil Obstat of Remy Lafort, Censor, and the Imprimatur of John Cardinal Farley, Archbishop of New York.

> **The name Lucifer originally denotes the planet Venus**, emphasizing its brilliance.... Metaphorically, the word is applied to the King of Babylon ... [and] **to Jesus Christ himself.**[501] *Catholic Encyclopedia* (emphasis added).

The Catholic Jesus is not the Lord of lords and King of kings of the Holy Bible, but is instead the infernal Lucifer. Blavatsky herself alludes to the fact that the Catholic Virgin Mary, the Catholic Jesus, and Lucifer are all one and the same god. She equated the Virgin Mary with the "Morning Star," which is in fact the title for Jesus found at Revelation 22:16. In witchcraft, heathen gods are often transposed, and a male god may take on the characteristics of a female goddess, or a god may take on both male and female characteristics. The androgyny of Baphomet (a/k/a Lucifer), who is depicted by Eliphas Levi in his infamous drawing with a male phallus and female breasts, is probably the most recognizable example of that fact.

Note that Baphomet is sitting on a globe and is pointing to two crescent moons with both his right and left hands. Levi describes Baphomet, among other things, as the "god of the primitive Gnostic schools" and as "the Christ also of the dissident priesthood."[502] Levi's reference to the "dissident priesthood" seems to be a reference to the Catholic priesthood. Is there support for the position that the Christ of the Catholic priesthood is Baphomet (a/k/a Satan and Lucifer)? Indeed, that support is found in the Catholic Encyclopedia, which defines Lucifer as both Venus and Jesus.[503]

Baphomet

Although the worship of the Virgin Mary is part and parcel of both Islam and Catholicism, oddly, both Roman Catholicism and Islam are misogynous religions. Women are oppressed and considered second class citizens with limited rights and authority in Islamic countries. In fact, Islamic countries have requirements that Islamic women cover their entire bodies head-to-toe when in public with garments known as burkas or chadors.[504]

The veiling of women is required by the Quran. We read in the Quran at Surat Al-Ahzab, 33:59:

253

> O Prophet! Tell your wives and your daughters and the women of the believers to draw their cloaks (veils) all over their bodies (i.e., screen themselves completely except the eyes or one eye to see the way). That will be better, that they should be known (as free respectable women) so as not to be annoyed. And Allah is Ever OftForgiving, Most Merciful.[505]

That command is reinforced in the Quran at Surat An-Nur, 24:31, where it states:

> And tell the believing women to lower their gaze (from looking at forbidden things), and protect their private parts (from illegal sexual acts, etc.) and not to show off their adornment except only that which is apparent (like palms of hands or one eye or both eyes for necessity to see the way, or outer dress like veil, gloves, head-cover, apron, etc.), and to draw their veils all over Juyubihinna (i.e. their bodies, faces, necks and bosoms, etc.) and not to reveal their adornment except to their husbands, their fathers, their sons, their husband's sons, their brothers or their brother's sons, or their sister's sons, or their (Muslim) women (i.e. their sisters in Islam), or the (female) slaves whom their right hands possess, or old male servants who lack vigour, or small children who have no sense of the shame of sex. And let them not stamp their feet so as to reveal what they hide of their adornment. And all of you beg Allah to forgive you all, O believers, that you may be successful.[506]

Islamic Chador

The parallels between the strict conduct and dress of women as outlined in the Quran and the strict conduct and dress for nuns are striking. Just as Islamic women are to "lower their gaze" as commanded in the Quran, so also cloistered Catholic nuns under their vow of chastity are prohibited from raising their eyes to look men in the face when speaking to them. Furthermore, nuns are also instructed to walk with downcast eyes.[507]

Catholic Nun Wearing Habit

Regarding dress, we can see an equivalent requirement for women under Islam as for Catholic nuns, who are required to cover their bodies head-to-toe with garments known as habits. While the practice with the Catholics is limited to nuns and not the entire female population, the principle is the same. The treatment of nuns, particularly cloistered nuns, is similar to the oppression suffered by women in Islamic countries.

There are Islamic laws (Sharia) that punish fornication. A woman who is accused of fornication can allege rape as a defense. The oppression of Islamic women, however, is so complete that if a woman is raped and she tries to seek justice, her allegation of rape will be turned on her and she will be prosecuted for fornication. The best that a woman who is raped can hope for is that she is not prosecuted for fornication. If she seeks justice by alleging rape, her allegation will be considered a confession and thus conclusive evidence of her fornication, for which she will then be prosecuted under Sharia law. The lesson for women in Islamic countries is that they must keep quiet about rape and only mention it if necessary as a defense against an allegation of fornication.

In 2014, an Austrian Islamic woman was raped while in Dubai by a Yemeni man in an underground parking garage. "When she reported it to police, she was arrested and told she could only escape being charged [with fornication] if she agreed to marry the man she said had attacked her."[508] The Austrian government intervened, and she was released from custody and flown back to Austria.

What happened to 13 year-old Aisha Duhulowa on October 30, 2008, in Somalia, is another appalling example of the injustice of the misogynous Sharia law.[509] Aisha was stoned to death for fornication. She sought justice after being gang raped. Her allegation of being gang raped was considered a confession to fornication. Her sentence was death by stoning, which took place in a stadium attended by approximately 1,000 people. Daniel Howden of *The Independent* reported the tragic event:

> [Aisha Duhulowa] was dragged into the stadium. She knew what was going to happen next, and witnesses saw her struggling and screaming.
>
> "What do you want from me?" she asked. Then she shouted "I'm not going, I'm not going. Don't kill me."
>
> But four men forced her into the hole and buried her up to her neck. Fifty men then set about stoning her to death. After 10 minutes she was dug up and two nurses checked to see if she was alive. She was. So they put her back in the ground and the stoning recommenced.[510]

Although rape is technically a crime in Islamic countries, the Islamic principle that the complaining rape victim can be prosecuted for fornication is a major impediment to bringing rape charges. The crime of fornication in Islamic countries is a crime almost exclusively enforced against women. To prove the crime of fornication there must be either a confession or four eye witnesses to the actual penetration. If the witnesses are women, there must be two women for each man, which means a total of eight witnesses to the penetration. Because of high burden of proof, fornication is almost never prosecuted against men. The Ottoman Empire recorded only one instance of a successful prosecution of a man for fornication in 440 years. While prosecution against men for fornication is rare, it is a charge that is frequently brought against women. If an unmarried woman becomes pregnant, she will almost certainly at least be imprisoned for fornication (as a *tazir* crime); if she confesses to the crime, she could be sentenced to death (as a *hadd* crime).

25 The Perverse Effect of Religious Misogyny

The misogyny of Catholicism and Islam may explain why homosexual pederasty is prevalent among the Catholic clergy and in the Islamic countries.[511] The sexual perversion that is part and parcel of the Catholic priesthood, has been caused by the unnatural prohibition on marriage, which is a doctrine of devils. (1 Timothy 4:1-3) That same sexual perversion has also been inculcated into the general Islamic community by the artificial separation of the sexes.

The undercurrent of misogyny in Islamic countries has caused the men to engage in unusual behavior. Because public interaction between the sexes is restricted, it is common to see men walking together holding hands in Islamic countries. Men holding hands with other men is so prevalent in Islamic countries that one Saudi businessman gave a western friend the following advice for blending into Saudi culture and thus avoiding being targeted for violence by Islamic militants: "Stroll like you have nowhere important to go, and if you see a friend's hand next to you, grab it."[512] The act of men holding hands as they walk is practiced by Muslim men who consider themselves heterosexual, and it is not considered a homosexual practice in Islamic countries. Such behavior, however, is symptomatic of a deeper problem in Muslim society. *The New York Times* reported:

[B]ecause the sexes are segregated, men rarely have the chance to touch or show affection toward a woman. "Arab culture has historically been segregated, so emotions and feelings are channeled to the same sex," said Musa Shteiwi, a sociology professor at the University of Jordan. "Men spend a lot of time together, and these customs grew out of that." ... "Holding hands is the warmest expression of affection between men," said Samir Khalaf, a sociology professor at American University of Beirut in Lebanon. ... Kissing cheeks, long handshakes and clutching hands are meant to reflect amity, devotion and most important, equality in status, noted Fuad Ishak Khuri, a social anthropologist, in his book, "The Body in Islamic Culture" (2001).[513]

What was the cause for *The New York Times* to write on that topic? President George W. Bush was photographed holding hands with Crown Prince Abdullah of Saudi Arabia in Crawford, Texas, in 2005.[514]

President George Bush Holding Hands With Crown Prince Abdullah of Saudi Arabia

The picture of Bush and Prince Abdullah was not a candid shot. It was arranged in advance to memorialize the hand-holding. It was for the purpose of furthering a sodomite political agenda. Most people do not know that President Bush, like his father before him, is a member of a satanic secret society known as Skull and Bones. Bush is completely onboard with the sodomite agenda.

President George

W. Bush, in his autobiography, *A Charge to Keep* stated: **"During my senior year I joined Skull and Bones, a secret society, so secret I can't say anything more."** What is so secret that he cannot speak any further about it? The secret is that in return for power, wealth, and fame, he must blindly obey his satanic masters in their antichrist conspiracy to enslave and rule the world. The initiation ceremony for Skull and Bones involves, but is not limited to, the inductees lying naked in a coffin and telling their deepest sexual secrets. According to Sherman H. Skolnick, new members of Skull and Bones also engage in homosexual acts while they lie in the coffin.[515] Anton LaVey, the founder of the Church of Satan, in his *Satanic Rituals: Companion to the Satanic Bible,* states that such a coffin ritual is a satanic ritual common in many pagan orders. During the ritual a powerful spiritual force charges through the participants transforming their lives dramatically. This powerful spiritual force is a devil. The participants in these ceremonies end up possessed by a devil.

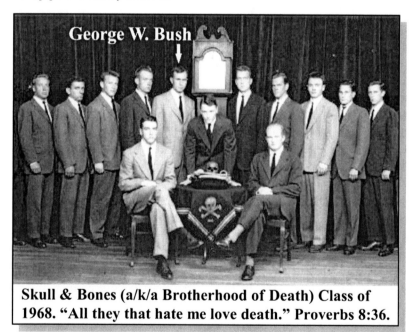

Skull & Bones (a/k/a Brotherhood of Death) Class of 1968. "All they that hate me love death." Proverbs 8:36.

Evidence indicates that the Order of Skull & Bones (a/k/a Brotherhood of Death) founded at Yale in 1832 is a chapter of the

Illuminati, which itself was originally founded in 1776 at the University of Ingolstadt in Germany.[516] From this we know that Skull & Bones is not American at all, but is a branch of a foreign secret society.[517]

The Skull & Bones use the Hegelian dialectic to change society into a totalitarian state. Under Hegel's dialectic there must be a conflict, either real or perceived, between a thesis and an antithesis which is resolved by a synthesis of the two. The secret societies create these conflicts in order to move society regressively away from Christ and Christian principles and toward Satan and satanic principles.[518]

The averred homosexual act committed by George Bush in the coffin during the skull and bones initiation ceremony has been alleged by some to be just one act in a long history of sodomy by Bush. Radio host and investigative journalist Sherman H. Skolnick alleged that George W. Bush is a sodomite.[519] Skolnick substantiated his claim by naming one of Bush's longtime sodomite male lovers (Victor Ashe). Before Kitty Kelley's book titled: *The Family: The Real Story of the Bush Dynasty* was to be published in 2004, Skolnick stated that publishing insiders informed him that her book would confirm that George Bush is a sodomite.[520] Kelley interviewed almost one thousand witnesses for her book on the Bush family. Skolnick's sources, apparently, were unreliable. While it is possible that early galleys of her book contained the proof of Bush's sexual deviance, the final version only alluded to him being considered unmanly as a male cheerleader at Yale. This author read Kelley's book and found no confirmation in it of George W. Bush being a sodomite. While Kelley may have uncovered such information, it never made it into the final published version of her book. Skolnick, who had a reputation for reliability, got that fact wrong.

While Sherman Skolnick in that one instance relied on an unreliable source, that does not necessarily mean that his underlying allegation, that George W. Bush is a sodomite, is wrong. Indeed, there is an eye-witness to Bush's sexual deviance, who independently corroborates Skolnick's allegation. Domina Leola McConnell is the eye-witness. She was a one time prostitute-for-hire and a 2006 Liberal Democratic candidate for Governor of Nevada.

McConnell alleged the following: "In 1984 I watched George W. Bush enthusiastically and expertly perform a homosexual act on another man, Victor Ashe."[521] McConnell further stated:"Other homo-erotic acts were also performed by then-private citizen George W. Bush. I know this because I performed one of them on him myself."[522]

Those revelations were to be detailed in an ebook titled, *Lustful Utterances*, which McConnell had scheduled to be published in 2007. From the time McConnell first made those allegations, she had been subjected to constant harassment and death threats. Apparently the threats were real, because McConnell disappeared in November 2007 and has not been heard from since. Her website, www.lustfulutterances.com, which at one time carried information about her forthcoming book, is now a dead link.[523] Her death ensured that the book would never be published.

McConnell was a threat to the sitting President, George W. Bush. One of the first things Kitty Kelley learned when researching her book is that the Bush family retaliates against anyone whom they view as a threat. People Kelley interviewed for her book about the Bushes were scared to death about retaliation. One person told her: "I want to live to see my grand-children."[524] Another man told Kelley: "You can't use my name. They'll come after me. The Bushes are thugs."[525] They knew the Bush family well, and their intimate knowledge of the Bush family created the singular emotion of fear.

Margie Schoedinger is another woman who has ended up dead after getting on the Bush enemies list. In December 2002, Schoedinger sued President George W. Bush for allegedly drugging and sexually assaulting her several times.[526] Schroedinger was not seeking publicity and only one media outlet reported on the case, *The Fort Bend Star*. Nine months after filing the rape charges against President George W. Bush, Schoedinger allegedly committed suicide. She died on September 22, 2003, of a gunshot to the head.

Some find it suspicious that Schoedinger would commit suicide that way. They conclude that it is unusual for women to shoot themselves in the head, because women are much more concerned about their appearance. Women usually choose to shoot themselves in the chest or ingest a lethal dose of drugs when committing suicide. While it is unusual for a woman to commit suicide by shooting herself in the head, it is not unheard of. In a study of 406 suicidal deaths by gunshot to the head, it was found that 18% of such persons committing suicide that way were female.[527] It is much more suspicious that this particular woman at the time of her death had a pending lawsuit alleging rape against the sitting President of the United States. President George W. Bush seems to have gained the most from her death. If her death is ruled a suicide, there is no further investigation. That is why assassins often try to make their murder victims appear to be the authors of their own demise.

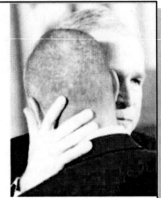

President George W. Bush hugging sodomite male escort Jeff Gannon (a/k/a Jeff Guckert).

Photos have surfaced showing President George W. Bush hugging Jeff Gannon (a/k/a Jeff Guckert). The photos were taken at a public forum, and so on the surface it seemed innocent enough. However, it was later discovered that Gannon was at that time a homosexual escort. Howard Kurtz of *The Washington Post* interviewed Gannon. "In the interview, Gannon did not dispute evidence that he has advertised himself as a $200-an-hour gay escort but would not specifically address such questions."[528]

It is certainly true that just because President Bush warmly hugged a male prostitute at the White House does not mean that the President knew who he was. There is, however, evidence suggesting that Gannon was at the White House at the specific request of President Bush. Between 2003 and 2005 Gannon was allowed access to the

White House grounds as a member of the press corps with no background investigation or credentials.[529] Gannon could not have passed the necessary FBI background check to get access to the White House. So how did he get in the White House? The incriminating fact is that the White House staff of George W. Bush arranged for Gannon to be given a new daily press pass each day. By doing that, they circumvented the security background check required for the press pool.[530] That was a deliberate evasion of the regular press credentialing that requires an FBI security check. Obviously, the White House staff knew that Gannon was a sodomite prostitute, otherwise they would not have made special provisions to circumvent the White House security protocol and sneak him into the White House. Clearly, President George W. Bush wanted Gannon in the White House and his staff saw that it was done.

It seems that sexual deviance is a Bush family value. Paul Joseph Watson reported for the *Jones Report* that President George W. Bush's father, President George H.W. Bush (also a member of Skull & Bones), found a way to get male prostitutes and children past White House security for sexual purposes.[531] Many of the young boys were flown to the White House from the Boys Town Catholic orphanage, which is near Omaha, Nebraska.[532] Watson summarizes the June 29, 1989 edition of *The Washington Times,* which detailed the nefarious

White House activity:

> On June 29, 1989, the Washington Times' Paul M. Rodriguez and George Archibald reported on a Washington D.C. prostitution ring that had intimate connections with the White House allegedly all the way up to President George H.W. Bush. According to the story, male prostitutes had been given access to the White House and the article also cited evidence of "abduction and use of minors for sexual perversion."[533]

It is notable that Kitty Kelley made no mention in her book of that very significant and incriminating evidence regarding President George H.W. Bush, revealed in Rodriguez and Archibald's report in *The Washington Times*. She certainly knew about it, as it was front page news, and she prides herself on the thoroughness of her research. It seems that Kitty Kelley and her publishers had limits on what they would reveal about the Bush family, which explains why she did not mention anything about the sodomy of George W. Bush.

God has unequivocally expressed his abhorrence of sodomy. "Thou shalt not lie with mankind, as with womankind: it is abomination." Leviticus 18:22. "If a man also lie with mankind, as he lieth with a woman, both of them have committed an abomination." Leviticus 20:13.

God was so angry with the abominable sin that "the Lord rained upon Sodom and upon Gomorrah brimstone and fire from the Lord out of heaven." Genesis 19:24. Sodomites to this day avoid calling their sin sodomy in order to conceal the memory of God's judgement upon Sodom and Gomorrah for such deviant conduct. It is common today to call their sinful lifestyle "gay," when there is nothing gay about it. God's view did not change with his coming as Jesus Christ. We read in 1 Corinthians 6:9-10:

> Know ye not that the unrighteous shall not inherit the kingdom of God? Be not deceived: neither fornicators, nor idolaters, nor adulterers, **nor effeminate, nor abusers of themselves with mankind**, nor thieves, nor covetous, nor drunkards, nor revilers, nor extortioners,

shall inherit the kingdom of God. 1 Corinthians 6:9-10 (emphasis added).

George W. Bush's political conduct confirmed the sodomy revelations of Skolnick and McKonnel. President George W. Bush used naive Christians to get elected, but he had nothing but contempt for Christians and their morally upright principles. David Kuo, who worked for President Bush in the White House, stated that Christians and their church leaders were used by President Bush for political purposes. Kuo wrote in his book, *Tempting Faith*, that "National Christian leaders received hugs and smiles in person and then were dismissed behind their backs and described as 'ridiculous,' 'out of control,' and just plain 'goofy.'"[534] The Christian leaders did not perceive they were being used and gave their blind support for President Bush. Indeed, while George W. Bush spoke a good game regarding his Christian values, his conduct revealed his real character. His actions as president reveal that he embraced the sodomite subculture. Texe Marrs explains:

> Many insiders snicker and laugh ha, ha, ha, at brain-dead Christian evangelicals who actually believe that George W. [Bush] is a God-fearing heterosexual, born again Christian. As David Kuo, former top White House adviser in the Bush Administration, reveals in his new book, Tempting Faith, the Bush White House team sneers and jokes about the evangelicals so easily deceived by the President. Kuo presents evidence that the Bush people view Christian evangelical leaders and their flocks as ridiculous, silly, nuts, even insane. To the Bush people, Christianity is a farce and Christians are easily duped idiots. ... Since assuming the presidency, George W. has surrounded himself with gay men. The White House is jokingly referred to as the "Pink House" by the Gay Community. First, there's Karl Rove, Bush's campaign chief. Rove's father was gay, and Rove himself is a queer. ... Bush appointed Ken Mehlman, a Jewish homosexual, as the Chairman of the Republican National Committee. Think of it—a homo as titular head of the entire Republican Party! Bush also named his gay roommate at Yale University, Tennessee's [former mayor of Knoxville] Victor Ashe,

Ambassador to Poland. As Global AIDS Coordinator, another Ambassador-rank position, Bush chose homosexual activist Mark R. Dybul. Secretary of State Condi Rice administered the oath of office to the new appointee, recognizing Dybul's gay lover and live-in partner, Jason. Condi, a reputed lesbian dominatrix, even permitted the Ambassador's homo partner, Jason, to hold the Bible upon which Dybul laid his hand while taking the oath of office. President Bush has more homosexuals in his Administration than Bill Clinton, and he's more than accommodated their "special needs." For example, Bush appointed a queer to be the new Ambassador to Romania, then approved the man's sodomite lover to fly off with him in a U.S. aircraft to Bucharest, the capital of that nation, where the gay Ambassador and his lover now contently shack-up together in an embassy-leased mansion, at U.S. taxpayers' expense. The two sodomites even attend official functions together. ... And there's more. George W. Bush was the first President to have formal public meetings in the Oval Office with the Log Cabin Republicans group—a merry band of GOP queers into politics.[535]

Marrs reveals the little known fact that George W. Bush's 2005 appointment to Chief Justice of the Supreme Court, John Roberts, in 1996 worked as a lawyer *pro bono* (free of charge) on behalf of sodomites to overturn Colorado's Constitutional provision that prevented sodomites from having any special protected status or preferential treatment beyond any other citizen under the laws of the state. Robert's efforts were instrumental in the success of the case, where the U.S. Supreme Court struck down the Colorado Constitutional provision in *Romer vs. Evans*[536]. Richard A. Serrano of the Los Angeles Times reported:

> The lawyer who asked for Roberts' help on the case, Walter A. Smith Jr., then head of the pro bono department at Hogan & Hartson, said Roberts didn't hesitate. "He said, 'Let's do it.' And it's illustrative of his open-mindedness, his fair-mindedness. He did a

brilliant job." Roberts did not mention his work on the case in his 67-page response to a Senate Judiciary Committee questionnaire, released Tuesday. The committee asked for "specific instances" in which he had performed pro bono work, how he had fulfilled those responsibilities, and the amount of time he had devoted to them.

Walter Smith claimed the omission by Roberts of his *pro bono* work on behalf of sodomites was probably just an oversight, because Roberts was not the chief litigator in *Romer vs. Evans*.[537] That excuse just does not pass the smell test. One does not have to be the chief litigator to be instrumental in preparing an appellate case for oral arguments. That is like the getaway driver in an armed robbery claiming that he forgot he took part in the robbery because he was only the getaway driver. How could Roberts not have remembered a case where he gave instrumental advice to the lead attorney and even spent hours playing the role of a Supreme Court Justice in order to prepare the litigators for their oral arguments? Serrano reveals:

> Jean Dubofsky, lead lawyer for the gay rights activists and a former Colorado Supreme Court justice, said that when she came to Washington to prepare for the U.S. Supreme Court presentation, she immediately was referred to Roberts. "Everybody said Roberts was one of the people I should talk to," Dubofsky said. "He has a better idea on how to make an effective argument to a court that is pretty conservative and hasn't been very receptive to gay rights."[538]

Dubofsky characterized Roberts' advice as "absolutely crucial." While Roberts may have deceived the Senate and the American people about his sodomite sympathies, President Bush knew all about it. Indeed, that was likely the reason Roberts was selected as Chief Justice. The country is now suffering under Roberts' most notable reprobate legal ruling in *National Federation of Independent Business v. Sebelius*,[539] wherein he upheld the constitutionality of Obamacare.

Karen Frazier Romero, in her book, *While They Slept*, opines that Obamacare is part of a centuries-old conspiracy by the Roman

Catholic Church:

> Healthcare in the United States is very important in the takeover plan by Satan's Jesuit Order. This too has been in the works for well over a hundred years. In 1888, Justin Fulton writes, "Is it a surprising fact, that every hospital in Washington is in the hands of Roman Catholics…" *Washington in the Lap of Rome*, Justin Fulton, Hardpress Publishing, 1888, page 87. The "Sisters of Mercy," which are Roman Catholic nuns, ran the hospitals at this time and there were countless stories of Protestants being denied care. These Protestants were "heretics" in their eyes, so it was doing the Church of Rome a great service by allowing them to die. The Reverend J.W. Parker of E-Street Baptist Church of Washington, D.C. related that his own brother was in a Washington hospital where the nuns were the nurses and he had asked for a drink of water in the night. He overheard the nun say, "He is a heretic; let him choke." There are other horror stories of those who were treated worse than a stray dog in the hospitals of Washington. Could it be that Obamacare will discriminate care for those who do not agree with the "standard" belief system set forth?[540]

Paul Campos reported for *Salon* that Chief Justice Roberts changed his vote at the last minute in the Obamacare case, thus giving the victory to the socialists.[541] It turns out that the principal dissenting opinion in *Sebelius*[542] was initially supposed to be the majority opinion striking down Obamacare as unconstitutional. Both the majority and three-quarters of the dissenting opinions were drafted by Roberts. The other conservative justices, as a silent protest over Roberts' duplicity, left the principal dissenting opinion unsigned; it simply lists their names, with no indication of authorship. Because the principal dissenting opinion was initially supposed to be the majority opinion, the majority opinion is not mentioned in the first 46 pages of that dissenting opinion. What would cause such a change in Roberts' opinion? Such an extreme change of opinion does not happen, except in the face of a compelling threat or reward. It is reasonable to conclude that Roberts was blackmailed; he was offered a carrot or a stick. He chose the carrot and immediately fled to the Roman Catholic enclave of Malta to receive it. According to Meghan Keneally of the Daily Mail, after rendering his Obamacare ruling, "Chief Justice John Roberts fled the country on Tuesday opting to take up temporary residence in an 'impregnable island fortress'."[543]

U.S. Supreme Court Chief Justice John Roberts arriving at the enclave of the Knights of Malta shortly after rendering his opinion upholding Obamacare.

Of course, we find the hidden hand of the papacy working behind the scenes to install a new socialist order in the United States. It is notable that Chief Justice John Roberts slunk off to Malta after authoring both the majority opinion and most of the dissenting opinion in an incomprehensible decision upholding Obamacare in *National Federation of Independent Business v. Sebelius*.[544] Malta is an Island in the Mediterranean that is the home of a Roman Catholic secret society known as the Knights of Malta. Texe Marrs explains:

> Universal socialized healthcare has long been the goal of the Vatican and its Secret Societies. So when U.S. Supreme Court Chief Justice John Roberts single-handedly forced United States citizens to accept President Obama's unsavory and heavily socialist "ObamaCare" legislation with his deciding (5-4) vote, the American judge, a devout Roman Catholic, won the immediate acclaim of his brothers in such secretive and infamous groups as the Knights of Malta and Opus Dei. Off to the "Impregnable Fortress" in Malta. Immediately after casting his vote and writing the majority opinion on ObamaCare, John Roberts told the Washington, D.C. press corps that, to escape the furor and controversy that erupted, he was heading to an "impregnable fortress to escape." Roberts choice of

words was carefully coded with secret and embedded meaning. That impregnable fortress, as it turns out, was to the Mediterranean island of Malta, the unofficial citadel of the papacy's Knights of Malta. It was to Malta where, after their stunning defeat in Jerusalem, the Knights and crusaders had retreated to what they referred to as their "impregnable fortress." It was on this same geographic island location where, in 1989, President George H. W. Bush and Soviet President Mikhail Gorbachev had met on ships in the harbor and forged the "New World Order." While the two leaders conferred on-ship, Gorby's wife, Raisa, dressed in a symbolic, Communist red-colored dress, was taken on a pilgrimage to the Knights of Malta's historic St. John's Chapel, where a statue of Jesus' mother, Mary, holds forth as the chosen icon. It sits on the exact spot where there were found ancient ruins of a great temple devoted to Goddess worship. At Malta, U.S. Judge Roberts was met by the top potentates of the Rome-headquartered Knights of Malta, including Grand Master Matthew Festig of Great Britain. Also on hand to congratulate Justice Roberts on his monumental socialist "achievement" was Herman Van Rompuy of Belgium, a Bilderberg leader who is currently the President of the European Council.[545]

Texe Marrs and others have alleged that Chief Justice Roberts is a sodomite.[546] This author revealed in his book, *Bloody Zion*, how politicians are often compromised through some hidden embarrassment of sufficiently criminal or repugnant nature that the targeted politician dares not allow it to be revealed. The targeted politician is threatened with exposure if he does not obey his socialist/Zionist political masters' dictates, which step-by-step move the world toward a new antichrist, socialist world order. The threat of exposure could very well account for Roberts' sudden (and otherwise unexplainable) change of opinion.

The strategy of political blackmail is perhaps most succinctly explained in paragraph three of Protocol 8 of the Protocols of the Learned Elders of Zion:

> For a time, until there will no longer be any risk in entrusting responsible posts in our State to our brother-Jews, we shall put them in the hands of persons whose past and reputation are such that between them and the people lies an abyss, persons who, in case of disobedience to our instructions, must face criminal charges or disappear - this in order to make them defend our interests to their last gasp.[547]

The strange last-moment change of opinion by Chief Justice Roberts, combined with his conduct of immediately thereafter leaving the country over the furor and arriving at the compound of the politically influential Knights of Malta, was bizarre in the extreme. His behavior has all the earmarks of political blackmail.

It is also known that President Barrack Obama is a sodomite, and that fact is no doubt used to keep him obedient to his Zionist masters. Jerome Corsi (Harvard, Ph.D.), reported for WorldNet Daily that "[f]ormer radical activist John Drew has said that when he met Obama when Obama was a student at Occidental College, he thought Obama and his then-Pakistani roommate were 'gay' lovers."[548] Indeed, Obama's sodomite activities were generally known in the gay community in the Chicago area. Corsi interviewed Kevin DuJan, who is the founder and editor of the Hillary Clinton-supporting website HillBuzz.org. DuJan told Corsi that "he has first-hand information from two different sources that 'Obama was personally involved in the gay bar scene.'"[549]

Investigative journalist Wayne Madsen, who formerly worked with the National Security Agency from 1984 to 1988 as a Navy intelligence analyst, confirmed what DuJan said. "'It is common knowledge in the Chicago gay community that Obama actively visited the gay bars and bathhouses in Chicago while he was an Illinois state senator,' Madsen told WND."[550]

There is more than just hearsay information about President Obama being a sodomite. Larry Sinclair, a sodomite himself, claimed that he had sex and used cocaine twice with Obama while Obama was an Illinois state senator.[551] Furthermore, Sinclair reveals that in October 2007, Donald Young told him that he was sexually involved with then-

United States Senator Barrack Obama.[552]

Donald Young, was the choir master at Trinity United Church of Christ, which was the church attended by Barrack Obama. That church was presided over at the time by the black racist preacher Jeremiah Wright. Young apparently knew too much. Donald Young was found murdered with multiple gunshot wounds on December 24, 2007, in his Chicago apartment.[553] Robbery was not the motive, as nothing was taken from the apartment. His Christmas presents were not touched. Young's murder was preceded by the November 17, 2007, execution-style murder of 25-year-old Larry Bland, another black gay member of the church attended by Barrack Obama.[554] Dead men tell no tales.

That strange hand-holding by Bush and Prince Abdullah is something that one would only expect among sodomites. It required the U.S. media to explain the conduct. No matter how it is spun to make it acceptable, *The New York Times* had to admit it was an accommodation for the custom of the segregation of the sexes in Islamic countries.

The New York Times did not dare to tell the whole story that the custom of Islamic men holding hands has a sexual meaning. The complete explanation would require the paper to reveal that the practice of Islamic men holding hands is a manifestation of the pervasive sodomite subculture caused by the misogyny of Islam. Jim Kouri, the Vice President and Public Information Officer of the National Association of Chiefs of Police explains:

> Those who believe in the sacredness and infallibility of the Koran adhere to the teaching that women are sub-human and quasi-slaves, and therefore Muslim men will look for relationships -- even sexual relationships -- with others of their own gender.[555]

Sodomy is rampant in Islamic countries. One of the principles of Islam is that unrelated men and women cannot socialize together. This has the tendency to divide a country into sexual camps, where men congregate with men and women with women. This artificial division of the sexes has given rise to a culture of sodomy in Islamic countries. In Islamic culture, being sodomized by men is viewed almost as a stage that boys must pass through. Nadya Labi, reporting for The Atlantic, wrote about the pervasive sodomite culture in Saudi Arabia:

> "Homosexuality is considered something one might pass by," he said. "It's to be understood as a stage of life, particularly at youth." This view of sexual behavior, in combination with the strict segregation of the sexes, serves to foster homosexual acts, shifting the stigma onto bottoms and allowing older men to excuse their younger behavior—their time as bottoms—as mere youthful transgressions.[556]

Young boys are viewed as prey for the lusts of Muslim men. Labi states:

> Yasmin, the student who told me about the lesbian enclave at her college, said that her 16-year-old brother, along with many boys his age, has been targeted by his male elders as a sexual object. "It's the land of sand and sodomites," she said. "The older men take advantage of the little boys." Dave, the American educator, puts it this way: "Let's say there's a group of men sitting around in a café. If a smooth-faced boy walks by, they all stop and make approving comments. They're just noting, 'That's a hot little number.'"[557]

This sodomite subculture is accommodated in Islamic countries. Labi explains how the child victim later grows up to become the victimizer:

> However much this may seem like sophistry, it is in keeping with a long-standing Muslim tradition of accommodating homosexual impulses, if not homosexual identity. In 19th-century Iran, a young beardless adolescent was considered an object of beauty—desired by men—who would grow naturally into an older bearded man who desired youthful males.[558]

Indeed, many homosexuals find that the Islamic countries offer them the perfect cover for their sodomy. Labi explains:

> Many gay expatriates say they feel more at home in the kingdom [of Saudi Arabia] than in their native lands. Jason, a South African educator who has lived in Jeddah since 2002, notes that although South Africa allows gay marriage, "it's as though there are more gays here."[559]

Labi states that the prevalence of sodomy in Saudi Arabia is so great that laws against such behavior are rarely or only selectively enforced.

> [T]hey believe the House of Saud isn't interested in a widespread hunt of homosexuals. For one thing, such an effort might expose members of the royal family to awkward scrutiny. "If they wanted to arrest all the gay people in Saudi Arabia," Misfir, my chat-room guide, told me—repeating what he says was a police officer's comment—"they'd have to put a fence around the whole country."[560]

In Islamic countries, the segregation of the sexes has contributed to rampant homosexual pederasty. In Afghanistan, for example, Islamic men engage in what is called "bacha bazi" (playing with boys), where they sexually exploit pre-pubescent boys, who are called "bacha," "dancing boys" and "chai boys." Islamic pederasts in Afghanistan see nothing morally wrong with sodomizing young boys. Jim Kouri explains:

> Even after marriage, many men keep their boy-lovers, according to former U.S. military personnel who served in Afghanistan. That helps explain why women are compelled to wear clothing that hides their faces and bodies and if they "sin" they are stoned to death in accordance with Islamic law. That same law also forbids homosexuality, but the pedophiles explain that it's not homosexuality since they aren't in love with their boys only fulfilling a bodily need.[561]

One Islamic pederast told Ernesto Londono, a reporter from the Washington Post, that the segregation of the sexes creates a culture that encourages even married men in Afghanistan to use dancing boys for their sexual pleasure.

> "You cannot take wives everywhere with you," he said, referring to the gender segregation in social settings that is traditional in Afghanistan. "You cannot take a wife with you to a party, but a boy you can take anywhere."[562]

Joel Brinkley explains the shock felt by the western military personnel who were exposed to the rampant pederasty in Afghanistan:

> Western forces fighting in southern Afghanistan had a problem. Too often, soldiers on patrol passed an older man walking hand-in-hand with a pretty young boy. Their behavior suggested he was not the boy's father. Then, British soldiers found that young Afghan men were actually trying to "touch and fondle them," military investigator Anna Maria Cardinalli told me. "The soldiers didn't understand." All of this was so disconcerting that the Defense Department hired Cardinalli, a social scientist, to examine this mystery. Her report, "Pashtun Sexuality," startled not even one Afghan. But Western forces were shocked - and repulsed. For centuries, Afghan men have taken boys, roughly 9 to 15 years old, as lovers. Some research suggests that half the Pashtun tribal members in Kandahar and other southern towns are bacha baz, the term for an older man with a boy lover. Literally it means "boy player." The men like to boast about it. "Having a boy has become a custom for us," Enayatullah, a 42-year-old in Baghlan province, told a Reuters reporter. "Whoever wants to show off should have a boy."[563]

Vlad Tepes also discovered the dismay and disgust of western soldiers deployed to Afghanistan, who were appalled by the pedophilia in the Islamic culture.

Former Canadian soldier Tyrel Braaten said that during his tour of duty in Afghanistan in 2006, he witnessed Afghan interpreters bringing young boys inside buildings at Forward Operating Base Wilson, a remote Canadian base outside Kandahar. The boys were then sodomized by the interpreters and Afghan soldiers, Braaten said. (Westhead [B] 2008) "The boy was no more than 12. He wore a wig, lipstick and perfume and was dressed in a flowing robe when an Afghan interpreter escorted him to the entrance of the Canadian base in remote Afghanistan. The bombardier was bewildered. He asked another interpreter standing next to him who the boy was. The interpreter shrugged that the boy was one of "the bitches." "I said, `What do you mean?' and he made the motion with his hips, like you know," said Braaten, 24. "I remember saying, 'Are we on Mars? Does this s— go on all the time?'"... Braaten said he heard the boy's cries from the building. ... (Westhead [A] 2008)[564]

The prevalence of pederasty in Afghanistan is a direct result of the misogyny of Islam. Joe Brinkley explains:

Sociologists and anthropologists say the problem results from perverse interpretation of Islamic law. Women are simply unapproachable. Afghan men cannot talk to an unrelated woman until after proposing marriage. Before then, they can't even look at a woman, except perhaps her feet. Otherwise she is covered, head to ankle. "How can you fall in love if you can't see her face," 29-year-old Mohammed Daud told reporters. "We can see the boys, so we can tell which are beautiful." Even after marriage, many men keep their boys, suggesting a loveless life at home. A favored Afghan expression goes: "Women are for children, boys are for pleasure." Fundamentalist imams, exaggerating a biblical passage on menstruation, teach that women are "unclean" and therefore distasteful. One married man even asked Cardinalli's team "how his wife could become pregnant," her report said.

When that was explained, he "reacted with disgust" and asked, "How could one feel desire to be with a woman, who God has made unclean?" That helps explain why women are hidden away - and stoned to death if they are perceived to have misbehaved. Islamic law also forbids homosexuality. But the pedophiles explain that away. It's not homosexuality, they aver, because they aren't in love with their boys.[565]

The culture of abuse perpetuates itself. The chai boys look toward the day when they can have their own chai boys. Brinkley states: "As one boy, in tow of a man he called 'my lord,' told the Reuters reporter: 'Once I grow up, I will be an owner, and I will have my own boys.'"[566]

Qhattab Khan, Sangin District Assistant Chief of Police in Afghanistan justified the rape of little boys: "'If they don't [*profane verb deleted*] the asses of those boys, what should they [*profane verb deleted*]?' he asks at one point. 'The [*profane noun deleted*] of their own grandmothers? Their asses were used before, and now they want to get what they are owed.'"[567] Kahn's attitude seems to be the accepted view of child rape among Afghanistani Muslims. Robert Long explains:

> The State Department has called bacha baazi a "widespread, culturally sanctioned form of male rape." For instance, one military intelligence reservist related a story about an Afghan colonel who stood before a judge after he hurt a chai boy by violently raping him: "His defense was, 'Honestly, who hasn't raped a chai boy? Ha ha ha.' The judge responds, 'You're right. Case dismissed.'" Cracking down on this practice is nearly impossible, as the main culprits are often the very law enforcement and military personnel that the U.S. works alongside. In the documentary "The Dancing Boys of Afghanistan" (2010), police officials insist that sex traffickers of young boys will be arrested; later that day, two of the same officers are filmed at a bacha baazi party.[568]

Keep in mind the Islamic pederasts are devout Muslims, who

take their religion seriously. For example, at the conclusion of the interview of the Islamic pederasts by reporter Ernesto Londono, the following exchange took place:

> "Are you Muslim?" one asked. I told them I am not. They asked me to convert then and there. Baffled, I told them I would think about it, and walked out.[569]

The Islamic religion is rather indefinite on the issue of pederasty, which may explain why it is so accepted. The Islamic Sunnah seems to prohibit homosexuality, however, some have alleged that the Quran alludes to pederasty as a reward for believers in heaven. For example, Quran Sura 52.24 states: "And round them shall go boys of theirs as if they were hidden pearls." See also, Quran Suras 56.17-18 and 76.19. The passages in the Quran are ambiguous enough to have alternative meanings, one innocent, the other deviant. Sodomites looking for justification for their conduct, interpret the passages in the Quran to justify sodomy.

One could argue that the passages in the Quran are being misinterpreted by the sodomites, because the licentious interpretation of those passages seems to conflict with the Sunnah. The apparent conflict between the Quran and the Sunnah, however, is not real. Under the Islamic religion, the Quran has primacy over the Sunnah. The seeming conflict between the Quran and the Sunnah on sodomy has been resolved by Muslims by interpreting the prohibition of homosexuality in the Sunnah in such a way that it does not altogether prohibit the practice of sodomy. Muslims have a very narrow definition of what it is to be a homosexual. In the Islamic culture, engaging in sodomy does not necessarily mean that one is a homosexual. Vlad Tepes explains that while homosexuality between men is said by many to be prohibited by Islam, Muslims justify sodomy of children, because there is no affection involved; it is simply a brutal subjugation of a weaker male by a stronger male. That interpretation brings the Sunnah in accord with the Quran. Raping boys is not considered prohibited homosexuality; it is accepted in Islamic culture. It seems that the above passages in the Quran give Islamic sodomites succor in justifying their conduct.

Islam may kill 'homosexuals' but homosexuality is

regarded as an affectionate/loving relationship between men while the rapes or other abuse of males for means of subjugation or humiliation are not a problem. Islam's text that is filled with loathing for women and the segregation of males and females creates the distorted social, emotional and psychological environment that breeds this unacceptable abuse of young boys or weaker males.[570]

Tepes reveals that pederasty is so ingrained in Islamic culture that famous Islamic poets extol the pleasures of pedophilia.

Indeed throughout the Arab/Islamic world sex with boys has been common. Many great Arabic poets glorified homosexuality with boys e.g., Abu Nuwas 'O the joy of sodomy! So now be sodomites you Arabs…Turn not away from it-therein is wondrous pleasure. Take some coy lad with kiss-curls twisting on his temple and ride him as he stands like some gazelle standing to her mate. A lad whom all can see girt with sword and belt not like your whore who has to go veiled…..Make for smooth faced boys and do your very best to mount them, for women are the mounts of devils! (Perfumed Garden and Thousand and one nights Abu Nuwas- cited in Circe 2007 Islam's lust and loathing of homosexuality).[571]

Vlad Tepes explains that the sexual abuse of young boys is prevalent throughout the Islamic countries.

Such abuse is not limited to Afghanistan but is widespread across the Islamic world. Pakistan: At least 95 percent of truck drivers in Pakistan consider indulging in sexual activities during their rest time as their main entertainment.[572]

Tepes gives an example of a terrible disfigurement of a young boy in Pakistan who refused the overtures of the Islamic religious cleric to sodomize him.

> Sexual abuse of boys is endemic in madrasses: On his hospital bed last week, 16-year-old Abid Tanoli sat listless and alone, half of his body covered by burns that all but destroyed both his eyes and left his face horribly disfigured.... The boy refused to have sex with a cleric, his teacher at a religious school or madrassa in Pakistan.
>
> Abid, who was 14 at the time, told neither parents nor friends what had happened because, he said, he was ashamed. A few days later, as he played with his brothers and sister at home, he said that his religious teacher – accompanied by three associates – broke into the house, bolted the door and threw acid over him, screaming: "This should be a lesson for your life."
>
> Religious authorities pressed the hospital to discharge Abid and offered his parents money to withdraw the charges. His father moved to a secret location for his safety.[573]

The horrifying man-on-boy pedophilia is endemic in Islamic countries. There are no voices in government, however, being raised in protest against it. Ernesto Londono reported for the *Washington Post*:

> But by and large, foreign powers in Afghanistan have refrained from drawing attention to the issue. ... "It is very sensitive and taboo in Afghanistan," said Hayatullah Jawad, head of the Afghan Human Rights Research and Advocacy Organization, who is based in the northern city of Mazar-e Sharif. "There are a lot of people involved in this case, but no one wants to talk about it." ... Afghan photojournalist Barat Ali Batoor, who spent months chronicling the plight of dancing boys. Some turn to drugs or alcohol, he said. ... When Batoor completed his project on dancing boys, he assumed that nongovernmental organizations would be eager to exhibit his work and raise awareness of the issue. To his surprise, none were. ... "They said: 'We don't want to make enemies in Afghanistan,'" he said,

> summarizing the general response. ... [Dee Brillenburg Wurth, a child-protection expert at the U.N. mission in Afghanistan stated]"It's rampant in certain areas," Wurth said. ... But, so far, the government has taken few meaningful steps to discourage the abuse of bachas. Wurth said she was not aware of any prosecutions. "A kid who is being sexually exploited, if he reports it, he will end up in prison," she said. "They become pariahs."[574]

Why are there no efforts to even begin to address such an abominable practice? Jim Kouri has uncovered the reason for the apathy over trying to put a stop to Islamic pederasty.

> Why is there hesitation on the part of Obama, Clinton, Panetta and others to discuss the widespread sexual assault of male children in Afghanistan? Could it be that it is politically incorrect to discuss any immoral and unlawful behavior on the part of Muslims? It's quite evident that U.S. politicians may bash Christians without fear of adverse effects on their political careers. But these same leaders will behave as if they are walking on egg shells to avoid even the hint of criticizing Muslims. In addition, there is always a hesitation to discuss man-on-boy sexual relationship for fear of mentioning the obvious: such a relationship is homosexual in nature.[575]

The lesbian, gay, bisexual, transgender (a/k/a LGBT) community together with the Islamic countries have such political sway, the topic of Islamic pederasty is quite simply off-limits. Michael Swift's 1987 Gay Manifesto reveals the dirty secret of the LGBT rights movement. The LGBT community wants the right to sodomize children. The Gay Manifesto brazenly states: "We shall sodomize your sons. ... We shall seduce them in your schools, ... in your locker rooms, ... in your youth groups. ... Your sons shall become our minions and do our bidding. They will be recast in our image."[576]

This predatory sexual agenda of the LGBT community has been confirmed by researchers. Former California State Assemblyman Steve

Baldwin researched the connection between the homosexual movement and child molestation. He published his findings in the Spring 2002 Regent University Law Review. Baldwin found that "[s]cientific studies confirm a strong pedophilic predisposition among homosexuals."[577] One 1988 study published in the *Archives of Sexual Behavior*, reported that 86% of pedophiles who victimized boys "described themselves as homosexual or bisexual."[578] Research statistics further show that homosexuals, as a population, molest children at a rate that is ten to twenty times greater than heterosexuals.[579] Those facts are well known in the homosexual community. San Francisco's leading homosexual newspaper, *The Sentinel*, bluntly states that "[t]he love between man and boys is at the foundation of homosexuality."[580]

Baldwin found that "the mainstream homosexual culture commonly promotes sex with children. Homosexual leaders repeatedly argue for the freedom to engage in consensual sex with children."[581] He determined that one of the principal aims of the LGBT rights movement is the legalization and promotion of child molestation. Mainstream LGBT organizations such as the International Lesbian and Gay Association (ILGA) and the National Coalition of Gay Organizations have passed many organizational resolutions calling for lowering or eliminating age of sexual consent laws, as a way to legalize pedophilia.[582]

Any campaign to stop pederasty will necessarily reveal the reprobation of Islam and interfere with the political aims of the LGBT rights movement. The LGBT community, in particular, has significant political influence. For example, President Barack Obama is a strident advocate of LGBT privileges.[583] David Axelrod, who was a top White House adviser to Barrack Obama, reveals in his book, *Believer: My Forty Years in Politics*, that Barack Obama outright lied to Americans when, in 2008, he stated that he opposed same-sex marriage.[584] Obama lied in order to gain the support of black church leaders during his campaign for President of the United States. Axelrod wrote in his book that Obama told him "I'm just not very good at bullshitting," after Obama was apparently dissatisfied with the quality of his dissimilation at a political event, where he stated that he opposed same-sex marriage. Axelrod admitted that he knew that Obama was in favor of same-sex marriages during the first presidential campaign, when Obama was publicly stating that he opposed same-sex marriages.

In 1996, Obama answered a political questionnaire, when running for the Illinois State Senate as follows: "I favor legalizing same-sex marriages, and would fight efforts to prohibit such marriages."[585] However, in 2008, when he was running for President, he lied about his true beliefs in order to get elected. Obama told Pastor Rick Warren, during a public interview at Saddleback Church: "I believe that marriage is a union between a man and a woman. ... For me as a Christian, it is also a sacred union ... you know, God's in the mix. ... I am not somebody who promotes same-sex marriage, but I do believe in civil unions."[586]

Once Obama was elected President, however, he began to act on his true political beliefs and jammed sodomites down the throats of federal agencies and the military. In June 2009, President Obama "expanded federal benefits for same-sex partners of federal employees and allowed same-sex domestic partners to apply for long-term care insurance."[587] In addition, on December 22, 2010, he signed the bill repealing the "don't ask, don't tell" military policy that previously prohibited sodomites in the military.[588] As a result of that bill, sodomites in the military can now engage in sodomy and openly proclaim that they are sodomites, without fear of court martial. Indeed, sodomites in the military have been given special privileges. For example, their same-sex-partners are allowed "military identification cards, commissary and exchange shopping privileges."[589]

On May 9, 2012, in an interview on ABC News, Obama stated: "It is important for me personally to go ahead and affirm that same-sex couples should be able to get married."[590] Until that announcement in 2012, Obama had been pretending not to favor same-sex marriage. He, in fact, had been in favor of same-sex marriage since at least 1996, and he said so at that time. For political purposes, he had been lying about his true beliefs. He made it seem as though his 2012 announcement was some kind of new political position, when in fact he was on record as having favored sodomite marriages 16 years earlier. As a result of the political influence of the LGBT community, the brutalization of the children in Islamic countries continues unabated, without a peep of protest from the U.S. government, non-government organizations, or the United Nations. In the end, what really matters is God's view of sodomy. "Then the Lord rained upon Sodom and upon Gomorrah brimstone and fire from the Lord out of heaven." Genesis 19:24.

26 Common Root of Catholicism and Islam

The misogyny and pederasty in both the Catholic priesthood and among Islamic males may be caused by the fact that both Islam and Catholicism are deviant phallic religions that flow from Babylon. All ancient mystery religions are based upon phallicism.[591] Phallicism is the pantheistic worship of procreation in nature, with a focus on genitalia. Phallicism is a fetish theology, wherein the generative principle is represented through images of phalli and yonis. That is why there is a phallic obelisk in St. Peter's Square and Islamic mosques are surrounded by phallic minarets.

The crescent moon cradle used in the monstrance (which is always in the form of a sunburst) to hold the Eucharist signifies the joining of the sun (Eucharist) with the moon (the crescent cradle). That same symbolism is found in Islam, where flags often depict a star and a crescent moon, which symbolizes the sun joining with the moon. In both the Catholic monstrance and the Islamic flags, the representation has an occult meaning that

Monstrance With Crescent Moon Cradle

celebrates the generative power of the procreative act where the sun is the lingam and the moon is the yoni.

Phallicism was the central theme of the ancient mystery religions flowing from Babylon. Martin Wagner explains:

Flag of Pakistan

> The phallus was an essential part in the rites and symbolism of the mysteries. Its office was to convey to the initiated a profound and sacred meaning. It was a common object of worship and of ornament. Originally it had no other meaning than that union of male and female upon which depended the procreation of life.[592]

> The gods were male and female, and the worship of the sexual was prominent in these cults. The religious ideas were based upon the sexual facts, and grew out of a profound veneration for the generative principle. Ritual prostitution which was possibly a decadence, was a recognized and wide spread institution, and grew out of a purely religious point of view. At the shrine of Baal and Astarte in Phoenicia and similar sanctuaries elsewhere, sexual intercourse was a part of the rite.[593]

Phallus worship is in fact the oldest form of idolatry. Wagner explains:

> Monumental, historical, and philological evidence shows that phallus worship is among the oldest, if not the oldest form of idolatry. Reverence for the phallus or for phallic emblems shows itself in the earliest historic remains of Babylonia, Assyria, India, China, Japan, Persia, Phrygia, Scandinavia, France, Spain, Great Britain, North and South America, Africa, and in the islands of the sea. Phallicism is the bond that unites all forms of idolatry into one great system. It is the essential principle that pervades them. It is the basis of tree worship, animal worship, serpent worship, sun worship, and man worship. It was the basis of the

mysteries of Phrygia, Egypt, Greece and Rome. It is the basis of all the mythology of the past ages, for as Weiss says "Freemasonry (Phallicism?) may be traced in all the mythology to the remotest part of the globe."[594]

What is the cause of the commonality of the theology and practices of Islam and Catholicism? Former Jesuit priest Alberto Rivera received a secret Vatican briefing from Jesuit Cardinal Augustine Bea. Cardinal Bea told Rivera that Islam was the creation of the Vatican.[595] Alberto Rivera first explained the rise of the papacy:

> Corruption, apathy, greed, cruelty, perversion and rebellion were eating at the Roman Empire, and it was ready to collapse. The persecution against Christians was useless as they continued to lay down their lives for the gospel of Christ.
>
> The only way Satan could stop this thrust was to create a counterfeit "Christian" religion to destroy the work of God. The solution was in Rome. Their religion had come from ancient Babylon and all it needed was a face-lift. This didn't happen overnight, but began in the writings of the 'early church fathers'.
>
> It was through their writings that a new religion would take shape. The statue of Jupiter in Rome was eventually called St. Peter, and the statue of Venus was changed to the Virgin Mary. The site chosen for its headquarters was on one of the seven hills called 'Vaticanus', the place of the divining serpent where the satanic temple of Janus stood.
>
> The great counterfeit religion was Roman Catholicism, called 'Mystery, Babylon the Great, the Mother of Harlots and Abominations of the Earth'- Revelation 17:5. She was raised up to block the gospel, slaughter the believers in Christ, establish religions, create wars and make the nations drunk with the wine of her fornication as we will see.[596]

The Roman whore of Babylon over time was faced with a serious problem. True Christians in North Africa who preached the gospel were winning Christian converts who refused to submit to the pope. The Vatican decided that they needed to create a messiah for the Arabs, who would be trained by Rome to wipe out biblical Christianity in Arab lands and capture Jerusalem for Rome.

Muhammad (surname: Mustafa) was born in 570 A.D. and died 632 A.D. When Muhammad was 25, he married a wealthy 40 year-old woman named Khadija. The interesting thing about Khadija is that she was living in a Roman Catholic convent prior to her marriage to Muhammad. Her cousin, Waraquah, who had tremendous influence over Muhammad, was also a Roman Catholic. Rivera states that Khadija was on a mission from Rome to find a charismatic Arab to lead a new religion. Muhammad was her man. Muhammad was subjected to intensive training for his "great calling" from Catholic teachers.

Muhammad was instructed that his enemies were Jews and that the only true Christians were Roman Catholics. Muhammad was taught that any persons calling themselves Christians who were not Roman Catholic, were actually wicked impostors who should be destroyed. "Muhammad began receiving 'divine revelations' and his wife's Catholic cousin Waraquah helped interpret them. From this came the Koran [a/k/a Quran]." Rivera stated:

> In the fifth year of Muhammad's mission, persecution came against his followers because they refused to worship the idols in the Kaaba.
>
> Muhammad instructed some of them to flee to Abysinnia where Negus, the Roman Catholic king accepted them because Muhammad's views on the virgin Mary were so close to Roman Catholic doctrine. These Muslims received protection from Catholic kings because of Muhammad's revelations.

Muhammad later conquered Mecca and the Kaaba was cleared of idols. History proves that before Islam came into existence, the Sabeans in Arabia worshiped the moon-god [Allah] who was married to the sun-god. They gave birth to three goddesses who were worshipped throughout the Arab world as "Daughters of Allah." An idol excavated at Hazor in Palestine in the 1950's shows Allah sitting on a throne with the crescent moon on his chest.[597]

Ancient Idol of the Moon Deity, Allah, With Crescent Moon on His Chest

Once Muhammad gained acceptance and Islam became the accepted religion among the Arabs, the pope issued bulls granting the Arab generals permission to invade and conquer the nations of North Africa. The Vatican helped to finance the massive Islamic armies in exchange for three things: 1) Eliminate Christians (true believers, which they called infidels) and Jews; 2) Protect the Augustinian Monks and Roman Catholics; 3) Conquer Jerusalem for the pope.

The power of Islam became tremendous, true Christians were slaughtered, and Jerusalem fell into their hands. Neither Roman Catholics nor their shrines were attacked. The Islamic armies conquered Jerusalem. When the pope asked for Jerusalem, he was surprised at their denial. The Arab generals had such military success they were not intimidated by the pope. Rome had lost control of Islam. The Islamic armies sought to conquer Europe. This required Rome to mount the bloody crusades to stem the Islamic tide. After centuries of fighting, there was an impasse that resulted in a concordat (treaty) between the Vatican and Islam. Rivera explains the terms of the concordat:

As a result, the Muslims were allowed to occupy Turkey in the "Christian" world, and the Catholics were allowed to occupy Lebanon in the Arab world. It was also agreed that the Muslims could build mosques in Catholic countries without interference as long as Roman Catholicism could flourish in Arab countries.

Cardinal Bea told us in Vatican briefings that both the Muslims and Roman Catholics agreed to block and destroy the efforts of their common enemy, Bible-believing Christian missionaries. Through these concordats, Satan blocked the children of Ishmael from a knowledge of Scripture and the truth.

A light control was kept on Muslims from the Ayatollah down through the Islamic priests, nuns and monks. The Vatican also engineers a campaign of hatred between the Muslim Arabs and the Jews. Before this, they had co-existed peacefully.

The Islamic community looks on the Bible-believing missionary as a devil who brings poison to the children of Allah. This explains years of ministry in those countries with little results.[598]

Rivera's account seems so fantastic and incredible; it is hard to believe. There is one way to verify its truth. He claims that as part of the concordat Catholic Churches would be allowed in Arab countries. Let us look at the most conservative Islamic country, Saudi Arabia (which follows the ultra-conservative Hanbali school of Sunni Islam) and see if the concordat is being put into force. Nina Shea, who is director of Hudson Institute's Center for Religious Freedom and co-author of *Persecuted: The Global Assault on Christians* states that "Saudi Arabia is the only state in the world to ban all churches and any other non-Muslim houses of worship."[599] She further stated that "[d]istributing Bibles in Saudi Arabia is illegal."[600] The persecution of Christian churches has continued unabated. For example, in September 2014, Benjamin Weinthal reported for Fox News that 28 people were arrested at a prayer meeting in a home church in Kafji, Saudi Arabia, by hard-line Islamists from the Commission for the Promotion of Virtue and Prevention of Vice.[601] The arrests were based solely upon the fact that the arrestees were practicing their Christian faith. Weinthal reported that "an article posted on the Arabic-language news website Akhbar 24 said the arrests came after the Kingdom's religious police got a tip about a home-based church."[602] It seems that the concordat is being enforced against bible-believing Christians.

What about the protection of the Catholic Church? In 2008, the Saudi Arabian government allegedly refused to allow the building of a Catholic Church in Saudi Arabia.[603] Shea, writing in 2014, claimed that the Catholic Church was among the persecuted churches. "Priests must go undercover, pretending to be cooks or mechanics, to celebrate underground Masses for the estimated 1.5 million Filipino, Indian and other Catholics working or living there."[604] Furthermore, the Roman Catholic Apostolic Vicariate of Northern Arabia explains on its website:

> As Saudi Arabia is home to Islam's holiest sites, it does not permit churches to be built, as a result there are no Christian churches or places of worship. Non-Islamic religion is not recognized and its public display or activity is prohibited.[605]

That suggests that there might not be a concordat that protects the Catholic Church in Islamic countries. Further checking, however, reveals that the alleged Catholic persecution is carefully contrived false propaganda. The persecution of churches is aimed solely at bible-believing Christians. The proof that the persecution of the Catholic Church is a myth is found on a Roman Catholic website that contains a worldwide directory of Roman Catholic Churches. Lo-and-behold, what do we find? There are listed the names, addresses, phone numbers, fax numbers, and web addresses of four (4) Roman Catholic churches in Riyadh, which is the capital city of Saudi Arabia.[606] That is not including the Lady of Fatima Catholic Church located at 1st Fahad Street, Ash Sharqiyah 31932, in the city of Khobar, Saudi Arabia. That is particularly notable, since even clandestine attempts at Christian worship by bible-believing Christians in secret home churches results in arrest if the Islamic authorities are tipped off. Yet, the Roman Catholic Church has openly publicized addresses for their churches. The Catholic Church, obviously, is not concerned about arrest or persecution in Saudi Arabia.

It seems that the Vatican is engaged in a sophisticated media deception designed to conceal their hidden hand behind the persecution of bible-believing Christians in Islamic countries. They are falsely portraying the persecution of Christian churches as including the Roman Catholic Church, when in fact the Roman Church can operate freely and openly. In fact, a review of the Catholic Church Directory reveals that there is not a single Islamic country that does not have a Catholic Church that is allowed to practice freely and openly. All the while, bible believing Christians are hunted down and persecuted. The fact that the Roman Catholic Churches are allowed to operate openly in Islamic countries supports Alberto Rivera's information that there is a concordat between Islam and the Vatican to allow Catholic Churches to operate in Islamic countries while those Islamic countries persecute the true Christian church.

Raymond Ibrahim and Scott Allswang revealed how the official Muslim theology calls for the elimination of biblical Christianity in Islamic countries, which makes it the perfect religion to do the dirty work for the Vatican in North Africa and the Middle East.

> The Grand Mufti of Saudi Arabia, one of the Islamic world's highest religious authorities, declared that it is "necessary to destroy all the churches of the region." He made his assertion in response to a question posed by a delegation from Kuwait, where a parliament member recently called for the "removal" of all churches: the delegation wanted to confirm Sharia's position on churches with the Grand Mufti, who "stressed that Kuwait was a part of the Arabian Peninsula, and therefore it is necessary to destroy all churches in it," basing his verdict on a saying (or hadith) of Muhammad.[607]

Upon visiting the global directory of Catholic churches we find that there are thriving Catholic churches in Kuwait in the cities of Ahmadi, Kuwait City, Moroni, and Salmiya.[608] The Catholic Churches proudly post their addresses, phone numbers, fax numbers, and websites. One of the Catholic churches, Our Lady of Arabia Catholic Church, even has its weekly Mass schedule posted on the directory.[609] The Roman Catholic churches seem not to have been affected at all by the fatwa from the Grand Mufti of Saudi Arabia calling for the elimination of all the churches in the region.

There have been instances where Catholic priests, nuns, and churches have been attacked by Muslims in Arab countries. However, such incidents seem to be collateral consequences of the confusion among the rank and file Muslims, who equate Catholicism with Christianity. Mobs, once set in motion, are hard to control. The real target of the Muslim attacks is biblical Christianity.

According to the U.S. State Department's International Religious Freedom Report for 2012, in Afghanistan "there are no public Christian churches."[610] The report states that, because there are no public churches, "Afghan Christians worship alone or in small congregations in private homes."[611] Oddly, the religious persecution of the Christian church in Afghanistan has increased since the arrival of U.S. troops. According to a news reports "Afghanistan has seen a decrease in religious liberty in the past decade, especially since American troops have been active there."[612] The U.S. Government was instrumental in drafting and installing the 2004 Constitution of Afghanistan, which provided for an inviolable Islamic state, with no freedom of religion. At the time the Constitution of Afghanistan was approved, the country was under U.S. Military occupation. It is almost as if part and parcel of the military mission was to remove any Christian influence. That has certainly been the effect. Raymond Ibrahim and Scott Allswang reported:

> Ten years after the U.S. invaded and overthrew the Taliban—at a cost of more than 1,700 U.S. military lives and $440 billion in taxpayer dollars—the State Department revealed that Afghanistan's last Christian church was destroyed. The report further makes clear that the Afghan government—installed by the U.S.—is partially responsible for such anti-Christian sentiments, for instance, by upholding apostasy laws, which make it a criminal offence for Muslims to convert to other religions.[613]

Apparently, the Catholic Church has been given a pass on the persecution. At the time the U.S. State Department reported that there were no longer any public churches in Afghanistan, there was (and still is today) a publicly listed Catholic Church in the capital city of Kabul, Afghanistan. The Catholic directory listing for the church includes its schedule of Masses for every day of the week, including 10 services on Sundays from 6:15 a.m to 12:00 p.m.[614] That open listing on the internet can be seen by any Afghanistan government official or Islamic leader, yet the church remains unmolested.

Certainly the U.S. State Department was aware of the existence of the Catholic church in Kabul when it announced that there were no public churches in Afghanistan. Why would the U.S. State Department make such a statement in the face of clear contrary evidence? One could hope that it is because the U.S. State Department did not consider the Catholic religion a Christian religion and therefore did not count it as such when stating that there were no Christian churches in Afghanistan. However, that certainly is not the reason the Catholic church in Kabul was not mentioned in the State Department report. The reason it was not mentioned is because to report that there was only one church in Afghanistan, a Catholic church, would reveal too much. That information would give away the fact that only Protestant churches were targeted for destruction. That must be kept secret. The evidence of the targeting and wiping out public Christian churches, while leaving Roman Catholic churches untouched, is yet more contemporary evidence that confirms the claim by former Jesuit Alberto Rivera of a secret concordat between the Vatican and Islamic leaders to act in concert against their common enemy, biblical Christianity.

Alberto Rivera's assertion regarding the secret concordat between Islam and the Vatican, wherein Catholics were allowed to occupy Lebanon in the Arab world, is also supported by the evidence. For example, since 1943, Lebanon has operated as a consociational government under an informal agreement known as the "National Pact," with power sharing between Maronite "Christians" (a Roman Catholic sect) and Muslims. This informal agreement was memorialized, with some changes, in the 1989 Taif Agreement, which gave more authority to the Muslim majority in Lebanon, but maintained the hegemony of the Catholic minority over the Lebanese government. In Lebanon, the President must be a Maronite "Christian." Furthermore, "Christians" are guaranteed at least 50% of the seats in the Lebanese Parliament, even though they make up less than 40% of the population.

27 Proving the Awful Disclosures of Maria Monk

Catholic nuns do not fare much better than Islamic women. Rosamond Culbertson revealed how the Catholic priests of Cuba in the early 19th century would persuade the deluded families of Cuba to give them their daughters to enter the convent. The religious and political power of the priests in Cuba was so absolute that the parents dared not refuse the request of the priests. "The young ladies are obliged to enter the convent whether it is their wish or not."[615] The young girls would enter the cloistered convent after solemn ceremony where they parade though the streets, followed by their families and hundreds of priests. Unknown to the families of the young girls, the priestly foxes were herding the innocent hens into the convent for their destruction. The priests talked freely when drunk in the presence of Rosamond Culbertson about how they had planned on ravishing the prettiest of the new nuns who had taken the veil.

Charlotte Keckler (a/k/a Charlotte Wells) (1889-1983) wrote an exposé revealing torture and abuse that she suffered during the twenty two years she spent in a cloistered convent.[616] She initially entered into the convent voluntarily thinking that she would be serving the Lord Jesus, but soon found that she was serving the very church of the devil. Once she became a cloistered nun, she found that she was imprisoned with no way out. After twenty-two years she finally found an opportunity and made her escape. Charlotte revealed that the Catholic priests use the cloistered convents as private brothels. The nuns often became pregnant from fornicating with the Catholic priests. Upon giving birth, the newborn baby is murdered.

Charlotte Keckler stated:

Many have said I exaggerate and that these things are not so, but I have yet to be hauled into court to refute the charges. They would have to open the cloisters and this they dare not do. After being snared in this rotten system for twenty-two years, I know whereof I speak. Normal young expectant mothers eagerly anticipate the arrival of their precious baby. Everything is ready, nursery, crib, clothing, and everyone is happy with her. By contrast, a little nun in the convent dreads the moment when she gives birth. The child is the product of a shameful, illicit union with a drunken priest which was forced on her. She knows from bitter experience that the baby will only be permitted to live four or five hours at the very most. It will never be cleaned or wrapped in a warm blanket for Mother Superior will put her hand over its mouth and pinch its nostrils to snuff out its life.

This is why there are lime pits in all the convents. Babies' bodies are tossed in these holes to be destroyed. Pray for the government to force the convents to open their doors to release the prisoners and let the whole world see what horrors are hidden behind those doors of cruel religious hypocrisy.

If this happens, I assure you that even the Catholic people will agree to the closing of the convents as they did in Mexico in 1934. They have no idea what is transpiring there either, or they would never expose their daughters to such barbarous debauchery and torture.

The convents in old Mexico have been turned into government museums which you can tour for a modest fee. You should go and see with your own eyes and touch with your hands the things of which I speak. Go

> down into the dungeons, through the tunnels and torture chambers and see all the fiendish devices, demonically conceived, to inflict suffering on the bodies of helpless nuns. See for yourself the cells in which nuns were locked each night and examine the beds, and the prayer boards.[617]

There are other nuns who have escaped cloistered nunneries and have exposed to the world the awful life of torture and abuse suffered by those poor cloistered nuns. There is the account of Sarah J. Richardson, *Life in the Grey Nunnery at Montreal*.[618] Probably the most famous account of torture and abuse in a cloistered nunnery is the 1836 book by Maria Monk, *Awful Disclosures of the Hotel Dieu Nunnery of Montreal*.[619] The disturbing accounts by Maria Monk brought howls of protest from Catholic authorities and defenders that her book was full of lies. It is notable, however, that the refutation was always limited to denunciation and attacks on her character. They dared not seek justice in open court, where the truth of the matter would be determined in public and under strict rules of evidence. The Catholic authorities' objective was to conceal the truth by trying to discredit Maria Monk, not reveal the truth by letting the world view the evidence. During her lifetime, Maria Monk's character was falsely attacked.

> Maria Monk, however, refused to be shaken in her testimony, and steadfastly avowed the truth of what she had written. To those who doubted or disbelieved her statements she made the following challenge.

> "Permit me," she said, "to go through the Hotel Dieu Nunnery at Montreal with some impartial ladies and gentlemen, and they may compare my account with the interior parts of the building, into which no other persons but the Roman Bishop and Priests are ever admitted; and if they do not find my description true, then discard me as an impostor. Bring me before a court of justice—there I am willing to meet Latargue, Duireme, Phelan, Bonin and Richards, and their wicked companions, and the Superior and any of the Nuns before a thousand men."[620]

The Catholic authorities did not dare to take Maria Monk up on her offer, as they knew it would have substantiated her charges. The nunnery was never opened to a tour by her accompanied by objective witnesses, nor were any of the resident nuns ever permitted to be interviewed. Instead, the Catholic church mounted a campaign of character assassination from a distance. To this day, there are websites devoted to discrediting Miss Monk. Why do they take such efforts, even today, to discredit Maria Monk? Because the abominations that still go on today inside the cloistered nunneries of the Catholic orders. Indeed, while Maria Monk's revelations were shocking enough, there were crimes committed inside the Hotel Dieu Nunnery that were so disturbing, Maria Monk could not bring herself to reveal them in her book. Maria solemnly declared that "there are crimes committed in the Hotel Dieu Nunnery too abominable to mention."[621]

Maria Monk's book was widely read and sold over three hundred thousand copies by 1860. Her book revealed the debauchery of the Catholic priests and the cruel rape, torture, murder, and infanticide taking place inside the cloistered nunnery. The Catholic Church was desperate to discredit her. They spread scurrilous lies about her. It is the common scheme of the Catholic priests to allege that an escaped nun is crazy and is therefore not to be believed.

It is common practice for the Catholic hierarchy to allege that a nun who escapes or is a threat is insane. For example, in 1846 Lady Superior Josepha and a Catholic priest named Calenski conspired to have the priest sexually seduce Barbara Ubryk, who was a newly veiled nun in the Carmelite nunnery in Cracow (a/k/a Krakow), Poland. Barbara resisted the advances of the priest and created a scene by her loud objection. The Lady Superior Josepha arrived at the scene, and by her conversation with the priest, Barbara discovered that the lady superior was working in concert with the priest. Barbara accused them both to their faces of their apparent lecherous conspiracy.

The priest and lady superior immediately took steps to keep Barbara quiet. Their first step was to spread word throughout the convent that the loud scene was because Barbara Ubryk had gone insane. They then locked her in a eight foot by six foot dungeon. There she remained for 21 years.[622] The other nuns knew that she was in the cell, but were afraid to do anything out of fear of the lady superior and the priest. They probably eased their consciences by convincing themselves of the truth of the allegation that Barbara was insane. Barbara was finally released by the intervention of a kind nun. The nun sneaked down to the cell and upon speaking to Barbara and being convinced that she was not insane got word to the police through an intermediary.[623]

The Catholic Bishop, upon being informed by the police of the allegation of Barbara's captivity, did not believe the allegation. The bishop thus gave the police permission to enter the convent, so that the allegation could be proven false. Upon opening the cell, the officer was shocked and disgusted with what he saw and sent for the bishop, so he could see Barbara's naked, skeletal condition for himself. Upon seeing the condition of Barbara, the bishop withdrew the protection of the Catholic Church from the priest and the lady superior and turned them over to the civil authorities. Calenski ended up committing suicide and the lady superior was criminally prosecuted and convicted.[624]

Wikipedia, the online encyclopedia, is typical of the libelous traducements of insanity against Maria Monk being spread even today.

> There is some evidence that Maria Monk had suffered a brain injury as a child. One possible result of this injury was that Monk was easily manipulated, and was not able to distinguish between fact and fantasy. It has been suggested that Maria Monk was manipulated into playing a role for profit by her publisher or her ghost writers.[625]

What is the source of the alleged head injury story? It was first floated in an false affidavit published in a book by Catholic priests, *Awful Exposure of the Atrocious Plot*, which was published to rebut Maria's book, *Awful Disclosures*. The false affidavit states in pertinent part: "At the age of about seven years, she broke a slate pencil in her head; that since that time her mental faculties were deranged."[626] The author of the affidavit is purported to be Maria Monk's mother. While Maria Monk's mother's name is affixed to the affidavit printed in the book, an original of the affidavit with her mother's signature has never been produced. Why not? Because Maria Monk's mother never signed the affidavit. After the book containing the affidavit was published,

Maria Monk's mother revealed that the affidavit was not written by her.[627] She stated that the affidavit was written by someone else; she did not sign the affidavit but was prevailed upon by the Catholic priests not to contest the contents of the affidavit.[628] The book in which the affidavit appeared was so full of provable libel against Maria Monk that it bore no author's name.[629] The book was the deceptive contrivance of the Jesuit priests of Montreal.

The book attacking Maria Monk was so shameful that no one would claim it as his work. The book is the source of the many false averments against Maria Monk that to this day have been used as the basis to assassinate her character and attack her credibility.

Pastor J.J. Slocum in his 1837 book, *Confirmation of Maria Monk's Disclosures Concerning the Hotel Dieu Nunnery*, explains how an innocuous childhood pencil incident was seized upon by the Catholic priests as their foundation for spinning a false yarn alleging that Maria Monk was not an escaped nun but was instead a crazy women only pretending to be a former nun.

> On page 73 [of the Catholic priest's book attacking Maria Monk], we have the celebrated pencil story. It is as follows: "It appears that Maria, while at school, had her ear perforated by a slate pencil, and that a piece of the pencil has remained in her ear to this day. Her sufferings arising from this cause have been acute, and have led to the supposition that her intellect has been from the time of the accident, seriously and badly affected. It is known to medical jurisconsults, that no question is of more difficult determination than that of alleged insanity. Thus it has happened that the cause of her malady still subsists, and that she still endures its effects." To say the least, this is a curious piece of historic knowledge. There are, however, two statements in it, which are as distant from truth, as the southern from the northern pole. First, the declaration that a piece of a slate pencil remains in her ear to this day, is too ridiculously false to deserve hardly a passing notice.

The origin of the story is this; when Maria Monk was quite a child, she and another little girl were at play, and they put each into the other's ear a piece of slate pencil. Maria says the piece in her ear remained for some time; but she declares, that she cannot positively tell, now, whether it was in her right, or in her left ear. The assertion, therefore, that it remains to this day in her ear, and that she still suffers from it, is destitute of the least semblance of truth. But we are told that the pencil remains, seriously affecting her intellect, and producing, if not absolute insanity, "strange flightiness and unaccountable irregularities." But to talk of an effect without a cause, is an absurdity; and in the present case we see that the alleged cause does not exist. Therefore the alleged effect cannot exist. If Maria Monk is insane, it is unaccountable that none of her friends in New York hare ever been able to discover the least indications of it. When her friends call to mind what she has passed through since she left the convent, they wonder that she has not been driven to insanity. Not one female in ten thousand would have endured the ordeal, through which she has been enabled to pass without injury. With an infant in her arms, she commenced the contest. She told her sad tale; but scarce anybody was prepared to believe it. It was too horrible for belief. Hence all about her was suspicion. Her circumstances were suspicious. She was examined, re-examined, and cross-examined by every sort of people. She has been persecuted by Catholics and by Protestants. Malice has directed against her its bitterest arrows of slander. Her feelings have been excited to the highest pitch for days and weeks, for she is naturally very excitable, being constitutionally sensitive. And yet, amidst all her excitements, she has never given any symptoms of insanity while she has been in New York. What confidence, therefore, can be reposed in the multipled charges of insanity which are made against her in the "Awful Exposure?" Sad indeed must be the predicament of truth, if it needs for its support such weapons.

> But this charge itself is one of the proofs of her having been a nun. It appears to be the standing order to charge upon every female who makes disclosures, disadvantageous to convents, madness and insanity. Rome set the example. Says Scipio de Ricci, "they say at Rome, to defend the Monks, that the two nuns are mad; but up to the present hour, no one has ever taken them for such." Thus [former nun] Miss Reed was mad or insane, and also [former nun] Miss Harrison, and now [former nun] Maria Monk.[630]

The Roman Catholic hierarchy has an established pattern of claiming that all former nuns who allege that they have escaped from nunneries are insane impostors. However, the suspicious conduct of the Catholic hierarchy and their provably false claims in response to the allegations of Maria Monk unintentionally testify to the truth of Maria Monk's allegations.

The Roman Catholic church denied that Maria Monk was ever a nun and that there were no hidden passages, as alleged by her, through which priests could enter the nunnery. Below is an account by Maria Monk of the murder of an infant, which the Catholic hierarchy simply could not allow to be known.

> It will be recollected, that I was informed immediately after receiving the veil, that infants were occasionally murdered in the Convent. I was one day in the nuns' private sick room, when I had an opportunity, unsought for, of witnessing deeds of such a nature. It was, perhaps, a month after the death of Saint Francis. Two little twin babes, the children of Sainte Catharine, were brought to a priest, who was in the room, for baptism. I was present while the ceremony was performed, with the Superior and several of the old nuns, whose names I never knew, they being called Ma tante, Aunt.
>
> The priests took turns in attending to confession and catechism in the Convent, usually three months at a time, though sometimes longer periods. The priest then on duty was Father Larkin. He is a good-looking

European, and has a brother who is a professor in the college. He baptized, and then put oil upon the heads of the infants, as is the custom after baptism. They were then taken, one after another, by one of the old nuns, in the presence of us all. She pressed her hand upon the mouth and nose of the first, so tight that it could not breathe, and in a few minutes, when the hand was removed, it was dead. She then took the other, and treated it in the same way. No sound was heard, and both the children were corpses. The greatest indifference was shown by all present during this operation; for all, as I well knew, were long accustomed to such scenes. The little bodies were then taken into the cellar, thrown into the pit I have mentioned, and covered with a quantity of lime.

I afterward saw another new-born infant treated in the same manner, in the same place; but the actors in the scene I choose not to name, nor the circumstances, as everything connected with it is of a peculiarly trying and painful nature to my own feelings.

These were the only instances of infanticide I witnessed; and it seemed to be merely owing to accident that I was then present. So far as I know, there were no pains taken to preserve secrecy on this subject; that is, I saw no attempt made to keep any of the inmates of the Convent in ignorance of the murder of children. On the contrary, others were told, as well as myself, on their first admission as veiled nuns, that all infants born in the place were baptized and killed, without loss of time; and I had been called to witness the murder of the three just mentioned, only because I happened to be in the room at the time.

That others were killed in the same manner during my stay in the nunnery, I am well assured.

How many there were I cannot tell, and having taken no account of those I heard of, I cannot speak with precision; I believe, however, that I learnt through nuns, that at least eighteen or twenty infants were smothered, and secretly buried in the cellar, while I was a nun.[631]

It has been known that the nunnery was altered by carpenters and masons to conceal the passages and cells revealed by Maria Monk, once her story became public knowledge. That conduct of concealing the hidden features of the nunnery is the best corroboration of the truth of Maria Monk's allegations. In the appendix to her book, it was revealed:

It is also a fact publicly avowed by certain Montreal Papists themselves, and extensively told in taunt and triumph, that they have been employed as masons and carpenters by the Roman Priests, since Maria Monk's visit to Montreal in August, 1835, expressly to alter various parts of the Hotel Dieu Convent, and to close up some of the subterraneous passages and cells in that nunnery. This circumstance is not pretended even to be disputed or doubted ... But the filling up and the concealment of the old apertures in the nunnery, by the order of the Roman Priests are scarcely less powerful corroborative proof of Maria Monk's delineations, than ocular and palpable demonstration.[632]

Maria Monk was informed that masons and carpenters had been employed to alter the nunnery since she left it and her story became public. Testimony from the workers proves that changes were made to the nunnery, but Maria opined that enough of the nunnery must have remained to substantiate her description. That is why the Catholic hierarchy never took her up on her challenge to allow her along with objective witnesses to tour the nunnery.

What could the Catholic Church do? Their initial refusal to agree to Maria Monk's challenge was suspicious and their explanation that the nature of a cloistered convent did not allow for public scrutiny simply was not believed. They were forced to do something to quell the public clamor that the convent be opened to inspection.

The Catholic hierarchy delayed for over a year while alterations were made to the nunnery and only then brought in observers, who were portrayed falsely as being objective, to view the newly altered nunnery. The people brought in to tour the nunnery could not be openly Roman Catholic; that would make the ruse too obvious. They decided upon William L. Stone, the Presbyterian editor of the *New York Commercial Advertiser* and a few other hand-picked observers. As expected, their hand-picked mouthpiece, Stone, published an article in his newspaper refuting the claims of Maria Monk regarding the layout of the nunnery. That was the whole purpose of Stone's guided tour.

Stone's deception is manifestly obvious to any informed reader. Stone claimed that he fully explored the entire Hotel Dieu Nunnery in three hours.[633] A knowledgeable architect, who was familiar with Hotel Dieu Nunnery, and in fact lived near it for 21 years, stated that anyone who thinks that they could fully explore the massive building in three hours is either a fool or a knave.[634] Stone was neither a fool nor a knave. Stone was a Freemason, accustomed to deception, who was practicing his craft of dissimulation.

Indeed, Stone admitted in a booklet he later published detailing his tour of the nunnery that he had not even read Maria Monk's book. "Of the truly 'Awful Disclosures' of Maria Monk, I had formed no very definite opinion previous to entering the province. Indeed, I had not read the book in any other manner than by occasional and very cursory glance at a few of its pages. Still I had read much *from* and *of* it, and heard much more."[635] (italics in original)

Stone was only a Protestant in name only, as his opinion was that the Catholic Church was a "Christian religion." He admitted that he found it difficult to believe Maria Monk's story. "The tale was most revolting, and it was not a little difficult to bring the mind to believe it possible, that even the most hardened of our species could be guilty, from year to year, of the frightful abominations charged by Miss Monk upon the priests and nuns of Montreal-much less the professed ministers of the Christian religion."[636] How could he make such a judgement without reading her book and assessing the evidence? Obviously, his opinion was preformed and based upon bias and prejudice.

Stone revealed his bias and the undue influence of the Catholic clerics over him by making the incredible assertion that "the whole town and province [of Montreal] disbelieved the narrative of Miss Monk."[637] That was so patently false, it could only have been a piece of propaganda that was inculcated to him by his Jesuit hosts. He was simply passing along the information with no thought to scrutinize its accuracy, because he understood his mission was not to inform but to pass along false propaganda. While the Catholics may have been afraid to say that they agreed with Maria Monk's account, they believed it to be true.

Stone's purpose of defending the Jesuit priests was clearly manifested in one particular lie he passed along from one of his hosts, Bishop M'Donald. Stone stated: "Bishop M'Donald is a Scotch gentleman of the old school; affable, intelligent, and for a Catholic, not intolerant. He allows his people to read the Bible, and gives away all that he can obtain for that object."[638] That patent falsehood conveyed by Stone was said to refute Maria Monk's claim that the priests taught the children in school not to read the bible. The Catholic Church is so famously the enemy of the word of God, the falsity of the claim made to Stone by the bishop of fidelity to the bible could only be believed by the most naive of persons. There is little doubt that Stone knew it was not true when he heard it. Stone was a willing participant in a charade.

Maria Monk gives the following account of her Catholic instruction when she was a student at the congregational nunnery, regarding the reading of the Holy Bible:

> Among the instructions given us by the priests, some of the most pointed were those directed against the Protestant Bible. They often enlarged upon the evil tendency of that book, and told us that but for it many a soul now condemned to hell, and suffering eternal punishment, might have been in happiness. They could not say any thing in its favour: for that would be speaking against religion and against God. They warned us against it, and represented it as a thing very dangerous to our souls. In confirmation of this, they would repeat some of the answers taught us at catechism, a few of which I will here give. We had little catechisms ("Le Petit Catechism") put into our

hands to study; but the priests soon began to teach us a new set of answers, which were not to be found in our books, and from some of which I received new ideas, and got, as I thought, important light on religious subjects, which confirmed me more and more in my belief in the Roman Catholic doctrines. These questions and answers I can still recall with tolerable accuracy, and some of them I will add here. I never have read them, as we were taught them only by word of mouth. ...

_Q_. "Why did not God make all the commandments?"

_A_. "Because man is not strong enough to keep them."

And another.

_Q_. "Why are men not to read the New Testament?"

_A_. "Because the mind of man is too limited and weak to understand what God has written."

These questions and answers are not to be found in the common catechisms in use in Montreal and other places where I have been, but all the children in the Congregational Nunnery were taught them, and many more not found in these books.[639]

The truth of Maria's account regarding the Catholic doctrinal biblio-animus is found in the official encyclicals issued by the mythically infallible popes, both before and after Maria Monk was catechized. On May 5, 1824, Pope Leo XII issued his encyclical *Ubi Primum* which exhorted the bishops to remind their flocks not to read the Bible. On May 24, 1829, Pope Pius VIII issued the encyclical *Traditi Humilitati,* which exhorted Catholics to check the spread of Bibles translated into the vernacular, because those Bibles endangered the "sacred" teachings of the Catholic Church. On May 8, 1844, Pope Gregory XVI issued his encyclical *Inter Praecipuas* in which he described Bible societies as plotting against the Catholic faith by providing Bibles to the common people, whom he referred to as "infidels."

The catechism to which Maria Monk referred was consistent with the official catholic doctrine of the Vatican. In view of those papal encyclicals, it seems a little ridiculous for the priests to pretend that the Catholic Church is trying to spread the word of God; particularly when everyone who has read the bible knows that at the turn of every page in the bible one finds an impeachment of Catholic dogma, and it is therefore clearly not in the Vatican's interest to see the word of God spread. In fact, when Stone described the books in the nun's quarters at the Hotel Dieu Nunnery, he did not mention once the presence of a bible, which one would think would be prominently displayed, if it was commonly used.

During a debate with a Protestant minister in the 19th century, a Catholic priest stated that "certain Protestants repeat that the [Catholic] Church forbids the reading of the Holy Bible by the people. That is a cowardly lie, and it is only the ignorant or the silly amongst Protestants who at present believe this ancient fabrication of heresy."[640] That priest called the pastors who made such allegations "unscrupulous" and their believing flocks "dupes." He gave the example of the availability of the Catholic versions of the bible in bookstores throughout Canada, the United States, and Europe as proof that the allegation that the Catholic Church suppresses the bible is not true.

The Catholic priest quoted in the debate above was Charles Chiniquy. He later left the Catholic priesthood and became one of the most famous Protestant preachers of the 19th century. Charles Chiniquy admitted that as a Catholic priest he had engaged in misleading statements like those in the above quoted debate. After Chiniquy left the Catholic Church, he explained that while Catholics are allowed to have bibles in Protestant countries, that is not the wish of the Catholic Church. The Catholic Church only permits such sales, because without political hegemony over a country, the Catholic Church must allow Catholics to possess Catholic bibles. However, Catholics are admonished by their priests never to interpret the scriptures according to their own understanding. A Catholic must always look to the "infallible" Church of Rome in all spiritual matters.

One major distinction between a Catholic mass and a Protestant service is that almost every Protestant can be seen carrying his bible to the service, whereas almost all Catholics will be walking into the Catholic Church building with empty hands. If a Catholic is carrying anything, it is usually a book called a Catholic missal. The missal looks like a bible, but it only contains the instructions, chants, and rituals of the Catholic Mass. Catholics will often say that the fact that they have in their home a Catholic Douay bible is evidence that it is a slanderous lie that the Catholic Church suppresses the bible. Chiniquy responds to that claim, and in doing so impeaches the position he took as a Roman Catholic priest; his response reveals the subtlety of his prior Catholic deception:

> To whom do they owe the privilege [of possessing a bible]? Is it the Church of Rome? Not at all. It is their Protestant friends, to the Protestant countries in which they live. Were they at Rome, they would be put in jail for the same thing allowed to them here. Then, if the Church of Rome permits the reading of the Scriptures, it is not because she likes that, but because she cannot help herself. The light is so near the eyes of the Roman Catholics of this country that it can't be entirely put out from them.[641]

How does Rome treat bible possession when it gains political hegemony? One example, out of many thousands, was the burning at the stake of William Tyndale in 1536, for the crime of translating the Holy Scriptures into English and making them available to the people.[642] In 1832, Rebecca Reed, as a candidate to be a nun, spent six months in the Ursuline Convent in Charlestown, Massachusetts, before escaping and exposing the cruelty and oppression of the nunnery. Miss Reed never saw a bible the entire time she was in the convent. All requests made by her to obtain a bible were ignored. She recalls the bishop stating that the laity were not qualified to expound on the scriptures and that only the successors of the apostles were authorized to interpret them.[643]

In order to understand why Maria Monk should be believed, one should understand how her revelations came to light. Maria Monk never spoke of her ordeal at the nunnery until she was taken ill at an almshouse and was not expected to live. Believing that she was near death, she summoned for the chaplain, Mr. Tappan, and told him that she had something to communicate to him, and that she could not die in peace without disclosing it. She then disclosed the horrors of her experience as a cloistered nun at the Hotel Dieu Nunnery.[644] She witnessed priestly fornication with the nuns, the killing of the resulting newborn infants, torture, and she was forced to assist in the murder of a fellow nun. She wanted to unburden her conscience about these abominations before she died. At the time she was still under the superstitious beliefs of the Roman Catholic religion and thought it was necessary to make an auricular confession in order to have her sins forgiven before death. She had no intention on making the matter public, as she was still under the superstitious Catholic belief that her auricular confession would be kept inviolably secret.

Maria Monk survived her illness, and upon recovery she was convinced to write her book documenting her ordeal. It is beyond belief that a person would tell a lie when she believed that she was at death's door, especially when nothing could be gained by it. Such a dying declaration is inherently trustworthy. It is an accepted maxim that no person wants to die with a lie on her lips. Poet Edward Young (1683-1765) succinctly stated the truth:"A death-bed is a detector of the heart."

After taking the veil in the nunnery, the nuns were renamed after Catholic saints. For example, Maria Monk was renamed Saint Eustace.[645] That name was given to her upon taking her vows and entering the cloistered order of nuns. Upon taking the veil as a cloistered nun, Maria was directed to take part in a ceremony where she laid in a coffin covered by a suffocating black cloth. The coffin had her new name engraved upon it: SAINT EUSTACE. The coffin was to be stored in a building on the convent grounds and used to bury her when she died.[646] Thus it was made clear to her that she could never leave the nunnery; her only release was through death. The founder of the Church of Satan, Anton LaVey, stated that coffin ceremonies are characteristic of satanic societies (e.g., Skull & Bones, a/k/a Brotherhood of Death). Below is Maria Monk's account of the Murder of a fellow nun known only to her as "Saint Francis:"

> I must now come to one deed, in which I had some part, and which I look back upon with greater horror

and pain, than any occurrences in the Convent, in which I was not the principal sufferer. It is not necessary for me to attempt to excuse myself in this or any other case. Those who have any disposition to judge fairly, will exercise their own judgment in making allowances for me, under the fear and force, the commands and examples, around me. I, therefore, shall confine myself, as usual, to the simple narrative of facts. The time was about five months after I took the veil; the weather was cool, perhaps in September or October. One day, the Superior sent for me and several other nuns, to receive her commands at a particular room. We found the Bishop and some priests with her; and speaking in an unusual tone of fierceness and authority, she said, "Go to the room for the Examination of Conscience, and drag Saint Francis up-stairs." Nothing more was necessary than this unusual command, with the tone and manner which, accompanied it, to excite in me most gloomy anticipation. It did not strike me as strange, that St. Francis should be in the room to which the Superior directed us. It was an apartment to which we were often sent to prepare for the communion, and to which we voluntarily went, whenever we felt the compunctions which our ignorance of duty, and the misinstructions we received, inclined us to seek relief from self-reproach. Indeed, I had seen her there a little before. What terrified me was, first, the Superior's angry manner, second, the expression she used, being a French term, whose peculiar use I had learnt in the Convent, and whose meaning is rather softened when translated into "drag"; third, the place to which we were directed to take the interesting young nun, and the persons assembled there as I supposed to condemn her. My fears were such, concerning the fate that awaited her, and my horror at the idea that she was in some way to be sacrificed, that I would have given anything to be allowed to stay where I was. But I feared the consequence of disobeying the Superior, and proceeded with the rest towards the room for the examination of conscience.

The room to which we were to proceed from that, was in the second story, and the place of many a scene of a shameful nature. It is sufficient for me to say, after what I have said in other parts of this book, that things had there occurred which made me regard the place with the greatest disgust. Saint Francis had appeared melancholy for some time. I well knew that she had cause, for she had been repeatedly subject to trials which I need not name—our common lot. When we reached the room where we had been bidden to seek her, I entered the door, my companions standing behind me, as the place was so small as hardly to hold five persons at a time. The young nun was standing alone near the middle of the room; she was probably about twenty, with light hair, blue eyes, and a very fair complexion. I spoke to her in a compassionate voice, but at the same time with such a decided manner, that she comprehended my full meaning.

"Saint Francis, we are sent for you."

Several others spoke kindly to her, but two addressed her very harshly. The poor creature turned round with a look of meekness, and without expressing any unwillingness or fear, without even speaking a word, resigned herself to our hands. The tears came into my eyes. I had not a moment's doubt that she considered her fate as sealed, and was already beyond the fear of death. She was conducted, or rather hurried to the staircase, which was near by, and then seized by her limbs and clothes, and in fact almost dragged up-stairs, in the sense the Superior had intended. I laid my own hands upon her—I took hold of her too, more gentle indeed than some of the rest; yet I encouraged and assisted them in carrying her. I could not avoid it. My refusal would not have saved her, nor prevented her being carried up; it would only have exposed me to some severe punishment, as I believed some of my companions, would have seized the first opportunity to complain of me.

All the way up the staircase, Saint Francis spoke not a word, nor made the slightest resistance. When we entered with her the room to which she was ordered, my heart sank within me. The Bishop, the Lady Superior, and five priests, namely, Bonin, Richards, Savage, and two others, I now ascertained, were assembled for her trial, on some charge of great importance.

When we had brought our prisoner before them, Father Richards began to question her, and she made ready but calm replies. I cannot pretend to give a connected account of what ensued: my feelings were wrought up to such a pitch, that I knew not what I did, nor what to do. I was under a terrible apprehension that, if I betrayed my feelings which almost overcame me, I should fall under the displeasure of the cold-blooded persecutors of my poor innocent sister; and this fear on the one hand, with the distress I felt for her on the other, rendered me almost frantic. As soon as I entered the room, I had stepped into a corner, on the left of the entrance, where I might partially support myself, by leaning against the wall, between the door and window. This support was all that prevented me from falling to the floor, for the confusion of my thoughts was so great, that only a few of the words I heard spoken on either side made any lasting impression upon me. I felt as if struck with some insupportable blow; and death would not have been more frightful to me. I am inclined to the belief, that Father Richards wished to shield the poor prisoner from the severity of her fate, by drawing from her expressions that might bear a favorable construction. He asked her, among other things, if she was not sorry for what she had been overheard to say, (for she had been betrayed by one of the nuns,) and if she would not prefer confinement in the cells, to the punishment which was threatened her.

But the Bishop soon interrupted him, and it was easy to perceive, that he considered her fate as sealed, and was determined she should not escape. In reply to some of the questions put to her, she was silent; to others I heard her voice reply that she did not repent of words she had uttered, though they had been reported by some of the nuns who had heard them; that she still wished to escape from the Convent; and that she had firmly resolved to resist every attempt to compel her to the commission of crimes which she detested. She added, that she would rather die than cause the murder of harmless babes.

"That is enough, finish her!" said the Bishop.

Two nuns instantly fell upon the young woman, and in obedience to directions, given by the Superior, prepared to execute her sentence.

She still maintained all the calmness and submission of a lamb. Some of those who took part in this transaction, I believe, were as unwilling as myself; but of others I can safely say, that I believe they delighted in it. Their conduct certainly exhibited a most blood-thirsty spirit. But, above all others present, and above all human fiends I ever saw, I think Sainte Hypolite was the most diabolical. She engaged in the horrid task with all alacrity, and assumed from choice the most revolting parts to be performed. She seized a gag, forced it into the mouth of the poor nun, and when it was fixed between her extended jaws, so as to keep them open at their greatest possible distance, took hold of the straps fastened at each end of the stick, crossed them behind the helpless head of the victim, and drew them tight through the loop prepared, as a fastening.

The bed which had always stood in one part of the room, still remained there; though the screen, which had usually been placed before it, and was made of thick muslin, with only a crevice through which a person behind might look out, had been folded up on its hinges in the form of a W, and placed in a corner. On the bed the prisoner was laid with her face upward, and then bound with cords, so that she could not move. In an instant another bed was thrown upon her. One of the priests, named Bonin, sprung like a fury first upon it, and stamped upon it, with all his force. He was speedily followed by the nuns, until there were as many upon the bed as could find room, and all did what they could, not only to smother, but to bruise her. Some stood up and jumped upon the poor girl with their feet, some with their knees, and others in different ways seemed to seek how they might best beat the breath out of her body, and mangle it, without coming in direct contact with it, or seeing the effects of their violence. During this time, my feelings were almost too strong to be endured. I felt stupefied, and was scarcely conscious of what I did. Still, fear for myself remained in a sufficient degree to induce me to some exertion, and I attempted to talk to those who stood next, partly that I might have an excuse for turning away from the dreadful scene.

After the lapse of fifteen or twenty minutes, and when it was presumed that the sufferer had been smothered, and crushed to death, Father Bonin and the nuns ceased to trample upon her, and stepped from the bed. All was motionless and silent beneath it.

They then began to laugh at such inhuman thoughts as occurred to some of them, rallying each other in the most unfeeling manner, and ridiculing me for the feelings which I in vain endeavored to conceal. They alluded to the resignation of our murdered companion, and one of them tauntingly said, "She would have made a good Catholic martyr." After spending some moments in such conversation, one of them asked if the corpse should be removed. The Superior said it had better remain a little while. After waiting a short time longer, the feather-bed was taken off, the cords unloosed, and the body taken by the nuns and dragged down stairs. I was informed that it was taken into the cellar, and thrown unceremoniously into the hole which I have already described, covered with a great quantity of lime, and afterwards sprinkled with a liquid, of the properties and name of which I am ignorant. This liquid I have seen poured into the hole from large bottles, after the necks were broken off, and have heard that it is used in France to prevent the effluvia rising from cemeteries.

I did not soon recover from the shock caused by this scene; indeed it still recurs to me, with most gloomy impressions. The next day there was a melancholy aspect over everything, and recreation time passed in the dullest manner; scarcely anything was said above a whisper.

I never heard much said afterward about Saint Francis.[647]

The verification of the truth of Maria Monk's book came in many forms, one of which was explained in an appendix to a second edition of Maria Monk's book:

We will however state one very recent occurrence, because it seems to us, that it alone is almost decisive of the controversy. A counselor of Quebec--his name is omitted merely from delicacy and prudential considerations--has been in New York since the publication of the "Awful Disclosures" His mind was so much influenced by the perusal of that volume, that he sought out the Authoress, and most closely searched into the credibility of her statements. Before the termination of the interview, that gentleman became so convinced of the truth of the picture which Maria Monk drew of the interior of the Canadian Nunneries, that he expressed himself to the following effect:—"My daughter, about 15 years of age, is in the Ursuline Convent at Quebec. I will return home immediately; and if I cannot remove her any other way, I will drag her out by the hair of her head, and raise a noise about their ears that shall not soon be quieted."

That gentleman did so return to Quebec, since which he has again visited New York; and he stated, that upon his arrival in Quebec, he went to the Convent, and instantly removed his daughter from the Ursuline Nunnery; from whom he ascertained, as far as she had been initiated into the mysteries, that Maria Monk's descriptions of Canadian Nunneries, are most minutely and undeniably accurate.[648]

When Maria Monk made her escape from the nunnery, she took refuge in the house of a woman named Lavalliere on Elizabeth street in Montreal; it was the second or third door from the corner of what is commonly called "the Bishop's Church." Madame Lavalliere when interviewed afterward confirmed that Maria Monk did arrive at her house at the time specified by Maria Monk, and that she was wearing the usual habiliments of a Nun. She stated that Maria made herself known to her as an escaped Nun. Madame Lavalliere stated that she provided her with other clothing; Madame Lavalliere afterward carried the nun's garments back to the Hotel Dieu Nunnery.[649]

Maria Monk was pregnant by a Catholic priest when she escaped from the nunnery. It was her desire to save her child from certain death that prompted her escape from the convent. She knew that the common practice in the nunnery was for a priest to baptize the newborn child and then to hand the infant over to a nun, who would put her hand over the infant's mouth and nose until it was suffocated to death.

After Maria escaped and then gave birth, she traveled to Montreal with some Protestants who were assisting her in seeking justice in the courts. The entire time after her escape she never let the name of the Catholic priest who was the father of her child pass her lips.[650] When Catholic priest Patrick Phelan (1795-1857)[651] found out that Maria Monk was in Montreal and seeking prosecution for the tortures and murders in the nunnery, he made the following statement in front of the entire Catholic congregation after a Catholic Mass over which he was officiating:

> There is a certain nun in this city who has left our faith, and joined the Protestants. She has a child of which she is ready to swear I am the father. She wishes in this way to take my gown from me. If I knew where to find her, I would put her in prison. I mention this to guard you against being deceived by what she may say. The Devil now has such hold upon people that there is danger lest some might believe her story.[652]

There are two notable things about Phelan's statement: 1) He admits that Maria Monk was a nun (a fact that has always been denied by the Catholic hierarchy); and 2) He claimed that Maria was alleging that he was the father. In fact, Maria had not identified him as the father of her child. Maria had only stated that the father of her child was a Catholic priest, whom she never named. She stated that the nunnery was visited by scores of priests, who regularly entered the nunnery for illicit sex with the nuns. Maria agreed that Phelan was the father of her child only after word reached her of Phelan's statement made before the church congregation. Phelan made the statement before the church congregation, because his guilty conscience assumed that Maria had revealed him as the father. Logic tells us that a denial of a crime by a person before he is alleged to have committed it, suggests a guilty conscience by the denier. Only the most negligent officer of the law would not investigate the denier to determine whether the denial is a false cover for guilt. Phelan's denial under such a circumstance certainly points to him as the true father of Maria Monk's child, and as such confirms the truth of Maria Monk's other allegations.

Samuel B. Smith, who was a former Catholic priest, published a booklet in 1836 titled, *Decisive Confirmation of the Awful Disclosures of Maria Monk*.[653] He knew that many of Maria Monk's claims are true, because when he was a Catholic priest, he was a superintendent of a nunnery in Kentucky.

The Catholic officials claimed that Maria Monk was never a Catholic nun. In his book, Samuel Smith reveals how he personally spoke with a witness who saw Maria Monk at the nunnery. The witness attended the congregational nunnery while she and Maria were only novices. The witness' family was able to get her out of the congregational nunnery after her brother when visiting her at the nunnery happened to see a priest put his arm around the neck of another nun and kiss her. This same witness was visiting an acquaintance in the publicly accessible area of the hospital that adjoined the black nunnery, when she saw Maria Monk serving the lunch. The witness was later determined to be Mrs. Hahn of Montreal.[654]

The priests alleged that they had an affidavit from Maria Monk's mother that stated Maria was never in the nunnery. The purported affidavit from Maria Monk's mother, does not bear her mother's signature. Maria Monk's mother wrote a letter to Maria, wherein she stated that she neither wrote nor signed the affidavit attributed to her. Maria's mother stated that she had been prevailed upon by the Catholic priests to allow it to go uncontradicted, but that it was written by someone else.[655] Maria's mother was known to be an alcoholic, who was putty in the manipulative hands of the Catholic priests and did not resist the priests efforts to destroy her daughter's credibility. The false affidavit prepared by the priests is impeached by what Maria's mother had told William Miller. Several years before Maria escaped, Maria's mother told a family friend, William Miller, that Maria was in the nunnery.

William Miller signed an affidavit under oath on March 3, 1836, stating that he knew Maria Monk when she was a child and attended school with her and her four brothers. He stated that his family and the Monk family were intimate friends, as his father had a high regard for Maria's father, Captain William Monk, who died suddenly from being poisoned. Miller stated that the "temper of his [Captain Monk's] wife was such, even at that time, as to cause much trouble."[656] In 1832, Miller left Montreal and moved to New York. He stated that "about a year afterward I visited Montreal, and on the day when the Governor reviewed the troops, I believe about the end of August, I called at the Government House, where I saw Mrs. Monk and several of the family. I inquired where Maria was, and she told me that she was in the nunnery."[657] Years later, after Maria's escape, Miller spoke with Maria and read her book. Miller concluded his sworn affidavit with: "I declare my personal knowledge of many facts stated in her book, and my full belief in the truth of her story, which, shocking as it is, cannot appear incredible to those persons acquainted with Canada."[658]

The Jesuits had other arrows in their quiver of deceit, and they shot them all at Maria Monk. The Jesuits were not going to confess guilt, and they could not allow the facts to be objectively examined, so they had to destroy the credibility of Maria Monk. They accomplished their goal only regarding the gullible masses. For those who examined closely the Jesuit evidence, it was apparent that it was completely manufactured.

Their efforts to destroy Maria Monk's credibility by assassinating her character has continued unabated to the present day. For example, the *Catholic Encyclopedia* lists Maria Monk among those the Catholic Church describes as "impostors." Included with Maria Monk by the *Catholic Encyclopedia* in the list of impostors is Charles Chiniquy. Charles Chiniquy was a former priest, who left the Catholic Church to become the most famous Protestant preacher of his time. For example, his 80th birthday was attended by 2,000 friends and followers, including many prominent citizens and ministers, who gave speeches lauding Chiniquy. His birthday celebration was reported on the front page of the Wednesday, July 31, 1889, edition of the *Chicago Tribune*. Incidently, Chiniquy's 80th birthday was five years after the publication of his book, *50 Years in the Church of Rome*. When Chiniquy died, his obituary appeared on the front page of the Tuesday, January 17, 1899, edition of *The New York Times*, with a eulogy praising his many accomplishments. According to the *Catholic Encyclopedia*, however, Chiniquy was an impostor. The *Catholic Encyclopedia* seeks to deceptively destroy Chiniquy's character and reputation, because they cannot allow him to be believed regarding his revelations about the involvement of the Roman Catholic Church in the assassination of Abraham Lincoln. The evidence proving that the Catholic Church orchestrated the assassination of President Lincoln will be discussed in more detail later in this book.

The Catholic Encyclopedia describes Maria Monk's book as being fueled by anti-Catholic prejudice, and implied that Maria was not a nun. The Catholic Encyclopedia claimed that Maria's account of the murders and immoralities inside the Hotel Dieu Nunnery had been "fully refuted from the very first by unimpeachable Protestant testimony, which proved that during the period of Maria Monk's alleged residence in the convent she was leading the life of a prostitute in the city."[659] Close scrutiny of the alleged "unimpeachable protestant evidence" shows it to be lacking in reliability, thin in substance, and not truly Protestant. The slightest waive of examination causes the smokescreen of deception to disappear, revealing behind it Jesuit priests fueling the illusion.

The Jesuits suborned perjury from loyal Catholics under their control. The Jesuits produced witnesses who claimed that Maria could not have been a nun in the Hotel Dieu Nunnery, because, they alleged, she worked as a prostitute for two years from 1832 to 1834, prior to entering the Magdalen Asylum in November 1834. The Jesuit false witnesses described Maria Monk during that period as having displaying "confirmed vagrancy," "strange frightiness and unaccountable irregularities," "insanity," "thievery,""lies," and "profligacy."[660]

The Jesuits were firing their arrows of deceit so haphazardly that they ended up shooting their own witnesses. One set of false witnesses contradicted other false witnesses. The Jesuits produced a different set of witnesses who alternatively claimed that for 15 months, from the spring of 1833 until July 1834, Maria was employed as a school teacher. The Jesuits would have people believe that Maria's employers were so derelict that they never noticed that the teacher they had hired to teach their children was an obviously insane, thieving, prostitute.[661]

The Jesuits had to account for the entire time Maria spent in the Hotel Dieu Nunnery. They desperately scraped the bottom of the societal barrel to find false witnesses who claimed that Maria Monk was employed as a servant girl in the Gouin family household from November 1831 until September 1832 in the small Canadien town of Sorel.[662] However, the witnesses that the Jesuits put forth were completely lacking in credibility. Charles Gouin was one of the Jesuit witnesses. Protestant minister J.J. Slocum summarized the character (or rather lack-thereof) of Charles Gouin: "Mr. Gouin is stated, by very respectable authority, to be a Roman Catholic, so far as he has any religion. A man notoriously destitute of moral principle; a bankrupt, owing much and paying little. He is described by his own friends, as 'an active conspirator, unworthy of confidence.'"[663]

Another false witness to Maria Monk's presence in Sorel as a servant girl was Mary Angelica Monk, who was no relation to Maria Monk. Pastor Slocum says of the character of that witness: "She is an impure woman; having been separated from her husband, on the ground of her criminal connection with a man by the name of Hall. Report also says, that she is very intimate with the notoriously profligate priest Kelly, of Sorel."[664]

The third witness in this trinity of deceit was one Martel Paul Hus Cournoier. J.J. Slocum explains the character of Cournier.

> The affidavit of this man has every appearance of having been fabricated, for the sole purpose of bolstering up, not only the testimony of Mr. Gouin and Mrs. [Mary Angelica] Monk, but also that of other individuals, to be examined hereafter. He is described by those who know him, "as an illiterate fellow, who can neither read nor write; an active speculator, of no property, little credit, reputation for virtue or integrity; having not long since debauched one of his own creed named Couthnay." He was convicted of perjury in the case of the King against Isaac Jones and others, for the murder of Louis Marcoux. If any man in Canada doubts the truth of this, he is referred to the legal registers of that Province, for the proof of it. Such, then, is the unprincipled character of Martel Paul: and I ask, what confidence can be reposed in the affidavit of such a perjured ignoramus?[665]

These witnesses alleged that for the ten months from November 1831 until September 1832, Maria Monk could not have been in the Hotel Dieu Nunnery, as Maria claimed, because she was working as a servant girl in the Gouin household in Sorel. The town of Sorel is on the banks of the St. Lawrence River, and at the time in 1832 only had fifteen hundred residents. In small towns during the 1800's, with no television or internet, social intercourse was much greater than it is today. Everybody knew everybody else living in small towns. Think about that. In that entire town of fifteen hundred people, the Jesuit priests could only produce a convicted perjurer, an adulterer, and a bankrupt as their star witnesses to prove that Maria Monk was in Sorel and not in the Hotel Diu Nunnery.

Maria Monk claimed that she had never been to Sorel. If Maria was not in the town of Sorel, it should be easy enough to establish by asking any of the remaining residents of Sorel. Pastor Slocum did just that. He determined that Maria Monk was telling the truth when she averred that she had never lived in Sorel, as was falsely claimed by the Jesuit priests. Pastor Slocum presents the testimony of a reputable merchant in Sorel, who lived near the home where Maria Monk was allegedly employed as servant girl.

> Mr. Buttery declared, that it was impossible for her [Maria Monk] to have resided in Sorel, as above stated, without his having had some knowledge of it. He was, therefore, decidedly of the opinion that she had never lived in that place. Mr. Buttery lives near Mr. Gouin's, And would of course have seen her, had she lived there for ten months.[666]

Pastor Slocum found a second witness, John Edler, who resided in Sorel and was often in the home of the Gouin's, where Maria Monk was alleged to have been employed as a servant girl. Mr. Edler states without equivocation that Maria Monk was not a servant girl in the Gouin home and was not a resident of Sorel as alleged by the Jesuit priests.

> The following testimony of Mr. John Edler, of New York, is decisive on the point. Mr. Edler first became acquainted with Maria Monk some time in the summer of 1836, in the city of New York. His statement is as follows: "I have friends, a grand-parent and a brother, residing in Sorel or William Henry, whom I have frequently visited in that place. My mother resided there before her decease. I am personally acquainted with Mr. Charles Grouin and his family, who keep a tavern in Sorel. Their residence is in the immediate vicinity of my relatives. On one occasion I resided with my connections in Sorel, for about the space of nine months, immediately preceding the commencement of the Cholera in July, 1832. During this period I was often at Mr. Gouin's, and personally knew the members of his household; and I am very certain that Maria

Monk, authoress of the "Awful Disclosures," was not, during this period of time, a member of Mr. Gouin's family, in any sense whatever. Nor did I ever hear of her living in Sorel, until I recently heard of it in New York. I first became acquainted with Maria Monk in New York, some three or four months since." Mr. Edler's testimony covers eight out of the ten months, during which time, Mr. Gouin says, that Maria Monk was a menial in his family. Mr. Edler, so far as I have been able to ascertain, is a young gentleman of veracity and industry. His statement, therefore, can be relied on as true. Since writing the above, a lady from Sorel has visited Maria Monk in New York. And she gives It as her decided opinion, that the authoress of the "Awful Disclosures" has never been a resident of Sorel, as testified by the priests' witnesses. Thus the evidence, that Charles Gouin, Mariel Paul Hus Cournoier, and Angelica Monk, have given false testimony, is constantly augmenting. It is evident, therefore, that Maria Monk, authoress of the "Awful Disclosures," has not resided in Sorel, as maintained by the priests and their perjured supporters.[667]

How is it that the Jesuits could so easily persuade someone to lie on their behalf? It is a Roman Catholic doctrine that has been the centuries-old ethic of the Catholic Church that it is permissible to lie in order to protect the Roman Catholic Church from scandal. The Jesuits permit the use of ambiguous terms to mislead a judge or outright lying under oath if the witness makes a mental reservation.[668] The Jesuits are so famous for deception that the term "Jesuitical" is defined in the Oxford Dictionary as: "Dissembling or equivocating, in the manner once associated with Jesuits."[669] Noah Webster's 1828 dictionary defines Jesuitical as: "Designing; cunning; deceitful; prevaricating."[670]

The Jesuits, and indeed all Catholic priestly orders, not only teach that it is permissible to lie to protect the Catholic Church from scandal, they have also devised a method for deception that persuades Catholics to lie who would otherwise be reticent to lie. The artifice of deception used by the priests is called "mental reservation."

Catholic priests teach that if one makes a mental reservation when telling a lie, the lie is not technically a lie. The Jesuits teach that it is not a sin if one silently, to himself, adds some qualification to the lying words he speaks. The Catholic priests teach that if the unspoken thought, when added to the spoken words, make the statement technically true, then it is not technically a lie.

For instance, hypothetically, a priest or nun could say falsely that Maria Monk was never a nun at the Hotel Dieu Nunnery, and make a mental reservation, thinking silently to themselves the words "prior to 1800." The mental reservation of "prior to 1800" if they were spoken would make the statement technically true, but the words are not spoken, and the listener does not hear the mental reservation. The listener only hears the false denial. According to the Catholic ethic, however, the mental reservation by the speaker makes his statement technically true and therefore not a lie, even though the spoken words that are heard are not true. It is this deceitful Jesuitical cunning that has required the U.S. Government to add to oaths and affirmations a clause that the person makes the affirmation "without any mental reservation or purpose of evasion."

Indeed, this Catholic ethic allowing mental reservation is still taught and practiced today. The Catholic ethic of mental reservation has become an issue in litigation over the rape of young children by Catholic priests. In one 2007 lawsuit in California, an elderly nun, under questioning by a lawyer, made statements that were inconsistent with the known facts. The lawyer was suspicious about her answers and asked her whether she subscribed to the practice of making "mental reservations." John Spano, reported for *The Los Angeles Times* that the lawyer "asked whether she was familiar with 'mental reservation'—a 700-year-old doctrine by which clerics may avoid telling the truth to protect the Catholic Church. She explained in her own way that it is 'to protect the church from scandal.' She said she subscribed to the doctrine."[671]

Spano reported that at least a half-dozen lawyers representing victims in sex abuse cases against priests in the Los Angeles Archdiocese have encountered Catholic witnesses using mental reservation as a means of deception.[672] Spano explained: "The doctrine has been used in modern times to 'claim that it is morally justifiable to lie in order to protect the reputation of the institutional church,' said Thomas P. Doyle, a Virginia priest who is an expert in canon law and has been widely consulted by lawyers for people who say they were victims of abuse."[673]

The lawyers representing the Catholic Church clearly understand the implications of bringing up the topic of mental reservation. The lawyers typically object to any discussion of the topic. Spano gives one instance: "A lawyer preparing one of the more than 500 claims of abuse against the Roman Catholic Archdiocese of Los Angeles asked a priest giving a sworn statement the same question [about making a mental reservation] earlier this month. His lawyer quickly intervened, telling the priest not to answer."[674] The lawyers representing the Roman Catholic Church are trying to avoid the type of answer given by a priest to Tim Hale, who is an attorney for victims of pedophile priests. Hale stated "that one priest answered yes without hesitation when asked if mental reservation 'is a doctrine that protects the church from scandal.'"[675]

Priests often came into the Hotel Dieu Nunnery through a secret passage from the nearby seminary to have their way with the nuns. Maria recounts an episode the very night that she took the veil to become a cloistered nun:

> Nothing important occurred until late in the afternoon, when, as I was sitting in the community-room, Father Dufrèsne called me out, saying he wished to speak with me. I feared what was his intention; but I dared not disobey. In a private apartment, he treated me in a brutal manner; and from two other priests I afterward received similar usage that evening. Father Dufrèsne afterward appeared again; and I was compelled to remain in company with him until morning.
>
> I am assured that the conduct of the priests in our Convent has never been exposed, and is not imagined by the people of the United States. This induces me to say what I do, notwithstanding the strong reasons I have to let it remain unknown. Still, I cannot force myself to speak on such subjects except in the most

brief manner.[676]

The nunneries are used as brothels by the priests who pimp out the nuns to wealthy Catholics seeking the thrill of illicit debauchery. Maria Monk and all nuns at the Hotel Dieu Nunnery took a vow "that all officers and citizens admitted into the nunnery in priests' dresses were to be obeyed in all things." Maria saw one man in the nunnery who was not a priest, but he was dressed up like a priest, whom she recognized as someone who lived only blocks from her mother's home. He told Maria that he had paid the priests $500 to gain access to the nunnery through the underground passageway. Clearly, he was there to take advantage of the nuns vow of obedience. He told Maria that many British officers were admitted to the nunnery in the same manner.[677]

Nuns take a vow of poverty, a vow of chastity, and a vow of obedience. In view of the vow of chastity, one might ask how is it that there is so much fornication in a nunnery that is sanctioned by the Catholic Church? There is a hierarchy in the vows. The solemn vow of obedience takes precedence over the vows of poverty and chastity. Obedience is to be given without question to a command from a superior. The priest is her superior. If a command violates either the vow of poverty or the vow of chastity, the other vows must yield to the vow of obedience. If, therefore, a priest demands sexual obedience from a nun, then she is obligated to suppress her vow of chastity and comply with the demand of the priest.[678] It is a deviant system that implicitly encourages debauchery.

The nuns were forced to submit to the priests' licentiousness through the centuries-old artifice of auricular confession. Maria Monk explains:

> The first time I went to confession after taking the veil, I found abundant evidence that the priests did not treat even that ceremony, which is called a solemn sacrament, with respect enough to lay aside the detestable and shameless character they so often showed on other occasions. The confessor sometimes sat in the room of examination of conscience, and sometimes in the Superior's room, and always alone, except the nun who was confessing. He had a common

chair placed in the middle of the floor, and instead of being placed behind a grate, or lattice, as in the chapel, had nothing before or around him. There were no spectators to observe him, and of course any such thing would have been unnecessary.

A number of nuns usually confessed on the same day, but only one could be admitted into the room at the time. They took their places just without the door, on their knees, and went through the preparation prescribed by the rules of confession; repeating certain prayers, which always occupy a considerable time. When one was ready, she rose from her knees, entered, and closed the door behind her; and no other one even dared touch the latch until she came out.

I shall not tell what was transacted at such times, under the pretense of confessing, and receiving absolution from sin: far more guilt was often incurred than pardoned; and crimes of a deep die were committed, while trifling irregularities, in childish ceremonies, were treated as serious offences. I cannot persuade myself to speak plainly on such a subject, as I must offend the virtuous ear. I can only say, that suspicion cannot do any injustice to the priests, because their sins cannot be exaggerated.[679]

The Catholic officials claimed that there was no tunnel leading to the Hotel Dieu Nunnery through which priests could clandestinely enter the nunnery, as claimed by Maria Monk. William Stone, of course, backed the Catholic claim and stated that "no such passage was ever heard of."[680] Stone emphasized that "no such passage exists."[681] Those statements by Stone were simply not true.

Samuel B. Smith spoke with a witness who saw the underground tunnel that led from the Hotel Dieu Nunnery across St. Joseph Street in the direction of the parish church and the priest's seminary. The witness saw this in the years 1813 or 1814 when workers were employed in digging a ditch for the conveyance of water pipes through the street. She stated that the tunnel was made of stone and about seven feet wide. She stated that it was about four feet beneath the surface of the ground.

Another witness saw a large tunnel exposed while a Catholic cathedral was being built between the Hotel Dieu Nunnery and the seminary. He stated that the tunnel crossed St. Joseph Street at the Hotel Dieu Nunnery and passed on in the direction of the seminary. Smith also talked to a former student at the seminary in Montreal who saw the entrance to the tunnel, which is accessed by way of the cellar under the yard in the rear of the seminary. The witnesses testimony of having seen the tunnel with their own eyes is strong evidence supporting Monk's credibility. That same testimony is also strong evidence that impeaches the credibility of the Catholic officials, who denied the existence of the tunnel.

On May 5, 1826, almost ten years before Maria Monk's revelations, the Boston Recorder published an account of the subterranean passage that ran from the seminary to the Hotel Dieu Convent. The article was republished in the Canadien papers, at which time it created a furor of indignation. The article stated in pertinent part: "In Montreal, a subterraneous pathway leads from the priests' residence to the two nunneries. At Three Rivers where the Jesuits' convent is on the opposite side of the street from the nunnery, a passage under the street formed a communication between the fraternity and the sisterhood."[682]

Mr. E. Sprague, in July 1836, spoke with a gentleman, who was formerly a Catholic, but had become a professed Christian. The man revealed to Sprague the following:

> "[H]e had been employed to labor in the cellars of the Priests' Seminary at Montreal, and while there engaged, he discovered a door in the wall of the cellar, which on opening, he found it connected with a passage under ground. He entered the passage, and passed through it until he came to some stairs, at the head of which was a trap door. From the direction and distance of the passage, he was perfectly certain that it must be a subterraneous communication between the seminary and the Convent. He further informed me that from the

testimony of many females, his relatives not excepted, that at confession, the priests were in the habit of asking the most licentious and revolting questions that could be propounded, not only to married ladies, but also to girls of 13 years. Likewise from the habiliments of the Nuns and their appearance at times, he was wholly confirmed in the belief that their course in the nunnery was any thing but virtuous. At the time of his making those disclosures Maria Monk had not written her book. I think testimony of this kind is powerfully corroborative, and that these things exist I fully believe.[683]

On or about 1836, Mr. W. Miller stated that it was common knowledge among those living nearby that there was an underground passage connecting the seminary with the Hotel Dieu Convent. Mr. Miller, himself, saw the underground passage uncovered when some workmen were excavating the area to install water and gas pipes. The workers who uncovered the underground passage went down into it, and a group of pedestrians gathered to observe it. After a short period, some priests from the seminary appeared and prevented any exploration of the tunnel and ordered it to be covered back over.[684]

On or about 1836, a Mr. Janes stated that he spent several years living in Montreal. He stated that in walking from his store to the Post-Office, he generally passed by the large Catholic cathedral under construction near the seminary. He stated that he witnessed the whole progress of the building, from the digging for the foundation to its completion. He estimated that on not less than one hundred occasions he saw the subterranean tunnel leading diagonally from the priests' seminary, across Saint Joseph Street to the Hotel Dieu Nunnery; it was large enough for persons to pass through.[685]

On or about 1836, Protestant minister George Bourne stated that he also saw the opened tunnel leading between the seminary and the convent at the excavation site during the construction of the Catholic cathedral. Mr. Bourne stated that the existence of the underground passage was generally known by the citizens of Montreal, because all who passed by the construction site could see it plainly.

Thomas Hogan was a student at the seminary before he changed his mind about becoming a priest. On October 6, 1836, he signed an affidavit under oath that revealed that there was an underground passage running from the seminary to the Hotel Dieu Convent, just as described by Maria Monk.

> Thomas Hogan, of the city of New York, being duly affirmed, doth say, —that in the year 1824, he was a resident of the city of Montreal, Lower Canada ; and that at that period, the existence of a subterranean passage between the seminary in Notre Dame street, and the Hotel Dieu Convent, was a matter of the most public notoriety; and that he himself has been in that passage, having entered it from the door in the seminary; and the said Hogan doth further depose, that to his own personal knowledge, the Roman priests were constantly in the practice of visiting the nuns for the purposes of licentious intercourse, by that secret passage. Affirmed the twenty-sixth day of October, 1836—before me. WM. H. BOGARDUS, Commissioner of Deeds.

William Stone also claimed that there had been no alterations of the nunnery. "No alteration whatever has been made within the Hotel Dieu Nunnery since the time Maria Monk says she left the place."[686] Stone emphasized that "[t]here have been no alterations either in the building within, or the vaults beneath, or the walls without."[687]

The aforementioned architect stated that Stone was completely "hoaxed" on that point by the Jesuits and nuns of Montreal. The architect, who was of the highest reputation and unimpeachable veracity, stated that he, along with 20 others, were working on an building adjacent to the Hotel Dieu Nunnery and could see from the scaffolding over the wall to the rear of the nunnery from Notre Dame street. He and the others were looking over the wall shortly after the publication of Maria Monk's revelations about the nunnery. He stated "there we saw, during last May, June, and July, between 15 and 20 men busily employed within the nunnery's outer walls, carrying in timber, stones, and mortar. The work went on briskly for three months; how much longer I do not profess to say."[688] He stated that the workers were occupied with carrying their materials inside the building and no work could be seen being done in that area on the outside. Indeed, it was general knowledge of the people living in Montreal around the Hotel Dieu Nunnery that the nunnery had undergone massive reconstruction after Maria Monk's allegations came to light.

In the course of Stone's attempt to play along with the charade he actually confirmed a statement that Maria Monk made about a door that was hidden from public view, and that she could only have known about if she was a nun in the Hotel Dieu Nunnery. Stone stated: "But here, true enough, we discovered what Maria calls 'a great, gloomy iron door!'"[689] Stone's purpose was to explain that Maria was wrong, because it was not in the same location averred by Maria and it did not conceal the burial pit described by Maria. Instead, Stone stated that behind the door he found a cellar containing a well and pump. The well and pump were constructed and installed that summer after Maria Monk's revelations. It was manifestly clear to any discerning inspection that it was a recently constructed well.[690] Indeed, there was no need for such a well, since there had always been two wells in the yard of the nunnery. The hastily built well was clearly unnecessary, except for the purpose of destroying and concealing the lime-pit used for eliminating the remains of murdered nuns and infants as described by Maria Monk.

Mass graves for murdered infants of nuns are a common feature in and around convents and have been uncovered in other countries. Former Jesuit priest, Alberto Rivera, revealed that frequently there are underground tunnels that link seminaries for priests with convents for nuns that facilitated the secret fornication between the nuns and priests. Rivera revealed that many mass grave sites for infants born to nuns and shortly thereafter murdered were discovered in Spain and Rome in and around convents and seminaries.[691] Infanticide is part of the overriding ethic of the Jesuits that the ends justify the means. The Jesuits believe that if one can get away with committing a crime without getting caught, it ceases to be a crime. Indeed, F. Xavier Makami, Prefect at the Jesuit College at Ro jen wrote that "successful crime ceases to be a crime. Success constitutes or absolves the guilty at its will."[692] Infanticide is justified by Jesuit theologians. Julia McNair Wright cites Jesuit authorities who justify infanticide, in order to protect the Roman church from scandal: "For the sake of concealing infamy and preserving reputations, infanticide is not only permitted but enjoined by Ariault in his propositions; by Marin, Theology, Tract 23; Castro Palms; Egidius; Bannez; Henriquez; and many other Jesuits."[693]

The Roman Catholic Church has a long and sordid history of secretly disposing in mass graves those who die under suspicious circumstances. In 1993, a mass grave containing 133 bodies was uncovered on the grounds of a previously closed Roman Catholic Magdalene laundry run at a nunnery north of Dublin, Ireland.[694] The so-called Magdalene Laundries were run by nuns and housed young girls, who were held in involuntary servitude. Many of the girls had died in the 1960s and 1970s. All of the remains found in the mass grave were girls who had died in the laundry, but the Roman Catholic Church could not identify 45 of the remains, and 80 of the deceased did not have death certificates as required by law. As the exhumation continued, 22 additional bodies were found making for a total of 155 bodies unearthed; who knows how many other bodies are buried in secret graves elsewhere on the property.

It is illegal in Ireland (and indeed almost every other civilized country) not to notify the government of a death occurring on your premises. The fact that the Catholic nunnery did not report the deaths suggests that they did not want the evidence of the cause of death, which would be manifested on the body, to be known by the authorities. The nunnery clearly had something to hide.

If a grave with the remains of a single unreported death were found on the property of an ordinary private citizen, there would be an immediate investigation, and it would become widely circulated news. The homeowner would be the focus of an unrelenting investigation into the cause of death. Those same rules do not apply to the Roman Catholic Church. The power of the Catholic Church is so absolute in Ireland that there has been no investigation into how the girls died, nor has there been (at the very least) an inquiry into why the Catholic Church did not report the deaths, as required by law.

Maria Monk learned the hard fact of the power of the Catholic Church, when she traveled to Canada in 1835 and sought to have the authorities investigate her allegations of torture, murder, and rape perpetrated within the Hotel Dieu Nunnery. The Canadien authorities were seemingly under the direction of the Roman Church. The authorities took her testimony, but would not take action. What the authorities did do was inform the Catholic hierarchy of the details recounted in Maria Monk's affidavit.[695] The Catholic Church responded by scouring the countryside for witnesses willing to perjure themselves to attack Maria Monk in defense of the Catholic Church. They also hatched a plan to abduct Maria Monk, which almost succeeded.[696]

Mr. Clary, a Protestant minister, stated that material alterations had been made to the Hotel Dieu Nunnery. In response to Stone's report Mr. Clary stated:

> He [Stone] said nothing about the recent building and repairing of stone walls within the enclosure of the convent, and which everybody who wishes can see, nor the new wall within the building, as mentioned privately by one of the former examiners-nor does he tell us that the well in the cellar was dug this summer, nor whether or not it is in exactly the same place that the cemetery, or hole for smothering nuns and infants is said to have been.[697]

William Stone made the absurd statement that Maria Monk is not to be believed, because she had no need to escape from the nunnery, as she was free to leave at any time. Stone stated: "But whence this great difficulty of escaping? There are plenty of doors and gates, and every nun has a key at her side."[698] Anyone who knows anything about cloistered nunneries could see through Stone's bold-faced lie. The very fact that the only former cloistered nuns who have ever left a nunnery have done so by escaping is testimony that nuns in cloistered nunneries are not free to leave and in fact are kept as prisoners.

Former cloistered nun, Charlotte Wells (real name: Charlotte Keckler) escaped her captivity. Prior to her death in 1983, she stated the following, which refutes the claim by the priests that the nuns can leave the cloistered nunnery at any time.

> No one imprisoned behind those walls ever comes out to tell the awful story. Priests will glibly pooh, pooh the idea that there is anything amiss. They will tell you that in this country and elsewhere sisters can walk out

of the convents anytime they please. That is a lie! I was shut up for twenty-two years and tried everything to escape. I even carried tablespoons to the dungeons and desperately dug in their dirt floors attempting to find a way out. Why a tablespoon? All the other tools were locked up or carefully supervised. They were used to dig the tunnels and underground chambers. Convents are constructed like prisons to thwart the escape of the nuns.[699]

Even today, Cloistered nuns are kept prisoner. They can never leave the nunnery. Once they agree to enter the cloister, their decision is irrevocable. Many of the poor nuns change their minds after realizing that they have entered into a hellish life of abuse, rape, torture, and murder. However, they are not allowed to leave.

In 2007, Diane Sawyer interviewed Mother Mary Francis, who was the mother superior at the cloistered convent of the Poor Clares order in Roswell, New Mexico. The mother superior told Diane Sawyer that the nuns "ordinarily" never leave the convent. In a voice-over, Diane Sawyer describes the cloistered nunnery and the ceremony of solemn vows and asks: "After this moment, what if you change your mind? Can you ever leave? What if you change your mind?" That voice-over question led into an interview with the mother superior, where she was asked by Diane Sawyer if "after you have taken the solemn perpetual vow can you then come in and say: 'not for me?'"[700] The mother superior, without hesitation, answered with an unequivocal "No," while emphatically shaking her head back and forth. The mother superior then added, "that would be a tragedy."[701]

The above program was posted on ABC's website. However, that part of the interview with the negative response from the mother superior was not part of the posting. The mother superior's response can only be viewed in a grainy duplicate on You Tube. Diane Sawyer seemed to have lost all curiosity after the mother superior's response. The mother superior's answer screams for a follow-up question, such as: "Would you use force to prevent a nun from leaving?" The implication from the mother superior's initial answer (although it was not said) is that force would be used to prevent a nun from leaving. Using force or the threat of force to keep someone confined against her will constitutes the crime of false imprisonment.

Diane Sawyer explained that when the nuns take their vow to enter the cloistered nunnery, they do so during a ceremony where they are portrayed as the bride of Christ. To leave the nunnery is theologically considered to be the equivalent of leaving their husband, Jesus Christ. Diane Sawyer explained in a voice-over that "we were told the spiritual consequences of leaving are considered dire, and in fact only the pope can give permission to dissolve marriage between a nun and Jesus."[702] So much for William Stone's incredible claim that the cloistered nuns are free to leave the convent at their will.

The priests consider themselves, *alter-Christos* (another Christ). They believe that they are in place of Christ on earth. According to their twisted theology, the priests are consummating the marriage between Christ and the nuns when they sexually assault the nuns in the convent.

William Stone inadvertently confirmed Maria Monk's story. Stone reveals the following, which at the time he probably thought was an insignificant detail. Stone explained: "Soon after we commenced our investigations, we were presented to the lady superior, at the door of her apartment, into which we were admitted. She was suffering from an attack of rheumatism. She is a lady of dignity and refinement of manner; somewhat advanced in years. She received us with the utmost urbanity, nay, with cordiality; and regretted not being able to accompany us through the institution."[703]

Stone had not read Maria Monk's book in its entirety and therefore did not know that he had inadvertently confirmed the description of the lady superior given by Maria Monk in her book. Maria Monk described the lady superior as suffering from swelled limbs that gave her great distress.

While in the nunnery, it was suddenly announced to Maria and the other nuns that the old superior was no longer there, being replaced, without explanation, by a new superior. "The lady he introduced to us was one of our oldest nuns, Saint Du ****, a very large, fleshy woman, with swelled limbs, which rendered her very slow in walking, and often gave her great distress."[704] She was the lady superior in residence when Maria Monk escaped from the cloistered nunnery. Maria's description matches precisely Stone's description of the lady superior. Indeed, she was so suffering when Stone arrived that she could not accompany them on their tour of the nunnery. Maria Monk documented the arthritic lady superior in her book before Stone visited the nunnery. The only way that Maria Monk could have known the condition of the lady superior of the Hotel Dieu Nunnery would be if she herself had been a nun in the convent and had seen her painful condition.

Furthermore, Maria Monk gave the specific names and physical descriptions of over one hundred priests whose parishes were scattered all over Canada. The only way in which Maria Monk could have possibly known that information was if she had personally seen those priests. That indicates that the priests were seen by her during their visits to the Hotel Dieu Nunnery when present there for sexual interludes with the nuns. As confirmation of these facts, she listed the names of the priests in the appendix to her later edition of her book. The significance of her descriptions of the priests is explained in the appendix.

> It is readily admitted, that any person could take one of the Ecclesiastical Registers of Lower Canada, and at his option mark any number of the Roman Priests in the catalogue, and impute to them any crime which he pleased. But if the accuser were closely examined, and among such a multitude of Priests, who in all their clothing are dressed alike, were called upon minutely to delineate them, it is morally impossible, that he could depict more than a hundred Priests dispersed from the borders of Upper Canada to Quebec, in as many different parishes, with the most perfect accuracy, unless he was personally and well acquainted with them.

> Maria Monk, however, does most accurately describe all the Priests in the preceding catalogue, and repeats them at the expiration of weeks and months; and the question is this: how is it possible that she could have become acquainted with so many of that body, and by what means can she so precisely depict their external appearance?—The startling, but the only plausible

answer which can be given to that question is this: that she has seen them in the Nunnery, whither, as she maintains, most of them constantly resorted for licentious intercourse with the Nuns.

One other connected fact may here be introduced. Maria Monk well knows the Lady Superior of the Charlestown Nunnery. That acquaintance could not have been made in the United States, because Saint Mary St. George as she called herself, or Sarah Burroughs, daughter of the notorious Stephen Burroughs, as is her real name, removed to Canada at the latter end of May, 1835; nor could it have been prior to the establishment of the Charlestown Nunnery, for at that period Maria Monk was a child, and was not in any Convent except merely as a scholar; and Mary St. George was at Quebec. How then did she become so familiar with that far-famed lady as to be able to describe her so exactly? The only answer is, that she derived her knowledge of the Charlestown Convent and of its Superior, from the intimations given, and from intercourse with that Nun in the Hotel Dieu Nunnery.[705]

Maria Monk was not an isolated historical anomaly; the sexual abuse of nuns by priests has spanned the centuries. Peter de Rosa in his book, *Vicars of Christ*, concluded that "[a] large part of the history of celibacy is the story of the degradation of women and – an invariable consequence – frequent abortions and infanticide. In the ninth century, many monasteries were the haunts of homosexuals; many convents were brothels in which babies were killed and buried. ... Promiscuity was rife in monasteries and convents. The great Ivo of Chartres (1040-1115) tells of whole convents with inmates who were nuns only in name. They had often been abandoned by their families and were really prostitutes."[706]

William H. Kennedy in his book, *Lucifer's Lodge*, explained that the sexual abuse of Catholic nuns continues unchecked today.

According to the 1996 survey of nuns in the United States (which was intentionally never published by the [Roman Catholic] Church but was leaked by some

Vatican insider), it is reported that a minimum of 34,000 Catholic nuns (about 40% of all American nuns) claim to have been sexually abused. Three of every four of these nuns claimed they were sexually victimized by a priest, nun, or other religious person. Two out of five nuns who stated they were sexually abused claimed that their exploitation included some form of genital contact. All nuns who claimed repeated sexual exploitation reported that they were pressured by religious superiors for sexual favors.[707]

There have been several recent reports written by senior members of women's religious orders that have documented the worldwide practice of priestly rape and sexual abuse of nuns.[708] The Vatican is unrepentant and has falsely characterized the sexual abuse of nuns by priests as being rare, isolated incidents.[709]

The European Parliament is not willing to go along with the Vatican denials. In 2001, the European Parliament approved an unprecedented motion that blamed the Vatican for rampant rapes suffered by nuns at the hands of Catholic priests in Africa.[710]

A Roman Catholic internet news agency, Zenit, reported:

The parliamentary motion, on the "Responsibility of the Vatican in Regard to the Violation of Human Rights by Catholic Priests," has no executive character but rather is intended as a "moral judgment."

It "condemns all the sexual violations against women, particularly against Catholic nuns. Likewise, it requests that the perpetrators of the crimes be arrested and handed over to justice."[711]

The above survey cited by Kennedy included all nuns in both open and cloistered orders. The sexual abuse in cloistered nunneries is much more prevalent, as those nuns are virtual prisoners in their convents. Margaret Shepherd (formerly a nun, Sister Magdalene Adelaide) describes the typical scene of the first experience of a young innocent cloistered nun being ravished by a priest of Rome.

> We leave the church, and, ascending twelve steps, find ourselves in a room comfortably furnished. A man in the guise of a priest of Rome is seated on a sofa. The door opens, and the young girl we noticed in the church enters the room, and, as with down-cast eyes she kneels to receive the priest's blessing, a look of loathing and fear pastes over her features. "Come and sit down here, my daughter; I desire to speak with you." With trembling steps the girl approaches the sofa, and the priest, taking her hand, says: " Why so fearful of me, my child?" And, drawing her down beside him, he places his arm around her waist; his hot, liquor-fumed breath fans her cheek. His coarse sensual lips are pressed to hers; she shrinks away in loathing; her womanly modesty is outraged; she struggles to liberate herself— too late! Poor, helpless girl, she has not sufficient physical strength to overcome the wretch that holds her; her piercing cries for help are not heard outside the room. Exhausted, she lies in the grasp of this spiritual father, and before she leaves the room her purity has been violated, and she becomes the toy and convenience of this "protector" (sic) of morality.[712]

Charlotte Wells (her real surname was Keckler[713]) spent 22 years (from approximately 1910 until 1932) in a cloistered nunnery, before she finally escaped to tell her story to the world. She explained how the nuns in the cloistered nunnery were helpless objects of sexual pleasure for the priests. When the nuns inevitably became pregnant, their babies were murdered shortly after birth, and the bodies of the babies were disposed of in lime pits.

> Here we are, a body of those little nuns. On this particular morning, the mother superior might say this, "We're all going to be lined up here." And I don't know what she's lining me up for. And then, you know, there might be ten others, there might be 15 others, and then she'll tell us all to strip and we have to take every stitch of our clothing off. ... And here we are, lined up, and here comes two or three Roman Catholic priests with liquor under their belts, and there they're going to

march in front of those nude girls and choose the girl they want to take to the cell with them. These are convents, cloistered convents, not open orders. The priest can do anything he wants to and hide behind the cloak of religion. Then that same Roman Catholic priest will go back into the Roman Catholic churches and there he'll say Mass, and there he'll go into the confessional box and make those poor people believe he can give them absolution from their sins when he's full of sin. When he's full of corruption and vice, still he acts as their God. What a terrible thing it is. And on it goes. ... Then sometimes the priests come and they get angry at us because we refuse to sin with them voluntarily. And you know, after all, the nuns bodies are broken after we're there awhile. And many, many the time, to have him strike you in the mouth is a terrible thing. I've had my front teeth knocked out. I know what it's all about. And then they get you down on the floor and then kick you in the stomach. Many of those precious little girls have babies under their heart, and it doesn't bother a priest to kick you in the stomach with a baby under your heart. He doesn't mind. The baby is going to be killed anyway because those babies are going to be born in the convent. ... They'll never bathe that baby's body, but he can only live four or five hours. And then the mother superior will take that baby and put her fingers in its nostrils, cover its mouth and snuff its little life out. ... And why do they build these lime pits in the convent? What is the reason for building them if it isn't to kill the babies? And that baby will be taken into the lime pit and chemical lime will be put over its body. And that's the end of babies.[714]

Charlotte Wells' testimony is belated corroboration of Maria Monk. The Catholic priests are the "natural brute beasts," to which God referred in 2 Peter 2:12. They are "made to be taken and destroyed," in hell by God, as they have "eyes full of adultery, and that cannot cease from sin; beguiling unstable souls: an heart they have exercised with covetous practices; cursed children: Which have forsaken the right way, and are gone astray. ... These are wells without water, clouds that are carried with a tempest; to whom the mist of darkness is reserved for ever. For when they speak great swelling words of vanity, they allure through the lusts of the flesh, through much wantonness." 2 Peter 2:14-15,17-18.

Furthermore, Maria Monk explained in detail her experience on Nun's Island, which is a Catholic monastic enclave on an Island in the Saint Lawrence River. Maria gave an account of how she was used as an unwitting accomplice in the poisoning of a priest by another priest, Patrick Phelan on Nun's Island.[715] Only those authorized by the mother superior, the rector of the seminary, or the bishop are allowed on the secretive Nun's Island. The Catholic hierarchy has by its silence loudly confirmed the authenticity of Maria Monk's account. Maria Monk was able to give a detailed description of the exterior and interior of the buildings, all of which are blocked from public view by a high wall surrounding the complex of buildings, which are situated on a secluded island. There is no way that Maria Monk would know the details of the layout of the complex of buildings unless she had been there. There has been no attempt to refute Maria's account of her stay on Nun's Island or detailed description of the layout of the buildings.

Final and irrefutable corroboration is found in an account that Maria Monk gave of an episode where she was abused in the Hotel Dieu Nunnery. The significance of the account is that it establishes facts that indisputably confirm that she was a nun at the Hotel Dieu Nunnery.

> The Superior ordered me to the cells, and a scene of violence commenced which I will not attempt to describe, nor the precise circumstances which led to it. Suffice it to say, that after exhausting my strength, by resisting as long as I could against several nuns, I had my hands drawn behind my back, a leathern band passed first round my thumbs, then round my hands, and then round my waist, and fastened. **This was drawn so tight that it cut through the flesh of my thumbs, making wounds, the scars of which still remain.** A gag was then forced into my mouth, not indeed so violently as it sometimes was, but roughly enough; after which I was taken by main force, and

carried down into the cellar, across it almost to the opposite extremity, and brought to the last of the second range of cells on the left hand. The door was opened, and I was thrown in with violence, and left alone, the door being immediately closed and bolted on the outside. The bare ground was under me, cold and hard as if it had been beaten down even. I lay still, in the position in which I had fallen, as it would have been difficult for me to move, confined as I was, and exhausted by my exertions; and the shock of my fall, and my wretched state of desperation and fear, disinclined me from any further attempt. I was in almost total darkness, there being nothing perceptible except a slight glimmer of light which came in through the little window far above me. How long I remained in that condition I can only conjecture. It seemed to me a long time, and must have been two or three hours. I did not move, expecting to die there, and in a state of distress which I cannot describe, from the tight bandage about my hands, and the gag holding my jaws apart at their greatest extension. I am confident I must have died before morning, if, as I then expected, I had been left there all night.

After a time, Maria was finally released from her bonds by the mother superior. Maria Monk explained the wounds that such abuse left on her body.

Among the marks which I still bear of the wounds received from penances and violence, are the scars left by the belt with which I repeatedly tortured myself, for the mortification of my spirit. These are most distinct on my side; for although the band, which was four or five inches in breadth, and extended round the waist, was stuck full of sharp iron points in all parts, it was sometimes crowded most against my side, by rocking in my chair, and the wounds were usually deeper there than anywhere else. My thumbs were several times cut severely by the tight drawing of the band used to

confine my arms, and the scars are still visible upon them. The rough gagging which I several times endured wounded my lips very much; for it was common, in that operation, to thrust the gag hard against the teeth, and catch one or both the lips, which were sometimes cut. The object was to stop the screams made by the offender as soon as possible; and some of the old nuns delighted in tormenting us. A gag was once forced into my mouth which had a large splinter upon it, and this cut through my under lip, in front, leaving to this day a scar about half an inch long. The same lip was several times wounded, as well as the other; but one day worse than ever, when a narrow piece was cut off from the left side of it, by being pinched between the gag and the under fore-teeth; and this has left an inequality in it which is still very observable.[716]

In Maria Monk's narrative we have the very evidence to either confirm or refute her allegations. If she was never in the nunnery, as the Catholic church alleges, she would not bear on her body the marks of the abuse she alleges. If the scars are present on her body, their imprint act as the seal of proof upon her allegations.

Were those scars on her body? The answer is yes. Minister J.J. Slocum stated that a respectable lady inspected Maria Monk for signs of scars from the leather belt lined with sharp points of which Maria spoke. The lady confirmed that Maria's body bore clearly evident scars of the pointed belt. The lady stated that "it looks distressing."[717] Further, Slocum could see for himself that "[t]he marks of gagging are seen on her lips; and there are scars also on her thumbs, which were 'cut severely by the tight drawing of the band used to confine her arms.'"[718]

Here we have on Maria's body the very imprint of truth that confirms her account of the abuse in the Hotel Dieu Nunnery. There is simply no other way to account the strange scaring manifest on Maria Monk's body other than according to Maria Monk's explanation. Those scars stood as silent witnesses corroborating the truth of Maria Monk's report.

28 Masonic Secret Agent

William L. Stone was a nominal Protestant, but he was not a true believer in Jesus Christ. Indeed, he may have been a secret Catholic sympathizer. Stone was the first superintendent of public schools in New York City. In his capacity as superintendent, he was allegedly considering using bibles in the public schools. Did he confer with the pastors of the Presbyterian Church, of which he was a member? No, he did not. Did he confer with the Protestant bible societies? No, he did not do that either. He instead conferred with a representative of an organization that thinks it is dangerous for the common man to read the bible. He conferred with the Roman Catholic Archbishop of New York, John Hughes. Conferring with an enemy of the bible is no way to get bibles into schools. Stone was portraying himself as a Protestant; his conduct of conferring with the Roman Catholic archbishop allows us to see a little of his wolf's fur beneath his sheep's clothing and his affinity for the Catholic Church.

Conferring with the Catholic archbishop about bibles is really only a hint of his fidelity to Rome. There is more. Another notable fact about Stone is that he was a Freemason. He later allegedly disavowed Freemasonry, because it became politically inexpedient to be a Freemason after the infamous Captain Morgan murder. Morgan was murdered by Freemasons for revealing Masonic secrets. It seems that Stone's disavowal of Freemasonry was, like so many others, only a pretended disavowal.

Stone's opinion on the uprightness of Freemasons in their

obligation to keep their oaths is still cited today in the authoritative *Mackey's Encyclopedia of Freemasonry*.[719] Would Freemasons cite Stone as an authority on Freemasonry if he had truly disavowed Freemasonry?

Stone's opinion on Masonic oaths, which is cited by *Mackey's Encyclopedia of Freemasonry,* was written by Stone after he allegedly left Freemasonry. His opinion on Masonic oaths was in the form of a letter to John Quincy Adams. That letter was originally published by Stone in his 1832 book titled: *Letters on Freemasonry and Anti-Freemasonry Addressed to the Honorable John Quincy Adams*. Stone's letter is not a condemnation of Freemasonry, but rather extols the (fictional) virtues of Freemasonry.

Stone opens that letter with the claim that "in behalf of all those virtuous and intelligent citizens with whom I have formerly associated as a Mason, utterly to disclaim any and all constructions of those obligations, at variance with the laws of God or man, or which conflict with a proper discharge of all moral, social, and religious duties of life."[720] Does that sound like a man who has truly disavowed Freemasonry? It sounds more like an advocate on behalf of Freemasonry. It is an age-old strategy to feign disavowal of membership in an organization as a way to lead the opposition to it and thereby undermine the effectiveness of that opposition. Stone as a supposed opponent of Freemasonry would be in the perfect position to limit the damage done to Freemasonry by the exposure of its secrets by Captain Morgan and the public uproar that ensued from his murder in consequence thereof. In the intelligence community this is called a "limited hangout," where certain information is acknowledged in a pretended opposition, in order to steer the opposition away from the whole truth that would damage the enterprise. Vladimir Lenin explained: "The best way to control the opposition is to lead it ourselves."

The letter written by Stone claims that the oaths of Masons do not mean what they say. One of the oaths in question, which is among the milder oaths, is the oath of the Master Mason, which Stone quotes: "Further do I promise and swear, that a Master Mason's secrets, given to me in charge as such, shall remain as secure and inviolable in my breast as in his own, when communicated to me, murder and treason excepted; and they left to my own election."[721] Stone claims that the last seven words of the oath are unfamiliar to him, and he further alleges that the oath does not allow a Mason to conceal the villainy of a fellow Mason. Stone states that "he is expressly to understand that nothing therein contained is to interfere with his political or religious principles; with his duty to God; or the laws of his country."[722] That is not true, and Stone knew it when he wrote it. In fact, the whole point of the oath is to keep the villainy of fellow Masons secret. Why else would there be mention of the specific crimes of murder and treason in the oath if it were not to cover for the villainy of fellow Freemasons? The *Handbook of Masonry* states flat out that a Mason must even commit perjury if necessary to conceal the crimes of a fellow Mason.[723] The blood oaths of fidelity to the secrets of Masonry were seen in operation by the obstruction of justice by Freemasons during the investigation into the Morgan murder. Stone, by his dissimulation, has impeached his credibility and revealed himself as a deceiving apologist for the Freemasons, while pretending to oppose them.

One might ask what is wrong with being a Freemason? Isn't Freemasonry just a fraternal organization? Freemasonry is a heathen religion. There is not only a link between Islam and Catholicism, but there is also a clear link between Islam and Freemasonry, and a link between Catholicism and Freemasonry. Indeed, the Vatican has a pattern of using Protestant Masons as its undercover agents. Freemason Billy Graham is probably the most famous example of that phenomenon. Graham's covert activities on behalf of the Vatican are detailed in this author's book, *The Anti-Gospel*.

James D. Shaw was the first to authoritatively expose Billy Graham's Masonic membership. Shaw was a former Freemason. He attained the rank of a 33rd Degree Freemason, Knight Commander of the Court of Honor, Past Worshipful Master, Blue Lodge, and Past Master of all Scottish Rite Bodies. Shaw was saved by the grace of God, left Freemasonry, and wrote a book titled *The Deadly Deception*. Shaw revealed that Billy Graham personally attended Shaw's ceremony of induction as a 33rd degree Mason. Only fellow 33rd degree Masons are allowed to attend such ceremonies.

Shaw explained in his 1988 book that one must be a 32nd degree Mason in good standing for six months before being eligible to become a member of the Ancient Arabic Order, Nobles of the Mystic Shrine (a/k/a Shriner). The Shrine is the "Show Army of Masonry."[724] Membership in the Shrine has since been opened up to any Master Mason.[725] When becoming a Shriner, the member takes a horrible blood oath before an altar upon which rests a Quran. The oath calls upon the person to accept having "his eyeballs pierced to the center with a sharp three edged blade"[726] should he reveal any of the secrets of the Shriners. The solemn oath is made to "Allah the God of Arab, Moslem and Mohammedan, the God of our fathers."[727] Shaw explains:

> Every Shriner, kneeling before the Koran, takes this oath in the name of Allah, and ackknowledges this pagan god of vengeance as his own ("the God of our Fathers"). And, in the ritual, he acknowledges Islam, the declared blood-enemy of Christianity, as the one true path. ("Whoso seeketh Islam earnestly seeks true direction.")[728]

Shriner Hat (a/k/a Fez)

Shriners proudly wear the red brimless hat, they call a fez. The fez is named after the Moroccan city of Fez, which was purportedly the site of many massacres of Jews and Christians by Muslims. The red color of the fez is allegedly attributed to the practice of the Muslim soldiers dipping their hats in the blood of the victims of the massacres.

There is no evidence that William Stone was a Shriner. The information about Shriners, however, is important because it reveals the link between Freemasonry and Islam. Shaikh Hatim Nakhoda states that **"both Islam and Masonry have the same root, neither contradicting the other."**[729] Nakhoda's statement on that can be considered authoritative, as he is a recognized expert in both Islam and Freemasonry. "Shaikh Hatim Nakhoda is a Past Master of Lodge St. Michael No. 2933 and a Past District Senior Grand Warden of the District Grand Lodge of the Eastern Archipelago. He is also a Past

Master of Lodge Singapore No 7178. In addition, he holds the rank of Past Assistant Grand Director of Ceremony in the Grand Lodge of Mark Master Masons of England and Wales and its Districts Overseas. He also carries the title Shaikh, which was conferred on him for his knowledge on Islam."[730] Another expert in Freemasonry, Albert Pike revealed in the doctrinal bible of freemasonry, *Morals and Dogma*: **"Masonry is a search for Light. That leads us directly back, as you see, to the Kabalah."**[731] Nakhoda states that "both Islam and Masonry have the same root." Albert Pike states that the root of Masonry is the Jewish Kabalah. The Jewish Kabbalah flowed from the occultism of ancient Babylon. Many of the degrees of Freemasonry were written by the Catholic Jesuits. Islam, Catholicism, and Judaism are all woven into the warp and woof of every degree of Freemasonry to form an occult amalgam. Freemasonry is a mixture of occult religions. It conceals the object of the worship beneath mystic liturgical veils; only those initiated into the highest degrees are given the secret behind the veil: Satan. The doctrines of Islam, Judaism, and Catholicism all spring from ancient Babylon and find a home in Freemasonry.

According to Nakhoda, the root of Islam is the same as that of Freemasonry. Albert Pike, the theological pontiff of Freemasonry, stated that the root of Freemasonry is that the god of Freemasonry is Lucifer.[732] Unless Nakhoda wants to contradict Albert Pike, he must admit that the god of Islam is Lucifer.

Martin L. Wagner conducted an objective and thorough study of Freemasonry and wrote a book about his findings titled *Freemasonry: An Interpretation.* Wagner's authoritative study of Freemasonry concludes that Freemasonry is not simply a fraternal organization, it is in fact a religion. What kind of religion is Masonry? Wagner interviewed many former Masons who quit Masonry because they discovered that the Masonic religion was antithetical to Christianity. "Its aim and tendency is to undermine their faith in the Lord Jesus Christ as their personal Saviour; that it alienates their affections and support from the church, and destroys their faith in the Bible as the word of God."[733]

The god of Freemasonry is the Great Architect of the Universe. In order to keep up the charade that the Masonic Great Architect of the Universe is the God of the bible, Freemasons conceal from the public the name of their god. Freemasons call their Great Architect of the Universe by the name *Jabulun*[734] (a/k/a *Jah-Bul-On*[735] or *Jah-Bel-On*[736]). That name is a cryptographic word that is based upon the abbreviated names for Jehovah (*Jah*), Baal (*Bel* or *Bul*), and Osiris (*On*).[737] The Freemasons blasphemously identify Jehovah, who is the God of the bible, as the Hebrew sun god.[738] The Freemasons join that name to Baal, who was the Assyrian sun god, to whom the Jews sacrificed their children. *See* Jeremiah 32:26-36. The sixteenth century demonologist John Weir identified Baal as a devil.[739] Osiris was the Egyptian sun god. There cannot be a joining of God with Baal, Osiris, or any other heathen god. "What concord hath Christ with Belial?" 2 Corinthians 6:15. The Prophet Elijah stated "if the Lord be God, follow him: but if Baal, then follow him." 1 Kings 18:21. There is only one God and salvation is solely by the grace of God through faith in Jesus Christ. "Neither is there salvation in any other: for there is none other name under heaven given among men, whereby we must be saved" Acts 4:12.

The cryptic title for the god of the Masons acts as a glyph to conceal the true god of Freemasonry, who is Lucifer. The Supreme Theological Pontiff of Freemasonry, Albert Pike, said that "[t]he doctrine of Satanism is heresy; and the true and pure philosophic religion is the belief in Lucifer, the equal of Adonay; but Lucifer, God of Light and God of Good, is struggling for humanity against Adonay, the God of Darkness and Evil."[740] The doctrines of Freemasonry are influenced to a great extent by Roman Catholic doctrine and history. In 1754 the first 25 degrees of the Scottish Rite of Freemasonry were written by the Jesuits in the College of Jesuits of Clermont in Paris, for the purpose of restoring to power the Jesuit controlled House of Stuart to the throne of England.[741] There are a series of degrees in the Masonic York Rite hierarchy known as the Order of Knights Templar. The Knights Templar was an organization founded in 1118 A.D. The Templars received papal sanction as a Catholic order (the Order of the Poor Knights of Christ) in 1128 and are recognized as the first Roman Catholic crusaders. The Templars were known as the "Militia of Christ." As explained by Nesta Webster, Freemasonry is an amalgam of the theology and secret practices of the Roman Catholic Templars and Cabalistic Jews.[742] Freemasonry is a phallic religion, like Islam and Catholicism. For more information on Freemasonry read this author's book, *Bloody Zion*.

Was William L. Stone's tour of the Montreal nunnery and pretended refutation of Maria Monk a fulfilment of his masonic blood oath of deception? The initiation into the Royal Arch (7th degree of the York Rite and 13th degree of the Scottish Rite) requires the initiate to drink wine from the top half of a human skull and take a blood oath not to reveal any of the secrets of Masonry and to lie and do anything else necessary to assist a fellow Mason in extricating himself from the consequences of committing any crime, including murder and treason. The *Handbook of Masonry* states that a Mason "must conceal all the crimes of your brother Masons ... and should you be summoned as a witness against a brother Mason be always sure to shield him ... It may be perjury to do this, it is true, but you're keeping your obligations."[743] According to the Roman Catholic publication Sodalitium, in 1961, Pope John XXIII reinstated the Knights of Malta and rescinded the prohibition of Roman Catholics holding membership in Freemasonry.[744]

While Pope John XXIII's edict was the first public permission given for Roman Catholics to become Freemasons, there were many Freemasons within the Catholic hierarchy for hundreds years prior to that, during which time there had been secret intercourse and cooperation. One notable Catholic Freemason was Pope John XXIII himself. French Freemason, Baron Yves Marsaudon, revealed that Roncalli (later elected Pope John XXIII) became a 33rd degree Freemason while a papal nuncio to France, between 1944 and 1953. During that time, Catholics were supposed to be prohibited from membership in Freemasonry. Baron Marsaudon was appointed by Pope John XXIII as head of the French branch of the Knights of Malta.[745] The fact that Pope John XXIII was a Freemason was confirmed by the Grand Master of the Grand Orient of Italy, who said in an interview for *30 Days* magazine: "As for that, it seems that John XXIII was initiated (into a Masonic lodge) in Paris and participated in the work of the Istanbul workshops."[746] (parenthetical in original)

Former Jesuit priest Alberto Rivera testified to the cooperation between the Jesuits and Freemasons. In one instance, Rivera was invited by high ranking Jesuit officials to a secret black Mass in Spain. At the event, River kneeled in obeisance to kiss a Jesuit official's ring.[747] The ring he kissed bore a masonic symbol, indicating that the Jesuit official was a Freemason.

Could Stone have been a Freemason on a secret assignment in service of Rome when he was given the tour of the Montreal nunnery? It is notable that Stone was one of very few persons who was ever allowed by the Catholic bishop inside the cloistered area of the nunnery to be given permission by the Catholic bishop to publish what he saw. That fact alone makes the whole affair suspicious. The Bishop refused all requests by Maria Monk to be allowed to bring in objective observers. Why was not Maria Monk, along with people of her choosing, allowed to tour the nunnery and document the event, as she requested? The answer is obvious. The whole point of Stone's tour was not to reveal but to conceal. As much as the Catholic authorities tried to rearrange the nunnery with new construction, they could not rebuild the building. They could not allow Monk to guide people to secret passages and to areas of the nunnery that only one who resided there would know about. Her knowledge of the building could have exposed the new construction.

After Stone's Article refuting Maria Monk appeared, a Protestant organization published a booklet, titled: *Evidence Demonstrating the Falsehoods of William L. Stone Concerning the Hotel Dieu Nunnery of Montreal*. That booklet reveals that while Stone publically maintained that his article was an accurate representation of what he saw at the nunnery, he had privately confessed that his article was a deception.[748]

Stone's mission to Montreal from the beginning was designed to refute the charges of Maria Monk. When Maria Monk first went public with her story, Stone's newspaper, the *New York Commercial Advertiser*, initially published articles in support of Maria Monk. However, because of pressure from some subscribers in Canada who cancelled subscriptions, and fearing the lost income from further cancellations, Stone's newspaper did an about face and changed its stance regarding Maria Monk. Stone's newspaper went from supporting Monk to suddenly calling her book-"a humbug."[749] Stone came to understand clearly that his Canadien subscribers were under the influence of the Catholic prelates, most of whom would cancel their subscriptions if ordered by them to do so. Stone's mission to tour the Hotel Dieu Nunnery in Montreal was for the purpose of placating the Catholic prelates and preventing his Catholic Canadien subscribers from cancelling their subscriptions.[750]

29   The Torture Room

Below is an excerpt from the 1858 book written by Sarah J. Richardson, *Life in the Grey Nunnery at Montreal*. Like Maria Monk, she was one of the few nuns to successfully escape from a cloistered nunnery and live to tell about it. The shocking revelations in the book are supported by six affidavits appended to the book attesting to the veracity and honesty of Sarah J. Richardson. Indeed, Sarah Richardson, herself, appended an affidavit to the book swearing under oath to its truth. She stated in pertinent part: "I, Sarah J. Richardson ... do solemnly swear, declare and say, that the foregoing pages contain a true and faithful history of my life before my marriage to the said Frederick S. Richardson, and that every statement made herein by me is true."[751]

The veracity of Sarah Richardson is significantly enhanced by the fact that she resisted every effort to convince her to publish her account of her life in the Grey Nunnery. She was afraid of certain death that would be orchestrated by the Romish priests. She stated: "For my life I would not do it. Not because I do not wish the world to know it, for I would gladly proclaim it wherever a Romanist is known, but it would be impossible for me to escape their hands should I make myself so public. They would most assuredly take my life."[752] Once she was married, however, she felt protected by her husband and therefore felt free to publically reveal in a book the horrors of the Grey Nunnery.

In addition to all of the other abuse that Sarah endured at the nunnery, she was one day sent to a torture room that was concealed in the bowels of the nunnery. Sarah made a trifling mistake for which she was to be punished. The pertinent part of her punishment required her to spend three days in a torture room. Until she was escorted to the torture room, she did not know that the room even existed at the nunnery. Sarah stated that the entrance to the torture room was so well hidden in the cellar of the nunnery that one could spend a lifetime in the nunnery and not know of its existence. Below is a narrative from chapter 17 of her book that recounts what Sarah saw in the torture room:

> I remember hearing a gentleman at the depot remark that the very enormity of the crimes committed by the Romanists, is their best protection. "For," said he, "some of their practices are so shockingly infamous they may not even be alluded to in the presence of the refined and the virtuous. And if the story of their guilt were told, who would believe the tale? Far easier would it be to call the whole a slanderous fabrication, than to believe that man can be so vile." This consideration led me to doubt the propriety of attempting a description of what I saw in that room. But I have engaged to give a faithful narrative of what transpired in the nunnery; and shall I leave out a part because it is so strange and monstrous, that people will not believe it? No. I will tell, without the least exaggeration what I saw, heard, and experienced. People may not credit the story now, but a day will surely come when they will know that I speak the truth.
>
> As I entered the room I was exceedingly shocked at the horrid spectacle that met my eye. I knew that fearful scenes were enacted in the subterranean cells, but I never imagined anything half so terrible as this. In various parts of the room I saw machines, and instruments of torture, and on some of them persons were confined who seemed to be suffering the most excruciating agony. I paused, utterly overcome with terror, and for a moment imagined that I was a witness to the torments, which, the priests say, are endured by the lost, in the world of woe. Was I to undergo such

tortures, and which of those infernal engines would be applied to me? I was not long in doubt. The priest took hold of me and put me into a machine that held me fast, while my feet rested on a piece of iron which was gradually heated until both feet were blistered. I think I must have been there fifteen minutes, but perhaps the time seemed longer than it was. He then took me out, put some ointment on my feet and left me.

I was now at liberty to examine more minutely the strange objects around me. There were some persons in the place whose punishment, like my own, was light compared with others. But near me lay one old lady extended on a rack. Her joints were all dislocated, and she was emaciated to the last degree. I do not suppose I can describe this rack, for I never saw anything like it. It looked like a gridiron but was long enough for the tallest man to lie upon. There were large rollers at each end, to which belts were attached, with a large lever to drive them back and forth. Upon this rack the poor woman was fastened in such a way, that when the levers were turned and the rollers made to revolve, every bone in her body was displaced. Then the violent strain would be relaxed, a little, and she was so very poor, her skin would sink into the joints and remain there till it mortified and corrupted.

It was enough to melt the hardest heart to witness her agony; but she bore it with a degree of fortitude and patience, I could not have supposed possible, had I not been compelled to behold it. When I entered the room she looked up and said, "Have you come to release me, or only to suffer with me?" I did not dare to reply, for the priest was there, but when he left us she exclaimed, "My child, let nothing induce you to believe this cursed religion. It will be the death of you, and that death, will be the death of a dog." I suppose she meant that they would kill me as they would a dog. She then asked, "Who put you here?" "My Father," said I. "He must have been a brute," said she, "or he never could have done it." At one time I happened to mention the name of God, when she fiercely exclaimed with gestures of contempt, "A God! You believe there is one, do you? Don't you suffer yourself to believe any such thing. Think you that a wise, merciful, and all powerful being would allow such a hell as this to exist? Would he suffer me to be torn from friends and home, from my poor children and all that my soul holds dear, to be confined in this den of iniquity, and tortured to death in this cruel manner? No, O, no. He would at once destroy these monsters in human form; he would not suffer them, for one moment, to breathe the pure air of heaven."

At another time she exclaimed, "O, my children! my poor motherless children! What will become of them? God of mercy, protect my children!" Thus, at one moment, she would say there was no God, and the next, pray to him for help. This did not surprise me, for she was in such intolerable misery she did not realize what she did say. Every few hours the priest came in, and gave the rollers a turn, when her joints would crack and--but I cannot describe it. The sight made me sick and faint at the time, as the recollection of it, does now. It seemed as though that man must have had a heart of adamant, or he could not have done it. She would shriek, and groan, and weep, but it did not affect him in the least. He was as calm, and deliberate as though he had a block of wood in his hands, instead of a human being. When I saw him coming, I once shook my head at her, to have her stop speaking; but when he was gone, she said, "Don't shake your head at me; I do not fear him. He can but kill me, and the quicker he does it the better. I would be glad if he would put an end to my misery at once, but that would be too merciful. He is determined to kill me by inches, and it makes no difference what I say to him."

She had no food, or drink, during the three days I was there, and the priest never spoke to her. He brought me my bread and water regularly, and I would gladly have given it to that poor woman if she would have taken it. But she would not accept the offer. It would only prolong her sufferings, and she wished to die. I do not suppose she could have lived, had she been taken out when I first saw her.

In another part of the room, a monk was under punishment. He was standing in some kind of a machine, with heavy weights attached to his feet, and a belt passed across his breast under his arms. He appeared to be in great distress, and no refreshment was furnished him while I was there.

On one side of the room, I observed a closet with a "slide door," as the nuns called them. There were several doors of this description in the building, so constructed as to slide back into the ceiling out of sight. Through this opening I could see an image resembling a monk; and whenever any one was put in there, they would shriek, and groan, and beg to be taken out, but I could not ascertain the cause of their suffering.

One day a nun was brought in to be punished. The priest led her up to the side of the room, and bade her put her fingers into some holes in the wall just large enough to admit them. She obeyed but immediately drew them back with a loud shriek. I looked to see what was the matter with her, and lo! every nail was torn from her fingers, which were bleeding profusely. How it was done, I do not know. Certainly, there was no visible cause for such a surprising effect. In all probability the fingers came in contact with the spring of some machine on the other side, or within the wall to which some sharp instrument was attached. I would give much to know just how it was constructed, and what the girl had done to subject herself to such a terrible and unheard-of punishment. But this, like many other things in that establishment, was wrapped in impenetrable mystery. God only knows when the veil will be removed, or whether it ever will be until the day when all secret things will be brought to light.[753]

30   The "Holy" Antichrist

The Pope takes the title of God the Father. For example, the *Catechism of the Catholic Church*, at § 10, refers to Pope John II as the "Holy Father, Pope John II." The pope goes by other majestic titles such as "Your Holiness." Pope John Paul II, himself, admitted that such titles are inimical to the Gospel. He even cited the Bible passage that condemns such practices. He simply explained that the Catholic traditions of men implicitly authorize this violation of God's commands.

> Have no fear when people call me the 'Vicar of Christ,' when they say to me 'Holy Father,' or 'Your Holiness,' or use titles similar to these, which seem even inimical to the Gospel. Christ declared: 'Call no one on earth your father; you have one Father in heaven. Do not be called 'Master;' you have but one master, the Messiah' (Mt 23:9-10). These expressions, nevertheless, have evolved out of a long tradition, becoming part of common usage. One must not be afraid of these words either. *Pope John Paul II.*[754]

The term "Holy Father" was used in the Holy Scripture only one time; it was used by Jesus the night before his crucifixion to refer to God the Father.

And now I am no more in the world, but these are in

> the world, and I come to thee. **Holy Father**, keep through thine own name those whom thou hast given me, that they may be one, as we are. (John 17:11)

Implicit in taking God's name is taking his position and authority. As Jesus said in John 14:28, God the Father is greater than Jesus.

> Ye have heard how I said unto you, I go away, and come again unto you. If ye loved me, ye would rejoice, because I said, I go unto the Father: for **my Father is greater than I.** (John 14:28)

By taking the title "Holy Father," the Pope is implicitly presenting himself as greater than Jesus Christ. Jesus Christ is God who came to earth in the flesh. Taking the title of "Holy Father" is a fulfilment of Paul's prophecy of the antichrist "[w]ho opposeth and exalteth himself above all that is called God, or that is worshipped; so that he as God sitteth in the temple of God, shewing himself that he is God." (2 Thessalonians 2:4)

Lucius Ferraris, a Franciscan Monk, in his authoritative work, *Prompta Bibliotheca Canonica*, states: "The Pope is of so great dignity and so exalted that he is not mere man, but as it were God, and the vicar of God."[755] Ferraris further states: "Hence the Pope is crowned with a triple crown, as king of heaven and of earth and of the lower regions."[756] Think about that. The pope claims to rule heaven; that means that he has authority in heaven over God Almighty. That is yet another fulfillment of the prophecy regarding the antichrist in 2 Thessalonians 2:4 which states that the antichrist will **"opposeth and exalteth himself above all that is called God, or that is worshipped."** (2 Thessalonians 2:4)

The arrogance of the pope who "exalteth himself above all that is called God" is so extreme, that he has delegated authority to his subordinate priests to order the Lord God Almighty Jesus Christ to obey their commands. The Catechism of the Council of Trent grants the Catholic priest *de jure* status equal to the Lord Jesus Christ. **"The priest is also one and the same, Christ the Lord."**[757] The Catholic practice, however, is that the priest has *de facto* authority above that of

Christ, since upon command of the Catholic priest, Jesus purportedly must obey their magical incantation, leave heaven, and enter the consecrated Eucharistic host during the Catholic Mass. **"Thus acting in the Person of Christ the Lord, he [the Catholic priest] changes the substance of the bread and wine into the true substance of His [Jesus'] body and blood."**[758] Under Catholic doctrine, the Catholic priests have power over God to conjure his presence upon command. What megalomania. What blasphemy!

The Catholic priests require their congregation to call them "father." What does God think of this practice? "And call no man your father upon the earth: for one is your Father, which is in heaven." (Matthew 23:9)

The very title "Pope" is a Latin word which means papa. It is the term used by small children to refer to their father. It is the Latin equivalent of "dada" or "daddy." In Aramaic Hebrew "papa" would be translated by some as "abba." Abba is used 3 times in the Holy Bible. Each time Abba refers to God the Father.

> And he said, **Abba, Father,** all things are possible unto thee; take away this cup from me: nevertheless not what I will, but what thou wilt. (Mark 14:36)

> For ye have not received the spirit of bondage again to fear; but ye have received the Spirit of adoption, whereby we cry, **Abba, Father.** (Romans 8:15)

> And because ye are sons, God hath sent forth the Spirit of his Son into your hearts, crying, **Abba, Father.** (Galatians 4:6)

As stated above, many view Abba as equivalent to "papa" or "dad." However, it should be noted that may not accurately reflect what Jesus was conveying. There is some debate over what exactly Abba means in the above passages. Clearly, it is an intimate, yet respectful, cry to God the Father. Notice the trusting humility connoted in Mark when Jesus calls God "Abba, Father." All the children of God who are saved by faith in Jesus Christ through God's grace can come to God the Father, with the same respect and intimacy that Jesus came to him, and cry "Abba, Father."

The doubts about what exactly the word Abba means explains why the King James translators, did not translate Abba with an equivalent English word. Regardless of the uncertainty over what Abba means, it seems that the pope of Rome is all to happy to be considered the 'papa' of his children in the Roman Catholic Church in the same way that God the Father is "Abba, Father" to his children. The Pope of Rome wants his subjects to humble themselves before him as trusting children. He is the papa of their faith. He has taken the name that is rightfully God's in his attempt to turn men from God to him. The Pope not only desires submission to his authority, but it is not uncommon for the Pope to humiliate his subjects by requiring them to kiss his feet.[759]
Such arrogance is the very opposite of the humility that is the calling of ministers of the true gospel.

> Whosoever therefore shall humble himself as this little child, the same is greatest in the kingdom of heaven. (Matthew 18:4)
>
> Verily I say unto you, Whosoever shall not receive the kingdom of God as a little child, he shall not enter therein. (Mark 10:15)

31 Supreme Druid

The ancient Romans were in general tolerant of the religions of other cultures as long as they were approved by the state. Rome had a council of priests which had charge of Rome's religious activities and passed on the acceptability of any religious belief.[760] The members of this early ecumenical council were called pontiffs.[761] Pontiff means bridge maker. The pontiffs considered themselves intermediaries between God (or the gods as the case may have been) and man.[762] Around 31 B.C. Caesar Augustus declared himself head of the council of priests.[763] Thereafter, the emperor of Rome was considered the Supreme Pontiff (*Pontifex Maximus*),[764] which was the high priest of the pagan religions of Rome.[765] He was also worshiped as a god.[766] The Roman Pontiff did not tolerate anyone who worshiped a god other than him. Consequently, Christians were persecuted for following the true God, Jesus

Where did Caesar get his concept of Potifex Maximus? When Rome conquered Britain, it borrowed many of the Druid customs. Caesar Augustus declared himself head of the council of priests (Pontifex Maximus), in imitation of the office of the Arch-Druid. Where did the Druids obtain their religious customs? Hislop explains that "[t]he Druidic system in all its parts was evidently the Babylonian system."[767]

When the Jews decided to create a rival to the Christian Church, they inculcated their paganized version of "Christianity" with the

Babylonian theology. It was an easy step to graft onto their Roman Church the office of Supreme Pontiff. The Pope is the successor to that pagan office and to this day claims the title of Supreme Pontiff. He even wears a triple crown, because he claims to rule as king over Heaven, Hell, and Earth. Hislop explains the Babylonian origins of this office of Supreme Pontiff:

> I have said that the Pope became the representative of Janus, who, it is evident, was none other than the Babylonian Messiah. If the reader only considers the blasphemous assumptions of the Papacy, he will see how exactly it has copied from its original. In the countries where the Babylonian system was most thoroughly developed, we find the Sovereign Pontiff of the Babylonian god invested with the very attributes now ascribed to the Pope. Is the Pope called "God upon earth," the "Vice-God," and "Vicar of Jesus Christ"? The King in Egypt, who was Sovereign Pontiff, was, says Wilkinson, regarded with the highest reverence as "THE REPRESENTATIVE OF THE DIVINITY ON EARTH."[768]

32 Denying Christ Has Come in the Flesh

John makes it clear in two passages that the antichrist will deny that Jesus Christ has come in the flesh.

For many deceivers are entered into the world, who confess not that Jesus Christ is come in the flesh. This is a deceiver and an antichrist. (2 John 1:7)

Hereby know ye the Spirit of God: Every spirit that confesseth that Jesus Christ is come in the flesh is of God: And every spirit that confesseth not that Jesus Christ is come in the flesh is not of God: and this is that spirit of antichrist, whereof ye have heard that it should come; and even now already is it in the world. (1 John 4:2-3)

Many take the view that the pope could not be the prophesied antichrist, because the pope does not deny that Jesus Christ has come in the flesh. Some hold the possibility that some future pope might be the antichrist but the present pope could not be the antichrist because he does not deny that Jesus has come in the flesh. An example is S. Michael Houdmann who is the Chief Executive Officer of GotQuestions.org, a bible answer website. In response to the question: "Is the pope, or the next pope, the antichrist?" Houdmann or a contributing editor responded on his bible answer website:

> The current Pope, Francis I, acknowledges Jesus as being from God and Jesus as coming in the flesh (see 1 John 4:2). While we disagree with Pope Francis I on numerous areas of Catholic doctrine, his view of the Person of Jesus Christ is biblical. Therefore, it's hard to believe that Pope Francis I is the Antichrist. While we believe it is possible for a Pope to be the Antichrist, the Bible does not give specific enough information to be dogmatic. A future Pope very well may be the Antichrist, or perhaps the Antichrist's false prophet (Revelation 13:11-17). If so, this future Pope will be clearly identified by a denial of Jesus as coming in the flesh.[769]

Others are more absolute and unequivocal and state that no pope could be the antichrist. "Since past and current Catholic Popes affirm that Jesus came in the flesh, it would be difficult to see how he could be the Antichrist."[770]

The pope himself paraphrases 1 John 4, telling people to look for the antichrist in the future who will deny Jesus. It seems that the pope is secure in the fact that people will not detect him as the antichrist if they look for someone who will deny Jesus. In January 2014, Pope Francis stated:

> John gives us a "simple" criterion to determine what is from God and what is from the Antichrist.
>
> "Every spirit that acknowledges Jesus Christ come in the flesh belongs to God, and every spirit that does not acknowledge Jesus does not belong to God," the Pope noted. "This is the spirit of the Antichrist."[771]

Does that settle it? Is the pope in the clear? Is it so apparent that the pope does not fulfill the test of John that the pope himself will cite that as the test of some future antichrist? Not so fast! Notice how clever the pope was in pointing people toward a future antichrist. The pope states that the future antichrist is the "spirit that does not acknowledge Jesus." In fact, that is not what John prophesied. John stated that **"every spirit that confesseth not that Jesus Christ is come in the flesh is not of God: and this is that spirit of antichrist."** Note the difference. The antichrist will deny that Jesus has come in the flesh. Pope Francis did not want his audience to use John's test to identify the antichrist.

The beast of Rome is so subtle! "The serpent was more subtil than any beast of the field." (Genesis 3:1) The pope hopes to subtly steer people away from looking into those who deny that Jesus has come in the flesh. Why? Because he knows it will lead people right to his door.

Steve Wohlberg explains how the Catholic doctrine of the immaculate conception of Mary fulfills the prophecy in the bible that the antichrist will deny that Jesus Christ has come in the flesh:

> The Bible says that a denial that "Jesus Christ is come in the flesh" is a definite mark of Antichrist. "Hereby know ye the Spirit of God: Every spirit that confesseth that Jesus Christ is come in the flesh is of God: And every spirit that confesseth not that Jesus Christ is come in the flesh is not of God: and this is that spirit of antichrist, whereof ye have heard that it should come; and even now already is it in the world (1 John 4:2, 3). Again we read, "For many deceivers are entered into the world, who confess not that Jesus Christ is come in the flesh. This is a deceiver and an antichrist" (2 John 7). This denial comes from those who are "deceivers," thus we should not expect it to be always open and obvious.
>
> The true Spirit of God, which is also called "the spirit of truth" (1 John 4:6), will always "confess" that Jesus Christ has come in the flesh. And this confession is more than simply a belief or statement that Jesus Christ is a real Person, that He came into the world two thousand years ago, lived a perfect life, and died on the cross for our sins. Amazingly, a person can confess all these things and yet still be "a deceiver and an

antichrist" (2 John 7). According to the Bible, the specific confession must be that Jesus Christ is come in *the flesh*. And this confession must be genuine. What does it mean that "Jesus Christ is come in the flesh"?

The Bible says about our Savior, "The Word was made flesh, and dwelt among us" (John 1:14). When the Son of God was "made flesh," He clothed His Divinity with humanity. Yet what kind of flesh did He clothe Himself with? Notice carefully, "Forasmuch then as the children are partakers of flesh and blood, he also himself likewise took part of *the same*" (Hebrews 2:14). This tells us clearly that Jesus Christ did not take upon Himself the flesh of Adam and Eve before they sinned, but rather that He took the flesh of the "children," which applies to fallen humanity. Read it again, "As the *children* are partakers of *flesh* and blood, he also himself likewise took part of *the same*" (Hebrews 2:14). Thus the Bible says that Jesus Christ took upon Himself the *same flesh* that we have. To deny this is the mark of Antichrist.

Why is this so important? Here's the reason. First of all, Hebrews 2:14,15 definitely connects the coming of Jesus Christ in the flesh with His high priestly ministry and with His present ability to save us from sin. Because Jesus came in the same flesh that we have, this made it possible for Him to be "in all points tempted *like as we are*, yet without sin." (Hebrews 4:15). Jesus took our flesh upon Himself, yet He never sinned. This means He overcame the flesh in our behalf! Then He ascended to heaven to become our great High Priest. "Seeing then that we have a great high priest, that is passed into the heavens, Jesus the Son of God, let us hold fast our profession [or confession]. For we have not a high priest which cannot be touched with the feeling of our infirmities; but was in all points tempted like as we are, yet without sin. Let us therefore come boldly unto the throne of grace, that we may obtain mercy, and find grace to help in time of need"

(Hebrews 4:14-16).

Hebrews 2:16,17 also firmly connects Jesus Christ's coming in the same nature that we have with His high priestly ministry and with His present ability to save us from sin. "For verily He took not on him the nature of angels [who are unfallen beings]; but he took on him the seed of Abraham [a fallen man]. Wherefore in all things it behoved him to be made like unto his brethren, that he might be a merciful and faithful high priest in things pertaining to God, to make reconciliation for the sins of the people. For in that he himself has suffered being tempted, he is able also to succour them that are tempted."

Once again the truth is established. Because Jesus Christ came in the same flesh and with the same nature that we have, He could be tempted in all points like as we are, and yet He never sinned. As our great High Priest, He is now fully able to sympathize with us in our weaknesses, to help us when we are tempted, and to supply sufficient grace that we also might overcome sin. Because Jesus Christ has come in the flesh, He is now waiting for us at the throne. His arms are open wide. Even though we are unworthy sinners, we may now "come boldly to the throne of grace" for mercy, forgiveness, and power. We need no other mediators. *This is all part of our confession.*

It was the teaching of all of the major Protestant Reformers that Papal Rome is the "little horn" (Daniel 7:8), the "beast" (Revelation 13:1), and "the man of sin" (2 Thessalonians 2:3) - the great Antichrist of Bible prophecy. Does the Roman Church truly teach and genuinely confess that "Jesus Christ is come in the flesh"? On the surface it may claim to do so, but let's take a closer look. One of the official doctrines, or "confessions," of the Roman Church is called the Immaculate Conception, which actually refers to the conception of Mary long before the birth of Christ.

This doctrine declares that when Mary was conceived in the womb of her own mother, she was miraculously preserved from all sin. Therefore her nature was "immaculate," or sinless, and thus different from the rest of humanity. In other words, Mary did not have the same flesh and nature that we have! According to the Papal Rome's official statements, when Jesus Christ was born, He took *Mary's nature, not ours*. Thus, in actuality, the Roman Church denies that "Jesus Christ has come in the flesh" (1 John 4:3).

Here's the proof:

"This is what the dogma of the Immaculate Conception confesses [this is their own word], as Pope Pius IX proclaimed in 1854: The most Blessed Virgin Mary was, from the first moment of her conception, by a singular grace and privilege of almighty God and by virtue of the merits of Jesus Christ, Savior of the human race, preserved immune from all stain of original sin." *Catechism of the Catholic Church*, p. 124 (1994).

As a consequence, according to the Roman Church, when Jesus Christ was born, He partook of *Mary's* [supposed immaculate] *nature, not ours*. The famous Cardinal Gibbons wrote: "In other words we affirm that the Second Person of the Blessed Trinity ...... by being born of the Virgin, [took] to Himself, from her maternal womb, a human nature of the same substance *with hers* ... a true human nature of the same substance with *her own*" (italics added). *The Faith of our Fathers*, by Cardinal Gibbons, p. 167. Quoted in *The Faith of Millions:* The Credentials of the Catholic Church, by Rev. John A. O'Brien, Ph. D., p. 441 (1955).

This doctrine of the Immaculate Conception and of the subsequent entrance of Jesus Christ into *Mary's* [supposed immaculate] *nature, not ours,* actually removes our Savior a step away from the rest of us. As a result of this dogma, and others, the Roman Church teaches that sinners cannot be saved by going directly to our heavenly Father through His Son, Jesus Christ (a Protestant doctrine). Instead, sinners must come to Jesus Christ *through* Mary, popes, priests, and saints - through the mediation of the Roman Catholic Church. By virtue of Mary's Immaculate Conception, "saving office," and "manifold intercession," she is now our "Advocate, Helper, Benefactress, and Mediatrix," who can supposedly "bring us the gifts of eternal salvation," and "deliver our souls from death." *Catechism of the Catholic Church,* p. 252. (1994).

Thus, in her official teachings, in spite of appearances, the Roman Church actually denies that "Jesus Christ has come in the flesh" (1 John 4:3), that is, in "the same" (Hebrews 2:14) flesh as the rest of us. No matter what she may claim, Rome's declaration that Mary is our "Advocate" and "Mediatrix" actually "denies the Father and the Son" (1 John 2:22). God's Word says, "...every spirit that confesseth not that Jesus Christ is come in *the flesh* is not of God: and this is that spirit of antichrist, whereof ye have heard that it should come; and even now already is it in the world (1 John 4:2, 3).

Dear friend, are you struggling with sin and with the temptations of your own flesh? I have good news for you. Not only did the Son of God die on the cross for all of your sins (1 Corinthians 15:3), but "Jesus Christ has come in *the flesh"* (1 John 4:2). He took your flesh and overcame it. And now, as our great High Priest, "he is able also to save them to the uttermost that come unto God by him, seeing he ever liveth to make intercession for them" (Hebrews 7:25). Because Jesus Christ has come in the flesh, He *alone* is our Savior and Intercessor. "There is one God, and *one mediator* between God and man, the Man Christ Jesus" (1 Timothy 2:5). To deny this is to deny that Jesus Christ has come in *the flesh,* which the Bible says is the special mark of the Antichrist.⁷⁷² (parenthetical brackets in original)

33 Queen of Heaven

The immaculately conceived Mary of the Roman Catholic Church is a different Mary from the Mary in the bible. In the bible, Mary is the handmaid of the Lord. See Luke 1:38. The immaculately conceived Mary of the Roman Catholic Church, however, is an imperious queen of heaven, who rules over all things.

The Catholic Mary (as distinguished from the biblical Mary) is a heathen goddess, who in 1950 was "infallibly" declared by Pope Pius XII to have been assumed body and soul into heaven and crowned **"Queen over all things."**

> Finally the Immaculate Virgin, preserved free from all stain of original sin, when the course of her earthly life was finished, was taken up body and soul into heavenly glory, and exalted by the Lord as **Queen over all things**, so that she might be the more fully conformed to her Son, the Lord of lords and conqueror of sin and death. Pope Pius XII -- Munificentissimus Deus, 1950.

The problem with that "infallible" pronouncement of the pope is that it is impossible for Mary to be "queen over all things." The Bible states unequivocally that Jesus Christ "is the blessed and **only Potentate**, the Lord of lords and King of kings." 1 Timothy 6:15. A potentate is a sovereign monarch.[773] Jesus Christ is the "only

Potentate." "Only" means only! There is not room in heaven for another Potentate. Mary, therefore, cannot be "queen over all things." Jesus is the **"only Potentate"** over all things! The Catholic Church also has a different gospel, with a different Jesus than that which is found in the bible. See 2 Corinthians 11:4. The Catholic Jesus is not the "only Potentate" in heaven.

Satan is using his Catholic Church and its doctrine of Mariolatry to attempt a futile spiritual *coup d'etat* to supplant Jesus and enthrone its Mary as the "Queen of Heaven." The Catholic Church is dedicated to the worship and service of "Mary," the queen of heaven. Jesus is ancillary and almost incidental to the worship of the Catholic queen of heaven. For example, the coin commemorating the pontificate of John Paul II has on the front has a declaration that he is the Pontifex Maximus. "On the reverse side is his papal heraldic shield. The large letter M on the shield stands for Mary, the mother of God. The words at the bottom 'TOTUS TUUS' are transposed and excerpted from a latin prayer composed by Saint Louis-Marie Grignion de Montfort: *tuus totus ego sum, et omnia mea tua sunt, O Virgo super omnia benedicta*, which in English reads 'I belong to you entirely, and all that I possess is yours, Virgin blessed above all.'"[774] The pope dedicates his fealty not to Jesus but to "Mary," the Catholic "Queen of Heaven."

In 1978, on the feast day of the Immaculate Conception, Pope John Paul II dedicated and entrusted the Roman Catholic Church and all its property not to their Catholic version of Jesus, but rather to their Catholic version of Mary:

> The Pope, at the beginning of his episcopal service in St. Peter's Chair in Rome, wishes to entrust the Church particularly to her in whom there was accomplished the stupendous and complete victory of good over evil, of love over hatred, of grace over sin; to her of whom Paul VI said that she is ' the beginning of the better world;' to the Blessed Virgin. He entrusts to her himself, as the servant of servants, and all those whom he serves, all those who serve with him. **He entrusts to her the Roman Church, as token and principle of all the churches in the world, in their universal unity. He entrusts it to her and offers it to her as her**

> **property.** Insegnamenti Giovanni Paolo II (1978), Vatican City: Libreria Editrice Vaticana, 313.[775]

The Catholic Church prays to Mary as a goddess. The practice of communicating with Mary is part and parcel of the general practice of praying to a pantheon of Catholic gods and goddesses, which the Catholic Church calls "saints," who purport to join along with Mary as the queen of heaven to answer the prayers of the faithful.

> The holy council... orders all bishops and others who have the official charge of teaching... to instruct... the faithful that the **saints**, reigning together with Christ, **pray to God for men** and women; **that it is good and useful to invoke them humbly and to have recourse to their prayers, to their help and assistance, in order to obtain favours from God** through his Son our lord Jesus Christ, who alone is our Redeemer and Saviour. Those who deny that the saints enjoying eternal happiness in heaven **are to be invoked**, or who claim that saints do not pray for human beings or that **calling upon them to pray for each of us** is idolatry or is opposed to the word of God and is prejudicial to the honour of Jesus Christ, the one Mediator between God and humankind; or who say that it is foolish to **make supplication orally or mentally to those who are reigning in heaven**; all those entertain impious thoughts. *THE GENERAL COUNCIL OF TRENT, TWENTY FIFTH SESSION, DECREE ON THE INVOCATION, THE VENERATION AND THE RELICS OF SAINTS AND ON SACRED IMAGES*, 1560.

> [The saints']... intercession is their most exalted service to God's plan. **We can and should ask them to intercede for us and for the whole world.** *CATECHISM OF THE CATHOLIC CHURCH*, § 2683, 1994.

One of the prophecies of John regarding the antichrist beast is that "he opened his mouth in blasphemy against God, to blaspheme his name, and his tabernacle, and them that dwell in heaven." (Revelation 13:6) Those that dwell in heaven are the saints. How can one blaspheme the saints that dwell in heaven? They are blasphemed by attributing to them the authority of God Almighty Jesus Christ to answer prayers. Prayers should only be given to Lord God Almighty Jesus Christ. Jesus is the only mediator between God and men. "For there is one God, and one mediator between God and men, the man Christ Jesus;" (1 Timothy 2:5)

One might argue: "Only God can be blasphemed. The saints aren't God. How is offering prayers to the saints, blaspheming the saints?"

Blaspheming the saints is similar in concept to the fact that the persecution of the church is the persecution of Jesus Christ himself. When Saul (later to become the Apostle Paul) persecuted the church. God knocked Saul to the ground, and Saul "said, Who art thou, Lord? And the Lord said, I am Jesus whom thou persecutest." (Acts 9:5) The persecution of the church is the persecution of Christ; in the same way, praying to the saints is blaspheming both God and his saints. It is a spiritual reality that "ye are all one in Christ Jesus." (Galatians 3:28)

In heaven, believers will have the imputed righteousness of Christ and all that goes with it.

> Behold, what manner of love the Father hath bestowed upon us, that we should be called the **sons of God**: therefore the world knoweth us not, because it knew him not. Beloved, **now are we the sons of God**, and it doth not yet appear what we shall be: but we know that, when he shall appear, **we shall be like him**; for we shall see him as he is. (1 John 3:1-2)

What does it mean to be like Christ? Each believer is part of the body of Christ. "Now ye are the body of Christ, and members in particular." (1 Corinthians 12:27) All saved Christians are one with Christ. "For both he that sanctifieth and they who are sanctified are **all of one**: for which cause he is not ashamed to call them brethren," (Hebrews 2:11)

We, who believe in Jesus Christ, were predestined to be glorified with Christ. "The Spirit itself beareth witness with our spirit, that **we are the children of God**: And if children, then heirs; heirs of God, and joint-heirs with Christ; if so be that we suffer with him, that **we may be also glorified together**." (Romans 8:16-17) "For whom he did foreknow, he also did predestinate to be conformed to the image of his Son, that he might be the firstborn among many brethren. Moreover whom he did predestinate, them he also called: and whom he called, them he also justified: and whom he justified, **them he also glorified**." (Romans 8:29-30)

Jesus made that point in John 14:20, where he said: "At that day ye shall know that I am in my Father, and ye in me, and I in you." (John 14:20) The prayers of Jesus are always answered by the Father. He prayed to the Father the following prayer:

> **That they all may be one; as thou, Father, art in me, and I in thee, that they also may be one in us**: that the world may believe that thou hast sent me. **And <u>the glory which thou gavest me I have given them</u>; that they may be one, even as we are one: I in them, and thou in me, that they may be made perfect in one**; and that the world may know that thou hast sent me, and **hast loved them, as thou hast loved me.** (John 17:21-23)

You see that all Christians are one with Christ. He is in us and we are in him. In John 17, Jesus states that the glory that the Father has given him he has given to those who believe in him. We are one with Jesus in glory. That means that when we go to heaven we will have the very glory of Jesus Christ.

Jesus himself states in John 17, that we will be "**<u>made perfect in one</u>**." What is the one with whom Christians are made perfect? Christians are made perfect in one with God! "We shall be like him; for we shall see him as he is." (1 John 3:2) In heaven, believers will have glorious bodies like that of Christ.

> For our conversation is in heaven; from whence also we look for the Saviour, the Lord Jesus Christ: **Who**

shall change our vile body, that it may be fashioned like unto his glorious body, according to the working whereby he is able even to subdue all things unto himself. (Philippians 3:20-21)

Those in heaven are one with Christ and thus have partaken of the divine nature. To pray to the saints is to blaspheme the saints, because they are part and parcel of the body of Christ.

According as his divine power hath given unto us all things that pertain unto life and godliness, through the knowledge of him that hath called us to glory and virtue: Whereby are given unto us exceeding great and precious promises: that by these ye might be **partakers of the divine nature**, having escaped the corruption that is in the world through lust. (2 Peter 1:3-4)

The prayers to the dead so-called "Catholic saints" are simply attempts to communicate with the dead. God has expressly commanded that we not attempt to communicate with the dead. To communicate with the dead is a sin called **necromancy**. There is only one mediator between man and God to whom we should pray, and that is Jesus Christ.

There shall not be found among you any one that maketh his son or his daughter to pass through the fire, or that useth divination, or an observer of times, or an enchanter, or a witch, Or a charmer, or a consulter with familiar spirits, or a wizard, or a **necromancer**. **For all that do these things are an abomination unto the LORD**: and because of these abominations the LORD thy God doth drive them out from before thee. (Deuteronomy 18:10-12)

The Catholic Church has a series of ritualistic mysteries that are recited after each of 15 Catholic "stations of the cross." These "mysteries" are said while counting beads that are called the rosary. The primary focus of the Catholic Rosary is not Jesus, it is Mary. Mary's role in Christ's birth, death, and resurrection is highlighted, exaggerated, and in some instances fabricated in 12 of the 15 "mysteries." In fact, the formal title of the Rosary is: "**The Roses of**

Prayer for the Queen of Heaven."[776] The prayers to Mary outnumber the supposed prayers to God by roughly 10 to 1. After each mystery is recited, Catholics say one "Our Father" prayer followed by ten "Hail Mary" prayers. The "Hail May" is a rote prayer to the Catholic goddess, whom they call Mary. They blaspheme God by praying to their Mary goddess and prove themselves heathen by repeating the blasphemous prayers over and over again. "But when ye pray, use not vain repetitions, as the heathen do: for they think that they shall be heard for their much speaking." (Matthew 6:7)

It is notable that the rosary said in honor of the queen of heaven has stations of the cross called "mysteries." There is a woman mentioned in the Bible whose very name is "mystery."

> And the woman was arrayed in purple and scarlet colour, and decked with gold and precious stones and pearls, having a golden cup in her hand full of abominations and filthiness of her fornication: And upon her forehead was a name written, **MYSTERY, BABYLON THE GREAT, THE MOTHER OF HARLOTS AND ABOMINATIONS OF THE EARTH.** (Revelation 17:4-5)

Later, when the Bible speaks of the destruction of the "mystery" harlot, the harlot says in her heart that she sits as a **"queen."**

> Reward her even as she rewarded you, and double unto her double according to her works: in the cup which she hath filled fill to her double. How much she hath glorified herself, and lived deliciously, so much torment and sorrow give her: **for she saith in her heart, I sit a queen**, and am no widow, and shall see no sorrow. Therefore shall her plagues come in one day, death, and mourning, and famine; and she shall be utterly burned with fire: for strong is the Lord God who judgeth her. (Revelation 18:6-8)

God reveals the mystery of the woman. God identifies the woman as a great city. "And the woman which thou sawest is that great city, which reigneth over the kings of the earth." (Revelation 17:18)

God also reveals the mystery of the woman.

> **I will tell thee the mystery of the woman**, and of the beast that carrieth her, which hath the seven heads and ten horns. The beast that thou sawest was, and is not; and shall ascend out of the bottomless pit, and go into perdition: and they that dwell on the earth shall wonder, whose names were not written in the book of life from the foundation of the world, when they behold the beast that was, and is not, and yet is. And here is the mind which hath wisdom. **The seven heads are seven mountains, on which the woman sitteth.** (Revelation 17:7-9)

So we know that the mystery harlot is a great city that sits on seven mountains. There is only one city that matches that description and that is Rome. Where are the mysterious seven mountains? Rome has traditionally been known as the city on seven hills or also "seven mountains." A mountain is simply a large mass of earth that rises above the common or adjacent land. It does not have to be of any definite altitude. Mountain accurately describes a large hill.[777] There is only one city that can meet the description of a city on seven mountains, Rome. Rome is famous for the seven mountains upon which it sits. The mountains are the Capitoline, the Quirinal, the Viminal, the Esquiline, the Caelian, the Avenue, and the Palatine.[778]

Alexander Hislop points out in his book The Two Babylons, that even pagan poets and orators, who would have no thought of elucidating biblical prophecy, described Rome as the city on seven hills.[779] Hislop quotes Virgil, who described Rome thusly: "Rome has both become the most beautiful (city) in the world, and alone has surround for herself seven heights with a wall."[780] Virgil died approximately 19 years before Christ was born and therefore long before the book of Revelation was written. Hislop also quotes poet Sextus Aurelius Propertius who describes Rome as "the lofty city on seven hills, which governs the entire world."[781] Notice how his description follows closely that which is contained in Revelation. "And the woman which thou sawest is that great city, which reigneth over the kings of the earth." (Revelation 17:18) Propertius died in 15 B.C. and so he would have had no knowledge of the book of Revelation which was written scores of years after his death. Marcus Valerius Martialis describes "the seven dominating mountains" of Rome.[782] Symmachus, the Prefect of Rome, introduced one friend of his to another by letter. In the letter he describes one friend as being *De septem montibus virum*, which translated means "a man from the seven mountains." That was equivalent in that day (circa 351-375 A.D.) to calling someone a *Civem Romanum*, which translated means "a Roman Citizen."[783]

Now that we have identified Rome as the location of the seven mountains, who is "Babylon the Great, the Mother of Harlots and Abominations of the Earth?" The Catholic Encyclopedia offers us a clue. It states that **"[i]t is within Rome, called the city of seven hills, that the entire Vatican State is now confined."**[784] The Vatican, being in Rome, is the great mother of harlots.

The glorification of the queen of heaven is in a sense a glorification by proxy of the Roman Catholic Church. That is why the Catholic hierarchy refers to their organization as "Mother Church."[785] It is true that the Catholic Church is a mother, **"THE MOTHER OF HARLOTS AND ABOMINATIONS OF THE EARTH."** (Revelation 17:4-5) That mother of harlots **"saith in her heart, I sit a queen."** Revelation 18:7. There is a spiritual parallel between the wicked harlot queen in the book of Revelation and Mary the queen of heaven glorified by the Catholic Church. The harlot of Revelation and Mary the queen of heaven both draw men from Jesus Christ, who "is the blessed and only Potentate, the Lord of lords and King of kings." 1 Timothy 6:15.

One of the "mysteries" recited during the Catholic rosary is called "the Fifth Glorious Mystery - The Coronation." In that mystery it is claimed by the Catholic Church that **"Mary is the Queen of Heaven."**

> Mary had served Jesus all her life. She had loved and served God with her whole heart and soul. She had never committed the slightest sin. So in heaven she was to have her reward. Body and soul, Mary entered heaven. Her Son, Jesus, met her and took her in His grateful arms. The heavenly Father said, "This is My dear devoted daughter." The Divine Son said, "This is

My dear faithful Mother." The Holy Spirit said, "This is my sweet, pure bride." And the saints and angels all cried, **"This is our Queen!"** So Jesus, the King of Kings, seated her on her throne. On her head He placed a glorious crown of stars. But Mary looked down to see her children on earth. For now she could help her sons and daughters to reach heaven. **Mary is the Queen of Heaven.** But she is our loving Mother who protects us with her power.[786]

One of the final prayers of the Rosary is a prayer to the Catholic goddess "Mary" called **"Hail Holy Queen."**

> **Hail, holy Queen**, Mother of Mercy! our life, our sweetness, and our hope! To thee do we cry, poor banished children of Eve; to thee so we send up our sighs, mourning and weeping in this valley, of tears. Turn, then, most gracious Advocate, thine eyes of mercy toward us; and after this our exile show unto us the blessed fruit of thy womb, Jesus; O clement, O loving, O sweet Virgin Mary.[787]

The Catholics also have other prayers not said during the rosary to their goddess, the Queen of Heaven:

> **Queen of heaven**, rejoice. Alleluia. The Son whom you were privileged to bear, Alleluia, has risen as he said, Alleluia. Pray to God for us, Alleluia. Rejoice and be glad, Virgin Mary, Alleluia. For the Lord has truly risen, Alleluia. O God, it was by the Resurrection of your Son, our Lord Jesus Christ, that you brought joy to the world. Grant that through the intercession of the Virgin Mary, his Mother, we may attain the joy of eternal life. Through Christ, our Lord. Amen.[788]

The Catholic "Mary" (queen of heaven) is viewed by the Roman Catholic Church as "the **restorer of the world that was lost, and the dispenser of all benefits** . . . the **most powerful mediator (mediatrix)** and **advocate (conciliatrix) for the whole world** . . . **above all others in sanctity and in union with Christ** . . . **the primary** minister in the distribution of the divine graces,"⁷⁸⁹ "the **beloved daughter of the Father and Temple of the Holy Spirit**,"⁷⁹⁰ "the mother of all the living,"⁷⁹¹ "the **new Eve**,"⁷⁹² "**Mother of the Church**,"⁷⁹³ "the '**Mother of Mercy**,' the **All Holy One**."⁷⁹⁴ She supposedly "**surpasses all creatures, both in heaven and on earth**,"⁷⁹⁵ conquered death and was ". . . raised body and soul to the glory of heaven, to **shine refulgent as Queen** at the right hand of her Son, the immortal King of ages."⁷⁹⁶ The Second Vatican Council subtly replaces Jesus Christ as the guardian over the church with Mary, whom they call the mother of the members of the church.

> [I]ndeed, she is clearly the **mother of the members of Christ since she has by her charity joined in bringing about the birth of believers in the Church** who are members of its head. Wherefore she is hailed as pre-eminent and as a wholly unique member of the Church, and as its type and outstanding model in faith and charity. The Catholic Church taught by the Holy Spirit, honours her with filial affection and **devotion as a most beloved mother**. THE SECOND VATICAN COUNCIL, 1964 (emphasis added).⁷⁹⁷

> What does God think of this Catholic goddess, Mary? Thou shalt worship the Lord thy God, and him **only** shalt thou serve. (Luke 4:8)

> Thou shalt have **no other gods** before me. . . . Thou shalt not bow down thyself to them nor serve them: for I the LORD thy God am a jealous God.. (Exodus 20:3-5)

When a woman praised Mary loudly, Jesus corrected her, making it clear that the woman who gave birth to him is not blessed above those who are saved by the grace of God.

> And it came to pass, as he spake these things, a certain woman of the company lifted up her voice, and said unto him, Blessed is the womb that bare thee, and the paps which thou hast sucked. But he said, Yea rather, blessed are they that hear the word of God, and keep it.

(Luke 11:27-28)

Roman Catholic Mariolatry is derived from the goddess worship performed by the Jews when they worship Matronita, the queen of heaven. For a more detailed discussion of the Judaic/Babylonian origins of the Roman Catholic Church read this author's book, *Solving the Mystery of BABYLON THE GREAT*. The Catholic Church has simply changed the name of the Jewish queen from Matronita to Mary. The Catholic Mary has nothing in common with the biblical Mary. The Catholic queen of heaven, however, has everything in common with the queen of heaven described in the Bible. In the Bible, God condemns homage and service to the queen of heaven.

> Seest thou not what they do in the cities of Judah and in the streets of Jerusalem? The children gather wood, and the fathers kindle the fire, and the women knead their dough, to make cakes to the **queen of heaven**, and to pour out drink offerings unto other gods, that they may provoke me to anger. Do they provoke me to anger? saith the LORD: do they not provoke themselves to the confusion of their own faces? Therefore thus saith the Lord GOD; Behold, mine anger and my fury shall be poured out upon this place, upon man, and upon beast, and upon the trees of the field, and upon the fruit of the ground; and it shall burn, and shall not be quenched. (Jeremiah 7:17-20)

Note how the ancient Jews were described by Jeremiah: "the women knead their dough, to make cakes to the queen of heaven." Jeremiah 7:18. Hislop states:

> The popular observances that still attend the period of its celebration amply confirm the testimony of history as to its Babylonian character. The hot cross buns of Good Friday, and the dyed eggs of Pasch or Easter Sunday, figured in the Chaldean rites just as they do now. The 'buns,' known too by that identical name, were used in the worship of the queen of heaven, the goddess Easter.[798]

Serving the queen of heaven is an abomination to God. There are consequences for that great sin against the Lord. In chapter 44 of Jeremiah we read that the Jews burned incense and served the **"queen of heaven."** This great sin kindled the fury and anger of the Lord, who responded by wasting and bringing desolation upon the cities of Judah, including Jerusalem. The Jews have not learned; they have inculcated their queen of heaven anew into their Roman Catholic Church.

As proof that the pope views Mary as the goddess of heaven, who has authority over even Jesus Christ, we have Pope Francis, during his inaugural homily, upon his installation as pope on March 19, 2013, calling on Mary to protect Jesus.

> Today too, amid so much darkness, we need to see the light of hope and to be men and women who bring hope to others. To protect creation ... **To protect Jesus with Mary**, to protect the whole of creation ... I implore the intercession of the Virgin Mary, Saint Joseph, Saints Peter and Paul, and Saint Francis, that the Holy Spirit may accompany my ministry, and I ask all of you to pray for me! Amen.[799]

To punctuate the heathen blasphemy, Pope Francis prays to "the Virgin Mary, Saint Joseph, Saints Peter and Paul, and Saint Francis."[800] There is no mention of Jesus. Pope Francis prays to supposedly godlike saints, to the exclusion of God Almighty, Jesus Christ. The Jesus of the pope is not the Jesus of the bible. Indeed, the Jesus of the pope is rather an impotent Jesus, who needs the protection of Mary, the Catholic goddess of heaven.

We read in Jeremiah that "Babylon hath been a golden cup in the LORD'S hand, that made all the earth drunken: the nations have drunken of her wine; therefore the nations are mad." (Jeremiah 51:7) Notice that language is very similar to what God states in Revelation regarding "BABYLON THE GREAT." She is described in Revelation as that great whore "[w]ith whom the kings of the earth have committed fornication, and the inhabitants of the earth have been made drunk with the wine of her fornication." (Revelation 17:2) God further describes her in the Book of Revelation:

For all nations have drunk of the wine of the wrath of her fornication, and the kings of the earth have committed fornication with her, and the merchants of the earth are waxed rich through the abundance of her delicacies." (Revelation 18:3)

Notice the commonality in the characteristics between the Babylon mentioned in Jeremiah, which was written sometime in the 6th Century B.C. and the Babylon in the book of Revelation, which was written sometime in the 1st century A.D. We have a span of approximately 700 years separating the descriptions and yet we have common elements. In Jeremiah, Babylon made all of the earth drunk by her wine, and in Revelation the kings and inhabitants of the earth have been made drunk with the wine of her fornication. It seems that this wine of Babylon is an intoxicating mixture that is born of fornication. Do we find any other clues from the bible as to what this fornication could be?

The bible gives us a clue. The Holy Bible depicts the church of Jesus as a chaste bride. Paul states of the Corinthian church: "For I am jealous over you with godly jealousy: for I have espoused you to one husband, that I may present you as a chaste virgin to Christ." (2 Corinthians 11:2) Obviously, chastity has nothing to do with the flesh. Paul is referring to spiritual purity.

The bride of Christ is described in Revelation as new Jerusalem, prepared as a bride for her husband. "And I John saw the holy city, new Jerusalem, coming down from God out of heaven, prepared as a bride adorned for her husband." (Revelation 21:2) Here we have the church symbolized as a chaste city adorned for her husband, who is Christ. How is she adorned? In Revelation 19:7-8 we read that she is adorned in fine linen. How different is that from the bejeweled city of Babylon who "was arrayed in purple and scarlet colour, and decked with gold and precious stones and pearls, having a golden cup in her hand full of abominations and filthiness of her fornication." Revelation 17:4.

The new Jerusalem is arrayed simply in fine linen. What does the fine linen signify? It is the "righteousness of saints."

Let us be glad and rejoice, and give honour to him: for

the marriage of the Lamb is come, and his wife hath made herself ready. And to her was granted that she should be arrayed in fine linen, clean and white: for the fine linen is the righteousness of saints. (Revelation 19:7-8)

The fine linen being the righteousness of the saints suggests that the purple and scarlet clothing and the gold and precious stones and pearls of the great whore of Babylon are symbolic of the wickedness of that religion. There is an unmistakable identity of the Roman Catholic hierarchy by the purple and scarlet ceremonial vestments worn by the Cardinals and the purple ceremonial vestments worn by the Bishops of Rome. This color scheme used by the church of Rome points directly to the Roman Catholic Church being not a chaste bride but rather the imperious whore of Babylon. God commands that his chosen people come out of the church of the great whore. See Revelation 18:4.

We have two very different women depicted in Revelation. Notice that in Revelation the chaste bride is "new" Jerusalem. That suggests that there is an "old" Jerusalem. Is there a link between the "old" Jerusalem" and the great whore of Babylon? When Israel was unfaithful to God he compared Israel to a harlot. In Ezekiel 16:15-37, the unfaithfulness of Israel is depicted, which parallels the sins of idolatry in the Catholic Church and demonstrates a common spiritual link between the religion of Israel and the religion of Rome. The commonality between the whore of Babylon in Revelation and the whore of Jerusalem depicted in Ezekiel is clear.

The great whore in Ezekiel is the same great whore in Revelation. God in Ezekiel has given us a clear clue as to the nature of the whore of Babylon. First, the reader must understand that Ezekiel is writing during his captivity in Babylon. Nebuchadnezzar, King of Babylon, conquered the city of Jerusalem and brought the Jews and the treasures of the city back to Babylon. 2 Kings 24:10-16. Ezekiel was one of the captives and described the corruption by the Jewish religious leaders who were adopting the heathen practices of the Babylonian religion. Ezekiel describes the origins of the harlot "old" Jerusalem of Judaism. That "old" Jerusalem is distinct from the chaste and holy "new" Jerusalem, which is made up of those who have been saved by the grace of God through faith in Jesus Christ. See Revelation 21:2.

Ezekiel explains that the whoredom of Jerusalem was following after the heathen religions by making images of men and worshiping those images. That is the same thing being done today in the Catholic church. The Jews were also sacrificing their children to their heathen idols. The great whore of Revelation is similarly "drunken with the blood of the saints, and with the blood of the martyrs of Jesus." (Revelation 17:6) There is an unmistakable common link between the spiritual whoredom of Church of Rome and the Jews of Jerusalem.

Jeremiah prophesied for the people to: "Flee out of the midst of Babylon, and deliver every man his soul: be not cut off in her iniquity; for this is the time of the LORD'S vengeance; he will render unto her a recompence. (Jeremiah 51:6)

John offered an identical prophecy to those in Babylon the Great: "And I heard another voice from heaven, saying, Come out of her, my people, that ye be not partakers of her sins, and that ye receive not of her plagues." (Revelation 18:4)

34 The Little Horn

The prophet Daniel had a vision, in which he beheld four beasts coming out of the sea. Beasts are used to represent kingdoms. The four kingdoms revealed by Daniel are prophesied to arise seriatim. Daniel notably describes an unusual little horn, which arises from the fourth beast. That little horn is distinct in nature from the other beasts.

> And four great beasts came up from the sea, diverse one from another. The first was like a lion, and had eagle's wings: I beheld till the wings thereof were plucked, and it was lifted up from the earth, and made stand upon the feet as a man, and a man's heart was given to it. And behold another beast, a second, like to a bear, and it raised up itself on one side, and it had three ribs in the mouth of it between the teeth of it: and they said thus unto it, Arise, devour much flesh. After this I beheld, and lo another, like a leopard, which had upon the back of it four wings of a fowl; the beast had also four heads; and dominion was given to it. After this I saw in the night visions, and behold a fourth beast, dreadful and terrible, and strong exceedingly; and it had great iron teeth: it devoured and brake in pieces, and stamped the residue with the feet of it: and it was diverse from all the beasts that were before it;

and it had ten horns. **I considered the horns, and, behold, there came up among them another little horn, before whom there were three of the first horns plucked up by the roots: and, behold, in this horn were eyes like the eyes of man, and a mouth speaking great things. I beheld till the thrones were cast down**, and the Ancient of days did sit, whose garment was white as snow, and the hair of his head like the pure wool: his throne was like the fiery flame, and his wheels as burning fire. (Daniel 7:3-9)

The meaning of the great beasts in his vision was explained to Daniel.

I Daniel was grieved in my spirit in the midst of my body, and the visions of my head troubled me. I came near unto one of them that stood by, and asked him the truth of all this. So he told me, and made me know the interpretation of the things. These great beasts, which are four, are four kings, which shall arise out of the earth. But the saints of the most High shall take the kingdom, and possess the kingdom for ever, even for ever and ever. Then I would know the truth of the fourth beast, which was diverse from all the others, exceeding dreadful, whose teeth were of iron, and his nails of brass; which devoured, brake in pieces, and stamped the residue with his feet; And of the ten horns that were in his head, and of the other which came up, and before whom three fell; even of that horn that had eyes, and a mouth that spake very great things, whose look was more stout than his fellows. I beheld, and the same horn made war with the saints, and prevailed against them; Until the Ancient of days came, and judgment was given to the saints of the most High; and the time came that the saints possessed the kingdom. Thus he said, **The fourth beast shall be the fourth kingdom upon earth, which shall be diverse from all kingdoms, and shall devour the whole earth, and shall tread it down, and break it in pieces. And the ten horns out of this kingdom are ten kings that** shall arise: and another shall rise after them; and he shall be diverse from the first, and he shall subdue three kings. **And he shall speak great words against the most High, and shall wear out the saints of the most High, and think to change times and laws: and they shall be given into his hand until a time and times and the dividing of time.** But the judgment shall sit, and they shall take away his dominion, to consume and to destroy it unto the end. And the kingdom and dominion, and the greatness of the kingdom under the whole heaven, shall be given to the people of the saints of the most High, whose kingdom is an everlasting kingdom, and all dominions shall serve and obey him. (Daniel 7:15-27)

The beasts in order of their historical appearance were Babylon (winged lion), Medio-Persia (bear), Greece (four headed winged leopard), and Rome (diverse terrible and strong beast with iron teeth).

The dreadful and terrible fourth beast which represented the Roman empire, had ten horns. The horns of the Roman beast are ten kingdoms which arose from that empire. After 476 AD ten kingdoms arose from the Roman empire: (1) Ostrogoths, (2) Visigoths, (3)Franks, (4) Vandals, (5) Suevi, (6) Alamani, (7) Anglosaxons, (8) Heruli, (9) Lombardi, and (10) Burgundians.

Daniel mentions that the little horn will spring out from among the ten horns and in the process three of the horns (kingdoms) will be plucked up by their roots. Daniel states that this little horn will have eyes like the eyes of a man and a mouth speaking great things. This new horn apparently is the antichrist, because Daniel explains that the horn will make war with the saints and will prevail against them until Christ, whom Daniel refers to as the "Ancient of days," shall come. Daniel explains that the little horn will be diverse from the other ten horns. Clearly, the religious nature of the papal Roman kingdom makes it diverse from any of the other kingdoms. The papal kingdom will wear out the saints of the most High and think to change the times and laws. As explained in a previous chapter on the Roman Catholic Church, it has changed the times by changing the sabbath from the seventh day of the week (Saturday) to the first day of the week

(Sunday). In addition, the Vatican has also changed the laws by deleting the second commandment against making and worshiping graven images and then splitting the last commandment into two commandments to make up for the missing commandment. This changing of God's laws and times is a fulfillment of the prophecy in Daniel chapter 7 regarding the beast, the antichrist.

Daniel states that the little horn had a look that was more stout than his fellows. That indicates that the antichrist has more power than the other kings. In fact, the pope was considered the source of the authority of kings. During the dark ages, it was the pope who crowned the kings of Europe. The following papal decrees illustrate clearly that the pope has a look more stout than his fellows.

> **[W]e hold upon this earth the place of God Almighty.** *Pope Leo XIII* (emphasis added).[801]
>
> [T]he Roman pontiff possess **primacy over the whole world**. *The Vatican Council*, Session IV, chapter III, July 18, 1870 (emphasis added).
>
> **[R]oyal power derives from the Pontifical authority.**[802] *Pope Innocent III.*
>
> **[T]emporal power should be subject to the spiritual.**[803] *Pope Boniface VII.*

The most notable detail provided by Daniel in his prophecy is that the little horn had "eyes like the eyes of man, and a mouth speaking **great things**." Daniel 7:8. What are the great things? John, in the book of Revelation, presents a parallel passage that states of the beast: "there was given unto him a mouth speaking **great things and blasphemies**." Revelation 13:5. It is also stated in Revelation that "upon his heads the name of **blasphemy**." Revelation 13:1. This is repeated in Revelation 17:3 where we read that John "saw a woman sit upon a scarlet coloured beast, full of names of **blasphemy**, having seven heads and ten horns."

John informs us that in addition to the "great things" the little horn of Daniel will speak blasphemies. Can we know what are these blasphemies? Can identifying the blasphemies identify the littler horn of Daniel, who is described as a beast in Revelation? In fact, identifying the blasphemies is a significant clue to identifying the antichrist. Mary Walsh explains how identifying the blasphemies in turn identifies the antichrist.

"And I saw a woman sit upon a scarlet-colored beast, full of names of blasphemy." According to this prophecy, the woman's mounting the beast indicates the pre-eminence which the apostate church would hold in civil affairs, as queen over the kings of the earth. The names of blasphemy referred to show the aspirations of the leader of the church in assuming the prerogatives of God.

Two ways of blaspheming, according to the Bible are these: (1) by claiming the power to forgive sins; and (2) by laying claim to be the Son of God. Christ was accused by the Pharisees of blasphemy when He forgave sin. "And when He saw their faith, He said unto him, Man, thy sins are forgiven thee. And the scribes and the Pharisees began to reason, saying, Who is this which speaks blasphemies? Who can forgive sins, but God alone?" Luke 5: 20, 21 Christ would have been guilty of blasphemy in claiming to forgive sins, if He had been a mere man, for God has never given that exclusive right to any human being.

The Roman Catholic Church claims that the power of absolution is invested in her priests: "Seek where you will, through heaven and earth, and you will find but one created being who can forgive the sinner, who can free him from the chains of hell, that extraordinary being is the priest, the [Roman] Catholic priest." Michael Muller, The Catholic Priest, Pages 78, 79. 'Who can forgive sins except God?' was the question which the Pharisees sneeringly asked. 'Who can forgive sins?' is the question which the Pharisees of the present day also ask, and I answer there is a man on earth that can forgive sins and that man is the [Roman] Catholic priest. Yes, beloved brethren, the priest not only declares that the sinner is forgiven, but he really forgives him. The priest raises his hand, he pronounces the word of absolution, and in an instant, quick as a flash of light, the chains of hell are burst asunder, and the sinner becomes a child of God. So great is the power of the priest that the judgments of heaven itself are subject to his decision." Michael Muller, The Catholic Priest, Pages 78, 79.

When the priest raises his hand over the penitent and pronounces the words of absolution, " I absolve thee," he is guilty of blasphemy.[804]

Mary Walsh has some theological beliefs that are not supported by the bible; however, she is absolutely correct on the fact that the claim of the Roman Church to forgive sins is fulfillment of the prophecy of John that the beast will speak "great things and blasphemies." Revelation 13:5. Who is Michael Muller cited by Mary Walsh as authority for the Catholic doctrine that the Catholic priest has authority to forgive sins? Muller was a nineteenth century Catholic priest of The Congregation of the Most Holy Redeemer, who was widely read and considered an authoritative Roman Catholic theologian on Catholic doctrine. Muller's books on Catholic theology were widely circulated and are still being published today.

Another blasphemy defined in the bible is claiming to be God. The Jews confronting Jesus clearly understood his claim to be Christ to be a claim to be God. When Jesus stated that he was Christ and that "ye shall see the Son of man sitting on the right hand of power, and coming in the clouds of heaven," (Mark 14:62) the Jews considered that blasphemy. "Then the high priest rent his clothes, and saith, What need we any further witnesses? Ye have heard the blasphemy: what think ye? And they all condemned him to be guilty of death." (Mark 14:63-64) Of course, Jesus is God Almighty and therefore was not guilty of blasphemy. However, anyone else who claims to be God commits blasphemy.

Pope John Paul II, in his 1995 book, Crossing the Threshold of Hope, stated unequivocally that the pope stands in place of God

Almighty Jesus Christ. That is the very blasphemy indicative of the antichrist as prophesied by John.

> Confronted with the Pope, one must make a choice. The leader of the Catholic Church is defined by the faith as the Vicar of Jesus Christ (and is accepted as such by believers). The Pope is considered the man on earth who represents the Son of God, who "takes the place" of the Second Person of the omnipotent God of the Trinity.[805]

Make no mistake about the meaning of what Pope John Paul II was saying. Pope Leo XIII claims for the popes to be in place of God Almighty. "We [popes] hold upon this earth the place of God Almighty."[806]

Pope Leo XIII's statement is not figurative. He intended to express that the popes have the position and authority of God Almighty on earth. Pope Leo XII made that point clear in the following allegedly infallible pronouncement, where he stated that all must obey and submit to the pope with the same submission and obedience owed to God himself:

> But the supreme teacher in the Church is the Roman Pontiff. Union of minds, therefore, requires, together with a perfect accord in the one faith, complete submission and obedience of will to the Church and to the Roman Pontiff, as to God Himself.[807]

Daniel indicates that the persecution by the Roman antichrist over the Christian churches was to last a time, times, and a dividing of time. It is not clear from that passage alone what is meant by the term times and times and dividing of time. In order to decipher what Daniel meant by that phrase it is necessary to study those sections of the Bible which deal with the persecution of Christ's church by the antichrist.

In Revelation we read the following passage.

> And there appeared a great wonder in heaven; a woman clothed with the sun, and the moon under her feet, and

upon her head a crown of twelve stars: And she being with child cried, travailing in birth, and pained to be delivered. And there appeared another wonder in heaven; and behold a great red dragon, having seven heads and ten horns, and seven crowns upon his heads. And his tail drew the third part of the stars of heaven, and did cast them to the earth: and the dragon stood before the woman which was ready to be delivered, for to devour her child as soon as it was born. And she brought forth a man child, who was to rule all nations with a rod of iron: and her child was caught up unto God, and to his throne. **And the woman fled into the wilderness, where she hath a place prepared of God, that they should feed her there a thousand two hundred and threescore days.** And there was war in heaven: Michael and his angels fought against the dragon; and the dragon fought and his angels, And prevailed not; neither was their place found any more in heaven. And the great dragon was cast out, that old serpent, called the Devil, and Satan, which deceiveth the whole world: he was cast out into the earth, and his angels were cast out with him. And I heard a loud voice saying in heaven, Now is come salvation, and strength, and the kingdom of our God, and the power of his Christ: for the accuser of our brethren is cast down, which accused them before our God day and night. And they overcame him by the blood of the Lamb, and by the word of their testimony; and they loved not their lives unto the death. Therefore rejoice, ye heavens, and ye that dwell in them. Woe to the inhabiters of the earth and of the sea! for the devil is come down unto you, having great wrath, because he knoweth that he hath but a short time. And when the dragon saw that he was cast unto the earth, he persecuted the woman which brought forth the man child. **And to the woman were given two wings of a great eagle, that she might fly into the wilderness, into her place, where she is nourished for a time, and times, and half a time, from the face of the serpent.** And the serpent cast out of his mouth water as a flood after the woman, that he might cause her to be carried away of the flood. And the earth helped the woman, and the earth opened her mouth, and swallowed up the flood which the dragon cast out of his mouth. And the dragon was wroth with the woman, and went to make war with the remnant of her seed, which keep the commandments of God, and have the testimony of Jesus Christ. (Revelation 12:1-17)

So we see that the woman, which represents the church, was protected for 1,260 days. What is the significance of the 1,260 days? God's prophetic calendar is a lunar calendar, in which the 12 months have 30 days each, totaling 360 days in a year. "**He appointed the moon for seasons**: the sun knoweth his going down." (Psalms 104:19) For example, If one looks at God's account of the Genesis flood, one sees that the flood began on the seventeenth day of the second month and ended exactly five months later on the seventeenth day of the seventh month. In a lunar calendar that would be exactly 150 days (5 months × 30 days per month = 150 days). In Genesis 7:24 we see that the duration of the flood was exactly 150 days. This demonstrates God's use of a 30 day lunar calendar. In fact, even today we divide a circle into 360 degrees, just as the lunar year has 360 days.

> In the six hundredth year of Noah's life, in the **second month, the seventeenth** day of the month, the same day were all the fountains of the great deep broken up, and the windows of heaven were opened. (Genesis 7:11)
>
> **And the waters prevailed upon the earth an hundred and fifty days**. (Genesis 7:24)
>
> And the ark rested in the **seventh month, on the seventeenth day of the month**, upon the mountains of Ararat. (Genesis 8:4)

According to God's prophetic calendar, three and one half years equals 1,260 days (30 days per month × 42 months). We see that this is confirmed in verse 14 of Revelation chapter 12, where God reveals that the woman will be protected from the serpent for a time (1) + times

+ (2) + half a time (½) = 3½ times. That is the same language used in Daniel 7:25, where it states: "And he shall speak great words against the most High, and shall wear out the saints of the most High, and think to change times and laws: and they shall be given into his hand until a time and times and the dividing of time." (Daniel 7:25) What are the 3 and one half times of Daniel? They are precisely three and one half years or 42 months or 1,260 days as prophesied in Revelation 12:6.

The 1,260 days do not, however, represent literal days. They are actually representative of 1,260 years. It is the number of years if one day equaled one year. Just as in Numbers 14:34, where God ordained that in his prophecy one day should equal one year. "After the number of the days in which ye searched the land, even forty days, **each day for a year**, shall ye bear your iniquities, even forty years, and ye shall know my breach of promise." *See also* Ezekiel 4:6: "And when thou hast accomplished them, lie again on thy right side, and thou shalt bear the iniquity of the house of Judah forty days: I have appointed thee **each day for a year**."

We see this forty two months of years again repeated later in Revelation.

> But the court which is without the temple leave out, and measure it not; for it is given unto the Gentiles: **and the holy city shall they tread under foot forty and two months**. And I will give power unto my two witnesses, and **they shall prophesy a thousand two hundred and threescore days**, clothed in sackcloth. (Revelation 11:2-3)

> And they worshipped the dragon which gave power unto the beast: and they worshipped the beast, saying, Who is like unto the beast? who is able to make war with him? **And there was given unto him a mouth speaking great things and blasphemies; and power was given unto him to continue forty and two months**. And he opened his mouth in blasphemy against God, to blaspheme his name, and his tabernacle, and them that dwell in heaven. And it was given unto him to make war with the saints, and to

overcome them: and power was given him over all kindreds, and tongues, and nations. And all that dwell upon the earth shall worship him, whose names are not written in the book of life of the Lamb slain from the foundation of the world. If any man have an ear, let him hear. (Revelation 13:4-9)

When is this 1260 years? Roman Emperor Justinian issued a decree in 533 making the bishop of Rome the head of all the churches. The decree took effect in 538 A.D. after the last of three kings were subdued. The Heruli were completely scattered in 493 A.D., the Vandals in 534 A.D. and the Ostrogoths in 538 A.D. The ascendency of the pope of Rome can be measured, according to Daniel's prophecy from 538 A.D., the date when the last of the three horns was finally uprooted and Vigilius took office as pope under the military protection of Belisarius. The defeat of the Ostrogoths in 538 A.D. put into effect Justinian's decree of 533, making the pope of Rome the head of all Christian churches and "corrector of heretics." The papacy from that date forward began to use the civil power of governments to further the propagation of its ecclesiastical power. Thus began what is known today as the dark ages, when Rome used the leverage of its supposed religious power and authority to control governments and persecute the Christian churches.

If we then begin our calculation from the ascendency of the pope of Rome, we start at 538 A.D., the date when the last of the three horns was finally uprooted, and move forward in history 1,260 years we cover the period of history so black with the superstition and brutality of the Roman Catholic Church that it is called even today the "dark ages." In the date that we come to that marks the end of this dark age is 1798 (538 A.D. + 1,260 years = 1798 A.D.).

What happened in 1798 that marked the end of the dark ages? Napoleon's General Berthier invaded Rome, took Pope Pius VI prisoner, and held him until his death. This freed Italy and Europe from the tyranny of the "Holy Roman Empire." This is the deadly wound that was suffered by the beast.

And I stood upon the sand of the sea, and saw a beast rise up out of the sea, having seven heads and ten horns, and upon his horns ten crowns, and upon his heads the name of blasphemy. And the beast which I saw was like unto a leopard, and his feet were as the feet of a bear, and his mouth as the mouth of a lion: and the dragon gave him his power, and his seat, and great authority. **And I saw one of his heads as it were wounded to death; and his deadly wound was healed**: and all the world wondered after the beast. (Revelation 13:1-3)

Note that the wound was healed. When was the beast's wound healed? The 1929 Lateran Treaty, wherein Mussolini and Rome reestablished the Vatican as a sovereign nation, with the "Holy" See the sole and exclusive governing authority. Other than Israel, the Roman Catholic Church is the only religion that is also a sovereign nation. A selected few of the 27 articles of the Lateran Treaty are listed below.

Article 1

Italy recognizes and reaffirms the principle established in the first Article of the Italian Constitution dated March 4, 1848, according to which the Catholic Apostolic Roman religion is the only State religion.

Article 2

Italy recognizes the sovereignty of the Holy See in international matters as an inherent attribute in conformity with its traditions and the requirements of its mission to the world.

Article 3

Italy recognizes the full ownership, exclusive dominion, and sovereign authority and jurisdiction of the Holy See over the Vatican as at present constituted, together with all its appurtenances and endowments, thus creating the Vatican City, for the special purposes and under the conditions hereinafter referred to.

Article 8

Considering the person of the Supreme Pontiff to be sacred and inviolable, Italy declares any attempt against His person or any incitement to commit such attempt to be punishable by the same penalties as all similar attempts and incitements to commit the same against the person of the King.

All offences or public insults committed within Italian territory against the person of the Supreme Pontiff, whether by means of speeches, acts, or writings, shall be punished in the same manner as offences and insults against the person of the King.

As prophesied in Daniel 7:23-24, the pope is a beast that is "diverse" from the other beasts. The mischief of the Roman beast will continue until the end of this world when Jesus returns.

And the devil that deceived them was cast into the lake of fire and brimstone, where the beast and the false prophet are, and shall be tormented day and night for ever and ever. (Revelation 20:10)

The 1,260 year prophecy is found later in Revelation. "And I will give power unto my two witnesses, and they shall prophesy a thousand two hundred and threescore days, clothed in sackcloth." (Revelation 11:3) Who are the two witnesses of God? When one understands that the time period is 1,260 years, it becomes clear that the witnesses could not be men. In the next verse is a clue as to the identity of the two witnesses. "These are the two olive trees, and the two candlesticks standing before the God of the earth." (Revelation 11:3-4) The two witnesses are described as two olive trees and two candlesticks standing before God.

And said unto me, What seest thou? And I said, I have looked, and behold a **candlestick all of gold**, with a bowl upon the top of it, and his seven lamps thereon, and seven pipes to the seven lamps, which are upon the top thereof: And **two olive trees** by it, one upon the right side of the bowl, and the other upon the left side thereof. So I answered and spake to the angel that talked with me, saying, What are these, my lord? Then the angel that talked with me answered and said unto me, Knowest thou not what these be? And I said, No, my lord. Then he answered and spake unto me, saying, **This is the word of the LORD** unto Zerubbabel, saying, Not by might, nor by power, but by my spirit, saith the LORD of hosts. (Zechariah 4:2-6)

The two candlesticks and two olive trees are the word of the LORD. The language used in Revelation chapter 11 is symbolic, it a prophesy of the suppression of the word of God during the 1,260 year reign of the pope during the dark ages. The word of God prophesied in sackcloth during that period, which is symbolic of the word of God being suppressed.

The Catholic Church has a long history of trying to keep God's word from the people. For example, at the *Council of Terragona* in 1234 A.D. the Roman Catholic Church prohibited anyone from possessing any part of the Old or New Testaments in any of the Romance languages (Portuguese, Spanish, Catalan, Provencal, French, Rhaeto-Romance, Italian, Sardinian, and Romanian). The council ruled that anyone owning a Bible was to turn it over to the local Catholic bishop to be burned. In 1229 at the *Council of Toulouse* (Pope Gregory IX presiding), the Catholic Church prohibited "laymen" from having the Holy Scriptures or translating them into the "vulgar tongue" (common language of the country). In 1551 the Catholic *Inquisitional Index of Valentia* forbade the Holy Bible to be translated into Spanish or any other "vernacular." In 1559 the Roman Catholic *Index Librorum Prohibitorum* (Index of Prohibited Books) required permission from the Catholic Church to read the Catholic version of the Bible; all Christian Bible versions were simply prohibited. On September 8, 1713, Pope Clement XI issued his Dogmatic Constitution, *Unigenitus,* which in part condemned as error the teaching that all people may read the Sacred Scripture. On May 5, 1824 Pope Leo XII issued his encyclical *Ubi Primum* which exhorted the bishops to remind their flocks not to read the Bible. On May 24, 1829 Pope Pius VIII issued the encyclical *Traditi Humilitati,* which exhorted Catholics to check the spread of Bibles translated into the vernacular, because those Bibles endangered the "sacred" teachings of the Catholic Church. On May 8, 1844, Pope Gregory XVI issued his encyclical *Inter Praecipuas* in which he described Bible societies as plotting against the Catholic faith by providing Bibles to the common people, whom he referred to as "infidels." On January 25, 1897 Pope Leo XIII issued his Apostolic Constitution *Officiorum ac Munerum* which prohibited all versions of the Bible in the vernacular tongue. The 1918 Catholic Code of Cannon Law, Index of Prohibited Books, Cannon 1385, § 1 prohibited publishing any edition of the Holy Scriptures without previous Catholic "ecclesiastical censorship." The 1983 Catholic Code of Cannon Law, Cannon 825, § 1 prohibits the publishing of the Sacred Scriptures without the permission of the Apostolic See or the Conference of Bishops.

The official doctrines of the Catholic Church prohibiting the publication, possession, or reading of the Holy Bible, were not a mere suggestions, they were enforced. For example, on October 6, 1536 at Vilvorde (outside Brussels, Belgium) William Tyndale was burned at the stake.[808] His crime was that he translated the Holy Scriptures into English and was making copies available to the people in violation of the rules of the Roman Catholic Church.[809]

Now that the deadly wound has been healed, the Supreme Pontiff has steadily regained his strength. His power is now concealed, but in the future his power will be manifested in all its evil splendor.

The picture below symbolizes the hidden power of the papacy in world affairs. They spent years planning the ceremony whereby the leaders of the member nations making up the European Union would sign the constitution of that union and thus hand over to a new European government the sovereignty of their countries. Everything was planned down to the last detail. Everything present at the ceremony was there for a purpose. So whom do you see wearing a triple crown with his condescending gaze overseeing the ceremony? Why it is none other than colossal statue of Pope Innocent X. The triple crown signifies the official teaching of the Roman Catholic Church that the pope of Rome rules over heaven, earth, and hell! The ceremony was dominated by the statue, with the dignitaries signing the constitution being relegated to a rather insignificant posture below the towering figure of the pope of Rome. This picture symbolizes the real power behind the European Union.

British Prime Minister Tony Blair Signing the Constitution of the European Union on 29 October 2004 at Rome's Capitoline Hill

35 Behold a White Horse

Read carefully the prophecy in Revelation 6:8 regarding the white horse and its rider. The color of the horse and the bow carried by the rider, taken together, reveal the papacy as the rider astride the white horse.

> And I saw, and behold a **white** horse: and he that sat on him had a **bow**; and a crown was given unto him: and he went forth conquering, and to conquer. Revelation 6:2.

First, consider the color of the horse (white) and juxtapose that against the woman who rides the scarlet beast, who is arrayed in scarlet and purple.

> So he carried me away in the spirit into the wilderness: and I saw a woman sit upon a **scarlet** coloured beast, full of names of blasphemy, having seven heads and ten horns. And the woman was arrayed in **purple** and **scarlet** colour, and decked with gold and precious stones and pearls, having a golden cup in her hand full of abominations and filthiness of her fornication: And upon her forehead was a name written, Mystery, Babylon The Great, The Mother Of Harlots And Abominations Of The Earth. Revelation 17:3-5.

The great harlot depicts the Roman Catholic Church with the

notable colors of the vestments of the cardinals being scarlet, and the color of the bishops' vestments being purple. When the cardinals elect a pope from among their members the newly elected pope takes off his scarlet vestments and dons the white vestments of the pope. The horse being white correlates to the pope's white vestments.

Patricia Treble, the royal specialist at Maclean's, explains that "[w]hen it comes to colours, white rules for the pope. It's reserved exclusively for popes, current and former. So the cassock, mozzetta (shoulder cape), mitre (tall pointed bishop's hat) and even the zucchetto (skullcap) are all white."[810] Treble's statement regarding "former" popes is an obvious reference to the recent resignation of the still-living Pope Benedict XVI, who was the first pope in almost 600 years to resign.

While the pope dons the white vestments reserved exclusively for him, he continues, from time-to-time, to wear the purple and scarlet that signifies Babylon the Great of Revelations 17:4. Treble states that "[o]n top of the plain white cassock, the pope's vestments will change with the liturgical calendar—so he'll often wear purple during Lent and Advent, gold on feast days such as Easter, and red on Good Friday and Palm Sunday."[811]

Cardinal Karol Wojtyla, wearing the scarlet sash and holding the scarlet zucchetto of a cardinal, pays homage to Pope John Paul I (left). After Pope John Paul I died, Cardinal Wojtyla was elevated to pope and took the title Pope John Paul II; he exchanged the scarlet of a cardinal and donned the white vestments of the pope. Pope John Paul II is seen seated on his ostentatious throne in the Vatican wearing the white papal vestments (right). The symbolism is unmistakable. The pope is the rider of the white horse of Revelation 6:2.

Notice that the rider of the horse in Revelation 6:2 is carrying a bow. The pope carries an unusual bowed crucifix in formal processions. The Merriam-Webster Dictionary defines the primary meaning of "bow" as "something bent into a simple curve."⁸¹² That is precisely what we see the popes carrying.

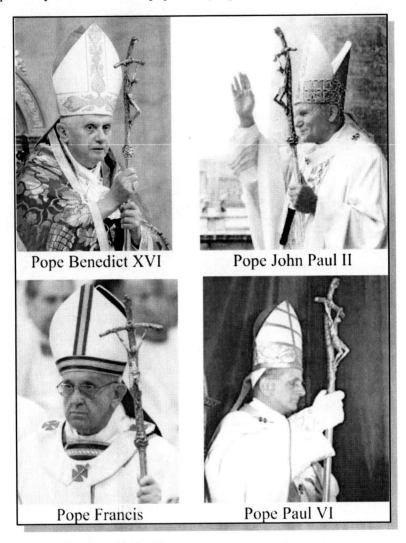

The pictures above depict a few of the many popes through history who have carried the bowed crucifix. That points directly to the pope of Rome as the rider of the white horse, who "had a bow." The bowed crucifix carried by the pope is a very unusual crucifix and is not found anywhere replicated in the Roman Catholic Church. Of all the thousands of idols in the thousands of Catholic churches throughout the world, there is not found a bowed crucifix. The bowed crucifix is reserved only for the pope, who is the prophesied rider of the white horse, who had a bow in Revelation 6:8.

Piers Compton states that the bowed crucifix with the distorted figure of Christ carried by the popes is the same sinister crucifix used by Satanists and sorcerers in the sixth century.[813] Compton states that there are woodcuts displayed in the Museum of Witchcraft in Bayonne, France, showing Satanists carrying the bowed crucifix.

Notice also that the rider on the horse is given a crown. A Crown signifies rule. The pope of Rome is given a special crown. Lucius Ferraris, a Franciscan Monk, in his authoritative work, *Prompta Bibliotheca Canonica*, states: "Hence the Pope is crowned with a triple crown, as king of heaven and of earth and of the lower regions."[814] In the picture at right we see Pope Pius XII wearing the triple tiara. During the coronation ceremony, upon the election of a new pope, the Pope is crowned with these words: "Take thou the tiara adorned with the triple crown, and know that thou art the father of princes and kings and the governor of the world"[815]

Pope Pius XII Wearing the Triple Crown as Ruler Over Heaven, Hell, and Earth

The authority of the pope to rule heaven, earth, and hell is based upon the official Catholic doctrinal premise expressed by Ferraris: "The Pope is of so great dignity and so exalted that he is not mere man, but as it were God, and the vicar of God."[816]

The purported sovereign rule of the pope over heaven, earth, and hell is symbolized in Catholic heraldry. Depicted on this page is the coat of arms for the Holy See. The term Holy See (Latin: *Sancta Sedes*) is what the Roman Catholic Church calls the seat of the pope and constitutes its ecclesiastical jurisdiction in Rome. Note the prominence of the triple crown, which signifies the universal rule of the pope over heaven, earth, and the lower regions (purgatory and hell). The crossed keys represent the keys to the gates of heaven, and signify the purported authority of the pope to allow or deny entry into heaven. "We declare, state and define that it is absolutely necessary for the salvation of all human beings that they submit to the Roman Pontiff."[817] *Bull Unum Sanctum,* Pope Boniface VIII, 1302.

36 Mark of the Beast

The Bible speaks of a beast whose number is the number of a man. "Here is wisdom. Let him that hath understanding count the number of the beast: for it is the number of a man; and his number is Six hundred threescore and six." (Revelation 13:18) The number is 666. The bible states that 666 is not only the number of a man but also the number of the beast's name. From this we know that the beast is a man whose name adds up to 666.

The Roman (Latin) letters are also Roman numerals. Latin, which was the official language of Rome and is also the official language of the Roman Catholic Church, is the logical first place to look for this number of the beast.

The Vatican is concerned that people will learn the mystery that the number of the beast points directly to the pope of Rome. In order to throw people off the trail of the pope they have proposed an alternative reading of the number of the beast as "616" in Revelation 13:18. The Roman Catholic Jerusalem Bible contains a footnote to Revelation 13:18 that states:

> Var. '616'. In both Greek and Hebr., letters are used as numbers, the values corresponding to the place in the alphabet; by adding up the values of component letters the total 'number of a person's name' is obtained. Some commentators point out that in Hebr., the letters of

Caesar Nero add up to 666, and in Greek, the letters of Caesar-God add up to 616 (an alternative reading).[818]

The Catholic editors of the Jerusalem Bible do not explain the source of the alternative reading of "616." They simply announce in a footnote that there is one. The alternative should be seen as what it is. It is an obvious deception formulated to mislead readers and cause them to doubt that the pope is the beast of Revelation.

People should not be looking for simply three 6's in a row; the number of the beast is the number **"six hundred threescore and six."** That means the beast's name must add up to six hundred sixty six.

According to the April 18, 1915, edition of *Our Sunday Visitor,* the largest circulated official Catholic publication in the United States, "[t]he letters inscribed in the pope's mitre are these: *Vicarius Filii Dei,* which is the Latin for the Vicar of the Son of God."[819] When a new pope is crowned, some allege it is with the words *"Vicarius Filii Dei,"* others claim it with the words *"Vicarius Christi."*

Vicarius Filii Dei was used to refer to Peter and the popes in the medieval document that the Roman Catholic Church composed to claim that the Emperor Constantine transferred authority over Rome and the western part of the Roman Empire to the Pope. The document is known as the Donation of Constantine. The Donation of Constantine has been proven to be forged by agencies of the Roman Catholic Church in the 8th century A.D.

The official title of the Pope written in classical Latin is **VICARIVS FILII DEI**. Notice that in classical Latin there is a V just before the S in *vicarius,* rather than a U. That is because there are only 23 letters in the classical Latin alphabet, it does not have the letters U, J, or W as in the English alphabet.[820] The V is used in classical Latin when making the U sound.[821] The values of Roman numerals are: D = 500, C = 100, L = 50, V = 5, I = 1. The values of the Roman numerals found in the Latin title for the Pope added together equals 666. V (used twice, 5 x 2 = 10) + C (100) + I (used 6 times, 1 x 6 = 6) + L (50) + D (500) = **666**.

The ubiquitous Universal Product Code (UPC) symbol contains

the number 666 hidden within the lines of the symbol. The UPC depicted on this page is typical of the most common UPC seen on goods in the marketplace of today. The UPC has two sets of numbers. Each set has distinct computer codes that are represented by two parallel lines per number. In the second set of codes, the number 6 is represented by two equally thin parallel lines (II).

Notice that there are three double lines in the UPC symbol that do not have an Arabic number to identify them. One set of lines are in the middle and there are two other sets of lines, one on each end. Those three sets of lines together represent the number 666. Look at any product in your home and you will see the same hidden code for the number 666.

The numbers that appear on either end of the UPC symbol on this page (6 and 3) correspond to the double line codes that are inside the double line codes for the end 6's. Note that there are two sets of line codes for the numbers 0-9. The first set is to the left of the middle double lines (II), and the second set is to the right of the middle double lines. The 3 sets of double lines without numbers are always the line codes for the number 6 from the second set of codes. As you will notice, the 6 from the first set of codes is represented by a thin line on the left with a thick line on the right, whereas the line code for 6 from the second set of codes is represented by two thin lines (II).

Why is it that the only lines that do not have an Arabic number identifying are the lines that together read 666? Because the UPC symbol is part of the groundwork being laid to control the world's commerce. The world's goods are being marked with the number of the beast. It is a hidden code so as not to alarm the slumbering masses. The Bible states that one day people will be marked with a similar code in their right hand or forehead and that refusal to receive the mark will preclude them from being able to buy or sell anything. "And that no man might buy or sell, save he that had the mark, or the name of the beast, or the number of his name." (Revelation 13:17)

The Bible does not state that the mark will be *on* peoples foreheads or *on* their right hands but *in* their right hands or *in* their foreheads. Implantable biochips that are capable of storing several megabytes of data equal to thousands of pages of information have already been developed.[822] These biochips allow the subject to be tracked and identified anywhere in the world. Could the present day UPC, with the hidden 666, be a key necessary to match a corresponding 666 code in an implantable biochip that would then allow a purchase of the item? Could it be that if there is no match, because the person has refused the 666 mark of the beast, then the person cannot purchase the item because "no man might buy or sell," unless he has the mark?

Once the governments of the world implement a mandatory identity card, it would only be a matter of time before the convenience of an implantable chip is accepted. How close are we? The failed Health Security Card proposed by President Clinton was manufactured by Drexler Technology Corporation, Mountain View, California and was in fact a data storage card capable of storing 2,000 pages of information, including fingerprints, voice prints, and pictures.[823]

The technology now exists to track persons and obtain massive amounts of information on them through an implantable chip. In 2004, the U.S. Food and Drug Administration approved the use of implantable radio frequency identification (RFID) chip in humans.[824] The chip readers can scan the chip for information from great distances and they have the capability to read hundreds (eventually thousands) of chips at one time.

The manufacturer, VeriChip, is touting its chip as an easy and secure way to ensure that a person has their important medical data available in an emergency. Thomas Green of The Register points out the obvious Orwellian dangers. "Indeed, the medical care angle looks like a warm-and-fuzzy gimmick to speed adoption so that other, potentially more sinister, applications might follow."[825]

It seems that the warm-and-fuzzy gimmick of using RFID chips in medical care is being pushed along by the U.S. Government. With the characteristic timing of a tyranny, Jill Fisher revealed that shortly before the VeriChip RFID was approved by the FDA for implantation into Humans,"in April 2004, President Bush issued an executive order calling for the incorporation of health information technology into all medical practices nationwide and the creation of a National Health Information Technology Coordinator to oversee the process."[826]

Fisher further reveals that VeriChip wasted no time in getting its implantable chip into hospitals. As of December 2005, the company had "agreements from 65 other medical facilities to begin implanting chips in patients in the near future.[827] The idea behind an RFID implant is that patients can carry their medical records (or, more accurately, an identifier to access their records) with them wherever they go."[828]

There has been much fear that the Obamacare law requires the implantation of RFID chips. The initial versions of the U.S. House of Representative health care bills (HR3200, HR3590, and HR4872) that eventually became Obamacare, did contain provisions for the discussed RFID chips. The language in those bills did not mandate the use of RFID chips, and only created a registry which would allow the Department of Health and Human Services to collect data about and from RFID chips. That RFID provisions did not make it into the final Obamacare Law. Do not rest so easy. Each new contrived or real national security issue can be used as an excuse for new legislation for such a mandate.

In a Fox Business article, Peter Andrews revealed the new ultra-secure microchip technology that is being introduced into credit cards. After discussing the benefits of the microchips and other "mobile wallet" technologies, Andrews concludes the article with the following ominous prognostication:

> And, of course, ultimately you may not need to wear or carry a device at all. Although nobody's proposing such a thing at the moment, the technology already exists that could allow you to have a radio frequency identification (RFID) chip implanted under your skin (maybe in that loose section between your thumb and your index finger), and one of those could, in the

future, provide payment and ID services.

Many Americans would be appalled at such a prospect. And the likelihood of it being offered anytime soon receded with the wave of outrage that occurred when some mistakenly believed that "Obamacare" would make these subcutaneous RFID chips mandatory. That turned out to be a myth, but the violent reaction to it means it would now take a brave innovator to even tentatively suggest their introduction. One day, however...[829]

In the Bible, God explains the consequences of worshiping the beast and receiving his mark:

> And the third angel followed them, saying with a loud voice, If any man worship the beast and his image, and receive his mark in his forehead, or in his hand, The same shall drink of the wine of the wrath of God, which is poured out without mixture into the cup of his indignation; and he shall be tormented with fire and brimstone in the presence of the holy angels, and in the presence of the Lamb: And the smoke of their torment ascendeth up for ever and ever: and they have no rest day nor night, who worship the beast and his image, and whosoever receiveth the mark of his name. (Revelation 14:9-11)

The Roman Catholic Church cannot allow the evidence that points to the pope as the antichrist, whose name is numbered 666, to go unchallenged. Patrick Madrid is an example of the defense by Roman Catholic theologians attempting to refute the evidence that their pope is the beast of Revelation. Madrid stated in Envoy, a Roman Catholic magazine: "Vicarius Filii Dei, or 'Vicar of the Son of God,' is not now, nor has it ever been, a title of the bishop of Rome."[830] Madrid claims that the title is a "fabrication." Madrid is an authoritative Catholic theologian whose writings have won the praises of the Catholic hierarchy, such as Cardinal Edward Egan, Archbishop of New York, Cardinal Francis George, Archbishop of Chicago, and Anthony M. Pilla, Archbishop of Cleveland.

Karl Keating, a prominent Catholic theologian and apologist, who is the founder and president of Catholic Answers, a Catholic apologetics and evangelization organization, stated in his book *Catholicism and Fundamentalism*: "Vicarius Filii Dei never has been used as a title by any Pope."[831]

Patrick Madrid goes even further to challenge anyone to prove that the pope has ever called himself or been referred to as "Vicar of the Son of God."(*Vicarius Filii Dei*):

> If the person making this claim disputes these facts, ask him to furnish even one example of a papal decree, ecclesiastical letter, conciliar statement, or any other official Catholic document in which the pope calls himself or is referred to as the "Vicar of the Son of God." He won't be able to find one, because none exist. Vicarius Filii Dei has never been a title of the pope.[832]

Would these eminent Catholic theologians risk their credibility in order to conceal the fact that the number of the beast points to the pope who has taken the title of "Vicar of the Son of God."(Vicarius Filii Dei)? It seems so. Let us examine the matter. Let the evidence speak for itself.

First let us look at what Madrid says about the aforementioned article in the April 18, 1915, edition of *Our Sunday Visitor*, which stated that "[t]he letters inscribed in the pope's mitre are these: *Vicarius Filii Dei,* which is the Latin for the Vicar of the Son of God."[833] Madrid states:

> I contacted Robert Lockwood, the president of Our Sunday Visitor, about this. He had personally gone through the OSV archives and reported that he had found no evidence that this quote ever appeared in any issue of the paper. Evidently, it had been removed from the archive. The error on the part of a newspaper staffer (and let's remember, the Catholic Church does not claim infallibility for journalists) was caught only after it had slipped into print, but the editor was obviously concerned about the incorrect answer being

perpetuated, so he expunged that issue from the archives.[834]

Here we have the editor stating that he could not find any evidence of that article ever appearing in any edition of *Our Sunday Visitor*. Why? Because that edition of the periodical was expunged from the archives. There was no evidence of the article, not because it had never been written, but instead because the president of the periodical admitted that the edition the article appeared in was remove from the archives and destroyed! Why would the OSV destroy the archived article? Because it let the cat out of the bag; it was evidence that the pope was the beast of Revelation.

Not to worry, Michael Scheifler was able to obtain a photocopy of the April 18, 1915 edition of Our Sunday Visitor, and he has posted it on the internet. It, in fact, contains the damning admission from an official Catholic publication that "[t]he letters inscribed in the pope's mitre are these: *Vicarius Filii Dei,* which is the Latin for the Vicar of the Son of God."[835]

Madrid also argues that the description in the Donation of Constantine indicating the title for the pope as *Vicarius Filii Dei* is not an official statement from the Roman Catholic Church, but is rather a statement from a Roman Emperor to the Roman Catholic Church. His argument is that, therefore, it is not an authoritative pronouncement by the Catholic Church. That is pure sophistry. Here is why.

The pertinent part of the Donation of Constantine, with the title of the pope as *Vicarius Filii Dei*, states in Latin:

> [U]t sicut B. Petrus in terris **Vicarius Filii Dei** esse videtur constitutus, ita et Pontifices, qui ipsius principis apostolorum gerunt vices, principatus potestatem amplius quam terrena imperialis nostrae serenitatis mansuetudo habere videtur, conscessam a nobis nostroque imperio obtineant.[836] (emphasis added)

Below is the English translation of the pertinent section quoted above from the Donation of Constantine:

> [A]s the Blessed Peter is seen to have been constituted **Vicar of the Son of God** on the earth, so the Pontiffs who are the representatives of that same chief of the apostles, should obtain from us and our empire the power of a supremacy greater than the clemency of our earthly imperial serenity is seen to have conceded to it.[837] (emphasis added)

Madrid's argument is that the Donation of Constantine was an edict from a Roman emperor and therefore cannot be attributed as an official Catholic title for the pope. His argument is a clever deception. The Donation of Constantine was not written by Constantine. It was forged by agencies of the Roman Catholic Church. It was then falsely portrayed by the Roman Catholic Church over a period of approximately 800 years as a genuine edict from Constantine. It is guile for Madrid to attempt to dismiss the Donation of Constantine as not being the statement of Roman Church. Michael Scheifler explains the portrayal by the Roman Catholic Church that the Donation of Constantine was genuine.

> The Donation of Constantine was cited in writing by no less than 10 Popes as proof of their civil authority and sovereignty over Rome, and what came to be known as the Papal States, which included a large portion of Italy. It was also eventually exposed as a pious fraud in 1440 by Laurentius Valla who proved the donation had to have been written several centuries after the death of Constantine (337 A.D.) The Vatican condemned Valla's scholarly work by listing it in the Index Librorum Prohibitorum, the Index of Prohibited Books of 1559 (a 1569 printing at Google books), and as late as 1580 the official edition of the Corpus Juris upheld the genuineness of the False Decretals. So the Donation of Constantine was held to be genuine for centuries.
>
> Catholics finally abandoned the defense of the authenticity of the Donation of Constantine shortly after Cesare Baronius published his Annales Ecclesiastici in 1592, which admitted the fraud, although the Donation and title Vicarius Filii Dei

continued to appear in Canon law and other Catholic publications well into the 19th century.[838]

Today, the Roman Catholic Church admits that the Donation of Constantine is a forgery, but tries to steer its authorship away from Rome itself and attribute its authorship to the Franks. The Catholic Church tries to steer the authorship away from the church to distance itself from the deception and to distance the pope from the number of the beast found in the title *Vicarius Filii Dei*. The Roman Church acknowledges that they had the world hoodwinked into believing the fraud of the Donation of Constantine, until Laurentius Valla ruined their scheme in 1440 by proving it to be a fraud. The following information is found in the Catholic Encyclopedia:

> Latin, Donatio Constantini. By this name is understood, since the end of the Middle Ages, a forged document of Emperor Constantine the Great, by which large privileges and rich possessions were conferred on the pope and the Roman Church. ... This document is without doubt a forgery, fabricated somewhere between the years 750 and 850. As early as the fifteenth century its falsity was known and demonstrated. ... It is so clearly a fabrication that there is no reason to wonder that, with the revival of historical criticism in the fifteenth century, the true character of the document was at once recognized. ... Many of the recent critical students of the document locate its composition at Rome and attribute the forgery to an ecclesiastic, their chief argument being an intrinsic one: this false document was composed in favour of the popes and of the Roman Church, therefore Rome itself must have had the chief interest in a forgery executed for a purpose so clearly expressed. Moreover, the sources of the document are chiefly Roman. Nevertheless, the earlier view of Zaccaria and others that the forgery originated in the Frankish Empire.... Most of the writers who locate at Rome itself the origin of the forgery maintain that it was intended principally to support the claims of the popes to secular power in Italy. ...The first pope who

> used it in an official act and relied upon, was Leo IX; in a letter of 1054 to Michael Cærularius, Patriarch of Constantinople, he cites the "Donatio" to show that the Holy See possessed both an earthly and a heavenly imperium, the royal priesthood. ... The medieval adversaries of the popes, on the other hand, never denied the validity of this appeal to the pretended donation of Constantine, but endeavoured to show that the legal deductions drawn from it were founded on false interpretations. The authenticity of the document, as already stated, was doubted by no one before the fifteenth century.[839]

Michael Scheifler explains the significance of the letter from Pope Leo IX to Michael Caerularius. "Pope Leo IX was asserting his primacy as the Bishop of Rome, and to that end he reproduced that portion of the donation containing vicarius filii Dei for the edification of the Greek Patriarch [Michael Caerularius]."[840] Pope Leo IX affirmed the genuineness of the Donation of Constantine as the basis for his claim of supremacy in authority over both Rome and Constantinople. The letter ultimately led to the schism between the Roman Catholic Church and the Greek Orthodox Church that remains today.

The Donation of Constantine is not the only evidence that the Roman Catholic Church has traditionally applied the title of *Vicarius Filii Dei* to the pope. In 1320 A.D., Augustino Trionfo of Ancona (Augustinus Triumphus) 1243-1328 A.D., published his treatise Titled *Summa de Potestate Ecclesiastica* (Summary On The Power Of The Church). Trionfo was commissioned by Pope John XXII to write *Summa de Potestate Ecclesiastica*, because he wanted a book that would explain and defend the ecclesiastical and temporal authority of the papacy.[841] Augustino dedicated the treatise to the same Pope, and it is considered the high water mark of papal pretensions.[842] Michael Scheifler quotes C.H. McIlwain and Michael Wilks, who stated of Augustino's treatise: "The Summa de potestate ecclesiastica of Augustinus Triumphus has been described as 'one of the half dozen most influential and most important books ever written' on the nature of the papal supremacy in the Middle ages."[843]

Augustino's treatise is considered an authoritative statement of

Catholic dogma on the ecclesiastical and political power of the pope of Rome. The 1582 printing has the official endorsement of F. Augustinus Fiuizanius Romanus, Sacrista, Et Ordinis Augustiniani, Vicarius Generalis, under the name of Pope Gregory XIII. The crest of Pope Gregory XIII, with the winged dragon, appears on the title page.[844]

On three occasions in Augustino's 1320 edition of *Summa de Potestate Ecclesiastica,* the pope is described as *"vicarius filii Dei."* The pope is further described two other times with the equivalent variant *"vicarius Dei filii"* and *"Dei filii vicarius."*[845] Each of those variations are simply a rearranging of the words and total 666, the number of the beast. In addition, there are eight other entries where different variants of that title are used to describe the pope, such as *"vicarius Dei," "Vicarius Christi,"* and *"vicarii Iesu Christi."*

Dr. Johannes Quasten (1900-1987), a renowned Catholic scholar, who was a Catholic monsignor and professor emeritus at The Catholic University of America, and who was recognized as one of the most eminent authorities in the field, wrote in response to a question about the authenticity of the title *Vicarius Filii Dei* that "[T]he title Vicarius Filii Dei as well as the title Vicarius Christi is very common as the title for the Pope."[846]

In fact, Pope Paul VI in his Decree of Paul VI elevating the Prefecture Apostolic of Bafia, Cameroon, to a Diocese used the equivalent variant *Dei Filii Vicarius* to describe his authority to do so.[847] Furthermore, Sheifler points out:

> In "Crossing The Threshold of Hope", by Pope John Paul II: First Chapter: "The Pope": A Scandal and a Mystery, page 3, you will find:
>
> "The Pope is considered the man on earth who represents the Son of God, who "takes the place" of the Second Person of the omnipotent God of the Trinity".
>
> If you directly translate "represents the Son of God" into Latin, the official language of the Church, you get "Vicarius Filii Dei".[848]

Allan Drisko summarizes his findings regarding the authenticity of *Vicarius Filii Dei* as the title for the pope of Rome:

> In the early collection of canon law, the *Decretum of Gratian*, first published in 1148, we read, (Latin) '*Beatus Petrus in terris **vicarious Filii Dei** videtur esse consitutus.*' Translated into English, it means, "Blessed Peter is seen to have been constituted **vicar of the Son of God** on earth." Furthermore, in the revised Corpus of Canon (sic), published by order of Pope Gregory XIII, it was to be corrected by, 'the plenitude of apostolic power,' so that it is, 'entirely freed from faults.' Therein we find the same statement as above [affirming *vicarious Filii Dei* as a moniker for the pope]. And I go on, when Lucius Ferraris wrote, *Prompta Bibliotheca* in 1755, he gave under the article 'Papa,' the title, ***Vicarius Filii Dei***, and cited the revised canon law as his authority. When his work was revised and published in Rome in 1890, the document and aforementioned title were retained! Moreover, the Catholic Encyclopedia says his work, 'will ever remain a precious mine of information' (1913, vol. 6, p.48).[849] (emphasis added)

Thus, Madrid's and Keating's claims that *Vicarius Filii Dei* has never been a title for the pope is shown to be false. The historical evidence is that *Vicarius Filii Dei* is a title that is by and for the papacy. The total of the letters in that name equals 666, which reveals the pope as the beast of Revelation.

37 Hiding the Antichrist

The belief that the pope is the antichrist was once virtually unanimous among Protestant denominations. For example, the Westminster Confession of Faith states:

> There is no other Head of the Church but the Lord Jesus Christ, nor can the Pope of Rome, in any sense, be head thereof, but is that antichrist, that man of sin, and Son of perdition, that exalteth himself in the Church against Christ and all that is called God.[850]

Other Protestant confessions of faith identified the pope as the antichrist, including but not limited to the Morland Confession of 1508 and 1535 (Waldenses) and the Helvetic Confession of 1536 (Switzerland).[851]

During the Reformation period, and thereafter, informed Christian writers and ministers have stated unequivocally that the pope is the prophesied antichrist. Reuel J. Schulz summarized the views of some of the theologians and ministers who studied the doctrines of the papacy and suffered under its tyranny and concluded that it was the prophesied antichrist:

> Eberhard II, archbishop of Salzburg, 1200-1246, did not look forward to the coming of an unidentified

individual antichrist. Instead, he looked back over the centuries since Rome's dismemberment and saw in the historical Papacy, as a system or succession, the fulfillment of the prophecies concerning Antichrist. He was excommunicated by the Pope and died under the ban in 1246. Michael of Cesena was one of the learned men on a list in John Foxe's "Book of Martyrs" who between 1331-1360 contended against the false claims of the pope. Michael declared the Pope "to be Antichrist, and the church of Rome to be the whore of Babylon, drunk with the blood of saints."

A century before Luther, John Wyclif, the noted English reformer, in his book, "The Mirror of Antichrist" referred repeatedly to the Pope as Antichrist. Lord Cobham, one of hundreds of thousands of Lollards" who sprang from the ministry of Wyclif, said of the pope: "I know him by the Scriptures to be the great antichrist, the son of perdition." Walter Brute, an associate of Wyclif, in 1391 was accused of claiming that "the Pope is Antichrist and a seducer of the people." Sir John Oldcastle, (1360-1417) was suspended in chains and slowly burned to death for speaking of the Pope in these words: "I know him by the Scriptures to be the great Antichrist, the Son of perdition...Rome is the very nest of Antichrist, and out of that nest come all the disciples of him."

The writings of John Huss (1369-1415), influenced by Wyclif, labeled the Pope as the Antichrist of which the Scriptures had warned. He constantly referred to Antichrist as the enemy of the church - not as a Jew, a pagan, or a Turk - but as a false confessor of the name of Christ. His uncompromising stand against the Antichrist of Bible prophecy led to his being burned to death. Andreas Osiander and Nicolas Von Amsdorf, contemporaries and colleagues of Luther, also were convinced that "the pope is the real, true Antichrist and not the vicar of Christ."

Even Philip Melancthon, the close associate of Luther who often has been faulted for his mild and compromising approach to doctrinal controversy, said: "Since it is certain that the pontiffs and the monks have forbidden marriage (cf. I Tim. 4:1-3), it is most manifest, and true without any doubt, that the Roman Pontiff, with his whole order and kingdom, is very Antichrist...Likewise in 2 Thess. 2, Paul clearly says that the man of sin will rule in the church exalting himself above the worship of God."

Other religious leaders who identified the Pope as Antichrist ... John Calvin (1509-1564), French reformer; John Knox (1505-1572) Scottish reformer; John Napier (1550-1617) Scottish mathematician and Protestant adherent; Huldreich Zwingli (1484-1531) Swiss reformer; Heinrich Bullinger (1504-1575); Theodor Bibliander (1504-1564) Swiss Bible scholar and translator; Alfonsus Conradus - in a 1560 commentary on Revelation insisted that Antichrist had already been revealed in the Papacy; William Tyndale (1484-1536) English Bible translator and martyr; Nicholas Ridley (1500-1555) English martyr who just before his execution spoke of Rome as "The seat of Satan; and the bishop of the same; that maintaineth the abominations thereof, is antichrist himself indeed."

Ridley's friend, John Bradford (1510-1555) also was martyred for his refusal to acknowledge the antichrist of Rome to be Christ's vicar-general and supreme head of the Catholic and universal church. He died at the stake for maintaining that the Papacy "undoubtedly (is) that great Antichrist, of whom the apostles do so much admonish us." John Hopper (1495-1555) another victim of England's "Bloody" Mary, also was burned at the stake for his resistance to the "wicked papistical religion of the bishop of Rome." Thomas Cranmer (1489-1556) died in the flames as he testified: "...as for the Pope, I refuse him as Christ's enemy and antichrist, with all his false doctrine."

Hugh Latimer (1490-1555); Thomas Becon (1511-1567), William Fluke (1538-1589) and John Jewel (1522-1571) also were involved in the 16th century English Reformation movement and made no bones about describing the Pope as the Antichrist, as did the preacher, Edwin Sandys (1519-1588) twenty-two of whose sermons have been preserved to our day. In his sermon on Isaiah 55:1 - "Ho, everyone that thirsteth, come ye to the waters...come ye, buy...without money and without price," he contrasted the Lord's invitation with that of the Papal Antichrist who requires money for his blessings."[852]

It was a dangerous thing during the dark ages to identify the pope as the antichrist. Such a statement was often met with horrible tortures and death. For example, Sir John Oldcastle (1360-1417), identified the pope as the antichrist and was sentenced to death for doing so. In 1417 he was dragged to St. Giles, suspended in chains, and slowly burned to death as his voice ascended in praise to God.[853]

John Huss (1369-1415) identified the Pope as the Antichrist as warned of in the scriptures. Pope Martin V issued a bull in 1418 in which he ordered the punishment of all who held to the teachings of John Wycliffe and John Huss.[854] Huss was condemned to death as a heretic after a trial on the charge of heresy presided over by Catholic prelates. The Catholic Bishop of Concordia announced the guilty verdict of heresy and the sentence of death. As was typical regarding Catholic ecclesiastical edicts, he was turned over to the secular authorities with the command: "Go take him" - *vade accipe eum* -" burn him as a heretic."[855]

The civil authorities then carried out the execution of Huss. Huss was put under the guard of 1,000 armed men and was surrounded by a vast crowd of spectators as he was led through a churchyard where his books were being burned. His hands were tied behind his back, and he was chained to a stake. A pile of fagots and straw were piled up around him to his neck. He was, at that time, given a final opportunity to recant his teachings, which were contrary to Catholic doctrine. Huss responded with resolute Christian courage: "In the same truth of the Gospel which I have written, taught and preached, drawing upon the sayings and positions of the holy doctors, I am ready to die today."[856] The combustibles were then lit, and as the flames consumed his body, Huss sang: *"Christe fili Dei vivi miserere mei"* which translated into Englsh means: "Christ, thou Son of the Living God, have mercy upon me."[857] Just before he died, he breathed the words: "Lord, into thy hands I commend my soul."[858]

John Wycliffe (a/k/a Wyclif) (1320-1384) was a noted English Reformer. Wycliffe taught that the persecuting little horn of Daniel had found fulfilment in the Papacy which arose out of the fourth kingdom, Rome.[859] Wycliffe identified the pope as the antichrist. The insane megalomania of the papacy is evidenced by the conduct of Pope Martin V. In 1428, Pope Martin V ordered the execution of Wycliffe. The problem for the pope was that Wycliffe had died a natural death over 40 years earlier, in 1384. The grave was no barrier to the evil vengeance of the pope. The devil-possessed pope ordered Wycliffe's corpse to be exhumed, burned, and the ashes cast into the River Swift in England.

Today, those that hold the belief that the pope is the antichrist are in the minority. In fact, nowadays it is viewed as radical and uncharitable for a Christian to say that the pope is the antichrist. How did such transformation take place among the Protestant denominations?

The change in the position of the Protestant denominations toward Rome was the direct result of a concerted campaign by agents of the Roman Catholic Church.[860] One of the methods used by the Roman Catholic theologians was to relegate much of the book of Revelation to some future time.[861] In 1590 a Roman Catholic Jesuit priest Francisco Ribera, in his 500 page commentary on the book of Revelation, placed the events of most of the book of Revelation in a period in the future just prior to the end of the world.[862] He claimed that the antichrist would be an individual who would not be manifested until very near the end of the world. He wrote that the antichrist would rebuild Jerusalem, abolish Christianity, deny Christ, persecute the church, and dominate the world for three and half years.[863]

Another Jesuit, Cardinal Robert Bellarmine (1554-1621), promoted Ribera's teachings.[864] Bellarmine was one of the most influential cardinals of his time. In 1930 he was canonized by Pope Pius XI as a Catholic saint and "Doctor of the Church." This Catholic interpretation of the book of Revelation did not become accepted in the Protestant denominations until a book titled *The Coming of the Messiah in Glory and Majesty* was published in 1812, 11 years after the death of its author.[865] The author of that book was another Jesuit by the name of Emanuel de Lacunza.

Part and parcel of the Catholic deception is the blasphemous interpretation of Daniel 9:27, where a supposed covenant of a future antichrist is substituted in place of the clear reference to the covenant of the Messiah (Jesus Christ) in Daniel 9:27. Most churches today have been hoodwinked into looking forward to a future antichrist, thus not perceiving the antichrist housed in the Vatican. Aurthur Pink is typical of Christians who have been inculcated into the anti-gospel designed to conceal the identity of the antichrist. Pink was convinced that the pope could not be the antichrist. Pink stated:

> The Antichrist will make a Covenant with the Jews. In Dan. 9:27 we read, "And he shall confirm the covenant with many for a week." The one referred to here as making this seven-year Covenant is "the Prince that shall come" of the previous verse, namely, the Antichrist, who will be the Head of the ten-kingdomed Empire. The nation with whom the Prince will make this covenant is the people of Daniel, as is clear from the context - see v. 24. But we know of no record upon the scroll of history of any pope having ever made a seven-year Covenant with the Jews![866]

Pink misinterprets the passage at Daniel 9:27. Pink follows the twisted view that the covenant for one week mentioned in that verse is a future seven year covenant made by a future antichrst, who has not yet made his appearance on the world stage. Daniel 9:24-27 states:

> Seventy weeks are determined upon thy people and upon thy holy city, to finish the transgression, and to make an end of sins, and to make reconciliation for iniquity, and to bring in everlasting righteousness, and to seal up the vision and prophecy, and to anoint the most Holy. Know therefore and understand, that from the going forth of the commandment to restore and to

build Jerusalem unto the **Messiah the Prince** shall be seven weeks, and threescore and two weeks: the street shall be built again, and the wall, even in troublous times. And after threescore and two weeks shall **Messiah** be cut off, but not for himself: and the people of the prince that shall come shall destroy the city and the sanctuary; and the end thereof shall be with a flood, and unto the end of the war desolations are determined. And **he** shall confirm the covenant with many for one week: and in the midst of the week **he** shall cause the sacrifice and the oblation to cease, and for the overspreading of abominations **he** shall make it desolate, even until the consummation, and that determined shall be poured upon the desolate. Daniel 9:24-27 (emphasis added).

The problem for Pink is that the passage in Daniel 9:27 that Pink is relying on for his doctrine does not support his construction. The passages in context states that "he" will confirm a "covenant." The "he" in that passage is not the antichrist, but is in fact Christ. Jesus has made a New Covenant. Jesus has caused the sacrifices and oblations to cease, since his sacrifice is the final sacrifice for our sins.

For finding fault with them, he saith, Behold, the days come, saith the Lord, when I will make a new covenant with the house of Israel and with the house of Judah. (Hebrews 8:8)

Jesus' ministry lasted 7 years as prophesied in Daniel 9:27: "he shall confirm the covenant with many for one week." Jesus was crucified in the midst of the 7 years (at the halfway point of three and a half years) as prophesied in Daniel 9:26: "After threescore and two weeks shall Messiah be cut off." That prophecy is repeated in Daniel 7:27: "In the midst of the week he shall cause the sacrifice and the oblation to cease." The gospel was spread and memorialized during the remaining years after his crucifixion, which is recounted in the book of Acts. The entire ministry of Jesus spanned 7 years and ended with the conclusion of the ministry of his apostles. The sacrifices were put to an end at the crucifixion of Jesus.

Jesus, when he had cried again with a loud voice, yielded up the ghost. And, behold, the veil of the temple was rent in twain from the top to the bottom; and the earth did quake, and the rocks rent. (Matthew 27:50-51)

Jesus' crucifixion was the focal point of the 70 weeks that were to "make an end of sins, and to make reconciliation for iniquity, and to bring in everlasting righteousness." Daniel 9:24. That rending of the veil in the old Temple recounted in Matthew 27:50-51 signified the end of the old covenant and its attendant sacrifices. The "he" in Daniel 9:27 who confirms the covenant with many for one week and in the midst of the week shall cause the sacrifice and oblation to cease is Jesus Christ:

And **he** shall confirm the covenant with many for one week: and in the midst of the week **he** shall cause the sacrifice and the oblation to cease, and for the overspreading of abominations he shall make it desolate, even until the consummation, and that determined shall be poured upon the desolate. (Daniel 9:27) (emphasis added)

The covenant referred to in Daniel 9:27 is the new covenant of Jesus Christ. Hebrews chapters 8 and 9 makes clear that the old law of animal sacrifice had passed away as the new covenant was being established. "In that he saith, A new covenant, he hath made the first old. Now that which decayeth and waxeth old is ready to vanish away." (Hebrews 8:13) That is the [new] covenant mentioned in Daniel 9, which is the same "holy covenant" in Daniel 11 that the antichrist shall have "indignation against."

Notice that in Daniel, chapter 9, verse 25 we see reference to "Messiah the Prince." In verse 26 we see reference to "Messiah" and "the prince." "The prince" in verse 26 is "Messiah" in that same verse and "Messiah the Prince" in verse 25. "He" in verse 27 is a reference to "the prince" in verse 26, who, as we have seen, is "Messiah the Prince."

Verse 24 of Daniel, chapter 9 states that "Seventy weeks are determined upon thy people and upon thy holy city, to finish the transgression, ..." The seventy weeks are broken into the first 7 weeks, followed by 62 weeks, followed by one week. The final (70th week) follows the second group of (62) weeks, which is the 69th week. And so Jesus was crucified in the midst of the 70th week, which was "after" the 69th week that is described as "after threescore and two weeks" because the first 7 weeks have to be added to the next 62 weeks. Jesus was crucified in the midst of the 70th week, which was "after" the 69th week. The seventy weeks fall sequentially one after another without a break. It is one of the great deceptions in the church that there is a parenthesis of an indeterminate interlude of time between the 69th and 70th weeks.

Many have concluded that the reference to "the people of the prince that shall come" in Daniel 9:26 must be a reference to Jews or Christians and could not be a reference to the Romans. That is a conclusion that is not supported by scripture. God has many people. In the bible you will find that God even calls Egypt "my people." "Whom the LORD of hosts shall bless, saying, Blessed be Egypt my people, and Assyria the work of my hands, and Israel mine inheritance." (Isaiah 19:25) God is the creator of all people and so all people are his people.

The whole point of the 70 weeks is to "to finish the transgression, and to make an end of sins, and to make reconciliation for iniquity, and to bring in everlasting righteousness, and to seal up the vision and prophecy, and to anoint the most Holy." Daniel 9:24. Can there be any other fulfillment of that than the covenant confirmed by Jesus at his crucifixion? "For this is my covenant unto them, when I shall take away their sins." (Romans 11:27)

38 Dual Destruction of the Antichrist

The destruction of the antichrist is prophesied to be a two stage process. First, "the Lord shall consume [the antchrist] with the spirit of his mouth," and second, he will "destroy [the antichrist] with the brightness of his coming:" (2 Thessalonians 2:8) Wylie explains:

> There is here a dual destruction suspended above Antichrist – a slow wasting first, for, it may be, centuries, and a sudden and utter extinction in the end. This duality in the doom of Antichrist has been noted in prophecy ever since its beginning. It is emphasised by Daniel. Speaking of the "little horn" which had a mouth speaking great things, eyes like the eyes of a man, a look more stout than his fellows, and which made war with the saints, and was to have dominion over them, "until a time, times, and the dividing of time," that is 1260 years, the prophet says. "The judgement shall sit, and they shall take away his dominion, to consume and destroy it unto the end" (Daniel 7:26) another proof, by the way, of identity between the "little horn" of Daniel, and the Antichrist of John.
>
> In the predicted doom of the Papacy there are thus two well-marked stages. There is, first, a gradual

consumption; and there is, second, a sudden and terrible destruction.

The "consumption," a slow and gradual process, is to be effected by the "spirit of his mouth," by which we understand the preaching of the Gospel. This consumption has been going on ever since the Bible was translated, and the Gospel began to be preached at the Reformation. Men have begun to see the errors of popery; its political props have been weakened, and in some instances struck from under it, and its hold generally on the nations of Christendom has been loosened; and thus the way has been prepared for the final stroke that will consummate its ruin. Great systems like the papacy, with their roots far down and spread wide around, cannot be plucked up while in their vigor without dislocating human society. They must be left to grow ripe and become rotten, and then the final stroke may be dealt them with safety to the church and the world.

When that hour shall have come then will the second part of the doom of the Papacy overtake it. The Lord shall "destroy" it "with the brightness of his coming." The form of the judgment is left vague, but enough is said to warrant us to conclude that it will be swift and final – it will come with lightning flash, and its holy vengeance will be so manifest that, to use the figure in the prophecy, it will irradiate both heaven and earth with a moral splendour.[867]

The translators of the Authorized (King James) Version of the Holy Bible knew the pope was the enemy of the gospel and that he desired to keep the people in ignorance of the gospel:

[W]e shall be traduced by Popish persons at home or abroad, who therefore will malign us, because we are poor instruments to make God's holy truth to be yet more and more known unto the people, whom they desire still to keep in ignorance and darkness.[868]

The King James translators had a sense that their work was part and parcel of the deadly blow that would be struck against the papal man of sin, and they said so:

> [T]he zeal of your Majesty towards the house of GOD, does not slack or go backward, but is more and more kindled, manifesting itself abroad in the furthest parts of Christendom, by writing in defense of the Truth, (which has given such a blow unto that man of Sin, as will not be healed).[869]

39 Identifying the False Prophet

In the book of Revelation, a second beast with an ominous character makes an appearance. The second beast is distinct from the papal antichrist, who is identified as the "first beast, whose deadly wound was healed." Revelation 13:14. Who is the mysterious second beast? First, let us look at his introduction onto the world stage as prophesied in Revelation 13.

> And I beheld another beast coming up out of the earth; and he had two horns like a lamb, and he spake as a dragon. And he exerciseth all the power of the first beast before him, and causeth the earth and them which dwell therein to worship the first beast, whose deadly wound was healed. And he doeth great wonders, so that he maketh fire come down from heaven on the earth in the sight of men, And deceiveth them that dwell on the earth by the means of those miracles which he had power to do in the sight of the beast; saying to them that dwell on the earth, that they should make an image to the beast, which had the wound by a sword, and did live. (Revelation 13:11-14)

This second beast is distinct from the antichrist beast. We know that because the second beast has those that dwell on the earth make an image to the beast that had the wound by the sword and was alive again. As we have seen, the antichrist was given a deadly wound in 1798 when

Napoleon's General Berthier invaded Rome, took Pope Pius VI prisoner, and held him until his death in fulfillment of the prophecy in Revelation 13:1-3.

This second beast has been described as the "false prophet" in Revelation 16:13, 19:20, and 20:10. The term "false prophet" is significant. It suggests that the second beast is Jewish. There is only one religious order who answers to the description of "false prophet," who has "two horns like a lamb," and speaks as a dragon. That is the Society of Jesus, otherwise known as the Jesuits. The head of the Jesuit order is the Jesuit General; he is so powerful and evil that he is commonly known as the "black pope."

The title of the Jesuit priesthood is significant. Jesus is often described as the lamb of God, while the second beast is described as having "two horns like a lamb, and he spake as a dragon." The Jesuits were instrumental in cursing the gospel of Jesus Christ through its authored doctrines in the Council of Trent and other anti-Christian dogma. That explains the description of the second beast in Revelation as speaking as a dragon. Who is the dragon? None other than Satan.

> And the great dragon was cast out, that old serpent, called the Devil, and Satan, which deceiveth the whole world: he was cast out into the earth, and his angels were cast out with him." (Revelation 12:9)

What most do not know is that the Jesuit order is a crypto-Jewish order of priests. While it may have gentile priests as members, it was founded by a Jew and today has close secret ties with other clandestine Jewish organizations. Benjamin Disraeli was a Jew and a former Prime Minister of England; he revealed that the first Jesuits were Jews.[870] Ignatius of Loyola's secretary, Polanco, was of Jewish descent and was the only person present at Loyola's deathbed. Ignatius Loyola himself was a crypto-Jew of the Occult Kabbalah. A crypto-Jew is a Jew who converts to another religion and outwardly embraces the new religion, while secretly maintaining Jewish practices.

James Lainez (J.G. 1558-1565), who succeeded Ignatius Loyola (J.G. 1541-1556) as the second Jesuit General, was also of Jewish descent. The third Jesuit General was Fransicso Borgia (J.G. 1565-

1572); he was followed by Eberhard Mercurian (J.G. 1573-1580), who was a Belgian Jew.[871] Robert Maryks has posted the names and biographies of approximately 390 Jews who are known to have been members of the Jesuit order.[872] One can be sure that Maryks' list is just the tip of the iceberg, since Jews sometimes go to extraordinary lengths to hide their Jewish heritage. The fact that Maryks does not include Eberhard Mercurian among the listed Jewish Jesuits is testimony to the incompleteness of his list. Jews were attracted to the Jesuit order and joined in large numbers.[873] Some of the most influential Jesuits in history, such as Francisco Ribera (1537-1591) and Emanuel Lacunza (1731-1801), were Jews. During the 5th General Congregation in 1593 of the 27 Jesuits who proposed changes to the Constitutions, 25 were of either Jewish or Moorish descent.[874] Many of the Jesuit doctrines are similar to those found in the Kabbalah and Babylonian Talmud. The Jesuits seem to fulfill the prophecies of the second beast in the book of Revelation.

John Torell explains the Jewish origins of the Jesuit order:

> The Illuminati order was not invented by Adam Weishaupt, but rather renewed and reformed. The first known Illuminati order (Alumbrado) was founded in 1492 by Spanish Jews, called "Marranos," who were also known as "crypto-Jews." With violent persecution in Spain and Portugal beginning in 1391, hundreds of thousands of Jews had been forced to convert to the faith of the Roman Catholic Church. Publicly they were now Roman Catholics, but secretly they practiced Judaism, including following the Talmud and the Cabala. The Marranos were able to teach their children secretly about Judaism, but in particular the Talmud and the Cabala, and this huge group of Jews has survived to this very day. After 1540 many Marranos opted to flee to England, Holland, France, the Ottoman empire (Turkey), Brazil and other places in South and Central America. The Marranos kept strong family ties and they became very wealthy and influential in the nations where they lived. But as is the custom with all Jewish people, it did not matter in what nation they lived, their loyalty was to themselves and Judaism.[875]

... In 1491 San Ignacio De Loyola was born in the Basque province of Guipuzcoa, Spain. His parents were Marranos and at the time of his birth the family was very wealthy. **As a young man he became a member of the Jewish Illuminati order in Spain. As a cover for his crypto Jewish activities, he became very active as a Roman Catholic.** On May 20, 1521, Ignatius (as he was now called) was wounded in a battle, and became a semi-cripple. Unable to succeed in the military and political arena, he started a quest for holiness and eventually ended up in Paris where he studied for the priesthood. In 1539 he had moved to Rome where he founded the "JESUIT ORDER," which was to become the most vile, bloody and persecuting order in the Roman Catholic Church. In 1540, the current Pope Paul III approved the order. At Loyola's death in 1556 there were more than 1000 members in the Jesuit order, located in a number of nations. [876]

Setting up the Jesuit order, Ignatius Loyola devised an elaborate spy system, so that no one in the order was safe. If there was any opposition, death would come swiftly. The Jesuit order not only became a destructive arm of the Roman Catholic Church; it also developed into a secret intelligence service. **While the Popes relied more and more on the Jesuits, they were unaware that the hard core leadership were Jewish, and that these Jews held membership in the Illuminati order which despised and hated the Roman Catholic Church.**[877]

The Jesuits were established by Ignatius of Loyola. Ignatius of Loyola was the leader of a secret occult organization known as the *Alumbrados* (Spanish for Illuminati).[878] On August 15, 1534, Loyola started a sister organization to the *Alumbrados*, which he called the Society of Jesus, it is more commonly known today as the Jesuits. Loyola was arrested by the Dominican order of Catholic inquisitors, who were concerned with his growing influence and power throughout Europe. Because of his influential allies among the principalities of Europe, he was granted an audience with the pope. Loyola promised the pope his allegiance and agreed to do the bidding of the papacy throughout the world. Pope Paul III formally approved the Jesuits as a Catholic religious order in his 1540 papal bull *Regimini Militantis Eccclesiae*.[879]

According to the Jesuit Catechism, the pope is equal to God in authority.

> Question 1: What is the Pope?
>
> Answer: He is the Vicar of Christ, KING OF KINGS, AND LORD OF LORDS, and there is but one and the same Judgment-Seat belonging to God and the Pope.[880]

Not surprisingly, the Jesuit Catechism places the authority of the pope above all kings and governments of the world.

> Question 2: Is the Pope above Kings?
>
> Answer: The Canon Law will tell you that the Pope is as far above Kings, as the Sun is greater than the Moon, upon which old Glossater took upon him to find out the distance; according to his astronomy he makes him to be above 7,744 times greater than any King, and for Kings, they are no more to be compared to the Pope, than lead is to gold.[881]

According to the Jesuit Catechism, even a common Roman Catholic priest, being an agent of the pope, has authority above kings.

> A common Priest is as much better than a King, as a man is better than a beast; nay, farther, that as much as God Almighty doth excel a Priest, so much doth a Priest excel a King.[882]

The fact that the founding Jesuits were crypto-Jews explains how the Talmudic philosophy that Gentiles are no more than animals compared to Jews is mirrored in the Jesuit theology when comparing the laity with the priesthood. Israel Shahak quotes from Rabbi Kook, who stated that "[t]he difference between a Jewish soul and souls of non-Jews - all of them in all different levels - is greater and deeper than the difference between a human soul and the souls of cattle."[883] In like manner, the Jesuit Catechism states:

> All Lay-men are no better than Horses, Mules, or Asses, and the Romanist himself hath but the honour to be a tame Ass, while the heretick is a wild one; nor do the Kings of the Popish persuasion get any more esteem from him than that they are the foremost or leading Asses with fine jangling bells about their necks.[884]

The crypto-Jewish Jesuit theology allows for no limit to the authority of the pope. Again, this theological superiority complex flows directly from the Jewish Talmud. In rabbinic Judaism, the Talmud has primacy and authority over God's word in the Old Testament.[885] For example, in the Talmud, Avodah Zarah 3B, it states that God spends part of his day studying the teachings of the Jewish rabbis found in the Talmud.[886] In like manner, the Jesuit Catechism allows for the pope to overrule the very word of God.

> Question: What if the Holy Scriptures command one thing, and the Pope another contrary to it?
>
> Answer: The Holy Scriptures must be thrown aside.[887]

Recall, that the Lord Jesus Christ is the word of God that became flesh.

> In the beginning was the Word, and the Word was with God, and the Word was God. The same was in the beginning with God. All things were made by him; and without him was not any thing made that was made. ... And the Word was made flesh, and dwelt among us, (and we beheld his glory, the glory as of the only begotten of the Father,) full of grace and truth. (John 1:1-3, 14)

The Jesuits blaspheme God and count him and his word as their sworn enemy. Hector Macpherson quotes from a Jesuit meeting at

Cheri, Italy in 1825:

> Then the Bible, that serpent which with head erect and eyes flashing, threatens us (the Jesuits) with its venom while it trails along the ground, shall be changed into a rod as soon as we (the Jesuits) are able to seize it...for three centuries past this cruel asp has left us no repose. You well know with what folds it entwines us and with what fangs it gnaws us.[888]

While the exoteric portrayal is that the pope has primacy over the Jesuit General, the esoteric true relationship is actually the reverse. Respected historian Francis Parkman succinctly explains the hierarchal relationship between the pope and the Jesuit General:

> The Jesuits, then as now, were the most forcible exponents of ultramontane principles. **The [Roman Catholic] Church to rule the world; the pope to rule the Church; the Jesuits to rule the Pope,** —such was and is the simple programme of the Order of Jesus; and to it they have held fast, except on a few rare occasions of misunderstanding with the Vicegerent of Christ.[889] (emphasis added)

Dave Hunt stated: "Like his predecessors, the new Superior General is a powerful man to whom even the Pope is subject."[890] Indeed, Pope Benedict XVI's confessor was Jesuit General Adolfo Nicolas.[891] Pope Benedict XVI resigned as pope, almost certainly under the advice of his confessor, the Jesuit General. After the extremely rare resignation, we find the unprecedented election of a Jesuit Vicar of Christ, Pope Francis. It appears that Pope Benedict XVI was persuaded to resign to make room for his successor. While having the Jesuit General as confessor is unusual, it seems that the confessor to the pope is always a Jesuit. According to Nino Lo Bello, "the Pope's confessor, an ordinary priest, must be a Jesuit: he must visit the Vatican once a week at a fixed time, and he alone may absolve the Pope of his sins."[892] The requirement that the confessor to the pope must be a Jesuit, attests to the control the Jesuit General has over the pope. His moniker, the black pope, signifies his esoteric but very real power over the white pope.

The influence of the Jews through the Jesuits in the Roman Catholic Church has been manifested from the beginning in Catholic doctrine. The Council of Trent was orchestrated by the Jesuits. It was an attack on Christianity, with anathema after anathema against Christian doctrine. The many curses from the Council of Trent fulfills the prophecy of John that the second beast (false prophet) "maketh fire come down from heaven on the earth in the sight of men, And deceiveth them that dwell on the earth." Revelation 13:13.

The Jesuits completely controlled the Council of Trent. It is notable that all of the "sole papal theologians" sent by the pope to the Council of Trent were Jesuits and three of those Jesuits are now known to have been Jews: Alfonso Salmerón, James (a/k/a Diego) Lainez, and Juan Alfonso Polanco.[893] It is curious that the Catholic Encyclopedia makes no mention of the involvement of Polanco at the Council of Trent.

The pagan Roman Catholic Church has been infiltrated by the Talmudic Jews, primarily, but not exclusively, through the Jesuit order. Notice the similarities between the imperious whorish woman in Ezekiel 16:14-40, which is apostate Israel, and the Roman Catholic harlot of Revelation 17. They are one and the same. The crypto-Jewish Jesuits of the Roman Catholic Church are modern day Pharisees.

James Lainez (a/k/a Diego Lainez), who was a crypto-Jew, was the most influential member of the Council of Trent and was responsible for many of the anathemas against Christians and biblical Christian doctrine. The influence of the crypto-Jewish Jesuits over the Council of Trent can be seen in the many curses issued by the council against those who follow orthodox Christian doctrine. For example, the Council of Trent Cannon XII curses all who believe the gospel that faith in Jesus Christ alone satisfies God as sufficient to remit the whole punishment for sin.[894] That is a direct attack on the gospel as contained in the Holy Bible. The bible states: "But if we walk in the light, as he is in the light, we have fellowship one with another, and the blood of Jesus Christ his Son cleanseth us from all sin." (1 John 1:7)

The *Extreme Oath of the Jesuits,* which is given to a Jesuit Priest when he is elevated to a position of command, contains the following provision: "I_____ declare and swear that his holiness, the Pope, is Christ's Vice-regent, and is the true and only head of the Catholic or Universal Church throughout the earth."[895] This fulfills the prophecy in John that the second beast "causeth the earth and them which dwell therein to worship the first beast, whose deadly wound was healed." Revelation 13:12. The Jesuits further wage spiritual war against Jesus Christ and his true church. The oath continues with:

> Therefore, to the utmost of my power, I shall and will defend this doctrine and his Holiness' right and customs against all usurpers of the heretical or Protestant authority. ... I do now renounce and disown any allegiance as due to any heretical king, prince or state named Protestant or Liberals, or obedience to any of their laws, magistrates or officers. ... I do further promise and declare, that I will, when opportunity presents, make and wage relentless war, secretly or openly, against all heretics, Protestants and Liberals, as I am directed to do to extirpate and exterminate them from the face of the whole earth, and that I will spare neither sex, age, nor condition, and that I will hang, waste, boil, flay, strangle, and bury alive these infamous heretics; rip up the stomachs and wombs of their women and crush their infants' heads against the wall, in order to annihilate forever their execrable race. ... That when the same cannot be done openly, I will secretly use the poison cup, the strangulation cord, the steel of the poinard, or the leaden bullet, regardless of the honor, rank, dignity or authority of the person or persons whatsoever may be their condition in life, either public or private, as I at any time may be directed so to do by any agent of the pope or superior of the brotherhood of the holy faith of the Society of Jesus.[896]

The Jesuits are the secret army of the Roman church; they are often referred to as the "pope's militia." The "Jesuit General" is unlike any other leader of a Catholic order, because the Jesuit General is independent of the Catholic Bishops and Cardinals; he answers directly to the Pope. Because of the power and influence of the Jesuit General, he is known as the "black pope." The Jesuit General has the purported authority to absolve persons of the sins of bigamy, murder, or any harm done to others as long as the matter is not publicly known and the cause of a scandal.[897] Pope Gregory XII gave the Jesuits the authority to deal in commerce and banking, which has made the order quite wealthy.[898] The popes have threatened princes, kings, and anyone else who interferes with the Jesuits with excommunication (*Latae Sententiae*).[899] In one of the most authoritative works on the Jesuits, J. Huber, professor of Catholic theology wrote: "Here is a proven fact: the Constitutions [of the Jesuits] repeat five hundred times that one must see Christ in the person of the [Jesuit] General."[900]

If the Jesuits are a Crypto-Jewish order that hates the Roman Catholic church, as alleged by Torell, why would it become a priestly order within that church and become its greatest defender with extreme oaths of obedience to the pope? Because, the Roman church offers the Jews an ideal cover from which to wage war against Christianity. This is evidenced by the fact that the Jesuits virtually controlled the Council of Trent, which produced anathema after anathema against bible believing Christians and fundamental Christian doctrine. This same Jesuit organization initially opposed the inquisition.[901] Why? Because the inquisition, in part, was initiated to root out crypto-Jewry inside the Catholic church. Of course, an organization founded and controlled by crypto-Jews would oppose a strategy that would expose its own Jewish core. Once the Jesuits gained control over the inquisition, however, their opinion changed.

The hierarchy of Orthodox Jews hate Gentiles; ostensibly Gentile organizations like the Roman church offer an ideal front from which to strike against the hated Christians. That is why God refers to the great harlot of Babylon as "MYSTERY." The Roman church appears to the world to be a gentile religious organization, yet it is to its core Jewish. As long at the Roman church does the bidding of the Jews, they will defend it. Once the Roman church is no longer useful, the Jews will shed it like a snake sheds its old skin.

It seems that the Jews have the destruction of the Roman church all planned out. The following is a passage from the THE PROTOCOLS OF THE LEARNED ELDERS OF ZION that seem to foretell the destruction of the Vatican by the nations of the world.

> When the time comes finally to destroy the papal court the finger of an invisible hand will point the nations towards this court. When, however, the nations fling themselves upon it, we shall come forward in the guise of its defenders as if to save excessive bloodshed. By this diversion we shall penetrate to its very bowels and be sure we shall never come out again until we have gnawed through the entire strength of this place.[902]

That is very similar to the prophecy found in the book of Revelation.

> And the ten horns which thou sawest upon the beast, **these shall hate the whore, and shall make her desolate and naked, and shall eat her flesh, and burn her with fire.** For God hath put in their hearts to fulfil his will, and to agree, and give their kingdom unto the beast, until the words of God shall be fulfilled. And the woman which thou sawest is that great city, which reigneth over the kings of the earth. (Revelation 17:16-18)

The horns of the beast are ten kings on the beast that is being ridden by the great harlot who sits on seven mountains (the Vatican). Revelation 17. The PROTOCOLS have set forth the planned destruction of the Vatican. The PROTOCOLS seem also to have provided for the entrance of their own special antichrist. "The King of the Jews will be the real pope of the universe, the patriarch of the international church."[903]

In fact, the Jesuits, the great defenders of the Catholic faith, have actually exercised their power to undermine the authority of the church and bring it to its knees. The Jesuits were the operating power behind the deadly wound suffered by the first beast (the pope). Revelations 13:3. The reason the Jesuits retaliated against the Catholic church was that the Jesuits were at one time dissolved as a Catholic order because of their subversive conduct. The political sedition of the Jesuits caused it to be banned from scores of countries. For example, in 1759 the Jesuits were banned throughout the Portuguese Empire.[904] In 1764 the Jesuits were outlawed in France, and in 1767 they were banned from Spain.⁹⁰⁵ On April 6, 1762 the French Parliament issued the following "statement of arrest" (indictment):

> The said Institute [Jesuits] is inadmissible in any civilised State, as its nature is hostile to all spiritual and temporal authority; it seeks to introduce into the Church and States, under the plausible veil of a religious Institute, not an Order truly desirous to spread evangelical perfection, but rather a political body working untiringly at usurping all authority, by all kinds of indirect, secret, and devious means. . . .[The Jesuits' doctrine is] perverse, a destroyer of all religious and honest principles, insulting to Christian morals, pernicious to civil society, hostile to the rights of the nation, the royal power, and even the security of the sovereigns and obedience of their subjects; suitable to stir up the greatest disturbances in the States, conceive and maintain the worst kind of corruption in men's hearts.⁹⁰⁶

The subversion of the European nations by the Jesuits became so great that an immense amount of military and political pressure was brought against the pope by the European nations. Finally, Pope Clement XIII decided on the 3rd of February 1769 to dissolve the Jesuits. While Jesuits are under an oath of allegiance to the pope, that oath is secondary to their extreme oath of allegiance to the Jesuit General:

> I do further promise and declare, that I will have no opinion or will of my own, or any mental reservation whatever, even as a corpse or cadaver [perinde ac cadaver] but unhesitatingly, obey each and very command that I may receive from my superiors in the Militia of the Pope and Jesus Christ.⁹⁰⁷

The night before Pope Clement XIII was to execute the dissolution, he suddenly fell ill and died. Prior to his death he cried out "I am dying . . . It is a very dangerous thing to attack the Jesuits."⁹⁰⁸ His successor, Pope Clement XIV, was also put under tremendous political pressure to dissolve the Jesuits, but he resisted doing so for three years until the political tension finally forced his hand. Pope Clement XIV issued the papal brief of dissolution, *Dominus ac Redemptor,* on August 16, 1773.[909] Pope Clement XIV knew the significance of such an act to the papacy; he exclaimed: "I have cut off my right hand."[910] In addition, Pope Clement XIV knew that by signing the brief dissolving the Jesuits he was signing his own death warrant. Soon after signing the brief the letters I.S.S.S.V. appeared on the palace walls in the Vatican.[911] Pope Clement XIV knew what it meant and explained that it stood for *In Settembre, Sara Sede Vacante.* Which translated means "in September, the See will be vacant (the pope will be dead)."[912] Pope Clement XIV was poisoned and died on September 22, 1774.[913]

Not coincidently, it was just three years after Pope Clement XIV's suppression of the Jesuits that the subversive organization the "Illuminati" was purportedly founded by a trained Jesuit named Adam Weishaupt in 1776.[914] Weishaupt was a Jew and a professor of canon law at Ingolstadt University, which was a Jesuit University and the center of the Jesuit counter-reformation.[915] Alberto Rivera, a former Jesuit priest, stated that the occult Illuminati organization was not founded by Weishaupt, as many believe, but in fact was established long before Weishaupt. The Illuminati is in fact a reincarnation of the ancient *Alumbrados*, whose one time leader was Ignatius of Loyola, the founder of the Jesuits.[916] The Illuminati was established by Lorenzo Ricco, the Jesuit General, in 1776, who used his disciple, Adam Weishaupt, as the front man for the new organization (which was really not new at all).[917] The Jesuits, having just been suppressed by the pope in 1773, found it necessary to establish the Illuminati, which was an alliance between the Jesuits and the very powerful Ashkenazi Jewish Banking House of Rothschild. The purpose of Weishaupt initially was to avenge the papal suppression of the Jesuits by rooting out all religion and overturning the governments of the world, bringing them under a single world government, controlled of course by the Illuminati, under the authority of their god. That world government is commonly referred to by the Illuminati as the "New World Order." The god of the Illuminati is Satan.[918]

Eric Jon Phelps in his book, *The Vatican Assassins*, explains:

> These 41 years [between their suppression in 1773 by Pope Clement XIV and their reestablishment by Pope

Pius VII in 1814] were absolutely golden for the Society of Jesus. For the Sons of Loyola punished all their enemies, including the Dominican priests, perfected the inner workings between themselves and Freemasonry, creating alliance between the house of Rothschild in establishing the illuminati; punished and absorbed the Knights of Malta . . . . They used the Orthodox Catherine of Russia and a Lutheran Frederick of Prussia to conquer and divide Poland, rendering the pope's Bull of Suppression of no effect in that Roman Catholic land. They caused the French Revolution, beheaded a Bourbon King and a Hapsburg Queen as punishment for being expelled from France and Austria. With Napoleon, the Freemason, they drove the Bourbons from their throne in Spain and the Braganzas from their throne in Portugal. They even attempted to take Palestine from the Moslems like the Crusaders of old.[919]

The company's most important victories were both religious and political. They deeply penetrated the Russian Orthodox Church and Germany's Lutheran Church, its Tubingen University specifically. Politically, they took control of the crown and the Bank of England. For this reason England, with Viscount Palmerston, would never go to war with France again, it would conduct the Pope's opium wars against people of China (just like the company, with its CIA and Mafia Commission is presently conducting a massive drug trade against the "heretic and liberal" people of the American Empire) . . . The Jesuits also captured the Papacy with the Vatican; along with its landed church properties the world over, and for this reason the Papal Caesar, occupying Satan's sacred office of the Papacy, would never suppress the Society of Jesus *ever again!*[920]

The secret Illuminati organization was the hidden guiding hand behind the brutal French Revolution of 1787, during which 300,000 people were massacred in a godless orgy of violence.[921] The rage by the

Jesuits and their reconstituted Illuminati culminated in 1798, with the capture of the pope himself. Napoleon's General Berthier invaded Rome, took Pope Pius VI prisoner, and held him until his death. Note that in Revelation 13, where the false prophet is introduced as a second great beast, the passages describe the first beast (the papacy) as the "beast, whose deadly wound was healed" (Revelation 13:14) and a second time as "the beast, which had the wound by a sword, and did live." (Revelation 13:12) It seems that John is trying to say that there is a link between the second beast (the false prophet) and the first beast (the papacy) who suffered the deadly wound, which was healed. The Jesuit rampage against the Vatican, and the resultant death of the pope in 1798 indicates that the deadly wound was caused by the second beast (the Jesuits). Indeed, the Jesuits did not surface as the militia of the pope until after God released the restraints put on his God-breathed holy word and allowed it to spread over the world. The spread of the true gospel during the Protestant Reformation was the ultimate cause of the deadly wound. The true gospel caused the scales of deception to fall from the eyes of kings and peasants alike. The Jesuits were merely the instruments through whom the blow was struck against the papacy.

The Roman Catholic church had learned its lesson. On August 7, 1814, the Jesuits were restored as a Catholic order by Pope Pius VII.[922] John Adams wrote to Thomas Jefferson in 1816 "I am not happy about the rebirth of the Jesuits. . . . Swarms of them will present themselves under more disguises ever taken by even a chief of the Bohemians, as printers, writers, publishers, school teachers, etc. If ever an association of people deserved eternal damnation, on this earth and in hell, it is the Society of Loyola. Yet, with our system of religious liberty, we can but offer them a refuge."[923] Thomas Jefferson answered Adams: "Like you, I object to the Jesuits' reestablishment which makes light give way to darkness."[924]

In 1835, Samuel Morse, the great inventor of the telegraph, echoed the concerns of Jefferson and Adams; he described the Jesuits and their threat to the United States as follows:

> And do Americans need to be told what *Jesuits* are? If any are ignorant, let them inform themselves of their history without delay: no time is to be lost: their workings are before you in every day's events: they are

a *secret* society, a sort of Masonic order, with superadded features of most revolting odiousness and a thousand times more dangerous. They are not confined to one class on society; they are not merely priests, or priests of one religious creed, they are merchants, and lawyers, and editors, and men of any profession, and no profession, having no outward badge (in this country) by which to be recognised; they are about in all your society. They can assume any character that of angels of light, or ministers of darkness, to accomplish their one great end, the *service* upon which they are sworn to *start at any moment, in any direction,* and for any service, commanded by the general of their order, bound to no family, community, or country, by the ordinary ties which bind men; and *sold for life* to the cause of the Roman Pontiff.[925]

The concerns of Morse, Adams, and Jefferson were justified; once being reestablished as a Catholic order the Jesuits did not miss a beat; during the 19th century they fomented revolutions throughout the world, attempting to bring to power oppressive despots whom they would then control. They were at one time or another expelled from Russia (1820), Belgium, Portugal (1834), the Italian states (1859), Spain (three times-1820, 1835, and 1868), Germany (1872), Guatemala (1872), Mexico (1873), Brazil (1874), Ecuador (1875), Colombia (1875), Costa Rica (1884), and France (twice-1880 and 1901).[926] They caused the Swiss Civil war in 1847; as a result they were banished from Switzerland in 1848.[927] Up until the year 2000, the Swiss Constitution (article 51) forbade the Jesuits from engaging in any cultural or educational activity in Switzerland.[928] In the year 2000 Switzerland ratified a new constitution, in which article 51 was removed. Those are just a sampling of the over 70 countries from which the Jesuits have been expelled for conducting subversive activities. The Jesuit subversion has continued to modern times, causing the Jesuits to be expelled from Haiti in 1964 and Burma in 1966.[929] To this day they are instigating communist revolutions in South America. The Jesuits' new brand of South American communism is known as "Liberation Theology."

Jesuits have a long and sordid history of distorting moral

obligations and practicing and advocating situational ethics. For example, God commands without exception that "Thou shalt not bear false witness against thy neighbor." Exodus 20:16. The Jesuits, on the other hand, permit the use of ambiguous terms to mislead a judge or outright lying under oath if the witness makes a mental reservation.[930] The Jesuits teach that if a young girl is pregnant, she may obtain an abortion if the pregnancy would bring dishonor to her or a member of the clergy.[931] They do not stop there; another Jesuit maxim states: "If a Father, yielding to temptation, abuses a woman and she publicises what has happened, and, because of it, dishonours him, this same Father can kill her to avoid disgrace."[932] That is not the only cause that is justification for murder. The Jesuits further teach that "[a] monk or a priest is allowed to kill those who are ready to slander him or his community."[933]

Immorality is not unique to the Jesuit order only. The doctrines of the Catholic Church allow for all sorts of situational ethics. Thomas Aquinas, who is considered a Catholic saint, declared in the 13th century that prostitution was necessary. He likened prostitution to a sewer, which keeps the filth from bubbling up into the palace. He stated that without prostitution society would be polluted by worse moral vice. Augustine, another Catholic saint, stated that "if you put down prostitution, license and pleasure will corrupt society."[934] Such is the Catholic ethic. In medieval times, the Catholic Church actually owned and operated brothels in Europe. Bishoprics regulated these houses of lust. Priests and monks were the major customers. It is from this accommodating ethic of licentiousness that William Kennedy finds the root of sex crimes by the Catholic clergy.

Thomas Aquinas, the most influential source of economic and theological doctrines for the Catholic Church, stated that it is lawful and not a sin for a man to steal another's property in order to fulfill a basic need. Aquinas' view was that all goods are community goods and therefore it is not a sin to take another's property when you need it.[935] That is in fact the official position of the Roman church today as expressed by the Second Vatican Council. "If one is in extreme necessity he has the right to procure for himself what he needs out of the riches of others."[936]

What is the authority for this ethic? It is found in the Talmud.

In *Baba Bathra 54b* it states: "The property of a heathen is on the same footing as desert land; whoever first occupies it acquires ownership."[937] Compare that to the eighth commandment of God: "Thou shalt not steal." Exodus 20:15. Furthermore, in *Baba Kamma 113b* it states that if one finds lost property it must be returned if the owner is a Jew; however if the owner is a gentile it can be kept. "It is to your brother that you make restoration, but you need not make restoration to a heathen."[938]

The Jesuits are zealous persecutors of Christians or anyone whom they view as an enemy of the Vatican. Jesuits take a solemn oath to destroy Protestant Christians and destroy any government that offers protection to Protestant Christians.[939] They are the natural enemies of liberty, their whole system is based on thoughtless, ruthless, blind obedience. Ignatius himself writing to his Jesuits in Portugal said: "We must see black as white if the church says so."[940] Jesuits are the subversive ambassadors of the Catholic Church, bringing chaos and ruin to all nations they infiltrate. They believe that "[t]he Catholic Church has the right and duty to kill heretics because it is by fire and sword that heresy can be extirpated. . . . Repentance cannot be allowed to save them, just as repentance is not allowed to save civil criminals; for the highest good of the church is the unity of the faith, and this cannot be preserved unless heretics are put to death."[941]

Alberto Rivera, a former Jesuit Priest, was saved by the grace of God and came out of the Jesuit priesthood. The Jesuits made numerous attempts to kill him before he could reveal the secrets of the Jesuits. He survived the attempts on his life and exposed much about sinister methods and motives of the Jesuits.

Franz Wernz, the Jesuit General from 1906-1915, stated that "[t]he Church can condemn heretics to death, for any rights they have are only through our tolerance, and these rights are apparent not real"[942] That view of heretics having no rights is very similar to the philosophy of the Jewish Talmud. Sanhedrin 57b provides that if a heathen robs another or a Jew the property must be returned. If, however, a Jew robs a heathen, the property does not have to be returned to the heathen.[943] That section of the Talmud also states that if a heathen murders another heathen or a Jew, the heathen should suffer the death penalty. If, however, a Jew kills a heathen "there is no death penalty."[944] For further information of the Jewish origins of the Roman Catholic Church read this author's book, *Solving the Mystery of BABYLON THE GREAT*.

Jesuit priests are subjected to certain "spiritual exercises" which were first devised by Ignatius Loyola. During the spiritual exercises the subject becomes possessed and controlled by a devil.

> We imbue into him spiritual forces which he would find very difficult to eliminate later, forces more lasting than all the best principles and doctrines; these forces can come up again to the surface, sometimes after years of not even mentioning them, and become so imperative that the will finds itself unable to oppose any obstacle, and has to follow their irresistible impulse.[945]

Between 1569 and 1605 the Jesuits orchestrated no less than eleven plots against Protestant England, which involved invasion, rebellion, and assassination. Each is known by the leader of the treachery: Ridolfi, Sanders, Gregory XIII, Campion, Parsons, Duke of Guise, Allen, Throgmorten, Parry, Babington, Sixtus V, Philip II of Spain, Yorke, Walpole, Southwell, and Guy Fawkes.[946]

In the 1586 "Babington plot" the Jesuits along with other Catholics planned to kill Protestant Queen Elizabeth I, place Catholic Mary Stuart, Queen of Scots on the throne of England and bring England under subjection to the Pope of Rome. That plot was discovered and Mary was executed for her troubles.[947]

After the failed Babington plot, the Pope, in league with Philip II of Spain, planned to invade England and bring it under papal control. In 1588 Spain brought the 136 ship Spanish Armada against England. The Sovereign God of the Universe whipped up a freak storm which devastated the Armada and allowed England with only 30 ships to defeat Spain after an eight hour sea battle.[948]

On November 5, 1605 Jesuit led Roman Catholic conspirators planned to kill King James I and the entire English Parliament by blowing up the House of Lords. They placed 20 barrels of gunpowder under the House of Lords. The plan was to blow up the house of Lords when the Lords, Commons, and King were all assembled on November 5, 1605 for the opening of Parliament.[949] The plot, however, was discovered and the conspirators were captured. To this day that event is simply referred to as the "Gunpowder Plot."[950] November 5th is a national holiday in England, commemorating the Catholic conspiracy in the Gunpowder Plot. The holiday is called Guy Fawkes Day; Guy Fawkes was one of the Gunpowder Plot conspirators.[951]

All nations should learn from the experience of Protestant England and understand the threat that Rome and the Jesuits pose to any free country. The Roman Catholic Church uses religious superstition to usurp the authority and undermine independence of any state. King Henry VIII cast off the yoke of Rome and declared that he was to be the head of the church in England.

In May 1538, the pope sought his revenge for the separation of the Church of England from Rome; the pope excommunicated all in Ireland who recognized the supremacy of the King of England or any ecclesiastical or civil power greater than that of the Roman Catholic Church. The events are recounted in the classic *Foxe's Book of Martyrs*:

> A short time after this, the pope sent over to Ireland (directed to the archbishop of Armagh and his clergy) a bull of excommunication against all who had, or should own the king's supremacy within the Irish nation; denouncing a curse on all of them, and theirs, who should not, within forty days, acknowledge to their confessors, that they had done amiss in so doing.
>
> Archbishop Browne gave notice of this in a letter dated, Dublin, May, 1538. Part of the form of confession, or vow, sent over to these Irish papists, ran as follows: "I do further declare him or her, father or mother, brother or sister, son or daughter, husband or wife, uncle or aunt, nephew or niece, kinsman or kinswoman, master or mistress, and all others, nearest or dearest relations, friend or acquaintance whatsoever, accursed, that either do or shall hold, for the time to come, any ecclesiastical or civil power above the

authority of the Mother Church; or that do or shall obey, for the time to come, any of her, the Mother of Churches' opposers or enemies, or contrary to the same, of which I have here sworn unto: so God, the Blessed Virgin, St. Peter, St. Paul, and the Holy Evangelists, help me," etc. is an exact agreement with the doctrines promulgated by the Councils of Lateran and Constance, which expressly declare that no favor should be shown to heretics, nor faith kept with them; that they ought to be excommunicated and condemned, and their estates confiscated, and that princes are obliged, by a solemn oath, to root them out of their respective dominions.[952]

The political and religious attacks against Protestant England by Rome continued up to and beyond 1641; in 1641 the beast of Rome planned a murderous insurrection in Ireland. The objective of the barbarous conspiracy was to murder all Protestants in Ireland, without exception. In this instance, as in many others, we find the Jesuits leading the murderous and maniacal charge. The Jesuits placed their hellish imprimatur on the massacre by beginning it on the feast day of their founder, Ignatius of Loyola. When the dust finally settled on the genocide, Rome had exterminated 150,000 innocent men, women, and children. This massacre illustrates the danger of a Roman Catholic majority in any country. No matter who seems to control the political reigns, when the lawful government is at odds with Rome there will be hell to pay. Rome is a master at mass insurrection through the incitation of base barbarians who have sold their soul to the superstition of the Roman cult.

The Irish genocide was planned and orchestrated from the Vatican. It was executed through the leadership of the Jesuits and the other priests of Rome. He who has eyes let him see through the pious facade of Rome. He who has understanding let him understand the danger posed by Rome and the Jesuits. The Roman Catholic Church never changes.

40 The Image of the Beast Comes Alive

The false prophet described in Revelation 16:13, 19:20, and 20:10 is introduced as a beast in Revelation 13:11-15. There is a mysterious prophecy regarding this beast in Revelation 13:15, in which he gives life to an image of another beast, who was introduced in Revelation 13:1. In order to understand that prophecy, we must understand its prelude. The first beast in Revelation 13:1 rose "out of the sea, having seven heads and ten horns, and upon his horns ten crowns, and upon his heads the name of blasphemy." God then reveals "another beast," in Revelation 13:11, who comes "up out of the earth; and he had two horns like a lamb, and he spake as a dragon." It is this second beast who, in Revelation 13:15, "had power to give life unto the image of the beast, that the image of the beast should both speak, and cause that as many as would not worship the image of the beast should be killed." What is the image of the beast? It is a graven image that is created by those on earth. Revelation 13:14 states that those that dwell on the earth are deceived and "make an image to the beast." It is that graven image to which the second beast had power to give life.

As we have seen, in a previous chapter, one of the heads on the first beast suffered a deadly wound. Revelation 13:3. That was the wound suffered by the papacy, which was later healed. The papacy made its first appearance in the bible as the little horn in Daniel 7:8: "there came up among them another little horn, before whom there were three of the first horns plucked up by the roots: and, behold, in this horn were eyes like the eyes of man, and a mouth speaking great things." In Daniel 7:20 we read how that "same horn made war with the saints, and prevailed against them."

The second beast of Revelation 13:11 represents the Jesuit General and his minion Jesuits. How does the second beast give life to the image of the first beast? The mystery is solved when we look back historically at the spiritual commonality between the kingdoms that made up the first beast. The first beast "was like unto a leopard, and his feet were as the feet of a bear, and his mouth as the mouth of a lion: and the dragon gave him his power, and his seat, and great authority." Revelation 13:2. Looking back to Daniel chapter 7 we read of three beasts: a lion, a bear, and a leopard. Daniel tells us that these three beasts are followed by a fourth dreadful beast, which had ten horns. Daniel describes "[t]hese great beasts, which are four, are four kings, which shall arise out of the earth." Daniel 7:17. The four beasts are the successive kingdoms of Babylon, Medo-Persia, Greece, and Rome. See Daniel 2:31-45; 8:20-24. As we saw in a previous chapter, the stout little horn that sprung from the Roman Empire is the papacy. That little horn "shall rise after them; and he shall be diverse from the first, and he shall subdue three kings. And he shall speak great words against the most High, and shall wear out the saints of the most High, and think to change times and laws." Daniel 7:24-25.

You may wonder what that all has to do with the image of the beast. An image is "a representation or similitude of any person or thing."[953] The image of the beast must represent the character of its constituent parts. The dragon gave his seat and authority to the beast. We know that dragon is "that old serpent, called the Devil, and Satan." Revelation 12:9. The beast of which the image is made is an amalgam of the kingdoms of Babylon (lion), Medo-Persia (bear), Greece (leopard), and Rome ("seven heads and ten horns, and upon his horns ten crowns"). Revelation 13:1-2. The second beast, identified in Revelation 13:11, gave life to the image of the first beast identified in Revelation 13:1. That image must represent the essence of the power and authority of the first beast.

God tells us that "the dragon gave him his power, and his seat, and great authority." Revelation 13:2. Therefore, the essence of the beast is the evil of the dragon, who we know is the evil spirit, Satan. In order for the image of the beast to be a true image, it must represent the nature of that beast. The real nature of the beast is spiritual evil. God gives us a hint as to where to look for this spiritual evil image by his description of the beast in Revelation 13:2. This spiritual evil image must have been evidenced in some way during the kingdoms of Babylon (lion), Medo-Persia (bear), Greece (leopard), and Rome ("seven heads and ten horns, and upon his horns ten crowns"). Revelation 13:1-2.

God states that the dragon gave his power and authority to that beast. God told us that to indicate that the image must represent the power behind those kingdoms. What is the power of a kingdom. All kingdoms seek to control and indeed try to subjugate its people. The one sure way to do that is through religious superstition. Throughout history, rulers have used religion as a means of controlling the population. That is what is behind the imagery in Revelation 17:3 where God describes the great harlot sitting astride a scarlet colored beast. That imagery depicts the control of the heathen religion over the governments of the world. In fact, we find God describing her relationship with the kings of the word as an illicit one, where she controls governments through spiritual seduction. She it is "[w]ith whom the kings of the earth have committed fornication and the inhabitants of the earth have been made drunk with the wine of her fornication." (Revelation 17:2) This phenomenon of spiritual seduction is particularly notable in Catholic countries. Without the approval of the Catholic hierarchy, no ruler in a Catholic country can reign long.

Tom Rushing explains how rulers use religion to control the people.

> Religion played an essential role in placating the masses. Before reading became popular, people went to their religious leaders and were told what was right and wrong and read to them selected text to confirm their assertions. The rulers made sure to keep close tabs on the religious leaders and rewarded and punished them according to the messages and influence they pushed on their congregations. If this sounds familiar, it should. This method continues to be used today. Perhaps the current administration is using it more than most have in a very long time however. Even today, the

people that I have met that are most steadfast in their faith in our rulers and question least their religion are the ones that do not bother to read more than what is recommended to them by their religious leaders. It continues to amaze me that most Christians have not read their bible at least once from cover to cover, but have no problem dedicating their lives and beliefs and their votes in accordance to their preacher's wishes without much deliberation. Religion is and has been perhaps the most effective tool of the ruling classes.[954]

Rushing's summary is not theory. Anyone who reads and understands history can see clearly how the popes throughout history held sway over the governments of the world by their control over the hearts and minds of the people. Zbigniew Brzezinski has revealed that the New World Order cannot come to power based solely upon politics and economics alone. Brzezinski is a Marxist communist who describes Marxism is "a victory of reason over belief."[955] He states that "Marxism represents a further vital and creative stage in the maturing of man's universal vision."[956] Brzezinski is an intellectual minion of the Zionist world conspiracy, a Rockefeller operative, and former National Security Advisor to President Jimmy Carter. The New World Order promoted by Brzezinski is a socialist/communist tyranny where the people are obedient "breeders." Brzezinski states that to bring about a New World Order, religion must be used to control the masses.[957]

Make no mistake about it, the Vatican is allied with very powerful forces, who are working toward a world government based upon the communist model. In a February 17, 1950, appearance before the U.S. Senate Committee on Foreign Relations, James Paul Warburg reportedly stated: "We shall have World Government, whether or not we like it. The only question is whether World Government will be achieved by conquest or consent." James Paul Warburg was the son of Paul Moritz Warburg and a financial adviser to Franklin D. Roosevelt. Paul Moritz Warburg was an influential Zionist Jew who is considered by historians to be the primary author of the Federal Reserve system. James Paul Warburg was also the nephew of both Felix Warburg and Jacob Schiff. Felix Warburg along with Otto Kahn took control of the powerful Jewish investment banking firm of Kuhn, Loeb & Co. after its chairman, Jacob Schiff, died in 1920. Kuhn, Loeb & Co. was instrumental in fostering the success of the communist revolution in Russia by pouring millions of dollars into it.

Socialism is the very essence of the Roman Catholic religion. The Roman Catholic Church has a long, but largely hidden, history of supporting communist, socialist, and fascist governments. It is not surprising that the Catholic Church would support communist regimes, since the political philosophy that permeates papal encyclicals and council edicts is that all property is common to all, and private ownership must be subordinate to that principle. The essence of communism, socialism, and fascism is that citizens do not have inalienable rights bestowed by God, but rather have group privileges bestowed by the state. In a communist state the government owns all property, in a fascist state the people own property but the government controls what the owner is allowed to do with the property. Pope Pius XI explains the Roman church's position:

> Provided the natural and divine law be observed, the public authority, in view of common good, may specify more accurately what is listed and what is illicit for property owners in the use of their possessions. History proves that the right of ownership, like other elements of social life, is not absolutely rigid.[958]

Pope Pius XI further stated:

> Socialism inclines toward and in a certain measure approaches the truths which Christian [Catholic] tradition has always held sacred; for it cannot be denied that its demands at times, come very near those that Christian reformers of society justly insist upon. Pius XI, *Quadragesimo Anno,* 109 (1931).[959]

The philosophy of collective state privileges found in communism, socialism, and fascism is also woven into the political fabric of the Catholic Church. It is the very nature of Catholicism. The political philosophy of collectivism flowed into the Catholic Church through Judaism, which obtained it directly from Babylon. It is not something that can be changed through a change in the Vatican leadership. The collective political philosophy is the inexorable product of the core doctrines of the Catholic religion. The Catholic leopard will not change its spots, because it cannot change its spots. When the beast comes to power, it will do so under the banner of a central and very powerful government that only recognizes collective privileges, whether it is communism, socialism, or fascism.

There is one religion that is feared by all tyrants: biblical Christianity. Why? Because, it sets the mind free from obedience to man-made dogma. It imbues the believer with the unction of the Holy Spirit. The Christian believer comes to understand that he is an autonomous soul, with God-given and inalienable individual rights to life, liberty, and property. Such an understanding is contrary to the system of group-privilege bestowed by the state. Biblical Christianity sets the mind and soul free from sin and ignorant obedience to the dictates of a government that tries to enslave the mind through superstitious religious mythology. For that reason, tyrannies based upon collectivism view Christians as a threat.

The bible is completely outside the control of government, whereas heathen religious dogma is used by the government as an opiate that keeps the masses obedient to the state. Karl Marx stated: "Religion is the opium of the people. Religion is a kind of spiritual gin."[960] Marx was absolutely correct when he called religion the opiate of the masses. Marx's statement parallels closely what God states about the religion of the great harlot of Revelation. "[A]ll nations have drunk of the wine of the wrath of her fornication." Revelation 18:3. In the very next clause we read how "the kings of the earth have committed fornication with her." Revelation 18:3. So we see that there is an intimate illicit spiritual coupling of religion and governments, wherein the people are made drunk and therefore malleable to the force of government.

Such is the case even in countries that are officially atheistic. For example, we see in communist Russia that the Russian Orthodox Church remains in power. How can that be? Because, the Orthodox Church has made an accommodation for the communist government and has agreed to anesthetize the people through its superstitious idolatry. This benefits the government, because it ensures that the people will be obedient and tolerate their oppression. Incidentally, while communist governments portray themselves as atheistic, in fact, they worship and serve a Satanic egregore. For more information on that fact, please read this author's book, *Bloody Zion*.

Initially, after the communists took power in Russia in 1917, the Russian Orthodox Church was brutally suppressed by the communist government. After 10 years, however, the communist government realized that it needed the influence of the Orthodox Church. In 1927, the Soviet government worked out an accord with the Orthodox Church. The Orthodox Church issued a declaration accepting as legitimate the communist authority over the Orthodox Church and pledged to cooperate with the government. The Russian Orthodox Church condemned political dissent. The agreement created a schism within the Orthodox Church, and there remained periods when the Orthodox Church was suppressed by the Russian government. Such conflict and treachery can always be expected when there is a dishonorable agreement.

Even Joseph Stalin turned to the Russian Orthodox Church to help intensify patriotic support for the war effort during World War II. While there is certainly no love lost between the communist government Russia and the Russian Orthodox Church, they have made accommodation for each other. They have found that they need each other. Such is the case with the relationship between all tyrannies and heathen religions.

The Roman Catholic Church wants to gather Russia back into its fold in the worst way. The Catholic Church is leveraging the apparition at Fatima to do that. Jesuit Bishop Pavol Hnilica reveals Pope John Paul's use of Fatima apparition of Mary to bring Russia back into the Roman Catholic fold.

> After his [Pope John Paul II] release from the hospital, I brought him a statue of Our Lady of Fatima which some German pilgrims, who had been in Rome during the assassination attempt, had brought from Fatima. They wanted to give it to the Holy Father as a present. For three months it was in my chapel. It was the most beautiful statue I had ever seen. It was hard for me to part with it when I presented it to the Holy Father. And what did he say to me? "Paul, in these three months I have come to understand that the only solution to all

the problems of the world, the deliverance from war, the deliverance from atheism, and from the defection from God, is the conversion of Russia. The conversion of Russia is the content and meaning of the message of Fatima. Not until then will the triumph of Mary come." The Holy Father had a chapel built on a hill on the eastern frontier of Poland - on the frontier of Russia - and put the statue there. The Mother of God looks toward Russia. But she wants us to look toward Russia as well.[961]

Pope John Paul II wants to draw Russia, which is already a collective government, into the Roman Catholic collective. It is foreseeable that at some future time there will be a healing of the schism between the Orthodox Church and the Roman Catholic Church. There are efforts being made today toward that end. Pope Francis and Patriarch Bartholomew I, who is the primary leader of Eastern Orthodox Christians, have announced that they plan on convening the Roman Catholic Church and the Orthodox Church for a synod at Nicea (modern day Iznik, Turkey) in 2025. The specific purpose of the synod was not announced, however, Patriarch Bartholomew gave an hint of an ecumenical purpose by stating that it was "to celebrate together, after 17 centuries, the first truly ecumenical synod."[962] Clearly, planning a synod 11 years in advance, suggests that the synod will be a conclusion (and not the start) of ecumenical agreements worked out in advance. It would seem that it is expected that the Rome and the Eastern Orthodox Church will mend their differences. No doubt, the Vatican will find a way to maintain the primacy of the papacy, which the Orthodox Church has contested over the centuries.

The Marian apparitions will likely be leveraged to mend the schism between the churches, because the Orthodox Church is just as devoted to the worship of Mary as is the Roman Catholic Church. The common worship of Mary will no doubt be the foundation for agreement. Jim Tetlow, Roger Oakland, and Brad Myers, in their book, *Queen of Rome, Queen of Islam, Queen of All*, explain:

> Marian devotion in the Eastern Church is enormous. For example, Roger Oakland has traveled to Russia over 30 times and has witnessed the widespread and

very visible Marian influence affecting every aspect of the Russian Orthodox Church. In Russia, icons and images of Mary are more prominent, numerous and attended to than any other figure. Dr. Kenneth Lawson has traveled throughout Eastern Europe researching and documenting the widespread devotion to Mary, particularly in the Eastern Orthodox Church. Ken has written a book entitled *The Mary Movement* in which he documents Mary's significant influence around the globe with many references to her exultation in Eastern Orthodoxy. Truly Mary could also be called Queen of the Orthodox Church.[963]

Organized religion is used to keep the people obedient to the oppression of government. It seems that the Marian apparitions are part of the spiritual intoxicant used against the masses to bring about obedience to the prophesied oppressive world government. *See* Revelation 13. Indeed, we read in Revelation how those who refuse to worship the image of the beast will be killed. Revelation 13:15. Throughout history, from the crucifixion of Jesus to the Roman Catholic inquisition, the religious authorities have used the force of government to punish deviation from their heathen orthodoxy. That will be the case once again, this time on a worldwide scale, when the beast comes to power.

The worship of the image further gives us a hint that the image is a religious idol of some kind. We are commanded to "flee from idolatry" 1 Corinthians 10:14. Why is God concerned over idols? Because behind every idol is a devil. 1 Corinthians 10:19-20. The worship of the image to the beast in Revelation is to be compelled. Indeed, "as many as would not worship the image of the beast should be killed." Revelation 13:15.

The use of an image and the worship of that image is rebellion against God. God commands: "Thou shalt not make unto thee any graven image, or any likeness of any thing that is in heaven above, or that is in the earth beneath, or that is in the water under the earth. Thou shalt not bow down thyself to them, nor serve them: for I the Lord thy God am a jealous God." Exodus 20:4-5.

Let us look to the religious images of Babylon, Medo-Persia, Greece, and Rome to see if we can find some commonality that will help us solve the mystery of the image of the beast. God's depiction of the great harlot in Revelation 17 gives us a hint to first look to the goddesses of Babylon, Medo-Persia, Greece, and Rome. Interestingly, we find commonality with the goddesses in those nations. The Babylonian goddesses Beltis or Mylitta was the corollary to the Medo-Persian goddess Anaita, who in turn the corollary to the Greek goddess Artemis, who in turn was the corollary to the Roman goddess Diana. In each of these cultures, the goddesses occupied the throne of the queen of heaven. Tetlow, Oakland, and Myers, reveal that virtually all heathen cultures throughout history had a goddess occupying the throne of the queen of heaven.[964]

Tetlow, Oakland, and Myers explain that the queen of heaven has gone by different names in different cultures, such as: Lilith, Minerva, Isis, Kwan-yin, Demeter, Gaia, Luna, Hectate, Aurora, Shing Moo, Holy Mother, White Buffalo Calf, Shakti, Hera, Innanna, Kali, Juno, Sophia, Ceres, Persephone, Aphrodite, Our Lady, Blessed Mother, etc.

Even Judaism has its corollary to Mary, the queen of heaven. The female goddess in Judaism is known as Shekinah. Shekinah is the Judaic moon goddess, whom the Romans called Diana and the Greeks called Artemis. Shekinah has manifold identities in Judaism. Shekinah is also known in Judaism as Malkuth and Miriam ha Kadosha. Miriam ha Kadosha in the Zohar 1:34a is called 'Moon of Israel.'[965] Shekinah is also equated with Matronita, who is both the Jewish warrior queen of heaven and innocent virgin.[966] As we have seen in a previous chapter, the Judaic mysteries are played out in the celebration of the Catholic Eucharistic celebration, where the Eucharist represents a trinity of goddesses and gods, including the moon goddess and sun god. In fact, the IHS symbol on the Eucharistic Host represents three heathen deities: Isis, Horus, and Seb.

As we have seen in a prior chapter, this queen of heaven is the heathen goddess that angered God when the Jews worshiped her in Jeremiah 7:17-20. The Roman Catholic Church has grafted this heathen goddess into its amalgamated religion, by simply changing the name from Diana, *et aliae,* to Mary. The roots of the goddess are found in

Babylon. Indeed, that is why the great harlot of Revelation is called "Babylon the Great." Revelation 17:5. The Catholic Mary (unlike the biblical Mary) is a heathen goddess, whom Pope Pius XII declared in 1950, to have been assumed body and soul into heaven and crowned **"queen over all things."** Even the formal title of the Catholic Rosary is: **"The Roses of Prayer for the Queen of Heaven."**[967] The Roman Church considers their unbiblical version of Mary to be their queen of heaven.[968]

The second beast in Revelation is seen to "give life unto the image of the beast, that the image of the beast should both speak." Revelation 14:15. If the second beast is the Jesuit General and his minions, we should find the Jesuits involved in the Marian apparitions. That is in fact what we find. Historian J. H. Merle D'Aubugine explained that apparitions were one of the foundational sources from which guidance was sought by the founder of the Jesuits, Ignatius Loyola.

> Visions came erelong to confirm Inigo [a/k/a Ignatius Loyola] in the convictions at which he had arrived. ... Inigo did not seek truth in the Holy Scriptures; but imagined in their place immediate communication with the world of spirits. ... Loyola at his time, bound himself to dreams and visions; and chimerical apparitions became the principle of his life and his faith.[969]

John A. Hardon gives further insight into the Marian apparitions that directed Ignatius Loyola. Hardon was a Jesuit priest and theologian who wrote over 40 books, including *Catholic Catechism: A Contemporary Catechism of the Catholic Church* (1975), which defined Catholic doctrine. Hardon's Catechism went through 26 printings and sold over one million copies. It was the normative standard for Catholic doctrine for almost 20 years, until the 1992 *Catechism of the Catholic Church* was published. Incidently, Hardon was a consultant on the 1992 Catechism. Hardon also wrote the *Modern Catholic Dictionary* (1980), which was a major Catholic reference dictionary. Hardon explains the significance of the thirty (30) recorded Marian apparitions that guided Ignatius Loyola.

It was during this period, while he [Ignatius Loyola] was still bedridden, that our Lady appeared to him. There are thirty recorded Marian apparitions and revelations in the life of Ignatius, so much so that at one point before he actually founded the Society of Jesus, he had thought of calling it, The Society of Mary. But he had no doubt that our Lady was the one who directed him to found the Society of Jesus. After our Lady's first appearance to Ignatius he got surprisingly healed, which confirmed him in his mission.[970]

Ignatius Loyola, however, was aware that some of the apparitions he saw were the devil in disguise. In his autobiography he states how one apparition had always appeared "most beautiful." However, on one occasion, "[t]here was a cross near which he was praying, and he noticed that near the cross the vision had lost some of its former beautiful color. He understood from this that the apparition was the work of the devil."[971] If Loyola could discern that a previously beautiful apparition was actually the devil in disguise, how could he have been so certain that the other apparitions purporting to be the Virgin Mary were not also the devil in disguise? In light of the evil doctrines born of the apparitions that formed the theology of the Jesuits, it is difficult to believe that Loyola did not understand that all of the apparitions were the devil in disguise.

From the beginning, the Jesuits were involved in the worship of Mary. Through their sub-society, *The Sodality of Our Lady*, they have promoted the worship of images and Marian apparitions. *The Sodality of Our Lady* is a Roman Catholic Marian Society, which was founded in 1563 by a Jesuit, Jean Leunis, at the Collegio Romano of the Society of Jesus and approved by the Holy See.[972] Pope Gregory XIII issued a Papal Bull in In 1584 granting *The Sodality of Our Lady* indulgences and establishing it as the mother Sodality.

With Marian apparitions giving intimate guidance to the Jesuit founder, it is not surprising that we find promotion of and involvement in Marian apparitions by other Jesuit priests. Greg Szymanski has discovered the strange personage of Jesuit Bishop Pavol Hnilica, who seemed always to be around to promote Marian apparitions. Szymanski asks: "Why Is Jesuit Bishop Pavol Hnilica Always Lurking In the Background When Mother Mary Appears?"[973] Jesuit Bishop Hnilica has worked tirelessly in spreading the message of Fatima. We find that Jesuit Bishop Hnilica accompanied Archbishop Kondrusiewicz on his visit to Fatima.[974] Furthermore, Jesuit Bishop Hnilica took Fatima documentation to Pope John Paul II during his convalescence in 1981.[975]

Who do we find declaring his acceptance of the Marian apparitions seen in Cairo, Egypt from 1968 to 1970? Not surprisingly, Jesuit priest, Dr. Henry Ayrout, who is the rector of the Catholic College de la Sainte Famille (Jesuit order) in Cairo. Ayrout said that whether Catholic or Orthodox, we are all her children and she loves us all equally and her apparitions at the Zeitoun Coptic Orthodox Church confirmed this notion.[976]

Not coincidently, a Jesuit priest, Luis Maria Andreu, was on hand at Garabandal, Spain, on August 8, 1961, to witness the ecstatic response of the four girls to whom the Marian apparition was manifested. The Jesuit also saw the Marian apparition as well as an unrevealed miracle that the Marian apparition promised to perform in order to confirm that she was the Virgin Mary. The Jesuit priest was present for the purpose of verifying the authenticity of the Marian apparition. He later stated that he believed in the authenticity of the apparition based upon what he saw. Within a day of his pronouncement the 36 year-old priest suddenly died.[977]

On September 1, 1991, an apparition of Mary calling herself "Our Lady of Light." appeared to five women in a field in Indiana. Later, on May 10, 1992, the apparition identified two priests by name that she said would be her "special ambassadors." Not surprisingly one of the two priests was a Jesuit priest, Donald Rinfret (1925-1997).[978]

Jesuit priest Edward J. Carter, S.J. (1929-2000), witnessed the Marian apparition of Our Lady on May 31, 1996, in an Ohio field. He continued be see her apparition and receive messages from it monthly until September 13, 1997. As an original member of the Board of Trustees of Our Lady of the Holy Spirit Center, he was dedicated to promoting the worship of Mary and the authenticity of Marian apparitions.[979]

This phenomenon of Jesuit involvement in Marian apparitions has been going on since the founding of the Jesuits. Marian apparitions was a devilish tool used to convert superstitious native populations to join the Roman Catholic Church. For example, Pierre-Jean DeSmet, one of three Jesuit priests who had founded St. Mary's Mission in Montana was on hand on Christmas eve in 1841 to counsel a young Indian boy who saw a bright apparition of Mary. That apparition was very helpful to the Jesuits in converting the local Indians to Roman Catholicism. The next day, Christmas, the boy and 150 Flathead Indians were baptized into the Catholic Church.[980] The apparitions give credibility and staying power to any Catholic Church or mission. Colleen Meyer, director of the historic St. Mary's Mission stated that "the reason St. Mary's Mission still stands today is because of miracles such as the apparition of the Blessed Mary."[981]

In keeping with its traditions, the Roman Catholic Church creates graven images of Mary, queen of heaven. The images of the Catholic queen of heaven are so common, few in the world have not seen them. Indeed, the Vatican gives primacy to Mary over Jesus. For example, Pope John Paul II stated in his book *Crossing The Threshold of Hope*: "After my election as Pope, as I became more involved in the problems of the universal Church, I came to have a similar conviction: On this universal level, if victory comes it will be brought by Mary. Christ will conquer through her, because he wants the Church's victories now and in the future to be linked to her."[982]

Pope John Paul II makes clear the primacy of Mary in the Catholic theology in the following prayer to Mary, he published: "To you [Mary] I give back all the fruits of my life and my ministry. To you I entrust the future of the Church; to you I offer my nation; in you do I trust and once more declare: *Totus Tuus*, Maria!"[983] Mary's absolute reign as queen of heaven under the Catholic theology is evidenced by Pope John Paul II's statement, "Totus Tuus, Maria," which means "Totally Yours Mary." The Catholic Church is not partially entrusted to Mary, it is totally entrusted to Mary, to the exclusion of all else, including Jesus. Notice that Pope John Paul II refers to the Catholic Church as "my nation." That is because the Vatican is a sovereign nation and all Roman Catholics are citizens of that nation.

Pope Paul II's successor, Pope Benedict XVI, continued the

theme of papal goddess worship. Shortly after being elevated to pope, on April 20, 2005, he stated during a Eucharistic celebration before the members of the College of Cardinals in the Sistine Chapel:

> To support me in my promise, I call on the motherly intercession of Mary Most Holy, in whose hands I place the present and future of the Church and of myself.[984]

Two days later, Pope Benedict XVI again reenforced the importance of Mary in an address before the College of Cardinals:

> I entrust all of us and the expectations, hopes and worries of the entire community of Christians to the Virgin Mother of God, who accompanied the steps of the newborn Church with her silent presence and comforted the faith of the Apostles. I ask you to walk under the motherly protection of Mary.[985]

Pope Benedict XVI continued the message of Mary worship in an address given on April 25, 2005:

> And let us pray to Mary, Mother of the Lord, so that she will enable us to feel her love as a woman and a mother, in which we can understand all of the depth of Christ's mystery.[986]

God, however, tells us to trust in him. "Trust in the LORD with all thine heart; and lean not unto thine own understanding. In all thy ways acknowledge Him, and He shall direct thy paths" (Proverbs 3:5-6).

The second beast is depicted in Revelation 13:15 as giving life to the image of the first beast. Has it been done? If so, when and how? It has been done, and it will continue to be done. It is being done by the devil through the apparitions of Mary, the queen of heaven.

During the apparitions, Mary appears as a living, breathing, three-dimensional woman enveloped in exquisite light.[987] Those viewing her apparition describe a beautiful, young woman glowing in radiant splendor as the queen of heaven. Accompanying the visions are often strange lights and glorious visions. On many occasions thousands of people have witnessed the apparitions and testified to seeing visions of angels, glowing orbs, tongues of fire, mysterious solar phenomena, and peculiar luminous clouds. Numerous miracles and physical healings have been reported at apparition sites around the globe.

During the apparitions the beautiful Mary speaks to people with decidedly unbiblical messages. The significant thing about the images is that they all resemble the standard Roman Catholic graven images that can be seen in virtually every Catholic Church throughout the world. These apparitions are truly a fulfillment of the prophecy of Revelation 13:15 that the second beast will "give life unto the image of the beast."

Let us catalogue some of the apparitions. In 1531, Mary appeared in an apparition to Juan Diego. That apparition is known today as Our Lady of Guadalupe. The site of the appearance of Mary at Guadalupe is visited by 15 to 20 million people each year. On December 12, 1999, which was the anniversary of the Virgin Mary's appearance, five million pilgrims visited the shrine to pay honor to the goddess known as "Our Lady."[988] Our Lady of Guadalupe is celebrated by all Catholic priests and bishops in the western hemisphere. Notably, Pope John Paul II elevated the anniversary of Our Lady of Guadalupe (December 12th) to a Roman Catholic "holy day."

In Bosnia, an estimated 30 million pilgrims have visited Medjugorje, since apparitions of the Blessed Virgin Mary began to appear there in 1981.[989] Many thousands of visitors have received message from the apparitions and have also seen other signs and wonders.

In Conyers, Georgia, Nancy Fowler saw a vison of the Virgin Mary.[990] She has since received up to 100,000 visitors to her farm on a single day. At the National Shrine Grotto of Our Lady of Lourdes, in Emmitsburg, Maryland, attendance has increased to 500,000 per year.[991] Keep in mind that the site in Maryland is to honor a series of Marian apparitions that took place in 1858 across the ocean in France. The city of Lourdes, France, hosts over five million pilgrims each year.

Millions, including four popes, have visited the Marian

apparition site in Knock, Ireland, known, accordingly, as "Our Lady of Knock."[992] In 1953, in Sabana Grande, Puerto Rico, the Virgin Mary reportedly appeared more than 30 times to several children. The site has become so popular to visitors that preparations are underway to build a statue of the Virgin Mary that will be twice as high as the Statue of Liberty in New York and will house a radio and TV station, a chapel, apartments, conference rooms, and even a food court.[993]

On May 13, 1917, At Fatima, Portugal, an apparition of the Virgin Mary appeared to three children, which they described as a "lady brighter than the sun." On the 13th of the month for five months thereafter the apparitions continued, until on October 13th 70,000 people assembled at the site in a rainstorm. Reportedly, the sun came out grew blindingly bright, danced around the sky and plunged to the earth. When the crowd came to its senses and it was over, the sun was shining in the sky and the rain had dried up.[994] Many who had been wet and muddy found their clothes dry and clean. Others who had been sick and crippled were reportedly healed.[995]

The fantastic sun dance has occurred at other Marian apparition sites. On April 23, 1991, the sun danced before a crowd of 100,000 in Puerto Rico. That was the 38th anniversary of the Marian apparitions there. It also happened on March 5, 1993, in the Philippines before a crowd of 300,000. In the 1980's, the miracle of the sun dance happened in El Cajas, Ecuador, in front of a crowd of 120,000. The sun dance has also happened at Marian apparition sites in Medjugorje, Bosnia; Denver, Colorado; Lubbock, Texas; and Conyers, Georgia.[996]

The total annual attendance of people on pilgrimages at Fatima each year is 4.5 million. In 1967, the 50th anniversary of the apparition, 1.5 million people gathered at Fatima. Rick Steves reports that "Pope John Paul II kicked off the construction of Fatima's grand new Church of the Holy Trinity with a stone from St. Peter's actual tomb in the Vatican. Completed in 2007, the huge new church can hold 9,000 devotees."[997]

The Marian apparition at Fatima is so important to the Catholic Church that Pope Francis has entrusted the Catholic Church, and indeed the world, to Mary as depicted in the apparition at Fatima. Francis X. Rocca reported that "[b]efore a congregation of more than 100,000 in

St. Peter's Square, Pope Francis formally entrusted the world to Mary. 'We are confident that each of us is precious in your sight,' the pope said Oct. 13, [2013] facing the statue of Mary that normally stands in the shrine at Fatima, Portugal. 'Guard our lives in your arms, bless and strengthen every desire for goodness.'"[998] October 13th was the anniversary of the last apparition of Mary to three shepherd children at Fatima in 1917. All three children have since been beatified as Catholic "saints" by the Roman Catholic Church. The adjacent picture shows Pope Francis engaging in idolatry as he pays homage to the graven image of "Our Lady of Fatima." Notice that the graven image is wearing a crown, emblematic of her status as "queen of heaven." Rocca reported that Pope Francis took the occasion to leverage the Marian apparitions at other sites throughout the world. "Later that night, Pope Francis sent a video message to faithful gathered at 10 Marian shrines around the world, stressing Mary's role as a bridge to her son."[999]

Pope Francis on October 13, 2013, paying homage to a graven image of Our Lady of Fatima, who is wearing the crown of the queen of heaven.

Tetlow, Oakland, and Myers reveal that "Marian apparitions from almost every state in America are being reported – many of these sites are drawing thousands. From New York City to San Francisco numerous reported visitations from the Queen of Heaven have been documented."[1000] In addition, Marian apparitions are accelerating in frequency. In 1967, *Newsweek* magazine reported that it documented over 400 apparitions of Mary throughout the world in the 20th century.[1001] That is greater than the number of Marian apparitions over the previous three centuries combined. The apparitions are not limited to only predominately Catholic countries. They are happening around the world, from Japan to Africa, from Korea to Australia, from Iraq to Israel, from Egypt to Syria.[1002]

It seems that the message from the apparitions is ecumenical and is particularly approving of the Roman Catholic theology. For example, the apparition of Mary at Medjugorje stated: "Tell this priest, tell everyone, that it is you who are divided on earth. The Muslims and the Orthodox, for the same reason as Catholics, are equal before my Son and I. You are all my children."[1003] Note that the message is to be given to Catholic priest and the message is that Muslims, Catholics, and Orthodox are all her children.

That is not the gospel. Jesus made it clear that only his elect are his children, and his elect are those that believe in him. God has elected certain to be saved by his grace through faith in Jesus Christ. Ephesians 1:3-9; 2:8-10. He imbues his elect with the faith needed to believe in Jesus. Romans 3:21-26; John 1:12-13. Catholics, Orthodox, or Muslims, if they remain as such, believe in a different Jesus than he who is in the bible. For example, one of the doctrines of Islam is that Allah had no son. The Quran at Sura 23:91 states in reference to Jesus that **"no son did Allah beget,"** and again at Sura 17:111: "All the praises and thanks be to **Allah, Who has not begotten a son.**" The bible states clearly that "[w]hosoever denieth the Son, the same hath not the Father: but he that acknowledgeth the Son hath the Father also." 1 John 2:23. Certainly, Jesus could save any person from that blasphemous religion, but once saved, they would come out of Islam, just as Jesus has commanded. Islam is one of the harlot children of the great harlot of Revelation. Jesus commands: "Come out of her, my people, that ye be not partakers of her sins, and that ye receive not of her plagues." Revelation 18:4. The point, however, is that by referring to Catholics, Muslim, and Orthodox adherents as her children, proves that the apparition is an unbiblical heathen goddess. Who is the goddess of the Marian apparitions? It is Satan. "And no marvel; for Satan himself is transformed into an angel of light." 2 Corinthians 11:14.

The spiritual seduction is so compelling that the apparitions have drawn in nominal Protestants. In Mexico, for example, some Protestant churches have incorporated the recognition of Our Lady of Guadalupe. According to Roman Catholic priest Francisco Schulte, a scholar at St. John's University in Collegeville, Minnesota, "Any church wanting to attract Latinos that doesn't take into account how deeply that message [of Our Lady of Guadalupe] is rooted in the Latino identity ... is pretty well doomed."[1004]

William Lobdell and Jennifer Mena, who are reporters for the *Los Angeles Times,* made an insightful observation in a 2003 article. "Our Lady of Guadalupe's appearance in non-Catholic services has scholars and others wondering whether the beloved apparition that has united Mexicans for nearly five centuries can bring together Christian denominations."[1005] Indeed, that is the whole purpose behind the apparitions. Satan wants to bring all denominations under the Catholic banner. That is why the message of all Marian apparitions is stridently ecumenical.

The infiltration of the heathen practice of Marian worship into nominal Protestant churches is not a fringe Latino phenomenon. R. Albert Mohler, Jr., President of the Southern Baptist Theological seminary reveals the following startling facts:

> The *Time* cover story is part of a larger phenomenon, with many mainline Protestants turning to a reconsideration of Mary and incorporating the veneration of Mary into personal devotions and corporate worship. Some are going so far as to acknowledge Mary as an intercessor, addressing prayers to her as well as to other saints. Surprisingly enough, some Protestants now argue that believers should pray to Mary, and should request her intercession.[1006]

The Marian Apparitions are convincing signs that even motivate Muslims to worship the goddess Mary. Muslims regularly make pilgrimages to Marian shrines. The shrine of Our Lady of Fatima in Portugal is one of those sites. Fatima is significant in Islam, as it was the name of Muhammad's favorite daughter, who Muhammad reportedly placed at the highest place in heaven after the Virgin Mary. Mary is highly esteemed in the Quran and Ahadith. Tetlow, Oakland, and Myers reveal that "in recent years apparitions of Mary have been reported in several Muslim nations including Iraq, Syria, Egypt, Turkey, and others.

Veneration has increased as more and more claim that they have experienced a miracle at a Marian shrine."[1007]

The apparitions seem to be part of Satan's plan to unite all religions under one banner to worship the image of the beast, the queen of heaven. Tetlow, Oakland, and Myers state that the phenomenal effect of the Marian apparitions affects adherents of all heathen religions

> Fatima may be the most famous Marian shrine where Muslims go to pray and pay homage to the Queen of Heaven, yet Fatima is hardly unique. In 2004, Reuters News Service wrote, in an article entitled "Twist of globalization: All faiths come together", that Hindus, Buddhists, Muslims and other pilgrims regularly worship at famous Roman Catholic shrines to the Virgin Mary. They drink holy water, light votive candles, and pray fervently to the Madonna. The article explains that many pilgrims venerate her like one of their own goddesses.[1008]

Millions find the Marian apparitions a compelling basis for the worship of Mary. *Life* magazine featured Mary on its cover in 1996. The magazine article, authored by Robert Sullivan, reveals the occurrences of 50 weeping Madonna statues within the prior two years and asked the questions: "Why are two billion Hail Marys said daily? Why did five million people, many non-Christian, visit Lourdes this year to drink the healing waters? Why did more than ten million trek to Guadalupe to pray to Our Lady? ... Why the apparitions? Why are Mary hymns creeping into Methodist songbooks? ... What is it about Mary?"[1009] Why indeed! Clearly, there is a very powerful spiritual influence behind the Marian apparitions. The issue is whether that influence is the Holy Spirit or the spirit of Beelzebub.

Tetlow, Oakland, and Myers explain just how effective the Marian apparitions are in cutting through religious boundaries in drawing all religions to the worship of Mary:

> One of the most widely witnessed series of apparitions occurred at a Coptic Orthodox church in Zeitoun, Egypt, a suburb of Cairo. People from many countries

and of varied religious backgrounds witnessed the apparitions from 1968 to1973. It is estimated that the total number of witnesses numbered in the millions! Muslims, Copts, Roman Catholics, Protestants, and others were united in their adoration of the Lady who seemed to be composed of light. Muslims chanted from the Koran: "Mary, God has chosen thee. And purified thee; He has chosen thee above all women." At Zeitoun, as well as countless other sites around the globe, the phenomenon draws together people from every conceivable background.[1010]

People seem to assume nowadays that all unexplainable wonders must be the work of God. In fact, Satan and his devils are capable of performing great wonders. In Exodus, we read how the Egyptian sorcerers were able to match the miracle of Aaron when Aaron cast his staff to the ground and it became a serpent.

> And Moses and Aaron went in unto Pharaoh, and they did so as the Lord had commanded: and Aaron cast down his rod before Pharaoh, and before his servants, and it became a serpent. Then Pharaoh also called the wise men and the sorcerers: now the magicians of Egypt, they also did in like manner with their enchantments. For they cast down every man his rod, and they became serpents: but Aaron's rod swallowed up their rods. Exodus 7:10-12.

It is Christians who are the fly-in-the-ointment for the Devil, because Christians know how to discern the works of the devil from the works of God. Christians are under a command to expose the works of darkness. "And have no fellowship with the unfruitful works of darkness, but rather reprove them." Ephesians 5:11.

That is why the second beast must compel the world to worship the image of the first beast. "And he had power to give life unto the image of the beast, that the image of the beast should both speak, and cause that as many as would not worship the image of the beast should be killed." Revelation 13:15. Without the threat of compulsion many would refuse to worship the image of the beast. Certainly, a born-again believer in Jesus Christ would refuse unto death.

Who do we find encouraging the worship of the images brought to life in the apparitions? None other than the pope of Rome. On May 11, 2005, Pope Benedict XVI exhorted all to "turn incessantly and with confidence" to the Virgin of Fatima. He stated: "Day after tomorrow, the liturgical memorial will be celebrated of the Blessed Virgin Mary of Fatima. Beloved, I exhort you to turn incessantly and with confidence to the Virgin, entrusting to her each one of your needs."[1011]

Pope Benedict XVI on May 13th 2005, only one month into his pontificate, placed the Roman Catholic Church into the maternal hands of Our Lady of Guadalupe. He did this before a white marble graven image of Our Lady of Guadalupe, which is located at the highest point of the Vatican Gardens. The following is a prayer by Pope Benedict XVI that he recited on that occasion:

> Holy Mary, who under the advocacy of Our Lady of Guadalupe, are invoked as mother of the men and women of the Mexican nation and of Latin America, encouraged by the love you inspire in us, we again place our lives in your maternal hands. You who are present in the Vatican Gardens, reign in the hearts of all mothers of the world and in our hearts. With great hope, we come to you and trust in you.[1012]

Our Lady of Guadalupe appeared in 1531 to seer Juan Diego, and remains one of the most popular Marian apparitions in the world.

Make no mistake about it, the pope is clearly putting the primary emphasis on the worship of Mary. He is elevating her as a goddess to the status of "queen of heaven." That is the very same "queen of heaven" which God condemned in Jeremiah 7:18.

> The children gather wood, and the fathers kindle the fire, and the women knead their dough, to make cakes to the **queen of heaven**, and to pour out drink offerings unto other gods, that they may **provoke me to anger**. (Jeremiah 7:18)

The pope brazenly ignores the warning of God and promotes the worship of the "queen of heaven." On August 25th 2005, during the Feast of the Assumption of Mary, Pope Benedict explained that the Catholic Mary is the "queen of heaven" and listed her powers as a goddess. He explained that she was assumed into heaven, in glory, body and soul, participates in the power of the Lord Jesus Christ, is always close, listens to us, hears our prayers, and knows our very hearts.

> Mary is taken up body and soul into the glory of heaven, and with God and in God she is **Queen of heaven and earth**... While she lived on this earth she could only be close to a few people... Being in God and with God, she is close to each one of us, knows our hearts, can hear our prayers, can help us with her motherly kindness... She always listens to us, and is always close to us, and being Mother of the Son, participates in the power of the Son and in his goodness. We can always entrust the whole of our lives to this Mother, who is not far from any one of us.

What does the pope mean that Mary "participates in the power of the Son?" The pope is clearly alluding to the Catholic theological position that Mary, as queen of heaven, is a goddess with the omnipotent power of God Almighty. You will never hear the pope ever utter the word "goddess" when referring to Mary. Indeed, Roman Catholic clerics will howl with indignation at the characterization of the Catholic Mary as a goddess. However, the theological pronouncements by the pope about Mary make clear that Mary is in fact the mother goddess of the Catholic Church, with primacy above that of Jesus Christ.

The Marian apparitions play a central role in promoting the Catholic goddess worship. Tetlow, Oakland, and Myers explain:

> In October 2000, John Paul ordered the miraculous statue of Our Lady of Fatima to the Vatican for the Great Jubilee. On Sunday October 8, Pope John Paul with 1,500 bishops – the largest group to assemble since Vatican II – entrusted humanity and the third millennium to Our Lady of Fatima. This is extremely

significant. Over one-third of the Catholic Church's bishops, and the pope himself, entrusted the world to the apparition known as Our Lady of Fatima![1013]

Indeed, the Marian apparitions seem to be working closely with the Roman Catholic Church in confirming its theology of goddess worship. For example, when concern was raised from all quarters over Pope Pius IX's 1854 brazen proclamation that Mary was immaculately conceived, just four years later, in 1858, a Marian apparition came to the rescue and announced to the world that she was "the immaculate conception."[1014] This supernatural confirmation of Pope Pius IX's announcement sealed the doctrine of the immaculate conception of Mary among Catholics.

Tetlow, Oakland, and Myers conclude that the Marian apparitions seem to be synchronized with the announcement of Catholic doctrine and act to guide and confirm those doctrines.

> Pius IX, Pius X, and Pius XII are among the long list of popes who relate the importance of the Queen of Heaven's apparitional manifestations, and how these supernatural appearances have helped guide the Roman Catholic Church through the centuries. ... Down through the centuries, Marian apparitions have guided popes, prelates, and Catholic saints. Apparitions have been vital in forming Church dogma. And apparitions have garnered the support of tens of millions of lay Catholics worldwide.[1015]

Proof that the Marian apparitions are Satanic is found in the fact that the Marian apparitions encourage and even demand those in its presence to worshiped it. In many instances, the seers are literally forced to their knees by a power emanating from the apparition.[1016] In addition, Tetlow, Oakland, and Myers explain that "the apparition of Mary at Lourdes, France; Guadalupe, Mexico; Beauraing, Belgium; Fatima, Portugal and many other sites, request[ed] that shrines or temples be built in her honor where the faithful may come and venerate her. It should be noted that the apparitions at the four sites mentioned above have received full approval by the Roman Catholic Church. The message is clear at all of the major apparition sites: The apparition of

Mary is worthy of worship, honor, and praise."[1017]

The Holy Bible, however, states that we are to only worship God. "Thou shalt worship the Lord thy God, and Him only shalt thou serve." (Matthew 4:10). When the apostle John fell to his feet to worship an angel the angel admonished him to only worship God.

> And I John saw these things, and heard them. And when I had heard and seen, I fell down to worship before the feet of the angel which shewed me these things. See thou do it not: for I am thy fellowservant, and of thy brethren the prophets, and of them which keep the sayings of this book: worship God." (Revelation 22:8-9)

When Satan appeared to Jesus and tempted him to worship him, Jesus rebuked Satan and told him to worship only God.

> Again, the devil taketh him up into an exceeding high mountain, and sheweth him all the kingdoms of the world, and the glory of them; And saith unto him, All these things will I give thee, if thou wilt fall down and worship me. Then saith Jesus unto him, Get thee hence, Satan: for it is written, **Thou shalt worship the Lord thy God, and him only shalt thou serve.** (Matthew 4:8-10)

Furthermore, the Marian apparitions advise the seers to whom it reveals itself to commit the sin of idolatry.

> As Mother I want to tell you that I am here with you, represented by the statue you have here. Each of my statues is a sign of a presence of mine and reminds you of your heavenly Mother. Therefore it must be honored and put in places of greater veneration ... you should look with love at every image of your heavenly Mother."[1018]

Tetlow, Oakland, and Myers explain the theological error of the idolatry that is advised by the demonic apparitions:

The apparition encourages her followers to make and honor graven images of her. Not once in the Bible do we find an obedient follower of the Lord making a graven image to venerate or bow or pray to. Not once. At many apparition sites, statues of Mary are carried and venerated in public processions. Marian followers even crawl to the statue of Mary on their knees (often bloody knees) – a show of reverence and worship toward the Queen of Heaven. Yet not one apparition that we have researched has ever discouraged this anti-biblical behavior. It should not come as a surprise that this idolatry is exactly what God warns against in the last days. We are told in the Book of Revelation, when God is pouring out His judgments on unrepentant mankind, that many continue to worship idols, and by extension, the demons which lurk behind them: "And the rest of the men which were not killed by these plagues yet repented not of the works of their hands, that they should not worship devils, and idols of gold, and silver, and brass, and stone, and of wood: which neither can see, nor hear, nor walk." (Revelation 9:20).[1019]

Indeed, the bible is clear that we should avoid the sin of idolatry. "Little children, keep yourselves from idols. Amen." (1 John 5:21) The Marian apparitions' advice to commit idolatry alone should be evidence enough that the apparitions are evil spirits.

Moreover, the messages from the Marian apparitions contain clearly unbiblical messages. The following is a message from a Marian apparition:

> I boldly assert that His suffering became my suffering, because His heart was mine. And just as Adam and Eve sold the world for an apple, so in a certain sense my Son and **I redeemed the world** with one heart. (bold emphasis added)[1020]

The Marian apparition states that she is the redeemer of the world. The Roman Catholic Church has stated that apparitional message comports with the official Catholic doctrine. The Holy Bible, however, states that God alone is the redeemer.

> As for our redeemer, the LORD of hosts is his name, the Holy One of Israel. (Isaiah 47:4)

> For Christ also hath once suffered for sins, the just for the unjust, that he might bring us to God, being put to death in the flesh, but quickened by the Spirit. (1 Peter 3:18)

The following is another apparitional statement of Mary, which incidently has been officially approved as Catholic doctrine by the Catholic Church:

> It is for this, that, as Mother, as Immaculate Mother, **Mediatrix of all Graces,** that I call you to this place...so that my union with you may be more intimate and vital, through the Holy Spirit, permitting you to live deeply in the spirit of the Gospel. (bold emphasis added)[1021]

The Marian apparition states that she is the "Mediatrix of all Graces." The Holy Bible, however, clearly states that Jesus is the "one" mediator between God and men, there is no other. "For there is one God, and **one mediator** between God and men, the **man Christ Jesus**." (1 Timothy 2:5)

Another Marian apparition adds to the blasphemy by claiming to be an advocate for us to God the Father:

> The world is degenerating, so much so, that it was necessary for the Father and the Son to send Me into the world, among all the peoples, in order to be their Advocate and to save them.[1022]

Mary cannot be an advocate before the Father to save men, as the demonic apparition claims, because only Jesus is our advocate before the Father. It is only Jesus that provided the propitiation that saves us from our sins.

> My little children, these things write I unto you, that ye sin not. And if any man sin, we have an advocate with the Father, Jesus Christ the righteous: And he is the propitiation for our sins: and not for ours only, but also for the sins of the whole world. (1 John 2:1-2)

> For God sent not his Son into the world to condemn the world; but that the world through him might be saved. (John 3:17)

The deception continues with the following unbiblical usurpation by a Marian apparition:

> Until I am acknowledged there where the Most Holy Trinity has willed me to be, I will not be able to exercise my power fully, in the maternal work of coredemption and of the universal mediation of graces. ... Sons, let yourselves be transformed by my powerful action as Mother, Mediatrix of Graces and Coredemptrix.[1023]

There is no coredemptrix as claimed by the demonic apparition. Jesus Christ is our only God and redeemer.

> And they sung a new song, saying, Thou art worthy to take the book, and to open the seals thereof: for thou wast slain, and hast redeemed us to God by thy blood out of every kindred, and tongue, and people, and nation. (Revelation 5:9)

> Thus saith the LORD the King of Israel, and his redeemer the LORD of hosts; I am the first, and I am the last; and beside me there is no God. (Isaiah 44:6)

It is notable that all of the apparitions of Mary take the same basic form and accord with the ubiquitous image of the Catholic Virgin Mary. That is a strong indication that the Marian apparitions are a fulfillment of the prophecy in Revelation 13:15 that the second beast will give life to the image of the first beast: "And he had power to give life unto the image of the beast, that the image of the beast should both speak, and cause that as many as would not worship the image of the beast should be killed." (Revelation 13:15) Furthermore, the allegiance to the beast will be accompanied by the mark of the beast.

> And he causeth all, both small and great, rich and poor, free and bond, to receive a mark in their right hand, or in their foreheads: And that no man might buy or sell, save he that had the mark, or the name of the beast, or the number of his name. Here is wisdom. Let him that hath understanding count the number of the beast: for it is the number of a man; and his number is Six hundred threescore and six. (Revelation 13:16-18)

The popular acceptance of the devilish doctrines of the Marian apparitions and the worship of their graven images is evidence that we are in the "latter times." "Now the Spirit speaketh expressly, that in the latter times some shall depart from the faith, giving heed to seducing spirits, and doctrines of devils." (1 Timothy 4:1)

41 The Great Harlot Seduces Protestant Churches

The Jesuits have used their secret agents in the Protestant churches to undermine the true gospel of Jesus Christ. One example, is Jacobus Arminius (1560-1609). His purpose was to undermine the preaching of the gospel of salvation by faith alone through grace alone in the Protestant churches. His mission was to replace the medicine of the sovereign grace of God with the poison of the sovereign free will of man. Under what became known as Arminianism, man has a free will to believe in Jesus unto salvation; therefore, man can decide at any time to reject the gospel and fall from grace to damnation. Arminianism was not a new and novel doctrine. It was simply repackaged doctrine historically known as Semi-Pelagianism. Semi-Pelagianism was promoted by a Jesuit priest named Luis de Molina. This doctrine became popularly known as Molinism.[1024]

The Roman Catholic church knew that Protestant Christians would never adopt Molinism if it were known to have sprung from a Jesuit priest, so they used Jacobus Arminius, an admirer of Molina, as a front man to introduce the free will anti-gospel into the Protestant churches.

The Catholic Church codified their semi-Pelagian anti-gospel at the Council of Trent (circa 1547), with accompanying curses against anyone who adheres to the bible doctrine of the sovereign grace of God.

> If anyone saith that, since Adam's sin, the free will of man is lost and extinguished; or that it is a thing with only a name, yea, a name without reality, a figment, in fine, introduced into the Church by Satan; let him be anathema. COUNCIL OF TRENT, SESSION VI, DECREE ON JUSTIFICATION, Canon V, January 13, 1547.

> If anyone saith that man's free will, moved and excited by God, by assenting to God exciting and calling, no wise cooperates towards disposing and preparing itself for obtaining the grace of justification; that it cannot refuse its consent, if it would, but that, as something inanimate, it does nothing whatever and is merely passive; let him be anathema. COUNCIL OF TRENT, SESSION IV, DECREE ON JUSTIFICATION, Canon IV, January 13, 1547.

> If anyone saith that by faith alone the impious is justified; in such wise as to mean that nothing else is required to cooperate in order to the obtaining the grace of justification, and that is not in any way necessary that he be prepared and disposed by the movement of his own will; let him be anathema. COUNCIL OF TRENT, SESSION VI, DECREE ON JUSTIFICATION, Canon IX, January 13, 1547.

Augustus Toplady, the author of the famous hymn *Rock of Ages*, documented that Jacobus Arminius was a secret agent of the Jesuits. Arminius' purpose was to infect the Christian church with the heathen Catholic doctrine of free will. Toplady wrote:

> The Jesuits were moulded into a regular body, towards the middle of the sixteenth century: toward the close of the same century, Arminius began to infest the Protestant churches. It needs therefore no great penetration, to discern from what source he drew his

poison. His journey to Rome (though Monsicur Bayle affects to make light of the inferences which were at that very time deduced from it) was not for nothing. If, however, any are disposed to believe, that Arminius imbibed his doctrines from the Socinians in Poland, with whom, it is certain, he was on terms of intimate friendship, I have no objection to splitting the difference: he might import some of his tenets from the Racovian brethren, and yet be indebted, for others, to the disciples of Loyola.[1025]

Toplady's conclusion was not just based upon circumstantial inference. The Jesuits themselves have revealed that Arminius was their secret agent sent to poison the doctrine of the Protestant churches. William Laud, the Archbishop of Canterbury, was working secretly with the Jesuits to infect the Church of England (Anglican Church) with Roman Catholic doctrine, including Arminianism. In 1638 Laud ordered the exclusive use of a "papistical" liturgy upon the Church of Scotland. It became known as "Laud's Liturgy." Laud was eventually found out, and in 1645 he was beheaded for treason against England. Toplady explains one of the papers found among Laud's effects after his death:

When archbishop Laud's papers were examined, a letter was found among them, thus endorsed with that prelate's own hand: "March, 1628. A Jesuit's Letter, sent to the Rector at Bruxels, about the ensuing Parliament." The design of this letter was to give the Superior of the Jesuits, then resident at Brussels, an account of the posture of civil and ecclesiastical affairs in England; an extract from it I shall here subjoin: "Father Rector, let not the damp of astonishment seize upon your ardent and zealous soul, in apprehending the sodaine and unexpected calling of a Parliament. We have now many strings to our bow. We have planted that soveraigne drugge Arminianisme, which we hope will purge the Protestants from their heresie; and it flourisheth and beares fruit in due season. For the better prevention of the Puritanes, the Arminians have already locked up the Duke's (of Buckingham) eares;

487

and we have those of our owne religion, which stand continually at the Duke's chamber, to see who goes in and out: we cannot be too circumspect and carefull in this regard. I am, at this time, transported with joy, to see how happily all instruments and means, as well great as lesser, co-operate unto our purposes. But, to return unto the maine fabricke:--OUR FOUNDATION IS ARMINIANISME. The Arminians and projectors, as it appears in the premises, affect mutation. This we second and enforce by probable arguments."[1026]

That letter found among Laud's belongings is proof, from a high Jesuit agent reporting to his superior at Brussels, that the very foundation of the effort to bring Protestant England back into the Catholic fold was to infect the Church of England with Catholic doctrine, and that the contagion of that infection was Arminianism. The writer proudly proclaimed virtual victory over Protestant England through the spiritual germ of Arminianism. **"We have planted that soveraigne drugge Arminianisme, which we hope will purge the Protestants from their heresie; and it flourisheth and beares fruit in due season."**[1027]

Arminianism springs from Rome and it draws all who adhere to it back to Rome. Toplady explains the significance of the documents found among Laud's belongings and the effect that the Catholic Arminian attack had on the Church of England:

> The "Sovereign drug, Arminianism," which said the Jesuit, "we (i.e. we Papists) have planted" in England, did indeed bid fair "to purge our Protestant Church effectually. How merrily Popery and Arminianism, at that time, danced hand in hand, may be learned from Tindal: "The churches were adorned with paintings, images, altar-pieces, & etc. and, instead of communion tables, altars were set up, and bowings to them and the sacramental elements enjoined. The predestinarian doctrines were forbid, not only to be preached, but to be printed; and the Arminian sense of the Articles was encouraged and propagated." The Jesuit, therefore, did not exult without cause. The "sovereign drug," so lately

> "planted," did indeed take deep root downward, and bring forth fruit upward, under the cherishing auspices of Charles and Laud. Heylyn, too, acknowledges that the state of things was truly described by another Jesuit of that age, who wrote: "Protestantism waxeth weary of itself. The doctrine (by the Arminians, who then sat at the helm) is altered in many things, for which their progenitors forsook the Church of Rome: as limbus patrum; prayer for the dead, and possibility of keeping God's commandments; and the accounting of Calvinism to be heresy at least, if not treason."[1028]

August Toplady reveals how Arminius himself acknowledged that his free will Semi-Pelagianism was completely in line with the Roman Catholic doctrine, and the Catholic Church considered predestination by the sovereign will of God as the arch-heresy against those Catholic doctrines. It is interesting that Arminius explains how the liberal branch of the Lutheran Church and the Anabaptists in his day were infected with the Semi-Pelagian heresy that undermined the grace of God; they were of one mind with Rome in their opposition against the gospel of God's grace. The Arminian free will tradition is still endemic in most Lutheran and Baptist churches today.

> Certain it is, that Arminius himself was sensible, how greatly the doctrine of predestination widens the distance between Protestantism and Popery. "There is no point of doctrines (says he) which the Papists, the Anabaptists, and the (new) Lutherans more fiercely oppose, nor by means of which they heap more discredit on the reformed churches, and bring the reformed system itself into more odium; for they (i.e. the Papists, & etc.) assert, that no fouler blasphemy against God can be thought or expressed, than is contained in the doctrine of predestination."[1029] For which reason, he advises the reformed world to discard predestination from their creed, in order that they may live on more brotherly terms with the Papists, the Anabaptists, and such like.[1030]

Arminianism is an anti-gospel. The anti-gospel is based on a myth that all men have a will that is free from the bondage of sin to choose whether to believe in Jesus. The Holy Bible, however, states that all men are spiritually dead and cannot believe in Jesus unless they are born again of the Holy Spirit. Ephesians 2:1-7; John 3:3-8. God has chosen his elect to be saved by his grace through faith in Jesus Christ. Ephesians 1:3-9; 2:8-10. God imbues his elect with the faith needed to believe in Jesus. Hebrews 12:2; John 1:12-13. The devil's false gospel contradicts the word of God and reverses the order of things. Under the anti-gospel, instead of a sovereign God choosing his elect, sovereign man decides whether to choose God. The calling of the Lord Jesus Christ is effectual; all who are chosen for salvation will believe in Jesus. John 6:37-44. The Arminian anti-gospel has a false Jesus, who only offers the possibility of salvation, with no assurance. The anti-gospel blasphemously makes God out to be a liar by denying the total depravity of man and the sovereign election of God. All who preach that false gospel are under a curse from God. Galatians 1:6-9. The error of Arminianism is discussed in detail in this author's book, *The Anti-Gospel*.

Ernest Reisinger explains that the theological error of the free will of man was the principal issue of the reformation:

> When most Christians think of the Reformation, the first thing that comes to their mind is justification by faith alone. There is good reason for that assumption; justification by faith alone was the key doctrine that came out of the Reformation; however, it was not the key issue at the foundation of the Reformation. A careful study of the historical facts will clearly show that the issue of man's will was at the heart of the theological difference between Martin Luther and the Roman Catholic Church.[1031]

The Roman Catholic anti-gospel has made new inroads since the reformation. Arminianism has been promoted by "Christian" luminaries all over the world including but not limited to John Wesley and Charles Finney of yesteryear to today's Billy Graham, Dave Hunt, Chuck Colson, Chuck Swindol, Chuck Smith, and Hank Hanegraff.

This Arminian gospel has today permeated most of the nominal

"Christian" churches. That anti-gospel is a direct attack on the sovereignty of God. Under the Arminian gospel, man is sovereign. The Arminian preachers speak of Jesus, but he is more an ornament to their theology. B.B. Warfield once observed of the Arminian theology of Charles Finney: "God might be eliminated from it entirely without essentially changing its character."[1032] Arminianism is a continuation of the seduction begun in the garden of Eden, where the serpent deceived Adam and Eve into eating of the fruit that would give them knowledge of good and evil. He told them "ye shall be as gods." Genesis 3:5.

A person seeking Christ is brought to the point where he cries out for help from God "Lord, I believe; help thou mine unbelief." Mark 9:24. However, a seeker exposed to the Arminian anti-gospel does not cry out for help from God, because he is convinced by the Arminian preacher that he does not need God to help him with his unbelief; it is all up to him and his own free will. He will be told that Jesus will not interfere with his free will decision.

The Arminian anti-gospel actually prevents true repentance from sin and turning toward God. Instead the seeker is told to look not to God for help with his unbelief, but rather that he has the power of his own free will to believe. Oh, they are told to believe in Jesus, but their belief is not in the Jesus of the Bible. In order to believe in the Jesus of the bible, a person must have the faith of the Jesus of the bible, not the faith of their free will. "But the scripture hath concluded all under sin, that the promise by **faith of Jesus** Christ might be **given to them that believe**." (Galatians 3:22)

Often a seeker is counseled by an Arminian pastor, who advises the seeker to recite a form statement. He is then told he is born again. However, there is no spiritual rebirth. The person is a counterfeit Christian who has a worldly belief in Jesus. That is not unlike the belief that even the devils have. James 2:19. That type of belief is not a saving faith. The counterfeit Christian goes through the motions of being a Christian, but his is just one of the many tares added to the wheat in the church. Tares look just like the wheat, but their end is quite different. Jesus explained this very phenomenon to his disciples in Mark 13.

As a result of the successful efforts of Arminius and other Jesuit agents, Molinism has since become popularized not as Molinism but as Arminianism.[1033] Many view Arminianism as an orthodox Christian view of Scripture, when in fact it is a corruption of the gospel that has been injected into the Protestant denominations by Jacobus Arminius. Arminianism is simply repackaged Roman Catholic, semi-Pelagian doctrine.[1034]

The Arminian gospel is a seduction designed to lead all back into the arms of Rome. Rome uses its Arminian spiritual offspring to seduce the ignorant back into its clutches. The Roman Catholic Church has been losing members, particularly in South America. In order to reverse this trend Roman Catholic pressed its undercover agents (both Arminians and so-called Calvinists) in the ranks of Protestant denominations to stem the tide of losses from its religion by convincing former Catholics to return to the spiritual bondage of the Catholic church.

One artifice recently used by the Roman Catholic Church/State and its Arminian agents is an agreement by highly respected leaders among Protestants with representatives of the Roman Catholic Church. This group met and hammered out a seductive agreement, which was announced in May 1994. The agreement was titled *Evangelicals and Catholics Together* (hereinafter, *ECT*).[1035]

The foundational principle of the entire document is that both Roman Catholicism and Christianity are religions of equivalent merit, and the doctrines in both should be accorded equal legitimacy under the common label "Christian."

The charlatan religious luminaries were not content with the ECT of May 1994. They came out in 1997 with yet another abomination, titled *The Gift of Salvation*.[1036]

Both *ECT* and *The Gift of Salvation* were Roman Catholic efforts to undermine the sovereign gospel of grace. The details of the Catholic strategy are documented in this author's book, *The Anti-Gospel*.

John Robbins explains the historical context of *ECT* and *The*

Gift of Salvation manifestos and their ultimate design and purpose:

> Rome realizes what the central theological issue is, and Rome is moving deliberately and effectively to heal the wound inflicted on her in the sixteenth century by the preaching of the Gospel. Rome apparently is finding plenty of eager dupes-useful idiots, Lenin called them-among the ersatz-evangelicals to accomplish its goal.
>
> The twentieth century has been an ecumenical century. Rome has moved as never before to heal its wound, and to incorporate all professors and churches within itself. These conversations, dialogues, and working relationships with non-Roman ecclesiastical organizations are far too numerous to list here; they have ranged from conversations with the Anglicans in Belgium in the 1920s, led by Cardinal Mercier, to continuous ecumenical efforts with the Lutherans, Anglicans, National Council and World Council of Churches, the charismatics and Pentecostals, the Eastern Orthodox Church, and the ersatz-evangelicals. Billy Graham, the most famous Arminian evangelist of the twentieth century, has sought and received the participation of Romanists in his "crusades" since the late 1950s. The Vatican intends to reinstate its monopoly, and many are worshiping the beast.
>
> The existence of groups like the Colson-Neuhaus Group [Principal authors of the *ECT* and *The Gift of Salvation* manifestos] is not new; what it demonstrates, however, is how thoroughly theologically corrupt the ersatz-evangelicals are. Christians have long known that the National Council of Churches, the World Council of Churches, the mainline denominations, and the charismatic movement are anti-Christian; now the Cassidy-Colson-Neuhaus Group is making it clear that ersatz-evangelicalism is fundamentally at one with Romanism. The Synod of Dordt condemned the Arminian theology of the ersatz-evangelicals as a

doctrine from the pit of Hell. Except for a scattered remnant, the American heirs of the Reformation have repudiated the faith of their fathers, they have abandoned the Gospel, and they are falling over each other in their eagerness to fawn before the beast. In the beast they see power and influence, success, respectability, fame, and riches - and they want to enjoy the things the beast can provide.[1037]

The papacy has continued in its deceptive strategy of entering into agreements with nominal Protestant ministers in order to undermine the biblical theology of the Protestant churches as a way to establish a single worldwide church, with the pope as head. In February 2014, Pope Francis addressed hundreds of Pentecostal pastors by way of a recorded message. The taped presentation was a brilliant piece of propaganda by the pope. During the presentation Pope Francis stated:

> We are kind of...permit me to say, separated. Separated because, it's sin that has separated us, all our sins. The misunderstandings throughout history. It has been a long road of sins that we all shared in. Who is to blame? We all share the blame. We have all sinned.[1038]

That is an astounding statement. Pope Francis is suggesting that the separation between the Catholic Church and the Protestant churches is due to a "misunderstanding." There is no misunderstanding. It is clear that for over 1,000 years the Roman Catholic church tortured and murdered millions of Christians because they refused to submit to the authority of the pope.

According to Pope Francis, though, the genocide of 150,000 Irish Christian men, women, and children in 1641 led by the Catholic clergy upon the orders from the papacy was just a "misunderstanding."[1039] Was it just a "misunderstanding" when upon the orders of the papacy between 50,000[1040] and 100,000[1041] French Protestants were massacred in Paris during the St. Bartholomew Day Massacre on August 24, 1572? According to Pope Francis, those victims shared in the blame for their massacre. That must mean that the Protestant victims deserved it. Does Pope Francis think that Pope Alexander III and the Lateran Council in 1179 just made a little "boo

boo" when they urged the use of force and established incentives for violence against Christians such as a two year remission of penance for those who murdered a "heretic?" Was it a misunderstanding, when in 1231 Pope Gregory IX formally established the papal inquisitional tribunal (*inquisitio haereticae pravitatis*)? Was it a "misunderstanding" in 1252, when Pope Innocent IV expressly authorized the use of torture against recalcitrant Christians.[1042] Was it just a misunderstanding when the Roman clergy tortured, mutilated, and burned at the stake millions of Christians, whom the Vatican considered "heretics?"[1043] Did the Roman clergy just misunderstand Thomas Aquinas (1226-1274), a Catholic "saint," when he wrote that "heretics [may] be justly slain once they are convicted."[1044]

The Pope Francis video monologue calling for reunion by the Protestants with Rome was introduced by Anthony Palmer, who is a leader in the ecumenical movement. Palmer considers Pope Francis his "friend, spiritual father and prayer partner."[1045] According to Palmer, doctrine is of little importance. The only thing of importance to Palmer is unity. Doctrinal purity is almost irrelevant. Palmer stated: "It's the glory that glues us together, not the doctrine. If you accept that the presence of God is in me and the presence of God is in you, that's all we need. God will sort out all our doctrines when we get upstairs."[1046]

Anthony Palmer explained how his wife was brought back into the Catholic fold: "When my wife saw that she could be Catholic, and Charismatic, and Evangelical, and Pentecostal, and it was absolutely accepted in the Catholic Church, she said that she would like to reconnect her roots with the Catholic culture. So she did."[1047]

Palmer then made a cryptic statement that has a very deep esoteric meaning: "I challenge you to find a bridge builder and back him."[1048] Those words were chosen very carefully. The pope carries the title of Supreme Pontiff, which means literally supreme bridge builder. Palmer is making an allusion to the pope in that statement. He is calling on people to back the "bridge builder," by which he means the pope.

How could a Protestant preacher advocate a return to Rome? Because Palmer claims that "we are not protesting the doctrine of salvation [taught] by the Catholic Church anymore ... we now preach the same Gospel."[1049] Is that true? According to Palmer, it is true. Palmer made an astounding statement: "Brothers and sisters, Luther's protest is over. Is yours?"[1050] Why does Palmer say that "Luther's protest is over?" Palmer was making reference to the 1999 Joint Declaration on the Doctrine of Justification between the Lutheran World Federation and the Vatican (hereinafter referred to JDDJ).[1051]

The delegation from the Lutheran World Federation was hoodwinked by the Vatican. That is being charitable. The Lutherans may have been deceived; however, it is more likely that they fully understood what they signed and are accomplices with the Vatican in ushering in a New World Order with a single universal (Catholic) religion. The Catholic church used every artifice of language and obfuscation to make it seem that they agreed with the Protestant view of justification by grace alone through faith alone. The Vatican, however, retained the traditional Catholic view of salvation by faith plus works. The salient point of the agreement appears in paragraph 13:

> Together we confess: By grace alone, in faith in Christ's saving work and not because of any merit on our part, we are accepted by God and receive the Holy Spirit, who renews our hearts while equipping and calling us to good works.[1052]

Upon first blush, it seems to be a biblically sound statement. However, "the serpent was more subtil than any beast of the field," and so also are the Catholic and Lutheran scribes subtle beasts. Notice the missing adjective. The statement says by grace alone but it does not say by faith alone. The JDDJ leaves room for works to be added to faith as a means of salvation. The so-called agreement is really a compromise of Christian doctrine by the Lutheran World Federation. The Catholic theologians used the artifice of reserving all things not agreed to in the document. Paragraph 5 of the agreement states that "[i]t does not cover all that either church teaches about justification."[1053] In particular, it does not cover the teaching of the Catholic church that salvation is merited by works.

In fact, the agreement reaffirms the continued validity of all of the Catholic Councils, in particular the Council of Trent, which contains over 100 curses against Christian biblical doctrines. The agreement opens in paragraph 1 with the following statement confirming the continued validity of the Council of Trent:

> Doctrinal condemnations were put forward both in the Lutheran Confessions and by the Roman Catholic Church's Council of Trent. **These condemnations are still valid today and thus have a church-dividing effect.**[1054]

Notably, the Lutheran Confessions were limited in a footnote with the following language:

> It should be noted that some Lutheran churches include only the Augsburg Confession and Luther's Small Catechism among their binding confessions. These texts contain no condemnations about justification in relation to the Roman Catholic Church.[1055]

According to the agreement, the Catholic condemnations against Christians remain "still valid," whereas the Lutheran confessions are limited to the Augsburg and Luther's Small Catechism which offer no condemnation of Catholic doctrine. The JDDJ contains deceptive sophistry. Paragraph 7 of the agreement has obfuscatory language, for which the Jesuits are known; it takes some discernment to decipher the crypto-linguistics of the JDDJ. The JDDJ states that the Catholic Church has not disavowed the condemnations it issued in its past ecclesiastical councils and papal bulls, but looks at them with new insight and in a new light.

> Like the dialogues themselves, this Joint Declaration rests on the conviction that in overcoming the earlier controversial questions and doctrinal condemnations, **the churches neither take the condemnations lightly nor do they disavow their own past**. On the contrary, this Declaration is shaped by the conviction that in their respective histories our churches have come to new insights. Developments have taken place which not only make possible, but also require the churches to examine the divisive questions and condemnations and see them in a new light.[1056]

That language in the JDDJ means that the curses issued by the Council of Trent against biblical Christian doctrine of salvation by the grace of God alone through faith in Jesus Christ alone are still in effect. Indeed, the Council of Trent has been a monument of Catholic dogma for almost 500 years and can never be repealed without destroying the very structure of the Catholic theology. The JDDJ cryptically states that the condemnations contained in the Catholic edicts remain and are "salutary warnings" that must be part of the Catholic teachings:

> Nothing is thereby taken away from the seriousness of the condemnations related to the doctrine of justification. Some were not simply pointless. They remain for us "salutary warnings" to which we must attend in our teaching and practice.[1057]

While the Catholic Church may try to deceive the unwary that it has changed, those who are familiar with Catholic dogma, know that the Catholic Church will not change. Indeed, the Catholic Church will not ever change, because it cannot ever change. It is ironclad Catholic dogma that the Catholic Church will not ever change its doctrine. Pope John Paul II stated: "Nothing ever changes in the eternal Catholic doctrine."[1058] Pope Benedict XV stated: "The Catholic Faith is such that nothing can be added to it, nothing taken away. Either it is held in its entirety, or rejected totally. This is the Catholic faith, which, unless a man believes faithfully and firmly, he cannot be saved."[1059] Pope Paul VI stated: "Under no circumstances can we conceive of the possibility of change, of evolution, or of any modification in matters of faith. The Creed remains always the same."[1060]

Paul T. McCain confirmed that there was not one iota of retreat in the joint declaration by the Vatican from the dogma of the Council of Trent:

> Was Trent set aside by the Joint Declaration on the Doctrine of Justification?
>
> No, quite the contrary. The Vatican was very careful to make it clear that it has not set aside the Council of Trent and that Trent still remains authoritative, binding dogma for the Roman Catholic Church. Cardinal

Cassidy, President of the Pontifical Council for Promoting Christianity Unity, the individual responsible in large part for Rome's involvement in the Joint Declaration, went out of his way to clarify this point in a press conference held when the JDDJ was signed. Here is what he had to say:

"Asked whether there was anything in the official common statement contrary to the Council of Trent, Cardinal Cassidy said: 'Absolutely not, otherwise how could we do it? We cannot do something contrary to an ecumenical council. There's nothing there that the Council of Trent condemns" (Ecumenical News International, 11/1/99).

With this statement by Cardinal Cassidy in mind, one is led to wonder how a document that is alleged to be a faithful Lutheran statement of justification contains nothing that Trent condemned.

What Did Trent Condemn?

Canon IX: If anyone says that the ungodly is justified by faith alone in such a way that he understands that nothing else is required which cooperates toward obtaining the grace of justification . . . let him be condemned.

Canon XII: If anyone says that justifying faith is nothing else than trust in divine mercy, which remits sin for Christ's sake, or that it is this trust alone by which we are justified, let him be condemned.

Canon XIV: If anyone says that a man is absolved and justified because . . . he confidently believes that he is absolved and justified . . . and that through this faith alone absolution and justification is effected, let him be condemned.

Note: These canons clearly indicate that something

more than trust in Christ is necessary for salvation.[1061]

Paragraph 13 does remove the curses issued by the Council of Trent, but does so only from the signatories to the agreement. Paragraph 13 states that "[i]n light of this consensus, the corresponding **doctrinal condemnations of the sixteenth century do not apply to today's partner.**"[1062] The sixteenth century curses against Christians and Christian doctrine issued by the Council of Trent do not apply to the Lutheran World Federation. Why? Because, by signing the JDDJ document, the Lutheran World Federation has disavowed the biblical doctrines that were the object of the curses from the Council of Trent. They have become a child of Rome. All who do not agree to sign the agreement remain under the curses of the Council of Trent.

One thing that is clearly expressed in the JDDJ is that the Vatican did not compromise on any of its established dogma. Paragraph 16 of the agreement reveals the core theology behind the agreement. It states: "All people are called by God to salvation in Christ." That statement reveals the sovereign drug of Arminianism, that makes the Protestants inebriated and unable resist the enticement back to Rome. The Lutheran World Federation was already under the influence of Arminianism. That is why the Lutheran World Federation found it so easy to agree with Rome. Arminians claim that God gives a "prevenient" grace to all men that frees their will and enables them to choose whether to believe in Jesus. Under Arminianism, those who choose to believe in Jesus can also, of their free will, choose to reject Jesus and lose the salvation that they had previously grasped.

The prevenient grace doctrine is biblically impossible. The bible states that "there is none that seeketh after God." Romans 3:11. To address man's depraved condition, God, by his grace, gives those he has chosen for salvation the faith of Jesus. Romans 3:21-26. It is only those whom God has elected for salvation who are the object of his grace. John 17:9-12. Once God gives his elect the faith to believe in Jesus, his elect will certainly believe in Jesus. John 6:39. The faith of God's elect is not left to the chance free will decisions of men. John 1:13. The claim by Arminians that all men are given a prevenient grace that frees their will to choose to believe in God is an unbiblical invention of the Vatican, who cannot tolerate the sovereign God.

The prevenient grace construct is a way to explain how man can have a free will after the fall. The problem with the prevenient grace myth is that it saves no one. Under the Arminian model, salvation requires an act of man's free will, aside from any influence by God other than his act of initially freeing the will through the (mythical) prevenient grace. Mark Herzer explains how prevenient grace is a necessary construct for the Arminians in order to keep the free will theory intact and at the same time acknowledge the fall of man.

> Their doctrine of prevenient grace is ultimately rooted in their insistence upon the absolute non-negotiable of their theology, namely, man must be free enough to accept or reject. They wish to be debtors to Free Will and we to Sovereign Grace. They argue that since prevenient grace came before our choice, therefore their theology is one of grace. But then again, this sort of argument was advanced by the Papists. It is true that this universal prevenient grace came before our choice; but it affected no one efficaciously. It led none to salvation. The efficacious act came from man who could accept or reject the prevenient grace. Man's choice is the sine qua non of their theology and not God's sovereign irresistible grace. We, on the other hand, declare, "Of Him are ye in Christ Jesus!"[1063]

Arminians had to come up with a theory to explain how man, who the bible states clearly is spiritually dead and enslaved to sin from the fall, could have a free will to believe in Jesus. It was out of this theological necessity that the myth of prevenient grace was born. Free will Arminianism is the root and branch of the Roman Catholic theology.

The very idea that "all people are called by God to salvation in Christ" is a direct attack on the grace of the gospel. That statement reveals what is truly meant in the JDDJ when it states that one is accepted by God "by grace alone." The grace to which the agreement refers is not to the grace spoken of in the gospel; it is rather a mythical prevenient grace.

Prevenient grace is not a grace that saves. The JDDJ was very careful to limit its statement in the agreement to say that the grace is given to one that is "accepted by God." Notice it did not say that the grace described in the JDDJ is a saving grace in and of itself. The JDDJ grace is a grace that it given to one who is merely "accepted by God." According to the language in the agreement, God accepts all people through his (prevenient) grace. It is from the point where everyone is "accepted by God" that all of those accepted persons must of their own free will decide to believe in God. That theological error is codified in section 2022 of the Catechism of the Catholic Church, which states: "The divine initiative in the work of grace precedes, prepares, and elicits the free response of man."[1064]

Part and parcel of that free will acceptance is the power to also exercise free will to reject Jesus Christ. In a response to the JDDJ, the Vatican confirmed that "the Catholic Church notes with satisfaction that n. 21 [of the JDDJ], in conformity with can. 4 of the Decree on Justification of the Council of Trent (DS 1554) states that man can refuse grace."[1065] That free will autonomy is degenerative and culminates in a theology of salvation by works. That is contrary to the effectual grace of the gospel where God chooses his elect for salvation and ensures that they are in fact saved. God's elect do not rely on their own faith born of their free will, but rather rely on "Jesus the author and finisher of our faith." Hebrews 12:2.

The ultimate goal of most Catholics is not heaven, but rather purgatory. Under Catholic dogma, only a very few can go straight to heaven. Catholics believe that those that do go directly to heaven can only do so as a reward for their own personal works of righteousness. That is directly contrary to the bible, which states that one is saved solely by God's grace, whereby the righteousness of Christ is imputed to his elect solely by the faith of Jesus. "But the scripture hath concluded all under sin, that the promise by **faith of Jesus** Christ might be **given** to them that believe." (Galatians 3:22) Paragraph 38 of the JDDJ states: "When Catholics affirm the 'meritorious' character of good works, they wish to say that, according to the biblical witness, a reward in heaven is promised to these works."[1066]

The Arminianism of the JDDJ is drawing other Protestant denominations founded upon a free will gospel back to the Vatican fold. In these end times, the mother of harlots is gathering her brood back home. On July 18, 2006, members of the World Methodist Council, meeting in Seoul, South Korea, voted unanimously to adopt the JDDJ.[1067] The Methodist church was founded by John Wesley, who was an ardent Arminian. Augustus Toplady had this to say about John Wesley: "I believe him to be the most rancourous hater of the gospel system that ever appeared in England." Toplady further said that Wesley "is still as dead to the feelings of shame as he is blind to the doctrines of God."

The Lutheran World Federation and World Methodist Council have abandoned the faith and have adopted the Romish dogma of imparted actual righteousness. Paragraph 22 of the JDDJ states: "We confess together that God forgives sin by grace and at the same time frees human beings from sin's enslaving power and imparts the gift of new life in Christ."[1068]

The Catholic Church has replaced the biblical doctrine of imputed righteousness, which is a forensic (legal) act of God, with the doctrine of imparted righteousness, which is an actual righteousness of the believer. Requiring actual righteousness for salvation is nothing less than salvation by works. Once it is decided that salvation is not legal, but instead involves imparted actual righteousness, that religion will necessarily require works of the "believers" to maintain their status as "believers."

Mark Herzer describes this doctrine of imparted righteousness as "unbiblical and not Protestant or evangelical. It is nothing less than the Romish notion of infused righteousness."[1069] Of course that is why it is in the JDDJ. The JDDJ is Catholic theology masquerading behind biblical language. The Roman Catholic mythology of infused righteousness is the foundation of their adding works to faith as the means of salvation. If one is infused with actual righteousness, then one must necessarily do good works in accordance with the infused actual righteousness. Imparted righteousness is an adjunct to Arminianism. Herzer calls imparted righteousness "Roman Catholicism in Protestant garb."[1070]

Christians trust in the righteousness of Christ being imputed to them, whereas Catholics and Protestant Arminians trust in the impartation of Christ's righteousness, which thus makes them holy and righteous in fact. The difference between imputed righteousness contained in the gospel and the Arminian imparted righteousness is explained by John Mark Hicks:

> This is no mere semantical difference. It is a fundamental disagreement concerning the ground of grace itself. It is the difference between being clothed in Christ's perfect righteousness and being clothed in our own partial righteousness voluntaristically . . . imputed to us. It is the difference between righteousness being wholly derived from Christ's work or righteousness partially derived from our own faith.[1071]

This doctrine that one can attain actual righteousness is the very error of the Jews. Catholics and their fellow travelers have a zeal for God, just as did the Jews, but it is not according to knowledge. Catholics try to establish their own righteousness, rather than rest in the imputed righteousness of Christ.

> For I bear them record that they have a zeal of God, but not according to knowledge. For they being ignorant of God's righteousness, and going about to establish their own righteousness, have not submitted themselves unto the righteousness of God. For Christ is the end of the law for righteousness to every one that believeth. Romans 10:2-4.

The error of the impartation of actual righteousness is apparent when one considers the fact that the atonement of Christ was a legal exchange. That means that the sins of the elect were imputed to Christ, and the righteousness of Christ was imputed to God's elect. 2 Corinthians 5:18-21. If, as required by the Arminian theology, there is an actual exchange (and not a forensic exchange), that would mean that the sinner becomes actually righteous, and it would also mean that Christ became actually sinful. That is blasphemy!

How is the righteousness imparted to the believer? According to the JDDJ it is through water baptism. Paragraph 30 of the JDDJ states: "Catholics hold that the grace of Jesus Christ imparted in baptism takes away all that is sin."[1072] The Lutheran World Federation and World Methodist Council have adopted the Catholic doctrine of baptismal regeneration. Paragraph 28 of the JDDJ states: "We confess together that in baptism the Holy Spirit unites one with Christ, justifies, and truly renews the person."[1073] The JDDJ is not speaking about the baptism of the Holy Spirit as promised in Mark 1:8, but water baptism. Paragraph 29 of the JDDJ clarifies that by stating that "the person who has been born anew by baptism and the Holy Spirit has this sin forgiven."[1074] Notice it doe not say "baptism of the Holy Spirit," but rather "baptism and the Holy Spirit." The baptism is not the baptism of the Holy Spirit, because it is something that must be added to the Holy Spirit.

The JDDJ is clearly making a reference to being saved through water baptism, which must be in addition to the Holy Spirit. Indeed it could mean nothing else, because if it did, it would violate the precepts of the Council of Trent, the Council of Florence, and the Catechism of the Catholic Church. Section 1214 of the Catechism of the Catholic Church states emphatically that when using the term baptism, it is meant to convey water baptism. Indeed, the Council of Trent ruled that "[i]f anyone says that true and natural water is not necessary for baptism and thus twists into some metaphor the words of our Lord Jesus Christ: Unless a man be born again of water and the Holy Ghost, let him be anathema."[1075] Section 1213 of the Catechism of the Catholic Church states that water baptism is the means by which God regenerates a Catholic and that person then becomes freed from sin.

> Holy Baptism is the basis of the whole Christian life, the gateway to life in the Spirit (*vitae spiritualis ianua*), and the door which gives access to the other sacraments. Through Baptism we are freed from sin and reborn as sons of God; we become members of Christ, are incorporated into the Church and made sharers in her mission: "Baptism is the sacrament of regeneration through water in the word."[1076]

The Lutheran World Federation and World Methodist Council agreement with the Vatican on the issue of baptism, means that they must necessarily agree with the Catholic Church that water baptism is the means by which one is regenerated and born again unto salvation.

The JDDJ is a significant step by the pope in bringing about a universal worldwide religion with him as the head, as is prophesied in Revelation.

> And they worshipped the dragon which gave power unto the beast: and they worshipped the beast, saying, Who is like unto the beast? who is able to make war with him? And there was given unto him a mouth speaking great things and blasphemies; and power was given unto him to continue forty and two months. And he opened his mouth in blasphemy against God, to blaspheme his name, and his tabernacle, and them that dwell in heaven. And it was given unto him to make war with the saints, and to overcome them: and power was given him over all kindreds, and tongues, and nations. And all that dwell upon the earth shall worship him, whose names are not written in the book of life of the Lamb slain from the foundation of the world. If any man have an ear, let him hear." (Revelation 13:4-9)

The Lutheran World Federation and World Methodist Council have been infected with Arminianism, which served as a Roman lever to pry them from their Protestant moorings and draw them back to Rome. Arminianism is a form of Catholicism, but it is a half-measure. Even an Arminian church today would not agree to bow down to idols, accept priests as having the authority of God to forgive sins, accept the pope in place of Christ on earth, worship Mary as a goddess, or believe that a piece of bread can be turned into God. While Arminian churches have compromised on the core doctrine of the bible, the sovereign grace of God, they have not yet gone the whole way and fully bloomed into the heathenism envisioned by the pope and his Jesuit minions. It would seem that the pope still has a significant hurdle before he can head a single worldwide Catholic religion to the exclusion of all others.

How is the pope going to convince the Arminian churches to swallow the full measure of the cup of spiritual fornication with Babylon the Great? The papacy will ultimately have to resort to force. There is no new thing under the sun. "The thing that hath been, it is that which shall be; and that which is done is that which shall be done: and there is no new thing under the sun." (Ecclesiastes 1:9) Pope Pius IX stated: "[It is error to believe that] the [Catholic] Church has not the power of using force, nor has she any temporal power, direct or indirect."[1077] The pope will simply dust off his tried and true system that has lain dormant for centuries; he will coopt the force of government to act as executioners of its judgements rendered in its ecclesiastical trials under the auspices of the office of the inquisition.

The arm of the Vatican that carried out the torture and murder of millions of Christians is still in operation today. After going through several name changes that redacted the ominous word "Inquisition" from its title, it has survived today under the title of "Congregation for the Doctrine of the Faith."[1078] It is the same office that presided over the ecclesiastical tortures and murders of those refusing to submit to the authority or dogma of the pope during the middle ages. The Congregation for the Doctrine of the Faith still holds weekly meetings today[1079] in its original Palace of the Inquisition, which is adjacent to the Vatican.[1080] The Grand Inquisitor, who is the chief enforcer of Catholic dogma, is viewed as an honored and powerful position within the Catholic hierarchy today.[1081] For example, one recent Grand Inquisitor, Joseph Cardinal Ratzinger, was able to use his significant political power within the curia to become elected Pope Bendedict XVI.

The Vatican is just laying the groundwork for its ascendance. History has shown that "Rome in the minority is a lamb. Rome as an equal is a fox. Rome in the majority is a tiger."[1082] The pope masquerades as a harmless lamb, but under that sheep's clothing is a ravenous beast, like unto that which possesses him. "Be sober, be vigilant; because your adversary the devil, as a roaring lion, walketh about, seeking whom he may devour:" 1 Peter 5:8. See also Matthew 7:15.

42 The Antichrist Orchestrates the Killing of Lincoln

The Vatican is both a sovereign state and the headquarters for a world religion. This structure was patterned upon Babylonian/Judaic principles. The Vatican is an independent and sovereign nation, with its own currency, Secretary of State and ambassadors.

Once a person is baptized into the Catholic Church he becomes a member of that church. When he is confirmed "[h]e becomes a citizen of the Church, able to assume the responsibility of that citizenship and to defend his faith against its enemies."[1083] Once confirmed the new citizen must be "prepared when called upon to fight for the faith of Christ."[1084] The citizens of the Roman Church must have "strength and fortitude to enable them, in the spiritual contest to fight manfully and resist their most wicked foes."[1085] He now becomes a "valiant combatant, he should be prepared to endure with unconquered spirit all adversaries for the name of Christ."[1086]

In contrast, Jesus made clear that his kingdom is not of this world, God's kingdom is spiritual.

> Jesus answered, **My kingdom is not of this world**: if my kingdom were of this world, then would my servants fight, that I should not be delivered to the

Jews: but now is my kingdom not from hence. (John 18:36)

Satan's kingdom is of this world. He has his citizens throughout the world. When a citizen must make a choice between obeying his country and obeying the Pope, according to the official Roman doctrine, he must obey the Pope. The Catholic Canon Law and Dogma has superiority over the constitution of the country. All federal and state government officials in the United States must swear or affirm to support the U.S. Constitution,[1087] but as far as the Roman Catholic Church is concerned, a Catholic's allegiance to the Pope comes first. In fact, in 1199 A.D. Pope Innocent III issued the Papal Bull *Vergentis in senium* in which he equated the "heresy" of violating Papal edicts and Roman Catholic doctrines to treason.[1088] In 1231 A.D. Pope Gregory IX issued Papal Bull *Excommunicamus* wherein he officially fixed the penalty for "heresy" against the Catholic Church as the death penalty.[1089]

During the Civil War, the Vatican was the only nation to recognize the sovereignty of the Southern Confederate States. How did this affect Catholic Union soldiers knowing that they were fighting a cause that was opposed by their spiritual leader, who they believed had authority to prevent their entry into heaven? Many Catholics fought with bravery and distinction, others abandoned the cause and turned traitor. Abraham Lincoln explains:

> Surely we have some brave and reliable Roman Catholic officials and soldiers in our armies, but they form an insignificant minority when compared with the Roman Catholic traitors against whom we have to guard ourselves, day and night. The fact is that the immense majority of Roman Catholic bishops, priests and laymen are rebels in heart, when they cannot be in fact; with very few exceptions, they are publicly in favor of slavery. *Abraham Lincoln, 1861.*[1090]

Contrast Catholic General Sheridan, whom Lincoln described as "worth a whole army by his ability, his patriotism, and his heroic courage,"[1091] with Catholic General Meade, who seems to have chosen allegiance to Rome over allegiance to the U.S. Lincoln recounts one episode:

> Meade has remained with us, and gained the bloody battle at Gettysburg. But how could he lose it, when he was surrounded by such heroes as Howard, Reynolds, Buford, Wadsworth, Cutler, Slocum, Sickles, Hancock, Barnes, etc. But it is evident that his Romanism superseded his patriotism after the battle. He let the army of Lee escape when he could easily have cut his retreat and forced him to surrender after losing nearly the half of his soldiers in the last three days' carnage. When Meade was to order the pursuit after the battle, a stranger came in haste to the headquarters, and that stranger was a disguised Jesuit. After ten minutes' conversation with him, Meade made such arrangements for the pursuit of the enemy that he escaped almost untouched with the loss of only two guns! *Abraham Lincoln*.[1092]

General Thomas Maley Harris presents hard statistics, which put meat on the bones of President Lincoln's words:

> In reply to the boast so freely made by Roman Catholic editors and orators that the Irish fought the battles of the civil war and saved the nation, the following document, received from the Pension department at Washington, is here given:
>
> Whole number of troops 2,128,200
>
> Natives of the United States 1,627,267
>
> Germans 189,817
>
> Irishmen 144,221
>
> British (other than Irish) 90,040
>
> Other foreigners and missions 87,855

The "Desertions" were as follows:

Natives of the United States . . . . 5 percent

Germans . . . . .10 percent

Irish Catholics . . . . 72 percent

British (Other than Irish) . . . . .7 percent

Other foreigners . . . . 7 percent

In other words: of the 144,000 Irishmen that enlisted. 104,000 deserted. And it is reliably stated that most of these desertions occurred after the recognition of the Confederacy by the Pope. It is also a fact that of the five percent of native Americans rated as deserters, 45 percent of the 5 percent were Catholics. --TOLEDO AMERICAN, as quoted on page 115 of "Why Am I An A.P.A."

This is a sufficient proof of the charge heretofore made that a good Roman Catholic can only be loyal to the Pope and so can never be loyal to our government, and to our Protestant institutions.

It is true that there were some able and brave Roman Catholic officers in the Union army, who were truly loyal to the cause; as also many in the ranks who were nominally members of the Roman Catholic Church: but these were they who had been educated in our free schools, and had thus become so imbued with the American Spirit, that they were no longer good Catholics. All honor to these!

Not only by desertions and resignations was Roman Catholic disloyalty made apparent, but more conspicuously by the draft riots that followed, the rioters being made up, almost entirely, of Irish Roman

Catholics. Archbishop Hughes posed as a Union man; and was so far trusted by President Lincoln, that he solicited his good offices at Rome, to prevent the Pope from giving recognition to the Confederate government; he being well aware of the consequences that would follow such recognition. The Archbishop proved a traitor to his trust; and the Pope's letter to Jefferson Davis followed closely on the heels of his visit to Rome, and resignations and desertions commenced. Then followed the terrible riots in New York City, when a draft became necessary to fill up our depleted ranks. For three fearful days and nights the city was terrorized by the violence of an Irish Catholic mob, right under the shadow of the Archbishop's palace. The Archbishop kept secluded in his palace, and as mute as a mouse, until notified by Mr. Lincoln that he would be held personally responsible for its continuance. He then came forth; and by a few kind words to the rioters, whom he addressed as his friends, the mob immediately dispersed, and order was restored. It only took a few words from him to accomplish what could not have been accomplished without much bloodshed, and perhaps the destruction of the city, by a military arm of our government; but mark those words were not spoken until it became necessary to the personal safety of the Archbishop. The traitor was here revealed. And now we come to the last desperate conspiracy to overthrow our government, and make the rebellion a success by a resort to the favorite policy of the Jesuits, that of assassination.[1093]

General Thomas Maley Harris concluded that the Roman Catholic Church was behind the conspiracy to assassinate President Lincoln.[1094] General Harris was a member of the Military Commission that tried and convicted the conspirators who assassinated President Lincoln. General Harris established a reputation for faithfulness, industriousness, intelligence, and efficiency. He was noted for his leadership in preparing his troops and leading them in battle. He was brevetted a major general for "gallant conduct in the assault on Petersburg." After the war, General Harris served one term as a representative in the West Virginia legislature, and was West Virginia's Adjutant General from 1869 to 1870.

General Harris wrote a book titled, *Rome's Responsibility for the Assassination of Abraham Lincoln*, wherein he gives an account of the conspiracy to assassinate President Lincoln. General Harris' account of the conspiracy is authoritative. In his capacity as a member of the commission, he dutifully heard and weighed the evidence, as he was called upon ultimately to render his judgement on the matter. He carefully listened to the 371 witnesses who testified under oath during the seven week trial of the conspirators. His judgement that the responsibility for the assassination of Abraham Lincoln rests with the Vatican in Rome is based in large part upon the evidence that was adduced during the trial of the conspirators.

The U.S. Military Commission that investigated the assassination of Abraham Lincoln and prosecuted the conspirators. General Thomas Maley Harris, is standing third from the left.

The Civil War was not the first war in which Roman Catholic soldiers showed that their allegiance to Rome outweighed their allegiance to the United States. The Irish Catholic soldiers during the Mexican-American War not only deserted, they committed treason by fighting with Mexico against their fellow Americans. Why would they do that? Former Catholic Priest, Emmett McLoughlin explained that Mexican General Santa Anna "hired an opportunistic Irish priest, Reverend Eugence McNamara, who infiltrated the American lines and convinced his co-religionists that their divinely chosen role was to fight by the side of their fellow-Catholics, the Mexicans, against the land-grabbing Protestant Yankees."[1095] The Handbook of Texas confirms this little-known episode of Catholic treason. "Mexican propaganda insinuated that the United States intended to destroy Catholicism in Mexico, and if Catholic soldiers fought on the side of the Americans, they would be warring against their own religion."[1096] Mexican General Santa Anna formed the Irish-Catholic deserters into a battalion that he called the San Patricio Battalion (English: Saint Patrick Battalion).

The San Patricio Battalion is celebrated by both Mexican and Irish Catholics today as a brave and highly principled group of soldiers. Indeed, it was announced recently that the San Patricio Battalion would be inducted into the Irish America Hall of Fame.[1097] Which is it, was the San Patricio Battalion a brave group of soldiers who were fighting against injustice or were they dupes of the Romish Church who were convinced by their superstitious religious beliefs to treasonously betray their country? Let us examine the facts. The oath taken by enlisted men during the Mexican-American War stated in pertinent part: "I, _____ do solemnly swear or affirm (as the case may be) that I will support the constitution of the United States ... to bear true allegiance to the United States of America, and to serve them honestly and faithfully, against all their enemies or opposers whatsoever, and to observe and obey the orders of the President of the United States of America, and the orders of the officers appointed over me."[1098] That oath is constitutionally required. The U.S. Constitution states that "all executive and judicial officers, both of the United States and of the several states, shall be bound by oath or affirmation, to support this Constitution."[1099] The San Patricio Battalion violated that constitutional oath. What honor can the Irish Catholics find in doing that? The violation of that oath by the San Patricio Battalion illustrates the tenuous nature of the loyalty of Roman Catholics to the United States. If it serves the purposes of Rome, Catholics will violate their solemn oath of allegiance to the United States and turn traitor.

Let us read a first-hand account of the shock felt by an American soldier who found his former comrades, still wearing their U.S. military uniforms, fighting alongside the enemy and shooting at him.

These men deluded by priests of their faith to violate

their oaths, ungratefully, in our own clothing and with our arms–at the battle of Cherubusco, near the City of Mexico–turned upon their former comrades and laid them low. It is impossible to estimate the felling of our men. At one time muskets were thrown aside and simply with the bayonet alone in hand, we met the enemy and captured over sixty of these deserters. There came an armistice, and during that armistice they were duly tried by court-martial, and, at Miscoac, in the presence of both armies, we hung thirty-two in good order.[1100]

All rabidly loyal Roman Catholics have the seed of treason planted in their hearts. Upon the order of a priest, that seed will germinate into full-bloom. They will not spare their neighbors or comrades. The draft riots of New York during the Civil war is another example of the Catholic sword of Damocles hanging over the U.S. Republic. A rampaging mob of approximately 50,000 Roman Catholic rioters raped, pillaged, and burned New York over a period of three days during July 13-15, 1863. That was ten days after the Battle at Gettysburg. The mob targeted Protestants, whom they called "heretics" and blacks.[1101] Emmett McLoughlin quotes from *The New York Daily Tribune* account of the arson of a Protestant's home, where it was reported that "in one instance, the crowd in attacking a house used as their watchword: 'Burn out the heretics.'"[1102] They murdered on sight any black person they came across regardless of sex or age. In fact, the mob set fire to different parts of an orphanage for black children in hopes of burning alive the 235 children trapped inside. A mob of two thousand Catholic men and women surrounded the orphanage and could be heard shouting: "Murder the damned monkeys" and "Wring the necks of the Lincolnites."[1103]

At all times during the rioting, Catholic priests could be seen walking untouched among the rioters. This did not go unnoticed. One Mr. Crowley tried to repair cut telegraph wires, but was afraid to risk traveling through the city controlled by the mob. He saw a passing carriage containing a Catholic priest, and when it stopped he got in it. The carriage was later surrounded by a mob of Catholic ruffians, who were about to do violence, but the ruffians suddenly went silent when they saw the priest inside the carriage; the carriage was allowed to pass unharmed.[1104] Emmitt McLoughlin stated that "many writers of the time felt that the New York riot was a deliberately incited act of treason, designed to mesh with riots, arson, and poisoning attempts in other Northern cities, in order to subdue the Northern will to fight on."[1105]

Indeed, at all times during the riot, it could have been quelled by the Roman Catholic Bishop Hughes. General Thomas Harris explained:

> For three fearful days and nights the city was terrorized by the violence of an Irish Catholic mob, right under the shadow of the Archbishop's palace. The Archbishop kept secluded in his palace, and as mute as a mouse, until notified by Mr. Lincoln that he would be held personally responsible for its continuance. He then came forth; and by a few kind words to the rioters, whom he addressed as his friends, the mob immediately dispersed, and order was restored. It only took a few words from him to accomplish what could not have been accomplished without much bloodshed, and perhaps the destruction of the city, by a military arm of our government; but mark those words were not spoken until it became necessary to the personal safety of the Archbishop.[1106]

Bishop Hughes was able to quell the rioters with a few words, which suggests complete control, even orchestration, of the mob. The Hughes control over the rioters brings to mind the threats made by Sister Mary St. George, the Mother Superior of the Ursuline Convent in Charlestown, Massachusets, to an incensed mob on August 11, 1834. Sister Mary John (formerly Elizabeth Harrison), had escaped from the Ursuline Convent. Just two years earlier, Rebecca Reed, who was a candidate to be a nun, also escaped from that same convent. Miss Reed revealed her involuntary captivity and the cruelty and oppression of the convent. The mother superior suspected Miss Reed's intentions of escaping and planned on surreptitiously spiriting her off to Canada, but Miss Reed escaped before the mother superior could carry out her plan. Miss Harrison was later convinced by the influence of Bishop Fenwick to return to the convent. However, a mob of citizens felt that she was inveigled back to the convent and was being held against her will.

Edward Cutter, who initially assisted Harrison upon her escape, testified in court that the mother superior threatened the mob that "the bishop had 20,000 of the vilest (or boldest) Irishmen under his control, who would tear down the houses of Mr. Cutter and others; and that the selectmen of the Charlestown might read the riot act till they were hoarse, and it would be of no use."[1107] That threat was the spark that set the mob in motion; it burned down the convent. The lady superior later testified in a prosecution of the rioters that "I told him, that the Right Reverend Bishop's influence over ten thousand brave Irishmen might lead to the destruction of his property and that of others."[1108] Samuel Morse explains the significance of her testimony: "Here we have the startling fact, acknowledged in a court of justice by the Superior of the Convent, that the Bishop has such influence over a mob of foreigners, that he can use them for vengeance, or restrain them at pleasure."[1109]

President Lincoln knew full well of the treachery of the Roman Catholic Church, and the Vatican viewed him as an implacable enemy who had to be eliminated. In addition, the Jewish money powers also had an interest in eliminating Lincoln. Lincoln in large part thwarted their efforts to gain huge profits from the civil war by printing the Lincoln greenbacks rather than borrowing the money at exorbitantly high interest rates from the bankers. Lincoln stated:

> The money powers prey upon the nation in times of peace and conspire against it in times of adversity. It is more despotic than a monarchy, more insolent than autocracy, and more selfish than bureaucracy. It denounces as public enemies all who question its methods or throw light upon its crimes. I have two great enemies, the Southern Army in front of me and the bankers in the rear. Of the two, the one at my rear is my greatest foe.

Charles Chiniquy, a former Catholic priest and close friend of Lincoln, revealed in his book, *Fifty Years in the Church of Rome,* that the most striking manifestation of the Catholic conspiracy came when in 1861 Civil War broke out in the U.S. Abraham Lincoln, with a wartime intelligence network second to none, knew the cause of the civil war: the pope of Rome and his deadly servants, the Jesuits. Paul Serup, in his well researched book, *Who Killed Abraham Lincoln?*, verifies Chiniquy's visits to the White House and his friendship with President Lincoln. Serup reveals an 1885 letter from President Lincoln's son, Robert Todd Lincoln, to Charles Chiniquy, which was sent after he received a copy of *Fifty Years in the Church of Rome* from Chiniquy. The letter attests to Lincoln's close friendship with Chiniquy.

> I beg you to accept my thanks for sending me your book and especially for the expression you use in your note in regards to my father. He made many friend [*sic*] in his life but plainly none were more than yourself. Most Sincerely Yours Robert Lincoln.[1110]

Letter from Robert Todd Lincoln to Charles Chiniquy, September 10, 1885, with transcription

My Dear Sir

I beg you to accept my thanks for sending your book and especially for the expression you use in your note in regards to my father. He made many friend in his life but plainly none were more than yourself.

Most Sincerely Yours
Robert Lincoln

The Chiniquy Collection

President Lincoln told Chiniquy: "I feel more and more that it is not against the South alone we are fighting, but against the Pope of Rome and his perfidious Jesuits, who are the principal rulers of the South."[1111] Lincoln further told Chiniquy on June 8, 1864:

> This war would never have been possible without the sinister influence of the Jesuits. We owe it to popery that we now see our land reddened with the blood of her noblest sons. Though there were great differences of opinion between the South and the North on the question of slavery, neither Jeff Davis nor any of the leading men of the Confederacy would have dared to attack the North, had they not relied on the promises of the Jesuits, that, under the mask of democracy the money and the arms of the Roman Catholics, even the arms of France, were at their disposal, if they would attack us.[1112]

President Lincoln further told Chiniquy about the alliance between the Pope of Rome and the Confederate leadership:

> From the beginning of our civil war, there has been, not a secret, but a public alliance, between the Pope of Rome and Jeff Davis. The pope and his Jesuits have advised, supported, and directed Jeff Davis on the land, from the first gun shot at Fort Sumter by the rabid Roman Catholic Beauregard. They are helping him on the sea by guiding and supporting the rabid Roman Catholic pirate, Semmes, on the ocean.[1113]

President Lincoln told Chiniquy how the Vatican was the real cause of the Civil War:

> It is with the Southern leaders of this civil war as with the big and small wheels of our railroad cars. Those who ignore the laws of mechanics are apt to think that the large, strong, and noisy wheels they see are the motive power, but they are mistaken. The real motive power is not seen; it is noiseless and well concealed in the dark, behind its iron walls. The motive power are

the few well-concealed pails of water heated into steam, which is itself directed by the noiseless, small, but unerring engineer's finger. The common people see and hear the big noisy wheels of the Confederacy's cars: they call them Jeff Davis, Lee, Toombs, Beauregard, Demmes, etc., and they honestly think they are the motive power, the first cause of our troubles. But this is a mistake. The true motive power is secreted behind the thick walls of the Vatican, the colleges and schools of the Jesuits, the convents of the nuns, and the confessional boxes of Rome.[1114]

President Lincoln kept his knowledge of the Catholic conspiracy secret from the public because of his concern that to reveal it would start a bloody religious war. Lincoln told Chiniquy:

I pity the priests, the bishops and the monks of Rome in the United States, when the people realize that they are, in great part, responsible for the tears and the blood shed in this war. I conceal what I know, for if the people knew the whole truth, this war would turn into a religious war, and at once, take a tenfold more savage and bloody character. It would become merciless as all religious wars are. It would become a war of extermination on both sides. The Protestants of both the North and the South would surely unite to exterminate the priests and the Jesuits if they could hear what Professor Morse has said to me of the plots made in the very city of Rome to destroy this republic, and if they could learn how the priests, the nuns, and the monks, which daily land on our shores under the pretext of preaching their religion, instructing the people in their schools, taking care of the sick in the hospitals are nothing else but the emissaries of the pope, of Napoleon, and the despots of Europe, to undermine our institutions, alienate the hearts of our people from our Constitution, and our laws, destroy our schools, and prepare a reign of anarchy as they have done in Ireland, in Mexico, in Spain, and wherever there are any people who want to be free.[1115]

President Lincoln knew that the Roman Catholic Church is an uncompromising enemy of the United States. Lincoln explained to Chiniquy:

> The Mormon and the Jesuit priests are equally the uncompromising enemies of our Constitution and our laws; but the more dangerous of the two is the Jesuit - the Romish priest, for he knows better how to conceal his hatred under the mask of friendship and public good; he is better trained to commit the most cruel an diabolical deeds for the glory of God. *Abraham Lincoln, June 10, 1864.*[1116]

> For it is now evident to me, that, with very few exceptions, every priest and every true Roman Catholic is a determined enemy of liberty. *Abraham Lincoln, 1861.*[1117]

Not only was the Romish church responsible for the Civil War, but the Jesuits inspired and planned the assassination of Lincoln. Lincoln knew that he was marked for death by Rome and the Jesuits, and he knew it was only a matter of time before they succeeded. Lincoln told Chiniquy:

> So many plots have already been made against my life, that it is a real miracle that they have all failed, when we consider that the great majority of them were in the hands of the skillful Roman Catholic murderers, evidently trained by Jesuits.[1118]

The Roman Catholic Church was the moving force behind the assassination of Lincoln. Ninety miles northwest of St. Paul, Minnesota, sits the small village of St. Joseph. It was settled by Roman Catholics, and in 1865 it had a college seminary for the education of Roman Catholic priests. On April 14, 1865, not later than 6:30 p.m., F.A. Conwell, chaplain of the First Minnesota Regiment, and Horace P. Bennet, were told by J.H. Linneman that President Lincoln and Secretary Seward were assassinated. Linneman was the landlord of the village hotel and in charge of the Roman Catholic friary and purveyor for the Roman Catholic priests.[1119] What is notable about the announcement by Linneman is that Lincoln had not yet been assassinated. Lincoln was not assassinated until approximately 10:00 p.m. Washington, D.C. time, the night of April 14, 1865.

Accounting for the time difference between St. Joseph, Minnesota, and Washington, D.C., the announcement by Linneman of the assassination of Abraham Lincoln, which he clearly learned from the Roman Catholic priests, indicates that the Roman Catholic priests of St. Joseph knew about the assassination of President Lincoln more than two hours before it happened. Both Conwell and Bennet prepared sworn affidavits setting forth the above facts. Linneman refused to sign an affidavit but did provide written verification of the facts. Linneman claimed that he did not know from whom he heard that Lincoln was assassinated; many accounted that lapse of memory as the reason that he was still alive to make a written statement.

Charles Chiniquy explains how it could be that Mr. Linneman knew of the assassination of President Lincoln over two hours before it took place:

> Naturally every one asked: "How could such news spread? Where is the source of such a rumour?" Mr. Linneman, who is a Roman Catholic, tells us that though he heard this from many in his store, and in the streets, he does not remember the name of a single one who told him that. And when we hear this from him, we understand why he did not dare to swear upon it, and shrank from the idea of perjuring himself. For every one feels that his memory cannot be so poor as that, when he remembers so well the names of the two strangers, Messrs. Conwell and Bennett, to whom he had announced the assassination of Lincoln, just seventeen years before. But if the memory of Mr. Linneman is so deficient on that subject, we can help him, and tell him with mathematical accuracy:
>
> "You got the news from your priests of St. Joseph! The conspiracy which cost the life of the martyred President was prepared by the priests of Washington, in the house of Mary Surratt, No. 541, H. Street. The

priests of St. Joseph were often visiting Washington, and boarding, probably, at Mrs. Surrat's, as the priests of Washington were often visiting their brother priests at St. Joseph. Those priests of Washington were in daily communication with their co-rebel priests of St. Joseph; they were their intimate friends. There were no secrets among them, as there are no secrets among priests. They are the members of the same body, the branches of the same tree. The details of the murder, as the day selected for its commission, were as well known among the priests of St. Joseph, as they were among those of Washington. The death of Lincoln was such a glorious event for those priests! That infamous apostate, Lincoln, who, baptized in the Holy Church, had rebelled against her, broken his oath of allegiance to the Pope, taken the very day of his baptism, and lived the life of an apostate! That infamous Lincoln, who had dared to fight against the Confederacy of the South after the Vicar of Christ had solemnly declared that their cause was just, legitimate and holy! That bloody tyrant, that godless and infamous man, was to receive, at last, the just chastisement of his crimes, the 14th of April! What glorious news!"

How could the priests conceal such a joyful event from their bosom friend, Mr. Linneman? He was their confidential man: he was their purveyor: he was their right hand man among the faithful of St. Joseph. They thought that they would be guilty of a want of confidence in their bosom friend, if they did not tell him all about the glorious event of that great day. But, of course, they requested him not to mention their names, if he would spread the joyful news among the devoted Roman Catholics who almost exclusively, formed the people of St. Joseph. Mr. Linneman has honourably and faithfully kept his promise never to reveal their names, and today, we have in our hand, the authentic testimonies signed by him that, though some body, the 14th of April, told him that President Lincoln was assassinated, he does not know who told him that!

But there is not a man of sound judgment who will have any doubt about that fact, the 14th of April, 1865, the priests of Rome knew and circulated the death of Lincoln four hours before its occurrence in their Roman Catholic town of St. Joseph, Minnesota. **But they could not circulate it without knowing it, and they could not know it, without belonging to the band of conspirators who assassinated President Lincoln.**[1120] (bold emphasis added)

Furthermore, the transcripts of the trial of the Lincoln assassination published by Ben Pitman contain clear proof that the plot to assassinate Lincoln was born in Rome and nurtured in the house of Mary Surratt, 561 H Street, Washington, D.C. There was a continual flow of Catholic priests who would rendezvous at the house as the assassination was being plotted. The priests were the personal friends and father confessors of John Wilkes Booth, John Surratt, Mrs. and Miss Surratt. Most of the principal conspirators in the Lincoln assassination plot and escape of Booth were Roman Catholic.[1121] Even John Wilkes Booth, who was raised a Protestant, converted to the Catholic religion. Edwin Sherman reveals that Booth was admitted into the Catholic Church in a private sacramental ceremony officiated by Roman Catholic Archbishop Spaulding three weeks prior to the assassination.[1122] That secret ceremony, presided over by the archbishop, was to impress upon Booth his important role in a special mission for the Catholic Church. The unusual secrecy of the ceremony was necessary to conceal the hidden hand of Rome in the assassination. When Booth was killed, he was found to be wearing a superstitious Catholic medal around his neck; which was clear evidence of his religious affiliation with Rome.

Elaborate steps were taken by the Roman Church to assist John Surratt in his escape. John Surratt was in Washington on April 14, 1865, helping Booth prepare for the assassination, which was carried out by Booth that day. Catholic priest Charles Boucher stated under oath that only a few days after the murder, John Surratt was sent to him by another Catholic priest "Father Lapierre." Boucher kept him hidden until the end of July. From July to September he was hidden by Lapierre in Montreal. When traveling on the steamer "Montreal" from Montreal to Quebec, Lapierre kept Suratt under lock and key in his cabin. On September 15, 1865, Lappierre and Surratt took the ocean steamer "Peruvian" to Europe. The doctor of the "Peruvian," L.I.A. McMillan, stated under oath that Catholic priest Lapierre introduced Surratt to him under the alias "McCarthy," and that Lapierre kept Surratt locked in his state room on the ship until the ship departed for Europe. Lapierre was the canon of Bishop Bourget of Montreal. The canon of the Bishop is the Bishop's confidential man; he eats with him, assists him with his counsel and receives his advice in every step of his life. According to the laws of the Roman Catholic Church, the canons are to the bishop what arms are to the body.[1123]

Once spiriting Surratt out of Canada to Europe, where do you suppose Surratt was finally found? He was found under the alias "Watson" in the 9th company of the pope's Zouaves. When the United States found Surratt, the pope was forced to pretend to withdraw his protection of him. Surratt was arrested by papal authorities. However, the arrest was only for appearances. Surratt was able to "escape" before American authorities could take custody of him. The papal authorities alleged unconvincingly that Surratt made his "escape" from Valletri Prison by jumping twenty three feet to a narrow precipice, while he was under the guard of six men. One of the papal guards recounted that "[a]s soon as the Lieutenant heard of the escape he ordered the entire party on watch under arrest, *but I recollect clearly that a smile of satisfaction played around his lips at the time, and I sincerely believe that he was in secret sympathy with Surratt.*"[1124] (italics in original). Two weeks after making his incredible escape from Valletri Prison, Surratt was captured and brought back to the United States for trial.

The Roman Catholic Church continued to support Surratt after his arrest. The first jury pool of 26 was composed of 16 Roman Catholics. At that time only ten percent of the population was Roman Catholic. Clearly, the jury pool had been rigged, and it was thrown out; with a new jury picked.[1125] There was a constant overt presence of many Jesuit priests in attendance each day during the trial. It was alleged on good evidence that there was surreptitious financial support from the Catholic Church for defense witnesses and Surratt's lawyers.[1126]

The evidence of Surratt's guilt was overwhelming, but Chiniquy explained that there was a hung jury because three of the jurors were Catholic and they had been "told by their father confessors that the most holy father, the pope, Gregory VII, had solemnly and infallibly declared that 'the killing of an heretic was no murder.'"[1127] The U.S. Government was forced to release Surratt.

John Surratt died on April 21, 1916. His funeral was held on the following Monday from his home on 1004 West Lanvale Street, Baltimore, Maryland. "A solemn High Requiem Mass was offered at St. Pius' Church by the pastor, the Reverend John E. Dunn, and John Harrison Surratt was laid to rest in Bonnie Brae Cemetery."[1128] Former Catholic priest Emmitt McLoughlin states that a Solemn High Requiem Mass, which is officiated by three priests, is usually reserved for the funerals of bishops, priests, or nuns. McLoughlin states: "The Solemn High Requiem Mass is not offered for ordinary spies, any more than for the sons of ordinary bartenders. When it is chanted at the funeral services of a layman, it is a token of recognition and appreciation for exceptional devotion or distinguished service to the Church. It was done for John Harrison Surratt. It must have been deserved."[1129]

John Surratt was honored by the Roman Catholic Church with a Solemn High Requiem Mass. That Solemn High Requiem Mass is the seal of approval by Rome on his performance as a conspirator in the assassination of President Lincoln. The implications could not be clearer, especially when the Solemn High Requiem Mass for Surratt is juxtaposed against the fact that the pope never even sent a message of condolence after the death of President Lincoln. There is not found among the collection of official condolences sent to the U.S. Government upon the death of Abraham Lincoln from every civilized country in the world anything from the pope of Rome expressing his condolences. Recall, that the pope claims to be the head of the universal church on earth; yet he did not send one word of sympathy for the loss of the leader of the greatest nation in the world. The pope's unique status as a religious leader would require such a message as a matter of course. Not doing so was not simply a diplomatic *faux pas*. It was a tacit expression of approval of the assassination.

The pope's silence after President Lincoln's death speaks loudly, particularly in light of the fact that there is not a record of a single word of criticism, disapproval, or regret from anyone in the Roman Catholic hierarchy for the participation of its clerics and the other Romanists in the conspiracy to assassinate President Lincoln. In particular, none of the Catholic priests who rendered the substantial assistance to John Surratt in his escape were ever disciplined by the Vatican for their complicity in the worst crime of the century. Such papal inaction is in bold relief to the formal recognition by the pope of the sovereign independence of the Confederate States of America during the Civil War; the only world leader to do so. The final imprimatur of the Vatican on the assassination of President Lincoln came with the Solemn High Requiem Mass given by the Roman Catholic Church for one of the assassins.

John Surratt, conspirator in the assassination of President Lincoln, photographed after the assassination while hiding out under the protection of the pope near Rome as member of the Papal Zouaves. The Papal Zouaves were an infantry force formed by Pope Pius IX to defend the Papal States.

The politicians in Washington concealed from the American public the hand of the Roman Catholic Church in the assassination of Lincoln. Charles Chiniquy in *Fifty Years in the Church of Rome* explains:

> The great fatal mistake of the American government in the prosecution of the assassins of Abraham Lincoln was to cover up the religious element of that terrible drama. But this was carefully avoided throughout the trial. Not long after the execution of the murderers, I went, incognito, to Washington to begin my investigation. I was not a little surprised to see that not a single one of the government men would discuss it with me except after I had given my word of honor that I would never mention their names. I saw, with a profound distress, that the influence of Rome was almost supreme in Washington. I could not find a single statesman who would dare to face that nefarious influence and fight it down.[1130]

President Lincoln was surrounded by enemies who were in the camp of Rome. Indeed, the pope would not have orchestrated the assassination without knowing that thereafter he would then have his agents in control of the U.S. Government. Those secret agents of the pope revealed themselves as they subtly undermined the investigation of the assassination. For Example, although the U.S. Government had been informed of the exact location of John Surratt, the U.S. Department of State instructed its consul in Liverpool, England, on October 13, 1865, that "no action be taken in regard to the arrest of the supposed John H. Surratt, at present."[1131] That order was in response to information from the consul that Surratt was hiding under the protection of Catholic officials at the Oratory of the Catholic Church of the Holy Cross in Liverpool. Surratt could have easily been arrested at that time, and the consul was seeking instructions on how to proceed with the arrest.

Further, on November 24, 1865, Secretary of War Edwin Stanton, under the authorization of President Andrew Johnson, revoked the reward for John Surratt, thus reducing the chances of public cooperation in apprehending him. Johnson and Stanton knew when they revoked the reward that Surratt was in Europe and that he planned on fleeing to Rome under the protection of the pope. Surratt fled to Rome, as planned. A year later Surratt was discovered hiding among the Papal Zouaves. Surratt would have gotten away and been safely protected by the papacy, but for the fact that he was discovered by an acquaintance from the U.S., Henri de Ste. Marie, who had also joined the Papal Zouaves. Ste. Marie first saw Surratt among the Papal Zouaves in the small town of Velletri, which is approximately 25 miles south of Rome. Ste. Marie recognized Surratt, who was going by the name Watson, and confronted him about his true identity. Surratt confessed to his true identity and to his

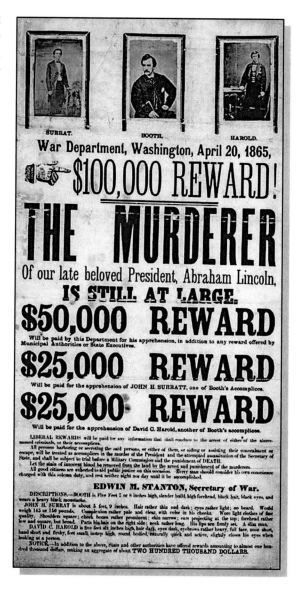

involvement in the Lincoln assassination. Ste. Marie submitted a sworn affidavit to the U.S. Minister to the Vatican, Rufus King, who in turn informed the Secretary of State that Surratt was hiding out among the Papal Zouaves. With Surratt's location widely known within the U.S. Government, the high officials in Washington could not continue to surreptitiously abet Surratt. The pope was forced to withdrew his protection; Surratt was then finally apprehended. Among other things, Ste. Marie stated the following in his sworn affidavit:

> He [Surratt] says he can get money in Rome at any time. I believe he is protected by the clergy and that the murder is the result of a deep laid plot, not only against the life of President Lincoln but against the existence of the republic, as we are aware that priesthood and royalty are and always have been opposed to liberty. That such men as Surratt, Booth, Weichmann, and others, should, of their own accord, plan and execute the infernal plot which resulted in the death of President Lincoln, is impossible. There are others behind the curtain who have pulled the strings to make these scoundrels act.[1132]

When he first met Ste. Marie years earlier in Maryland, Surratt expressed his successionist sentiments, with which Ste. Marie did not agree. They went their separate ways, and Ste. Marie joined the Union Army. Apparently, Ste. Marie was a Roman Catholic, however, he did not seem to completely adhere to Catholicism. His affidavit indicates that he had a negative opinion of the Vatican. He had formed an opinion that the plot to assassinate President Lincoln ran deep into the recesses of the Vatican. Ste. Marie viewed the assassination of President Lincoln as part of a Catholic plot against the U.S. Republic.

Ste. Marie's strident condemnation of the Roman clerics for their involvement in the plot suggests that he was not a tried and true member of the Papal Zouaves. His seeming status as an ardent defender of the Catholic Church as a member of the Zouaves does not match his statements in opposition to the tyranny of Rome. A member of the Zouaves heard Ste. Marie, upon his arrival at his battalion, persistently asking questions about whether any Americans were in the Papal Zouaves.[1133] That suggests that Ste. Marie joined the Papal Zouaves because he was on a secret mission to track down Surratt. He probably had information that Surratt could be found among the Papal Zouaves. Whether Ste. Marie was on a personal mission (perhaps seeking the advertised reward) or was supported by a U.S. Government agency is not clear. It is common for government agencies to maintain the confidentiality of their secret assets and informants.

Ste. Marie is an example of a courageous Roman Catholic who put the love for his country before his allegiance to the Church of Rome. There are many in the Roman Church like him, who are disgusted with the corruption of the Catholic Church. Most Catholics, however, are paralyzed from acting, by the superstitions of the Catholic Church. The remedy is the gospel of Jesus Christ. The gospel must be spread to all, so that those precious souls can be reached and freed from their spiritual bondage. That is the fervent prayer of this author and the primary purpose of this book.

So disgusted were members of the U.S. Congress with the deliberately dilatory conduct of the executive branch in capturing John Surratt, that the Judiciary Committee for the House of Representatives investigated the matter and on March 2, 1867, issued a report, which concluded that "due diligence in the arrest of John H. Surratt, was not exercised by the Executive Department of the government."[1134]

The congressional committee stated that the testimony given by the Secretary of State, the Secretary of War, and others before the committee "does not, in the opinion of your committee, excuse the great delay in arresting a person charged with complicity in the assassination of the late President Abraham Lincoln."[1135] The congressional committee found "[t]hat from the reception of the communications of [the U.S. Resident Minister to the Vatican] Mr. [Rufus] King, August 8th, 1866, to October 16th, 1866, no steps were taken, either to identify or procure the arrest of Surratt, then known to be in the Military service of the Pope."[1136]

Early on, the U.S. government had information of the exact location of Surratt when he first arrived in Liverpool, England. Surratt was known to be hiding out at the Oratory of the Roman Catholic Church of the Holy Cross. Congress determined that, while knowing this, "the Executive did not send any detective or agent to Liverpool to identify Surratt, or trace his movements, notwithstanding there was ample opportunity for doing so."[1137] Indeed, it was much worse, the U.S. Department of State issued orders to its consul in Liverpool telling him to take no action to arrest Surratt. Such conduct can only be described as aiding and abetting Surratt's escape.

What possible excuse could any member of the executive

branch have for telling the American consul in Liverpool that "no action should be taken to arrest of the supposed John Surratt?" Congress wanted to know the answer to that question. They called witnesses from the executive branch to explain themselves. The Second Assistant Secretary of State, William Hunter, was the Acting Secretary of State who sent the "no action" dispatch. Hunter testified before Congress that he sent the "no action" order to Liverpool because he was told by the Chief Clerk of the Department of State, Robert S. Chew, that Judge Advocate Holt and Secretary of War Stanton were of the opinion that "the arrest of Surratt should not be made at that time."[1138]

Robert Chew, in turn, testified that he showed Secretary Stanton the September 27, 1865, dispatch (#538) from the consul in Liverpool indicating that the consul had taken an affidavit from a witness who knew Surratt and that Surratt was expected to arrive in Liverpool within the next day or two. The witness was clearly well acquainted with Surratt, as he stated in his affidavit that he expected Surratt to visit him in Liverpool.[1139] Chew testified that Stanton told him upon reading the dispatch that "he did not think it necessary that any action should be taken in the case at present."[1140]

Three (3) days after sending the first dispatch (#538), the U.S. Consul in Liverpool sent another dispatch (#539) on September 30, 1865, to Secretary of State Seward, giving Surratt's exact location in Liverpool at the oratory of the Roman Catholic Church of the Holy Cross. While the testimony of Stanton involved his review of dispatch #538, the State Department also had in its possession dispatch #539. In fact, when issuing the order to take no action to arrest Surratt, in his October 13, 1865, dispatch, Acting Secretary of State William Hunter stated in the body of the dispatch that "your despatches from 533 to 541, inclusive, have been received."[1141]

Secretary Stanton disputed Robert Chew's account and denied that he ever told Chew that "he did not think it necessary that any action should be taken in the case at present," as Chew testified.[1142] Stanton testified that he did not give any instructions to Chew at the time Chew showed him the dispatch. Stanton stated that he told Chew he would "consider the matter, and if any instructions occurred to me which I ought to give they would be given before the next steamer. My opinion or advice was not asked by Mr. Chew at that time."[1143] Stanton testified that he was later called upon to give instructions, to which he stated that he "expressed the opinion that identity should be established before an arrest was made."[1144] Stanton told Congress that he did not instruct Chew not to take action to arrest Surratt. Stanton claimed that Mr. Chew "certainly mistook what I said."[1145]

Secretary Stanton's story was simply not credible, and Congress did not buy it for a minute. Congress ruled that there was no excuse for the delay in arresting Surratt. Stanton's testimony regarding the "no action" instructions should not be viewed in a vacuum. It was part of a pattern of conduct by Stanton that seemed designed to allow Surratt to achieve his goal of getting to Rome. For example, his "no action" instructions were followed five weeks later by his revocation of the reward for the arrest of Surratt.

The reward was posted on April 20, 1865, and revoked seven months later, on November 24, 1865. What was Stanton's explanation for revoking the reward for Surratt? Incredibly, Stanton testified that he revoked the reward because he was satisfied that Surratt was no longer in the United States, and if he were arrested overseas it was likely to be by a foreign government official. Stanton testified that he did not think that a foreign official should claim the reward. He further stated that if the reward was withdrawn it would make Surratt think that the U.S. government had given up the chase and return to the United Sates to be arrested.[1146]

Stanton's explanation is simply ridiculous. Stanton was one of the most intelligent lawyers in the country. Indeed, Stanton's intelligence and skill as a lawyer was the reason that President Lincoln selected him to be the U.S. Secretary of War. Stanton knew when he testified that it is an established precedent in the law that if a public official apprehends a suspect while in the performance of his official duties, he is ineligible to claim any reward for the capture.[1147] Government officials are ineligible for rewards, because such officials should not need further pecuniary incentives to perform a job they are already paid to do.

That is not to say that Stanton could not violate that principle in his discretion, which he did on several occasions. For example, he gave a substantial portion of the reward for capturing Booth to the head of the U.S. Government Intelligence Service, Lafayette Baker, and to his subordinate, Colonel Everton Conger. Conger also received a quick promotion and was later appointed a federal judge. Those arguably improper payments were probably bribes to keep them quiet about what they knew. We will read later that they knew plenty.

The strangest reward was given to Major James O'Beirne. He received $3,000 of the reward money and a promotion to the rank of general by Stanton. O'Beirne, to the untrained eye, seemingly did nothing to earn the money or promotion. Mark Hageman explains the mystery: "Upon closer inspection, perhaps it was where O'Beirne was stationed in Maryland that counted most [for his promotion and reward]. His men were guarding the very escape route through Maryland which Booth took, one where the assassin galloped past outpost after outpost without being challenged, stopped, or questioned."[1148] Apparently, Stanton was rewarding Major O'Beirne for a job well-done.

While Stanton violated the general principle that government officials are ineligible for government rewards, that does not mean that he could not stand on the principle to refuse to grant a reward to a foreign official. He could certainly have done that without revoking the reward. Stanton's revocation of the reward for Surratt's arrest had only the effect of removing a pecuniary motive for persons who were not government officials. Those are the very persons the U.S. government still needed to encourage to assist in Surratt's apprehension. The reward revocation had the effect of making it more likely that Surratt would get away. The reason Stanton gave Congress for revoking the reward was not based in reality, and Stanton knew it.

If the reason given by Stanton for the reward revocation was false, that means that Stanton had some nefarious ulterior motive for revoking the reward. Furthermore, Congress found that when Stanton was informed by his consul in Montreal that Surratt would soon take a ship to Liverpool, Stanton was being purposely dilatory when he made no effort to send a detective to pursue Surratt. His decision not to pursue Surratt must be viewed in the face of an October 25, 1865, dispatch from U.S. Consul to Montreal, John Potter, pleading for the government to send a detective to Liverpool to apprehend Surratt. Potter stated: "If an officer could proceed to England in this ship, I have no doubt but that Surratt's arrest might be effected."[1149]

Stanton's alleged strategy of lulling Surratt back to the United States by revoking the reward, thus making Surratt think that the government had given up the chase is absurd. When Stanton revoked the reward he had already been informed that Surratt planned on traveling to Rome to hide out under the protection of the pope. It makes no sense to revoke a reward for the apprehension of a murderer after only seven months, especially one that is aimed at the apprehension of an assassin of the President of the United States. It is silly to suggest that upon learning that the reward was revoked that Surratt would think that the coast was clear for his return to the United States.

Stanton sent no detectives to apprehend Surratt, he sent orders that officials in England should take no steps to arrest Surratt, and he revoked the reward for Surratt's arrest. He did all of those things at a time when he knew exactly where Surratt was located. He then gave incredible reasons for his actions and disputed the sworn testimony of those that contradicted his account. Stanton's conduct suggests that he was using his position as Secretary of State to aid and abet the Vatican in its efforts to secure Surratt's escape. There is a word to describe the conduct of a person who adheres to the enemies of the United States and gives aide and comfort to them—TREASON.[1150]

Congress not only condemned the dilatory conduct of the Andrew Johnson administration in apprehending Surratt, it forced President Johnson to break off diplomatic ties with the Vatican. Congress saw clearly the involvement of the Vatican in the assassination of President Lincoln. Consequently, Congress responded on February 28, 1867, by passing a law providing that no federal funds could be used to maintain a diplomatic mission with the Vatican.

Congress passed the legislation breaking diplomatic ties with the Vatican before it issued its report condemning the shameful behavior of the executive branch. Andrew Johnson was not going to break off diplomatic ties with the Vatican, so Congress did it for him. Cutting off funding forced President Andrew Johnson to withdraw his minister to the Vatican, Rufus King, and caused the U.S. to break off diplomatic relations with the Holy See. Diplomatic relations were not restored between the U.S. and the Holy See until 117 years later, under the Ronald Reagan administration in 1984.[1151]

Conspirators being hung for the assassination of President Lincoln. From left to right: Mary Surratt, Lewis Powell (a/k/a Payne), David Harold, and David Atzerodt. Three of the other conspirators, Michael O'Laughlen, Samuel Arnold, and Dr. Samuel Mudd were sentenced to life terms in prison. Edmund Spangler was sentenced to a prison term of six years. O'Laughlen died in prison of yellow fever in 1867. Despite the triumph of justice in the military trial, Rome's influence still ran deep in the U.S. Government. In 1869, President Andrew Johnson pardoned Arnold, Mudd, and Spangler. Johnson and Stanton had previously (November 1865) revoked the reward for the arrest of John Surratt and other conspirators. Despite Johnson's and Stanton's efforts to impede John Surratt's capture, Surratt was ultimately arrested.

Secretary of War Stanton had an animus toward Lincoln. Durbin Blakeslee recounts one episode, where in an unguarded moment Stanton allowed his feelings toward Lincoln to come out. The incident displays Stanton's animosity toward Lincoln and at the same time the sublime character and good nature of President Lincoln:

> One day Stanton sharply rebuked Judge Advocate General Joseph Holt for a mission he had undertaken on behalf of the President, saying: "Well, all I have to say is, we've got to get rid of that baboon at the White House!" When the story was repeated to the President, he refused to even consider Stanton's comment an insult, saying "that is no insult, it an expression of opinion; and what troubles me most about it is that Stanton said it and Stanton is usually right."[1152]

In the end, Stanton accomplished his desire "to get rid of that baboon at the White House." The apparent collusion by high officials in the executive branch of government with Rome culminated in President Johnson's 1869 pardons of the convicted conspirators, Samuel Arnold, Dr. Samuel Mudd, and Edmund Spangler.

Compare the pardon by Johnson of Arnold, Mudd, and Spangler, with Johnson's refusal for a reprieve of the death sentences of the other prisoners. Edwin Sherman explains the inconsistency. He alleges that the chief conspirators in the assassination, which included Johnson, orchestrated a swift execution of the prisoners to ensure that no further information would come out that might lead to the real power behind the assassination.[1153] The conspirators were ordered to be hung within 48 hours of their death sentences. Strict orders were given that the condemned prisoners were only to be attended by their spiritual advisors, no newspaper reporters would be allowed into the cells of the condemned prisoners, and that no further information or any confession or statement of any kind should be elicited from the prisoners. It is a well known fact that a prisoners sentenced to death will betray their former comrades in crime in an attempt to save their necks or delay the execution. That suspicious order of cutting off all communication with the condemned prisoners was clearly designed to conceal any revelations that might assist in capturing other unknown conspirators. President Johnson refused a request by Mary Surratt's lawyer to grant a reprieve of the her death sentence, and after doing that he (Johnson) gave imperative orders that he would receive no one on the day of the execution, thus ensuring that he would not be importuned to interfere with the executions. Furthermore, the Jesuit priests made no efforts to seek a reprieve for their penitents. It was only after Mary Surratt's execution that Catholic priests spoke in defense of Mary Surratt. The conspirators behind the scenes simply could not take the chance that the condemned prisoners might regret their actions, decide to unburden their consciences before the world, and say something that would lead to the secret personages and organizations behind the assassination.

It seems that Johnson had a habit of granting pardons to the enemies of the Republic. Albert Pike, the "Sovereign Grand Commander of the Ancient and Accepted Scottish Rite of Freemasonry of the Southern Jurisdiction, U.S.A.," was a war criminal who fled to Canada to avoid prosecution; he was reportedly convicted *in absentia* for treason. However, on April 22, 1866, Pike was granted a pardon by President Andrew Johnson. The next day Pike allegedly visited the president in the White House.

General Gordon Granger was present at another 1867 meeting between Pike and Johnson after the initiation of impeachment proceedings against Johnson. General Granger testified before Congress that Johnson and Pike discussed Masonry and that he understood from the conversation that Pike was Johnson's superior in Masonry. Shortly thereafter, on June 20, 1867, a delegation of Masons granted Johnson the fourth through the 32nd degrees of the Scottish Rite of Masonry in his bedroom at the White House.[1154]

Johnson's Masonic connections paid off. A little known fact about the impeachment vote at the Senate trial of President Johnson is that Senator Edmund G. Ross' "not guilty" vote decided the matter. Who was Senator Ross? Darrell L. Aldridge who is a "Worshipful Master" Freemason, writing for the Louisiana Lodge of Research reveals that "in 1859 Edmund G. Ross had been made a master mason in Topeka Lodge No. 12."[1155] Aldridge refers to President Johnson as "Brother Andrew Johnson," thus indicating his worthiness as a Mason in distress to get help from a brother Mason, in this case, Edmund G. Ross. Freemason Aldridge describes the vote of Masonic Senator Ross during the impeachment trial of Masonic President Johnson as follows:

The impeachment trial of Bro. Andrew Johnson was a nasty affair from beginning to end. ... It was a dramatic moment in the Senate of the United States on May 16, 1886, when Bro. Salmon P. Chase, Chief Justice of the Supreme Court, presiding at the trial called for the final vote. "How say you Senator Ross, is the respondent Andrew Johnson, President of the United States guilty or not guilty of a high misdemeanor as charged in this article of impeachment?" There was no sound, hardly a movement throughout the Senate chamber, as Ross rose to cast the final vote. [Out of a total number of 54 Senators], the count stood at thirty-five for conviction [thirty-six were needed], eighteen not guilty – Ross's vote would be decisive. Against the wall was a chart depicting how each of the Senators had voted. Saying "not guilty" Ross sat down. With these two words his political career ended. He returned to Kansas where he and his family were socially ostracized and ignored. By practicing the cardinal virtues of Masonry – fortitude, prudence, temperance, and justice, a great Mason chose to sacrifice a career in the Senate. His one vote was very important.[1156]

James A. Marples, another Freemason writing on behalf of *The Sottish Rite Journal,* lauds Ross for his courage in voting against the impeachment of his brother Mason. "In his lifetime, Bro. Edmund G. Ross had taken many oaths and obligations to do the right thing: first, as a Mason; second, as a U.S. Senator; third, as a U.S. Senator in the capacity as a juror in the impeachment trial of President Johnson."[1157] The Masonic oath mentioned by Marples includes the obligation to help a brother Mason, in this case, President Johnson. The *Handbook of Masonry* states that a Mason must conceal the crimes of a fellow Mason.[1158] The Masonic oath includes an obligation to commit perjury, if it is necessary to protect a brother Mason.

Ross had no choice in the matter. He was bound by his Masonic blood oath to vote "not guilty" on the impeachment charges against a brother Mason, regardless of whether that brother Mason was in the right or in the wrong. That irrelevance of justice under the Masonic oath is illustrated by the Royal Arch, or Seventh Degree oath, which states, in pertinent part: "I furthermore promise and swear, that I will assist a Companion Royal Arch Mason when I see him engaged in any difficulty, and will espouse his cause so far as to extricate him from the same, whether he be right or wrong."[1159]

On the day of the assassination of President Lincoln, April 14, 1865, John Wilkes Booth, stopped at the Kirkwood where Vice President Andrew Johnson was staying. Booth left a message in the box of William Browning, who was Johnson's secretary. Browning found the note in his box when he returned at approximately 5:00 p.m. that day. The note stated: "Don't wish to disturb you; are you at home? J. Wilkes Booth."

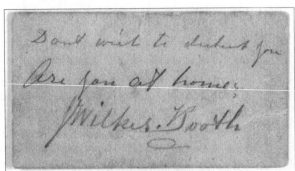

Actual note written By John Wilkes Booth and left for Vice President Andrew Johnson on the day President Lincoln was assassinated.

Abraham Lincoln's widow, Mary Todd Lincoln, thought the note left by Booth for Johnson implicated Johnson in the assassination of her beloved husband. She wrote a letter on March 15, 1866, to her friend, Sally Ore, wherein she expressed her suspicions about Johnson:

> My own intense misery has been augmented by the same thought—that, that miserable inebriate Johnson, had cognizance of my husband's death—Why, was that card of Booth found in his box, some acquaintance certainly existed—I have been deeply impressed, with the harrowing thought, that he, had an understanding with the conspirators & they knew their man. Did not Booth say, "There is one thing, he would not tell." There is said, to be honor, among thieves. No one ever heard of Johnson, regretting my sainted husband's death, he never wrote me a line of condolence, and

behaved in the most brutal way. ... As sure, as you & I live, Johnson, had some hand, in all this.[1160]

What is significant is that her suspicions of Johnson were not based alone upon the note left by Booth. She also cited Johnson's "brutal" behavior, and his failure to show the least bit of commiseration for her loss. It is astounding that the Vice President of the United States, who is suddenly elevated to President by the assassination of that President would not at least write a letter of condolence to the President's widow. That is very suspicious indeed, particularly in light of the fact that his elevation to President was only on account of the Assassination of Abraham Lincoln.

Clearly, Booth left that message for Johnson, knowing that he was going to assassinate President Lincoln that day. Booth's intent seemed to be to purposely implicate Johnson in the assassination. If Johnson was not involved in the assassination, it would mean that Booth was being malicious. That does not make sense. It is more likely that Johnson was involved in the conspiracy and Booth was instructed to leave the note to Johnson by the masterminds of plot. Why would they do such a thing? The following is speculation by this author. It could be that the conspirators could not trust Johnson, and they had to have something to hold over him to ensure that he kept his end of the bargain. His most important role would be to use the high office of the President of the United States to limit the investigation, thus ensuring the command and control of the conspiracy would not be implicated. There was too much to lose if Johnson failed to act on their behalf. Johnson was a notoriously unreliable drunk. He was the weak link. But he was the Vice President, and willing to get rid of President Lincoln to ascend to the Presidency. Johnson was unreliable, but they were stuck with him.

If Johnson double-crossed them, it would be too late after a double-cross to repair the damage. They had to make Johnson feel vulnerable. The note was designed as a thread; Johnson would be in constant fear that if that thread was pulled it would unravel Johnson's involvement in the conspiracy. The note was designed to keep Johnson in a state of concern for his own well being. The note was little evidence in and of itself. Its purpose, however, was not evidence; its purpose was as a phantom to scare Johnson into obedience out of fear that if he did not keep up his end of the conspiracy, the Catholic assets in the government and press would retaliate and reveal more damning evidence that would expose Johnson. The Catholic assets gave little notice to the note, since Johnson apparently kept his end of the bargain.

There were other strange occurrences on and after the assassination. After Booth was killed, his diary was seized from his body and turned over to Stanton. Before it was given to Stanton, Lafayette Baker, who was the head of the Union Intelligence Service, counted the exact number of pages in the presence of Colonel Everton J. Conger. Baker studied the diary at great length and took notes. He then had Colonel Conger accompany him as a witness as Baker delivered the diary directly to Stanton. Clearly, Baker did not trust Stanton, and as the intelligence chief, he was in a position to have solid evidence about Stanton's untrustworthiness. Baker's counting and confirming the number of the pages before turning it over to Stanton suggests that he saw something in the diary that gave him reason to suspect Stanton would try to tear out certain pages. Stanton had possession of the diary from that time until it was next seen. A year later that diary would implicate Stanton in the conspiracy, not by what it said, but by what it did not say. Mark Hageman explains:

> In 1867, the Attorney General attempted to build a case against John Surratt. He was informed that Stanton was in possession of Booth's diary and he asked that the Secretary of War turn it over. Stanton refused. The Attorney General insisted, officially ordering him to do so. The diary Stanton relinquished was missing eighteen pages. The Attorney General wanted to know where the missing pages had gone. Stanton said he had turned over the diary just as he had received it. Lafayette Baker and Colonel Conger were called in. Both reluctantly stated that the missing pages were present when they turned over Booth's diary to Stanton. What information did those pages contain?[1161]

Baker knew what the diary said, but dead men tell no tales. Baker died 18 months later. A modern-day professor at Indiana State University, Ray A. Neff, used an atomic absorption spectrophotometer to analyze several hairs from Baker's corpse. Professor Neff concluded that Baker died of Arsenic poisoning. Baker's brother in law, Wally Pollack, who worked for the U.S. War Department, brought Baker beer on regular intervals, prior to Baker's death. Those beer deliveries were indicated in Baker's wife's detailed diary. The time frame of the deliveries corresponded to the gradually elevated levels of toxins in Baker's hair samples.

Emanuel Hertz reveals a strange event in 1923 that further confirms that the conspiracy to assassinate President Lincoln ran to the highest levels of the U.S. Government. Before Abraham Lincoln's son, Robert Todd Lincoln, turned over President Lincoln's papers to the Library of Congress, he purged many of the papers that implicated high cabinet officials in treason. Hertz explains what he was told by a friend of the then deceased Horace G. Young, President of the Delaware & Hudson Railroad:

> "Horace G. Young was an intimate friend of Robert T. Lincoln, and he and Mr. Lincoln were accustomed to spend part of each summer together. A few years before Mr. [Robert Todd] Lincoln's death, Mr. Young went as usual to visit him at Mr. Lincoln's home in Manchester, Vermont. On arriving at the house he found Mr. Lincoln in a room surrounded by a number of large boxes and with many papers scattered about the floor, and with the ashes of many burnt papers visible in the fireplace. Mr. Young asked Mr. Lincoln what he was doing, and Mr. Lincoln replied that he was destroying some of the private papers and letters of his father, Abraham Lincoln. Mr. Young at once remonstrated with Mr. Lincoln and said that no one had any right to destroy such papers, Mr. Lincoln least of all. Mr. Lincoln replied that he did not intend to continue his destruction since **the papers he was destroying contained the documentary evidence of the treason of a member of Lincoln's Cabinet, and that he thought it was best for all that such evidence be destroyed.** Mr. Young immediately visited Dr. [Nicholas Murray] Butler, who was in town, and told him what Robert T. Lincoln was doing. Dr. Butler promptly called on Robert T. Lincoln and argued and

pleaded with him and finally prevailed upon him to desist and place the papers where they would be safe in order that they might be preserved for posterity."

Dr. Butler's own account (in a letter to the writer [Emanuel Hertz], dated November 5, 1937) of the incident is as follows: "It was Mr. Horace G. Young, then at Manchester, Vermont, who brought to my attention within a few hours after I arrived from Europe the fact that Robert Lincoln was about to burn a collection of his father's papers, and that he, Mr. Young, had been unable to persuade him not to do so. I went immediately to his house and had a most earnest discussion of the whole subject with Mr. Lincoln in his library. I went so far as to insist that the papers did not belong to him, since his father had belonged to the country for half a century and the papers therefore belonged to the country also. Robert Lincoln finally acceded to my urgent and insistent request for the preservation of the papers and sent them under seal to the Library of Congress, there to remain unopened for fifty years.

"Subsequently, Senator Beveridge, then engaged on his Life of Lincoln, having heard of the incident, asked me to procure for him opportunity to examine these papers. I have the correspondence with Robert Lincoln in which he declined flatly to grant Beveridge's request."[1162] (emphasis added)

43 The Antichrist Targets the USA

The political intrigue of the pope during the Civil War and his assassination of President Lincoln reveal the antichrist conspiracy against the United States. The papacy has not given up on its plan for world religious conquest. The United States is an impediment to the plans of the papacy for world dominion.

No European power has the military might to conquer the United States. How then do they expect to destroy this great country? In 1835, Samuel Morse, contributing inventor of the single wire telegraph and co-developer of the "Morse Code," revealed one of the strategies of the Vatican being that of subversion rather than violent conquest. The Catholic church has a long term plan to flood the United States with Roman Catholic immigrants.[1163]

Samuel Morse stated: "The ratio of increase of Popery is the exact ratio of decrease of civil liberty."[1164] That is because the authoritarianism of the papacy is incompatible with the concept of God-given individual rights. Cardinal Giuseppe Melchior Sarto (later elevated to Pope Pius X) stated that "when one speaks of the Pope, it is not necessary to examine, but to obey ... no rights must be set up against the rights of the Holy Father."[1165]

Samuel Morse revealed the Catholic political conspiracy against the United States under the cloak of a religious mission in his 1835 work, *Foreign Conspiracy Against the Liberties of the United States*.[1166]

The liberty enjoyed in the United States by its republican form of government is viewed as a direct threat to the despotic governments of the world including the Vatican.

What threat does the United States pose to the tyrannies of the world? Samuel Morse answered that question as follows:

> Is it asked, Why should the Holy Alliance feel interested in the destruction of transatlantic liberty? I answer, the silent but powerful and increasing influence of our institutions on Europe, is reason enough. The example alone of prosperity which we exhibit in such strong contrast to the enslaved, priest-ridden, tax burdened despotisms of the old world, is sufficient to keep those countries in perpetual agitation. How can it be otherwise? Will a sick man, long despairing of cure, learn that there is a remedy for him, and not desire to procure it? Will one born to think a dungeon his natural home, learn through his grated bars, that man may be free and not struggle to obtain his liberty? And what do the people of Europe behold in this country? They witness the successful experiment of a free government; a government for the *people*; without rulers *de jure divino,* (by divine right:) having no hereditary privileged classes; a government exhibiting good order and obedience to law, without an armed police and secrecy tribunals; a government out of debt; a people industrious, enterprising, thriving in all their interests; without monopolies; a people religious without an establishment; moral and honest without the terrors of the confessional or the inquisition; a people not harmed by the uncontrolled liberty of the press, and freedom of opinion; a people that read what they please, and think, and judge, and act for themselves; a people enjoying the most unbounded security of person and property; among whom domestic conspiracies are unknown where the poor and rich have equal justice; a people social and hospitable; exerting all their energies in schemes of public and private benefit without other control than

mutual forbearance. A government so contrasted in all points with absolute governments, must, and does engage the intense solicitude, both of the rulers and people of the old world. Every revolution that has occurred in Europe for the last half century has been in a greater or less degree the consequences of our own glorious revolution. The great political truths there promulgated to the world, are the deed of the disorders and conspiracies, and revolutions of Europe, from the first French revolution, down to the present time. They are the throes of the internal life, breaking the bands of darkness with which superstition and despotism have hitherto bound the nations struggling into the light of a new age. Can despotism know all this, and not feel it necessary to do something to counteract the evil?[1167]

In 1855 the Duke of Richmond admitted to the conspiracy against the United States, which he explained thusly:

[The United States] will be destroyed, it ought not, and will not be permitted to exist . . . and so long as it exists, no prince will be safe upon the throne; and the sovereigns of Europe are aware of it, and they have determined upon its destruction, and come to an understanding upon this subject, and have decided on the means to accomplish it; and they will eventually succeed by subversion rather than conquest. As the low and surplus population of the different nations of Europe will be carried into that country, it is and will be a receptacle for the bad and disaffected population of Europe, when they are not wanted for soldiers, or to supply the navies, and the European governments will favor such course. This will create a surplus and majority of low population, who are so very easily excited and they will bring with them their principles, and in nine cases out of ten, adhere to their ancient and former governments, laws, manners, and religion, and will transmit them to their posterity, and in many cases propagate them among the natives. These men will become citizens and by the Constitution and laws will be invested with the right of suffrage. The different grades of society will then be created by the elevation of a few and by degrading many, and thus a heterogeneous population will then be formed, speaking different languages, and of different religions and sentiments, and to make them act, think, and feel alike in political affairs, will be like mixing oil and water; hence discord, dissension, anarchy and civil war will ensue, and some popular individual will assume the government and restore order, and the sovereigns of Europe, the immigrants, and many of the natives will sustain him.[1168]

Keep in mind that the above quote was written in 1855. Since then, the Jesuits and their fellow popish conspirators have used that very strategy to gradually corrupt the government of the United States to act more like the tyrannies of the world. As explained by Dr. John Robbins:

Roman Catholic economic thought, as developed by the popes in their encyclicals and by Roman Church-State councils, has been a contributor to if not the only source of, several forms of anticapitalist political and economic organization during the long hegemony of the Roman Church-State. Among these forms are
(1) feudalism and guild socialism in Europe during the Middle Ages;
(2) fascism in Italy, Spain, Portugal, Croatia, and Latin America in the twentieth century;
(3) Nazism in Germany in the twentieth century;
(4) interventionism and redistributive state in the West, including United States in the twentieth century; and
(5) liberation theology in Latin America and Africa in the twentieth century.[1169]

Austria's Prince Metternich (1773-1859) was both Chancellor and Foreign Minister of the Austrian Empire, under Austrian Emperors Francis I and Ferdinand I. Prince Metternich was grievously concerned with the increased liberty brought about by the Protestant theology that guided the principles of government in the United States. Leo Hirrel states that "[v]isitors to Vienna reported that he spent many hours studying maps of the United Stated in an effort to decide how to handle the threat."[1170] Prince Metternich soon directed a grand conspiracy aimed at subverting American liberties. The primary method of subversion was mass immigration of Catholics into the U.S., subsidized by the Austrian Leopold Society. Another thing that the Leopold Society did was fund the immigration of Catholic priests into the United States.

Why would a foreign diplomat care to increase the population of Catholics and spread the religious influence of the Catholic Church? Prince Metternich did not want to spread the Catholic religion because he was a religious man. Rather, he wanted to spread the Catholic political influence, because he knew that the spread of the Catholic religion would work to undermine the political and civil liberties of the people. The Catholic priests were being sent on a subversive political mission.

Why would a European diplomat care about the liberties of a country across an ocean on another continent? Because, Metternich knew that the existence of the freedoms in the United States would cause dissatisfaction within his country with their more limited freedoms. The Austrian emperor would be forced to limit oppression in order to ensure there was not a rebellion. Protestant Christianity was a clear and present danger to both monarchies and the Roman Catholic Church. Indeed, monarchy is the very nature of the Roman Catholic Church. The Vatican officially describes itself as follows: "Vatican City State is governed as an absolute monarchy. The Head of State is the Pope who holds full legislative, executive and judicial powers."[1171]

Once the population of Catholics increased, they became a potent political force under the control of the Roman Catholic Church. The Catholic vote could be promised to an unprincipled politician. The politician, thereafter, was under the complete control of Rome. The *Quarterly Christian Spectator* warned its readers of the impending danger: "The system is so well arranged in some parts of the country that a bishop or priest can state before an election what number of people he can bring to the polls for the person he advocates."[1172] The *New York Observer*, under the editorship of Sidney Morse, pointed out that while the voters were under the control of priests, those priests were in turn under the control of the papacy, which meant that our elections were under the influence of a foreign power. "Let an emergency arise, in which his Holiness at Rome shall think it worth his while to interfere, and swift as a telegraphic dispatch and unseen signal will be made across the ocean, and repeated over our land; all factions and subdivisions among Romanists in America will come to the polls in a solid phalanx."[1173]

The flood of Catholics, bringing with them their superstitious religion and their blind obedience to Papal political instructions, did not go unnoticed by patriotic liberty-loving Americans. They could see clearly the increased influence of Rome over the elections of public officials by guaranteeing to politicians a Catholic block of votes. Native Protestants realized that in order to stem this threat to their liberties, they must also vote as a single block. Protestant Americans formed the Native American Party (1845-1855) and the American Party (1855-1860). The American Party's Presidential Nominee in 1856 was former U.S. President Millard Fillmore. That brief period of Protestant American political reaction to the influx of Catholic immigrants and their block voting in elections is commonly known as the "Know-Nothing" movement. The movement only lasted approximately 15 years and then died out. The United States, with few exceptions, has ever since been guided by politicians who owe their political success to their allegiance to Rome. As a result, the United States is being transformed from a decentralized land of liberty, where the people ruled, to a centralized land of oppression, ruled by autocrats.

When Charles Chiniquy was still a Catholic priest he attended a large conclave of Catholic priests and bishops in the Spring of 1852 in Buffalo, New York. At the meeting, D'Arcy McGee, then editor of The Freeman's Journal, official Journal of the Bishop of New York, proposed that the Catholic Church encourage Catholic immigrants to settle in the great plains of the United States as a way to gain political hegemony over the country. His plan, however, was rejected by the Catholic hierarchy. The Catholic Church, instead, planned on controlling the United Sates by bringing in hoards of Catholic immigrants into the large cities. Chiniquy explains what he witnessed at the 1852 Buffalo meeting:

He [D'Arcy McGee] vainly spoke with a burning

eloquence for his pet scheme. The majority coldly answered him: "We are determined, like you, to take possession of the United States and rule them; but we cannot do that without acting secretly and with the utmost wisdom. If our plans are known, they will surely be defeated. What does a skillful general do when he wants to conquer a country? Does he scatter his soldiers over the farm lands, and spend their energy and power in ploughing the fields and sowing grain? No! he keeps them well united around his banners, and marches at their head, to the conquest of the strongholds, the rich and powerful cities. The farming countries then submit and become the price of his victory without moving a finger to subdue them. So it is with us. Silently and patiently, we must mass our Roman Catholics in the great cities of the United States, remembering that the vote of a poor journeyman, though he be covered with rags, has as much weight in the scale of power as the millionaire Astor, and that if we have two votes against his one, he will become as powerless as an oyster. Let us then multiply our votes; let us call our poor but faithful Irish Catholics from every corner of the world, and gather them into the very hearts of those proud citadels which the Yankees are so rapidly building under the names of Washington, New York, Boston, Chicago, Buffalo, Albany, Troy, Cincinnati, ect. Under the shadows of those great cities, the Americans consider themselves a giant and unconquerable race. They look upon the poor Irish Catholic people with supreme contempt, as only fit to dig their canals, sweep their streets and work in their kitchens. Let no one awake those sleeping lions, today. Let us pray God that they may sleep and dream their sweet dreams, a few years more. How sad will their awakening be, when with our out-numbering votes, we will turn them for ever, from every position of honour, power and profit! What will those hypocritical and godless sons and daughters of the fanatical Pilgrim Fathers say, when not a single judge, not a single teacher, not a single policeman, will be elected if he be not a devoted Irish Roman Catholic? What will those so-called giants think of their matchless shrewdness and ability, when not a single Senator or member of congress will be chosen, if he be not submitted to our holy father the Pope! What a sad figure those Protestant Yankees will cut when we will not only elect the President, but fill and command the armies, man the navies and hold the keys of the public treasury? It will then be time for our faithful Irish people to give up their grog shops, in order to become the judges and governors of the land. Then, our poor and humble mechanics will leave their damp ditches and muddy streets, to rule the cities in all their departments, from the stately mansion of Mayor to the more humble, though not less noble position of teacher.

"Then, yes! then, we will rule the United States, and lay them at the feet of the Vicar of Jesus Christ, that he may put an end to their godless system of education, and impious laws of liberty of conscience which are an insult to God and man!"

D'Arcy McGee was left almost alone when the votes were taken. From that, the Catholic priests, with the most admirable ability and success, have gathered their Irish legions into the great cities of the United States, and the American people must be very blind indeed, if they do not see that if they do nothing to prevent it, the day is very near when the Jesuits will rule their country, from the magnificent White House at Washington to the humblest civil and military department of this vast Republic. They are already the masters of New York, Baltimore, Chicago, St. Paul, New Orleans, Mobile, Savannah, Cincinnati, Albany, Troy, Milwaukee, St. Louis, San Francisco, etc. Yes! San Francisco, the rich, the great queen of the Pacific, is in the hands of the Jesuits![1174]

That is a strategy that one can see taking place to this very day with the flood of illegal immigrants from Latin America, most notably

Mexico. Approximately 70% of illegal immigrants in the United States today are Roman Catholic. According to the Department of Homeland Security (DHS), in 2013 there were approximately 11.5 illegal aliens in the United States. The National Association of Former Border Patrol Officers (NAFBPO) alleges that DHS is under-reporting the actual number of illegal immigrants. NAFBPO states that there are approximately 18-20 million illegal aliens in the United States.[1175]

Roman Catholic Cardinal Roger Mahony of Los Angeles advised his priests to defy a proposed 2006 immigration bill if it became law. The immigration bill, among other things, called for building more detention centers, building another wall along the U.S.-Mexico border, and increasing penalties for violations of the immigration laws. In the end, the law was never passed by Congress. Karen Frazier Romero explains:

> The Vatican has been increasing the Roman Catholic population through immigration, both legal and illegal. Cardinal Roger Mahony of Los Angeles has been a key player in lobbying for the continued influx of immigrants into the United States, even calling all priests to "defy the law" if the immigration bill is passed![1176]

Kevin Appleby, Director of Migration and Refugee Policy for the U.S. Conference of Catholic Bishops, advocates amnesty for illegal aliens, but without actually using that word. Appleby also avoids using the term "illegal alien." He instead refers to illegal aliens as "undocumented" and "working without papers." Appleby stated:

> First of all, we need to look at how we're going to address the 11 million undocumented that are currently in the country, that are in the shadows, they're in an underground economy, that are working in important industries that help our economy grow, and we do not recognize any of their rights, we do not extend them the protection of the law, and we believe that there should be a program that allows them to come out of the shadows.

> We think this is the only way that we're going to get a hold of who is in the country working without papers, and we think it's good policy because it's pro-economy because it stabilizes our workforce and it ensures employers that you're going to have a stable workforce.
>
> And what's especially important to bishops is it's pro-family, is that it allows immigrant families to stay together.[1177]

Interestingly, Appleby admits that the Catholic Church has directly benefitted from a liberal immigration policy. He and the Catholic bishops, no doubt, expect that the Catholic Church will benefit further from an amnesty program for illegal aliens.

> Our church has grown as the country has grown with the wide-range of immigrant populations that have come over the years. Italians, Irish, even those some Eastern Europe recently [sic], Vietnamese from Southeast Asia have helped grown [sic] our church and made it a culturally diverse church that's reflective of our nation, so we're really in concert with the nation as an immigrant nation.[1178]

Appleby admitted that the Roman Catholic Church as an organization is presently giving aid and comfort to illegal aliens. He stated that is the reason that he and the bishops objected to the provisions in the proposed 2006 bill. The bill provided criminal penalties for anyone who knowingly transports, harbors, conceals, or assists an illegal alien to remain in the United States. Appleby explained the Catholic Church's objection to the proposed law:

> You can be assisting someone who might be undocumented with a cup of soup, with any sort of food or meal, a shelter for the night. And it could be interpreted by a judge and by prosecutors that you're assisting them to remain in the United States.
>
> Again, pastoral services, if we're providing pastoral care to immigrants who may be undocumented,

whether that be allowing them to come to mass, providing them other types of advice and spiritual counseling, again, a judge or a prosecutor could interpret that as saying we're assisting them to remain in the United States because we're welcoming them into our spiritual community.[1179]

Cardinal Mahony and the Catholic hierarchy want to encourage and give aid and comfort to the illegal immigrants from Mexico, because, according to the 2010 Mexican census figures, 91% of Mexicans are Roman Catholic. Granting the millions of illegal aliens in the United States amnesty, and ultimately citizenship, would significantly change the political landscape of the United States. Karen Frazier Romero explains the economic and political threat:

> Faithful Roman Catholics are forbidden by Church law to use any kind of birth control besides what they refer to as "natural family planning." Most who use this method will tell you that it is not very effective! What does this mean for the United States? Well, for example, Frosty Wooldridge writes, "Mexico will grow from its current 104 million people to well over 300 million in this century. If Mexicans can't find a better life in their home country in 2007—30, 40 to 50 million will stream over U.S. borders in the coming years." You do the math; 30-50 million Roman Catholic Mexican immigrants who do not use birth control could mean disastrous results for our country and its citizens in the form of over population, the economy and not to mention the Roman Catholic majority it gives the Church of Rome here in America![1180]

The Roman Catholic Church has been using its political influence to ram through immigration reform legislation, which will give amnesty to most of those illegal aliens. "The United States Conference of Catholic Bishops (USCCB) opposes 'enforcement only' immigration policies and supports comprehensive immigration reform."[1181] Of course, the pope supports the U.S. Catholic Bishop's position on immigration reform.[1182] Indeed, they are following his orders. If the immigration reform legislation passes, it will change the political landscape significantly toward the socialist/fascist ideals of group privileges flowing from the government and away from Christian constitutional principles of individual rights that flow from God.

The comprehensive immigration reform (which is a euphemism for amnesty) advocated by the Catholic Church will make instant citizens of illegal aliens and tip the political scales significantly toward further erosion of liberty in the United States. There will be a huge new obedient block of Roman Catholic voters who will elect officials who will pander to the fascist/socialist agenda and further disintegrate biblical Christian values.

The pope claims dominion over all kings and all kingdoms. The pope wants to rule the world. However, the pope cannot rule a country like the United States where there is no king. In order to accomplish the goal of ruling the world he must destroy the United States as we know it. The pope and his fellow despots cannot conquer us by force of arms yet, so they have set upon our gradual destruction by the artifice of a religious mission. Like the proverbial Trojan horse, the Jesuit immigration into the United States is in reality an invasion by the secret army of the pope. In the mid 1800's the power that was most interested in the destruction of the U.S. was Austria, which funded the invasion into the U.S. of the Jesuits, whose mission was to secretly undermine our republic. Morse had this to say about the conspiracy:

> Yes; these Foreign despots are suddenly stirred up to combine and promote the greater activity of Popery in this county; and this, too, just after they had been convinced of the truth, or, more properly speaking, had their memories quickened with it, that *Popery is utterly opposed to Republican liberty.*[1183]

The official pronouncements of the Catholic Church in the United States, going back over 100 years, confirm the fact that the Catholic Church is antagonistic to liberty. "If Catholics ever gain a sufficient numerical majority in this country, religious freedom is at an end. So our enemies say, so we believe." *The Shepherd of the Valley* (official journal of the Bishop of St. Louis, Nov. 23, 1851).[1184] "No man has a right to choose his religion." *New York Freeman* (official Journal of Bishop Hughes, Jan. 26, 1852).[1185] "The Church . . . does not, and cannot accept, or in any degree favor, liberty in the Protestant sense of liberty." *Catholic World* (April 1870).[1186]

Pope Pius IX on December 8, 1864 issued an encyclical letter *Quanta Cura,* containing the *Syllabus Errorum,* in which he condemned freedom of conscience as "an insane folly" and freedom of the press as "a pestiferous error, which cannot be sufficiently detested."[1187] In the *Syllabus Errorum* Pope Pius stated: "No man is free to embrace and profess that religion which he believes to be true, guided by the light of reason."[1188] Pope Gregory XVI (1831-46) viewed freedom of conscience and the press as absurd and mad concepts, not only within the church but in society as a whole.[1189]

How effective can such a plot be to subvert the liberties of the United States? Isn't the Roman Catholic institution just a religion? Samuel Morse explains:

> Popery is a *Political system, despotic* in its organization, *anti-democratic* and *ant-republican,* and cannot therefore co-exist with American republicanism.
>
> The ratio of *increase of Popery* is the exact ratio of *decrease of civil liberty.*
>
> The *dominance of Popery* in the United States is the *certain destruction of our free institutions.*
>
> Popery, by its organization, is wholly under the control of a FOREIGN DESPOTIC SOVEREIGN.[1190]

The foundation of the Romish church is blind obedience; the foundation of the United States is Liberty. As Richard Thompson, former U.S. Secretary of the Navy, stated in his book *The Papacy and the Civil Power:* "Nothing is plainer than that, if the principles of the Church of Rome prevail here, our Constitution would necessarily fall. The two cannot exist together. They are in open and direct antagonism with the fundamental theory of our government and of all popular government everywhere."[1191] The papacy must destroy the United States Constitution in order to impose her will and claim of ownership on

America. Our First Amendment to the U.S. Constitution provides that: "congress shall make no law respecting an establishment of religion, or prohibiting the free exercise thereof." That single principle alone makes the United States a mortal enemy of the Vatican. Pope Pius IX in his 1864 *Syllabus Errorum* stated: "The [Roman] Church ought to be in union with the state, and the State ought to be in union with the [Roman] Church. . . . **It is necessary even in the present day that the Catholic religion shall be held as the only religion of the State, to the exclusion of all other forms of worship."**[1192] The Roman Catholic Church will not tolerate freedom of religion; its history demonstrates its intolerance of other religions and the future, sadly, will confirm its intolerance. When the Catholic Church is insufficiently powerful, it acts as a harmless lamb, biding its time until it becomes more powerful. The Catholic Church is trying to gain political hegemony in the United States by increasing the population of obedient Catholics through illegal immigration. James A. Wylie explains that when the Catholic Church determines it has sufficient power, it will then throw off its sheep's clothing and reveal itself as a ravening wolf.

> The Roman Church has made it the solemn duty of all her members to destroy all Protestants when they are able to do so without danger to themselves. Bannes, a Dominican, determines "that Catholics in England and Saxony are excused from rising up against their Protestant princes with their subjects, because they commonly are not powerful enough, and the attempt in such circumstances would expose them to great danger." (In. ii. 2; Thom. 9-12, art. ii.) Belarmine, one of their greatest authorities, is equally frank and explicit. He says, "If it were possible to root out the heretics, without doubt, they are to be destroyed root and branch; but if it cannot be done, because they are stronger than we, and there be danger that if they should oppose us that we should be worsted, then we are to be quiet." (De Laicis, lib.iii. cap. 22.) The two latest Popes, Pius IX and Leo XIII in their public manifestos, claim the same formidable power; but they prudently postpone the exercise of it till the arrival of a happier day to the Papacy.[1193]

Pope Martin V (1417-1431) ordered the King of Poland to exterminate the Hussites. The Hussites were followers of John Huss who was a Christian burned at the stake by the Catholic authorities in 1418. Reading the words of Pope Martin V drives home that the Vatican is an enemy of liberty and all the principles of Protestantism.

> Know that the interests of the Holy See and those of your crown, make it duty to exterminate the Hussites. Remember that these impious persons dare proclaim principles of equality; they maintain that all Christians are brethren and God has not given to privileged men the right of ruling nations; they hold that Christ came on Earth to abolish slavery; they call the people to liberty, that is to the annihilation of kings and priests. While there is still time, then, turn your forces against Bohemia; burn, massacre, make deserts everywhere, for nothing could be more agreeable to God, or more useful to the cause of kings, than the extermination of the Hussites.[1194]

Former Catholic priest Emmitt McLoughlin explains that the papacy draws its strength from the principle of the "divine right of kings," of which the pope claims primacy. In the United States, however, the government is based upon the Protestant principle of the "consent of the governed."[1195] The two principles are antithetical. McLoughlin states that the animosity born by those irreconcilable differences was the driving force behind the pope's conspiracy to assassinate President Lincoln. Abraham Lincoln personified the great success of the Protestant principles of government despised and loathed by the pope.[1196]

Under the United States Constitution, the people are free and supreme, subject only to God, and the government officials are servants of the people. In the Catholic Church, on the other hand, the pope claims a divine right to rule as supreme over all mortals and kings, and the people are slaves to obey his commands as the "infallible Vicar of Christ." The two systems cannot coexist, they are antithetical polar opposites. If Rome is to rule, it must destroy the United States.

Marquis de Lafayette was convinced of the Roman conspiracy.

He said that "[i]f the liberties of the American people are ever destroyed, they will fall by the hands of the Catholic clergy."[1197]

Indeed, the ascension of the papacy in the world necessarily brings with it a concomitant erosion of liberty. Everywhere in the world where the Roman church has hegemony, there is found a powerful state stamping out freedom and standing at the ready to do the bidding of the papacy to persecute the true church of Jesus Christ. While it appears to the people in Catholic countries that the state is independent and sovereign, that is not truly the case. The papacy holds the reigns of government, as is depicted in Revelation, where the great Roman whore, decked in purple and scarlet, is described riding the beast of government.

> [A]nd I saw a woman sit upon a scarlet coloured beast, full of names of blasphemy, having seven heads and ten horns. And the woman was arrayed in purple and scarlet colour, and decked with gold and precious stones and pearls, having a golden cup in her hand full of abominations and filthiness of her fornication: And upon her forehead was a name written, MYSTERY, BABYLON THE GREAT, THE MOTHER OF HARLOTS AND ABOMINATIONS OF THE EARTH. And I saw the woman drunken with the blood of the saints, and with the blood of the martyrs of Jesus: and when I saw her, I wondered with great admiration. (Revelation 17:3-6)

Those of Gods's elect who are still in the Roman Catholic Church are ordered by God to come out of that great harlot church.

> And I heard another voice from heaven, saying, **Come out of her, my people, that ye be not partakers of her sins, and that ye receive not of her plagues**. For her sins have reached unto heaven, and God hath remembered her iniquities. Reward her even as she rewarded you, and double unto her double according to her works: in the cup which she hath filled fill to her double. (Revelation 18:4-6)

Endnotes

1. Hypocrisy, Merriam-Webster, http://www.merriam-webster.com/dictionary/hypocrisy (last visited on June 1, 2014).

2. Hypocrisy, American Dictionary of the English Language (1828), http://webstersdictionary1828.com/.

3. J. A. Wylie, The Papacy is the Antichrist, A Demonstration, at 14 (1888), available at http://www.historicism.net/readingmaterials/thepapacy.pdf.

4. J. A. Wylie, The Papacy is the Antichrist, A Demonstration, at 14 (1888), available at http://www.historicism.net/readingmaterials/thepapacy.pdf.

5. J. A. Wylie, The Papacy is the Antichrist, A Demonstration, at 14 (1888), available at http://www.historicism.net/readingmaterials/thepapacy.pdf.

6. J. A. Wylie, The Papacy is the Antichrist, at 16.

7. J. A. Wylie, The Papacy is the Antichrist, at 16.

8. J. A. Wylie, The Papacy is the Antichrist, at 12.

9. Pope Boniface VIII, Bull Unum Sanctum, November 18, 1302, available at New Advent Catholic Encyclopedia, http://www.newadvent.org/library/docs_bo08us.htm.

10. Mark Binelli, Pope Francis, The Times They Are A-Changin', Rolling Stone, at 37, February 13, 2014.

11. J. A. Wylie, The Papacy is the Antichrist, A Demonstration, at 11 (1888), available at http://www.historicism.net/readingmaterials/thepapacy.pdf.

12. NOAH WEBSTER, AMERICAN DICTIONARY OF THE ENGLISH LANGUAGE (1st ed. 1828) republished by Foundation for American Christian Education, San Francisco, California.

13. Oxford University Press (1979).

14. J. A. Wylie, The Papacy is the Antichrist, at 12.

15. J. A. Wylie, The Papacy is the Antichrist, A Demonstration, at 11 (1888), available at http://www.historicism.net/readingmaterials/thepapacy.pdf.

16. JOHN PAUL II, CROSSING THE THRESHOLD OF HOPE, p. 12, 1994.

17. Maas, Anthony. "Antichrist." The Catholic Encyclopedia. Vol. 1. New York: Robert Appleton Company, 1907. 17 Mar. 2014 <http://www.newadvent.org/cathen/01559a.htm>.

18. A. Wylie, The Papacy is the Antichrist, at 18.

19. A. Wylie, The Papacy is the Antichrist, at 20.

20. A. Wylie, The Papacy is the Antichrist, at 20.

21. CATECHISM OF THE CATHOLIC CHURCH, § 881-882 (1994).

22. The Inverted Cross, http://www.jesus-is-lord.com/anti5.htm (last visited on

May 31. 2008).

23. Russell R. Boedeker, Albert Pike: Trilogy of Thoughts, Pietre-Stones, Review of Freemasonry, September 15, 2007, http://www.freemasons-freemasonry.com/albert_pike.html.

24. Russell R. Boedeker, Albert Pike: Trilogy of Thoughts, Pietre-Stones, Review of Freemasonry, September 15, 2007, http://www.freemasons-freemasonry.com/albert_pike.html.

25. Russell R. Boedeker, Albert Pike: Trilogy of Thoughts, Pietre-Stones, Review of Freemasonry, September 15, 2007, http://www.freemasons-freemasonry.com/albert_pike.html.

26. The Symbolism of Freemasonry, http://www.theforbiddenknowledge.com/hardtruth/pagen_alter_four.htm#N_4_, quoting Albert Pike, Morals and Dogmas, page 819.

27. David Bay, Freemasonry - Two Organizations, One Visible, the Other Invisible, http://www.cuttingedge.org/FREE001a.html, quoting Albert Pike, Morals and Dogma, p. 104-05.

28. Albert Pike, Morals and Dogma, p.819, quoted at http://ritualabusefree.org/Immorals%20and%20Dogma.htm (last visited on August 3, 2014).

29. Ian R. K. Paisley, The Pope is the Antichrist, http://www.ianpaisley.org/antichrist.asp (last visited on February 20, 2014).

30. COUNCIL OF TRENT, SESSION VI, DECREE ON JUSTIFICATION, Canon XXIV, January 13, 1547.

31. COUNCIL OF TRENT, DOCTRINE ON THE SACRAMENT OF PENANCE, Canon XII, November 25, 1551.

32. COUNCIL OF TRENT, SESSION VI, DECREE ON JUSTIFICATION, Canon XXX, January 13, 1547.

33. DAVE HUNT, A WOMAN RIDES THE BEAST, Harvest House Publishers, p. 89 (1994) (quoting Austin Flannery, O.P., gen. ed., *Vatican II, The Conciliar and Post Conciliar Documents*, rev. ed. (Costello Publishing 1988), vol. 1, p. 412).

34. CATECHISM OF THE CATHOLIC CHURCH § 846 (1994) (emphasis added).

35. DECLARATION "DOMINUS IESUS" ON THE UNICITY AND SALVIFIC UNIVERSALITY OF JESUS CHRIST AND THE CHURCH, *Rome, from the Offices of the Congregation for the Doctrine of the Faith, August 6, 2000.*

36. The Canons and Decrees of the Ecumenical Council of Trent, 25th Session, December 4, 1563., Under the Pontiff, Pius IV, available at https://history.hanover.edu/texts/trent/ct25.html.

37. Margaret Shepherd, My Life in the Convent: or The Marvelous Personal Experiences of Margaret Shepherd, 216-218 (1892), https://archive.org/details/mylifeinconvento00shepuoft.

38. Margaret Shepherd, My Life in the Convent: or The Marvelous Personal Experiences of Margaret

Shepherd, 216-218 (1892), https://archive.org/details/mylifeinconvento00shepuoft.

39. Barbara Aho, MYSTERY, BABYLON THE GREAT, CATHOLIC OR JEWISH?, http://watch.pair.com/mystery-babylon.html (last visited on April 4, 2014).

40. David Goldenberg, 10 Secrets of the Vatican Exposed, The Week, March 13, 2013, http://theweek.com/article/index/241233/10-secrets-of-the-vatican-exposed.

41. Mark Binelli, Pope Francis, The Times They Are A-Changin', Rolling Stone, at 37, February 13, 2014.

42. As Cardinals Gather to Elect Pope, Catholic Officials Break into a Sweat over News That Priests Share €23m Building with Huge Gay Sauna, The Independent, 11 March 2013, http://www.independent.co.uk/news/world/europe/as-cardinals-gather-to-elect-pope-catholic-officials-break-into-a-sweat-over-news-that-priests-share-23m-building-with-huge-gay-sauna-8529670.html.

43. John Hooper, Papal Resignation Linked to Inquiry into 'Vatican Gay Officials', Says Paper, The Guardian, 21 February 2013, http://www.theguardian.com/world/2013/feb/21/pope-retired-amid-gay-bishop-blackmail-inquiry.

44. Rachel Donadio, On Gay Priests, Pope Francis Asks, 'Who Am I to Judge?', The New York Times, July 29, 2013, available at http://www.nytimes.com/2013/07/30/world/europe/pope-francis-gay-priests.html?pagewanted=all&_r=0.

45. Catholic Synod: Vatican Family Review Signals Shift on Homosexuality, BBC, October 13, 2014, http://www.bbc.com/news/world-europe-29603496.

46. Catholic Synod: Vatican Family Review Signals Shift on Homosexuality, BBC, October 13, 2014, http://www.bbc.com/news/world-europe-29603496.

47. John Thavis, a Pastoral Earthquake at the Synod, October 13, 2014, http://www.johnthavis.com/a-pastoral-earthquake-at-the-synod#.VDvimZVOE9W.

48. John Thavis, a Pastoral Earthquake at the Synod, October 13, 2014, http://www.johnthavis.com/a-pastoral-earthquake-at-the-synod#.VDvimZVOE9W.

49. John Thavis, a Pastoral Earthquake at the Synod, October 13, 2014, http://www.johnthavis.com/a-pastoral-earthquake-at-the-synod#.VDvimZVOE9W.

50. Nicole Winfield and Daniela Petroff, Bishops Split Over Welcoming Gays, Associated Press, Fredericksburg Free Lance Star, at page A7, October 19, 2014.

51. Conservative US Cardinal Demoted by Pope, He Tells Buzzfeed, MSN News, http://www.msn.com/en-us/news/world/conservative-us-cardinal-demoted-by-pope-he-tells-buzzfeed/ar-BB9OCXz (last visited on October 19, 2014).

52. Conservative US Cardinal Demoted by Pope, He Tells Buzzfeed, MSN News, supra.

53. Bill Donohue, Attempts to Censor Donohue Fail, The Catholic League, April 1, 2010, http://www.catholicleague.org/attempts-to-censor-donohue-fail/.

54. Vatican: Former Ambassador To Dominican Republic Covered By Diplomatic Immunity In Abuse Investigation, Associated Press, Fox News Latino, January 11, 2014, http://latino.foxnews.com/latino/news/2014/01/11/vatican-former-ambassador-to-dominican-republic-covered-by-diplomatic-immunity/.

55. Tom Kington, Pope Calls on Catholic Church to 'Repair Injustice' of Sexual Abuse, The Guardian, December 20, 2010, http://www.theguardian.com/world/2010/dec/20/pope-catholic-church-child-abuse-scandal.

56. Tom Kington, Pope Calls on Catholic Church to 'Repair Injustice' of Sexual Abuse, The Guardian, December 20, 2010, http://www.theguardian.com/world/2010/dec/20/pope-catholic-church-child-abuse-scandal.

57. Tom Kington, Pope Calls on Catholic Church to 'Repair Injustice' of Sexual Abuse, The Guardian, December 20, 2010, http://www.theguardian.com/world/2010/dec/20/pope-catholic-church-child-abuse-scandal.

58. Benjamin Radford, Pope Blames 1970s Society for Pedophile Priests, Live Science, December 21, 2010, http://www.livescience.com/9179-pope-blames-1970s-society-pedophile-priests.html.

59. Benjamin Radford, Pope Blames 1970s Society for Pedophile Priests, Live Science, December 21, 2010, http://www.livescience.com/9179-pope-blames-1970s-society-pedophile-priests.html.

60. Archbishop Jozef Wesolowski's Extradition Declined: Former Papal Nuncio Accused Of Sex Abuse Remains In Vatican, Huffington Post, January 11, 2014, http://www.huffingtonpost.com/2014/01/10/archbishop-jozef-wesolowski-extradition_n_4577241.html.

61. Vatican: Former Ambassador To Dominican Republic Covered By Diplomatic Immunity In Abuse Investigation, Associated Press, Fox News Latino, January 11, 2014, http://latino.foxnews.com/latino/news/2014/01/11/vatican-former-ambassador-to-dominican-republic-covered-by-diplomatic-immunity/.

62. Vatican Slammed by UN Human Rights Committee Over Sex Abuse, The Associated Press, Feb 05, 2014, http://www.cbc.ca/news/world/vatican-slammed-by-un-human-rights-committee-over-sex-abuse-1.2523737.

63. Edited by Henry Makow, UN Peddles Illuminati's Heterophobic Program, April 9, 2014, http://henrymakow.com/2014/04/UN-Peddles-Illuminati-Sexual-Agenda%20.html.

64. Leonard and Squires, Pope Benedict, Telegraph, April 9, 2010, supra.

65. Sex Crimes Cover-Up By Vatican?, *CBS Evening News*, August 6, 2003, http://www.cbsnews.com/stories/2003/08/06/eveningnews/main566978.shtml (website address current as of

August 10, 2003).

66. FROM THE SUPREME AND HOLY CONGREGATION FOR THE HOLY OFFICE FOR ALL PATRIARCHS, ARCHBISHOPS, BISHOPS, AND OTHER DIOCESAN ORDINARIES "EVEN OF THE ORIENTAL RITE," Instruction on the Manner of Proceeding in Cases of Solicitation, ¶ 11 (1962) (marked: CONFIDENTIAL).

67. FROM THE SUPREME AND HOLY CONGREGATION FOR THE HOLY OFFICE FOR ALL PATRIARCHS, ARCHBISHOPS, BISHOPS, AND OTHER DIOCESAN ORDINARIES "EVEN OF THE ORIENTAL RITE," Instruction on the Manner of Proceeding in Cases of Solicitation, ¶ 11 (1962) (marked: CONFIDENTIAL).

68. FROM THE SUPREME AND HOLY CONGREGATION FOR THE HOLY OFFICE FOR ALL PATRIARCHS, ARCHBISHOPS, BISHOPS, AND OTHER DIOCESAN ORDINARIES "EVEN OF THE ORIENTAL RITE," Instruction on the Manner of Proceeding in Cases of Solicitation, ¶ 11 (1962) (marked: CONFIDENTIAL).

69. FROM THE SUPREME AND HOLY CONGREGATION FOR THE HOLY OFFICE FOR ALL PATRIARCHS, ARCHBISHOPS, BISHOPS, AND OTHER DIOCESAN ORDINARIES "EVEN OF THE ORIENTAL RITE," Instruction on the Manner of Proceeding in Cases of Solicitation, Title V, The Worst Crime, ¶ 71 (1962) (marked: CONFIDENTIAL).

70. FROM THE SUPREME AND HOLY CONGREGATION FOR THE HOLY OFFICE FOR ALL PATRIARCHS, ARCHBISHOPS, BISHOPS,

AND OTHER DIOCESAN ORDINARIES "EVEN OF THE ORIENTAL RITE," Instruction on the Manner of Proceeding in Cases of Solicitation, Title V, The Worst Crime, ¶ 73 (1962) (marked: CONFIDENTIAL).

71. FROM THE SUPREME AND HOLY CONGREGATION FOR THE HOLY OFFICE FOR ALL PATRIARCHS, ARCHBISHOPS, BISHOPS, AND OTHER DIOCESAN ORDINARIES "EVEN OF THE ORIENTAL RITE," Instruction on the Manner of Proceeding in Cases of Solicitation, Appendix, The Formula for Taking an Oath to Exercise One's Office Faithfully and to Observe the Secret of the Holy Office, Formula A (1962) (marked: CONFIDENTIAL).

72. FROM THE SUPREME AND HOLY CONGREGATION FOR THE HOLY OFFICE FOR ALL PATRIARCHS, ARCHBISHOPS, BISHOPS, AND OTHER DIOCESAN ORDINARIES "EVEN OF THE ORIENTAL RITE," Instruction on the Manner of Proceeding in Cases of Solicitation, ¶ 13 (1962) (marked: CONFIDENTIAL).

73. FROM THE SUPREME AND HOLY CONGREGATION FOR THE HOLY OFFICE FOR ALL PATRIARCHS, ARCHBISHOPS, BISHOPS, AND OTHER DIOCESAN ORDINARIES "EVEN OF THE ORIENTAL RITE," Instruction on the Manner of Proceeding in Cases of Solicitation, Title Number One, ¶ 16 (1962) (marked: CONFIDENTIAL).

74. FROM THE SUPREME AND HOLY CONGREGATION FOR THE HOLY OFFICE FOR ALL PATRIARCHS, ARCHBISHOPS, BISHOPS, AND OTHER DIOCESAN ORDINARIES "EVEN OF THE ORIENTAL RITE," Instruction on the Manner of

Proceeding in Cases of Solicitation, Appendix, Way of Undertaking the Entire Investigation, Note 1, Formula G (1962) (marked: CONFIDENTIAL).

75. FROM THE SUPREME AND HOLY CONGREGATION FOR THE HOLY OFFICE FOR ALL PATRIARCHS, ARCHBISHOPS, BISHOPS, AND OTHER DIOCESAN ORDINARIES "EVEN OF THE ORIENTAL RITE," Instruction on the Manner of Proceeding in Cases of Solicitation, ¶ 52 (1962) (marked: CONFIDENTIAL).

76. Sex Crimes Cover-Up By Vatican?, *CBS Evening News*, August 6, 2003, http://www.cbsnews.com/stories/2003/08/06/eveningnews/main566978.shtml (website address current as of August 10, 2003).

77. Michael Powell and Lois Romano, *Roman Catholic Church Shifts Legal Strategy: Aggressive Litigation Replaces Quiet Settlements, Washington Post*, May 13, 2002, http://www.washingtonpost.com/wp-dyn/articles/A8117-2002May12.html (web page current as of May 14, 2002.

78. Michael Powell and Lois Romano, *Roman Catholic Church Shifts Legal Strategy: Aggressive Litigation Replaces Quiet Settlements, Washington Post*, May 13, 2002, http://www.washingtonpost.com/wp-dyn/articles/A8117-2002May12.html (web page current as of May 14, 2002.

79. DAVE HUNT, A WOMAN RIDES THE BEAST, Harvest House Publishers, p. 168 (1994).

80.DAVE HUNT, A WOMAN RIDES THE BEAST, Harvest House Publishers, p. 164 (1994).

81.*Id.* at p. 172.

82.*Id.* at pp. 172-173 (quoting National Catholic Reporter, p. 9, January 7, 1994).

83.*Id.* at p. 173.

84.*Diocese OKs $23 Million Payout in Abuse Case,* Chicago Tribune, July 11, 1998.

85.*Paper Says Ex-Priest Admitted Sex Abuse to Pope,* The New York Times, October 25, 1992.

86.Declan White, *Scandal of Vatican and Pervert Priest; Church Knew for 7 Years that He was a Molester; Vatican were Aware in 1987 of Sex Crimes of Father Brendan Smith,* The People, December 4, 1994.

87.Michael McCord, *Fortier Guilty in Altar Boy Sex Assaults . . .,* The Union Leader(Manchester, N.H.), August 5, 1998.

88.Walter Robinson, *A 'Grieving' Law Apologizes for the Assignment of Geoghan,* The Boston Globe, January 10, 2002, http://www.boston.com/globe/spotlight/geoghan/01100 2_law.htm (current as of April 4, 2002).

89.*Ex-Sudbury Priest Accused of Abuse: Local Man Claims the Cardinal Tried to Quash Allegations about 'Father B',* The Metro West Daily News, AP, Boston, April 5, 2002.
http://www.metrowestdailynews.com/news/local_regio nal/ap_priestabuse0405002.htm (current as of April 6,

2002).

90. Elizabeth Mehren, Boston Archdiocese 'Sacrificed the Children,' *Toronto Star*, July 24 2003.

91. Elizabeth Mehren, Boston Archdiocese 'Sacrificed the Children,' *Toronto Star*, July 24 2003.

92. Elizabeth Mehren, Boston Archdiocese 'Sacrificed the Children,' *Toronto Star*, July 24 2003.

93. Don Lattin, Molestation Victim Protests Vatican Service, *San Francisco Chronicle*, April 11, 2005, http://sfgate.com/cgi-bin/article.cgi?file=/chronicle/archive/2005/04/11/rome11.TMP (web address current as of May 5, 2005).

94. Elizabeth Mehren, Boston Archdiocese 'Sacrificed the Children,' *Toronto Star*, July 24 2003.

95. Elizabeth Mehren, Boston Archdiocese 'Sacrificed the Children,' *Toronto Star*, July 24 2003.

96. U.S. House of Representatives, 8th District of Wisconsin, Press Release, U.S. House Passes Rep. Green "Two Strikes Bill," http://www.house.gov/markgreen/PRESS/2000/July00News/NR072500TwoStrikesPassage.htm (website address current as of August 16, 2003). See also http://www.geocities.com/Wellesley/2726/Molester.html (website address current as of August 16, 2003); Jon Donenberg, Keller Attacks Johnson's Vote On 1987 Bill, The Daily Illini Online, October 3, 2000, http://www.dailyillini.com/oct00/oct03/news/printer/news01.shtml (website address current as of August 16, 2003).

97. Boston Archdiocese Offers 55 Million Dollars to Settle Lawsuits, *Boston Associated Press, Fox 23 News,* WXXA, Albany, NY, www.fox23news.com, August 11, 2003.

98. Philip Pullella, Pope Immunity: Vatican Will Protect Benedict From Sexual Abuse Prosecution, Reuters, 02/17/2013, http://www.huffingtonpost.com/2013/02/17/pope-immunity_n_2708518.html.

99. JOHN W. DECAMP, THE FRANKLIN COVER-UP, pp. 151-56 (1996).

100. JOHN W. DECAMP, THE FRANKLIN COVER-UP, pp. 283-85 (1996).

101. *The Tampa Tribune,* May 5, 1996.

102. DAVE HUNT, A WOMAN RIDES THE BEAST, Harvest House Publishers, p. 174 (1994) (quoting National Catholic Reporter, pp. 6-7, September 17, 1993).

103. *The Associated Press,* March 20, 1992.

104. DAVE HUNT, A WOMAN RIDES THE BEAST, Harvest House Publishers, p. 172 (1994).

105. *The Associated Press,* March 20, 1992.

106. Deborah Zabarenko, *Study Finds 10,600 Children Abused by U.S. Priests*, Reuters, February 27, 2004.

107. *Key Figures From a Catholic Abuse Survey,* Guardian Unlimited, Associated Press, February 27, 2004.

108.Deborah Zabarenko, *Study Finds 10,600 Children Abused by U.S. Priests*, Reuters, February 27, 2004.

109.*U.S. Church Reports 11,000 Abuse Complaints*, Globe and Mail, Associated Press, February 27, 2004.

110.Deborah Zabarenko, *Study Finds 10,600 Children Abused by U.S. Priests*, Reuters, February 27, 2004.

111.*U.S. Church Reports 11,000 Abuse Complaints*, Globe and Mail, Associated Press, February 27, 2004.

112.*Key Figures From a Catholic Abuse Survey*, Guardian Unlimited, Associated Press, February 27, 2004.

113.*Key Figures From a Catholic Abuse Survey*, Guardian Unlimited, Associated Press, February 27, 2004.

114.*Key Figures From a Catholic Abuse Survey*, Guardian Unlimited, Associated Press, February 27, 2004.

115.DAVE HUNT, A WOMAN RIDES THE BEAST, Harvest House Publishers, p. 172 (1994).

116.U.S. House of Representatives, 8th District of Wisconsin, Press Release, U.S. House Passes Rep. Green "Two Strikes Bill," http://www.house.gov/markgreen/PRESS/2000/July00News/NR072500TwoStrikesPassage.htm (website address current as of August 16, 2003). See also http://www.geocities.com/Wellesley/2726/Molester.html (website address current as of August 16, 2003); Jon Donenberg, Keller Attacks Johnson's Vote On 1987 Bill, The Daily Illini Online, October 3, 2000, http://www.dailyillini.com/oct00/oct03/news/printer/ne

ws01.shtml (website address current as of August 16, 2003).

117. Jason Berry, Vatican a Conflicted Attitude Toward Gays, Los Angeles Times, August 1, 1999, http://www.soulforce.org/catholics.html (web address current as of April 27, 2002). Notice: soulforce.org is a pro-sodomite website.

118. Cardinal in Vatican Accused of Sexual Abuse Cover-Up, ABC News, April 26, 2002, http://www.abcnews.go.com/sections/2020/DailyNews/2020_Vatican_coverup_020426.html (web address current as of April 27, 2002).

119. Jason Berry, Clergy Sex Abuse - the Trail Leads to Rome, http://www.peak.org/~snapper/News_Vatican/VATICAN_BackPage_3.htm (web address current as of April 27, 2002).

120. Jason Berry, Vatican a Conflicted Attitude Toward Gays, Los Angeles Times, August 1, 1999, http://www.soulforce.org/catholics.html (web address current as of April 27, 2002). Notice: soulforce.org is a pro-sodomite website.

121. Brian Ross, Priestly Sin, Cover-Up, Powerful Cardinal in Vatican Accused of Sexual Abuse Cover-Up, ABC News, April 26, 2002, http://www.abcnews.go.com/sections/2020/DailyNews/2020_Vatican_coverup_020426.html (web address current as of April 27, 2002).

122. Jason Berry, Vatican a Conflicted Attitude Toward Gays, Los Angeles Times, August 1, 1999, http://www.soulforce.org/catholics.html (web address

current as of April 27, 2002). Notice: soulforce.org is a pro-sodomite website.

123. Ann Rodgers-melnick, Pedophile Priest Problem Blamed on Church Leadership, Pittsburgh Post-Gazette, http://www.post-gazette.com/world/20020324priests0324p1.asp (web address current as of April 27, 2002).

124. Brian Ross, Priestly Sin, Cover-Up, Powerful Cardinal in Vatican Accused of Sexual Abuse Cover-Up, ABC News, April 26, 2002, http://www.abcnews.go.com/sections/2020/DailyNews/2020_Vatican_coverup_020426.html (web address current as of April 27, 2002).

125. Brian Ross, Priestly Sin, Cover-Up, Powerful Cardinal in Vatican Accused of Sexual Abuse Cover-Up, ABC News, April 26, 2002, http://www.abcnews.go.com/sections/2020/DailyNews/2020_Vatican_coverup_020426.html (web address current as of April 27, 2002).

126. Michael Sheridan, Father Marcial Maciel, Was My Dad, and He Sexually Abused me, Raul Gonzalez Claims in Lawsuit, New York Daily News, June 22, 2010, http://www.nydailynews.com/news/national/father-marcial-maciel-dad-sexually-abused-raul-gonzalez-claims-lawsuit-article-1.181520.

127. Michael Sheridan, Father Marcial Maciel, Was My Dad, and He Sexually Abused me, Raul Gonzalez Claims in Lawsuit, New York Daily News, June 22, 2010, http://www.nydailynews.com/news/national/father-marcial-maciel-dad-sexually-abused-raul-gonzalez-claims-

lawsuit-article-1.181520.

128. Jason Berry, Son of Former Legionaries Leader Arrested in Mexico for Extortion, National Catholic Reporter, October 23, 2012, http://ncronline.org/news/son-former-legionaries-leader-arrested-mexico-extortion.
http://ncronline.org/news/son-former-legionaries-leader-arrested-mexico-extortion.

129. Jason Berry, Son of Former Legionaries Leader Arrested in Mexico for Extortion, National Catholic Reporter, October 23, 2012, http://ncronline.org/news/son-former-legionaries-leader-arrested-mexico-extortion.
http://ncronline.org/news/son-former-legionaries-leader-arrested-mexico-extortion.

130. Emilio Godoy, Pope Rewrites Epitaph for Legion of Christ Founder, Inter Press Service News Agency, May 3, 2010, http://www.ipsnews.net/2010/05/pope-rewrites-epitaph-for-legion-of-christ-founder/.

131. Jason Berry, Son of Former Legionaries Leader Arrested in Mexico for Extortion, National Catholic Reporter, October 23, 2012, http://ncronline.org/news/son-former-legionaries-leader-arrested-mexico-extortion.
http://ncronline.org/news/son-former-legionaries-leader-arrested-mexico-extortion.

132. Richard Owen, *Chief exorcist Father Gabriele Amorth says Devil is in the Vatican*, The Times, March 11, 2010, http://www.timesonline.co.uk/tol/comment/faith/article7056689.ece.

133. Richard Owen, *Chief exorcist Father Gabriele Amorth says Devil is in the Vatican*, The Times, March 11, 2010, http://www.timesonline.co.uk/tol/comment/faith/article7056689.ece.

134. quoted in SIDNEY HUNTER, IS ALBERTO FOR REAL?, p. 63 (1988).

135. St. Catherine of Siena, SCS, p. 201 - 202, p. 222, quoted in Apostolic Digest, by Michael Malone, Book 5: "The Book of Obedience", Chapter 1: "There is No Salvation Without Personal Submission to the Pope." http://c950485.r85.cf2.rackcdn.com/appalling-papal-proclamations.pdf.

136. William H. Kennedy, Lucifer's Lodge, at 9 (2004).

137. William H. Kennedy, Lucifer's Lodge, at 14 (2004).

138. Kennedy, Lucifer's Lodge, at 36.

139. Ma. Ceres P. Doyo, Cambodian Cnn Hero Exposed as Fraud, June 5, 2014, http://opinion.inquirer.net/75294/cambodian-cnn-hero-exposed-as-fraud.

140. Simon Marks, Somaly Mam: The Holy Saint (and Sinner) of Sex Trafficking, Newsweek, May 21, 2014, http://www.newsweek.com/2014/05/30/somaly-mam-holy-saint-and-sinner-sex-trafficking-251642.html.

141. Simon Marks, Somaly Mam: The Holy Saint (and Sinner) of Sex Trafficking, Newsweek, May 21, 2014, http://www.newsweek.com/2014/05/30/somaly-mam-holy-saint-and-sinner-sex-trafficking-251642.html.

142. Trafficking in Persons Report 20015, U.S. Department of State, at 22, http://www.state.gov/documents/organization/47255.pdf.

143. Jay Nelson, Killer Priest Convicted but Denial Continues, http://www.renegadecatholic.com/blog/2006/05/killer-priest-convicted/ (last visited on June 16, 2014).

144. The Murder of Sr. Margaret Ann Pahl, Clergy Ritual Abuse Illuminated, http://archives.weirdload.com/cra.html (last visited on June 16, 2014).

145. Mark Reiter, Priest Named in Lawsuit That Alleges Ritual Abuse, Toledo Blade, April 21, 2005, http://archives.weirdload.com/cra.html.

146. Michael D. Sallah and Mitch Weiss, Dark Allegations Arise Amid Probe of Nun's Slaying, Authorities Expand Investigation to Claims of Ritualistic Sex Abuse, Toledo Blade, February 20, 2005, http://archives.weirdload.com/cra.html.

147. Michael D. Sallah and Mitch Weiss, Dark Allegations Arise Amid Probe of Nun's Slaying, Authorities Expand Investigation to Claims of Ritualistic Sex Abuse, Toledo Blade, February 20, 2005, http://archives.weirdload.com/cra.html.

148. Michael D. Sallah and Mitch Weiss, Dark Allegations Arise Amid Probe of Nun's Slaying, Authorities Expand Investigation to Claims of Ritualistic Sex Abuse, Toledo Blade, February 20, 2005, http://archives.weirdload.com/cra.html.

149. Kennedy, Lucifer's Lodge, at 43.

150. Kennedy, Lucifer's Lodge, at 47.

151. Kennedy, Lucifer's Lodge, at 50.

152. Kennedy, Lucifer's Lodge, at 52.

153. Kennedy, Lucifer's Lodge, at 63.

154. Kennedy, Lucifer's Lodge, at 77.

155. Kennedy, Lucifer's Lodge, at 73-74.

156. Kennedy, Lucifer's Lodge, at 204 Kennedy, Lucifer's Lodge, at 70..

157. Kennedy, Lucifer's Lodge, at 86.

158. Kennedy, Lucifer's Lodge, at 64.

159. Kennedy, Lucifer's Lodge, at 66-67.

160. CNN LARRY KING LIVE, Encore Presentation: Interview With John Walsh, July 15, 2003, http://transcripts.cnn.com/TRANSCRIPTS/0307/15/lkl.00.html. See also Kennedy, Lucifer's Lodge, at 67.

161. Kennedy, Lucifer's Lodge, at 148.

162. Kennedy, Lucifer's Lodge, at 154.

163. Kennedy, Lucifer's Lodge, at 154.

164. Kennedy, Lucifer's Lodge, at 68.

165. Kennedy, Lucifer's Lodge, at 70.

166. Kennedy, Lucifer's Lodge, at 70.

167. Kennedy, Lucifer's Lodge, at 95.

168. Kennedy, Lucifer's Lodge, at 98.

169. Is the priest "another Christ" when he says Holy Mass, hears confessions, etc.?, Catholic Answers, http://www.catholic.com/quickquestions/is-the-priest-another-christ-when-he-says-holy-mass-hears-confessions-etc (last visited on June 16, 2014).

170. The *Opus Sanctorum Angelorum*, http://www.vatican.va/roman_curia/congregations/cfaith/documents/rc_con_cfaith_doc_20110316_nota-opus-angelorum_en.html (last visited on June 17, 2014).

171. The Priest: Christ Present Among Us, http://www.opusangelorum.org/crusade/priestamongus.html (last visited on June 17, 2014).

172. Constitution on the Sacred Liturgy Sacrosanctum Concilium Solemnly Promulgated by His Holiness Pope Paul VI on December 4, 1963, http://www.vatican.va/archive/hist_councils/ii_vatican_council/documents/vat-ii_const_19631204_sacrosanctum-concilium_en.html.

173. Letter Dominicae Cenae of the Supreme Pontiff John Paul II to All the Bishops of the Church on the Mystery and Worship of the Eucharist, http://www.vatican.va/holy_father/john_paul_ii/letters/documents/hf_jp-ii_let_24021980_dominicae-cenae_en.html (last visited on June 17, 2014).

174. Maria Monk, Awful Disclosures, at 21-24 (1836).

175. Kennedy, Lucifer's Lodge, at 183.

176. Kennedy, Lucifer's Lodge, at 183.

177. Kennedy, Lucifer's Lodge, at 199.

178. FROM THE SUPREME AND HOLY CONGREGATION FOR THE HOLY OFFICE FOR ALL PATRIARCHS, ARCHBISHOPS, BISHOPS, AND OTHER DIOCESAN ORDINARIES "EVEN OF THE ORIENTAL RITE," Instruction on the Manner of Proceeding in Cases of Solicitation, ¶ 11 (1962) (marked: CONFIDENTIAL).

179. FROM THE SUPREME AND HOLY CONGREGATION FOR THE HOLY OFFICE FOR ALL PATRIARCHS, ARCHBISHOPS, BISHOPS, AND OTHER DIOCESAN ORDINARIES "EVEN OF THE ORIENTAL RITE," Instruction on the Manner of Proceeding in Cases of Solicitation, ¶ 11 (1962) (marked: CONFIDENTIAL).

180. Sex Crimes Cover-Up By Vatican?, *CBS Evening News*, August 6, 2003, http://www.cbsnews.com/stories/2003/08/06/eveningnews/main566978.shtml (website address current as of August 10, 2003).

181. Patrick Reilly, *Assessing the Catholic Campaign for Human Development, Human Events,* November 20, 1998.

182. *Id.*

183. *Id.*

184. *Id.*

185. *Id.*

186. Katheryn Jean Lopez, *Catholic Campaign for Human Development: Still Entranced by Leftist*

Activism, Despite Growing Unrest, Human Events, November 10, 2000.

187.*Id.*

188.*Id.*

189.*Id.*

190.*Id.*

191.KERRI HOUSTON AND PATRICIA FAVA, ALL GORE, AMERICA IN THE BALANCE, p. 59 (2000).

192.CATECHISM OF THE CATHOLIC CHURCH, § 2131, 1994.

193.Lucius Ferraris, "Papa," art. 2, Prompta Bibliotheca Canonica, Juridica, Moralis, Theologica, Ascetica, Polemica, Rubristica, Historica. ("Handy Library"), Vol. 5, published in Petit-Montrouge (Paris) by J. P. Migne, 1858 edition, column 1823, Latin.

194.Decret. Par Distinct 96 Ch. 7 Edit Lugd. 1661, quoted in Josiah Pratt, The Church Historians of England: Reformation Period, at 159, 1856. http://www.orthodoxchristianity.net/forum/index.php?topic=11778.0;imode. Alberto Rivera, who was given access to the Vatican archives when he was a Jesuit priest, and quoted language very similar to the statement from Pope Nicholas's statement, but he quoted it as part of the Pope Boniface VIII's *Bull Unum Sanctum*. ALBERTO RIVERA, THE GODFATHERS, Chick Publications, p. 32, 1982 (quoting The Registers of Boniface VIII, The Vatican Archives, L. Fol. 387 and THE CATHOLIC ENCYCLOPEDIA, Encyclopedia Press (1913)).

195. The Canons and Decrees of the Ecumenical Council of Trent, 25th Session, December 4, 1563., Under the Pontiff, Pius IV, available at https://history.hanover.edu/texts/trent/ct25.html.

196. The New American, Dark Dealings in the Vatican?, at p. 24, March 3, 1997.

197. Satanism in the Vatican, http://www.jesus-is-savior.com/False%20Religions/Roman%20Catholicism/SS/anti3.htm (last visited on December 12, 2010).

198. The New American, The Catholic Church in Crisis, p. 39, June 9, 1997.

199. The New American, Dark Dealings in the Vatican?, at p. 24, March 3, 1997.

200. *Id.*

201. CATECHISM OF THE CATHOLIC CHURCH, PART THREE LIFE IN CHRIST, SECTION TWO, THE TEN COMMANDMENTS, available at http://www.vatican.va/archive/ccc_css/archive/catechism/command.htm (last visited on February 23, 2014).

202. CATECHISM OF THE CATHOLIC CHURCH § 2051, p. 551 (1994).

203. CATECHISM OF THE CATHOLIC CHURCH, PART THREE LIFE IN CHRIST, SECTION TWO, THE TEN COMMANDMENTS, available at http://www.vatican.va/archive/ccc_css/archive/catechism/command.htm (last visited on February 23, 2014).

204. *Id.* at § 2051, p.552.

205. *Id.* at § 2175.

206. CATECHISM OF THE CATHOLIC CHURCH, § 2185 (1994).

207. Walter Veith, Denominational Testimony, Protestant Testimony of the Sabbath Change, September 9, 2009, http://amazingdiscoveries.org/S-deception-Sabbath_Sunday_denominations, citing Isaac Williams, Plain Sermons on the Catechism, Volume 1:334, 336.

208. Walter Veith, Denominational Testimony, Protestant Testimony of the Sabbath Change, September 9, 2009, http://amazingdiscoveries.org/S-deception-Sabbath_Sunday_denominations, citing Lionel Beere, Church and People, 1947.

209. Walter Veith, Denominational Testimony, Protestant Testimony of the Sabbath Change, September 9, 2009, http://amazingdiscoveries.org/S-deception-Sabbath_Sunday_denominations, citing Manual of Christian Doctrine:127.

210. S. Michael Houdmann, Did Constantine change the Sabbath from Saturday to Sunday?, http://www.gotquestions.org/Constantine-Sabbath.html (last visited April 25, 2014) (quoting, Codex Justinianus lib. 3, tit. 12, 3; trans. in Philip Schaff, *History of the Christian Church*, Vol. 3, p. 380, note 1).

211. Catechism of the Catholic Church, § 2174, http://www.vatican.va/archive/ENG0015/__P7O.HTM, (last visited on April 25, 2014), citing St. Justin, I

Apol. 67: PG 6, 429 and 432.

212. How The Sabbath Was Changed, http://www.sabbathtruth.com/sabbath-history/how-the-sabbath-was-changed (last visited on April 25, 2014) quoting, Dr. Gilbert Murray, History of Christianity in the Light of Modern Knowledge.

213. William Dollarhide, the 1752 Calendar Change in North America, http://www.rootsweb.ancestry.com/~cacvgs2/Articles/Misc/calendar_change.pdf (last visited on April 5, 2014).

214. Evangelical Christendom, Vol. 49, January 1, 1895, pg. 15, the organ of the Evangelical Alliance, published in London by J. S. Phillips. See also, Catholique Nationale, July 13, 1895 (Reported in the Protestant Church Review of October 3, and November 14th, 1895, and the India Watchman, in The Friend, A Religious And Literary Journal, Volume LXIX, 1896, Philadelphia, pg. 154.). Daniel and the Revelation: The Chart of Prophecy and Our Place In It, A Study of the Historical and Futurist Interpretation, by Joseph Tanner, published in London by Hodder and Stoughton, 1898, pages 153, 154. Michael Scheifler, The Curious Case of Cardinal Sarto's Homily, http://biblelight.net/Sarto-homily.htm (last visited on March 17, 2014).

215. Sydney F. Smith, S.J., Does the Pope Claim to be God?, Publications of the Catholic Truth Society, at 11 (1896).

216. Steve Wohlberg, Antichrist Appeals, Is Antichrist Only One Man?, http://www.whitehorsemedia.com/articles/?d=42 (last

visited on March 1, 2014).

217. A. Wylie, The Papacy is the Antichrist, at 32-33.

218. ORDERED BY THE COUNCIL OF TRENT, EDITED UNDER ST. CHARLES BORROMEO, PUBLISHED BY DECREE OF POPE ST. PIUS V, 1566, TAN Books, p. 258, 1982.

219. *See* CHINIQUY, THE PRIEST, THE WOMAN, AND THE CONFESSIONAL, Chick Publications.

220. Rosamond Culbertson, A Narrative of the Captivity and Sufferings of an American Female Under the Popish Priests, in the Island of Cuba; With a Full Disclosure of Their Manners and Customs, at 48 (1837).

221. Margaret Shepherd, My Life in the Convent: or The Marvelous Personal Experiences of Margaret Shepherd, 216 (1892), https://archive.org/details/mylifeinconvento00shepuoft.

222. Amazing Statements Regarding the Roman Catholic Church, Let There Be Light Ministries, http://www.lightministries.com/id524.htm (last visited on June 19, 2014), quoting Pope Paul VI, as in turn quoted in The Apostolic Digest, by Michael Malone, Book 6: "The Book of Sentimental Excuses", Chapter 4: "The Dogmas of Faith Admit No Alteration Whatsoever," quoting St. Alphonsus De Liguori, True Spouse of Christ, p 352, Benziger Brothers, NY.

223. A. Wylie, The Papacy is the Antichrist, at 36-38.

224. A. Wylie, The Papacy is the Antichrist, at 36-38.

225. A. Wylie, The Papacy is the Antichrist, at 36-38.

226. Catechism of the Catholic Church, § 1461, 1994.

227. Compendium of the Catechism of the Catholic Church, §§ 297-298, http://www.vatican.va/archive/compendium_ccc/documents/archive_2005_compendium-ccc_en.html (last visited on July 27, 2014). The Forgiveness of Sins, Catholic Answers, http://www.catholic.com/tracts/the-forgiveness-of-sins (last visited on July 27, 2014).

228. Remit, Merriam Webster Dictionary, http://www.merriam-webster.com/dictionary/remit (last visited on July 26, 2010).

229. CATECHISM OF THE CATHOLIC CHURCH, §§ 1579-1580 (1994).

230. *See* CATECHISM OF THE CATHOLIC CHURCH, §§ 540, 1438, 2043 (1994).

231. ROBERT McCLORY, POWER AND THE PAPACY, LIGUORI PUBLISHING, p. 66, 1997.

232. Roman Catholic Priest David S. Phelan, The Western Watchman (St. Louis: Western Watchman Publishing Company), June 10, 1915, http://www.sotruth.org/spirit_of_truth_027.htm.

233. ORDERED BY THE COUNCIL OF TRENT, EDITED UNDER ST. CHARLES BORROMEO, PUBLISHED BY DECREE OF POPE ST. PIUS V, 1566, TAN Books, 1982 at p. 233.

234. WILLIAM AND SHARON SCHNOEBELEN, LUCIFER DETHRONED, p. 56-58 (1993).

235. *Id.* at p.141.

236. WILLIAM AND SHARON SCHNOEBELEN, LUCIFER DETHRONED, p. 259-66 (1993).

237. *Id.* at p. 264.

238. PETER J. ELLIOTT, CEREMONIES OF THE MODERN ROMAN RITE, Ignatius Press, § 663, p. 245 (1994).

239. PETER J. ELLIOTT, CEREMONIES OF THE MODERN ROMAN RITE, Ignatius Press, p. 264 (1994).

240. THE CATECHISM OF THE CATHOLIC CHURCH, § 1367, 1994.

241. THE CATECHISM OF THE CATHOLIC CHURCH, § 1364, 1994.

242. THE CATECHISM OF THE COUNCIL OF TRENT, *Ordered By the Council of Trent, Edited Under St. Charles Borromeo, Published by Decree of Pope St. Pius V* (emphasis added), p. 258 (1982).

243. THE CATECHISM OF THE COUNCIL OF TRENT, *Ordered By the Council of Trent, Edited Under St. Charles Borromeo, Published by Decree of Pope St. Pius V* (emphasis added), p. 258 (1982).

244. Fortescue, A. (1910). Liturgy. In The Catholic Encyclopedia. New York: Robert Appleton Company. Retrieved February 19, 2010 from New Advent: http://www.newadvent.org/cathen/09306a.htm.

245. Joseph Cardinal Ratzinger, The Reservation of the Blessed Sacrament, Institute for Sacred Architecture, Volume 12, Fall/Winter 2006, *available at* http://www.sacredarchitecture.org/articles/reservation_

of_the_blessed_sacrament/.

246. Letter from Bishop Mengeling to David Moss, President of the *Association of Hebrew Catholics*, dated March 19, 1982, http://www.hebrewcatholic.net/wp-content/uploads/2013/05/bishopmengelingle.gif.

247. The Catechism of the Catholic Church, § 97 (2003).

248. Michael Hoffman, *Judaism Discovered*, at 266-67 (2008).

249. Michael Hoffman, *Judaism Discovered*, at 268 (2008).

250. Michael Hoffman, *Judaism Discovered*, at 239 (2008).

251. Michael Hoffman, *Judaism Discovered*, at 240 (2008).

252. Michael Hoffman, *Judaism Discovered*, at 240 (2008).

253. Laura Ellen Shulman, Judaism, Jewish *Mysticism Kabbalah and the Sefirot* (March 13, 2007), *at* http://www.nvcc.edu/home/lshulman/Rel232/resource/sefirot.htm.

254. Athol Bloomer, *The Eucharist and The Jewish Mystical Tradition • Part 1*, Association of Hebrew Catholics, *at* http://hebrewcatholic.org/PrayerandSpirituality/eucharistjewishm.html (originally published in The Hebrew Catholic #77, pp 15-18 (Summer-Fall 2002)).

255. Athol Bloomer, *The Eucharist and The Jewish Mystical Tradition • Part 1*, Association of Hebrew Catholics, *at* http://hebrewcatholic.org/PrayerandSpirituality/eucharistjewishm.html (originally published in The Hebrew Catholic #77, pp 15-18 (Summer-Fall 2002)).

256. Yesod, Jewish Virtual Library, *at* http://www.jewishvirtuallibrary.org/jsource/Judaism/Yesod.html (last visited on March 2, 2010).

257. Athol Bloomer, *The Eucharist and The Jewish Mystical Tradition • Part 1*, Association of Hebrew Catholics, at http://www.hebrewcatholic.net (originally published in The Hebrew Catholic #77, pp 15-18 (Summer-Fall 2002)).

258. Athol Bloomer, *The Eucharist and The Jewish Mystical Tradition • Part 1*.

259. Athol Bloomer, *The Eucharist and The Jewish Mystical Tradition • Part 1*.

260. Athol Bloomer, *The Eucharist and The Jewish Mystical Tradition • Part 1*.

261. Athol Bloomer, *The Eucharist and The Jewish Mystical Tradition • Part 1*.

262. Dan Cohn-Sherbok and Lavinia Cohn-Sherbok, Jewish and Christian Mysticism: An Introduction, at 167 (1994).

263. Rabbi Eli Mallon, M.Ed., LMSW, Shir ha-Shirim: The Song of Songs, April, 23, 2011, http://rabbielimallon.wordpress.com/2011/04/23/4-23-11-shir-ha-shirim-the-song-of-songs/, quoting, Schochet, J. Immanuel, transl. and ed.; Tzva'at

ha-Rivash (The Ethical Will of the Baal Shem Tov); section 68; Kehot Publication Society.

264. Rabbi Eli Mallon, M.Ed., LMSW, Shir ha-Shirim: The Song of Songs, April, 23, 2011, http://rabbielimallon.wordpress.com/2011/04/23/4-23-11-shir-ha-shirim-the-song-of-songs/.

265. Francis and the Shekinah, Call Me Jorge, May 25, 2014, http://callmejorgebergoglio.blogspot.com/2014/05/francis-shekinah.html. See also, Brother Nathaniel Enlightens Us: Satan at the "Wailing Wall," http://givingpsychologyaway.com/?tag=davening and http://www.realjewnews.com/?p=798.

266. Brother Nathaniel Kapner, Satan at the Wailing Wall, February 13, 2013, http://www.realjewnews.com/?p=798.

267. Rabbi Michael Leo Samuel, Davening at Victoria's Secret, San Diego Jewish Herald, 27 December 2013, http://www.sdjewishworld.com/2013/12/27/davening-at-victorias-secret/, quoting Jacob I. Schochet, Tzavat HaRivash (Brooklyn, NY: Kehot Publication, 1998), pp.54-55.

268. Rabbi Michael Leo Samuel, Davening at Victoria's Secret, San Diego Jewish Herald, 27 December 2013, http://www.sdjewishworld.com/2013/12/27/davening-at-victorias-secret/, quoting Jacob I. Schochet, Tzavat HaRivash (Brooklyn, NY: Kehot Publication, 1998), pp.54-55.

269. Athol Bloomer, *The Eucharist and The Jewish Mystical Tradition • Part 2*, Association of Hebrew Catholics, http://www.hebrewcatholic.net/eucharist-jewish-mystical-tradition-part-2/ (last visited on April 6, 2014).

270. Athol Bloomer, *The Eucharist and The Jewish Mystical Tradition • Part 2*, Association of Hebrew Catholics, *at* http://hebrewcatholic.org/PrayerandSpirituality/eucharistjewisht.html (originally published in The Hebrew Catholic #78 (Winter-Spring 2003)).

271. Athol Bloomer, The Eucharist and The Jewish Mystical Tradition • Part 2, http://www.hebrewcatholic.net/eucharist-jewish-mystical-tradition-part-2/.

272. Athol Bloomer, *The Eucharist and The Jewish Mystical Tradition • Part 3*, Association of Hebrew Catholics, *at* http://hebrewcatholic.org/HCLives/Bloomer-Athol/eucharistandjewi.html, (originally published in The Hebrew Catholic #80 (Spring/Summer 2004)). See also Tiferet, Jewish Virtual Library, at http://www.jewishvirtuallibrary.org/jsource/Judaism/Tiferet.html (last visited on March 3, 2010).

273. Athol Bloomer, *The Eucharist and The Jewish Mystical Tradition • Part 3*, Association of Hebrew Catholics, *at* http://hebrewcatholic.org/HCLives/Bloomer-Athol/eucharistandjewi.html, (originally published in The Hebrew Catholic #80 (Spring/Summer 2004)).

274. Alexander Hislop, *The Two Babylons*, at 160 (1959).

275. Acharya S, *Osiris The Lord: Out of Egypt*, at http://www.truthbeknown.com/osiris.htm (last visited on March 4, 2010) (excerpt from Acharya S, *Suns of God: Krishna, Buddha and Christ Unveiled*).

276. George A. Barton, *Tammuz and Osiris*, Journal of the American Oriental Society, Vol. 35, (1915), pp. 213-223, available at http://www.jstor.org/stable/592647.

277. Acharya S, *Osiris The Lord: Out of Egypt*, at http://www.truthbeknown.com/osiris.htm (last visited on March 4, 2010) (excerpt from Acharya S, *Suns of God: Krishna, Buddha and Christ Unveiled*).

278. Acharya S, *Osiris The Lord: Out of Egypt*, at http://www.truthbeknown.com/osiris.htm (last visited on March 4, 2010) (excerpt from Acharya S, *Suns of God: Krishna, Buddha and Christ Unveiled*).

279. Images of the Nile and Egypt, *at* http://www.thenileandegypt.com/deities.html (last visited on March 3, 2010).

280. Images of the Nile and Egypt, *at* http://www.thenileandegypt.com/deities.html (last visited on March 3, 2010).

281. Athol Bloomer, *The Eucharist and The Jewish Mystical Tradition • Part 2*, Association of Hebrew Catholics, *at* http://hebrewcatholic.org/PrayerandSpirituality/eucharistjewisht.html (originally published in The Hebrew Catholic #78 (Winter-Spring 2003)).

282. Aharon Yosef, A Catholic Jew Pontificates, *Miriam ha Kedosha the Lady Moon of Israel*, January

10, 2008, *at* http://aronbengilad.blogspot.com/2008/01/miriam-hakedosha-lady-moon-of-israel.html.

283. Michael Hoffman, *Judaism Discovered*, at 269 (2008).

284. See also, Sketch of Chalice and Eucharistic host from SymbolDictionary.net, Religious Symbols, A Visual Glossary, *at* http://symboldictionary.net/?p=2090 (last visited on March 3, 2010).

285. Alexander Hislop, *The Two Babylons*, at 164 (1959).

286. Alexander Hislop, *The Two Babylons*, at 160 (1959).

287. Alexander Hislop, *The Two Babylons*, at 163 (1959).

288. Athol Bloomer, *The Eucharist and The Jewish Mystical Tradition • Part 3*, Association of Hebrew Catholics, *at* http://hebrewcatholic.org/HCLives/Bloomer-Athol/eucharistandjewi.html, (originally published in The Hebrew Catholic #80 (Spring/Summer 2004)). See also Tiferet, Jewish Virtual Library, at http://www.jewishvirtuallibrary.org/jsource/Judaism/Tiferet.html (last visited on March 3, 2010).

289. Alexander Hislop, *The Two Babylons*, at 232 (1959).

290. Alexander Hislop, *The Two Babylons*, at 232 (1959).

291. Alexander Hislop, *The Two Babylons*, at 232 (1959).

292. Michael Hoffman, *Judaism Discovered*, at 791 (2008) (citing The Zohar III, 282a).

293. Alter Breads, BSPA, Quality Alter Breads Since 1910, http://altarbreadsbspa.com/altarbreads/ (last visited on April 6, 2014).

294. Alexander Hislop, *The Two Babylons*, at 164 (1959).

295. Ryan Erlenbush, What does IHS stand for? The meaning of the Holy Name of Jesus, January 3, 2012, http://newtheologicalmovement.blogspot.com/2012/01/what-does-ihs-stand-for-meaning-of-holy.html.

296. Maere, R. (1910). IHS. In The Catholic Encyclopedia. New York: Robert Appleton Company. Retrieved October 26, 2012 from New Advent: http://www.newadvent.org/cathen/07649a.htm. Ecclesiastical approbation. Nihil Obstat. June 1, 1910. Remy Lafort, S.T.D., Censor. Imprimatur. +John Cardinal Farley, Archbishop of New York.

297. Maere, R. (1910). IHS. In The Catholic Encyclopedia. New York: Robert Appleton Company. Retrieved October 26, 2012 from New Advent: http://www.newadvent.org/cathen/07649a.htm. Ecclesiastical approbation. Nihil Obstat. June 1, 1910. Remy Lafort, S.T.D., Censor. Imprimatur. +John Cardinal Farley, Archbishop of New York.

298. Maere, R. (1910). IHS. In The Catholic Encyclopedia. New York: Robert Appleton Company. Retrieved October 26, 2012 from New Advent:

http://www.newadvent.org/cathen/07649a.htm.
Ecclesiastical approbation. Nihil Obstat. June 1, 1910.
Remy Lafort, S.T.D., Censor. Imprimatur. +John Cardinal Farley, Archbishop of New York.

299. Holweck, F. (1910). Holy Name of Jesus. In The Catholic Encyclopedia. New York: Robert Appleton Company. Retrieved October 26, 2012 from New Advent: http://www.newadvent.org/cathen/07421a.htm.
Ecclesiastical approbation. Nihil Obstat. June 1, 1910.
Remy Lafort, S.T.D., Censor. Imprimatur. +John Cardinal Farley, Archbishop of New York.

300. Maere, R. (1910). IHS. In The Catholic Encyclopedia. New York: Robert Appleton Company. Retrieved October 26, 2012 from New Advent: http://www.newadvent.org/cathen/07649a.htm.
Ecclesiastical approbation. Nihil Obstat. June 1, 1910.
Remy Lafort, S.T.D., Censor. Imprimatur. +John Cardinal Farley, Archbishop of New York.

301. Ryan Erlenbush, What does IHS stand for? The meaning of the Holy Name of Jesus, January 3, 2012, http://newtheologicalmovement.blogspot.com/2012/01/what-does-ihs-stand-for-meaning-of-holy.html.

302. Ron Byerly, IHS, http://www.eyeoftheneedle.net/Church%20Traditions/ihs.htm (last visited on October 26, 2012).

303. See Michael Hoffman, *Judaism Discovered*, at 184 (2008).

304. CATECHISM OF THE CATHOLIC CHURCH § 839 (1994) (footnotes omitted, emphasis added).

305. CATECHISM OF THE CATHOLIC CHURCH § 839 (1994) (footnotes omitted, internal quotation marks omitted).

306. Michael L. Rodkinson: The History of the Talmud; http://www.come-and-hear.com/talmud/rodkin_ii3.htm l#E27 (web address current as of February 8, 2004).

307. Michael Hoffman & Alan R. Critchley, The Truth About the Talmud, http://www.hoffman-info.com/talmudtruth.html (current as of September 12, 2001).

308. Michael Hoffman & Alan R. Critchley, The Truth About the Talmud, http://www.hoffman-info.com/talmudtruth.html (current as of September 12, 2001).

309. Michael Hoffman & Alan R. Critchley, The Truth About the Talmud, http://www.hoffman-info.com/talmudtruth.html (current as of September 12, 2001).

310. Michael Hoffman, *Judaism Discovered*, at 534 (2008).

311. Michael Hoffman, *Judaism Discovered*, at 196 (2008).

312. Light of Truth in a World of Dark, http://lightoftruth.tumblr.com/post/25395978741/video-of-benedict-xvi-invoking-satan-in-front-of (last visited on March 16, 2014).

313. Light of Truth in a World of Dark, http://lightoftruth.tumblr.com/post/25395978741/video-of-benedict-xvi-invoking-satan-in-front-of (last visited on March 16, 2014).

314. Light of Truth in a World of Dark, http://lightoftruth.tumblr.com/post/25395978741/video-of-benedict-xvi-invoking-satan-in-front-of (last visited on March 16, 2014).

315. Lucifer Invoked at the Vatican, http://www.youtube.com/watch?v=caTodjoE2b0 (last visited on March 16, 2014).

316. Maas, Anthony. "Lucifer." The Catholic Encyclopedia. Vol. 9. New York: Robert Appleton Company, 1910. 13 Apr. 2014 <http://www.newadvent.org/cathen/09410a.htm>.

317. SAMUEL C. GIPP, AN UNDERSTANDABLE HISTORY OF THE BIBLE, p. 70 (1987).

318. *Id.*

319. *Id.* at p. 71.

320. *Id.* at p. 70.

321. *Id.* at p. 71.

322. *Id.* at p. 70.

323. *Id.* at p. 71.

324. *Id.*

325. *Id.* at p. 72.

326. LES GARRETT, WHICH BIBLE CAN WE TRUST?, p. 151 (1982).

327. G.A. RIPLINGER, BLIND GUIDES, p. 19.

328. G.A. RIPLINGER, BLIND GUIDES, p. 19.

329. Company History: Zondervan Corporation, http://www.answers.com/topic/zondervan (last visited on April 5, 2010).

330. G. A. RIPLINGER, THE LANGUAGE OF THE KING JAMES BIBLE, p. 114 (1998).

331. G.A. RIPLINGER, NEW AGE BIBLE VERSIONS, p. 2 (1993).

332. G. A. RIPLINGER, THE LANGUAGE OF THE KING JAMES BIBLE, p. 128 (1998).

333. Company History: Zondervan Corporation, http://www.answers.com/topic/zondervan (last visited on April 5, 2010).

334. Anton La Vey, Satanic Bible, Harper Collins, *available at* http://www.harpercollins.com/book/index.aspx?isbn=9780380015399 (on sale 12/1/1976); NIV Bible, Harper Collins *available at* http://www.harpercollins.com/books/9780310949862/NIV_Bible/index.aspx.

335. G. A. RIPLINGER, THE LANGUAGE OF THE KING JAMES BIBLE, p. 128 (1998).

336. G. A. RIPLINGER, THE LANGUAGE OF THE KING JAMES BIBLE, p. 128 (1998).

337. Michael Hoffman II, Secret Societies and Psychological Warfare, at p. 75 (2001).

338. Michael Hoffman II, Secret Societies and Psychological Warfare, at p. 75 (2001).

339. ALBERT PIKE, MORALS AND DOGMA OF THE ANCIENT AND ACCEPTED SCOTTISH RITE OF FREEMASONRY, p. 205 (1871).

340. DES GRIFFIN, THE FOURTH REICH OF THE RICH, p. 70 (1993).

341. JAMES R. WHITE, THE ROMAN CATHOLIC CONTROVERSY, p. 187, 1996 (quoting *Indulgentiarum Doctrina,* January 1, 1967).

342. CATECHISM OF THE CATHOLIC CHURCH, §§ 1030-1031 (1994).

343. COUNCIL OF TRENT, SESSION VI, DECREE ON JUSTIFICATION, Canon XXX, January 13, 1547 (emphasis added).

344. AVRO MANHATTAN, THE VATICAN BILLIONS, Chick Publications (1983).

345. DAVE HUNT, A WOMAN RIDES THE BEAST, p. 240 (1994).

346. *Id.* at 239.

347. *Id.*

348. *Id.* at 240.

349. AVRO MANHATTAN, THE VATICAN BILLIONS, p. 184 (1983).

350. *Id.*

351. *Id.* at p. 184.

352. *Id* at 185.

353.Jack Chick, SMOKESCREENS, http://www.acts2.com/thebibletruth/Online%20Books/SMOKESCREENS.pdf (web address current as of September 23, 2003).

354.*Id.* at 187.

355.*Id.* at p. 188.

356.*Id.* at p. 188.

357.*Id.* at p. 178-179.

358.DAVE HUNT, A WOMAN RIDES THE BEAST, p.241 (1994).

359.AVRO MANAHATTAN, THE VATICAN BILLIONS, Chick Publications, p.41 (1983).

360.Rosamond Culbertson, A Narrative of the Captivity and Sufferings of an American Female Under the Popish Priests, in the Island of Cuba; With a Full Disclosure of Their Manners and Customs (1837).

361.CATECHISM OF THE CATHOLIC CHURCH, § 1471-73 (1994).

362.*Id.* at § 1471.

363.AVRO MANAHATTAN, THE VATICAN BILLIONS, Chick Publications, p.183 (1983).

364.*Id.* at p. 57-65.

365.PETER J. ELLIOTT, CEREMONIES OF THE MODERN ROMAN RITE, Ignatius Press, § 369, p. 135 (1994).

366. RALPH E. WOODROW, BABYLON MYSTERY RELIGION, p. 61 (1966).

367. J.A. Wylie, The Papacy is the Antichrist, Chapter XI (1888).

368. A. Wylie, The Papacy is the Antichrist, at 35.

369. The Papal Bull *In Coena Domini*, With a Short Introduction (1848), Roman Catholic Church.

370. A.W. Pink, A Study of Dispensationalism, http://www.pbministries.org/books/pink/Dispensationalism/ (last visited on March 1, 2014).

371. Arthur W. Pink, The Antichrist, available at http://www.biblebelievers.com/Pink/antichrist01.htm (last visited on March 1, 2014).

372. THE COMPACT EDITION OF THE OXFORD ENGLISH DICTIONARY, COMPLETE TEXT REDUCED MICROGRAPHICALLY, OXFORD UNIVERSITY PRESS (1979). *See also,* NOAH WEBSTER, AMERICAN DICTIONARY OF THE ENGLISH LANGUAGE (1828).

373. THE COMPACT EDITION OF THE OXFORD ENGLISH DICTIONARY, COMPLETE TEXT REDUCED MICROGRAPHICALLY, OXFORD UNIVERSITY PRESS (1979).

374. NOAH WEBSTER, AMERICAN DICTIONARY OF THE ENGLISH LANGUAGE (1828).

375. NOAH WEBSTER, AMERICAN DICTIONARY OF THE ENGLISH LANGUAGE (1828). *See also,* D.P. SIMPSON, CASSELL'S LATIN DICTIONARY p. 500-01 (1982).

376. D.P. SIMPSON, CASSELL'S LATIN DICTIONARY p. 501 (1982).

377. PAUL ENNS, THE MOODY HANDBOOK OF THEOLOGY, p. 113, 333-34, 391-92 (1989).

378. *Id.* at 389-94.

379. *Id.* at 392.

380. A. Wylie, The Papacy is the Antichrist, at 38-39.

381. Noah Webster, AMERICAN DICTIONARY OF THE ENGLISH LANGUAGE, *Cardinal* (1828). See also Online Etymology Dictionary, *Cardinal, at* http://www.etymonline.com/index.php?term=cardinal (last visited on March 16, 2010).

382. Jewish Encyclopedia, High Priest, *available at* http://www.jewishencyclopedia.com/view.jsp?artid=721&letter=H&search=high%20priest (last visited on March 16, 2010).

383. Jewish Encyclopeidia, Sanhedrin, *available at* http://www.jewishencyclopedia.com/view.jsp?artid=229&letter=S&search=sanhedrin (last visited on March 16, 2010).

384. Sägmüller, J.B. (1908). Cardinal. In The Catholic Encyclopedia. New York: Robert Appleton Company. Retrieved March 16, 2010 from New Advent: http://www.newadvent.org/cathen/03333b.htm.

385. The High Priest and His Garments, http://www.domini.org/tabern/highprst.htm (last visited on March 16, 2010).

386. CATECHISM OF THE CATHOLIC CHURCH, § 830-831, 1994.

387. Arthur W. Pink, The Antichrist, available at http://www.ccel.org/ccel/pink/antichrist.pdf and http://www.biblebelievers.com/Pink/antichrist04.htm (last visited on February 24, 2014).

388. A. Wylie, The Papacy is the Antichrist, at 44.

389. A. Wylie, The Papacy is the Antichrist, at 45-46.

390. ALBERTO RIVERA, FOUR HORSEMEN, Chick Publications, p. 25, 1985 (quoting AVRO MANHATTAN, VATICAN IMPERIALISM IN THE 20th CENTURY, p. 76.). *See also*, JOHN W. ROBBINS, ECCLESIASTICAL MEGALOMANIA, at p. 132 (1999).

391. CATECHISM OF THE CATHOLIC CHURCH, § 2034-2035, 1994.

392. Medieval Sourcebook: Boniface VIII, Unam Sanctam, 1302, http://www.fordham.edu/halsall/source/b8-unam.asp. See also, ALBERTO RIVERA, THE GODFATHERS, Chick Publications, p. 32, 1982 (quoting The Registers of Boniface VIII, The Vatican Archives, L. Fol. 387 and THE CATHOLIC ENCYCLOPEDIA, Encyclopedia Press (1913)).

393. Decret. Par Distinct 96 Ch. 7 Edit Lugd. 1661, quoted in Josiah Pratt, The Church Historians of England: Reformation Period, at 159, 1856. http://www.orthodoxchristianity.net/forum/index.php?topic=11778.0;imode. Alberto Rivera, who was given access to the Vatican archives when he was a Jesuit priest, and quoted language very similar to the statement from

Pope Nicholas's statement, but he quoted it as part of the Pope Boniface VIII's *Bull Unum Sanctum*. ALBERTO RIVERA, THE GODFATHERS, Chick Publications, p. 32, 1982 (quoting The Registers of Boniface VIII, The Vatican Archives, L. Fol. 387 and THE CATHOLIC ENCYCLOPEDIA, Encyclopedia Press (1913)).

394. Decretals of Gregory IX, Bk. 1, Ch. 3, http://christianitybeliefs.org/end-times-deceptions/pope-quotes-verify-they-are-antichrist-son-of-perdition/.

395. Roman Catholic Priest David S. Phelan, The Western Watchman (St. Louis: Western Watchman Publishing Company), June 10, 1915, http://www.sotruth.org/spirit_of_truth_027.htm.

396. Papal Bull Unum Sanctum, November 18, 1302, http://www.americancatholictruthsociety.com/docs/unamsanctum.htm. See also, Papal Bull Unum Sanctum, November 18, 1302, Papal Encyclicals Online, http://www.papalencyclicals.net/Bon08/B8unam.htm.

397. Barclay, Chapter XXVII, p. 218, "Cities Petrus Bertanous." http://www.orthodoxchristianity.net/forum/index.php?topic=11778.0;imode.

398. ALBERTO RIVERA, DOUBLE CROSS, Chick publications, p. 27, 1981(quoting THE GREAT ENCYCLICAL LETTERS OF POPE LEO XIII, p. 304, Benziger Brothers (1903). See also, Praeclara Gratulationis Publicae, The Reunion of Christendom, Apostolic Letter of Pope Leo XIII, June 20, 1894, Papal Encyclicals Online, available at http://www.papalencyclicals.net/Leo13/l13praec.htm.

399. Decret. Par Distinct 96 Ch. 7 Edit Lugd. 1661, quoted in Josiah Pratt, The Church Historians of England: Reformation Period, at 159, 1856. http://www.orthodoxchristianity.net/forum/index.php?topic=11778.0;imode. Alberto Rivera, who was given access to the Vatican archives when he was a Jesuit priest, and quoted language very similar to the statement from Pope Nicholas's statement, but he quoted it as part of the Pope Boniface VIII's *Bull Unum Sanctum*. ALBERTO RIVERA, THE GODFATHERS, Chick Publications, p. 32, 1982 (quoting The Registers of Boniface VIII, The Vatican Archives, L. Fol. 387 and THE CATHOLIC ENCYCLOPEDIA, Encyclopedia Press (1913)).

400. Alexander Hislop, The light of prophecy let in on the dark places of the papacy (London: William Whyte and Co., 1846): 91 and Letters between a Catholic and a Protestant on the doctrines of the Church of Rome originally published in Borrow's Worcester Journal (Worcester Journal, 1827): 29. http://rekindlingthereformation.com/R-Pope_Rome_blasphemy_power_Jesus.html.

401. The Gloss of Extravagantes of Pope John XXII, Cum. Inter, title 14, chapter 4, "Ad Callem Sexti Decretalium", Column 140 (Paris, 1685). In an Antwerp edition of the Extravagantes, the words, Dominum Deum Nostrum Papam ("Our Lord God the Pope") can be found in column 153. http://rekindlingthereformation.com/R-Pope_Rome_blasphemy_power_Jesus.html.

402. Post-Synodal Apostolic Exhortation, *Vita Consecrata* Of the Holy Father John Paul II, March 25, 1996, http://www.vatican.va/holy_father/john_paul_ii/apost_

exhortations/documents/hf_jp-ii_exh_25031996_vita-consecrata_en.html.

403.G.A. RIPLER, NEW AGE BIBLE VERSIONS, p. 134 (1993).

404.*Id.*

405.RALPH E. WOODROW, BABYLON MYSTERY RELIGION, p. 72, 1966.

406.COLLIER'S ENCYCLOPEDIA, volume 19, p. 239 (1991).

407.STEWART PEROWNE, ROMAN MYTHOLOGY, p. 125-26, 1969.

408.COLLIER'S ENCYCLOPEDIA, volume 13, p. 38 (1991).

409.ENCYCLOPEDIA AMERICANA, volume 15, p. 193 (1998).

410.*Id.*

411.COLLIER'S ENCYCLOPEDIA, volume 13, p. 38 (1991).

412.COLLIER'S ENCYCLOPEDIA, volume 3, p. 644 (1991).

413.EDMOND PARIS, CONVERT OR DIE!, Chick Publications, p. 5.

414.RALPH E. WOODROW, BABYLON MYSTERY RELIGION, p. 100, 1966.

415. Joseph Jenkins, Saint Bartholomew Day's Massacre, Father Joe, http://fatherjoe.wordpress.com/instructions/debates/anti-catholicism/saint-bartholomew-day%E2%80%99s-massacre/ (last visited on March 29, 2014).

416. The Christian's Monthly Magazine and Universal Review, January to June, 1844, at 341, http://books.google.com/books?id=bOgEAAAAQAAJ&pg=PA341&lpg=PA341&dq=vgonottorum+strages&source=bl&ots=6pX5QdbPn8&sig=k3r1pELxsl6AoG8CFINg8wKDCFI&hl=en&sa=X&ei=JG03U6DsN7OrsASQ8oDYDw&ved=0CD0Q6AEwBg#v=onepage&q=vgonottorum%20strages&f=false (last visited on March 29, 2014).

417. Vasari's Mural Commemorating the Massacre of Protestant Christians on St. Bartholomew's Day, High Plains Parson, February 13, 2014, http://highplainsparson.wordpress.com/2014/02/13/vasaris-mural-commemorating-the-massacre-of-protestant-christians-on-st-bartholomews-day/

418. Joseph Jenkins, Saint Bartholomew Day's Massacre, Father Joe, http://fatherjoe.wordpress.com/instructions/debates/anti-catholicism/saint-bartholomew-day%E2%80%99s-massacre/ (last visited on March 29, 2014).

419. Michael Scheifler, The Red Dragon and Rome, http://biblelight.net/dragon.htm (last visited on March 29, 2014).

420. CORRADO PALLRNBERG, INSIDE THE VATICAN, p. 180-81, 1960.

421. ENCYCLOPEDIA BRITANNICA, volume 6, p. 329, 1998.

422. ENCYCLOPEDIA AMERICANA, volume 15, p.194 (1998).

423. DAVE HUNT, A WOMAN RIDES THE BEAST, p. 261, 1994.

424. COLLIER'S ENCYCLOPEDIA, volume 13, p. 40 (1991).

425. DAVE HUNT, A WOMAN RIDES THE BEAST, p. 261, 1994.

426. *Id.*

427. *Id.*

428. JOHN W. ROBBINS, ECCLESIASTICAL MEGALOMANIA, p. 113 (1999).

429. DAVE HUNT, A WOMAN RIDES THE BEAST, Harvest House Publishers, p. 89 (1994) (quoting Austin Flannery, O.P., gen. ed., *Vatican II, The Conciliar and Post Conciliar Documents*, rev. ed. (Costello Publishing 1988), vol. 1, p. 412).

430. CATECHISM OF THE CATHOLIC CHURCH § 846 (1994) (emphasis added).

431. *Id.* at § 881-882.

432. A. Wylie, The Papacy is the Antichrist, at 36-37.

433. JOHN PAUL II, CROSSING THE THRESHOLD OF HOPE, p. 11, 1994.

434. ALBERTO RIVERA, DOUBLE CROSS, Chick publications, p. 27, 1981(quoting THE GREAT ENCYCLICAL LETTERS OF POPE LEO XIII, p. 304, Benziger Brothers (1903).

435. Las Angeles Times, December 12, 1984 (quoted by Arthur Noble, The Pope's 'Apology' the First Great Laugh of the New Millennium, http://www.ianpaisley.org/article.asp?ArtKey=apology).

436. ORDERED BY THE COUNCIL OF TRENT, EDITED UNDER ST. CHARLES BORROMEO, PUBLISHED BY DECREE OF POPE ST. PIUS V, 1566, TAN Books, p. 331, 1982.

437. AVRO MANAHATTAN, THE VATICAN BILLIONS, Chick Publications, p.183 (1983).

438. AVRO MANAHATTAN, THE VATICAN BILLIONS, Chick Publications, p.41 (1983).

439. RALPH E. WOODROW, BABYLON MYSTERY RELIGION, p. 72, 1966.

440. COLLIER'S ENCYCLOPEDIA, volume 19, p. 239 (1991).

441. Medieval Sourcebook: Boniface VIII, Unam Sanctam, 1302, http://www.fordham.edu/halsall/source/b8-unam.asp. See also, ALBERTO RIVERA, THE GODFATHERS, Chick Publications, p. 32, 1982 (quoting The Registers of Boniface VIII, The Vatican Archives, L. Fol. 387 and THE CATHOLIC ENCYCLOPEDIA, Encyclopedia Press (1913)).

442.A letter from Cardinal Giuseppe Sarto (who became Pope Pius X in 1903) as quoted in Publications of the Catholic Truth Society Volume 29 (Catholic Truth Society: 1896): 11.

443.The Pontifical Biblical Commission, *The Jewish People and Their Sacred Scriptures in the Christian Bible*, section II A 7, 2002, http://www.vatican.va/roman_curia/congregations/cfaith/pcb_documents/rc_con_cfaith_doc_20020212_popolo-ebraico_en.html#5.%20The%20Unity%20of%20God%27s%20Plan%20and%20the%20Idea%20of%20Fulfilment

444.CATECHISM OF THE CATHOLIC CHURCH, § 882, 1994.

445.CATECHISM OF THE CATHOLIC CHURCH § 841 (1994).

446.T.A. McMahon, Catholicism & Islam: Ties That Bind,
Reaching Catholics For Christ, http://www.reachingcatholics.org/cath_islam.html (last visited on March 11, 2014).

447.Joseph Jenkins, Pope John Paul II Kisses the Koran,
http://fatherjoe.wordpress.com/instructions/debates/anti-catholicism/pope-john-paul-ii-kisses-the-koran/ (last visited on March 29, 2014).

448.Richard Bennett, Pope Francis Shows His True Colors,
http://www.trinityfoundation.org/journal.php?id=294#ftn15 (last visited on April 23, 2014).

449. Abdullahi Ahmed An-Na'im, Toward an Islamic Reformation: Civil Liberties, Human Rights, and International Law, Syracuse University Press, 1996, p. 183, http://books.google.com/books?id=U4e7Ph4lXzUC&pg=PA183#v=onepage&q&f=false. Kecia Ali and Oliver Leaman, Islam: the key concepts, Routledge, 2008, p. 10, http://books.google.com/books?id=H5-CdzqmuXsC&pg=PA10 .

450. Sir Muhammad Zafrulla Khan, Punishment of Apostasy in Islam, Opinions of Jurists, Ahmadiyya Muslim Community, http://www.alislam.org/books/apostacy/17.html (last visited on May 29, 2013).

451. Gamal El-Banna: A lifetime of Islamic Call, Al-Ahram Weekly Online, 8 April 2009, Issue # 941, http://weekly.ahram.org.eg/2009/941/intrvw.htm.

452. S. A. Rahman, Punishment of Apostasy in Islam, at 133, 2007. ISBN 978-983-9541-49-6. http://books.google.com.ph/books?id=L4fsYtFf5AoC&pg=PA132#v=onepage&q&f=false.

453. Benjamin Weinthal, Egyptian Court Sentences Christian Family to 15 Years for Converting from Islam, Fox News, January 16, 2013, http://www.foxnews.com/world/2013/01/16/egyptian-court-sentences-entire-family-to-15-years-for-converting-to/.

454. Robert Spencer, Abdul Rahman: Death for Apostasy, Human Events, 10/22/2006, http://www.humanevents.com/2006/10/22/abdul-rahman-death-for-apostasy/.

Afghan Clerics Call Christian Convert 'Apostate', Associated Press, March 24, 2006, http://www.foxnews.com/story/0,2933,188986,00.html.

455. Lisa Daftari, Iran Court Convicts Christian Pastor Convert to Death, Fox News, February 22, 2012, http://www.foxnews.com/world/2012/02/22/iran-court-convicts-christian-pastor-convert-to-death/.

456. Anugrah Kumar, Pastor Youcef Nadarkhani Still Alive; Execution Claim False, Says Group, The Christian Post, March 9, 2013, http://www.christianpost.com/news/pastor-youcef-nadarkhani-still-alive-group-says-refuting-execution-claim-91542/.

457. Anugrah Kumar, Pastor Youcef Nadarkhani Still Alive; Execution Claim False, Says Group, The Christian Post, March 9, 2013, http://www.christianpost.com/news/pastor-youcef-nadarkhani-still-alive-group-says-refuting-execution-claim-91542/.

458. Paul Marshal, The War on Christians, The Weekly Standard, June 23, 2014.

459. Former Muslims United, http://formermuslimsunited.org/apostasy-from-islam/al-azhar-fatwa/ (last visited on May 31, 2013).

460. Former Muslims United, http://formermuslimsunited.org/apostasy-from-islam/al-azhar-fatwa/ (last visited on May 31, 2013).

461. Unofficial English Translation of the Constitution of Egypt, 2014,

http://www.sis.gov.eg/Newvr/Dustor-en001.pdf.

462.Saudi Arabia-Constitution, http://www.servat.unibe.ch/icl/sa00000_.html.

463.Saudi Arabia-Constitution, http://www.servat.unibe.ch/icl/sa00000_.html.

464.Constitution of Afghanistan, http://www.afghan-web.com/politics/current_constituti on.html.

465.Constitution of Afghanistan, http://www.afghanembassy.com.pl/afg/images/pliki/Th eConstitution.pdf.

466.Constitution of Afghanistan, http://www.afghanembassy.com.pl/afg/images/pliki/Th eConstitution.pdf.

467.Pakistan Penal Code (Act XLV of 1860), Amended by: Protection of Women (Criminal Laws Amendment) Act, 2006,Criminal Laws (Amendment) Act, 2004 (I of 2005),Criminal Law (Amendment) Ordinance (LXXXV of 2002),Criminal Laws (Reforms) Ordinance (LXXXVI of 2002), http://www.pakistani.org/pakistan/legislation/1860/act XLVof1860.html.

468.Religious Persecution of Ahmadiyya Muslim Community, Section 295C Pakistan Criminal Code, http://www.thepersecution.org/archive/10_c.html (last visited on October 24, 2013).

469.Pakistan Minorities Minister Shahbaz Bhatti Shot Dead, BBC News, South Asia, 2 March 2011, http://www.bbc.co.uk/news/world-south-asia-1261756 2.

470. Pakistan Minorities Minister Shahbaz Bhatti Shot Dead, BBC News, South Asia, 2 March 2011, http://www.bbc.co.uk/news/world-south-asia-12617562.

471. Abdul Waheed Wafa and Carlotta Gall, Afghan Court Backs Prison Term for Blasphemy, The New York Times, March 11, 2009, http://www.nytimes.com/2009/03/12/world/asia/12afghan.html?_r=2&ref=world&.

472. International Religious Freedom Report, U.S. State Department, 2007.http://www.state.gov/j/drl/rls/irf/2007/90137.htm.

473. International Religious Freedom Report, U.S. State Department, 2007.

474. Quran, http://quran.com/20 (last visited on April 8, 2014).

475. Edward Williams Lane, Arabic-English Lexicon, 1863, http://www.tyndalearchive.com/tabs/lane/.

476. Andrew C. McCarthy, Thank God for McCain -- Allahu Akbar!, National Review, September 13, 2013, http://www.nationalreview.com/corner/357511/thank-god-mccain-allahu-akbar-andrew-c-mccarthy.

477. Raymond Ibrahim, Scott Allswang, Muslim Persecution of Christians: April, Faith Defenders, http://faithdefenders.com/islamupdates/Muslim-Persecution-of-Christians-April.html (last visited on June 6, 2014).

478. Raymond Ibrahim, Scott Allswang, Muslim Persecution of Christians: February, Faith Defenders, http://faithdefenders.com/islamupdates/Muslim-Persec

ution-of-Christians-February.html (last visited on June 6, 2014).

479. Raymond Ibrahim, Scott Allswang, Muslim Persecution of Christians: July, http://faithdefenders.com/islamupdates/Muslim-Persecution-of-Christians-July.html (last visited on June 6, 2014).

480. See generally, Juan Eduardo Campo, Encyclopedia of Islam, at 34, 2009, http://books.google.com/books?id=OZbyz_Hr-eIC&printsec=frontcover#v=onepage&q&f=false.

481. Patrick Glenn, Legal Traditions of the World, at 181, 2010.

482. *Encyclopedia of Religion and Ethics*, edited by James Hastings, M.A., D.D., with the assistance of John A. Selbie, M.A., D.D., and other scholars [Charles Scribner's Sons, New York; T. & T. Clark, Edinburgh, 1908], Volume I. A-Art, p. 326. http://books.google.com/books?id=uiJBAQAAIAAJ&printsec=frontcover#v=onepage&q&f=false.

483. E.g., Ibn Ishaq, Sirat Rasul Allah, (translated by A. Guillaume under the title, The Life of Muhammad), pp. 165-167. http://www.inthenameofallah.org/Satanic%20Verses.html (last visited on May 23, 2013).

484. Sam Shamoun, The Quran, Allah and Plurality Issues, http://www.answering-islam.org/Shamoun/allah_plurality.htm (last visited on June 6, 2014).

485. Sam Shamoun, The Quran, Allah and Plurality Issues, http://www.answering-islam.org/Shamoun/allah_plurality.htm (last visited on June 6, 2014).

486. Kahn, Islamic Law, at 18 (citing Cyril Glasse, *The Concise Encyclopedia of Islam* (Harper and Row, 1989), 228–232.).

487. Robert Morey, The Islamic Invasion, at 49, citing Mohammedanism: An Historical Survey (New York: Mentor Books, 1955), p.38.

488. Robert Morey, The Islamic Invasion, at 50, citing Arthur Jeffery, ed,, Islam: Muhammad, and His Religion (New York: The Liberal Arts Press, 1958), p. 85.

489. Morey, at 50, citing Arabic Lexicographical Miscellanies by J. Blau in the Journal of Semitic Studies, Vol. XVII, #2, 1972, pp. 173-190, and Hastings' Encyclopedia of Religion and Ethics, 1908, I:326.

490. Morey at 50.

491. Morey at 50, citing Encyclopedia of Religion, Thomas O'Brian, Consuela Aherne, I:117 (Washington DC, Corpus Pub., 1979). See also, Robert A. Morey, Islam Unveiled: The True Desert Storm (Shermans Dlae, PA: The Scholars Press, 1991),p. 46.

492. T.E. Wilder, The Desert Pagans, Contra Mundum, No. 3, Spring 1992, http://www.contra-mundum.org/cm/reviews/tw_desert.pdf, review of Islam Unveiled: The True Desert Storm, by Robert A. Morey (Shermans Dale, PA: The

Scholars Press, 1991) 179 pages, index, bibliography.

493. Mary and the Moslems: Fulton J. Sheen 1952, http://forums.catholic.com/showthread.php?t=509468.

494. Bukhari, Anbiya, 44; Muslim, Fada'il, trad. 146, 147. See also, Juan Eduardo Campo, Encyclopedia of Islam (Infobase Publishing 2009 ISBN 978-1-43812696-8), p. 559.

495. George Sale, Koran, commonly called the Alcoran of Mohammed, chapter 3, p. 39, http://posner.library.cmu.edu/Posner/books/pages.cgi?call=297_K84K_1734&layout=vol0/part0/copy0&file=0258.

496. T.A. McMahon, Catholicism & Islam: Ties That Bind,
Reaching Catholics For Christ,
http://www.reachingcatholics.org/cath_islam.html (last visited on March 11, 2014).

497. Catechism of the Catholic Church, § 499.

498. See Aliah Schleifer, MARY, THE MOTHER OF JESUS, Mary's perpetual virginity, http://answering-islam.org/Index/ (last visited on April 11, 2014).

499. Madame Helena Blavatsky, THE HISTORY OF A PLANET, Blavatsky Net - Theosophy, http://www.blavatsky.net/blavatsky/arts/HistoryOfAPlanet.htm (last visited on April 13, 2014).

500. Maas, Anthony. "Lucifer." The Catholic Encyclopedia. Vol. 9. New York: Robert Appleton Company, 1910. 13 Apr. 2014 <http://www.newadvent.org/cathen/09410a.htm>.

501.Maas, Anthony. "Lucifer." The Catholic Encyclopedia. Vol. 9. New York: Robert Appleton Company, 1910. 13 Apr. 2014 <http://www.newadvent.org/cathen/09410a.htm>.

502.Michael Osiris Snuffin, Devil of the Astral Light: Eliphas Levi's Baphomet, 2009, http://hermetic.com/osiris/levibaphomet.htm, quoting, Eliphas Levi, Transcendental Magick, page 308.

503.Maas, Anthony. "Lucifer." The Catholic Encyclopedia. Vol. 9. New York: Robert Appleton Company, 1910. 13 Apr. 2014 <http://www.newadvent.org/cathen/09410a.htm>.

504.https://www.flickr.com/photos/samira888/.

505.Quran, Surat Al-Ahzab, 33:59, Muhsin Khan English translation, http://quran.com/33 (last visited on June 2, 2014).

506.Quran, Surat An-Nur, 24:31, Muhsin Khan English translation, http://quran.com/24 (last visited on June 2, 2104).

507.Ford Hendrickson, The Black Convent Slave, at 21 (1914), https://archive.org/details/blackconventsla00hendgoog.

508.Luke Garratt, Austrian Rape Victim Was Arrested for Having Sex Outside of Marriage in Uae When She Reported the Crime... and Told She Had to Marry Her Attacker, Daily Mail, January 31, 2014, http://www.dailymail.co.uk/news/article-2549707/Austrian-rape-victim-arrested-having-sex-outside-marriage-UAE-reported-crime-told-MARRY-attacker.html.

509. Hasan Mahmud, How Sharia Law Punishes Raped Women, http://www.ahl-alquran.com/English/show_article.php?main_id=6157 (last visited on April 15, 2014).

510. Daniel Howden, 'Don't Kill Me,' She Screamed. Then They Stoned Her to Death, The Independent, November 9, 2008, http://www.independent.co.uk/news/world/africa/don't-kill-me-she-screamed-then-they-stoned-her-to-death-1003462.html.

511. Pedophilia in Islam, http://www.faithfreedom.org/Gallery/16.htm (last visited on April 12, 2014). Shaista Gohr, The Hypocrisy of Child Abuse in Many Muslim Countries, The Guardian, April 24, 2010, http://www.theguardian.com/commentisfree/2010/apr/25/middle-east-child-abuse-pederasty. Jim Kouri, Afghan Pedophilia: a Way of Life, Say U.S. Soldiers and Journalists, The Examiner, January 19, 2012, http://www.examiner.com/article/afghan-pedophilia-a-way-of-life-say-u-s-soldiers-and-journalists.

512. Why Arab Men Hold Hands, The New York Times, May 1, 2005, http://www.nytimes.com/2005/05/01/weekinreview/01basics.html?_r=0.

513. Why Arab Men Hold Hands, The New York Times, May 1, 2005, http://www.nytimes.com/2005/05/01/weekinreview/01basics.html?_r=0.

514. Photograph by Jason Reed of Reuters.

515. Sherman H. Skolnick, The Overthrow Of The American Republic - Part 15, September 4, 2002, http://www.rense.com/general28/skolover15.htm.

516. ANTHONY C. SUTTON, AMERICA'S SECRET ESTABLISHMENT, AN INTRODUCTION TO THE ORDER OF SKULL & BONES, at p. 212 (1986).

517. ANTHONY C. SUTTON, AMERICA'S SECRET ESTABLISHMENT, AN INTRODUCTION TO THE ORDER OF SKULL & BONES, at p. 212 (1986).

518. See generally, David Bay, Secret Societies Killed Jesus Christ, www.cuttingedge.org http://home.talkcity.com/InspirationAv/jforjesus/secret_societies.html (current as of October 1, 2001).

519. Sherman H. Skolnick, The Overthrow Of The American Republic - Part 15, September 4, 2002, http://www.rense.com/general28/skolover15.htm.

520. Sherman H. Skolnick, Bush Bisexuality Asserted In Scorching New Book, UPDATE New Book Further Confirms Our Independent Investigations!, September 7, 2004, http://www.rense.com/general57/newbook.htm.

521. Paul Joseph Watson, Bush Homosexual Allegations Resurface In New Book, Jones Report, September 24, 2007, http://www.jonesreport.com/articles/240907_bush_homosexual.html.

522. Paul Joseph Watson, Bush Homosexual Allegations Resurface In New Book, Jones Report, September 24, 2007,

http://www.jonesreport.com/articles/240907_bush_homosexual.html.

523. See an archived page at: Lustful Utterances by Domina Leola McConnell, https://web.archive.org/web/20070831134737/http://politics.lustfulutterances.com/.

524. Kitty Kelley, The Family, The Real Story of the Bush Dynasty, Author's Note, The Bush Family, at XX, January 6, 2012, http://www.smokershistory.com/Bush.html (last visited on May 16, 2014).

525. Kitty Kelley, Author's Notes on The Family, The Bush Family, January 6, 2012, http://www.smokershistory.com/Bush.html (last visited on May 16, 2014).

526. Jackson Thoreau, The Strange Death of the Woman Who Filed a Rape Lawsuit Against Bush, http://www.opednews.com/thoreau1103bush_rape_suicide.htm (last visited on May 16, 2014).

527. Blumenthal R., Suicidal Gunshot Wounds to the Head: a Retrospective Review of 406 Cases, December 28, 2007, http://www.ncbi.nlm.nih.gov/pubmed/18043013.

528. Howard Kurtz, Jeff Gannon Admits Past 'Mistakes,' Berates Critics, The Washington Post, February 19, 2005, http://www.washingtonpost.com/wp-dyn/articles/A36733-2005Feb18.html.

529. Paul Joseph Watson, Bush Homosexual Allegations Resurface In New Book, Jones Report,

September 24, 2007, http://www.jonesreport.com/articles/240907_bush_homosexual.html.

530. Jeff Gannon: Media Prostitute: Pimping to Power, http://www.oilempire.us/jeffgannon.html (last visited on May 16, 2014).

531. Paul Joseph Watson, Bush Homosexual Allegations Resurface In New Book, Jones Report, September 24, 2007, http://www.jonesreport.com/articles/240907_bush_homosexual.html. See article at Paul M. Rodriguez and George Archibald, Homosexual Prostitution Inquiry Ensnares VIPs with Reagan, Bush 'Call Boys' Took Midnight Tour of White House, June 29, 1989, http://www.wanttoknow.info/890629washingtontimesfranklin.

532. JOHN W. DECAMP, THE FRANKLIN COVER-UP, pp. 151-56 (1996).

533. Paul Joseph Watson, Bush Homosexual Allegations Resurface In New Book, Jones Report, September 24, 2007, http://www.jonesreport.com/articles/240907_bush_homosexual.html.

534. David Kuo, Tempting Faith, at 230 (2006).

535. Texe Marrs, White House Bordello, Power of Prophecy, Exclusive Intelligence Examiner Report, http://www.texemarrs.com/122006/white_house_bordello.htm (last visited on May 21, 2014).

536. 517 US 620 (1996).

537. 517 US 620 (1996).

538. Richard A. Serrano, Roberts Donated Help to Gay Rights Case, Los Angeles Times, August 4, 2005, http://articles.latimes.com/2005/aug/04/nation/na-roberts4.

539. 567 US 1 (2012).

540. Karen Frazier Romero, While They Slept (2014).

541. Paul Campos, Roberts Wrote both Obamacare Opinions, Salon, July 3, 2012, http://www.salon.com/2012/07/03/roberts_wrote_both_obamacare_opinions/.

542. 567 US 1 (2012).

543. Meghan Keneally, after Joking about Heading to Malta to Escape Criticism....Chief Justice Roberts Heads to Malta as it Emerges That He May Have Written for AND Against Opinions on Obamacare, Daily Mail, July 3, 2012, http://www.dailymail.co.uk/news/article-2168451/Chief-Justice-Roberts-heads-Malta-emerges-written-AND-opinions-Obamacare.html

544. 567 US 1 (2012).

545. Texe Marrs, Supreme Court Justice John Roberts Lauded by Knights of Malta for "ObamaCare" Vote, Power of Prophecy, Special Report, http://www.texemarrs.com/072012/roberts_lauded_by_knights_of_malta.htm (last visited on May 27, 2014).

546. Texe Marrs, White House Bordello, Power of Prophecy, Exclusive Intelligence Examiner Report, http://www.texemarrs.com/122006/white_house_bordello.htm (last visited on May 21, 2014).

547. Protocols of the Learned Elders of Zion, Protocol 8, http://www.biblebelievers.org.au/przion3.htm#PROTOCOL%20No.%208 (Last visited on August 22, 2012).

548. Jerome R. Corsi, Trinity Church Members Reveal Obama Shocker!, WorldNet Daily, http://www.wnd.com/2012/10/trinity-church-members-reveal-obama-shocker/ (last visited on October 4, 2012).

549. Jerome R. Corsi, Claim: Obama Hid 'Gay Life' to Become President, WorldNet Daily, http://www.wnd.com/2012/09/claim-obama-hid-gay-life-to-become-president/ (last visited on October 4, 2012).

550. Jerome R. Corsi, Claim: Obama Hid 'Gay Life' to Become President, WorldNet Daily, http://www.wnd.com/2012/09/claim-obama-hid-gay-life-to-become-president/ (last visited on October 4, 2012).

551. Jerome R. Corsi, Trinity Church Members Reveal Obama Shocker!, WorldNet Daily, http://www.wnd.com/2012/10/trinity-church-members-reveal-obama-shocker/ (last visited on October 4, 2012).

552. Jerome R. Corsi, Trinity Church Members Reveal Obama Shocker!, WorldNet Daily, http://www.wnd.com/2012/10/trinity-church-members-reveal-obama-shocker/ (last visited on October 4, 2012).

553. Jerome R. Corsi, Trinity Church Members Reveal Obama Shocker!, WorldNet Daily,

http://www.wnd.com/2012/10/trinity-church-members-reveal-obama-shocker/ (last visited on October 4, 2012).

554. Jerome R. Corsi, Trinity Church Members Reveal Obama Shocker!, WorldNet Daily, http://www.wnd.com/2012/10/trinity-church-members-reveal-obama-shocker/ (last visited on October 4, 2012).

555. Afghan Pedophilia: A way of Life, Say U.S. Soldiers and Journalists, Law Enforcement Examiner, January 19, 2012, http://www.examiner.com/article/afghan-pedophilia-a-way-of-life-say-u-s-soldiers-and-journalists.

556. Nadya Labi, The Kingdom in the Closet, The Atlantic, May 1, 2007, http://www.theatlantic.com/magazine/archive/2007/05/the-kingdom-in-the-closet/305774/.

557. Nadya Labi, The Kingdom in the Closet, The Atlantic, May 1, 2007, http://www.theatlantic.com/magazine/archive/2007/05/the-kingdom-in-the-closet/305774/.

558. Nadya Labi, The Kingdom in the Closet, The Atlantic, May 1, 2007, http://www.theatlantic.com/magazine/archive/2007/05/the-kingdom-in-the-closet/305774/.

559. Nadya Labi, The Kingdom in the Closet, The Atlantic, May 1, 2007, http://www.theatlantic.com/magazine/archive/2007/05/the-kingdom-in-the-closet/305774/.

560. Nadya Labi, The Kingdom in the Closet, The Atlantic, May 1, 2007, http://www.theatlantic.com/magazine/archive/2007/05/the-kingdom-in-the-closet/305774/.

561. Afghan Pedophilia: A way of Life, Say U.S. Soldiers and Journalists, Law Enforcement Examiner, January 19, 2012, http://www.examiner.com/article/afghan-pedophilia-a-way-of-life-say-u-s-soldiers-and-journalists.

562. Ernesto Londono, Afghanistan Sees Rise in 'Dancing Boys' Exploitation, Washington Post, April 4, 2012, http://www.washingtonpost.com/world/asia_pacific/afganistans-dancing-boys-are-invisible-victims/2012/04/04/gIQAyreSwS_story.html.

563. Joel Brinkley, Afghanistan's Dirty Little Secret, SFGate, August 29, 2010, http://www.sfgate.com/opinion/brinkley/article/Afghanistan-s-dirty-little-secret-3176762.php.

564. Vlad Tepes, Western Complicity in the Rape of Boys in the Islamic World, August 12, 2011, http://vladtepesblog.com/2011/08/12/western-complicity-in-the-rape-of-boys-in-the-islamic-world/.

565. Joel Brinkley, Afghanistan's Dirty Little Secret, SFGate, August 29, 2010, http://www.sfgate.com/opinion/brinkley/article/Afghanistan-s-dirty-little-secret-3176762.php.

566. Joel Brinkley, Afghanistan's Dirty Little Secret, SFGate, August 29, 2010, http://www.sfgate.com/opinion/brinkley/article/Afghanistan-s-dirty-little-secret-3176762.php.

567. Robert Long, Routine Child Rape by Afghan Police, The American Conservative, July 10, 2013, http://www.theamericanconservative.com/routine-child-rape-by-afghan-police/.

568. Robert Long, Routine Child Rape by Afghan Police, The American Conservative, July 10, 2013, http://www.theamericanconservative.com/routine-child-rape-by-afghan-police/.

569. Ernesto Londono, Afghanistan's 'Dancing Boys': Behind the Story, Washington Post, April 5, 2012, http://www.washingtonpost.com/blogs/blogpost/post/afghanistans-dancing-boys-behind-the-story/2012/04/05/gIQAFXzJxS_blog.html.

570. Vlad Tepes, Western Complicity in the Rape of Boys in the Islamic World, August 12, 2011, http://vladtepesblog.com/2011/08/12/western-complicity-in-the-rape-of-boys-in-the-islamic-world/.

571. Vlad Tepes, Western Complicity in the Rape of Boys in the Islamic World, August 12, 2011, http://vladtepesblog.com/2011/08/12/western-complicity-in-the-rape-of-boys-in-the-islamic-world/.

572. Vlad Tepes, Western Complicity in the Rape of Boys in the Islamic World, August 12, 2011, http://vladtepesblog.com/2011/08/12/western-complicity-in-the-rape-of-boys-in-the-islamic-world/.

573. Vlad Tepes, Western Complicity in the Rape of Boys in the Islamic World, August 12, 2011, http://vladtepesblog.com/2011/08/12/western-complicity-in-the-rape-of-boys-in-the-islamic-world/.

574. Ernesto Londono, Afghanistan Sees Rise in 'Dancing Boys' Exploitation, Washington Post, April 4, 2012, http://www.washingtonpost.com/world/asia_pacific/afganistans-dancing-boys-are-invisible-victims/2012/04/04/gIQAyreSwS_story.html.

575. Afghan Pedophilia: A way of Life, Say U.S. Soldiers and Journalists, Law Enforcement Examiner, January 19, 2012, http://www.examiner.com/article/afghan-pedophilia-a-way-of-life-say-u-s-soldiers-and-journalists.

576. Michael Swift's 1987 Gay Manifesto, http://www.blessedcause.org/protest/Gay%20Manifesto.htm.

577. Steve Baldwin, Child Molestation and the Homosexual Movement, 14 REGENT L. REV. 267, 278 (2002), http://www.mega.nu/ampp/baldwin_pedophilia_homosexuality.pdf.

578. Baldwin, supra, at 271, 278 citing W.D. Erickson et al., *Behavior Patterns of Child Molesters*, 17 ARCHIVES SEXUAL BEHAV., at 83 (1988).

579. Baldwin, supra, at 278.

580. Baldwin, supra, at 274.

581. Baldwin, supra, at 268.

582. Baldwin, supra, at 272-73, 277.

583. President Obama and the LGBT Community, White House, https://www.whitehouse.gov/lgbt (last visited on March 18, 2015).

584. Zeke J. Miller, Axelrod: Obama Misled Nation When He Opposed Gay Marriage In 2008, TIME, February 10, 2015, http://time.com/3702584/gay-marriage-axelrod-obama/

585. Obama's past Statements on Same-Sex Marriage, Fox News, May 9, 2012, http://www.foxnews.com.

586. Jim Hoft, Obama Lied to Christian Leader Rick Warren on Gay Marriage Just to Get Elected, February 11, 2015, http://www.thegatewaypundit.com.

587. Protecting LGBT Individuals from Discrimination, https://www.whitehouse.gov/issues/civil-rights/discrimination (last visited on March 18, 2015).

588. Don't Ask, Don't Tell is Repealed, U.S. Department of Defense, http://www.defense.gov/home/features/2010/0610_dadt/ (last visited on March 18, 2015).

589. By Karen Parrish, Same-sex Couples Can Claim New Benefits by October, American Forces Press Service, February 11, 2013, http://www.defense.gov/News/NewsArticle.aspx?ID=119260.

590. Obama's past Statements on Same-Sex Marriage, Fox News, May 9, 2012.

591. Martin L. Wagner, Freemasonry: An Interpretation, at 210 (1912), available at http://www.mindserpent.com/American_History/organization/mason/freemasonry/freemasonry.html.

592. Wagner, at 220.

593. Wagner, at 221-22

594. Wagner, at 258-59, quoting Weiss, Obelisk and Freemasonry, p. 40.

595. Jack Chick, The Prophet, Alberto Part Six, Chick Publications, 1988.

596. Jack Chick, The Prophet, Alberto Part Six, Chick Publications, 1988, http://www.redicecreations.com/specialreports/2006/04apr/catholicislam.html.

597. Jack Chick, The Prophet, Alberto Part Six, Chick Publications, 1988, http://www.redicecreations.com/specialreports/2006/04apr/catholicislam.html.

598. Jack Chick, The Prophet, Alberto Part Six, Chick Publications, 1988, http://www.redicecreations.com/specialreports/2006/04apr/catholicislam.html.

599. Nina Shea, Obama and the Churches of Saudi Arabia, The Christian Post, March 21, 2014, http://www.christianpost.com/news/obama-and-the-churches-of-saudi-arabia-116526/.

600. Nina Shea, Obama and the Churches of Saudi Arabia, The Christian Post, March 21, 2014, http://www.christianpost.com/news/obama-and-the-churches-of-saudi-arabia-116526/.

601. Benjamin Weinthal, Saudi Anti-Christian Sweep Prompts Calls for US Involvement, Fox News, September 10, 2014, http://www.foxnews.com/world/2014/09/10/saudi-anti-christian-sweep-prompts-calls-for-us-involvement/.

602. Benjamin Weinthal, Saudi Anti-Christian Sweep Prompts Calls for US Involvement, Fox News, September 10, 2014, http://www.foxnews.com/world/2014/09/10/saudi-anti-christian-sweep-prompts-calls-for-us-involvement/.

603. Hugh McNichol, Saudi Arabia Says No To A Catholic Church: The Islamic Fear of Freedom of Religion, March 26, 2008, http://www.pewsitter.com/view_news_id_7306.php.

604. Nina Shea, Obama and the Churches of Saudi Arabia, The Christian Post, March 21, 2014, http://www.christianpost.com/news/obama-and-the-churches-of-saudi-arabia-116526/.

605. Roman Catholic Apostolic Vicariate of Northern Arabia, http://www.avona.org/saudi/saudi_about.htm# (last visited on April 12, 2014).

606. The Catholic Directory, http://www.thecatholicdirectory.com.

607. Raymond Ibrahim, Scott Allswang, Muslim Persecution of Christians: March, http://faithdefenders.com/islamupdates/Muslim-Persecution-of-Christians-March.html (last visited on June 6, 2014).

608. The Catholic Directory, http://www.thecatholicdirectory.com/directory.cfm?fuseaction=show_country&country=KW (last visited on June 6, 2014).

609. The Catholic Directory, http://www.thecatholicdirectory.com/directory.cfm?fuseaction=display_site_info&siteid=112577 (last visited

on June 6, 2014).

610. International Religious Freedom Report for 2012, Afghanistan, U.S. State Department, Bureau of Democracy, Human Rights, and Labor, http://www.state.gov/j/drl/rls/irf/religiousfreedom/index.htm?year=2012&dlid=208422.

611. International Religious Freedom Report for 2012, Afghanistan, U.S. State Department, Bureau of Democracy, Human Rights, and Labor, http://www.state.gov/j/drl/rls/irf/religiousfreedom/index.htm?year=2012&dlid=208422.

612. Christian Churches Officially Extinct in Afghanistan, Charisma News, http://www.charismanews.com/world/32161-christian-churches-officially-extinct-in-afghanistan (last visited June 6, 2014).

613. Raymond Ibrahim, Scott Allswang, Muslim Persecution of Christians: October, http://faithdefenders.com/islamupdates/Muslim-Persecution-of-Christians-October.html (last visited on June 6, 2014).

614. Catholic Directory, http://www.thecatholicdirectory.com/directory.cfm?fuseaction=display_site_info&siteid=75953 (last visited on June 6, 2014). See also, Internet Archive showing a Catholic Church in Kabul, Afghanistan, on January 7, 2011, December 17, 2012, and October 28, 2013, https://web.archive.org/web/20111011134300/http://www.thecatholicdirectory.com/directory.cfm?fuseaction=show_country&country=AF (last visited on June 6, 2014).

615. Rosamond Culbertson, A Narrative of the Captivity and Sufferings of an American Female Under the Popish Priests, in the Island of Cuba; With a Full Disclosure of Their Manners and Customs, at 72 (1837).

616. Sister Charlotte (as told to Sister Nilah), From Convent to Pentecost, My Escape From the Cloistered Convent, 1999. See also, The Sister Charlotte Keckler Story, The Horrors Deep Within The Church Of Rome, http://jesus-messiah.com/charlotte/html/charlotte.html (last visited on April 15, 2014).

617. David A. Plaisted, Estimates of the Number Killed by the Papacy in the Middle Ages and Later, 2006, http://predoc.org/docs/index-10153.html?page=9.

618. Sarah J. Richardson, Life in the Grey Nunnery at Montreal, 1858, http://www.gutenberg.org/ebooks/5734, also available at https://archive.org/details/cihm_47296 (last visited on April 15, 2014).

619. Maria Monk, Awful Disclosures of the Hotel Dieu Nunnery of Montreal, 1836, http://www.reformation.org/maria-monk.html.

620. Maria Monk, Awful Disclosures of the Hotel Dieu Nunnery of Montreal, 1836, http://www.reformation.org/maria-monk.html.

621. Maria Monk, Further Disclosures, at 89 (1837), addendum to J.J. Slocum, Confirmation of Maria Monk's Disclosures Concerning the Hotel Dieu Nunnery, http://ssoc.selfip.com:81/texts/1839__slocum__confirmation_of_maria_monks_disclosures.pdf.

622. Barbara Ubryk, The Convent Horror, The Story of of Barbara Ubryk, Twenty-One Years in a Convent Dungeon Eight Feet Long, Six Feet Wide, from Official Records, Excerpted from the enlarged 1957 Edition, http://www.jesus-is-lord.com/barbara.htm.

623. Ford Hendrickson, The Black Convent Slave, at 77-115 (1914), https://archive.org/details/blackconventsla00hendgoog.

624. Ford Hendrickson, The Black Convent Slave, at 77-115 (1914), https://archive.org/details/blackconventsla00hendgoog.

625. Maria Monk, Wikipedia, http://en.wikipedia.org/wiki/Maria_Monk#cite_note-3 (last visited on May 31, 2014).

626. Awful Exposure of the Atrocious Plot, at 126-129 (1836).

627. Maria Monk, Account of Attempt to Abduct Maria Monk, 1837, at 18, addendum to J.J. Slocum, Confirmation of Maria Monk's Disclosures Concerning the Hotel Dieu Nunnery, http://ssoc.selfip.com:81/texts/1839__slocum___confirmation_of_maria_monks_disclosures.pdf.

628. Maria Monk, Account of Attempt to Abduct Maria Monk, 1837, at 18, addendum to J.J. Slocum, Confirmation of Maria Monk's Disclosures Concerning the Hotel Dieu Nunnery, http://ssoc.selfip.com:81/texts/1839__slocum___confirmation_of_maria_monks_disclosures.pdf.

629. Awful Exposure of the Atrocious Plot (1836).

630. J.J. Slocum, Confirmation of Maria Monk's Disclosures Concerning the Hotel Dieu Nunnery, 30-32, (1837) http://ssoc.selfip.com:81/texts/1839__slocum___confirmation_of_maria_monks_disclosures.pdf.

631. Maria Monk, Awful Disclosures (with supplemental appendix), at 155-157 (1836).

632. Maria Monk, Maria Monk, Awful Disclosures (with supplemental appendix), at 344 (1836).

633. *Falsehoods of William L. Stone*, at 15, https://archive.org/details/cihm_57287.

634. *Falsehoods of William L. Stone*, at 20, https://archive.org/details/cihm_57287.

635. William L. Stone, Maria Monk and the Nunnery of the Hotel Dieu, Being an Account of a Visit to the Convents of Montreal and Refutation of the "Awful Disclosures," 1836, at 8-9, https://archive.org/details/cihm_37485.

636. William L. Stone, Maria Monk and the Nunnery of the Hotel Dieu, Being an Account of a Visit to the Convents of Montreal and Refutation of the "Awful Disclosures," 1836, at 9, https://archive.org/details/cihm_37485

637. William L. Stone, Maria Monk and the Nunnery of the Hotel Dieu, Being an Account of a Visit to the Convents of Montreal and Refutation of the "Awful Disclosures," 1836, at 11, https://archive.org/details/cihm_37485

638. Stone, Refutation of the "Awful Disclosures," at 18.

639. Maria Monk, Maria Monk, Awful Disclosures (with supplemental appendix), at 18 (1836) (French language recitation deleted).

640. Paul Serup, Who Killed Abraham Lincoln?, at 228 (2008).

641. Paul Serup, Who Killed Abraham Lincoln?, at 228-29 (2008), quoting The Life and Labours Of the Reverend Father Chiniquy, at 5 (1861).

642. LES GARETT, WHICH BIBLE CAN WE TRUST?, p. 16 (1982); *See also,* COLLIER'S ENCYCLOPEDIA, volume 22, p. 563.

643. Rebecca Theresa Reed, Six Months in a Convent, at 133 (1835).

644. Samuel B. Smith, Decisive Confirmation of the Awful Disclosures of Maria Monk, 1836, https://archive.org/details/cihm_60942.

645. Patrick Phelan, Dictionary of Canadien Biography, http://www.biographi.ca/en/bio.php?id_nbr=4133 (last visited on May 10, 2014).

646. Maria Monk, Maria Monk, Awful Disclosures (with supplemental appendix), at 45-46 (1836).

647. Maria Monk, Awful Disclosures (with supplemental appendix), at 97-104 (1836).

648. Maria Monk, Maria Monk, Awful Disclosures (with supplemental appendix), at 345 (1836).

649. Maria Monk, Maria Monk, Awful Disclosures (with supplemental appendix), at 338 (1836).

650. Maria Monk, Maria Monk, Awful Disclosures (with supplemental appendix), at 312 (1836).

651. Patrick Phelan, Dictionary of Canadien Biography, http://www.biographi.ca/en/bio.php?id_nbr=4133 (last visited on May 10, 2014).

652. Maria Monk, Maria Monk, Awful Disclosures (with supplemental appendix), at 346 (1836).

653. Samuel B. Smith, Decisive Confirmation of the Awful Disclosures of Maria Monk, 1836, https://archive.org/details/cihm_60942.

654. *Evidence Demonstrating the Falsehoods of William L. Stone Concerning the Hotel Dieu Nunnery of Montreal*, 1837, at 24-25, https://archive.org/details/cihm_57287.

655. Maria Monk, Account of Attempt to Abduct Maria Monk, 1837, at 18, addendum to J.J. Slocum, Confirmation of Maria Monk's Disclosures Concerning the Hotel Dieu Nunnery, http://ssoc.selfip.com:81/texts/1839__slocum___confirmation_of_maria_monks_disclosures.pdf.

656. Maria Monk, Maria Monk, Awful Disclosures (with supplemental appendix), at 367 (1836).

657. Maria Monk, Maria Monk, Awful Disclosures (with supplemental appendix), at 367 (1836).

658. Maria Monk, Maria Monk, Awful Disclosures (with supplemental appendix), at 367 (1836).

659. Thurston, Herbert. "Impostors." The Catholic Encyclopedia. Vol. 7. New York: Robert Appleton Company, 1910. 17 May 2014

<http://www.newadvent.org/cathen/07698b.htm>.

660. J.J. Slocum, Confirmation of Maria Monk's Disclosures Concerning the Hotel Dieu Nunnery, 1837, at 28, http://ssoc.selfip.com:81/texts/1839_slocum_confirmation_of_maria_monks_disclosures.pdf.

661. J.J. Slocum, Confirmation of Maria Monk's Disclosures Concerning the Hotel Dieu Nunnery, 1837, at 28.

662. J.J. Slocum, Confirmation of Maria Monk's Disclosures Concerning the Hotel Dieu Nunnery, 1837, at 42.

663. J.J. Slocum, Confirmation of Maria Monk's Disclosures Concerning the Hotel Dieu Nunnery, 1837, at 42.

664. J.J. Slocum, Confirmation of Maria Monk's Disclosures Concerning the Hotel Dieu Nunnery, 1837, at 42.

665. J.J. Slocum, Confirmation of Maria Monk's Disclosures Concerning the Hotel Dieu Nunnery, 1837, at 43.

666. J.J. Slocum, Confirmation of Maria Monk's Disclosures Concerning the Hotel Dieu Nunnery, 1837, at 44-45.

667. J.J. Slocum, Confirmation of Maria Monk's Disclosures Concerning the Hotel Dieu Nunnery, 1837, at 45-46.

668. EDMOND PARIS, THE SECRET HISTORY OF THE JESUITS, p. 64 (1975).

669. Jesuitical, Oxford Dictionary, http://www.oxforddictionaries.com/definition/english/Jesuitical (last visited on May 8, 2014).

670. Jesuitical, Noah Webster, American Dictionary of the English Language, 1828, http://webstersdictionary1828.com/.

671. John Spano, Catholic Doctrine Is Cited in Priest Sex Abuse Cases, Los Angeles Times, March 26, 2007, http://articles.latimes.com/2007/mar/26/local/me-priest26.

672. John Spano, Catholic Doctrine Is Cited in Priest Sex Abuse Cases, Los Angeles Times, March 26, 2007, http://articles.latimes.com/2007/mar/26/local/me-priest26.

673. John Spano, Catholic Doctrine Is Cited in Priest Sex Abuse Cases, Los Angeles Times, March 26, 2007, http://articles.latimes.com/2007/mar/26/local/me-priest26.

674. John Spano, Catholic Doctrine Is Cited in Priest Sex Abuse Cases, Los Angeles Times, March 26, 2007, http://articles.latimes.com/2007/mar/26/local/me-priest26.

675. Would a Priest or Bishop Lie under Oath? Mental Reservation Debated in Court Wednesday Re Church Witnesses Refusing to Answer in Depositions, City of Angels, May 17, 2007, http://www.bishop-accountability.org/news2007/05_06

/2007_05_17_CityOfAngels_.htm.

676. Maria Monk, Awful Disclosures (with supplemental appendix), at 53 (1836).

677. Maria Monk, Further Disclosures, at 134-135 (1837), addendum to J.J. Slocum, Confirmation of Maria Monk's Disclosures Concerning the Hotel Dieu Nunnery, http://ssoc.selfip.com:81/texts/1839__slocum___confirmation_of_maria_monks_disclosures.pdf.

678. Ford Hendrickson, The Black Convent Slave, at 23 (1914), https://archive.org/details/blackconventsla00hendgoog.

679. Maria Monk, Awful Disclosures (with supplemental appendix), at 108-109 (1836).

680. Stone, Refutation of the "Awful Disclosures," at 31.

681. Stone, Refutation of the "Awful Disclosures," at 32.

682. *Falsehoods of William L. Stone*, at 5-6.

683. *Falsehoods of William L. Stone*, at 7.

684. *Falsehoods of William L. Stone*, at 8.

685. *Falsehoods of William L. Stone*, at 8.

686. *Falsehoods of William L. Stone*, at 18.

687. *Falsehoods of William L. Stone*, at 4.

688. *Falsehoods of William L. Stone*, at 19.

689. Stone, Refutation of the "Awful Disclosures," at 28.

690. *Falsehoods of William L. Stone*, at 12.

691. Alberto Rivera, ALBERTO, at 12 (1979).

692. Julia McNair Wright, Secrets of the Convent and Confessional, footnote at 254-255 (1876).

693. Julia McNair Wright, Secrets of the Convent and Confessional, footnote at 254 (1876).

694. Sam Jordison, Magedine Laundries, February 5, 2014, http://samdjordison.blogspot.com/2013/02/magdalene-laundries.html.

695. Maria Monk, Account of The Attempts to Abduct Maria Monk (1837), at 4, addendum to J.J. Slocum, Confirmation of Maria Monk's Disclosures Concerning the Hotel Dieu Nunnery, http://ssoc.selfip.com:81/texts/1839__slocum___confirmation_of_maria_monks_disclosures.pdf.

696. Maria Monk, Account of The Attempts to Abduct Maria Monk (1837), addendum to J.J. Slocum, Confirmation of Maria Monk's Disclosures Concerning the Hotel Dieu Nunnery, http://ssoc.selfip.com:81/texts/1839__slocum___confirmation_of_maria_monks_disclosures.pdf.

697. J.J. Slocum, Confirmation of Maria Monk's Disclosures Concerning the Hotel Dieu Nunnery, 1837, at 82.

698. William L. Stone, Maria Monk and the Nunnery of the Hotel Dieu, Being an Account of a Visit to the

Convents of Montreal and Refutation of the "Awful Disclosures," 1836, at 31, https://archive.org/details/cihm_37485

699. The Sister Charlotte Keckler Story, November 28, 2011, http://wesdancin.wordpress.com/2011/11/28/the-sister-charlotte-keckler-story-the-horrors-deep-within-the-church-of-rome-get-this-to-every-female-male-woman-man-of-all-ages-all-parents-all-grand-parents-2/.

700. Personal Sacrifices for Faith, ABC 20/20, May 11, 2007, https://www.youtube.com/watch?v=Tm_8MUct7VA.

701. Personal Sacrifices for Faith, ABC 20/20, May 11, 2007, https://www.youtube.com/watch?v=Tm_8MUct7VA.

702. Personal Sacrifices for Faith, ABC 20/20, May 11, 2007, https://www.youtube.com/watch?v=Tm_8MUct7VA.

703. Stone, Refutation of the "Awful Disclosures," at 25.

704. Maria Monk, Maria Monk, Awful Disclosures (with supplemental appendix), at 160 (1836) (French language recitation deleted).

705. Maria Monk, Maria Monk, Awful Disclosures (with supplemental appendix), at 351-52 (1836) (French language recitation deleted).

706. Darryl Eberhart, Sexual Abuse in the Roman Catholic Church, October 16, 2009, http://www.toughissues.org/handoutsnew/Sexual%20Abuse.htm, quoting Peter de Rosa, Vicars of Christ, at

404 and 408 (1988).

707. Darryl Eberhart, Sexual Abuse in the Roman Catholic Church, October 16, 2009, http://www.toughissues.org/handoutsnew/Sexual%20Abuse.htm, quoting William H. Kennedy, Lucifer's Lodge: Satanic Ritual Abuse in the Catholic Church, at 179 (2009), who in turn quoted the Boston Globe, January 1, 2002.

708. The Nuns' Stories, Vatican Condemned for Abuse of Nuns by Priests, http://archives.weirdload.com/nuns.html (Last visited on April 17, 2014).

709. The Nuns' Stories, Vatican Condemned for Abuse of Nuns by Priests, http://archives.weirdload.com/nuns.html (Last visited on April 17, 2014).

710. European Parliament Assails Vatican Over Abuse Cases, April 6, 2001, http://www.zenit.org/en/articles/european-parliament-assails-vatican-over-abuse-cases.

711. European Parliament Assails Vatican Over Abuse Cases, April 6, 2001, http://www.zenit.org/en/articles/european-parliament-assails-vatican-over-abuse-cases.

712. Margaret Shepherd, My Life in the Convent: or The Marvelous Personal Experiences of Margaret Shepherd, 206-207 (1892), https://archive.org/details/mylifeinconvento00shepuoft.

713. The Sister Charlotte Keckler Story, November 28, 2011,

http://wesdancin.wordpress.com/2011/11/28/the-sister-charlotte-keckler-story-the-horrors-deep-within-the-church-of-rome-get-this-to-every-female-male-woman-man-of-all-ages-all-parents-all-grand-parents-2/.

714. The Testimony of Charlotte Wells, http://www.jesus-is-lord.com/charlot1.htm (last visited on May 12, 2014). See also, From Convent to Pentecost, My Escape From the Cloistered Convent, As told to Sister Nilah by Sister Charlotte (1999).

715. Maria Monk, Further Disclosures, at 144, et. seq.(1837), addendum to J.J. Slocum, Confirmation of Maria Monk's Disclosures Concerning the Hotel Dieu Nunnery, http://ssoc.selfip.com:81/texts/1839__slocum___confirmation_of_maria_monks_disclosures.pdf

716. Maria Monk, Awful Disclosures (with supplemental appendix), at 148 (1836).

717. J.J. Slocum, Confirmation of Maria Monk's Disclosures Concerning the Hotel Dieu Nunnery, at 121 (1837).

718. J.J. Slocum, Confirmation of Maria Monk's Disclosures Concerning the Hotel Dieu Nunnery, at 121 (1837).

719. Mackey's Encyclopedia of Freemasonry, http://www.masonicdictionary.com/oath.html (last visited on April 17, 2014).

720. William L. Stone, Letters on Freemasonry and Anti-Freemasonry Addressed to the Honorable John Quincy Adams, 1832, at 66.

721. William L. Stone, Letters on Freemasonry and Anti-Freemasonry Addressed to the Honorable John Quincy Adams, 1832, at 67.

722. William L. Stone, Letters on Freemasonry and Anti-Freemasonry Addressed to the Honorable John Quincy Adams, 1832, at 68.

723. JIM SHAW (33rd Degree Mason, Knight Commander of the Court of Honor, Past Worshipful Master of the Blue Lodge, Past Master of All Scottish Rite Bodies) and TOM MCKENNEY, THE DEADLY DECEPTION, Freemasonry Exposed by One of Its Top Leaders, p. 137 (1988).

724. Tom C. Mckenney, 33 Degrees of Deception.

725. AMRAN Shriners, How to Become a Shriner, http://www.amranshriners.us/history/history05.htm (last visited on April 21, 2014).

726. Jim Shaw & Tom McKenny, The Deadly Deception, 1988, at 75-76.

727. Jim Shaw & Tom McKenny, The Deadly Deception, 1988, at 75.

728. Jim Shaw & Tom McKenny, The Deadly Deception, 1988, at 76, n. 2.

729. Shaikh Hatim Nakhoda, ISLAM AND FREEMASONRY, http://www.freemasons-freemasonry.com/islam_freemasonry.html (last visited on April 22, 2014).

730. Shaikh Hatim Nakhoda, ISLAM AND FREEMASONRY, http://www.freemasons-freemasonry.com/islam_freem

asonry.html (last visited on April 22, 2014).

731. ALBERT PIKE, MORALS AND DOGMA OF THE ANCIENT AND ACCEPTED SCOTTISH RITE OF FREEMASONRY, p. 741 (1871).

732. DES GRIFFIN, THE FOURTH REICH OF THE RICH, p. 70 (1993).

733. Martin L. Wagner, Freemasonry: An Interpretation, at 85-86 (1912), available at http://www.mindserpent.com/American_History/organization/mason/freemasonry/freemasonry.html.

734. Wagner, at 338.

735. Stephen Knight, The Brotherhood, at 236 (1986).

736. Wagner, at 338.

737. Knight, at 236.

738. Wagner, at 338.

739. Knight, at 236.

740. DES GRIFFIN, THE FOURTH REICH OF THE RICH, p. 70 (1993).

741. ERIC JON PHELPS, VATICAN ASSASSINS: "WOUNDED IN THE HOUSE OF MY FRIENDS," p. 180 (2001).

742. NESTA WEBSTER, SECRET SOCIETIES AND SUBVERSIVE MOVEMENTS, http://web.archive.org/web/20021005055527/http://www.plausiblefutures.com/text/SS.html (website address current as of 2-28-05) (footnotes contained in original

text omitted).

743. JIM SHAW (33rd Degree Mason, Knight Commander of the Court of Honor, Past Worshipful Master of the Blue Lodge, Past Master of All Scottish Rite Bodies) and TOM MCKENNEY, THE DEADLY DECEPTION, Freemasonry Exposed by One of Its Top Leaders, p. 137 (1988).

744. Barbara Aho, *Mystery, Babylon the Great - Catholic or Jewish?*, Watch Unto Prayer, at http://watch.pair.com/mystery-babylon.html (last visited on February 8, 2010) (citing "The Pope of the Council, Part 19: John XXIII and Masonry," Sodalitium, October/November 1996).

745. The Scandals and Heresies of John XXIII, http://www.mostholyfamilymonastery.com/13_JohnX XIII.pdf, citing Paul I. Murphy and R. Rene Arlington, La Popessa, 1983, pp. 332-333.

746. The Scandals and Heresies of John XXIII, http://www.mostholyfamilymonastery.com/13_JohnX XIII.pdf, quoting Giovanni Cubeddu, 30 Days, Issue No. 2-1994., p. 25. See also, Mary Ball Martinez, The Undermining of the Catholic Church, Hillmac, Mexico, 1999, p. 117.

747. Alberto Rivera, Alberto, Part One, at 27.

748. *Evidence Demonstrating the Falsehoods of William L. Stone Concerning the Hotel Dieu Nunnery of Montreal*, 1837, at 2, https://archive.org/details/cihm_57287.

749. *Evidence Demonstrating the Falsehoods of William L. Stone Concerning the Hotel Dieu Nunnery*

of Montreal, 1837, at 3, https://archive.org/details/cihm_57287.

750.*Evidence Demonstrating the Falsehoods of William L. Stone Concerning the Hotel Dieu Nunnery of Montreal*, 1837, at 3, https://archive.org/details/cihm_57287.

751.Sarah J. Richardson, Life in the Grey Nunnery at Montreal, 212 (1858).

752.Sarah J. Richardson, Life in the Grey Nunnery at Montreal, 209 (1858).

753.Sarah J. Richardson, Life in the Grey Nunnery at Montreal, 134-139 (1858).

754.*Id.* at p. 6.

755.Lucius Ferraris, "Papa," art. 2, Prompta Bibliotheca Canonica, Juridica, Moralis, Theologica, Ascetica, Polemica, Rubristica, Historica. ("Handy Library"), Vol. 5, published in Petit-Montrouge (Paris) by J. P. Migne, 1858 edition, column 1823, Latin. http://www.aloha.net/~mikesch/claims.htm.

756.Lucius Ferraris, "Papa," art. 2, Prompta Bibliotheca Canonica, Juridica, Moralis, Theologica, Ascetica, Polemica, Rubristica, Historica. ("Handy Library"), Vol. 5, published in Petit-Montrouge (Paris) by J. P. Migne, 1858 edition, column 1823, Latin. http://www.aloha.net/~mikesch/claims.htm.

757.*CATECHISM OF THE COUNCIL OF TRENT, ORDERED BY THE COUNCIL OF TRENT, EDITED UNDER ST. CHARLES BORROMEO, PUBLISHED BY DECREE OF POPE ST. PIUS V,* 1566, TAN Books, p. 258, 1982.

758.*CATECHISM OF THE COUNCIL OF TRENT*, ORDERED BY THE COUNCIL OF TRENT, EDITED UNDER ST. CHARLES BORROMEO, PUBLISHED BY DECREE OF POPE ST. PIUS V, 1566, TAN Books, p. 258, 1982.

759.*E.g.*, W. GRINTON BERRY, FOXE'S BOOK OF MARTYRS, p. 357.

760.GERARDUS D. BOUW, GEOCENTRICITY, p. 153 (1992).

761.*Id.*

762.*Id.*

763.*Id.*

764.RALPH E. WOODROW, BABYLON MYSTERY RELIGION, p. 72, 1966.

765.COLLIER'S ENCYCLOPEDIA, volume 19, p. 239 (1991).

766.STEWART PEROWNE, ROMAN MYTHOLOGY, p. 125-26, 1969.

767.Alexander Hislop, *The Two Babylons* (1959), *available at* http://www.biblebelievers.com/babylon/sect23.htm.

768.Alexander Hislop, *The Two Babylons*, at 211 (1959).

769.S. Michael Houdmann, Is the pope, or the next pope, the antichrist? http://www.gotquestions.org/pope-antichrist.html (last visited on March 1, 2014).

770. Is the Antichrist the current Pope, or a future Pope?, http://www.compellingtruth.org/pope-antichrist.html (last visited on March 1, 2014).

771. Elise Harris, Pope Francis: The Path of Humility Leads Christians to Jesus, National Catholic Register, January 8, 2014, http://www.ncregister.com/daily-news/pope-francis-the-path-of-humility-leads-christians-to-jesus/#ixzz2q1GfTW00. See also, Nick Donnelly, Pope Francis Talks about the Antichrist Following His Earlier Reference to Mgr Benson's Novel 'Lord of the World', Protect the Pope, January 10th, 2014, http://protectthepope.com/?p=9668.

772. Steve Wohlberg, The Antichrist Chronicles, What Prophecy Teachers Have Left Behind! (Part 11), http://www.endtimeinsights.com/AntichristFlesh.html (website address current as of August 14, 2003).

773. THE RANDOM HOUSE DICTIONARY OF THE ENGLISH LANGUAGE, unabridged edition, 1973.

774. Salvation is Obtained From . . . Mary?, http://www.aloha.net/~mikesch/mary.htm (web address current as of April 3, 2005), quoting Arthur Burton Calkins, TOTUS TUUS, pp.21, 27, Academy of the Immaculate, New Bedford, Massachusetts, ISBN 0-9635345-0-5, Nihil Obstat and Imprimatur of the Catholic Church.

775. Salvation is Obtained From . . . Mary?, http://www.aloha.net/~mikesch/mary.htm (web address current as of April 3, 2005), quoting Arthur Burton Calkins, TOTUS TUUS, pp.21, 27, Academy of the Immaculate, New Bedford, Massachusetts, ISBN 0-

9635345-0-5, Nihil Obstat and Imprimatur of the Catholic Church.

776.The Rosary, Roses of Prayer for The Queen of Heaven, Daniel A. Lord, S.J., Nihil Obstat Athur J. Scanlan S.T.D: Censor Liborum, Imprimatur + Francis J. Spellman, D.D. Archbishop, New York, http://www.truecatholic.org/rosary.htm (web address current as of March 20, 2005).

777.NOAH WEBSTER, AMERICAN DICTIONARY OF THE ENGLISH LANGUAGE (1st ed. 1828) republished by Foundation for American Christian Education, San Francisco, California.

778.COLLIER'S ENCYCLOPEDIA, volume 20, p. 169 (1991).

779.Alexander Hislop, *The Two Babylons*, at 2 (1959).

780.Alexander Hislop, *The Two Babylons*, at 2 (1959).

781.Alexander Hislop, *The Two Babylons*, at 2 (1959).

782.Alexander Hislop, *The Two Babylons*, at 2 (1959).

783.Alexander Hislop, *The Two Babylons*, at 2 (1959).

784.G.A. RIPLINGER, NEW AGE BIBLE VERSIONS, p. 133 (1993).

785.*E.g., CATECHISM OF THE CATHOLIC CHURCH*, §§ 105, 1141,1163, 1203, 1249, 1667 (1997), http://www.scborromeo.org/index2.htm (web address current as of March 22, 2005).

786.The Rosary, Roses of Prayer for The Queen of Heaven, Daniel A. Lord, S.J., Nihil Obstat Athur J.

Scanlan S.T.D: Censor Liborum, Imprimatur + Francis J. Spellman, D.D. Archbishop, New York, http://www.truecatholic.org/rosary.htm (web address current as of March 20, 2005).

787. Rosary Meditations, http://www.cfalive.org/ReadRosary.htm (web address current as of March 20, 2005).

788. Prayer to Mary, Queen of Heaven, http://www.catholic-forum.com/saints/pray0421.htm (web address current as of March 20, 2005).

789. J.NEUNER, S.J & J. DUPUIS, S.J., THE CHRISTIAN FAITH IN THE DOCTRINAL DOCUMENTS OF THE CATHOLIC CHURCH, PIUS X, ENCYCLICAL LETTER *AD DIEM* § 712 (6th ed. 1996).

790. J.NEUNER, S.J & J. DUPUIS, S.J., THE CHRISTIAN FAITH IN THE DOCTRINAL DOCUMENTS OF THE CATHOLIC CHURCH, THE SECOND VATICAL COUNCIL, DOGMATIC CONSTITUTION *LUMEN GENTIUM,* § 716a (6th ed. 1996).

791. CATECHISM OF THE CATHOLIC CHURCH, § 2679, 1994.

792. J.NEUNER, S.J & J. DUPUIS, S.J., THE CHRISTIAN FAITH IN THE DOCTRINAL DOCUMENTS OF THE CATHOLIC CHURCH, THE SECOND VATICAL COUNCIL, DOGMATIC CONSTITUTION *LUMEN GENTIUM,* § 718a (6th ed. 1996).

793. *Id.* at § 718b.

794. CATECHISM OF THE CATHOLIC CHURCH, § 2677, 1994.

795. J.NEUNER, S.J & J. DUPUIS, S.J., THE CHRISTIAN FAITH IN THE DOCTRINAL DOCUMENTS OF THE CATHOLIC CHURCH, THE SECOND VATICAL COUNCIL, DOGMATIC CONSTITUTION *LUMEN GENTIUM,* § 716a (6th ed. 1996).

796. J.NEUNER, S.J & J. DUPUIS, S.J., THE CHRISTIAN FAITH IN THE DOCTRINAL DOCUMENTS OF THE CATHOLIC CHURCH, § 713, PIUS XII, APOSTOLIC CONSTITUTION, *MUNIFICENTISSIMUS DEUS* (6th ed. 1996).

797. J.NEUNER, S.J & J. DUPUIS, S.J., THE CHRISTIAN FAITH IN THE DOCTRINAL DOCUMENTS OF THE CATHOLIC CHURCH, § 716a (6th ed. 1996).

798. ALEXANDER HISLOP, THE TWO BABYLONS (1916), *available at* http://www.biblebelievers.com/babylon/sect32.htm.

799. Mass, Imposition of the Pallium and Bestowal of the Fisherman's Ring for the Beginning of the Petrine Ministry of the Bishop of Rome, Homily of Pope Francis, Saint Peter's Square, Tuesday, 19 March 2013, http://w2.vatican.va/content/francesco/en/homilies/2013/documents/papa-francesco_20130319_omelia-inizio-pontificato.html.

800. Mass, Imposition of the Pallium and Bestowal of the Fisherman's Ring for the Beginning of the Petrine Ministry of the Bishop of Rome, Homily of Pope Francis, Saint Peter's Square, Tuesday, 19 March 2013,

http://w2.vatican.va/content/francesco/en/homilies/2013/documents/papa-francesco_20130319_omelia-inizio-pontificato.html.

801. ALBERTO RIVERA, DOUBLE CROSS, Chick publications, p. 27, 1981(quoting THE GREAT ENCYCLICAL LETTERS OF POPE LEO XIII, p. 304, Benziger Brothers (1903).

802. G.A. RIPLER, NEW AGE BIBLE VERSIONS, p. 134 (1993).

803. *Id.*

804. Mary E. Walsh, the Wine of Roman Babylon, 1945, available at http://www.friendsofsabbath.org/Further_Research/Paganism%20&%20RCC/The%20Wine%20of%20Roman%20Babylon.pdf.

805. Pope John Paul II, Crossing the Threshold of Hope, 1995, http://frcoulter.com/books/CrossingThresholdHope/chap1.html.

806. Pope Leo XIII, Apostolic Exhortation Praeclara Gratulationis Publicae (The Reunion of Christendom), dated June 20, 1894, trans. in The Great Encyclical Letters of Pope Leo XIII (New York: Benziger, 1903), paragraph 5, page 304.
http://www.aloha.net/~mikesch/claims.htm.

807. Pope Leo XIII, Encyclical Letter, Sapientiae Christianae (On the Chief Duties of Christians as Citizens), dated January 10, 1890, trans. in The Great Encyclical Letters of Pope Leo XIII (New York: Benziger, 1903), p. 193.

http://www.aloha.net/~mikesch/claims.htm.

808. LES GARETT, WHICH BIBLE CAN WE TRUST?, p. 16 (1982); *See also,* COLLIER'S ENCYCLOPEDIA, volume 22, p. 563.

809. *Id.*

810. Patricia Treble, Dressing a Pope from Head to Toe, What Francis Has to Look Forward To, Sartorially Speaking, Maclean's, March 19, 2013, http://www.macleans.ca/news/world/dressing-a-pope-from-head-to-toe/.

811. Patricia Treble, Dressing a Pope from Head to Toe, What Francis Has to Look Forward To, Sartorially Speaking, Maclean's, March 19, 2013, http://www.macleans.ca/news/world/dressing-a-pope-from-head-to-toe/.

812. Merriam-Webster Dictionary, Bow, http://www.merriam-webster.com/dictionary/bow (last visited on March 7, 2014).

813. Piers Compton, The Broken Cross, 1983, http://www.watchmenfaithministries.com/images/Broken_Cross_-_The_Hidden_Hand_in_the_Vatican.pdf.

814. Lucius Ferraris, "Papa," art. 2, in his Prompta Bibliotheca Canonica, Juridica, Moralis, Theologica, Ascetica, Polemica, Rubristica, Historica. ("Handy Library"), Vol. 5, published in Petit-Montrouge (Paris) by J. P. Migne, 1858 edition, column 1823, Latin. http://www.aloha.net/~mikesch/claims.htm.

815. ALBERTO RIVERA, FOUR HORSEMEN, Chick Publications, p. 25, 1985 (quoting AVRO MANHATTAN, VATICAN IMPERIALISM IN THE 20th CENTURY, p. 76.). *See also*, JOHN W. ROBBINS, ECCLESIASTICAL MEGALOMANIA, at p. 132 (1999).

816. Lucius Ferraris, "Papa," art. 2, in his Prompta Bibliotheca Canonica, Juridica, Moralis, Theologica, Ascetica, Polemica, Rubristica, Historica. ("Handy Library"), Vol. 5, published in Petit-Montrouge (Paris) by J. P. Migne, 1858 edition, column 1823, Latin. http://www.aloha.net/~mikesch/claims.htm.

817. Medieval Sourcebook: Boniface VIII, Unam Sanctam, 1302, http://www.fordham.edu/halsall/source/b8-unam.asp. See also, ALBERTO RIVERA, THE GODFATHERS, Chick Publications, p. 32, 1982 (quoting The Registers of Boniface VIII, The Vatican Archives, L. Fol. 387 and THE CATHOLIC ENCYCLOPEDIA, Encyclopedia Press (1913)).

818. The Jerusalem Bible, Revelation 13:18, at footnote h, (1966), *Nihil Obstat*: Lionel Swain, S.T.L., L.S.S., *Imprimatur*: John Cardinal Heenan, Westminster, July 4, 1966.

819. *Our Sunday Visitor,* April 18, 1915. The publication is still being published today: 200 Noll Plaza, Huntington, Indiana, 46750, (800) 348-2440.

820. D.P. SIMPSON, CASSELL'S LATIN DICTIONARY, p. 621, 1968.

821. COLLIER'S ENCYCLOPEDIA, volume 1, p. 592-96 (1991).

822. TEXE MARRS, PROJECT L.U.C.I.D., Living Truth Publishers (1996) (citing Antony Sutton, "Why Clinton Wants Universal Health Care," Phoenix Letter, Vol. 13, No. 10, October 1994).

823. *Id.* at p. 88.

824. Thomas C Greene, Feds Approve Human RFID Implants, The Register, 14 Oct 2004, http://www.theregister.co.uk/2004/10/14/human_rfid_implants/.

825. Thomas C Greene, Feds Approve Human RFID Implants, The Register, 14 Oct 2004, http://www.theregister.co.uk/2004/10/14/human_rfid_implants/.

826. Fisher, Jill A. 2006 "Indoor Positioning and Digital Management: Emerging Surveillance Regimes in Hospitals." In T. Monahan (Ed, Surveillance and Security: Technological Politics and Power in Everyday Life (pp. 77-88). New York: Routledge. Available at: http://www.jillfisher.net/papers/rfid.pdf.

827. Fisher, Jill A. 2006 "Indoor Positioning and Digital Management: Emerging Surveillance Regimes in Hospitals." In T. Monahan (Ed, Surveillance and Security: Technological Politics and Power in Everyday Life (pp. 77-88). New York: Routledge. Available at: http://www.jillfisher.net/papers/rfid.pdf.

828. Fisher, Jill A. 2006 "Indoor Positioning and Digital Management: Emerging Surveillance Regimes in Hospitals." In T. Monahan (Ed, Surveillance and Security: Technological Politics and Power in Everyday Life (pp. 77-88). New York: Routledge. Available at: http://www.jillfisher.net/papers/rfid.pdf.

829.Peter Andrew, Big New Changes Unveiled for Credit Cards, Fox Business, March 25, 2014, http://www.foxbusiness.com/personal-finance/2014/03/24/big-new-changes-unveiled-for-credit-cards/.

830.Patrick Madrid, Pope Fiction, Envoy, March/April 1998, http://web.archive.org/web/20031002094908/http://www.envoymagazine.com/backissues/2.2/mar_apr98_coverstory.html (last visited on March 10, 2014).

831.Karl Keating, Catholicism and Fundamentalism, 1988, pg 221, http://biblelight.net/envoy.htm#23sept.

832.Patrick Madrid, Pope Fiction, Envoy, March/April 1998, http://web.archive.org/web/20031002094908/http://www.envoymagazine.com/backissues/2.2/mar_apr98_coverstory.html (last visited on March 10, 2014).

833.*Our Sunday Visitor,* April 18, 1915. The publication is still being published today: 200 Noll Plaza, Huntington, Indiana, 46750, (800) 348-2440.

834.Patrick Madrid, More Vicarius Thrills, Envoy, http://biblelight.net/envoy.htm#23sept (last visited on March 10, 2014).

835.*Our Sunday Visitor,* April 18, 1915. http://biblelight.net/Sources/OSV%20Apr%2018%201915.pdf. The publication is still being published today: 200 Noll Plaza, Huntington, Indiana, 46750, (800) 348-2440.

836.Michael Scheifler, VICARIUS FILII DEI, 666, The Number of the Beast, http://biblelight.net/666.htm#OFFICIAL (last visited on March 10, 2014).

837. Michael Scheifler, VICARIUS FILII DEI, 666, The Number of the Beast, http://biblelight.net/666.htm#OFFICIAL (last visited on March 10, 2014).

838. Michael Scheifler, VICARIUS FILII DEI, 666, The Number of the Beast, http://biblelight.net/666.htm#OFFICIAL (last visited on March 10, 2014).

839. Kirsch, Johann Peter. "Donation of Constantine." The Catholic Encyclopedia. Vol. 5. New York: Robert Appleton Company, 1909. 11 Mar. 2014 <http://www.newadvent.org/cathen/05118a.htm>. Nihil Obstat. May 1, 1909. Remy Lafort, Censor. Imprimatur. +John M. Farley, Archbishop of New York.

840. Michael Scheifler, VICARIUS FILII DEI, 666, The Number of the Beast, http://biblelight.net/666.htm#OFFICIAL (last visited on March 10, 2014).

841. Michael Scheifler, VICARIUS FILII DEI, 666, The Number of the Beast, http://biblelight.net/666.htm#OFFICIAL (last visited on March 10, 2014).

842. Michael Scheifler, VICARIUS FILII DEI, 666, The Number of the Beast, http://biblelight.net/666.htm#OFFICIAL (last visited on March 10, 2014).

843. Michael Scheifler, VICARIUS FILII DEI, 666, The Number of the Beast,

http://biblelight.net/666.htm#OFFICIAL (last visited on March 10, 2014), quoting C. H. McIlwain, The Growth of Political Thought in the West (London, 1932), p. 278. — The Problem of Sovereignty in the Later Middle Ages: The Papal Monarchy with Augustinus Triumphus and the Publicists by Michael Wilks, Cambridge University Press, 2008, ISBN 052107018X, 9780521070188, p. 2.

844. Michael Scheifler, VICARIUS FILII DEI, 666, The Number of the Beast, http://biblelight.net/666.htm#OFFICIAL (last visited on March 10, 2014).

845. Michael Scheifler, VICARIUS FILII DEI, 666, The Number of the Beast, http://biblelight.net/666.htm#OFFICIAL (last visited on March 10, 2014).

846. Robert Franklin Correia, The Search to Document and Authenticate Vicarius Filii Dei, http://biblelight.net/vicarius-filii-dei-documentation.htm (last visited on March 12, 2014).

847. Michael Scheifler, VICARIUS FILII DEI, 666, The Number of the Beast, http://biblelight.net/666.htm#OFFICIAL (last visited on March 10, 2014). Acta Apostolicae Sedis, Commentarium Officiale, vol. LX (1968), n. 6, pp. 317-319. Libreria Editrice Vaticana. ISBN 8820960680, 9788820960681.

848. VICARIUS FILII DEI and 666, Response to a Challenge by Patrick Madrid of Envoy Magazine, http://biblelight.net/envoy.htm#23sept (last visited on March 10, 2014).

849. Michael Sheifler, VICARIUS FILII DEI and 666, Response to a Challenge by Patrick Madrid of Envoy Magazine, http://www.biblelight.net/envoy.htm (last visited on March 13, 2014).

850. Westminster Confession of Faith, Chapter XXV, Paragraph VI.

851. JOHN L. BRAY, THE MAN OF SIN OF II THESSALONIANS 2, p. 8 (1997) (Incidentally, Bray does not believe that the pope of Rome is the man of sin mentioned in II Thessalonians 2. He quotes from some of the traditional Protestant confessions of faith only to explain the historical Protestant view. While his survey of the historical confessions of faith is accurate, he is wrong regarding his conclusion about the pope.).

852. Reuel J. Schulz, The Pope is the Antichrist? or !, http://www.wlsessays.net/files/SchulzPope.pdf (last visited on March 17, 2014).

853. What Reformers Said About the Antichrist, Christian Assemblies International, http://www.cai.org/bible-studies/historical-interpretation, citing Foxe, Acts and Movements, Vol.1, p.636-641.

854. What Reformers Said About the Antichrist, Christian Assemblies International, http://www.cai.org/bible-studies/historical-interpretation, citing Leroy Edwin Froom, The Prophetic Faith of Our Fathers, vol.2, p.121.

855. David Schley Schaff, John Huss: His Life, Teachings and Death, 1915, at 255.

856. David Schley Schaff, John Huss: His Life, Teachings and Death, 1915, at 257.

857. David Schley Schaff, John Huss: His Life, Teachings and Death, 1915, at 257.

858. David Schley Schaff, John Huss: His Life, Teachings and Death, 1915, at 257.

859. What Reformers Said About the Antichrist, Christian Assemblies International, http://www.cai.org/bible-studies/historical-interpretation, citing Leroy Edwin Froom, The Prophetic Faith of our Fathers, vol.2, p.445 (1948) and Guinness, Romanism and the Reformation, p.134.

860. JOHN L. BRAY, MILLENNIUM - THE BIG QUESTION, P. 59 (1984) (quoting ERNEST R. SANDEEN, THE ROOTS OF FUNDAMENTALISM, p. 37 (1970)).

861. JOHN L. BRAY, MILLENNIUM - THE BIG QUESTION, P. 59 (1984) (quoting ERNEST R. SANDEEN, THE ROOTS OF FUNDAMENTALISM, p. 37 (1970)); WILLIAM R. KIMBALL, THE RAPTURE, A Question of Timing, p. 31 (1985) (OSWALD T. ALLIS, PROPHECY AND THE CHURCH, p. 297).

862. WILLIAM R. KIMBALL, THE RAPTURE, A Question of Timing, p. 31 (1985).

863. *Id.*

864. WILLIAM R. KIMBALL, THE RAPTURE, A Question of Timing, p. 31 (1985) (quoting LEROY E. FROOM, THE PROPHETIC FAITH OF OUR FATHERS, vol. 2, p. 495).

865. WILLIAM R. KIMBALL, THE RAPTURE, A Question of Timing, p. 32 (1985).

866. Arthur W. Pink, The Antichrist, available at http://www.ccel.org/ccel/pink/antichrist.pdf and http://www.biblebelievers.com/Pink/antichrist04.htm (last visited on February 24, 2014).

867. A. Wylie, The Papacy is the Antichrist, at 48.

868. Epistle Dedicatory, The Holy Bible, Authorized (King James) Version, 1611 Edition.

869. Epistle Dedicatory, The Holy Bible, Authorized (King James) Version, 1611 Edition.

870. Anti-Zion, Jews on the Jewish Question, http://www.diac.com/~bkennedy/az/A-E.html (current as of September 10, 2001).

871. Edith Starr Miller (Lady Queenborough), Occult Theocrasy, p. 319 (1933).

872. Robert Maryks, *Jesuits of Jewish Ancestry. A Biographical Dictionary* (2008), at http://sites.google.com/a/jewishjesuits.com/www/.

873. Ivan Fraser, Protocols of the Learned Elders of Zion, Proofs of an Ancient Conspiracy, http://www.vegan.swinternet.co.uk/articles/conspiracies/protocols_proof.html (current as of September 10, 2001).

874. Barbara Aho, *Mystery, Babylon the Great - Catholic or Jewish?, Part III, The Jesuits*, Watch Unto Prayer, *at* http://watch.pair.com/mystery-babylon.html (last visited on February 8, 2010).

875.John S. Torell, European-American Evangelical Association, July 1999, http://www.eaec.org/NL99jul.htm (current as of October 2, 2001).

876.John S. Torell, European-American Evangelical Association, July 1999, http://www.eaec.org/NL99jul.htm (current as of October 2, 2001).

877.John S. Torell, European-American Evangelical Association, July 1999, http://www.eaec.org/NL99jul.htm (current as of October 2, 2001).

878.MANFRED BARTHEL, THE JESUITS, HISTORY AND LEGEND OF THE SOCIETY OF JESUS, p. 16 (1984).

879.COLLIER'S ENCYCLOPEDIA, vol. 13, p. 550 (1992).

880.Roy Livesey, Understanding the New Age, at 104 (1989), quoting the Jesuit Catechism.

881.Roy Livesey, Understanding the New Age, at 104 (1989).

882.Roy Livesey, Understanding the New Age, at 104 (1989).

883.Peter Myers, *Israel Shahak on Jewish Fundamentalism and Militarism* (September 12, 2001), at http://www.mailstar.net/shahak2.html.

884.Roy Livesey, Understanding the New Age, at 104 (1989).

885. Michael Hoffman & Alan R. Critchley, The Truth About the Talmud, http://www.hoffman-info.com/talmudtruth.html (current as of September 12, 2001).

886. Michael A. Hoffman II, *Judaism's Strange God's*, at 79 (2000).

887. Roy Livesey, Understanding the New Age, at 104 (1989).

888. Catholics and the Jesuits, http://www.1611kingjamesbible.com/catholic_jesuits.html/, quoting Hector Macpherson, The Jesuits in History, Ozark Book Publishers, Appendix 1 (1997).

889. Francis Parkman, The Works of Francis Parkman, The Old Regime in Canada, France & England in North America, Volume 1 of 2, 153-154 (1897).

890. Dave Hunt, A Woman Rides the Beast (Eugene: Harvest House Publishers, 1994), quoted in The Jesuit Vatican New World Order, October 24, 2012, http://vaticannewworldorder.blogspot.com/2012/10/the-black-pope-wolf-in-sheeps-clothing.html.

891. The Jesuit Vatican New World Order, October 24, 2012, http://vaticannewworldorder.blogspot.com/2012/10/the-black-pope-wolf-in-sheeps-clothing.html.

892. Nino Lo Bello, The Vatican Empire (New York: Trident Press, 1968), quoted in The Jesuit Vatican New World Order, October 24, 2012, http://vaticannewworldorder.blogspot.com/2012/10/the-black-pope-wolf-in-sheeps-clothing.html.

893. Robert Maryks, *Jesuits of Jewish Ancestry. A Biographical Dictionary* (2008), at http://sites.google.com/a/jewishjesuits.com/www/.

894. COUNCIL OF TRENT, DOCTRINE ON THE SACRAMENT OF PENANCE, Canon XII, November 25, 1551.

895. ALBERTO RIVERA, DOUBLE CROSS, Chick Publications, p. 12, 1981. *See also,* EDWIN A. SHERMAN, THE ENGINEER CORPS OF HELL, Library of Congress catalog card # 66-43354, p. 118 (1883); Congressional Record, House Bill 1523, contested election case of Eugene C. Bonniwell against Thos. S. Butler, February 15, 1913, at pp. 3215-16; BURKE MCCARTY, THE SUPPRESSED TRUTH ABOUT THE ASSASSINATION OF ABRAHAM LINCOLN, at pp. 14-16.

896. ALBERTO RIVERA, DOUBLE CROSS, Chick Publications, p. 12, 1981. *See also,* EDWIN A. SHERMAN, THE ENGINEER CORPS OF HELL, Library of Congress catalog card # 66-43354, p. 118 (1883); Congressional Record, House Bill 1523, contested election case of Eugene C. Bonniwell against Thos. S. Butler, February 15, 1913, at pp. 3215-16; BURKE MCCARTY, THE SUPPRESSED TRUTH ABOUT THE ASSASSINATION OF ABRAHAM LINCOLN, at pp. 14-16.

897. EDMOND PARIS, THE SECRET HISTORY OF THE JESUITS, p. 29 (1975).

898. *Id.*

899. *Id.*

900. EDMOND PARIS, THE SECRET HISTORY OF THE JESUITS, p. 26 (1975).

901. Barbara Aho, *Mystery, Babylon the Great - Catholic or Jewish?, Part III, The Jesuits*, Watch Unto Prayer, *at* http://watch.pair.com/mystery-babylon.html (last visited on February 8, 2010) (quoting Maurice Pinay, *The Plot Against the Church, Chapter Thirty-Nine, Jewish-Freemasonic Infiltration into the Jesuit Order*, http://www.catholicvoice.co.uk/pinay/part4d.htm (last visited February 10, 2010)).

902. THE PROTOCOLS OF THE LEARNED ELDERS OF ZION, Paragraph 3, Protocol 17, http://www.thewinds.org/library/protocols_of_zion.html (current as of September 9, 2001).

903. THE PROTOCOLS OF THE LEARNED ELDERS OF ZION, Paragraph 4, Protocol 17, http://www.thewinds.org/library/protocols_of_zion.html (current as of September 9, 2001).

904. COLLIER'S ENCYCLOPEDIA, volume 13, p. 550 (1991).

905. COLLIER'S ENCYCLOPEDIA, volume 13, p. 550 (1991).

906. EDMOND PARIS, THE SECRET HISTORY OF THE JESUITS, p. 69 (1975).

907. ALBERTO RIVERA, DOUBLE CROSS, Chick Publications, p. 12, 1981. *See also,* EDWIN A. SHERMAN, THE ENGINEER CORPS OF HELL, Library of Congress catalog card # 66-43354, p. 118 (1883); Congressional Record, House Bill 1523,

contested election case of Eugene C. Bonniwell against Thos. S. Butler, February 15, 1913, at pp. 3215-16; BURKE MCCARTY, THE SUPPRESSED TRUTH ABOUT THE ASSASSINATION OF ABRAHAM LINCOLN, at pp. 14-16.

908.EDMOND PARIS, THE SECRET HISTORY OF THE JESUITS, p. 70 (1975).

909.COLLIER'S ENCYCLOPEDIA, volume 13, p. 550 (1991); *see also,* EDMOND PARIS, THE SECRET HISTORY OF THE JESUITS, p. 70 (1975).

910.EDMOND PARIS, THE SECRET HISTORY OF THE JESUITS, p. 73 (1975).

911.EDMOND PARIS, THE SECRET HISTORY OF THE JESUITS, p. 70 (1975).

912.*Id.* at 70-71.

913.*Id.* at 71.

914.COLLIER'S ENCYCLOPEDIA, volume 12, p. 516 (1991).

915.SIDNEY HUNTER, IS ALBERTO FOR REAL?, p. 21 (1991); *see also,* EDMOND PARIS, THE SECRET HISTORY OF THE JESUITS, p. 35 (1975).

916.SIDNEY HUNTER, IS ALBERTO FOR REAL?, Chick Publications, p. 21-23 (1988).

917.ERIC JON PHELPS, VATICAN ASSASSINS: "WOUNDED IN THE HOUSE OF MY FRIENDS," P. 206 (2001).

918. WILLIAM STILL, NEW WORLD ORDER, The Ancient Plan of Secret Societies, p. 79 (1990).

919. ERIC JON PHELPS, VATICAN ASSASSINS: "WOUNDED IN THE HOUSE OF MY FRIENDS," p. 205 (2001).

920. ERIC JON PHELPS, VATICAN ASSASSINS: "WOUNDED IN THE HOUSE OF MY FRIENDS," p. 205 (2001).

921. WILLIAM STILL, NEW WORLD ORDER, The Ancient Plan of Secret Societies, pp. 81-91 (1990).

922. COLLIER'S ENCYCLOPEDIA, volume 13, p. 550 (1991).

923. EDMOND PARIS, THE SECRET HISTORY OF THE JESUITS, p. 75 (1975).

924. *Id.*

925. SAMUEL FINLEY BREESE MORSE, IMMINENT DANGERS TO THE FREE INSTITUTIONS OF THE UNITED STATES THROUGH FOREIGN IMMIGRATION AND THE PRESENT STATE OF THE NATURALIZATION LAWS, p. 9-10 (1835).

926. COLLIER'S ENCYCLOPEDIA, vol. 13, p. 550 (1991).

927. *Id.*

928. *Id. See also,* EDMOND PARIS, THE SECRET HISTORY OF THE JESUITS, p. 39 (1975).

929.COLLIER'S ENCYCLOPEDIA, volume 13, p. 550 (1991).

930.PARIS at p. 64.

931.PARIS at p. 65.

932.PARIS at p. 65.

933.PARIS at p. 65.

934.Kennedy, Lucifer's Lodge, at 101.

935.JOHN W. ROBBINS, ECCLESIASTICAL MEGALOMANIA, at p. 32 (1999) (quoting *Summa Theologiae*, ii-ii, 7th article).

936. JOHN W. ROBBINS, ECCLESIASTICAL MEGALOMANIA, at p. 40 (1999) (quoting The Second Vatican Council, *Gaudium et Spes, Pastoral Constitution on the Church in the Modern World,* at p. 69 (1965)).

937.Babylonian Talmud, *Tractate Baba Bathra, Folio 54b* (1961), *available at* http://www.come-and-hear.com/bababathra/bababathra_54.html.

938.Babylonian Talmud, *Tractate Baba Kamma, Folio 113b*, Translated into English with Notes, Glossary and Indices by E. W. Kirzner, M.A., Ph.D., M.Sc, under the Editorship of Rabbi Dr I. Epstein, B.A., Ph.D., D. Lit. (1961), *available at* http://www.come-and-hear.com/babakamma/babakamma_113.html.

939.J. E. C. SHEPHERD, THE BABINGTON PLOT, Wittenburg Publications, p.14, 1987.

940. EDMOND PARIS, THE SECRET HISTORY OF THE JESUITS, p. 26 (1975).

941. J. E. C. SHEPHERD, THE BABINGTON PLOT, Wittenburg Publications, p.16, 1987 (quoting Marianus de Luce, S.J., Professor Canon Law, Gregorian University of Rome, *Institutes of Public Ecclesiastical Law,* with personal commendation from Pope Leo XIII, 1901).

942. EDMOND PARIS, THE SECRET HISTORY OF THE JESUITS, Chick Publications, p. 166-167, 1975.

943. Babylonian Talmud: *Tractate Sanhedrin, Folio 57b*, Sanhedrin Translated into English with Notes, Glossary and Indices Chapters I - VI by Jacob Shachter, Chapters VII - XI
by H. Freedman, B.A., Ph.D., Under the Editorship of Rabbi Dr I. Epstein B.A., Ph.D., D. Lit. (1961), *available at*
http://www.come-and-hear.com/sanhedrin/sanhedrin_57.html (the section actually uses the word "Cuthean," but an endnote explains: "'Cuthean' (Samaritan) was here substituted by the censor for the original goy (heathen).").

944. Babylonian Talmud: *Tractate Sanhedrin, Folio 57b*, Sanhedrin Translated into English with Notes, Glossary and Indices Chapters I - VI by Jacob Shachter, Chapters VII - XI
by H. Freedman, B.A., Ph.D., Under the Editorship of Rabbi Dr I. Epstein B.A., Ph.D., D. Lit. (1961), *available at*
http://www.come-and-hear.com/sanhedrin/sanhedrin_57.html (the section actually uses the word "Cuthean," but an endnote explains: "'Cuthean' (Samaritan) was here substituted by the censor for the original goy

(heathen)."").

945. EDMOND PARIS, THE SECRET HISTORY OF THE JESUITS, p. 21 (1975) (quoting *H. Boehmer*, professor at the University of Bonn, *Les Jesuits* (1910)).

946. J. E. C. SHEPHERD, THE BABINGTON PLOT, Wittenburg Publications, p.118, 1987.

947. J. E. C. SHEPHERD, THE BABINGTON PLOT, Wittenburg Publications, 1987.

948. *Id.* at p. 104-117. *See also* COLLIER'S ENCYCLOPEDIA, volume 9, p. 97 (1991). *See also,* LES GARRETT, WHICH BIBLE CAN WE TRUST?, p. 60 (1982).

949. COLLIER'S ENCYCLOPEDIA, volume 9, p. 620 (1991).

950. COLLIER'S ENCYCLOPEDIA, volume 11, p. 536 (1991).

951. COLLIER'S ENCYCLOPEDIA, volume 12, p. 192 (1991).

952. FOXE'S BOOK OF MARTYRS, edited by William Byron Forbush, http://www.ccel.org/foxe/martyrs/fox117.htm.

953. Image, American Dictionary of the English Language, Noah Webster, 1828.

954. Tom Rushing, Controlling the Masses: From Religion to Bernaise, August 30, 2006. http://www.informationclearinghouse.info/article14763.htm.

955. Zbigniew Brzezinski, Between Two Ages: America's Role in the Technetronic Era, at 72, quoted by Alan Stang, Your New President, Zbig Brother, News With Views, October 29, 2008, http://www.newswithviews.com/Stang/alan170.htm.

956. Donn deGrand Pre, Barbarians Inside the Gates, Book Two, The Vipers Venom, at 187 (2002), quoting Zbigniew Brzezinski, Between Two Ages: America's Role in the Technetronic Era (1970).

957. Texe Marrs, The Illuminati Builds Tower of Infamy, http://www.texemarrs.com/012005/illuminati_builds_tower_of_infamy.htm (last visited on October 7, 2012).

958. JOHN W. ROBBINS, ECCLESIASTICAL MEGALOMANIA, at p. 41 (1999) (quoting Pius XI, *Quadragesimo Anno, On Social Reconstruction,* p. 25 (1931).

959. JOHN W. ROBBINS, ECCLESIASTICAL MEGALOMANIA, at p. 67 (1999).

960. Dr. David Livingston, Religion: an "Opiate of the People"?, http://www.davelivingston.com/opiate.htm (last visited on October 20, 2014), quoting Lenin, Selected Works, XI: 658.

961. The Testimony of Bishop Hnilica, http://www.christendom-awake.org/pages/ttindalr/hnilica.htm (last visited on October 20, 2014).

962. Emma Green, Christian Leaders May Return to Nicaea: What Does It Mean?, The Atlantic, May 31, 2014, http://www.theatlantic.com/international/archive/2014/

05/what-does-it-mean-that-there-will-be-a-new-council-of-nicaea/371943/.

963. Jim Tetlow, Roger Oakland, and Brad Myers, Queen of Rome, Queen of Islam, Queen of All, at 41 (2006).

964. Jim Tetlow, Roger Oakland, and Brad Myers, Queen of Rome, Queen of Islam, Queen of All, at 43 (2006).

965. Athol Bloomer, *The Eucharist and The Jewish Mystical Tradition • Part 2*, Association of Hebrew Catholics, *at* http://hebrewcatholic.org/PrayerandSpirituality/eucharistjewisht.html (originally published in The Hebrew Catholic #78 (Winter-Spring 2003)).

966. Aharon Yosef, A Catholic Jew Pontificates, *Miriam ha Kedosha the Lady Moon of Israel*, January 10, 2008, *at* http://aronbengilad.blogspot.com/2008/01/miriam-hakedosha-lady-moon-of-israel.html.

967. The Rosary, Roses of Prayer for The Queen of Heaven, Daniel A. Lord, S.J., Nihil Obstat Athur J. Scanlan S.T.D: Censor Liborum, Imprimatur + Francis J. Spellman, D.D. Archbishop, New York, http://www.truecatholic.org/rosary.htm (web address current as of March 20, 2005).

968. The Rosary, Roses of Prayer for The Queen of Heaven, Daniel A. Lord, S.J., Nihil Obstat Athur J. Scanlan S.T.D: Censor Liborum, Imprimatur + Francis J. Spellman, D.D. Archbishop, New York, http://www.truecatholic.org/rosary.htm (web address current as of March 20, 2005).

969. Ignatius of Loyola and Martin Luther, Amazing Discoveries, April 21, 2010, http://amazingdiscoveries.org/R-Jesuits_Ignatius_Loyola_Luther, quoting J.H. Merle D'Aubugine, D.D., History of the Reformation of the Sixteenth Century (Grand Rapids, MI: Baker Book House, reproduced from London 1846 edition in 1976).

970. John A. Hardon, S.J., Saint Ignatius Loyola - Jesuit Saint, The Real Presence Association, http://www.therealpresence.org/archives/Saints/Saints013.htm (last visited on October 23, 2014).

971. Ignatius Loyola, The Autobiography of St. Ignatius, at 57-58 (1900), *Imprimatur*, Michael Augustine, Archbishop of New York. *Nihil obstat*, Edwardus I. Purbrick, S.J., *Præpositus Provincialis Provinciæ Marylandiæ Neo-Eboracensis*.

972. Sodality of Our Lady, The History of Sodality, http://www.sodality.ie/index.php?option=com_content&view=article&id=71:history&catid=38:demo-slideshow (last visited on October 19, 2014). See also, O'Malley, J W 1993, 'The First Jesuits', Harvard University Press, Cambridge, Massachusetts, p. 197.

973. Greg Szymanski, Mother Mary Apparitions, And The Jesuits Miracles And Phony Mother Mary Apparitions Equal Big Money, April 22, 2006, http://www.rense.com/general70/d3nt.htm.

974. The Testimony of Bishop Hnilica, http://www.christendom-awake.org/pages/ttindalr/hnilica.htm (last visited on October 20, 2014).

975. The Testimony of Bishop Hnilica, http://www.christendom-awake.org/pages/ttindalr/hnili

ca.htm (last visited on October 20, 2014).

976. The Apparitions Of The Blessed Holy Virgin Mary To Millions In The Coptic Orthodox Church Named After Her, In Zeitoun, Cairo, Egypt (1968-1970), http://www.zeitun-eg.org/zeitoun1.htm (last visited on October 22, 2014).

977. Sandra L. Zimdars-Swartz, Encountering Mary: From La Salette to Medjugorje, Princeton University Press, at 226-27 (1991).

978. Our Lady of Light, http://www.ourladyoflight.org/history.htm (last visited on October 22, 2014).

979. Our Lady of Light, http://www.ourladyoflight.org/history.htm (last visited on October 22, 2014).

980. Kim Briggeman, Montana's Own Christmas Miracle a Salish Boy's Vision, December 24, 2010, http://missoulian.com/news/local/montana-s-own-chris tmas-miracle-a-salish-boy-s-vision/article_e3799ab6-0f ce-11e0-af79-001cc4c002e0.html.

981. Kim Briggeman, Montana's Own Christmas Miracle a Salish Boy's Vision, December 24, 2010, http://missoulian.com/news/local/montana-s-own-chris tmas-miracle-a-salish-boy-s-vision/article_e3799ab6-0f ce-11e0-af79-001cc4c002e0.html.

982. Jim Tetlow, Roger Oakland, and Brad Myers, Queen of Rome, Queen of Islam, Queen of All, at 20 (2006), quoting Pope John Paul II, Vittorio Messori, editor, Crossing The Threshold of Hope, New York, Alfred A. Knopf, Borzoi Book, 1994, p. 220-21.

983. Jim Tetlow, Roger Oakland, and Brad Myers, Queen of Rome, Queen of Islam, Queen of All, at 21 (2006), quoting "Pope Entrusts His Mission to Mary," Online posting from Aug. 19, 2002: www.zenit.org, April 16, 2005.

984. Jim Tetlow, at 18, quoting "Marian Thoughts of Pope Benedict XVI," Online posting: www.udayton.edu/mary/popessaying.html, University of Dayton's Marian Page, Dec. 4, 2005.

985. Jim Tetlow, at 18, quoting "Marian Thoughts of Pope Benedict XVI," Online posting: www.udayton.edu/mary/popessaying.html, University of Dayton's Marian Page, Dec. 4, 2005.

986. Jim Tetlow, at 18, quoting "Marian Thoughts of Pope Benedict XVI," Online posting: www.udayton.edu/mary/popessaying.html, University of Dayton's Marian Page, Dec. 4, 2005.

987. Jim Tetlow, Roger Oakland, and Brad Myers, Queen of Rome, Queen of Islam, Queen of All, at 5 (2006).

988. Jim Tetlow, Roger Oakland, and Brad Myers, Queen of Rome, Queen of Islam, Queen of All, at 5 (2006), citing "5 Million Pilgrims Visit Virgin's Shrine," Orange County Register, Dec. 13, 1999, p. 20.

989. Tetlow, at 6, citing "5 Million Pilgrims Visit Virgin's Shrine," Orange County Register, Dec. 13, 1999, p. 20. Wayne Weible, The Final Harvest, Brewster, MA, Paraclette Press, 1999, p. xiv.

990. Tetlow, at 6, citing "Virgin Mary's Messenger Draws Huge Crowd for Final Sermon," Los Angeles

Times, Oct. 14, 1998, p. A16.

991. Tetlow, at 7, citing Thomas Petrisko, Call of the Ages, Santa Barbara, CA, Queenship Publishing, 1995, p. xxix. Message received by Barbara Ruess, Marienfried, Germany, June 25, 1946.

992. Tetlow, at 7, citing Knock: The Apparition Gable From 1879 To the Present, Cashin Printing Services, pp. 3, 19.

993. Tetlow, at 7, citing Steve Beauclair, "Skyscraper statue slated for Sabana Grande: $42 million Virgin Mary part of Mystical City," Caribbean Business, Feb. 26, 1998, Late News cover story. Note: The 305 foot high statue will be set on a 1,200 foot base, giving a structure whose total height is 1,500 feet.

994. Rick Steves, Witnessing the Power of Faith in Fátima, Portugal, https://www.ricksteves.com/watch-read-listen/read/articles/witnessing-the-power-of-faith-in-fatima (last visited on October 16, 2014).

995. Tetlow at 14, quoting Our Lady of Fatima's Peace Plan From Heaven, Tan Books and Publishers, Inc., 1983, pp. 7-8.

996. Tetlow at 14.

997. Rick Steves, Witnessing the Power of Faith in Fátima, Portugal, https://www.ricksteves.com/watch-read-listen/read/articles/witnessing-the-power-of-faith-in-fatima (last visited on October 16, 2014).

998. Francis X. Rocca, Pope Dedicates World to Mary, The Tablet, October 16, 2013,

http://thetablet.org/pope-dedicates-world-to-mary/.

999. Francis X. Rocca, Pope Dedicates World to Mary, The Tablet, October 16, 2013, http://thetablet.org/pope-dedicates-world-to-mary/.

1000. Tetlow, at 7.

1001. Tetlow at 8, citing Kenneth L. Woodward, "Hail, Mary," Newsweek, Aug. 25, 1997, p. 50.

1002. Tetlow at 8.

1003. Tetlow at 10, quoting Richard J. Beyer, Medjugorje Day By Day, Notre Dame, IN., Ave Maria Press, 1993, April 6th meditation.

1004. William Lobdell and Jennifer Mena, "Our Lady: Not Just for Catholics," Los Angeles Times, Dec. 12, 2003, p. B-1.

1005. William Lobdell and Jennifer Mena, "Our Lady: Not Just for Catholics," Los Angeles Times, Dec. 12, 2003, p. B-1, available at http://articles.latimes.com/2003/dec/12/local/me-guadalupe12.

1006. R. Albert Mohler, Jr., The Christian Post, "Mary for Protestants? A New Look at an Old Question," March 18, 2005.

1007. Tetlow at 36.

1008. Tetlow at 36, quoting ExpressIndia website, Reuters, Online posting: www.expressindia.com/fullstory.php?newsid=35246&headline=Twist~of~globalisation:~All~faiths~come~together, August 20, 2004, accessed Nov. 11, 2005.

1009. Tetlow at 13, quoting Robert Sullivan, "The Mystery of Mary," Life Magazine, Dec., 1996, p. 45.

1010. Tetlow at 12.

1011. Tetlow at 18, quoting "Marian Thoughts of Pope Benedict XVI," Online posting: www.udayton.edu/mary/popessaying.html, University of Dayton's Marian Page, Dec. 4, 2005.

1012. Tetlow at 19, quoting "Our Lady of Guadalupe Receives Papal Visit – We Place Our Lives in Your Maternal Hands." Online posting: www.zenit.org, May 13, 2005.

1013. Tetlow at 21, citing "Vatican Dossier – John Paul II Entrusts Third Millennium To Mary," Online posting: www.zenit.org, June 6, 2001. Go to Archives and click on Oct. 8, 2000.

1014. Tetlow at 23.

1015. Tetlow at 24, 27.

1016. Tetlow at 61.

1017. Tetlow at 61.

1018. Tetlow at 57, quoting Paul A. Mihalik, The Virgin Mary, Fr. Gobbi and the Year 2000, Santa Barbara, CA, 1998, p. 34. Message number 441i to Father Gobbi.

1019. Tetlow at 65.

1020. Tetlow at 56, quoting Petrisko, Call of the Ages, p. 247. Message to St. Bridget of Sweden, 14th century.

1021. Tetlow at 57, quoting Sister Margaret Catherine Sims, CSJ, Apparitions in Betania, Venezuela: Mary, Virgin and Mother of Reconciliation of All People, Framingham, MA,
Medjugorje Messengers, 1992, p. 42. Message given to Maria Esperanza in Betania, Venezuela.

1022. Tetlow at 57, quoting Kunzli, p. 51. Message given to Ida Peerdeman of Amsterdam, Holland on April 29, 1951.

1023. Tetlow at 57-58, quoting Gobbi, pp. 264-265. Message given to Father Gobbi, June 14, 1980.

1024. MICHAEL BUNKER, SWARMS OF LOCUSTS, *The Jesuit Attack on the Faith,* pg. 44 (2002).

1025. Augustus Toplady, Aminianism, http://www.apuritansmind.com/Arminianism/Augustus Toplady%20Arminianism.htm (web address current as of September 18, 2005).

1026. Augustus Toplady, Aminianism, http://www.apuritansmind.com/Arminianism/Augustus Toplady%20Arminianism.htm (web address current as of September 18, 2005).

1027. Augustus Toplady, Aminianism, http://www.apuritansmind.com/Arminianism/Augustus Toplady%20Arminianism.htm (web address current as of September 18, 2005).

1028. Augustus Toplady, Aminianism, http://www.apuritansmind.com/Arminianism/Augustus Toplady%20Arminianism.htm (web address current as of September 18, 2005).

1029. Arminius, in Oper. P.115. Ludg. 1629. (See book for Latin.).

1030. Augustus Toplady, *Arminianism: The Road to Rome!*, http://www.swrb.com/newslett/actualNLs/RHNarmin.htm (last visited on October 23, 2011).

1031. Ernest Reisinger, God's Will, Man's Will, and Free Will, http://www.founders.org/FJ25/article2.html (web address current as of September 11, 2005).

1032. Nick Bibile, God's Grace or the Free Will of Man, http://www.sounddoctrine.net/Nick/freewill.htm (last visited on September 15, 2011).

1033. MICHAEL BUNKER, SWARMS OF LOCUSTS, *The Jesuit Attack on the Faith,* pg. 42-52 (2002).

1034. MICHAEL BUNKER, SWARMS OF LOCUSTS, *The Jesuit Attack on the Faith,* pg. 47 (2002).

1035. Evangelicals and Catholics Together, The Christian Mission in the Third Millennium, http://www.leaderu.com/ftissues/ft9405/articles/mission.html (web address current as of October 27, 2005).

1036. The Gift of Salvation, http://www.firstthings.com/ftissues/ft9801/articles/gift.html (web address current as of November 7, 2005).

1037. John W. Robbins, *Healing the Mortal Wound*, The Trinity Foundation, http://www.trinityfoundation.org/journal.php?id=146 (last visited on October 13, 2011).

1038.Pope to Copeland: Catholics and Charismatics must Spiritually Unite, Stand Up For The Truth, http://standupforthetruth.com/2014/02/pope-to-copeland-catholics-and-charismatics-must-spiritually-unite/ (last visited on April 27, 2014).

1039.FOXE'S BOOK OF MARTYRS, edited by William Byron Forbush, http://www.ccel.org/foxe/martyrs/fox117.htm.

1040.COLLIER'S ENCYCLOPEDIA, volume 3, p. 644 (1991).

1041.EDMOND PARIS, CONVERT OR DIE!, Chick Publications, p. 5.

1042.COLLIER'S ENCYCLOPEDIA, volume 13, p. 38 (1991).

1043.ENCYCLOPEDIA AMERICANA, volume 15, p. 193 (1998).

1044.COLLIER'S ENCYCLOPEDIA, volume 13, p. 38 (1991).

1045.False Ecumenical Unity Robs Christ: Pope, Kenneth Copeland & Bishop Tony Palmer Unite Catholics, Charismatics & No Longer Protestant Anglicans, February 34, 2014, http://ratherexposethem.blogspot.com/2014/02/false-ecumenical-unity-robs-christ-pope.html.

1046.False Ecumenical Unity Robs Christ: Pope, Kenneth Copeland & Bishop Tony Palmer Unite Catholics, Charismatics & No Longer Protestant Anglicans, February 34, 2014, http://ratherexposethem.blogspot.com/2014/02/false-ecumenical-unity-robs-christ-pope.html.

1047.False Ecumenical Unity Robs Christ: Pope, Kenneth Copeland & Bishop Tony Palmer Unite Catholics, Charismatics & No Longer Protestant Anglicans, February 34, 2014, http://ratherexposethem.blogspot.com/2014/02/false-ecumenical-unity-robs-christ-pope.html.

1048.False Ecumenical Unity Robs Christ: Pope, Kenneth Copeland & Bishop Tony Palmer Unite Catholics, Charismatics & No Longer Protestant Anglicans, February 34, 2014, http://ratherexposethem.blogspot.com/2014/02/false-ecumenical-unity-robs-christ-pope.html.

1049.Katy Schiffer, Pope Francis to Pentecostal Conference: Tears of Love, Spiritual Hugs, February 20, 2014, http://www.patheos.com/blogs/kathyschiffer/2014/02/pope-francis-to-pentecostal-conference-tears-of-love-spiritual-hugs/.

1050.Pope to Copeland: Catholics and Charismatics must Spiritually Unite, Stand Up For The Truth, http://standupforthetruth.com/2014/02/pope-to-copeland-catholics-and-charismatics-must-spiritually-unite/ (last visited on April 27, 2014).

1051.Joint Declaration on the Doctrine of Justification by the Lutheran World Federation and the Catholic Church, http://www.vatican.va/roman_curia/pontifical_councils/chrstuni/documents/rc_pc_chrstuni_doc_31101999_cath-luth-joint-declaration_en.html#_ftnref3 (last visited on April 28, 2014).

1052.Joint Declaration on the Doctrine of Justification by the Lutheran World Federation and the Catholic

Church, at paragraph 15, http://www.vatican.va/roman_curia/pontifical_councils/chrstuni/documents/rc_pc_chrstuni_doc_31101999_cath-luth-joint-declaration_en.html#_ftnref3 (last visited on April 28, 2014).

1053. Joint Declaration on the Doctrine of Justification by the Lutheran World Federation and the Catholic Church, at paragraph 5, http://www.vatican.va/roman_curia/pontifical_councils/chrstuni/documents/rc_pc_chrstuni_doc_31101999_cath-luth-joint-declaration_en.html#_ftnref3 (last visited on April 28, 2014).

1054. Joint Declaration on the Doctrine of Justification by the Lutheran World Federation and the Catholic Church, at paragraph 1.

1055. Joint Declaration on the Doctrine of Justification by the Lutheran World Federation and the Catholic Church, at paragraph 1, n.3.

1056. Joint Declaration on the Doctrine of Justification by the Lutheran World Federation and the Catholic Church, at paragraph 7.

1057. Joint Declaration on the Doctrine of Justification by the Lutheran World Federation and the Catholic Church, at paragraph 42.

1058. Amazing Statements Regarding the Roman Catholic Church, Let There Be Light Ministries, http://www.lightministries.com/id524.htm (last visited on June 19, 2014), quoting Pope John Paul II, LOR, #49, December 9, 1992, (quoted in The Apostolic Digest, by Michael Malone, Book 6: "The Book of Sentimental Excuses", Chapter 4: "The Dogmas of

Faith Admit No Alteration Whatsoever").

1059. Amazing Statements Regarding the Roman Catholic Church, Let There Be Light Ministries, http://www.lightministries.com/id524.htm (last visited on June 19, 2014), quoting Pope Benedict XV, Ad Beatissimi, PTC:761, (quoted in The Apostolic Digest, by Michael Malone, Book 6: "The Book of Sentimental Excuses", Chapter 4: "The Dogmas of Faith Admit No Alteration Whatsoever").

1060. Amazing Statements Regarding the Roman Catholic Church, Let There Be Light Ministries, http://www.lightministries.com/id524.htm (last visited on June 19, 2014), quoting Pope Paul VI, as in turn quoted in The Apostolic Digest, by Michael Malone, Book 6: "The Book of Sentimental Excuses", Chapter 4: "The Dogmas of Faith Admit No Alteration Whatsoever."

1061. Paul T. McCain, Betrayal of the Gospel, The Joint Declaration on the Doctrine of Justification, http://www.firstthings.com/index.php?permalink=blogs&blog=firstthoughts&year=2010&month=03&&entry_permalink=a-betrayal-of-the-gospel-the-joint-declaration-on-the-doctrine-of-justification (last visited on April 29, 2014).

1062. Joint Declaration on the Doctrine of Justification by the Lutheran World Federation and the Catholic Church, at paragraph 13.

1063. Mark Herzer, *Arminianism Exposed*, http://www.the-highway.com/Arminianism_Exposed2.html (last visited on October 25, 2011).

1064. Catechism of the Catholic Church, § 2022, http://www.vatican.va/archive/ccc_css/archive/catechism/p3s1c3a2.htm.

1065. The Catholic Church and the Lutheran World Federation On the Doctrine of Justification, http://web.archive.org/web/20001004124921/http://www.vatican.va/roman_curia/pontifical_councils/chrstuni/documents/rc_pc_chrstuni_doc_01081998_off-answer-catholic_en.html (last visited on April 30, 2014).

1066. Joint Declaration on the Doctrine of Justification by the Lutheran World Federation and the Catholic Church, at paragraph 38.

1067. Pontifical Council for Promoting Christian Unity the World Methodist Council Statement of Association With the Joint Declaration on the Doctrine of Justification(accompanied by the Official Common Affirmation signed by Representatives of the Catholic Church, the Lutheran World Federation and the World Methodist Council) Seoul, South Korea, 23 July 2006, http://www.vatican.va/roman_curia/pontifical_councils/chrstuni/meth-council-docs/rc_pc_chrstuni_doc_20060723_text-association_en.html.

1068. Joint Declaration on the Doctrine of Justification by the Lutheran World Federation and the Catholic Church, at paragraph 22.

1069. Mark Herzer, *Arminianism Exposed*, http://www.the-highway.com/Arminianism_Exposed2.html (last visited on October 25, 2011).

1070. Mark Herzer, *Arminianism Exposed*, http://www.the-highway.com/Arminianism_Exposed2.html (last visited on October 25, 2011).

1071. Mark Herzer, *Arminianism Exposed*, http://www.the-highway.com/Arminianism_Exposed2.html (last visited on October 25, 2011), quoting John Mark Hicks, "The Righteousness of Saving Faith: Arminian Versus Remonstrant Grace," Evangelical Journal 9.1 (1991) 34. John Hicks did his doctoral work on this very issue. See The Theology of Grace in the Though of Jacobus Arminius and Philip van Limborch: A Study in the Development of Seventeenth Century Dutch Arminianism (Ph.d. Dissertation, Westminster Theological Seminary, 1985).

1072. Joint Declaration on the Doctrine of Justification by the Lutheran World Federation and the Catholic Church, at paragraph 30.

1073. Joint Declaration on the Doctrine of Justification by the Lutheran World Federation and the Catholic Church, at paragraph 28.

1074. Joint Declaration on the Doctrine of Justification by the Lutheran World Federation and the Catholic Church, at paragraph 29.

1075. THE COUNCIL OF TRENT, Session VII - Celebrated on the third day of March 1547, under Pope Paul III, Baptism, Cannon 2, http://www.ewtn.com/library/councils/trent7.htm#3.

1076. Catechism of the Catholic Church, § 1213, http://www.vatican.va/archive/ccc_css/archive/catechism/p2s2c1a1.htm (last visited on May 1, 2014).

1077. Pope Pius IX, The Syllabus (of Errors), Issued in 1864, Section V, Errors Concerning the Church and Her Rights, #24, http://www.ewtn.com/library/PAPALDOC/P9SYLL.H

TM. (last visited on June 19, 2014), quoted in Amazing Statements Regarding the Roman Catholic Church, Let There Be Light Ministries, http://www.lightministries.com/id524.htm (last visited on June 19, 2014).

1078. ENCYCLOPEDIA AMERICANA, volume 15, p.194 (1998).

1079. COLLIER'S ENCYCLOPEDIA, volume 13, p. 40 (1991).

1080. DAVE HUNT, A WOMAN RIDES THE BEAST, p. 261, 1994.

1081. *Id.*

1082. Religious Intolerance, http://www.cuttingedge.org/articles/RC112.htm (last visited on May 1, 2014).

1083. ALBERTO RIVERA, THE FOUR HORSEMEN, Chick publications, p. 7, 1985 (quoting JESSIE CORRIGAN PEGIS, A PRACTICAL CATHOLIC DICTIONARY, p. 67 (1957)).

1084. CATECHISM OF THE COUNCIL OF TRENT, ORDERED BY THE COUNCIL OF TRENT, EDITED UNDER ST. CHARLES BORROMEO, PUBLISHED BY DECREE OF POPE ST. PIUS V, 1566, TAN Books, 1982 at p. 208.

1085. *Id.* at p. 211.

1086. *Id.* at p. 212.

1087. U.S. CONST. article VI.

1088. EDWARD PETERS, INQUISITION, p. 48, 1989.

1089. *Id.* at p. 56.

1090. CHARLES CHINIQUY, FIFTY YEARS IN THE CHURCH OF ROME, Chick Publications, p. 295 (1985) republished from the 1886 edition.

1091. CHARLES CHINIQUY, FIFTY YEARS IN THE CHURCH OF ROME, Chick Publications, p. 298 (1985) republished from the 1886 edition.

1092. CHARLES CHINIQUY, FIFTY YEARS IN THE CHURCH OF ROME, Chick Publications, p. 298 (1985), republished from the 1886 edition.

1093. Thomas M. Harris, Rome's Responsibility for the Assassination of Abraham Lincoln, With an Appendix Containing Conversations Between Abraham Lincoln and Charles Chiniquy, at 19-21 (1897), Great Mountain Publishing.

1094. Thomas M. Harris, Rome's Responsibility for the Assassination of Abraham Lincoln, at 19-21 (1897), Great Mountain Publishing.

1095. Emett McLoughlin, Emett McLoughlin's An Inquiry Into the Assassination of Abraham Lincoln, at 40 (1963).

1096. Pam Nordstrom, "SAN PATRICIO BATTALION," Handbook of Texas Online (http://www.tshaonline.org/handbook/online/articles/qis01), accessed March 21, 2015. Uploaded on June 15, 2010. Published by the Texas State Historical Association.

1097. Matt Skwiat, San Patricios Will Be Inducted Into the Irish America Hall of Fame, Irish America, http://irishamerica.com/2013/08/san-patricios-will-be-inducted-into-the-irish-america-hall-of-fame/ (last visited on March 22, 2015).

1098. Oaths of Enlistment and Oaths of Office, http://www.history.army.mil/html/faq/oaths.html (last visited on March 22, 2015).

1099. U.S. Const. art. VII cl. 3.

1100. Emett McLoughlin, Emett McLoughlin's An Inquiry Into the Assassination of Abraham Lincoln, at 41 (1963), quoting John T. Christian, America or Rome, Which?, Baptist Book Concern, Louisville, Kentucky, at 86 (1895).

1101. McLoughlin, at 53.

1102. McLoughlin, at 53, quoting New York Daily Tribune, July 18, 1863.

1103. McLoughlin, at 52, quoting Harpers Weekly, August 1, 1863.

1104. McLoughlin, at 58.

1105. McLoughlin, at 58.

1106. Thomas M. Harris, Rome's Responsibility for the Assassination of Abraham Lincoln, With an Appendix Containing Conversations Between Abraham Lincoln and Charles Chiniquy, at 21 (1897), Great Mountain Publishing.

1107. Samuel Morse, Foreign Conspiracy Against the Liberties of the United States, at 148 (1841).

1108. Samuel Morse, Foreign Conspiracy Against the Liberties of the United States, at 148 (1841).

1109. Samuel Morse, Foreign Conspiracy Against the Liberties of the United States, at 148 (1841).

1110. Paul Serup, Who Killed Abraham Lincoln, at 27-28, figure 10, and 198 (2008), Letter from Robert Todd Lincoln to Charles Chiniquy. September 10, 1885, citing The Lincoln Writings of Charles P.T. Chiniquy, p. 24, 25, Robert Todd Lincoln to Charles Chiniquy, September 10, 1885, The Chiniquy Collection.

1111. The Murder of Abraham Lincoln, Planned and executed by Jesuit Priests, 1893. Available at https://ia600503.us.archive.org/0/items/murderofabraham l00chin/murderofabrahaml00chin.pdf.

1112. Charles Chiniquy, Fifty Years in the Church of Rome, at 296, 1 Also v886. http://ia700407.us.archive.org/12/items/fiftyyearsinchu r00chin/fiftyyearsinchur00chin.pdf.

1113. Chiniquy, at 299.

1114. Chiniquy, at 305.

1115. Chiniquy, at 297.

1116. Chiniquy, at 300.

1117. Chiniquy, at 300.

1118. Chiniquy, at 302.

1119. The Murder of Abraham Lincoln, Planned and executed by Jesuit Priests, 1893. Available at https://ia600503.us.archive.org/0/items/murderofabraham

aml00chin/murderofabrahaml00chin.pdf.

1120.Charles Chiniquy, 50 Years in the Church of Rome, Chapter 61 (1886), http://jesus-is-lord.com/fifty13.htm#CHAPTER 61.

1121.Chiniquy, at 311.

1122.Edwin A. Sherman, Engineer Corps of Hell, at 213 (circa 1882).

1123.Chiniquy, at 314.

1124.Edwin A. Sherman, Engineer Corps of Hell, at 230 (circa 1882).

1125.Emett McLoughlin, Emett McLoughlin's An Inquiry Into the Assassination of Abraham Lincoln, at 148-49 (1963).

1126.Emett McLoughlin, Emett McLoughlin's An Inquiry Into the Assassination of Abraham Lincoln, at 148-49 (1963).

1127.Chiniquy, at 314.

1128.Alfred Isaacson, John Surratt and the Lincoln Assassination Plot, Maryland Historical Magazine, Vol. 52, No. 4, December 1957, 316, 342, citing The Baltimore Sun, April 22, 1916, http://msa.maryland.gov/megafile/msa/speccol/sc5800/sc5881/000001/000000/000208/pdf/msa_sc_5881_1_208.pdf.

1129.Emett McLoughlin, Emett McLoughlin's An Inquiry Into the Assassination of Abraham Lincoln, at 157 (1963).

1130. Chiniquy, at 312.

1131. Burke McCarty, The Suppressed Truth About the Assassination of Abraham Lincoln, at 171-72 (1922), http://www.spirituallysmart.com/lincoln10.htm (last visited on December 2014). 39th Congress, Second Session, House of Representatives, Judiciary Committee Report No. 33, https://ia600406.us.archive.org/6/items/johnhsurrattrepo00wood/johnhsurrattrepo00wood.pdf.

1132. Emett McLoughlin, Emett McLoughlin's An Inquiry Into the Assassination of Abraham Lincoln, at 142 (1963).

1133. Edwin A. Sherman, Engineer Corps of Hell, at 229 (circa 1882).

1134. Burke McCarty, at 178-79.

1135. Burke McCarty, at 178-79.

1136. Burke McCarty, at 178-79.

1137. Burke McCarty, at 178-79.

1138. Sworn Testimony of Second Assistant Secretary of State, William Hunter, 39th Congress, Second Session, House of Representatives, Judiciary Committee Report No. 33, at 10, March 2, 1867, https://ia600406.us.archive.org/6/items/johnhsurrattrepo00wood/johnhsurrattrepo00wood.pdf.

1139. September 27, 1865, Dispatch #538, from A. Wilding, U.S. Consul to Liverpool, John H. Surratt: message from the President of the United States, transmitting a report of the Secretary of State relating to the discovery and arrest of John H. Surratt, http://archive.org/stream/johnhsurrattmess00unit/johnhsurrattmess00unit_djvu.txt.

1140. Sworn Testimony of Chief Clerk of the Department of State, Robert S. Chew, 39th Congress, Second Session, House of Representatives, Judiciary Committee Report No. 33, at 12, March 2, 1867, https://ia600406.us.archive.org/6/items/johnhsurrattrepo00wood/johnhsurrattrepo00wood.pdf.

1141. October 13, 1865, Dispatch #476, from William Hunter, Acting Secretary of State, to A. Wilding, U.S. Consul to Liverpool, John H. Surratt: message from the President of the United States, transmitting a report of the Secretary of State relating to the discovery and arrest of John H. Surratt, http://archive.org/stream/johnhsurrattmess00unit/johnhsurrattmess00unit_djvu.txt.

1142. Sworn Testimony of Chief Clerk of the Department of State, Robert S. Chew, 39th Congress, Second Session, House of Representatives, Judiciary Committee Report No. 33, at 12, March 2, 1867, https://ia600406.us.archive.org/6/items/johnhsurrattrepo00wood/johnhsurrattrepo00wood.pdf.

1143. Sworn Testimony of Secretary of War, Edwin M. Stanton, 39th Congress, Second Session, House of Representatives, Judiciary Committee Report No. 33, at 12-13, March 2, 1867, https://ia600406.us.archive.org/6/items/johnhsurrattrepo00wood/johnhsurrattrepo00wood.pdf.

1144. Sworn Testimony of Secretary of War, Edwin M. Stanton, 39th Congress, Second Session, House of Representatives, Judiciary Committee Report No. 33, at 12-13, March 2, 1867, https://ia600406.us.archive.org/6/items/johnhsurrattrepo00wood/johnhsurrattrepo00wood.pdf.

1145. Sworn Testimony of Secretary of War, Edwin M. Stanton, 39th Congress, Second Session, House of Representatives, Judiciary Committee Report No. 33, at 12-13, March 2, 1867, https://ia600406.us.archive.org/6/items/johnhsurrattrepo00wood/johnhsurrattrepo00wood.pdf.

1146. Sworn Testimony of Secretary of War, Edwin M. Stanton, 39th Congress, Second Session, House of Representatives, Judiciary Committee Report No. 33, at 3, March 2, 1867, https://ia600406.us.archive.org/6/items/johnhsurrattrepo00wood/johnhsurrattrepo00wood.pdf.

1147. E.g., 22 U.S. Code § 2708 (f).

1148. Mark Hageman, Lafayette Baker, AKA: Sam Munson, Union Spymaster (Self-Proclaimed Chief of U.S. Intelligence) During American Civil War (1826 - 1868), Signal Corps Association, http://www.civilwarsignals.org/pages/spy/lafayettebaker.html (last visited on March 20, 2015).

1149. October 25, 1865, Dispatch #236, from U.S. Consul, John F. Potter to Secretary of State William Seward, John H. Surratt: message from the President of the United States, transmitting a report of the Secretary of State relating to the discovery and arrest of John H. Surratt, http://archive.org/stream/johnhsurrattmess00unit/johnhsurrattmess00unit_djvu.txt.

1150. U.S. Const. Art. III, § 3.

1151. Steven R. Weisman, U.S. and Vatican Restore Full Ties after 117 Years, New York Times, January 11, 1984, http://www.nytimes.com/1984/01/11/world/us-and-vatican-restore-full-ties-after-117-years.html.

1152. Abraham Lincoln and Edwin Stanton, The Lincoln Institute, citing Rufus Rockwell Wilson, editor, Intimate Memories of Lincoln, p. 435 (Dr. Francis Durbin Blakeslee), http://abrahamlincolnsclassroom.org/abraham-lincolns-contemporaries/abraham-lincoln-and-edwin-stanton/ (last visited on March 28, 2015). See also, Donald T. Philips, Lincoln on Leadership.

1153. Edwin A. Sherman, Engineer Corps of Hell, at 212 (circa 1882).

1154. WILLIAM STILL, NEW WORLD ORDER, The Ancient Plan of Secret Societies, p. 123 (1990).

1155. Darrell L. Aldridge, The First Presidential Impeachment Trial – May 1868, http://louisianalodgeofresearch.org/papers/14THE%20FIRST%20PRESIDENTIAL%20IMPEACHMENT%20TRIAL.pdf (last visited on March 25, 2015).

1156. Darrell L. Aldridge, The First Presidential Impeachment Trial – May 1868.

1157. James A. Marples, Rose Hill, Kansas, The Scottish Rite Journal, http://srjarchives.tripod.com/1998-03/marples.htm (last visited on March 24, 2015).

1158. JIM SHAW (33rd Degree Mason, Knight Commander of the Court of Honor, Past Worshipful

Master of the Blue Lodge, Past Master of All Scottish Rite Bodies) and TOM MCKENNEY, THE DEADLY DECEPTION, Freemasonry Exposed by One of Its Top Leaders, p. 137 (1988).

1159. James Hahn, Religious Titles And Oaths Used By Masons, quoting Revised Duncan's Ritual of Freemasonry Complete, p. 230, http://www.truthmagazine.com/archives/volume24/TM024277.html (last visited on March 25, 2015).

1160. Letter to her friend, Sally Orne, March 15, 1866. http://rogerjnorton.com/Lincoln90.html. See also, John Wilkes Booth, Right Or Wrong, God Judge Me: The Writings of John Wilkes Booth, Edited by John Rhodenamel and Louise Taper, at 146, n.2., quoting Mary Todd Lincoln: Her Life and Letters by Justin G. Turner and Linda Levitt Turner (New York, Alfred A. Knopf, 1972), p.345.

1161. Mark Hageman, Lafayette Baker, AKA: Sam Munson, Union Spymaster (Self-Proclaimed Chief of U.S. Intelligence) During American Civil War (1826 - 1868), Signal Corps Association, http://www.civilwarsignals.org/pages/spy/lafayettebaker.html (last visited on March 20, 2015).

1162. Emanuel Hertz, The Hidden Lincoln, from the Letters and Papers of William H. Herndon, at 17-18 (1940), https://archive.org/stream/hiddenlincoln006356mbp#page/n37/mode/2up.

1163. SAMUEL F.B. MORSE, IMMINENT DANGERS TO THE FREE INSTITUTIONS OF THE UNITED STATES THROUGH FOREIGN IMMIGRATION (1835).

1164.SAMUEL FINLEY BREESE MORSE, FOREIGN CONSPIRACY AGAINST THE LIBERTIES OF THE UNITED STATES: THE NUMBERS OF BRUTUS, p. 118-119 (1835).

1165.Evangelical Christendom, Vol. 49, January 1, 1895, pg. 15, the organ of the Evangelical Alliance, published in London by J. S. Phillips. See also, Catholique Nationale, July 13, 1895 (Reported in the Protestant Church Review of October 3, and November 14th, 1895, and the India Watchman, in The Friend, A Religious And Literary Journal, Volume LXIX, 1896, Philadelphia, pg. 154.). Daniel and the Revelation: The Chart of Prophecy and Our Place In It, A Study of the Historical and Futurist Interpretation, by Joseph Tanner, published in London by Hodder and Stoughton, 1898, pages 153, 154. Michael Scheifler, The Curious Case of Cardinal Sarto's Homily, http://biblelight.net/Sarto-homily.htm (last visited on March 17, 2014).

1166.CHARLES CHINIQUY, FIFTY YEARS IN THE CHURCH OF ROME, Chick Publications, p. 285 (1985) republished from the 1886 edition.

1167.SAMUEL FINLEY BREESE MORSE, FOREIGN CONSPIRACY AGAINST THE LIBERTIES OF THE UNITED STATES: THE NUMBERS OF BRUTUS, p. 19-21 (1835).

1168.ERIC JON PHELPS, VATICAN ASSASSINS: "WOUNDED IN THE HOUSE OF MY FRIENDS," P. 305-06 (2001) (quoting J. WAYNE LAURENS, THE CRISIS: OR, THE ENEMIES OF AMERICA UNMASKED (1855)).

1169. JOHN W. ROBBINS, ECCLESIASTICAL MEGALOMANIA, at p. 30 (1999).

1170. Leo Hirrel, Children of Wrath: New School Calvinism and Antebellum Reform, at 112 (1998).

1171. Vatican City State, State Departments, http://www.vaticanstate.va/content/vaticanstate/en/stato-e-governo/organi-dello-stato.html (last visited on March 18, 2015).

1172. Leo Hirrel, Children of Wrath: New School Calvinism and Antebellum Reform, at 112 (1998).

1173. Leo Hirrel, Children of Wrath: New School Calvinism and Antebellum Reform, at 113 (1998).

1174. Charles Chiniquy, 50 Years in the Church of Rome, Chapter 59 (1886), http://www.biblebelievers.com/chiniquy/cc50_ch59.html.

1175. Matthew Boyle, Border Patrol Agent Assoc. Claims Far More than 11 Million Illegal Aliens in America, 9 September 2013, http://www.breitbart.com/Big-Government/2013/09/09/Border-Patrol-agents-Millions-more-than-just-11-million-illegal-aliens-in-America.

1176. Karen Frazier Romero, While They Slept (2014), citing L.A. Cardinal Mahony Attacks Immigration Bill, NPR, March 5, 2006, http://www.npr.org/templates/story/story.php?storyId=5246128.

1177. L.A. Cardinal Mahony Attacks Immigration Bill, NPR, March 5, 2006, http://www.npr.org/templates/story/story.php?storyId=

5246128.

1178.L.A. Cardinal Mahony Attacks Immigration Bill, NPR, March 5, 2006, http://www.npr.org/templates/story/story.php?storyId=5246128.

1179.L.A. Cardinal Mahony Attacks Immigration Bill, NPR, March 5, 2006, http://www.npr.org/templates/story/story.php?storyId=5246128.

1180.Karen Frazier Romero, While They Slept (2014).

1181.Catholic Church's Position on Immigration Reform, August 2013, http://www.usccb.org/issues-and-action/human-life-and-dignity/immigration/churchteachingonimmigrationreform.cfm.

1182.Victor L. Simpson, Associated Press, Pope Benedict XVI Backs U.S. Bishops' Commitment To Immigration Reform, May 18, 2012, http://www.huffingtonpost.com/2012/05/18/pope-benedict-immigration-reform_n_1526954.html.

1183.SAMUEL FINLEY BREESE MORSE, IMMINENT DANGERS TO THE FREE INSTITUTIONS OF THE UNITED STATES THROUGH FOREIGN IMMIGRATION AND THE PRESENT STATE OF THE NATURALIZATION LAWS, p. 8-9 (1835).

1184.CHARLES CHINIQUY, FIFTY YEARS IN THE CHURCH OF ROME, Chick Publications, p. 285 (1985) republished from the 1886 edition.

1185.*Id.*

1186.*Id.*

1187.DAVE HUNT, A WOMAN RIDES THE BEAST, p. 55 (1994), quoting J.H. IGNAZ VON DOLLINGER, THE POPE AND THE COUNCIL, p. 21 (London 1869).

1188.JOHN W. ROBBINS, ECCLESIASTICAL MEGALOMANIA, p. 143 (1999).

1189.DAVE HUNT, A WOMAN RIDES THE BEAST, p. 123 (1994).

1190.SAMUEL FINLEY BREESE MORSE, p. 118-119 (1835).

1191.CHARLES CHINIQUY, FIFTY YEARS IN THE CHURCH OF ROME, Chick Publications, p. 285 (1985) republished from the 1886 edition.

1192.JOHN W. ROBBINS at 143-44.

1193.J.A. Wylie, The Papacy is the Antichrist, Chapter XIV (1888).

1194.JOHN W. ROBBINS at p. 134.

1195.Emett McLoughlin, Emett McLoughlin's An Inquiry Into the Assassination of Abraham Lincoln, at 24 (1963).

1196.Emett McLoughlin, at 26.

1197.CHARLES CHINIQUY, FIFTY YEARS IN THE CHURCH OF ROME, Chick Publications, p. 288.

Other books available from Great Mountain Publishing:

9/11-Enemies Foreign and Domestic
ISBN-13: 978-0983262732

9/11-Enemies Foreign and Domestic proves beyond a reasonable doubt that the U.S. Government's conspiracy theory of the attacks on September 11, 2001, is a preposterous cover story. The evidence in 9/11-Enemies Foreign and Domestic has been suppressed from the official government reports and censored from the mass media. The evidence proves that powerful Zionists ordered the 9/11 attacks, which were perpetrated by Israel's Mossad, aided and abetted by treacherous high officials in the U.S. Government. 9/11-Enemies Foreign and Domestic identifies the traitors by name and details their subversive crimes. There is sufficient evidence in 9/11-Enemies Foreign and Domestic to indict important officials of the U.S. Government for high treason. The reader will understand how the U.S. Government really works and what Sir John Harrington (1561-1612) meant when he said: "Treason doth never prosper: what's the reason? Why if it prosper, none dare call it treason." There are millions of Americans who have taken an oath to defend the U.S. Constitution against all enemies foreign and domestic. The mass media, which is under the control of a disloyal cabal, keeps those patriotic Americans ignorant of the traitors among them. J. Edgar Hoover, former Director of the FBI, explained: "The individual is handicapped by coming face-to-face with a conspiracy so monstrous-he simply cannot believe it exists." 9/11-Enemies Foreign and Domestic erases any doubt about the existence of the monstrous conspiracy described by Hoover and arms the reader with the knowledge required to save our great nation. "My people are destroyed for lack of knowledge." Hosea 4:6.

Solving the Mystery of BABYLON THE GREAT
ISBN-13: 978-0983262701

"Attorney and Christian researcher Edward Hendrie investigates and reveals one of the greatest exposés of all time. . . . a book you don't want to miss. Solving the Mystery of Babylon the Great is packed with documentation. Never before have the crypto-Jews who seized the reins of power in Rome been put under such intense scrutiny." Texe Marrs, Power of Prophecy. The evidence presented in this book leads to the ineluctable conclusion that the Roman Catholic Church was established by crypto-Jews as a false "Christian" front for a Judaic/Babylonian religion. That religion is the core of a world conspiracy against man and God. That is not a conspiracy theory based upon speculation, but rather the hard truth based upon authoritative evidence, which is documented in this book. Texe Marrs explains in his foreword to the book: "Who is Mystery Babylon? What is the meaning of the sinister symbols found in these passages? Which city is being described as the 'great city' so full of sin and decadence, and who are its citizens? Why do the woman and beast of Revelation seek the destruction of the holy people, the saints and martyrs of Jesus? What does it all mean for you and me today? Solving the Mystery of Babylon the Great answers these questions and more. Edward Hendrie's discoveries are not based on prejudice but on solid evidence aligned forthrightly with the 'whole counsel of God.' He does not condone nor will he be a part of any project in which Bible verses are taken out of context, or in which scriptures are twisted to mean what they do not say. Again and again you will find that Mr. Hendrie documents his assertions, backing up what he says with historical facts and proofs. Most important is that he buttresses his findings with scriptural understanding. The foundation for his research is sturdy because it is based on the bedrock of God's unshakeable Word."

The Anti-Gospel
ISBN-13: 978-0983262749

Edward Hendrie uses God's word to strip the sheep's clothing from false Christian ministers and expose them as ravening wolves preaching an anti-gospel. The anti-gospel is based on a myth that all men have a will that is free from the bondage of sin to choose whether to believe in Jesus. The Holy Bible, however, states that all men are spiritually dead and cannot believe in Jesus unless they are born again of the Holy Spirit. Ephesians 2:1-7; John 3:3-8. God has chosen his elect to be saved by his grace through faith in Jesus Christ. Ephesians 1:3-9; 2:8-10. God imbues his elect with the faith needed to believe in Jesus. Hebrews 12:2; John 1:12-13. The devil's false gospel contradicts the word of God and reverses the order of things. Under the anti-gospel, instead of a sovereign God choosing his elect, sovereign man decides whether to choose God. The calling of the Lord Jesus Christ is effectual; all who are chosen for salvation will believe in Jesus. John 6:37-44. The anti-gospel has a false Jesus, who only offers the possibility of salvation, with no assurance. The anti-gospel blasphemously makes God out to be a liar by denying the total depravity of man and the sovereign election of God. All who preach that false gospel are under a curse from God. Galatians 1:6-9.

Bloody Zion
ISBN-13: 978-0983262763

Jesus told Pontius Pilate: "My kingdom is not of this world." John 18:36. God has a spiritual Zion that is in a heavenly Jerusalem. Hebrews 12:22; Revelation 21:10. Jesus Christ is the chief corner stone laid by God in Zion. 1 Peter 2:6. Those who believe in Jesus Christ are living stones in the spiritual house of God. 1 Peter 2:5; Ephesians 2:20-22. Believers are in Jesus and Jesus is in believers. John 14:20; 17:20-23. All who are elected by God to believe in Jesus Christ are part of the heavenly Zion, without regard to whether they are Jews or Gentiles. Romans 10:12. Satan is a great adversary of God, who has created his own mystery religions. During the Babylonian captivity (2 Chronicles 36:20), an occult society of Jews replaced God's commands with Satan's Babylonian dogma. Their new religion became Judaism. Jesus explained the corruption of the Judaic religion: "Howbeit in vain do they worship me, teaching for doctrines the commandments of men." Mark 7:7. Jesus revealed the Satanic origin of Judaism when he stated: "Ye are of your father the devil, and the lusts of your father ye will do." John 8:44. Babylonian Judaism remains the religion of the Jews today. Satan has infected many nominal "Christian" denominations with his Babylonian occultism, which has given rise to "Christian" Zionism. "Christian" Zionism advocates a counterfeit, earthly Zion, within which fleshly Jews take primacy over the spiritual church of Jesus Christ. This book exposes "Christian" Zionism as a false gospel and subversive political movement that sustains Israel's war against God and man.

Murder, Rape, and Torture in a Catholic Nunnery
ISBN-13: 978-1-943056-00-2

There has probably not been a person more maligned by the powerful forces of the Roman Catholic Church than Maria Monk. In 1836 she published the famous book, *Awful Disclosures of the Hotel Dieu Nunnery of Montreal*. In that book, she told of murder, rape, and torture behind the walls of the cloistered nunnery. Because the evidence was verifiably true, the Catholic hierarchy found it necessary to fabricate evidence and suborn perjury in an attempt to destroy the credibility of Maria Monk. The Catholic Church has kept up the character assassination of Maria Monk now for over 175 years. Even today, there can be found on the internet websites devoted to libeling Maria Monk. Edward Hendrie has examined the evidence and set it forth for the readers to decide for themselves whether Maria Monk was an impostor, as claimed by the Roman Catholic Church, or whether she was a brave victim. An objective view of the evidence leads to the ineluctable conclusion that Maria Monk told the truth about what happened behind the walls of the Hotel Dieu Nunnery of Montreal. The Roman Catholic Church, which is the most powerful religious and political organization in the world, has engaged in an unceasing campaign of vilification against Maria Monk. Their crusade against Maria Monk, however, can only affect the opinion of the uninformed. It cannot change the evidence. The evidence speaks clearly to those who will look at the case objectively. The evidence reveals that the much maligned Maria Monk was a reliable witness who made awful but accurate disclosures about life in a cloistered nunnery.

What Shall I Do to Inherit Eternal Life?
ISBN-13: 978-0983262770

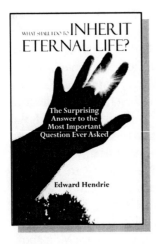

A certain ruler posed to Jesus the most important question ever asked: "Good Master, what shall I do to inherit eternal life?" (Luke 18:18) The man came to the right person. Jesus is God, and therefore his answer to that question is authoritative. This book examines Jesus' surprising answer and definitively explains how one inherits eternal life. This is a book about God's revelation to man. Except for the Holy Bible, this is the most important book you will ever read.

Rome's Responsibility for the Assassination of Abraham Lincoln, With an Appendix Containing Conversations Between Abraham Lincoln and Charles Chiniquy
ISBN-13: 978-0983262794

The author of this book, General Thomas Maley Harris, was a medical doctor, who recruited and served as commander of the Tenth West Virginia Volunteers during the Civil War. He rose in rank through meritorious service to become a brigadier general in the Union Army. General Harris established a reputation for faithfulness, industriousness, intelligence, and efficiency. He was noted for his leadership in preparing his troops and leading them in battle. He was brevetted a major general for "gallant conduct in the assault on Petersburg." After the Civil War, General Harris served one term as a representative in the West Virginia legislature, and was West Virginia's Adjutant General from 1869 to 1870. General Harris was a member of the Military Commission that tried and convicted the conspirators who assassinated President Abraham Lincoln. He had first hand knowledge of the sworn testimony of the witnesses in that trial.

This book summarizes the salient evidence brought out during the military trial and adds information from other sources to present before the public the ineluctable conclusion that the assassination of Abraham Lincoln was the work of the Roman Catholic Church. The Roman Catholic Church has been largely successful in suppressing the circulation of this book. This book has never been given a place on bookstore shelves, as it exposed too much for the Roman Catholic hierarchy to tolerate. Any display of this book would bring an instant boycott of the bookstore. It is only now, in the age of the internet, where the marketplace of ideas has been opened wide, that this book can be found by those searching for the truth of who was behind the assassination of Abraham Lincoln.

The above books can be ordered from bookstores and from internet sites, including, but not limited to: www.antichristconspiracy.com, www.lulu.com, www.911enemies.com, www.mysterybabylonthegreat.net, www.antigospel.com, https://play.google.com, www.barnesandnoble.com, and www.amazon.com.

Edward Hendrie
edwardhendrie@gmail.com

CPSIA information can be obtained at www.ICGtesting.com
Printed in the USA
BVOW03s1208170515

400694BV00017B/600/P